ALGORITHMS IN SNOBOL4

JAMES F. GIMPEL
Bell Telephone Laboratories

A WILEY-INTERSCIENCE PUBLICATION
JOHN WILEY & SONS,
New York • London • Sydney • Toronto

Published by John Wiley & Sons, Inc.

Copyright © 1976 by Bell Telephone Labs., Inc.

All rights reserved. Published simultaneously in Canada.

No part of this book may be reproduced by any means, nor transmitted, nor translated into a machine language without the written permission of the publisher.

Library of Congress Cataloging in Publication Data:
Gimpel, James F.
  Algorithms in SNOBOL4.

  Bibliography: p.
  Includes index.
  1. SNOBOL (Computer program language) I. Title.
QA76.73.S6G55   001.6'424   75-33850
ISBN 0-471-30213-9

Printed in the United States of America

10 9 8 7 6 5 4 3 2 1

To Anna

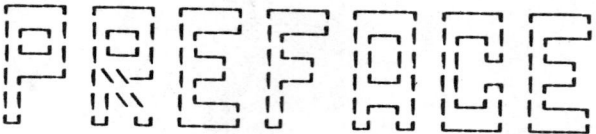

When I first began collecting SNOBOL4 programs for a book, I had two major misgivings. First, I wondered whether there would be enough material and second, I wondered whether the programs would be sufficiently nonobvious to warrant publication. Both fears slowly evaporated. On the one hand, the range of SNOBOL4 applications is as wide as the spectrum of computer uses and this, it seems, is well-nigh inexhaustible. Indeed, an entire book of algorithms and algorithmic techniques has recently appeared [Aho et al, 1974] in which the range of applications and techniques when intersected with that of my own book approximates the empty set. It gives one pause to contemplate the complement of both sets. In the end, I had a considerable amount of material left over and so my one fear was baseless.

As to my other concern, I was happy to discover in the course of writing the book many new and nonobvious ways of programming in SNOBOL4 (not all of my own discovery) so that I can now be confident that the collection of routines are more than merely exercises in the use of the language. Indeed, some routines or techniques were previously believed to be impossible to write in SNOBOL4. For example, employing SNOBOL4 patterns directly in the compilation process, dynamically loading SNOBOL4 functions on a call basis, and determining the compilation numbers of statements compiled at execution time are three problems encountered during the development of production programs which were previously thought simply not doable in the language. These are relatively easily achievable by techniques described in this book (see Programs L_ONE (18.2), DEXTERN (14.2) and LPROG (11.5) respectively). Since I have been a SNOBOL programmer for over a decade and since I am still discovering how to do things in the language, the reader may conclude either that I am a dunce or that the designers of SNOBOL4 have created a very flexible and powerful language that deserves further study and wider use. The remainder of the book will convince him, I hope, that it is the latter and not the former.

Another, less prominent, concern was the relative obscurity of the SNOBOL4 language. While more widely used and available than most languages, it is not so ubiquitous as say Fortran or Cobol. For a variety of reasons such as cheaper machines it is not hard to visualize a future in which SNOBOL4, or at least a SNOBOL4-like approach to life, will play a more prominent role. Also the quest for simplicity of programming may ultimately be achieved by way of semantic richness rather than by feature elimination.

Viewed most generally, the book is a collection of algorithms with SNOBOL4 used as a communication vehicle. The algorithms are decidedly oriented toward the nonnumerical as this is SNOBOL4's forte and as such tend to supplement other published algorithms such as those appearing in the Communications of the ACM which, due to the reliance on Fortran and Algol, are primarily mathematical in nature. Because of its nonnumerical character, the book should be especially helpful to artisans in the humanities and in business applications as well as to the information scientists to whom the work is primarily addressed. The reader is assumed to know or be learning SNOBOL4 and if his knowledge in this respect is a little weak he should be willing to consult an appropriate manual or primer for reference. Little or no assumption is made with respect to his knowledge of other areas of computer science and mathematics.

As a collection of SNOBOL4 algorithms, the book lends itself for direct use by the growing number of SNOBOL4 programmers who may use the programs as is, or modify them to suit their particular application. To further this end, virtually all programs are written as functions with a conscientiously applied naming system so that they can be simply 'plugged in' to existing programs without disturbing things. Hence another purpose is served, i.e., to foster and illustrate a technique of well-structured modular programming which is all too frequently lacking in many SNOBOL4 programs. There is currently great interest and for good reason in goto-less structured programs and while the control structures of SNOBOL4 prohibit adherence to the letter of this dictum, the examples in this book serve to carry out its spirit.

The SNOBOL4 programmer will find much information of an implementation nature not available elsewhere. Most of this is intended to guide him in the writing of more efficient programs but some SNOBOL4 lore is included for his general information. An effort has been made to describe pattern matching more fully and comprehensively than it has been heretofore as this has been one of the murkier aspects of the language.

Finally, the large number of SNOBOL4 example programs should complement well a SNOBOL4 primer or manual in teaching the language. This author's experience has been that programming languages as well as natural languages are most easily taught by varied and intriguing examples. Not only is interest heightened and motivation increased, but the example carries the student forward on a familiar framework and provides a convenient gestalt for later recall. Because of this use as a supplementary text, various features of the language are compartmentalized in the early chapters so that their introduction can be synchronized with a course of instruction. In fact the author has used notes from this book very successfully in teaching a course in nonnumerical programming to members of the staff at Bell Laboratories and to graduate students at Stevens Institute of Technology. A number of exercises have been included to extend its usefulness in the classroom as well as to suggest possible modifications of the routines themselves.

The alert reader will note that the book was prepared by a computer. This was done to permit the automatic testing of the programs. To remain faithful to this idea, all figures, titling, paragraph illumination, etc. were done without succumbing to the temptation of later touchup. Chapter 10 describes in detail some of the routines used in the book's production.

The programs, as presented, are directly applicable to the IBM 360 implementation of SNOBOL4 and SPITBOL. In virtually all cases, these programs can be used with SNOBOL4 processors (including SITBOL) on other machines without change or, at most, by a transliteration of characters.

The writing style has been chosen to be direct, informal and sometimes even cheerful. It is hoped that occasional lapses into whimsy (not expunged by the final version) do not disturb the reader; the intent is not so much to amuse as to present a welcome relief to the frankly difficult task of reading and interpreting programs.

A number of individuals have contributed in one way or another to the production of this book. Thanks go to Frank Boesch, Len Bosack, Fran Brophy, Steve Chen, Bob Dewar, Ralph Griswold, Scott Guthrey, Dave Hanson, Cass Lewart, J. C. Noll, Ivan Polonsky, Mark Rochkind, Larry Samberg, Dick Stone, and Jane Walsh. A special appreciation goes to Ralph Griswold who taught a Computer Science course at the University of Arizona from an early computerized draft of Chapters 2-5 and provided valuable feedback. I am flattered that he was able to expand on this material to produce an excellent and very readable book [Griswold 1974a]. Those having difficulty reading the early chapters here may wish to consult this text.

Finally, thanks go to the management and staff of Bell Laboratories whose consent, cooperation and computers have made this text possible.

James F. Gimpel
Holmdel, New Jersey
May 1, 1975

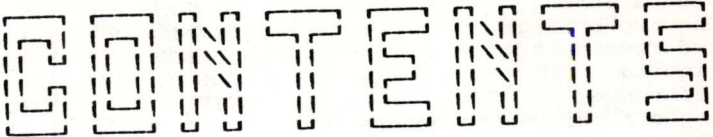

Preface vi

Contents ix

1. Preliminaries 1

    Algorithms and programs
    SNOBOL4 origins
    The future
    SNOBOL4 implementations
    SNOBOL4 foibles
    Structured programming
    Conventions

2. Conversions 22

Upper-case to lower case	UPLO	2.1
BCD code to EBCDIC code	BCD_EBCDIC	2.2
Arabic to Roman	ROMAN	2.3
Base 10 to arbitrary base	BASE10	2.5
Arbitrary base to base 10	BASE10	2.5
Character string to hexadecimal	HEX	2.6
The inverse of HEX	CH	2.7
Day of the week from date	DAY	2.8
Month, day, year from day number	MDY	2.9
Spelled out form of an integer	SPELL	2.10

3. Basic String Functions 41

Ordering the characters of a string	ORDER	3.1
Padding (left	LPAD	3.2
and right)	RPAD	3.3
Counting substring occurrences	COUNT	3.4
Rotating a string	ROTATER	3.5
String transformations		

Reversing a string	REVERSE	3.6
Blending two strings	BLEND	3.7
Balanced reversals	BALREV	3.8
Substringing	SUBSTR	3.9
Set difference	DIFF	3.10
Skimming off unique characters	SKIM	3.11
Lexical comparison	LEXGT	3.12
Alphabetic comparison	AGT	3.13
Swapping variable values	SWAP	3.14
String replacement	REPL	3.15
String quoting	QUOTE	3.16

4. Basic Array Functions   63

Converting strings to arrays	CRACK	4.1
Converting arrays to strings	STRINGOUT	4.2
Sequencing	SEQ	4.3
Array operators	AOPA	4.4
Array searching	FIND	4.5
Array subscripting	AI	4.6
Array truncation	TRUNC	4.7
Array concatenation	CATA	4.8

5. Basic List Processing   79

Read a list	READL	5.1
Read a list in reverse	READRL	5.2
Reverse a list	REVL	5.3
Retrieve the last item of a list	LAST	5.4
Stack manipulation	PUSH	5.5
	POP	5.6
	TOP	5.7
Copying a list	COPYL	5.8
Obtaining the field of a structure	FLD	5.9
Visiting nodes of a list	VISIT	5.10

6. Pattern Theory   99

Patterns and cursors
Nonlinear patterns
Fundamental properties of patterns
Scanning
ARBNO
Recursive patterns

7. Pattern Matching Implementation 121

    Path diagrams
    Derived patterns
    The scanning algorithm - SCAN
    Heuristics
    Compounds
    Unevaluated expressions

8. Pattern Construction 145

Extending BREAK	BREAKREM	8.1
	BREAKX	8.2
Matching balanced strings	BAL	8.3
	FASTBAL	8.4
Pattern complementation	NOT	8.5
Picking off the first alternative	ONCE	8.6
Trouble-free pattern predicates	TEST	8.7
Matching a similar string	LIKE	8.8
Speeding up alternation	OR	8.10
Matching a PL/I statement	PLI.STMT	8.11
Matching OS/360 assembler input	ASM360	8.12

9. Input / Output 166

Pattern-based reading	READ	9.1
Reading Fortran source	FORTREAD	9.2
Reading text	PARAGRAPH	9.3
Reading trees	TREEREAD	9.4
Multi-file reading	MFREAD	9.6
Outputting lines	PUT	9.7
Outputting Fortran source	FORTPUT	9.8
Peeling off SNOBOL4 source segments	PEEL	9.9
Outputting SNOBOL4 source	SNOPUT	9.10

10. Paragraph Formatting 188

Backspace normalization	BNORM	10.1
Image Normalization	INORM	10.2
Line extraction	LINE	10.3
Padding with blanks	PAD	10.4
Measuring the print width	SPACING	10.5
Determining the minimum print width	MINP	10.6
Hyphenation	HYPHENATE	10.7
Determining the printed image	IMAGE	10.8

11. Implementation and Timing   224

```
Symbol tables
Types of compilers
Floating storage
Anatomy of a processor
Determing the clock resolution    RESOLUTION   11.1
Timing program sections           TIMER        11.2
Determining the processor         SYSTEM       11.3
Anatomy of a SNOBOL4 statement
Timing the garbage collector      TIMEGC       11.4
The inner loop
Determining the length of your host  LPROG     11.5
Obtaining a frequency profile     FPROFILE     11.6
Obtaining a time profile          TPROFILE     11.7
```

12. Permutations   255

```
Permutation records
Determining the Ith permutation   PERMUTATION  12.1
Trotter's algorithm               PERM         12.2
String permutations               PERMS        12.3
Permutations with repeated elements  REORDER   12.4
Lexicographic permutations        LPERM        12.5
Inverting a permutation           IP           12.6
```

13. Sorting   274

```
Comparison sorts
  Interchange sorting
    A bubble sort                 BSORT        13.1
    Hoare's QUICKSORT             HSORT        13.2
  Merging
    A linked-list sort            LSORT        13.3
    Sorting by merging arrays     MSORT        13.4
    A frequency sort              FRSORT       13.5
  Selection sorting
    A tournament (and table) sort TSORT        13.6
  Insertion sorting
    A quick and dirty sort        SSORT        13.7
    A tree sort                   INSERT       13.8
    Linearizing the tree          LINEARIZE    13.9
    A backwards insertion sort    INSERTB      13.10
Distributive sorts
```

14. Function Functions   301

Defining an expression	DEXP	14.1
Dynamically loadable functions	DEXTERN	14.2
Self-defined function tracing	FTRACE	14.3
Changing the universe at function crossings	INSULATE	14.4
Large-scale redefinition	REDEFINE	14.5
Arithmetic on physical quantities	PHYSICAL	14.6
Co-routines and state functions		
State-function definition	STATEF	14.7
Multiple stacks	STACK	14.8

15. Numbers   318

Combinations	COMB	15.1
Combinatorial number system	DECOMB	15.2
Infinite precision arithmetic	INFINIP	15.3
Reals and mixed mode		
Reals to integer	FLOOR	15.4
	CEIL	15.5
Transcendental functions		
Finding the square root	SQRT	15.6
The trigonometric functions	TRIG	15.7
The inverse trigonometrics	ARC	15.8
Logarithms	LOG	15.9
Raising to powers	RAISE	15.10

16. Stochastic Strings   341

A random number generator	RANDOM	16.1
A more random generator	RAMM	16.2
Randomly permuted strings	RPERMUTE	16.3
Oneway ciphers	ONEWAY	16.4
Random character (in context)	RCHAR	16.5
Random words	RWORD	16.6
Random selection (with weights)	RSELECT	16.7
Random sentence generation	RSENTENCE	16.8
Random poetry	RPOEM	16.9
Simulation		
Baseball simulation	RSEASON	16.10
Random story generation	RSTORY	16.11

17. Games — 374

Gaming phrases	PHRASE	17.1
Gaming dialogue	QUEST	17.2
The stone game	STONE	17.3
Tick-tack-toe	TICTACTOE	17.4
Game theory		
Functions for card-playing	CARDPAK	17.5
A poker evaluation function	POKEV	17.6
Optimal poker	POKER	17.7

18. Assemblers, Compilers and Macros — 405

An assembler for a simple machine	ASM	18.1
Compiling using SNOBOL4		
A compiler for a simple language	L_ONE	18.2
Partitioning the compiler		
Blank removal in Fortran	BLANKS	18.3
Converting to Polish notation	POL	18.4
A pattern to match a tree	TREE	18.5
Translating from Polish to an intermediate form	TR	18.6
Code generation from 4-tuples	TUPLE	18.7
A general purpose macro processor	GPM	18.8

Solutions to odd-numbered exercises — 441

Appendix A - Cross references of functions — 460

References — 469

Index — 478

ALGORITHMS IN SNOBOL4

CHAPTER ONE

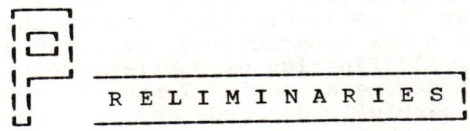

```
┌─────────────────────────────────────┐
│              CONTENTS               │
│                                     │
│      Algorithms and Programs        │
│                                     │
│      SNOBOL4 Origins                │
│                                     │
│      The Future                     │
│                                     │
│      SNOBOL4 Implementations        │
│                                     │
│      SNOBOL4 Foibles                │
│                                     │
│      Structured Programming         │
│                                     │
│      Conventions                    │
└─────────────────────────────────────┘
```

Algorithms and Programs

An algorithm is a sequence of self-evident steps for carrying out some activity. A familiar example of an algorithm is the procedure for 'long' multiplication which multiplies two numbers which are bigger than the operands in a memorized table. The notion of algorithm is actually quite old going back several thousand years B.C. [Knuth 1972], and the word 'algorithm' has a long and convoluted etymology [Knuth Vol.1, p. 1-2].

We say an algorithm is composed of "self-evident steps" to rule out some such phrases as "add salt to taste", or "apply sward to mainskee according to Fig. 3". That is, each step can be mechanically carried out without assistance from a human being. But it is interesting to note that the definition of algorithm is not a rigorous one, since no one can ever give an all-inclusive definition of "self-evident step". What we generally do is devise a special language within which each operation is carefully defined, and this language is used to express all algorithms. Thus we can devise a special machine language as was done by Knuth [Vol. 1-3], or we may devise a matching and replacement operation as was done by Markov [1954], or invent a dialect of some existing language, such as Pidgin ALGOL [Aho et al, 1974], or we may use an existing programming language, such as is used in the Algorithms section of the Communications of the ACM. In this book we will use an existing language, viz. SNOBOL4 [Griswold et al, 1971].

This means that our collection of techniques are not merely algorithms, they are programs as well. Since there is some question (not to mention controversy) as to the distinction between algorithm and program [ACM Algorithm Letters, 1966 and ACM Forum, 1974-1975], it is perhaps worth our trouble to consider these two notions. An algorithm is a method, distinct from any external form, and distinct from any language. On the other hand, a program is a sequence of characters which will implement some process. For example, we may say that a program is 332 characters long, but we may not say such a thing about an algorithm, because an algorithm may be implemented in several different languages producing programs of various lengths. To communicate the algorithm to another human being, we generally require its formulation in terms of concrete symbols. Any such formulation may be said to be a program. Hence, on the surface at least, the notions of algorithm and program would seem to bear the same relationship to each other as the notions of function and expression in mathematics. That is, one is a representation of the other. However, the analogy is somewhat imperfect. Programs are generally written to be run on a digital computer, and, as such, tend to communicate an algorithm to a machine, as opposed to another human being. Programs are a medium whereby a process is effected, and hence are, as it were, part of the machinery. We may therefore expect them to reflect idiosyncrasies not part of the original pure algorithmic notion. That is, programs may be dirty. On the other hand, programs, when coupled with an appropriate linguistic processor, can actually carry out the activity for which they are designed. In short, they work.

Although in principle an algorithm is independent of the particular language in which it is expressed, in practice, this is an impossibility. This is because, as the notion of self-evident step varies, the techniques employed to carry out an overall activity will vary. Thus, a method to compute a hash function will depend on what arithmetic operations (such as division) are available. Random number generators will depend not only on what operations are present, but on whether some forms of arithmetic overflow are permitted. Certainly, string algorithms implemented in a Markov language such as SNOBOL4, which permit string scanning as a fundamental operation, will appear entirely different than when written in some other language. This is unavoidable and is, of course, one of the purposes of a text like this one.

There is currently heightened interest in both algorithms and in programs. For example, there is a famous problem in graph theory called the Koenigsberg Bridge Problem. The problem calls for a path leading across all edges (bridges) of a graph without traveling along any edge twice. A constructive procedure for finding such a path was furnished by Euler in 1736; this has long been regarded as the starting point of modern graph theory. However, it was not until 1973 [Edmonds and Johnson] that anyone specified a method for finding such a path in an amount of time proportional to the number of edges. This particular example is only typical of a general trend. We are no longer content with knowing that a procedure can be carried out, nor even with *how* such a procedure can be carried out. The thrust of much computer science activity is in determining how effective a particular algorithm is, and in carefully specifying an algorithm to maximize efficiency.

Another area of waxing interest is in determining the proper form of a program. Virtually unheard of five years ago, the term 'structured programming' has captured the fancy of the computing fraternity and, at this writing, is perhaps the most used (and abused) term in the literature's lexicon. While the term means many things to many people, the general idea is that many of the ills plaguing the software industry are traceable to the fact that we are incapable of properly structuring large complex tasks. While we can study the strategy of structuring from a language-independent point of view, many of the tactics in forming clear and cogent code depend on the particular tools at one's disposal. Hence, another purpose of this text is to discuss and present methods of organizing, i.e., structuring, SNOBOL4 programs.

Chapter 1 - Preliminaries

> **¶¶¶¶ NOBOL4 ORIGINS**
> ¶
> ¶¶¶¶
> ¶
> ¶¶¶¶

Programs written in SNOBOL4 tend to be oriented toward the manipulation of strings. A string is a sequence of characters and a character is any of the various letters, digits, logograms and punctuation symbols (including the blank) that one might punch on cards or type on an electronic terminal. The stream of characters you are reading now is an example of a string. It has, in fact, been subjected to some of the algorithms to be described in this book.

String processing includes the testing, comparing, scanning, rearranging, transliterating, transforming, inserting, crunching, and deletion of strings. Since programs and data are normally entered into a digital computer in the form of strings and since all data printed is in this form, it might seem that string processing is, and always has been, in the forefront of computer studies. But this is hardly the case. Historically, string processing has been something of a step-child of computation.

The computer was initially perceived as a machine whose primary purpose was performing numerical computations. Getting numbers and programs into the machine was considered incidental to computing rather than occupying any central role. In fact, to program an early machine, one did not use characters at all, but wired up a plug board. A single program took weeks of effort. Humans began to realize that they were more like slaves to the machine than high-priests as they were forced to do an inordinate amount of work just to keep the machine busy. Alt [1972] recalls that, as early as 1947, the team of programmers for the ENIAC discovered a method whereby they could enter programs by merely dialing digits rather than wiring plug boards. To do this they wired the plug-board control permanently in such a way that the machine read the digits and performed associated instructions in much the same way that a modern interpreter might do. This seems to be the world's first higher level language. At any rate, the machine slowed by a factor of five but the technique was the preferred one thereafter. Why? Was it because men are lazy and they want the machine to do <u>all</u> the work? Well, there is a way to express this less argumentatively. The machine was so successful at performing arithmetic that the bottle-neck shifted away from calculations with numbers to the logistics of presenting the problems to the machine. In many ways this problem is still with us.

Peripheral devices for reading characters from paper tape and cards had existed for some time and it did not take long before such devices were attached to the machine for input/output. More importantly, machines were beginning to be designed with the stored-program concept which meant that plug boards did not have to be wired for each different program. Rather, like the trick used with the ENIAC, the machine would translate numbers into instructions, but with the important difference that the numbers did not have to be set manually. They could be read from some external device or they could be computed; in particular, they could be produced by some other program and the Great Age of computer languages was born. From this point on, the evolution of machine design gave way to an evolution of languages, in much the same way that human biological evolution has given way to a cultural evolution. Although the components have changed to give us cheaper, smaller, more efficient machines, the machine organization has remained essentially the same (the Von Neumann Machine). In this organization main storage consists of an aggregate of words each addressable by some assigned number. The data within this storage is entirely unstructured as seen by the hardware. Complex data such as strings, patterns, arrays, etc. are only such in the eyes of the software, not as viewed by the hardware.

The first programming languages were, of course, assembly languages in which generally there is a one-to-one correspondence between lines in the source language and machine instructions. The assembler's job is essentially to translate from names (suitable to humans) to numbers (suitable to machine). This is unnatural for a machine to do and it was resolved essentially by a mechanism known as a symbol table (see Chapter 11). The use and disposition of a symbol table is key to the implementation and understanding of many programming languages in addition to assemblers.

A rather impressive advance was made by the Fortran language which was developed in the mid-1950's. This language was so well designed that today it is perhaps the most widely used programming language in spite of regular denunciations by the academic community. Fortran opened up computation to a large number of programmers who would need to know nothing or very little of the internal organization of the machine in order to start programming (although they usually wind up having to know a great deal). Now an important point to note in connection with Fortran is its peculiarly numerical orientation. The tools provided to the Fortran programmer were totally different than the tools required by the system programmers who had to write assemblers, operating systems and the Fortran compiler itself. Fortran had, for example, a rich mathematical library containing trigonometric functions, exponentiation, etc. which the writers of Fortran had absolutely no need for; on the other hand, Fortran lacked string, character, bit and address data objects which are essential to 'systems' work. Although a step away from the numerical was made in that the language gave the machines the ability to accept programs in human style, it was assumed that the end use would be 'number crunching'.

The first non-numerical language of consequence was IPL [Newell 1957]. This language was developed as a by-product of some experiments in artificial intelligence by Newell, Shaw and Simon in which an attempt was made to mimic the thinking patterns of human beings. In particular, the mental processes involved in theorem-proving were explored [Feigenbaum and Feldman 1963]. IPL is a list-processing language. All data is in the form of lists; the components of a list may be other lists or basic non-decomposable units which are actually addresses referenced symbolically as in an assembler. Numerous built-in functions are available to manipulate lists. In fact, an IPL program is itself a list. The arch-difficulty of IPL is its syntax which is forbiddingly like assembly language.

IPL was soon followed by LISP [McCarthy 1960] which overcame some of the syntactic difficulties of IPL. Rather than place components of a list vertically down the page with symbolic reference to sublists, LISP provided a more abbreviated horizontal notation with nested parenthetical expressions to denote sublists. Moreover, the basic nondecomposible unit, called the atom in LISP, was a string. In LISP, large strings were represented as lists of atoms, and atoms, as their name suggests, could not be decomposed.

A list was the first data object whose size was not fixed for the duration of the program but which could vary as required. Lists are particularly useful in problem areas which are not well understood and cannot, or at least, have not been reduced to easily computable mathematical formulas. Hence list structures have been a favorite form of data for artificial intelligence applications.

COMIT is often considered the first true string processing language. Unlike LISP, the strings of COMIT can be arbitrarily manipulated not by rearranging pointers between fixed strings but by completely rearranging the characters (and hang the cost). With COMIT the string had become a data object; a variable (of sorts) could range over the entire set of strings. These variables were called 'shelves' and were referenced by shelf number. A very powerful process called pattern matching could be applied to such strings and matched substrings could be replaced by other strings. COMIT has one major deficiency; one may not use ordinary common names such as S, LIST, or BILL to denote variables as one might do with numerical variables in Fortran or even assembly language.

The pattern matching notation entered COMIT by way of linguistics where the notation is quite old. The notation was studied in depth by Markov [1954] who treated the replacement operation as a fundamental algorithmic component and showed that all computations were possible using replacement alone. Languages such as COMIT and SNOBOL4 are sometimes referred to as Markov languages even though there is no evident historical connection.

Early work at Bell Laboratories in string processing included the development of a language called SCL (Symbolic Communication Language) by Lee, et al [1962]. SCL extended the facilities of COMIT for string processing but had several deficiencies including an ungainly assembly-language syntax and the absence of variable names (as in COMIT). SCL had certain unique and valuable features such as a run-time compilation and execution of strings, but its most valuable contribution was that it provided a gestation period for SNOBOL.

SNOBOL [Farber et al, 1964] combined two very important ideas, the string processing and pattern matching of COMIT and the symbolic referencing of variables. Thus for the first time in any major language (and possibly ever), a programmer could write:

$$A = B\ C$$

to indicate in a simple and natural way that the string B concatenated with the string C is to be assigned to the string A without disturbing the values of either B or C. The pattern matching operation of COMIT could be invoked in a similarly convenient and concise fashion. Thus for the first time, strings of characters could be manipulated with the notational ease that Fortran provided for numbers.

Unlike Fortran, however, no simple easy translation existed into machine orders. On the IBM 7090, on which SNOBOL was first implemented, concatenation was a complex process requiring the shifting of characters through an ungainly accumulator. Also, the use of variables whose values cannot be destroyed complicates further the operation of concatenation. Thus, we cannot merely direct a pointer from B to C to effect the above concatenation as this would alter B. We cannot copy C onto the tail end of B as this would destroy other data. Rather, a separate section of core is allocated, the strings B and C are copied in, and a pointer is directed from A to the new storage. Since storage is being generated continuously, a process of storage recovery (garbage collection) is required. Thus, the apparent simplicity requires a rather considerable software system to support it. It is not surprising that it appeared relatively late on the programming scene.

SNOBOL's successors, SNOBOL3 [Farber et al 1966] and SNOBOL4 [Griswold et al 1968], while retaining the simple and powerful notation of the original SNOBOL, greatly extended and generalized its facilities. In fact, it is no longer accurate to characterize SNOBOL4 as a string language, since its facilities extend considerably beyond string manipulation.

%%% he Future   How well may we expect SNOBOL4 to fare in the future? Certainly, this is an intriguing question to ask of any language and one which is extremely difficult to answer. To a first approximation, the success of the language will depend on the future importance of nonnumeric data processing. Although numerical programming will doubtlessly increase in the future, non-numerical processing should increase even faster. This is due to the economics of the situation. A computer can multiply two 8-digit numbers together in approximately 6 microseconds whereas it takes a human about 60 seconds. The computer is therefore 10^7 times (or 7 orders of magnitude) faster at this activity than humans. On the other hand, to take a typical string-processing problem, a computer, carefully programmed, will require about two milliseconds to scan a paragraph containing 1000 characters for some string such as 'ALPHA', whereas a human will require approximately 20 seconds. Hence, the machine for the non-numeric problem is only 10^4 (or 4 orders of magnitude) faster than the human. Hence, the machine is better at numerical processing by about 3 orders of magnitude. Since historically computers have been much more expensive than humans it is understandable that they have been applied mostly in those areas with a strong arithmetic flavor.

Another factor to consider in comparing the two kinds of processing is input/output (i/o). Two numbers that are multiplied together typically do not come from typed data but are the result of other computations within the machine. But the string that is being scanned for the word 'ALPHA' has generally entered the machine from some i/o device such as disk, tape or terminal. If we consider disk as typical we find that this device transmits 10,000 characters in a total time of about 100 milliseconds so that our paragraph to be scanned requires 10 milliseconds. Multi-programming operating systems help somewhat to alleviate the problems of delay time due to disk i/o by transferring control to another resident program while i/o is in progress but the program doing i/o must remain resident in main storage thereby consuming resources. If we add a factor for the inefficiency of the transfer of control process and the time expended in transporting the characters from the main storage receiving stations (i/o buffers) into work areas we arrive at a figure very much like ten milliseconds anyway. The net effect is that if the string to be scanned is also read and written we increase the cost of string processing by another order of magnitude.

Another difficulty with string processing that has helped hinder its more rapid development is that string operations are by no means standardized at the machine level. Thus, string processing is not only slower, it is more complicated. In Fortran, the statement:

$$X = Y * Z$$

results in three instructions, LOAD Y, MULTIPLY by Z, and STORE into X. No such corresponding instruction sequence can be produced for typical SNOBOL4 operations such as pattern matching or concatenation. Not only do these operations require more instructions but the methods vary from machine to machine. To begin with, the method of representing strings varies [Madnick 1967]. Representational decisions such as whether to store one character per word or several characters per word may depend on machine characteristics such as whether characters are directly addressable. Another important difference is how string values are bound (assigned) to variables. For example, in PL/I the only very efficient string representation is to allocate a given storage area of maximum size for each string variable. On the other hand, an implementation of the SNOBOL4 language requires that a pointer be associated with each variable which points to the actual characters. This may seem like a minor difference but it is not; in the PL/I approach a simple string assignment such as:

$$S1 = S2$$

results in copying the string. In SNOBOL4, only the address is copied. However, the latter method implies the necessity to garbage collect whereas the former does not. That is, if S1's pointer is overwritten by another pointer, the old string pointed to by S1 may no longer be needed. Experience shows that we cannot afford the luxury of retaining every string ever referenced in a string-processing application, and so, obsolete strings must be discarded.

Even fixing on a common data representation, the method of scanning a string S for a substring, say 'ALPHA', can vary considerably. The IBM 360/370 contains a TRT* instruction which enables the machine to quickly scan a string for one of a set of characters. Thus, we might rapidly scan the string S for the lead character 'A' thus increasing the scan rate. But time is required to set up this rapid scanning. For short strings or for strings containing many A's it would be more economical not to use this special scan. Even given the rapid scan ability, it is not clear that 'A' should be the character searched for. If we assume that P's occur less frequently than A's then a rapid scan for the letter 'P' should be made. Given any such 'P' we can then check for the characters 'AL' directly before and 'HA' directly after.

The setup tradeoff is not unique to the 360/370 architecture. For many machines a fast inner loop can be written to test for a specific character that will be faster than a loop to test for an arbitrary character (which is, say, in a register). If one is willing to invest time in forming characterizations of the subject string (the string being scanned) one can perform a kind of hash test [Harrison 1971] which is very fast. This is inefficient, however, unless the subject string will be scanned repeatedly.

The complexity involved in specifying string algorithms becomes significant in several ways. The languages for string processing must call functions rather than compile in-line code and the linkage overhead further slows down computation. In fact, most implementations tend to be interpretive which greatly reduces the speed of numerical operations if, for simplicity, these are also treated interpretively. Complex language processors cannot be built as rapidly and any string

---

*TRT stands for TRanslate and Test. This is a misnomer; 'Scan and Test' would have been better.

language will experience more difficulty in being reproduced on some other machine. When a processor, such as the macro implementation of SNOBOL4, attempts to be machine-independent, it must sacrifice efficiency significantly. For example, the macro implementation of SNOBOL4 will scan a string for a substring at the rate of 40 microseconds per character (on the IBM 360/Mod 65) a full order of magnitude slower than is possible on that machine essentially because of its machine independence. The most efficient utilization of any machine for typical string operations requires in general a complete restructuring of the program and this tends to inhibit the rapid spread of any language.

The complexity issue becomes important when one realizes that the very great strides in producing economical computation in the last several years have come in the form of minicomputers and microcomputers. These machines tend to be small, new and, as is characteristic of a new industry, exhibit a relatively large number of different designs. All three factors tend to work against a large ambitious SNOBOL-like language.

As the early ENIAC programmers discovered, however, very few problems are so purely numerical that the machine can be casually fed problems and spew out answers. In fact, most of what mankind wants done is non-numerical and is difficult if not impossible to program. By contrast, those problems which are very numerical have probably already been programmed or are embedded so intricately in an essentially non-numerical setting that the numerical part can't be brought easily to the machine. To consider just one example, the filling out of one's income tax can be done conversationally from a computer terminal; the amount of computation that must be performed is insignificant compared to the total programming required to make the system usable by the 'unwashed' (naive) user. Hence, if we are to extend the application of computers to new areas there will surely be much about these areas that is non-numerical.

| **** NOBOL4 Implementations |
| ** |
| **** | changeover
| ** | was written
| **** | In this way,

SNOBOL4 was developed during a period of computer changeover at Bell Laboratories and so the language was written in a system of macros [Griswold 1972]. In this way, the language could relatively easily be transported to the new machine (whatever it was going to be). This had the fortunate consequence of making SNOBOL4 transferrable to other different machines with far less difficulty and with much greater faithfulness to the original design than would otherwise have been possible. This implementation is usually referred to as the MAcro ImplementatioN of SNOBOL4; we will refer to it throughout as MAINBOL.

While MAINBOL is relatively portable, it is also inefficient. This is due primarily to its machine independence. A fair estimate of the cost of machine independence in the case of SNOBOL4 is a factor of two in both space and time.

SPITBOL [Dewar 1971] was developed to overcome the inefficiencies of SNOBOL4, at least for the IBM 360. By writing exclusively in assembly language, by developing new techniques for string handling and storage management, and by compiling executable code rather than running interpretively, SPITBOL was able to better the running speed of MAINBOL by a factor of 7 (this was a median figure of 21 programs tested at Bell Laboratories). SPITBOL is also smaller than MAINBOL by a factor of two. It should also be pointed out that SPITBOL not only did not compromise with the language which so often happens when a language is reimplemented from scratch, but actually extended the language in several significant ways.

The SITBOL processor [Gimpel 1973a & 1974] is a completely new implementation of the SNOBOL4 language for the PDP-10. SITBOL benefitted greatly from the SPITBOL experience, using and improving upon the implementation innovations of SPITBOL. Although SITBOL is an interpreter, it is faster than MAINBOL by a factor of from 3 to 5 and is smaller by a factor of 3. SITBOL is upward compatible with both SNOBOL4 and SPITBOL and contains many language enhancements as well. These three implementations are discussed more fully in Chapter 11.

While these are the only implementations that can claim to support a full SNOBOL4, the FASBOL implementation [Santos 1971] should also be mentioned. This ambitious project is intended to produce a compiler for SNOBOL4 that, in addition to obtaining high speed, supports separate subroutine compilation, compiled patterns and in-line arithmetic. FASBOL, however, lacks several SNOBOL4 features and many of the programs in this book will therefore not run under that system.

```
┌─────────────────────┐
│ %%%% NOBOL4 foibles │
│ %                   │
│ %%%% ┌──────────────┘
│ %    │
│ %%%% │
└──────┘
```
Winston Churchill's famous statement about democracy can be made with particular aptness about SNOBOL4. It is the worst of all programming languages, except for all the rest. By this we mean that SNOBOL4 is a very effective programming language not because it is free of blemish, it actually has quite a few, but because of the many valuable features which it _does_ have. In my own experience, unless the problem is totally numerical, a SNOBOL4 program will be at most half as large as one written in some other language to achieve the same effect. In some cases the reduction in size and complexity is indeed dramatic. SNOBOL4 achieves this code condensation by providing a number of facilities simply not available in most other languages. These include pattern matching which is so rich as to amount to a language within a language. The storage allocation facility, while conceptually simple, completely frees the user from concern over the detailed disposition of data objects. All data objects are represented by a descriptor of fixed size.

This makes it possible to have heterogenous arrays, declaration-free variables and structures, and, most importantly, it allows data objects to be freely transferred between calling and called functions. The historic tendency of interpreters to include symbol tables during execution leads to a number of facilities not normally available. These include indirect referencing, indirect goto's, dynamic definition of functions and structures and, the ultimate source of freedom and flexibility, the ability to compile and execute arbitrary strings. It has a comprehensive tracing and error recovery facility and the ability, through numerous keywords, to provide the user with all sorts of information concerning his running program.

In general, the power and flexibility of SNOBOL4 are unequaled. While the language can be abused, as many languages can be, it has many features which, properly employed, enable large programs to be written with a minimum of difficulty.

This is not to suggest that the language is entirely free of defect. As in any ambitious project of SNOBOL4's magnitude, there are many minor deficiencies. Moreover, merely knowing about them does the language designer no good. Liabilities get 'frozen' into a language since it is impolitic to make non-compatible changes. For casual SNOBOL4 programming we may ignore many of these deficiencies. When composing large programs, however, it is much more important to develop a systematic approach and we must confront these defects squarely.

As remarked by Dunn [1973], a language which is very inefficient can be a burden to use even though the application, such as bootstrapping, is not nominally one demanding high efficiency. Dunn was critical of SNOBOL4 in this regard but his remarks were actually directed to a specific implementation, MAINBOL. As Hanson [1973] remarks, the inefficiencies noted in using MAINBOL do not apply to SPITBOL and SITBOL. Our remarks in this critique will be directed only to the SNOBOL4 language as described by Griswold et al [1971] and not to any particular implementation

1. Perhaps the most noted deficiency of SNOBOL4, especially in an age when the goto is harangued daily, is the lack of good control structures. They are admittedly primitive [Griswold 1974]. There is no IF ... THEN ... ELSE, and no repetition element such as the Fortran DO. One is forced to use many goto's and to invent unique label names. This is a bother and conventions must be adopted. It is not, however, as detrimental to good programming practice as one might think, since it generates dependency on the use of the function which is a superior control structure anyway. See the remarks on Structured Programming.

2. A number of difficulties involve pattern matching. Pattern matching is a complex process and to be used fully requires a comprehensive understanding on the part of the user. For this

reason two chapters in this book are devoted to a theoretical and practical treatment of the subject. But aside from the learning problem there are residual difficulties. One of these is the <u>one-character assumption</u> which we discuss more fully in Chapter 7. The statement below:

HERE   S   LEN(1) $ C   LEN(1) $ D   *LGT(C,D)   =   D C   :S(HERE)

should sort the string S as it repeatedly swaps any consecutive pair of characters not in the correct lexicographic order. Unfortunately, if the last two characters are out of order they are never swapped because the pattern matching mechanism assumes that *LGT(C,D) matches at least one character and that therefore the entire pattern requires at least three characters and that it would be a waste of time to try the pattern on merely two characters. The manual will say to use FULLSCAN mode to circumvent this but, as we will argue later, mode switching is not good practice for large programs.

Predicates may be employed within patterns in spite of the one-character assumption if one employs a trick. See Prog. 8.7.

<u>3.</u> Another heuristic that gives problems is the length-failure, or futility heuristic. Under this assumption, the very natural back-referencing operation becomes virtually unusable. For example, the pattern matching statement:

                S   LEN(3) $ X   ARB   *X

examines the string S for a pair of identical three-character substrings, if it would only work. The first three characters of S are assigned to X and this string is searched for in the remainder of S. Upon failing, the next three characters of S should be assigned to X and the search should continue. This will not happen, however. When *X does not match by reason that there are insufficient characters remaining in S, it signals 'length failure' or 'futility' (See Chapter 7 for a more detailed discussion of these terms). The scanner believes that it can immediately halt all processing and so it does. The result is that, unless the first of the pair of three-character strings begins with the first character, the pattern fails. The error can be cured by FULLSCAN. As indicated in the preceding paragraph, however, this introduces other problems.

<u>4.</u> <u>Pattern building,</u> as distinct from matching, also causes some problems. The pattern matching statement:

                S   LEN(N) . K   =

removes the first N characters from the string S and assigns them to the variable K. Unfortunately, the pattern must be constructed each time the statement is executed. The cost of building the pattern with the concomitant garbage collection will require more time than the pattern match itself. A solution is

$$P = LEN(*N) \, . \, K$$
$$.$$
$$.$$
$$S \quad P \quad =$$

Although this can serve to remove the pattern-building operation from the 'inner loop', it creates several other problems. One has to think up a unique name (P just won't do in a large program). The statement bearing the pattern definition is separated from the statement bearing the match. This can cause difficulties when trying to decipher a large program. The side-effect of setting the variable K without any apparent indication at the pattern match is poor practice. Finally, the use of *N is awkward. The novice tends to overuse the deferred expression and begins to use it where it produces errors. In short, the language becomes more confusing, difficult to learn and error prone.

<u>5.</u> It should be possible in any language to write a function whose behavior will be <u>invariant</u> with respect to its environment. The language that comes closest to this ideal is Fortran with its separately compiled subprogram. SNOBOL4 tends to be worse than others in this respect. For example, the function X(S), below, will return its string argument rotated one character to the right.

```
        DEFINE('ROT(S)T')              :(ROT_END)
ROT     S  RPOS(1) LEN(1) . T =
        ROT = T S                      :(RETURN)
ROT_END
```

This function will behave properly provided (1) LEN, RPOS, binary '.' and concatenation have not been redefined, (2) RETURN has not been redefined, (3) the &ANCHOR mode has not been set, (4) ROT is not used as a label outside the program, and (5) neither ROT, S nor T have been I/O associated.

<u>6.</u> SNOBOL4 contains no block structure so that problems of <u>scope</u> emerge. For example, the function INC(NAME), defined below, will increment the named variable. Also, COUNT will record the number of times the function was called.

```
        DEFINE('INC(NAME)')            :(INC_END)
INC     COUNT = COUNT + 1
        $NAME = $NAME + 1              :(RETURN)
INC_END
```

If COUNT is used outside the function, its current value can be destroyed. That is, there is no way to isolate this use of COUNT from any other that might exist in a program. One may designate that COUNT is local (a misnomer, 'temporary' would be better) to the function. But this would mean that the value of COUNT would be saved before entering the function and restored on return and hence could not be used to count the number of calls.

The named variable being incremented by INC may not be arbitrary. If it were COUNT, then it will be incremented twice. If it were INC, then it would be incremented once, but on return its old value would be restored. If it were NAME, there would be an attempt to add 1 to the string 'NAME' resulting in a fatal error.

7. <u>Function definition</u> is unusually flexible in SNOBOL4, but, as has been noted by Abrahams [1974], it also leads to difficulties. Since function definition is dynamic, the DEFINE must be executed; but where should it be placed? If the DEFINE is placed in some initialization section separated from the body of the function by some distance, programs become difficult to follow. To place the DEFINE adjacent to the body of the function, which is good practice, it is necessary to use a hop-around construct as we have done above with ROT(A) and INC(NAME). But this is troublesome and wastes space. Execution time space is required for: (1) the string bearing the function prototype, (2) the code required for the DEFINE, the hop-around and the target of the hop, and (3) the string bearing the hop-around label. The third item above is explained more fully below.

8. By means of the <u>indirect goto</u> it is possible to do a multi-way branch. For example:

: ($TRIM(INPUT))

will read a label and go to it. But this requires that every label must be in the symbol table at run-time. Not only must the physical characters of each label be present but an amount of additional storage to house other data associated with a name. This additional information averages about 32 characters across several implementations. A 40-character storage penalty for each label is considerable for large programs.

9. In SNOBOL4, INPUT/OUTPUT is markedly clean and uncluttered; but it generally lacks facilities. If one is only transmitting strings to sequential files, SNOBOL4 is adequate. However, no special facilities exist for printing columns of numbers or for doing direct-access I/O. Output media intended for human viewing is really two dimensional and merely outputting strings is inadequate. Although an extension to the language was made in this regard [Gimpel 1972a] space limitations have excluded it from most implementations.

10. The statement

X = X * .1

results in a strange error. One must write '0.1', not '.1', because <u>unary '.'</u> is an operator, which should be applied to a variable, not a value such as 1.

11. There are several <u>precedence</u> anomolies. In virtually all programming languages, the operators '/' and '*' have the same precedence and associate to the left. In SNOBOL4, '*' has a higher precedence than '/'.

The precedence of concatenation is one of the lowest whereas it should be one of the highest. Thus,

                A B + C

is parsed as A (B + C).

The two highest precedence binary operators, viz. '¬' and '?' associate differently. The first associates to the right and the second associates to the left. What is one then to make of:

                A ¬ B ? C

12. SNOBOL4 usurps the characters '<' and '>' for bracketing which renders them unusable as operators. This means one must use the relatively primitive: GT(X,Y), GE(X,Y), etc. But square brackets are available, at least in ASCII, for the purpose and these are unused.

13. The use of a blank to denote <u>concatenation</u> seems to force the language to require surrounding binary operators with blanks. Thus, it is a mistake in SNOBOL4 to write 'A+B'; one must write 'A + B'. This causes learning problems.

The blank operator also requires placing a function call adjacent to its arguments. A common mistake for beginners, for example, is to write:

                TRIM (INPUT)

and wonder why the TRIM function didn't work. No error can be signalled for this sequence, of course, which dutifully prepends the input with the current value of the variable TRIM which is probably null.

14. To compound the learning difficulties, the blank binary operator is also used to denote pattern matching. If one is teaching SNOBOL4 one must explain why the sixth blank below denotes pattern matching while the others denote concatentation.

              ((A B C) A B C) A B C

15. While SNOBOL4 is more than just a string language, the facilities of the language are geared much more for string processing than any other kind. For example, although SNOBOL4 contains <u>arrays</u> there is no way to automatically sequence through an array as one can by pattern matching a string or as is possible with APL. Worse, SNOBOL4 does not even contain a conventional repetition element like the DO-loop. Also, the tracing facilities, while quite useful for strings yield little information with arrays. When accessing strings to do fairly complex activities one does not mind paying a small interpretive overhead since this is a relatively small part of the overall computation. But the interpretive overhead of array processing can be several times the cost of accessing the array. The net result is that although SNOBOL4 contains arrays, it is not very good at processing them. One is much better off in some other language. Similar remarks may be made with perhaps less force about the programmer-defined datatype.

<u>16.</u> There is some <u>language clutter</u> which could be removed. In particular &TRIM, &INPUT and &OUTPUT were introduced into the language to overcome implementation inefficiencies of MAINBOL. The &ANCHOR keyword invites unstructured programming and should be abolished. The VALUE function was a nice idea but was defined incorrectly and, in its current form, is useless. I know of no serious uses of the SUCCEED pattern but, if needed, one could use ARBNO(NULL) were it not for the fact that SNOBOL4 attempts to 'protect' you from having a null argument to ARBNO.

<u>17.</u> Although essential for some applications, <u>FENCE and ABORT</u> are difficult to learn and use and do not compound very well. A NOT function would have been better. See chapters 6-8 in this respect.

It is hoped that the reader has not by now come to the conclusion that SNOBOL4 is an utter abomination. With care and foresight many of these deficiencies can not only be overcome but turned to advantage. We will see ample evidence of this in this and the remaining chapters. It is also the writer's hope that this catalog of defects can serve to dispel the notion that a recognition of a language's strengths is tantamount to being in love with the language and hence blind to its flaws. (This happens frequently but it is not a universal phenomenon.)

Having thusly disposed of the bath water, and assuming that we still have our baby, we may proceed to the important topic of:

```
┌─────────────────────────────┐
│ ％％％％  tructured Programming │
│ ％                           │
│ ％％％％                       │
│    ％                        │
│ ％％％％                       │
└─────────────────────────────┘
```
An unsophisticated programmer, in a surge of programming frenzy, will write a large program straight-out over several pages which will exhibit no evidence of structure. Such programs generally prove to be bitterly difficult to debug and modify. Dijkstra [1968] cited the over use of the goto as one of the most flagrant abuses in such run-on programs. Willy-nilly transfers of control from one program segment to another results in a mangle of spaghetti-like confusion. In fact, the abuse has become so

great that a controversy has arisen over whether the goto should be _permitted at all_ by a programming language.

It is this writer's contention that improper use of the goto is a symptom rather than a cause of poor structuring. To properly structure a large program it must be decomposed into smaller subroutines (or, equivalently, functions, procedures, etc.). Subroutinizing reduces the overall size of a program since the same section of code may be referred to by several different statements. It also allows greater flexibility in the writing of a program since it is often unclear at the start where an important subactivity will be needed. But the most important aspect of subroutinizing is the structure it endows the overall program. With reasonably well-defined interfaces between subroutines, the complexity of a large program becomes merely the sum of the complexity of the individual component routines, not the product or some higher order function. Under such circumstances, the subroutine call becomes the primary method of inter-routine transfers of control. Intra-routine transfers of control can quite comfortably be made with the goto. In fact, many algorithms described in a half dozen or so English statements use the goto as a means of making more precise that which might otherwise be ambiguous. Far from being inherently evil, the goto is a powerful, and the most basic, control element. It is perhaps because of this power that it can so easily be abused.

But whereas we may elect to keep the goto as a control element of last resort, it is not generally the best control structure for all circumstances. In particular, the IF ... THEN ... ELSE ... sequence as well as a repetition structure (such as the Fortran DO) are ideal in many instances. Their absence in SNOBOL4 has led some critics to be unkind to the language. To a certain extent the deficiency is real, but is ameliorated considerably by what may be called the implicit iteration of pattern matching. Thus, the statement:

$$S \quad ' \; ' \; = \; ''$$

which removes the first blank from the string S contains an implicit iteration over the characters of the string S. The result is a statement which is considerably easier to understand than an explicit sequencing. Thus the reason for the lack of conventional control structures in SNOBOL4 is that the need for them is not felt so acutely. As confirmation of this supposition, APL, with its many forms of implicit array iteration, also lacks the standard control structures (other than the goto).

It would not be correct to conclude that to write large programs in SNOBOL4 we subroutinize everything in sight and let it go at that. Certain conventions must be followed with respect to names of labels, global variables, keywords, etc. so that separately written subroutines can co-exist comfortably. A system of conventions of this kind is followed in writing the individual functions in this book so that they indeed can be joined together without mutually interfering with each other. Many of the routines, in fact, call each other and the text processor which produced this book is a rather large assemblage (over 3000 statements) of functions which in some cases are identical to routines described and in all cases were written according to the conventions advocated.

Conventions In order to write well-structured programs in SNOBOL4 it is rather more important to establish a system of conventions than in other languages. This is because the language does not support separately-compiled functions and hence there is a potential problem with name conflicts. Another problem has to do with mode switches. For example, if we write a function which uses pattern matching, we are not generally free to set the mode of &ANCHOR. To do so would set the mode of &ANCHOR for the calling routine. But how can the called function know which setting exists for the &ANCHOR switch? There are only two ways out of this dilemma; either the called routine saves the old value of &ANCHOR, assigns it a new value, and restores the old value before returning, or it makes an assumption as to what its value will be and all routines live by that assumption. The first method is clearly too awkward and is made more odious by the thought that we would have to do the same for &FULLSCAN as well. Hence, our routines will assume these keywords to contain certain values. There are perhaps good reasons to always assume &ANCHOR to be on and/or to assume &FULLSCAN to be on, but we will abide by the convention that they always have their default value of 0 (off).

It is possible to vary the value of variables having preassigned (pattern) values such as ARB, BAL, FAIL, etc. However, it should be obvious that it is poor practice to change these values for normal programming. The only exception may be to modify ARB (and other patterns) in an upperward compatible way for debugging purposes. For example, if we set:

           ARB = ARB $ OUTPUT

at the beginning of the program then every string matched by ARB will be printed. Since such a modification only produces an upward compatible side-effect, and since the change is only temporary, no ill can come of it.

It is also poor practice to redefine built-in operators and functions unless they are done in an upward compatible manner. For example, since the SIZE function is not pre-defined for array arguments it is not necessarily poor practice to redefine the SIZE function so that if the argument is an array it will return the number of elements in the array (a function which is very possible to write in SNOBOL4). On the other hand to redefine SIZE where it is already defined is to produce the sort of global change in the language which makes subroutinizing difficult.

How should names be kept separate to avoid collision? Conflicts can occur with names of functions, variables, and labels. Since the number of functions are relatively small (a few hundred at most) there is generally no problem here. The names of functions in this book were generally chosen after English words and if this is the case conflicts are readily apparent.

Variable-name conflicts could be a severe problem if one does not subroutinize. If one does, the problem virtually disappears. One simply designates the variables to be temporary to some given procedure. If the functions are kept short enough no problems arise. It's occasionally necessary to use global variables. Here potential conflicts can arise unless one is careful. We will use the general policy of designating such global names with a name bearing one of the special characters '.' or '_'. This tends to reduce the possibility of collision. We will typically use the '.' in a pattern name to suggest that a variable is being assigned a value. Thus we may write:

```
           LEN1.T  =  LEN(1) . T
```

and the name becomes a convenient mnemonic. In fact if this is not done a strong argument can be made that the use of a pre-defined pattern is too obscuring to be used as a general programming practice.

To keep labels from conflicting we will employ the usual practice of appending an identifying suffix to some convenient root. Thus, for function ALPHA, we can use labels ALPHA_1, ALPHA_2, etc. Labels such as LOOP or DONE are obviously poor practice except for examples or in a main routine but we always shudder a bit when forced to contemplate them.

We will rely a great deal on the following convention for defining functions. The DEFINE function must be _executed_ in SNOBOL4 before a function can be defined. For well-structured programs, the body of the function should be adjacent to the function definition. The function body should not be entered other than via a function call. Hence we will use a _hop-around_ convention. To define the function ALPHA() we write:

```
          DEFINE('ALPHA()')
          Initialization for ALPHA
                                                   :(ALPHA_END)
ALPHA

          Function body of ALPHA

ALPHA_END
```

As indicated here, unless we have special reasons for doing otherwise the entry label will be the same as the name of the function. Following the call to DEFINE(), we have what is termed the _initialization section_. Here we may assign patterns to variables, initialize tables, etc. The initialization section is especially helpful in SNOBOL4 since for efficiency reasons many patterns should be defined 'out-of-line'. The ability to perform initializing computations on a per-function basis is not generally available in most programming languages. Hence, the hop-around technique, which at first appears to be a cumbersome apparatus for overcoming a language deficiency, becomes a language asset for structuring one's programs.

Other conventions are as follows. Although the initial value of each variable is the null string, we will not generally use this fact. Hence, the initialization section is free to modify any variable not used globally (i.e., one whose name does not contain one of the special characters '.' or '_'). An exception is the variable NULL whose value is never changed. Of course any variable which is a temporary variable of a function will be automatically assigned the null string before function entry and this fact will be used throughout.

Occasionally a transfer is made to the label ERROR. It is not necessarily presumed that a label named ERROR actually appears in the source program. If a branch is attempted to some undefined label, the program will halt and an appropriate diagnostic will be given. This will indicate where the error occurred. It is also helpful in this regard and in general to always set &DUMP on (=1) at the start of the program as this can provide vital clues as to the source of any error. It is easy enough to turn the &DUMP off if the program terminates normally.

CHAPTER TWO

CONVERSIONS

CONTENTS

UPLO	2.1
BCD_EBCDIC	2.2
ROMAN	2.3
BASEB	2.4
BASE10	2.5
HEX	2.6
CH	2.7
DAY	2.8
MDY	2.9
SPELL	2.10

Program 2.1 - UPLO

This chapter covers basic conversions of a kind frequently needed in a computer environment. We are presenting this material first, not necessarily because it is the easiest but because it is relatively unsophisticated. That is, the intent of a program that does a conversion will probably be clear even if nothing else is. SNOBOL4 is a good language to represent conversion algorithms because frequently the objects converted are strings. This is natural because we are normally converting between two external representations of the same thing and the way we represent things externally is most often via strings of characters.

Program 2.1 UPLO

UPLO is a program for converting all upper case characters within a string to lower case and vice versa. Thus UPLO('UPlo') will return 'upLO'. In all cases, characters which cannot be converted are <u>left unchanged</u>. The program assumes the IBM 360 EBCDIC encoding of characters [IBM360a; Appendix F]. There are many uses for such a program owing to the relative difficulty of keypunching lower case letters and the growing use of printers with lower case graphics.

> UPLO(S) will convert upper case to lower case and vice versa. The argument S is an arbitrary string. Nonalphabetic characters are ignored.

```
                DEFINE('UPLO(S)')
```

> The first problem is to obtain the sequence of lower case letters. This is done by a computation to avoid having to type lower case letters in the program itself. The computation depends on the fact that the upper case letters and the lower case letters are arranged in an identical pattern on the EBCDIC chart. The only difference is that the lower case letters are in the 3rd quadrant (Q3) of &ALPHABET and the uppers are in the 4th quadrant (Q4).

```
           &ALPHABET   LEN(128)  LEN(64) . Q3 LEN(64) . Q4
           UPPERS_  =  'ABCDEFGHIJKLMNOPQRSTUVWXYZ'
           LOWERS_  =  REPLACE(UPPERS_,Q4,Q3)
           UP_LO    =  UPPERS_ LOWERS_
           LO_UP    =  LOWERS_ UPPERS_
                                              :(UPLO_END)
```

> Then the function UPLO merely consists of a call to the REPLACE function.

```
UPLO       UPLO   =  REPLACE(S, UP_LO, LO_UP)       :(RETURN)
UPLO_END
```

Epilogue

As discussed in chapter one, we will generally begin a function with a call to DEFINE. Following this is the initialization section. Here we initialize variables such as UP_LO so that subsequent execution is fast. After initialization a transfer around the function body is made to a label which is normally the function name followed by '_END' (UPLO_END in our example). When the function is called, execution normally begins at the statement labeled with the same name as the name of the function (UPLO in this example).

The encoding of UPLO depends on the arrangement of characters in the string &ALPHABET. The characters shown in the box below are the result of printing &ALPHABET on the printer used to produce this book.

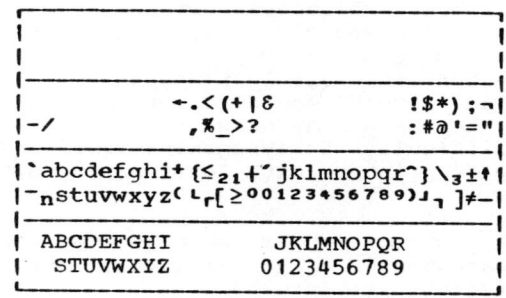

In EBCDIC, &ALPHABET contains 256 characters which may be regarded as consisting of four quadrants of 64 characters each. In the above, each quadrant is printed in a separate sector as two lines of 32 characters each. It is easy to see from this table that the relative positions of the upper and lower case alphabets in their respective quadrants is the same. Hence it is possible to obtain the lower case alphabet from the upper case by a simple replacement.

Although UPLO is character-code dependent, it can easily be modified for ASCII [ASCII]. In this case, &ALPHABET contains 128 characters whose printing graphics are shown (in order) below.

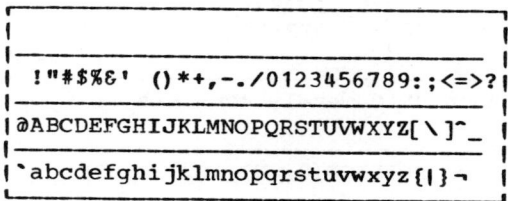

UPLO can be modified to operate with such an &ALPHABET by changing five numbers.

```
┌─────────────────┐
││   Program    ││
││     2.2      ││
││  BCD_EBCDIC  ││
└─────────────────┘
```
The transition to the 3rd generation brought with it, for IBM users, a character conversion problem. The old 6-bit BCD code was replaced by an expanded 8-bit code. One disadvantage of the older code was that business and scientific users had different graphics for the same card code. In particular, the 5 characters #∂%<& known only to the business users had the same card code respectively as ='()+ which were known only to the scientific user. These two sets diverged in the 3rd generation. The fortunate business users saw no change, but the scientific user (such as the FORTRAN programmer) suddenly found lots of strange characters in his source program.

In such cases one would like to write a program to convert an input deck with these 5 commercial characters into the scientific equivalents. One such program is Program 2.2; it appears on one line and in the days when we were converting to 3rd generation, I found it convenient to carry such a card on my person as a ready answer for anyone wishing to know the whereabouts of a program for translating BCD to EBCDIC.

```
┌─────────────────────────────────────────────────────────────────┐
│ This is a complete program to convert BCD card code to          │
│ EBCDIC card code.  Input cards will be read in, converted,      │
│ and punched.  When no more cards remain the program             │
│ terminates.                                                     │
└─────────────────────────────────────────────────────────────────┘
```
L   PUNCH = REPLACE(INPUT, "#∂%<&", "='()+")   :S(L)   ;END

Epilogue
─────────

This is a neat and compact example of the use of the REPLACE function. A card is read in and any character of the second argument found in this card is replaced by the corresponding character in the 3rd argument. The REPLACE function is fast, proceeding at machine speeds (on the IBM 360-70 a 256-byte table is set up, after which a single instruction (TR) translates the entire string [IBM360a]). The REPLACE function is not only extremely useful for such transliterations but, as we shall see in the next chapter, can be used for permuting and rearranging characters as well.

```
┌─────────────────┐
││   Program    ││
││     2.3      ││
││    ROMAN     ││
└─────────────────┘
```
ROMAN will convert its argument, assumed to be an integer, into Roman numeral format. Thus, ROMAN(256) returns 'CCLVI'. Though a classic problem in string manipulation, the reader may wonder about the utility of such a program (are we going to use SNOBOL4 to print tombstones?). But there is one

common application in which such an algorithm is essential, viz. a text formatter which must number pages preceding the first with Roman numerals. In such cases it is customary to perform computations (such as adding one for each page) in the normal Arabic system before converting. In this example, the Roman numeral would normally appear in lower case. This conversion, if necessary, can be done using UPLO, Program 2.1.

Although it occasionally happens that we wish to convert from Arabic to Roman we almost never want to do the reverse so that we will be content here with going in one direction only.

```
| ROMAN(N)  will  return a string equal to the Roman numeral |
| equivalent of the integer N.  N is assumed to be less than |
| 4000 and nonnegative.                                      |
```

```
              DEFINE('ROMAN(N)T')                    :(ROMAN_END)
| Entry point:  remove the last digit and call it T.           |
ROMAN      N    RPOS(1)   LEN(1) . T =            :F(RETURN)
| Convert T to its equivalent Roman form.  Then append it to |
| the Romanized form of the preceding digits  multiplied  by |
| 10.                                                        |

              '0,1I,2II,3III,4IV,5V,6VI,7VII,8VIII,9IX,'
+          T     BREAK(',') . T                   :F(FRETURN)
           ROMAN = REPLACE(ROMAN(N), 'IVXLCDM', 'XLCDM**') T
+                                                 :S(RETURN) F(FRETURN)
ROMAN_END
```

Epilogue

The big trick here is to realize that it is relatively easy to multiply a Roman number by 10 by merely doing a transliteration of its symbols into the next higher 'octave'. This is done by REPLACE. Another trick which reduces the size of the program is to compact a set of information into a long string and use SNOBOL4's powerful pattern matching to extract the information.

This is not the fastest encoding of ROMAN. There was no effort to economize on time because it may be presumed that the use of ROMAN is infrequent. If anything, an effort was made to reduce the size of the program in order to minimize storage consumption. This is good practice for seldomly used code.

Programs 2.4 & 2.5 - BASEB & BASE10

```
┌─────────────────────┐
│ │   Programs     │ │
│ │   2.4 & 2.5    │ │
│ │ BASEB & BASE10 │ │
└─────────────────────┘
```

The decimal system in common use to represent numbers is a positional system, meaning that the value of a digit depends on its position. Generally, in a positional number system, the numeral

$$a_1 a_2 \ldots a_n$$

represents the number

$$a_1 B^{n-1} + a_2 B^{n-2} + \ldots + a_n$$

where B is some integer called the base. The decimal system uses B = 10. A positional system can represent arbitrarily large quantities with only a finite number (equal to B) of symbols. This is in contrast to the Roman numbers where the value of a symbol depends on the symbol itself and not on its position. Hence, for arbitrarily large numbers, we need arbitrarily many symbols.

Though our current decimal system was introduced in Europe by the Arabs in the 9th Century, the system did not flourish there until the 16th Century Spanish merchants were humiliated by the arithmetic prowess of the stone-age Mayan Indians who were using a base 20 positional system. See Von Hagen [1960].

The growth of computer systems in which base 2 arithmetic is used internally to represent numeric quantities has drawn attention to the representation of numbers in various bases and has led to the need in many cases to convert from one base to another.

In this section we include two routines for base conversion. BASEB(N,B) will convert integer N into its representation in base B. Thus, BASEB(15,3) will return '120' as this is the base 3 representation of 15. Conversely, BASE10(N,B) will convert the numeral N in base B to the equivalent decimal number. Thus BASE10('120',3) will return '15'. This is customarily written

$$(120)_3 = 15$$

where the absence of an explicit base indication implies base 10.

To convert N from base b_1 to base b_2 we could combine the functions thusly:

$$BASEB(BASE10(N, b_1), b_2)$$

The characters used to indicate digits higher than 9 are the letters of the alphabet with A equal to 10, B equal to 11, etc. This seems to be the most common method of denoting the higher digits. On the other hand, there are dissenters who

Chapter 2 - CONVERSIONS

say that this encoding is unnatural in that the even letters
(B, D, F, etc.) correspond to odd numbers (11, 13, 15, ...)
whereas the odd letters (A, C, E, ...) correspond to even numbers (10, 12, 14, ...). These people might prefer the letters
'XABC.. rather than 'ABC... another method might be to use
some arbitrary sequence from the end of the alphabet such as
'UVWXYZ' rather than 'ABCDEF'. In either case, the functions
BASEB and BASE10 can be modified to suit by changing the value
of the global variable BASEB_ALPHA.

| BASEB(N,B) will convert the integer N to its base B representation. B may be any positive integer ≤36.

```
            DEFINE('BASEB(N,B)R,C')
    BASEB_ALPHA   =   '0123456789ABCDEFGHIJKLMNOPQRSTUVWXYZ'
                                                   :(BASEB_END)
```

| Entry point and top of loop: If N is zero we are done

```
BASEB           EQ(N,0)                              :S(RETURN)
```

| Obtain the base-B representation (C) of the least
| significant digit of N.

```
            R  =  REMDR(N,B)
            BASEB_ALPHA   TAB(*R)   LEN(1) . C    :F(ERROR)
```

| Tack result onto previous value, update N and loop.

```
            BASEB  =  C BASEB
            N   =   N / B                           :(BASEB)
BASEB_END
```

| BASE10(N,B) will convert the string N assumed to be a
| numeral expressed in base B arithmetic to decimal (base
| 10).

```
            DEFINE('BASE10(N,B)T')
    BASEB_ALPHA   =   '0123456789ABCDEFGHIJKLMNOPQRSTUVWXYZ'
                                                  :(BASE10_END)
```

| Entry point and top of loop. Find first digit in N and
| determine its value in base 10.

```
BASE10       N   LEN(1) . T   =                      :F(RETURN)
             BASEB_ALPHA   BREAK(*T)   @T            :F(ERROR)
```

| Then use standard conversion algorithm for converting to
| base 10.

```
            BASE10  =  (BASE10 * B) + T             :(BASE10)
BASE10_END
```

Epilogue

In BASEB, the search for the representation of the Rth character is done using the pattern

$$\text{TAB}(*R) \quad \text{LEN}(1) \quad . \quad C$$

This pattern is identical in performance to the pattern

$$\text{TAB}(R) \quad \text{LEN}(1) \quad . \quad C$$

Strangely enough, the former is faster in SPITBOL. This is because TAB(*R) LEN(1) . C is a constant valued pattern and can be pre-evaluated, whereas the same pattern without the '*' is not constant. It requires more time, in general, to form the pattern than it does to do the pattern match so that much has been gained. A similar remark can be made about the pattern matching statement involving BREAK(*T) immediately following label BASE10.

In SNOBOL4, similar considerations apply except that the programmer must pre-evaluate his own expressions; the compiler will not do it for him. Thus

$$\text{CONVERT\_R} = \text{TAB}(*R) \quad \text{LEN}(1) \quad . \quad C$$

. . .

$$\text{BASEB\_ALPHA} \quad \text{CONVERT\_R}$$

would yield a more efficient rendition, in SNOBOL4, of the function BASEB. This is recommended if speed is of importance. The pattern CONVERT_R could be defined in the initialization section of the function thereby keeping the pattern associated with the function. But note that

$$\text{CONVERT\_R} = \text{TAB}(R) \quad \text{LEN}(1) \quad . \quad C$$

. . .

$$\text{BASEB\_ALPHA} \quad \text{CONVERT\_R}$$

would not be valid because the pattern CONVERT_R would be using the value of R at the time of assignment and not at the time of the pattern match.

We will not always use a deferred form such as TAB(*R) but will generally prefer TAB(R). This is simpler and is not implementation dependent. It is always easy enough to modify the function so that a pattern is not continually being generated. Choosing the path of least resistance, as we will tend to do, has another advantage. For those programs for which space is more important than time, pre-defining the pattern is actually less efficient for the pattern must then occupy space continuously and not merely when it is needed.

```
┌─────────────────┐
│ │ Program   │ │   To a human being a character is some
│ │   2.6     │ │   geometric configuration, but to a machine it
│ │   HEX     │ │   is just a sequence of bits.  On the IBM
└─────────────────┘   360-370 series machines, a character is a
sequence of 8 bits. For example, the pattern of bits represen-
ting the letter A is
```

$$11000001$$

it is obviously more convenient to write these 8 bits in base 16 notation so that A comes out looking like

$$C1$$

HEX(S) is a function which will accept a string of characters and return a string of hexadecimal digits representing its internal representation. Thus

$$HEX('ABA')$$

returns 'C1C2C1'.

All characters have an 8-bit code and all 8-bit codes represent some character, but not all characters are printable. Thus the SNOBOL4 keyword &ALPHABET is a string of all the 8-bit characters starting with 00000000 and going on up to 11111111 (in numerical order). If this string were to be printed (as we did earlier) most of the characters would appear blank. The graphical image printed is a function of the printer. The IBM 1403 printer has room for at most 240 graphics. Moreover, to increase printing speed there are many duplications of the more frequently appearing characters. The net result is that there are seldom more than 100 graphics in &ALPHABET. Thus, an important use of HEX is for processing data which is not character oriented and is therefore not easily dealt with in terms of characters. For example, suppose we wish to scan the input text for 2 consecutive occurrences of the hexadecimal constant 50. Then the following statement would perform the scan

```
            HEX(INPUT)    POS(0) ARBNO(LEN(2))   '5050'
```

┌───┐
│ HEX(S) will return the hexadecimal (internal) representa-   │
│ tion of the string S.   │
└───┘

```
                  DEFINE('HEX(S)')
```
┌───┐
│ Prepare tables of the 1st and 2nd hex digits.   │
└───┘

```
              H       = '0123456789ABCDEF'
              HEX_2ND = DUPL(H,16)
HEX_1         H LEN(1) . T =                         :F(HEX_END)
              HEX_1ST = HEX_1ST DUPL(T,16)           :(HEX_1)
```

Program 2.7 - CH

```
                                                                Page 31
┌─────────────────────────────────────────────────────────────────────┐
│ Entry point:  Form the first and second digits separately           │
│ and then blend them.                                                │
└─────────────────────────────────────────────────────────────────────┘
HEX              HEX    =  BLEND(REPLACE(S, &ALPHABET, HEX_1ST),
+                          REPLACE(S, &ALPHABET, HEX_2ND))   :(RETURN)
HEX_END
```

Names referenced by HEX:	Name	Type	Where defined
	BLEND	Function	Program 3.7

Epilogue

We have taken an unusual approach in encoding HEX. It might seem at first that it would be better to prepare some table which would yield the correct pair of characters for every character in the &ALPHABET. But we have already noted how fast REPLACE can be so that we can obtain either hex digit extremely quickly. The question remains as to how we may swiftly merge the 2 character sequences. This we do by the program BLEND (Program 3.7) which merges 2 equi-length strings. As we shall see, BLEND also uses the REPLACE function in an unobvious way and is quite rapid.

```
┌─────────────────┐
││   Program    ││   CH(H) will take a string of hexadecimal
││     2.7      ││   digits (H) and convert them to the cor-
││     CH       ││   responding character sequence. Thus
└─────────────────┘   CH('C1C2') will return 'AB'. CH is the in-
verse of HEX so that CH(HEX(S)) = S. The conversion provided
by CH can be useful for obtaining characters that can be prin-
ted but not typed. Thus CH('818283') returns 'abc'.
```

```
┌─────────────────────────────────────────────────────────────────────┐
│ CH(HEX) will convert the sequence of hexadecimal digits             │
│ into the corresponding character string. CH is the inverse          │
│ of HEX.                                                             │
└─────────────────────────────────────────────────────────────────────┘

                 DEFINE('CH(HEX)T,C,N')
                                                           :(CH_END)
┌─────────────────────────────────────────────────────────────────────┐
│ Entry point: Remove 2 characters from string HEX. Then              │
│ convert to decimal (using BASE10) and retrieve the indexed          │
│ character from the &ALPHABET.                                       │
└─────────────────────────────────────────────────────────────────────┘
CH               HEX    LEN(2) . T    =              :F(RETURN)
                 C    = BASE10(T,16)
                 &ALPHABET   LEN(C)   LEN(1) . C
                 CH   = CH C                          :(CH)
CH_END
```

Names referenced by CH:	Name	Type	Where defined
	BASE10	Function	Program 2.5

Page 32   Chapter 2 - CONVERSIONS

Epilogue

The method used to program CH is to treat each pair of hexadecimal characters as a number in base 16. This number can be converted to decimal using BASE10 (Program 2.5). This decimal number can then be used to index into the keyword &ALPHABET.

```
| Program |
|   2.8   |
|   DAY   |
```
DAY will return the day of the week given some date. Thus DAY('3/24/71') will return 'WEDNESDAY', and DAY(DATE()) will return the current day. As an added bonus, the global variable D will be set to an integer between 0 and 6 inclusive to give a numeric indication of the day. If a year other than one from the 20th century is intended then a 4-digit year must be given as in DAY('3/24/1825'). If the year is missing, the current year is assumed. Thus:

'CHRISTMAS FALLS ON ' DAY('12/25') ' THIS YEAR.'

will be a sematically correct string when evaluated, no matter in what year it is evaluated.

The program assumes the Gregorian Calendar and will accept dates for any date from the 2nd century onward (i.e. after 100 A.D.). The extrapolation into the time period before the Gregorian calendar went into effect (1588), however, will not agree with historical records.

It is interesting to note that the revision of the calendar followed on the heels of the discoveries of Indian civilizations in the New World whose elaborate and involved calendrics are said to be even more accurate than our present Gregorian calendar (see Morley [1956] for example).

```
| DAY(DATE) will return the day of the week appropriate to
| the given DATE.  DATE is given as month/day/year.
```

DEFINE('DAY(DATE)M,Y')

```
| YEAR_ is the number of days in a year.  YEAR_4, CENT_ and
| CENT_4 are the number of days in the cyclic time periods
| of respectively 4 years, a century and 4 centuries.
```

```
         YEAR_   =  365
         YEAR_4  =  4 * YEAR_ + 1
         CENT_   =  (25 * YEAR_4) - 1
         CENT_4  =  4 * CENT_ + 1
         DAY_ZERO =  2
                                              :(DAY_END)
```

```
| First extract the month, day, and year.  If the year is
| null the current year (obtained from DATE) is used.  Then
```

Program 2.8 - DAY

```
                    '19' is prepended if the year is only 2 characters long.

DAY            DATE          BREAK('/') . M     LEN(1)
+                    (BREAK('/') . D  LEN(1)    REM . Y  |  REM . D)
                     (IDENT(Y,'')   DATE())     '/' ARB '/'  REM . Y
                     Y  =  EQ(SIZE(Y),2)        '19'  Y
```

The number of days since March 0, 0000 will be computed.
First compute the number of whole months and the number of
whole years since that date.

```
                     M  =  LE(M,2)    M + 12                    :F(DAY_1)
                     Y  =  Y - 1
DAY_1                M  =  M - 3
```

Now add an appropriate number of days for each cyclic year
period. Note: integer divided by integer yields integer.

```
DAY_2   DAY = (Y / 400) * CENT_4 + (REMDR(Y,400) / 100) * CENT_
.        + (REMDR(Y,100) / 4) * YEAR_4 + REMDR(Y,4) * YEAR_
```

Now add an appropriate amount for the month (note that 153
is the number of days in a 5-month period), the day, and
an initializing constant. This value is taken modulo 7
and a search is made based on that value.

```
                     DAY = DAY + ((153 * M) + 2) / 5 + D + DAY_ZERO
                     D   = REMDR(DAY,7)
                     '0SUN1MON2TUES3WEDNES4THURS5FRI6SATUR7'
+                    D  BREAK('01234567') . DAY
                     DAY = DAY   'DAY'                          :(RETURN)
DAY_END
```

<u>Epilogue</u>

This program was modified for SNOBOL4 from an Algol program by
Tantzen [1963]. His version is slightly more efficient and we
leave this refinement as an exercise.

The program is done by a computation; it could also have been
done by a look-up procedure in which a string might contain a
month-day sequence in which the proper number of days are associated with each month. In general, this would have been
easier and less error-prone but would not have been as
efficient.

A very clever scheme is used to obtain the number of days that
a given month is worth. It is recognized that if we start in
March, the number of days per month is given by the sequence
31 30 31 30 31 which repeats itself for effectively the
remainder of the March - March year. The computation:

$$\frac{153 * M + 2}{5}$$

is so calculated as to yield precisely the correct number of days.

```
┌─────────────────┐
││  Program     ││   MDY(Y,D) will convert a year,day date into a
││    2.9       ││   month/day/year date. For example MDY(71,83)
││    MDY       ││   will return '3/24/71'. The global variables
└─────────────────┘   M and D are set to equal the month and day
```
respectively. MDY is useful in an environment where the system computes days but not months (such as OS 360).

> MDY(Y,D) will convert its argument which is given as year
> , day into month/day/year format.

```
                DEFINE('MDY(Y,DY)X,T')
```

> Set up 2 tables to be searched. One showing cumulative
> days vs. month (DAY_MONTH) for normal years and one for
> leap years (LY_DAY_MONTH).

```
+           DAY_MONTH    = '(334,12)(304,11)(273,10)(243,9)'
    '(212,8)(181,7)(151,6)(120,5)(90,4)(59,3)(31,2)(0,1)'
+           LY_DAY_MONTH = '(335,12)(305,11)(274,10)(244,9)'
    '(213,8)(182,7)(152,6)(121,5)(91,4)(60,3)(31,2)(0,1)'
```

> Set up a pattern to search the tables.

```
        I        = SPAN('0123456789')
        SEARCH.X.M = '(' I $ X *GT(DY,X) ',' I $ M    :(MDY_END)
```

> Entry point: Set up the proper table in T. Use leap year
> table if Y is either (divisible by 400) or (divisible by 4
> but not 100).

```
MDY    T = EQ(REMDR(Y,400),0) LY_DAY_MONTH    :S(MDY_1)
       T = EQ(REMDR(Y,100),0) DAY_MONTH       :S(MDY_1)
       T = EQ(REMDR(Y , 4),0) LY_DAY_MONTH    :S(MDY_1)
       T = DAY_MONTH
```

> Then search the table for the current month (M) and the
> number of days (X) associated with that month. Fail if DY
> is not a valid day.

```
MDY_1       T     SEARCH.X.M                      :F(FRETURN)
            D   = DY - X
            GT(D, 31)                             :S(FRETURN)
            MDY = M '/' D '/' Y                   :(RETURN)
MDY_END
```

Epilogue

We have written this program in terms of a 'table-look-up' procedure (actually string look-up would be more correct). But we could have done this by computational methods by turning

Program 2.10 - SPELL   Page 35

the DAY function around and 'pointing it backward'. This we invite the reader to try as an Exercise.

```
| | Program | |
| |  2.10   | |
| |  SPELL  | |
```
SPELL(N) will return an English phrase designating the integer N. Thus SPELL(13) will return 'THIRTEEN'. SPELL will convert all integers from 0 to 999999999 (a thousand million - 1). SPELL can easily be extended to handle larger ranges; see Exercise 2.16. One obvious application of SPELL is in writing checks.

```
            DEFINE('SPELL(N)M')              :(SPELL_END)
```

| Entry Point: Fan out to one of several labels depending on the value of N.

```
SPELL        GE(N,1000)                      :S(SPELL_1000)
             GE(N,100)                       :S(SPELL_100)
             GE(N,20)                        :S(SPELL_20)
             GE(N,13)                        :S(SPELL_13)
```

| Here if N is 12 or less; look its value up in a table.

```
         ('1ONE,2TWO,3THREE,4FOUR,5FIVE,6SIX,7SEVEN,8EIGHT,9NINE,'
      +  '10TEN,11ELEVEN,12TWELVE,')  N ARB . SPELL ','  :(RETURN)
```

| Here to do the teens. It will be simpler to do the tens version and substitute 'TEEN' for 'TY' afterward.

```
SPELL_13   N 1 LEN(1) . M
           SPELL = SPELL(M 0)
           SPELL   'TY'  =  'TEEN'
           SPELL   'FOR' =  'FOUR'               :(RETURN)
```

| Here to handle all compounds from 20 through 99. Just look up the root in a table and add the suffix 'TY'. Then call SPELL recursively to handle the units.

```
SPELL_20   N LEN(1) . M =
           '2TWEN,3THIR,4FOR,5FIF,6SIX,7SEVEN,8EIGH,9NINE,'
      +    M BREAK(',') . SPELL
           SPELL = SPELL 'TY'
           SPELL = NE(N,0) SPELL '-' SPELL(N)    :(RETURN)
```

| Hundreds are handled by converting the hundreds and tens recursively.

```
SPELL_100  N LEN(1) . M =
           SPELL = SPELL(M) ' HUNDRED'
           SPELL = NE(N,0) SPELL ' AND ' SPELL(N)  :(RETURN)
```

| For numbers over 1000, remove all but the last three digits of N assigning them to M. Convert M, 'multiply' it

| by 1000 and 'add' N.

```
SPELL_1000
        N    RTAB(3) . M   =
        SPELL  =  SPELL(M)
        SPELL     'THOUSAND'   =    'MILLION'
        SPELL  =  SPELL ' THOUSAND'
        SPELL  =  NE(N,0) SPELL ' AND ' SPELL(N)   : (RETURN)
SPELL_END
```

Epilogue

SPELL was written to be small rather than fast and uses recursion quite liberally and effectively to render a smaller and more readable program.

???
????????????????????????? EXERCISES ???????????????????????
???

| Exercise 2.1 | Using strings prepared in the initialization section of UPLO write a function UP() which will convert any lower case in its argument to upper case.

| Exercise 2.2 | Given the function UPLO() and a function UP() which converts lower case to upper case, write a function LO() which converts upper case to lower case.

| Exercise 2.3 | Given a paragraph in P assumed keypunched in upper case, use UPLO to convert P into lower case except that the first character of every sentence should remain capitalized. The first nonblank character is regarded as the beginning of the first sentence. Subsequent sentences are marked by a period followed by at least 2 blanks. (This requires only two statements.)

| Exercise 2.4 | Write a function (ARABIC) to convert a number in the Roman representation to one in standard (base 10) notation.

| Exercise 2.5 | Let $\{x\}$ be the smallest integer $\geq$ the real number x (sometimes referred to as the ceiling of x). Thus

$$\{1.5\} = 2$$
$$\{2.0\} = 2$$
$$\{-9.5\} = -9$$

Exercises for chapter 2

With the help of functions defined in this section write SNOBOL4 expressions equivalent to

$$\{\log_2 K\}$$

$$\{\log_n K\}$$

where K and n are positive integers.

Exercise 2.6 The Mayan Indians used a base 20 positional number system. The figures for the digits 0 thru 19 were built up systematically as in the table below.

Arabic form	Mayan equiv	Arabic form	Mayan equiv
0	0	10	||
1	.	11	||.
2	..	12	||..
3	...	13	||...
4	....	14	||....
5	|	15	|||
6	|.	16	|||.
7	|..	17	|||..
8	|...	18	|||...
9	|....	19	|||....

Hence the number 752 would be represented as

. \|\|\|.. \|\|..

Here the digits are run from left to right in descending significance whereas the Mayans would allign their digits vertically. Also the dots ran in a direction orthogonal to the bars. One has a great deal more freedom in these matters if one is merely carving the figures out of stone.

The exercise is, given the integer N write a loop to convert N to its Mayan form. This can be done in 4 statements (without using the functions defined in this chapter).

Exercise 2.7 A hypothetical machine has a word size of 32 bits represented as $b_1 b_2 \ldots b_{32}$. The bits have the following meaning when representing floating point.

S: b_1 (sign)   0:positive, 1:negative

E: $\{b_2 \ldots b_{11}\}$ exponent of 2 in excess 1024 notation

Chapter 2 - CONVERSIONS

F: $\{b_{12} \ldots b_{32}\}$ fractional part with decimal point to the left of b_{12}.

Hence a floating point number will have the value:

$$V = (-1)^S \frac{F}{2^{21}} 2^{(E-1024)}$$

Write a function (using the base conversion algorithms) to convert an eight-hexadecimal-digit machine word into a floating point number.

Exercise 2.8 Extend the routines BASEB and BASE10 to handle decimal points. Assume a global cell PRECISION which will hold the number of digits of precision required in the fraction. Allow BASEB and BASE10 to call themselves recursively.

Exercise 2.9 What statements would have to be modified if BASEB and BASE10 were to be extended to unlimited-precision arithmetic?

Exercise 2.10 Let Y, N and M be integers.

a) Show that:

$$\text{REMDR}(Y, N*M) / N = (Y/N) - (Y/(M*N))*M$$

and hence that line labeled DAY_2 in Program 2.8 can be rewritten:

DAY_2   DAY = (Y / 400) * K1 + (Y / 100) * K2
             + (Y / 4) * K3 + Y * K4

where K1, K2, K3, K4 are values which can be precomputed.

b) Compute K1, K2, K3, K4.

Exercise 2.11 Suppose there are 64 characters in &ALPHABET. Rewrite HEX so that it returns the base-8 representation of a string. Call the function OCTAL.

Exercise 2.12 In writing a compiler it is sometimes necessary to manipulate bits since the instruction is formed as a sequence of bits.

Exercises for chapter 2 — Page 39

a) Set the Nth bit of a string S to 1. Assume the bits are numbered starting with 0 and ending with 8 * SIZE(S) - 1 (This assumes 8 bits per character).

b) Invert the Nth bit of a string S.

Exercise 2.13 Using DAY, determine whether a given date is valid. For example, 2/29/1973 is invalid.

Exercise 2.14 Using DAY, write a program which prints a calendar for the month M and year Y.

Exercise 2.15 Given that the number of days since March 0 is (153*M+2)/5 where M is the number of whole months since that date, write an expression for the number of whole months given the number of days. Using this formula rewrite MDY as a computation.

Exercise 2.16 Assuming that a billion is a thousand million, add a single statement to SPELL to increase the range of convertable numbers to a thousand billion - 1.

Exercise 2.17 In the U.S. the terms billion, trillion, quadrillion, quintillion, sextillion, septillion and octillion refer to the numbers 1000 million, 1000^2 million, 1000^3 million,..., 1000^7 million respectively whereas in Great Britain these terms refer respectively to million^2, million^3, million^4,..., million^8. Extend SPELL so that it will convert its argument up to the octillions in the British system. Note that SNOBOL4 integers don't go that high so assume the input is string and don't use arithmetic operators (like GE) on anything too big.

Exercise 2.18 Pick a number; count the letters in its spelled-out form and you produce a new number. For example 13 is spelled 'THIRTEEN' and hence transforms into 8. This transformation has the interesting property that its repeated application will cause every number to converge rapidly to 4. For example, starting with 13, the sequence

13 8 5 4 4 4 4 ...

is produced. Write a program to determine the smallest integer between 0 and 10000 which requires the most steps to converge to 4 (the integer is 113 and it requires 6 steps).

Exercise 2.19 — The musical scale is given by the following sequence of 12 notes.

C C# D D# E F# G G# A A# B

Given a number N between 1 and 12, write a single pattern-matching statement to assign the Nth note (a one or two character string) to the variable NOTE.

CHAPTER THREE

BASIC

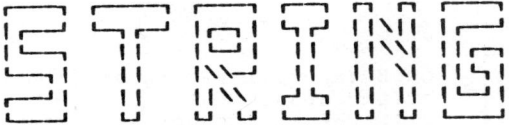

FUNCTIONS

```
CONTENTS

ORDER  ..................... 3.1
LPAD   ..................... 3.2
RPAD   ..................... 3.3
COUNT  ..................... 3.4
ROTATER .................... 3.5
REVERSE .................... 3.6
BLEND  ..................... 3.7
BALREV ..................... 3.8
SUBSTR ..................... 3.9
DIFF   ..................... 3.10
SKIM   ..................... 3.11
LEXGT  ..................... 3.12
AGT    ..................... 3.13
SWAP   ..................... 3.14
REPL   ..................... 3.15
QUOTE  ..................... 3.16
```

NOBOL4 represents strings by a pointer to string storage. One of the consequences of this storage management philosophy is that the cost of string assignment is relatively low. That is, it costs very little to interchange string values among variables. In particular it is relatively inexpensive to pass string values to and from functions.

The functions presented in this chapter all are fairly short utility-like functions which operate primarily with strings. We will see most of these functions later in the book where they will serve as lemma-like procedures to make larger programs more understandable.

```
|| Program ||    ORDER(S) will return an alphabetized version
||   3.1    ||   of its argument S.  Thus,   ORDER('ORDER')
||  ORDER   ||   will return 'DEORR'. The alphabetic ordering
                 of  characters  is  determined, as usual, by
&ALPHABET. To modify the ordering produced by ORDER the state-
ment containing this keyword should be replaced.  ORDER, as we
will see, has many uses.  For example, it furnishes  an  easy
way to check for set equality.
```

| ORDER(S) will put the characters of its argument in al- |
| phabetic order. |

```
              DEFINE('ORDER(S) T,HIGHS,S1')
                                                 : (ORDER_END)
```

| Entry Point: Extract a character (T) from S; obtain (in |
| HIGHS) characters alphabetically ≥ the extracted charac- |
| ter.   Then scan ORDER for the first occurrence of one of |
| these higher characters. |

```
ORDER     S     LEN(1) . T =                    :F(RETURN)
                &ALPHABET  BREAK(T)  REM . HIGHS
                CRDER    (BREAK(HIGHS) | REM) . S1 = S1 T   :(ORDER)
ORDER_END
```

Epilogue

ORDER is essentially a sorting routine and as such it is an insertion sort.   Characters are extracted one at a time from the argument S and are inserted in order into the growing string ORDER.

Program 3.4 - COUNT   Page 43

```
|| Programs     ||    (available in SPITBOL and SITBOL) LPAD
|| 3.2 & 3.3    ||    and RPAD are useful in formatting line
|| LPAD & RPAD  ||    output.  They are patterned after the
                      built-in  functions  in SPITBOL and are
```
included here for use with SNOBOL4. LPAD will pad on the left
to fill out a string to the required field width and RPAD will
pad on the right. Thus

             OUTPUT = RPAD(S1,60)   LPAD(S2,60)

will place string S1 on the left and string S2 on the extreme
right of a computer printout page that happens to be 120
characters wide. Both functions may be called with a 3rd argument to indicate a pad character other than a blank.

```
| LPAD(S,N,C)  will pad string S on the left with character
| C until the string is N characters long.  S is returned if
| it is ≥ N characters long.   C is  taken  to  be  ' '  if
| unspecified.
```

```
           DEFINE('LPAD(S,N,C)')           :(LPAD_END)
LPAD       LPAD  =  GE(SIZE(S),N) S         :S(RETURN)
           C  =  IDENT(C)  ' '
           LPAD  =  DUPL(C, N - SIZE(S)) S  :(RETURN)
LPAD_END
```

```
| RPAD(S,N,C)  pads on the right rather than on the left but
| its behaviour is otherwise the same as LPAD.
```

```
           DEFINE('RPAD(S,N,C)')           :(RPAD_END)
RPAD       RPAD  =  GE(SIZE(S), N) S        :S(RETURN)
           C  =  IDENT(C)  ' '
           RPAD  =  S DUPL(C, N - SIZE(S)) :(RETURN)
RPAD_END
```

```
|| Program  ||  COUNT(S1,S2) will count the number of occur-
|| 3.4      ||  rences of string  S2  in  S1.   Overlapping
|| COUNT    ||  occurrences  of  S1 are counted as separate
                occurrences. Thus COUNT('MISSISSIPPI', 'SI')
```
returns 2, and COUNT('AAA', 'AA') also returns 2. If a substring is not found the function effectively returns a zero
(actually the null string).

```
| COUNT(S1,S2)   counts  the number of occurrences of string
| S2 in string S1.
```

              DEFINE('COUNT(S1,S2) FIRST,REST,P')
                                             :(COUNT_END)

```
| Entry point:  Set up pattern P to scan S1.  P makes rapid
| scan for first character of S2 and then checks to see if
```

Chapter 3 - STRING FUNCTIONS

```
|  S2 matches.                                                            |

COUNT           S2      LEN(1) . FIRST    REM . REST       :F(RETURN)
                P  =    POS(0)   BREAKX(FIRST)   S2

|  Find  and remove all characters up to an occurrence of S2.  |
|  If found put all but first character of S2 back onto S1.    |

COUNT_1         S1      P  =  REST                          :F(RETURN)
                        COUNT  =  COUNT + 1                 :(COUNT_1)
COUNT_END
```

Names referenced	Name	Type	Where defined
by COUNT:	BREAKX	Function	Program 8.2

Epilogue

The simple-minded approach to this problem is to simply scan the string S1 for an occurrence of the string S2, removing all that precedes the substring and repeating the process until no more occurrences are found. A faster technique (used here) is to use the high speed operation of the BREAK function which scans across a string at machine speeds looking for one of a class of characters. If successful, then and only then is the entire word (S2) matched. To employ BREAK in this way it is convenient to use BREAKX which is defined in Program 8.2 (BREAKX is a built-in function in SPITBOL but not available in SNOBOL4). BREAKX, unlike BREAK, has implicit alternatives. If a pattern to its right (its subsequent) fails, it will try again, picking up one character to the right of where it left off.

```
||  Program  ||    ROTATER(S,N) will rotate the string S  right
||    3.5    ||    by N characters. If N is negative the rota-
||  ROTATER  ||    tion  will   be  to   the   left.    Thus
                   ROTATER('ABCD',1) will return 'DABC'.

|  ROTATER(S,N)  will rotate the string S right by N  charac- |
|  ters.  If N is negative, S will be rotated to the left.    |

           DEFINE('ROTATER(S,N)S1')                :(ROTATER_END)

|  Entry point:  If S is null, return.                                    |

ROTATER         IDENT(S)                                    :S(RETURN)

|  Reduce  number  of positions to be rotated modulo SIZE(S). |
|  Note REMDR preserves the sign of N.  If N is negative, use |
|  complement.                                                |

                N  =   REMDR(N,  SIZE(S))
                N  =   LT(N,0)   SIZE(S)  -  N
```

Program 3.6 - REVERSE   Page 45

| Perform the rotation and return |

```
              S     RTAB(N) . S  REM . S1  =  S1  S
              ROTATER  =  S                              :(RETURN)
ROTATER_END
```

| Program | (available in SPITBOL and SITBOL) REVERSE(S)
| 3.6 | will return S with its characters reversed.
| REVERSE | Thus   REVERSE('SERUTAN')   will   return
                'NATURES'.   One use of REVERSE is to effec-
tively reverse the order of pattern matching. For example, if
one wishes to replace the <u>last</u> occurrence of the substring SS
in the string S with the string R one can write:

```
              S  =  REVERSE(S)
              S    REVERSE(SS)   =   REVERSE(R)
              S  =  REVERSE(S)
```

| REVERSE(S) will reverse the sequence of characters in the |
| string S and return the result. |

```
              DEFINE('REVERSE(S)A1,A2,L')
```

| Initialize REV_ALPHA to hold the reversed alphabet. |

```
              TEMP    =  &ALPHABET
REV_1         TEMP    LEN(1) . T  =                  :F(REVERSE_END)
              REV_ALPHA  =  T REV_ALPHA              :(REV_1)
```

| Entry point: For oversize strings go to REVERSE_1. Also |
| ignore null strings. |

```
REVERSE       L  =  SIZE(S)
              GT(L,256)                              :S(REVERSE_1)
              LE(L,0)                                :S(RETURN)
```

| Take the first L characters of &ALPHABET and the last L |
| characters of the reversed alphabet and issue a REPLACE. |

```
              &ALPHABET   TAB(*L) . A1
              REV_ALPHA   RTAB(*L) REM . A2
              REVERSE  =  REPLACE(A2,A1,S)           :(RETURN)
```

| Divide and Conquer. |

```
REVERSE_1     S    LEN(256) . A1 REM . A2
              REVERSE  =  REVERSE(A2) REVERSE(A1)    :(RETURN)
REVERSE_END
```

Page 46   Chapter 3   -   STRING FUNCTIONS

Epilogue

The method used to perform the reversal follows a suggestion
by Morris Siegel. It transforms a string, not by setting up
the last 2 arguments of REPLACE and effecting a transliteration, but by setting up the first 2 arguments to accomplish a
rearrangement. We will elaborate on this before continuing to
the next function.

```
 ****  tring Transformations
 *
 ****
   *
 ****
```
A *string transformation* is any
function which accepts a
string as argument and returns a string as value.
As a humble example, TRIM(S) is a transformation
which produces a string without trailing blanks.
Special kinds of transformations exist which are
either interesting in their own right or can be programmed to
run very rapidly.

A *homomorphism* is a transformation T such that

$$T(S_1 \; S_2) = T(S_1) \; T(S_2) \qquad (3.1)$$

That is, the transformation of the concatenation is equal to
the concatenation of the transformations. Said another way,
the transformation is context free. Since any string S can
ultimately be decomposed into characters, $c_1 c_2 \ldots c_n$ we have

$$T(S) = T(c_1) \; T(c_2) \ldots T(c_n) \qquad (3.2)$$

And from this last equation we can see that a homomorphism is
completely characterized by the transformation on individual
characters. Let $a_1 a_2 \ldots a_n$ be a list of all the characters
of the alphabet. Then the set of strings $\{T(a_1), T(a_2), \ldots, T(a_n)\}$
identify completely and unambiguously the transforma-
tion T.

A *transliteration* is an important special case of a homomorphism in that each of the strings $\{T(a_1), T(a_2), \ldots, T(a_n)\}$
is a character. If T is a transliteration then T can be
programmed in SNOBOL4 as:

$$T(S) = \text{REPLACE}(S, \&ALPHABET, T(\&ALPHABET)) \qquad (3.3)$$

In this way any transliteration can be programmed to run very
swiftly merely by obtaining the transliteration of &ALPHABET.
We have seen a number of examples of transliterations.
Programs UPLO (2.1), BCD_EBCDIC(2.2) and HEX(2.6) all make use
of REPLACE to perform the transliteration.

Consider the following statement

$$S = \text{REPLACE}(S, S_1, S_2) \qquad (3.4)$$

Here S_1 and S_2 are two equi-length strings which describe a
transliteration on the string S. In fact, only those charac-

ters which appear in S_1 undergo a change. If we subject &ALPHABET to such a transliteration to obtain

$$TT = REPLACE(\&ALPHABET, S_1, S_2) \quad (3.5)$$

we can use the result to effect the same transliteration on S as in (3.4).

$$S = REPLACE(S, \&ALPHABET, TT) \quad (3.6)$$

A <u>k-transformation</u> is a string transformation that operates only on strings of length k and is undefined for strings of other length. (Its domain is said to consist of the strings of length k.) For example, the permutation (1 3 2) which rearranges the 2nd and 3rd characters of a string of length 3 is a 3-transformation since it only applies to strings of length 3.

A <u>positional transformation</u> is a k-transformation in which the output is some rearrangement of the characters of the input string with the properties that 1) characters in some positions of the input string may be dropped, while others may appear several times and 2) constant characters may be added into some fixed positions of the output string. But in any case the disposition of a character depends on its position and not its value. More formally, the positional transformation on strings of length k can be described as:

$$T(c_1 \; c_2 \; ... \; c_k) = t_1 \; c_{i_1} \; t_2 \; c_{i_2} \; ... \; t_n \; c_{i_n} \; t_{n+1}$$

where $t_1, t_2, ...$ are constant strings depending only on the transformation and $i_1, i_2, ..., i_n$ are constant integers chosen from the set $\{1, 2, ..., k\}$.

An example of a positional transformation is depicted graphically in Figure 3.1. It transforms a restricted class of English words into the corresponding 'piglatin'. Thus DIG becomes IGDAY, DOG becomes OGDAY and CAT becomes ATCAY. In general, it permutes a 3-character string and appends an 'AY'.

Another example of a positional transformation, one chosen from a more practical point of view, is the translation from ASCII to EBCDIC (see [IBM360a], App. F and [ASCII]). This transformation is indicated graphically in Figure 3.2. It, for example, transforms the ASCII code 1010101 to 10110101.

A call to the replace function $REPLACE(S_1, S_2, S_3)$ is said to be <u>well-defined</u> if S_2 is as long as S_3. If repeated characters exist in S_2 the last appearance of each character will indicate the mapping. In this latter case the operation of the

Page 48   Chapter 3 - STRING FUNCTIONS

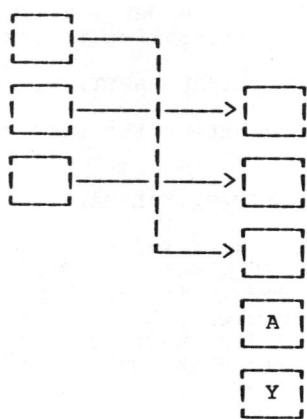

Figure 3.1

A positional transformation that translates three-character words into their pig-latin equivalent.

function would not be ambiguous although the programmer's motives might be.

As we have described earlier, every transformation T defined as

$$T(S) = REPLACE(S, S_1, S_2)$$

is a transliteration provided the operation is well-defined. Also, as has been previously noted, any transliteration T can be written as $REPLACE(S, S_1, S_2)$ for some S_1, S_2. Hence the set of all transliterations are identical with the set of all REPLACE's with given 2nd and 3rd arguments.

In a considerably less obvious way, the positional transformations can also be implemented by the REPLACE function.

For any strings S_1, S_2, the transformation defined as

$$T(S) = REPLACE(S_1, S_2, S)$$

is a positional k-transformation on S where k is the size of S_2.

Conversely, any positional transformation satisfying certain size constraints can be written as a REPLACE. Let P(S) be a positional k-transformation. Let S_1 be a string composed of k different characters none of which are included in the constant characters of the mapping. Then we can express P as

String Transformations   Page 49

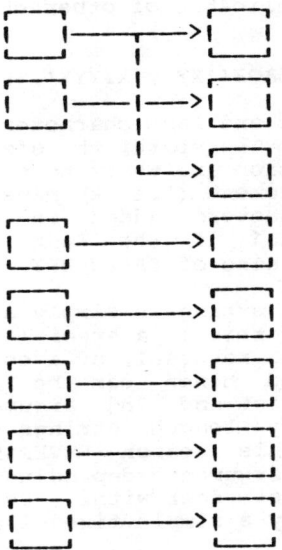

Figure 3.2

A positional transformation for converting ASCII to EBCDIC.

$$P(S) = REPLACE(P(S_1), S_1, S)$$

Like the transliterations, we need only obtain the positional transformation for one model string to set up a high speed program for transforming all strings in the domain.

As an example, the transformation indicated in Figure 3.1 can be expressed as

REPLACE('OGDAY','DOG',S)

As another example the transformation indicated in Figure 3.2 can be expressed as

REPLACE('12134567', '1234567', S)

The characters in the model string must all be different from any constant characters added to the string. Moreover, the characters in the model string must all be different from each other except that characters corresponding to positions that are dropped may be duplicates of other characters which follow them. Thus

REPLACE('XY','XYYYY',S)

will extract the first and last characters from S provided S is 5 characters long. Therefore, the size constraints imposed by the REPLACE function are that the total number of characters in the second argument (i.e. k) plus the number of different constant characters added in the mapping minus the positions ignored plus 1 if the last position is ignored should not exceed the size of &ALPHABET.

A *permutation* of a string is simply a rearrangement of its characters and clearly this is a special case of a positional transformation. String reversal, of a constant length string, is a permutation and hence can be accomplished by using REPLACE with suitable 1st and 2nd arguments. But string-reversal of arbitrary length strings represents a class of permutations and for this reason REVERSE must prepare appropriate 1st and 2nd arguments depending on the particular k-transformation it must deal with. But this preparation is rapidly accomplished by a simple fixed-length pattern matching operation.

```
| | Program | |
| |   3.7   | |
| |  BLEND  | |
```
BLEND(X,Y) will merge the two strings X and Y taking the first character from X, the 2nd from Y, the 3rd from X, etc. Thus BLEND('ABC','123') equals 'A1B2C3'. BLEND has been used previously by the HEX function (Program 2.6) and is an example of a class of positional transformations which can be programmed to run quite rapidly. The 2 strings X and Y are either the same length or X is one character longer than Y. Thus BLEND('CHAPTER', DUPL(' ',6)) will return 'C H A P T E R'. BLEND's of strings not satisfying these constraints are undefined.

```
| BLEND(S1,S2) will blend the two (equi-length) strings S1 |
| and S2 such that every other character is taken from each |
| string. Thus BLEND('ABC','123') will return 'A1B2C3'.    |
```

DEFINE('BLEND(S1,S2)T1,T2,ABC,XYZ,L1,L2')

```
| Prepare in BLENDED_ALPHABET a blend of the lower and upper |
| halves of &ALPHABET.                                       |
```

```
             &ALPHABET   LEN(128) . ABC   LEN(128) . XYZ
BLE_1        ABC   LEN(1) . T1   =              :F(BLEND_END)
             XYZ   LEN(1) . T2   =
             BLENDED_ALPHABET   =   BLENDED_ALPHABET   T1 T2
                                                     :(BLE_1)
```

Program 3.8 - BALREV

| Entry point: If S1 is too large, subdivide and recurse. |

```
BLEND     L1   =   SIZE(S1)
          GT(L1,128)                              :F(BLEND_1)
          EQ(L1,0)                                :S(RETURN)
          S1       LEN(128) . S1    REM . T1
          S2       LEN(128) . S2    REM . T2
          BLEND =  REPLACE(BLENDED_ALPHABET,&ALPHABET,S1 S2)
+                  BLEND(T1,T2)                   :(RETURN)
```

| Otherwise prepare AXBYCZ to be a BLEND of ABC and XYZ and
| to be as long as the string to be returned. These strings
| serve as a template for a positional transformation of the
| combined string S1 S2.

```
BLEND_1   L2   =   SIZE(S2)
          &ALPHABET         LEN(*L1) . ABC   TAB(128)    LEN(*L2) . XYZ
          BLENDED_ALPHABET  LEN(*(L1 + L2))  . AXBYCZ
          BLEND  =  REPLACE(AXBYCZ, ABC XYZ, S1 S2)
                                                  :(RETURN)
BLEND_END
```

Epilogue

The initialization section of BLEND prepares a string BLENDED_ALPHABET which thereafter is used to obtain templates for a positional transformation. For very large strings BLEND is called recursively. As in REVERSE, this is done because of limitations in the size of &ALPHABET rather than due to any difficulties or limitations in handling long strings in SNOBOL4. A slightly faster version of BLEND can be achieved by nonrecursive methods but it seems hardly worth it.

```
|| Program  ||
||   3.8    ||
|| BALREV   ||
```
BALREV(S) will return the balanced reversal of the string S. That is, the characters of S are reversed and the parenthesis are interchanged. For example, BALREV('F(X)') is '(X)F' rather than ')X(F' as would be returned by REVERSE. BALREV can be used to reverse the order of scanning in an environment in which BAL plays a role in the pattern matching. For example

          S   '(' BAL . E   ')'

will find the first parenthesized expression in S, whereas

          BALREV(S)   '(' BAL . E   ')'
          E   =   BALREV(E)

will set E to be the _last_ parenthesized expression in S.

Chapter 3 - STRING FUNCTIONS

> BALREV(S) will return the balanced reversal of S.

```
            DEFINE('BALREV(S)')                     :(BALREV_END)
BALREV      BALREV = REPLACE(REVERSE(S), ')(', '()')
                                                    :(RETURN)
BALREV_END
```

Names referenced	Name	Type	Where defined
by BALREV:	REVERSE	Function	Program 3.6

Epilogue

BALREV is not of interest because it offers a challenge to one's program-writing abilities but rather because of the general notion of balanced reversal that it introduces and the fact that we will have occasion to make use of the function in later chapters. It is also of interest in that it provides in one line of code not only a useful function but one which uses both a transliteration and a positional transformation.

```
|| Program ||
||   3.9   ||
||  SUBSTR ||
```
(available in SPITBOL and SITBOL) SUBSTR(S,I,L) will return a substring of the string S beginning at character I and extending for L characters. If such a string is not properly included in S then SUBSTR fails. The SUBSTR function was patterned after the function by the same name in PL/I. Although the taking of a substring is a capability implicit in the pattern-matching facilities of SNOBOL4, its availablity as a function offers another dimension to this most fundamental of string operations.

> SUBSTR(S,I,L) returns a substring of length L beginning at the Ith character of S.

```
            DEFINE('SUBSTR(S,I,L)')              :(SUBSTR_END)
SUBSTR      S LEN(*(I - 1)) LEN(*L) . SUBSTR  :S(RETURN)F(FRETURN)
SUBSTR_END
```

```
|| Program ||
||  3.10   ||
||  DIFF   ||
```
We may regard a string as a set of characters if we ignore duplicates and their ordering. The fundamental set operations are union, intersection and complementation. String concatenation gives us union. Intersection can be obtained from union if we also have complementation. Complementation can be obtained if we have the universe string (set of all characters) and set difference. &ALPHABET serves as the universe and DIFF(S1,S2) will return the set difference, S1 - S2. That is, DIFF(S1,S2) returns a string containing all those characters that are in S1 and not S2.

Program 3.11 - SKIM

```
            DEFINE('DIFF(S1,S2)')                    : (DIFF_END)
```
> Entry point: set DIFF to S1 and then remove any consecu-
> tive string of S2 characters.

```
DIFF       DIFF   =   S1
           IDENT(S2,NULL)                            :S(RETURN)
           S2  =  SPAN(S2)
DIFF_1     DIFF   S2  =                              :S(DIFF_1)F(RETURN)
DIFF_END
```

	Program	
	3.11	
	SKIM	

SKIM(S) 'skims off' the first appearance of each different character of S and returns the result. Thus SKIM('MISSISSIPPI') returns 'MISP'.

```
            DEFINE('SKIM(S)C')                       : (SKIM_END)
```
> Entry point: Remove character from S and if not already
> in SKIM, put it there and repeat.

```
SKIM       S   LEN(1) . C  =                         :F(RETURN)
           SKIM    C                                 :S(SKIM_D)
           SKIM  =  SKIM  C                          :(SKIM)
```
> But if C was found in SKIM, it may be prudent to remove
> all characters already SKIM'ed from S.

```
SKIM_D     S  =  DIFF(S, SKIM)                       :(SKIM)
SKIM_END
```

Names referenced	Name	Type	Where defined
by SKIM:	DIFF	Function	Program 3.10

Epilogue

SKIM is slightly more complicated than it has to be. The line at SKIM_D is not strictly necessary and the statement that branches to SKIM_D could as well branch to SKIM. But for efficiency purposes it is better to remove already-skimmed characters in the wholesale manner of DIFF rather than painfully, one at a time. The technique used in SKIM is to call DIFF whenever an old character is found. This will be an improvement even if it takes relatively long to call DIFF. If the ratio of times of calling DIFF vs. going through the loop is 5, then it will pay if as few as 5 characters are removed from DIFF. It is possible, however, that the calls to DIFF are too frequent. It may be better to call DIFF only when, say, 2 characters in a row have already been found.

Page 54   Chapter 3   -   STRING FUNCTIONS

```
┌─────────────────┐
││   Program    ││    There   exists a built-in function in SNOBOL4
││    3.12      ││    called LGT.  LGT(S1,S2) is a predicate which
││    LEXGT     ││    will    succeed   if  string   S1  is   lexically
└─────────────────┘    greater  than   S2  and  fail  otherwise.   The
determination  of  lexical ordering  is based  on &ALPHABET  which
is  machine  dependent  and  may  not  represent  the  desired
ordering.   In  particular  the  lower  case  alphabet   appears
separate  from   the upper case alphabet so that  all upper case
letters are regarded as greater than all lower  case  letters.
Thus, 'Arabic' is considered greater than 'zebra'.   The func-
tion   LEXGT which we define below will differ from LGT in that
the  lexical  ordering will not be based on &ALPHABET but   on  a
user-supplied transliteration table: LEX_TT.
```

```
| LEXGT(S1,S2)  is a predicate  to determine   whether   S1   is |
| lexically  greater   than   S2  according  to a user-supplied  |
| transliteration table in LEX_TT.                               |
```

          DEFINE('LEXGT(S1,S2)')

```
| As an example, we will initialize LEX_TT to a  value  such |
| that  upper and lower case letters of the same letter will |
| be regarded as being adjacent.   Also letters will compare |
| lower  than  anything  else.   First form, in ALPHA, the  new |
| alphabetic ordering.                                       |
```

          ALPHA   =   BLEND(LOWERS_,UPPERS_)
 +   DIFF(&ALPHABET, LOWERS_ UPPERS_)

```
| Now transform this string to form a transliteration table. |
```

          LEX_TT =   REPLACE(&ALPHABET, ALPHA, &ALPHABET)
                                                  : (LEXGT_END)

```
| Entry point:  translate and compare.                       |
```

LEXGT   LGT(REPLACE(S1, &ALPHABET, LEX_TT),
+   REPLACE(S2, &ALPHABET, LEX_TT))
+   :S(RETURN) F(FRETURN)
LEXGT_END

Names referenced   Name   Type   Where defined
by LEXGT: BLEND *   Function   Program 3.7
                       UPPERS_ *   String   Program 2.1
                       LOWERS_ *   String   Program 2.1
                       DIFF *   Function   Program 3.10
 * indicates name is referenced in the initialization section.

Epilogue

We have effectively modified LGT by modifying its arguments.
In many problems this could be carried one step further for
greater efficiency.   Assume that all the data that would ever

Program 3.13 - AGT   Page 55

appear for comparison purposes is coming from the normal input
stream (under INPUT). We could convert characters as they were
being read in via a statement such as

         L = REPLACE(INPUT, &ALPHABET, LEX_TT)

But were we to do this we must be careful in using pattern
matching so that all character strings used to specify patterns were also mapped in the same way. Thus to match the line
L for 'CAT' we would have to write:

         L   REPLACE('CAT', &ALPHABET, LEX_TT)

```
|| Program ||
||   3.13  ||
||   AGT   ||
```
One might suspect that LEXGT provides maximum flexibility in the comparison of
strings, since one may supply one's own alphabet. But it does not handle the important
case in which certain distinct characters are to be regarded
as identical for comparison purposes. In particular, the lower
case 'a' and upper case 'A' are normally regarded as equal for
dictionary purposes. LEXGT would sort words
'able,Afghan,artist' as 'able,artist,Afghan' which is not the
dictionary ordering. AGT(S1,S2) will compare 2 strings and
return success if S1 is alphabetically greater than S2. AGT
is blind to the distinction between upper and lower case.
Otherwise it accepts the ordering implied by &ALPHABET.

| AGT(S1,S2) is a predicate to determine if S1 is al- |
| phabetically greater than S2. Upper and lower case ver- |
| sions of the same letter are regarded as equal. |

```
          DEFINE('AGT(S1,S2)')
      AGT_TT  =  REPLACE(&ALPHABET, UPPERS_, LOWERS_)
                                               :(AGT_END)
AGT       LGT( REPLACE(S1, &ALPHABET, AGT_TT),
+              REPLACE(S2, &ALPHABET, AGT_TT))
+                                :S(RETURN) F(FRETURN)
AGT_END
```

Names referenced	Name	Type	Where defined
by AGT:	UPPERS_ *	String	Program 2.1
	LOWERS_ *	String	Program 2.1

* indicates name is referenced in the initialization section.

Epilogue

AGT and LEXGT provide 2 distinct means whereby one may alter
the effective behaviour of LGT. If necessary, these 2 methods
may be combined into one suitably-designed call to REPLACE.
We leave this as an exercise.

Chapter 3 - STRING FUNCTIONS

```
|  Program  |     SWAP(NAME1,NAME2) will swap the values of
|   3.14    |     the named variables. Thus, SWAP(.N,.M) will
|   SWAP    |     interchange the values of N and M.
```

```
             DEFINE('SWAP(SWAP_ARG1,SWAP_ARG2)')     :(SWAP_END)
SWAP         SWAP       = $SWAP_ARG1
             $SWAP_ARG1 = $SWAP_ARG2
             $SWAP_ARG2 = SWAP
             SWAP       =                             :(RETURN)
SWAP_END
```

Epilogue

The names of the arguments to SWAP were deliberately chosen strange so as to avoid collision with the outside world. The variable SWAP is set to null before returning because otherwise a value would be returned and it is conceivable that in some cases this would not be desirable.

```
|  Program  |     REPL(S1,S2,S3) will do a string-by-string
|   3.15    |     replacement (as opposed to a character-by-
|   REPL    |     character replacement ala REPLACE) on the
                  string S1.  The string S1 is scanned for
```
instances of the string S2 and each is replaced by S3. Portions of S1 already scanned and the replaced string are not reexamined for instances of S2.

```
             DEFINE('REPL(S1,S2,S3) C,T,FINDC')       :(REPL_END)
```

| Entry point: Define pattern FINDC which will do a fast scan for the initial character. |

```
REPL         S2 LEN(1) . C =                          :F(FRETURN)
             FINDC = BREAK(C) . T LEN(1)
             S2 = POS(0) S2
```

| Top of loop: First remove the prefix, T; then test for S2. |

```
REPL_1       S1   FINDC =                             :F(REPL_2)
             S1   S2    =                             :F(REPL_3)
             REPL =     REPL T S3                     :(REPL_1)
REPL_3       REPL =     REPL T C                      :(REPL_1)
```

| Return point: The lead character, C, was not found in S1. |

```
REPL_2       REPL = REPL S1                           :(RETURN)
REPL_END
```

Names referenced	Name	Type	Where defined
by REPL:	BREAKX	Function	Program 8.2

Epilogue

like the function COUNT, the technique used to speed the search is to do a fast scan (at BREAK speeds) for the initial character. Other than this, the coding is straightforward but surprisingly lengthy.

```
| |   Program  | |
| |   3.16     | |
| |   QUOTE    | |
```

QUOTE(S) will convert its argument to a string which will resemble a SNOBOL4 expression which, when evaluated, will yield the original string. In the simplest case QUOTE(S) will place the string S between apostrophes. However, if S contains apostrophes, QUOTE will enclose these within double quotes. Thus

           OUTPUT = QUOTE("DON'T")

will print

                  'DON' "'" 'T'

Note that EVAL(QUOTE(S)) is always equal to S. QUOTE is useful when preparing code. An example is given in RSELECT (Prog. 16.7).

```
          DEFINE('QUOTE(S) S1,Q,QQ')              :(QUOTE_END)
```
| Entry point: The only thing that gives us any trouble is the single quote. If we find one we must wrap it in double quotes and offset it with blanks. |

```
QUOTE      Q' = "'"  ;  QQ = '"'
           QUOTE = Q REPL(S, Q, ' ' QQ Q QQ ' ' Q) Q   :(RETURN)
QUOTE_END
```

Names referenced	Name	Type	Where defined
by QUOTE:	REPL	Function	Program 3.15

???
???????????????????????? EXERCISES ????????????????????????????
???

| Exercise 3.1 | Write RPAD in terms of LPAD and REVERSE.

| Exercise 3.2 | Write RPAD in terms of LPAD and ROTATER. Assume that SIZE(S) ≤ N.

Chapter 3 - STRING FUNCTIONS

| Exercise 3.3 | Write a function CENTER(S,N,C) for centering
                  objects within a field of width N.

| Exercise 3.4 | Use the REPLACE function and BLEND to
                  rapidly extract every other character from
the string S, starting with the first (Assume that SIZE(S) is
less than 2 * SIZE(&ALPHABET) and can be even or odd). This
can be done in 2 statements.

| Exercise 3.5 | a) Determine S_1 and S_2 so that
                  REPLACE(S_1,S_2,S) realizes the positional
transformation shown in Figure 3.3.

b) What is the fewest number of different characters needed
in S_1 and S_2.

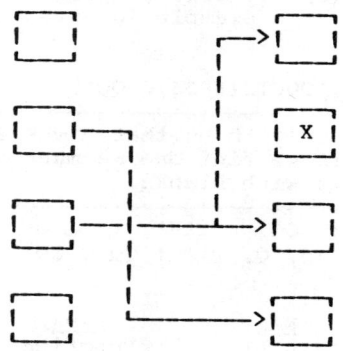

Figure 3.3

| Exercise 3.6 | a) Using REPLACE, obtain the last charac-
                  ter of string S.
b) In a similar way extract the Kth character.

Exercises for chapter 3   Page 59

| Exercise 3.7 | Some cyphers (called Transpositional) serve
                   to encode text by rearranging characters
(see for example Smith [1955]). The message is written in a
rectangular matrix horizontally from left to right. The
encoding is obtained by reading vertically. Thus, if the
matrix is 2x6 and the message is

                         ATTACK
                         ATDAWN

the encoding is

                       AATTTDAACWKN

a) Write a function TPOS(S,H,W) to encode the string S.   H
is the height and W is the width of the matrix and S is assumed to be exactly H * W characters long.

b) Using TPOS, find S_1 & S_2 such that REPLACE(S_1, S_2, S)
will convert all strings of length H * W (Assume that H * W
does not exceed SIZE(&ALPHABET)).

c) Using the scheme of b) write a function ENCODE which will
encode arbitrary length strings. Trailing characters are
ignored. Thus, if the matrix is 7x3 and the message is

                         THEBRIT
                         ISHAREC
                         OMING

then the encoding is

                    'TIOHSMEHIBANRRGIETC'

(Hint: assume some character exists, say colon (:), which will
never appear in the string to be encoded).

| Exercise 3.8 | a) Extend BLEND(X,Y) so that if string X is
                    n times longer than string Y then the
characters of Y will be inserted at every (n+1)st position.
Thus BLEND('ABCDEF', '123') will return 'AB1CD2EF3'. For efficiency purposes, a table of templates may be stored for the
positional transformations.

b) How would the new BLEND be used in the encoding of TPOS
(see Exercise 3.7).

| Exercise 3.9 | Assuming a function OR(S1,S2) is available
                   for ORing the bits of the equi-length
character strings S1 and S2 (at high speeds). Rewrite CH
(Program 2.7) so that it performs at high speed using the
REPLACE function.

Chapter 3 - STRING FUNCTIONS

| Exercise 3.10 | E contains a string representing a Fortran arithmetic expression which consists, possibly, of the sum or difference of expressions E1 and E2. Keeping in mind that Fortran associates operators from left to right, parse E assigning to E1 and E2 the proper values. If E is not of this form go to label NOT.

| Exercise 3.11 | Design a 'worst-case' (time-wise) string argument for SKIM that is 20 characters long.

| Exercise 3.12 | Any string may be said to denote a set of characters, viz. the set of which it consists. Assuming that the strings denoting sets may have duplicate characters, write an expression to express the a) union and b) intersection of 2 sets S1 and S2. c) Write an expression to indicate the negation of S. d) Write an expression which succeeds if set S1 equals set S2.

| Exercise 3.13 | Write an expression which will succeed if there are no duplicate characters in the string S (you may use functions defined in this chapter).

| Exercise 3.14 | Write an expression to obtain the set of characters that occur exactly once in a string S.

| Exercise 3.15 | (a) Remove leading 0's from a string by means of TRIM, REPLACE, and REVERSE. (b) Remove leading 0's from a numeric string S (one capable of being converted to integer) by means of a single operator.

| Exercise 3.16 | AGT and LEXGT represent 2 methods of effectively modifying the lexical comparison. To generalize, let the string ALPHA denote an alphabetic ordering as follows. Sets of equal letters are enclosed in parenthesis. Otherwise the lowest to the highest character are ordered left to right. Characters not in ALPHA may occur in any order. Thus

ALPHA = '(Aa)(Bb)(Cc)(Dd)(Ee)...(Zz)0123456789'

would describe an ordering in which all the alphabetics appear before the numerics and in which the alphabetics are grouped in their normal order. (a) Write a program to convert a string such as ALPHA into a pair of strings A1 and A2 such that

LGT(REPLACE(S1,A1,A2) , REPLACE(S2,A1,A2))

will compare strings S1 and S2.

(b) If parenthesis themselves are to be included in the characters to be explicitly ordered a difficulty arises. Establishes escape conventions for parens and modify your conversion program accordingly.

| Exercise 3.17 | What 3 variables may not be swapped using SWAP? (Prog. 3.14)

| Exercise 3.18 | Assume that input text, contained in the string S, is a personalized message to some one or some organization. Within S, and embedded within paired #'s are SNOBOL4 expressions to be evaluated on an individual basis. The rest of the text is constant for each message. This text may have quotes embedded within it but not #'s. Compose, in Q, a SNOBOL4 expression which when evaluated will yield the desired string. For example if S is:

        DEAR MR. #NAME#:

then a correct translation is

        'DEAR MR. ' NAME ':'

| Exercise 3.19 | State which of the following are homomorphisms (h) and which of the homomorphisms are also transliterations (ht). (a) UPLO, (b) BCD_EBCDIC, (c) ROMAN, (d) HEX, (e) CH, (f) QUOTE

| Exercise 3.20 | Some systems accept abreviations of all command names. For example, DEL, DE or even D would be acceptable abreviations for the DELETE command provided this uniquely specified the command. Given a list of commands in the string CMD such as:

        CMD = ',ALLOCATE,AUGMENT,BEGIN,CHANGE, ... '

write a function C(S) which will determine if a given string S uniquely specifies a command. If it does C should return the command. If it does not it should fail. Hint: using COUNT (Prog. 3.4) the body of the routine can be written in one statement.

| Exercise 3.21 | Assume that X and Y are string-valued. In one statement, swap X and Y without using a third variable.

Chapter 3 - STRING FUNCTIONS

Exercise 3.22 | What is the value of SIZE(QUOTE(QUOTE('X')))?

CHAPTER FOUR

BASIC

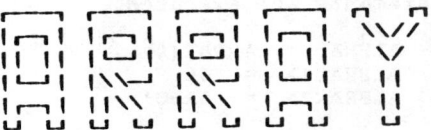

FUNCTIONS

CONTENTS

CRACK 4.1

STRINGOUT 4.2

SEQ 4.3

AOPA 4.4

FIND 4.5

AI 4.6

TRUNC 4.7

CATA 4.8

Chapter 4 - ARRAY FUNCTIONS

       hile strings are convenient for representing input data and for economizing on search time when scanning for patterns, arrays are quite useful when it is necessary to randomly alter selected portions of the interior of the structure. Arrays are also convenient when dealing with sequences of things other than characters, such as numbers, patterns, and strings themselves.

To effectively use the array facility in SNOBOL4 it is important to have some conception as to how arrays are implemented. The 3 statements below allocate an array and assign values to its first 2 elements. Figure 4.1 indicates the data configuration after the statements are executed.

```
        ALPHA    =   ARRAY(4)
        ALPHA<1> =   16
        ALPHA<2> =   'ABC'
```

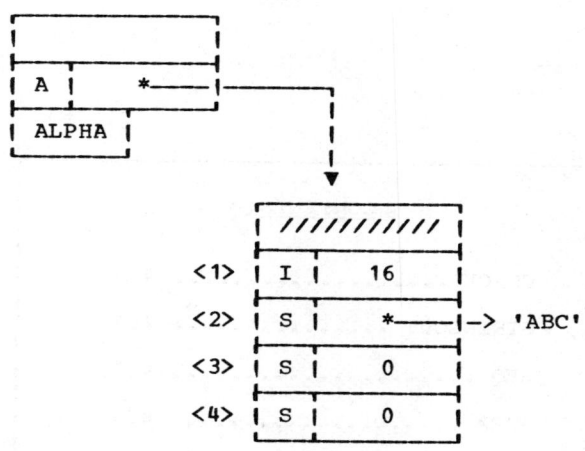

Figure 4.1

The data configuration after an array allocation and 2 element assignments.

Chapter 4 - ARRAY FUNCTIONS

The array is a data object of type ARRAY (denoted by A in the datatype field of the descriptor in the variable ALPHA). The data object has information (denoted by cross hatching) to indicate its physical extent and upper and lower bounds. In addition, for every array element, there is one descriptor. Hence, each array element may be assigned a data object of any datatype; also, the objects may be of mixed type as the example illustrates. Thus, an array in SNOBOL4 is more properly regarded as an array of variables rather than as an array of data. The default value of array elements is the null string denoted by (S,0) in the figure.

Since an array is a value, it may readily be passed from variable to variable. The data configuration resulting from the following statements is indicated in Figure 4.2.

```
          BETA   =  ALPHA
          BETA<1> =  3.7
```

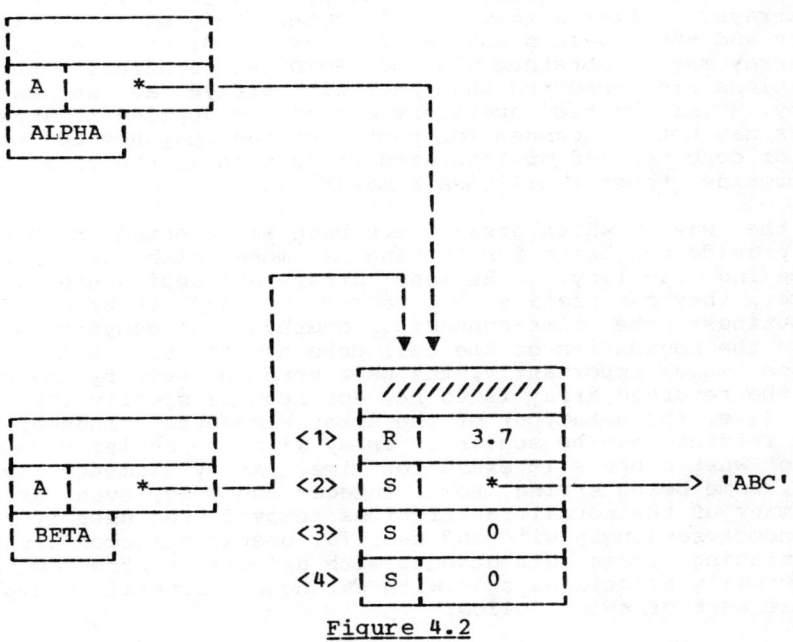

Figure 4.2

The data configuration after an array assignment (to BETA) and one element assignment.

Chapter 4 - ARRAY FUNCTIONS

The assignment to BETA is accomplished only by copying the descriptor in ALPHA, not by copying the array. Thus, a reference to BETA<1> becomes also a reference to ALPHA<1>, so that modification of BETA<1> implies modification of ALPHA<1>. This sort of collision can be avoided by use of the COPY function. Figure 4.3 illustrates the data configuration which results by executing the following 2 statements in place of the above 2.

```
         BETA    = COPY(ALPHA)
         BETA<1> = 3.7
```

The array elements are variables and hence may be assigned any data objects as value, including an array. For example

```
         ALPHA<2> = BETA
```

will result in the data configuration shown in Figure 4.4.

Compared with the rather rich string-handling facilities in SNOBOL4 there is a relative lack of such facility with respect to arrays. Arrays may be allocated; they may be assigned values and these values may later be examined; and the size of the array may be obtained via the PROTOTYPE function. But few operations are supported that deal with arrays as an entire entity. Arithmetic operators may not be applied to arrays. Arrays may not be scanned for patterns; they may not be trimmed, or concatenated or truncated other than as the programmer may provide these facilities himself.

But the way in which arrays have been implemented in SNOBOL4 does provide the basis for forming a more elaborate array-processing facility. Because arrays are represented via a pointer, they can readily be passed to and returned from subroutines; the time-consuming overhead of copying arrays across the boundaries of the call does not exist. Also, and perhaps more importantly, the user need not specify the size that the returned array is to be, nor need he specify the nature (i.e. the datatype) of the array elements. Indeed, the value returned may be scalar or array with the decision depending on what happens at execution time. Array elements may be mixed, some being string, some, integer and some, even array. With many of the normal restrictions removed, the user if free to concoct seemingly wild and fanciful operations upon arrays, manipulating these data objects with a degree of freedom that one normally associates only with strings. Several examples of this sort of thing follow.

The use of descriptor notation can be cumbersome in dealing with an array of simple objects such as integers, reals or strings. Hence, where the meaning is otherwise clear, we will display an array of data objects in the simplified notation shown in Figure 4.5b.

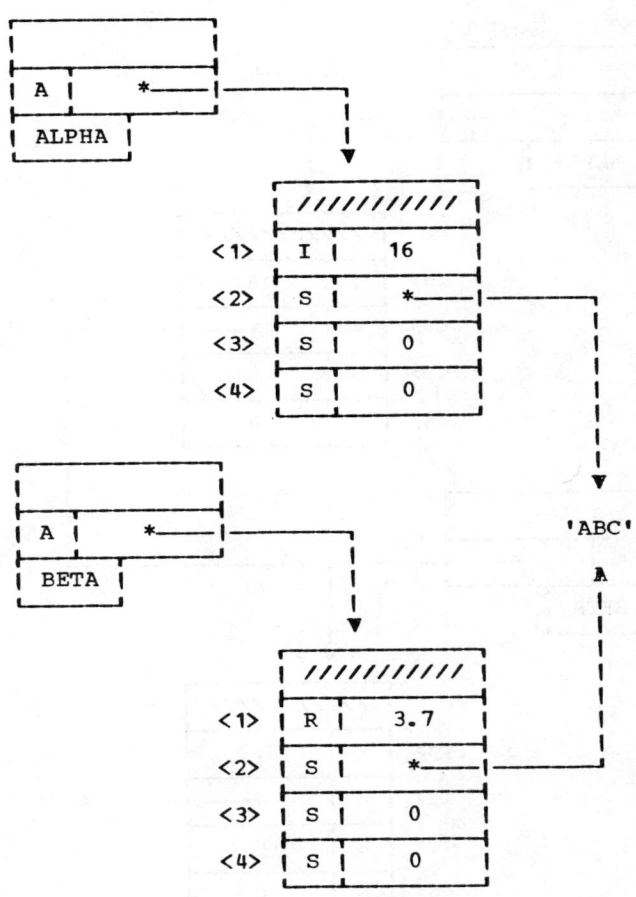

Figure 4.3

This figure illustrates the effect of the COPY function as contrasted with assignment.

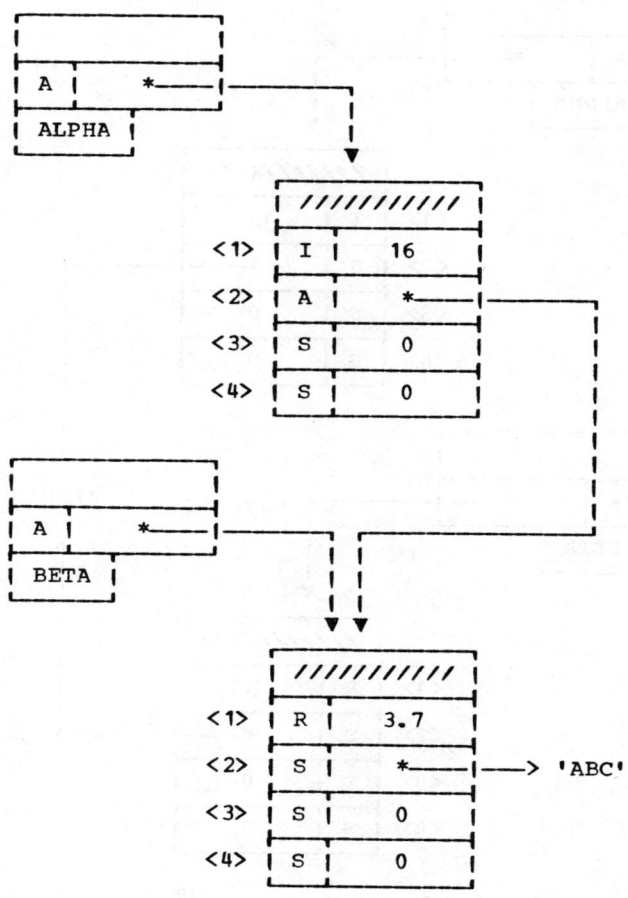

Figure 4.4

The result of executing ALPHA<2> = BETA.

Program 4.1 - CRACK

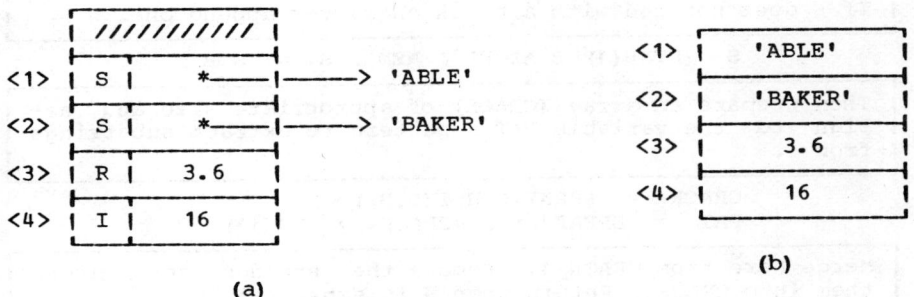

(a)   (b)

Figure 4.5

(a) shows the descriptor representation of an array. (b) shows a simplified representation for the same array.

```
|| Program  ||
||   4.1    ||
||  CRACK   ||
```
CRACK(S,B) is used to 'crack' open the string S and assign its contents to an array. This array is returned. B is a break character which serves to separate items in the string. The caller has the option of ending the string S with a break character. If none exists, CRACK will append one before further processing. Thus

          CRACK('ABLE BAKER CHARLIE',' ')

will return the array

```
        <1> |  'ABLE'   |
        <2> |  'BAKER'  |
        <3> | 'CHARLIE' |
```

If B is null, the individual characters are cracked apart.

| CRACK(S,B)   will convert from string to array breaking at |
| the character B. |

              DEFINE('CRACK(S,B)I,PAT')   : (CRACK_END)

| Entry point: If B is null branch off to CRACK_1. |

CRACK   IDENT(B,NULL)   :S(CRACK_1)

> If S does not end with a break character append one.

```
          S     RTAB(1) B ABORT  | REM . S  =  S B
```

> Then prepare an array (CRACK) of appropriate size and assign to the variable PAT a pattern to extract substrings from S.

```
          CRACK  =  ARRAY(COUNT(S,B))
          PAT    =  BREAK(B) . *CRACK<I>   LEN(1)
```

> Merge here from CRACK_1. Remove the strings and insert them into CRACK. Return when S is exhausted.

```
CRACK_2   I  =  I + 1
          S     PAT  =                         :S(CRACK_2) F(RETURN)
```

> If no break character, allocate CRACK and assign pattern to PAT. This pattern will strip individual characters from S.

```
CRACK_1   CRACK  =  ARRAY(SIZE(S))
          PAT    =  LEN(1) . *CRACK<I>           :(CRACK_2)
CRACK_END
```

Names referenced by CRACK:	Name	Type	Where defined
	COUNT	Function	Program 3.4

```
| |  Program    | |
| |    4.2      | |
| |  STRINGOUT  | |
```

STRINGOUT(A,SEP) will serve to convert from array to string. SEP contains a separation string to be inserted between strings of the array A. Thus if A is an array with values

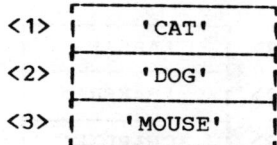

then STRINGOUT(A,',') will return 'CAT,DOG,MOUSE'. A is assumed to be singly dimensioned with lower bound 1 and composed of strings or items which can be concatenated. Note that STRINGOUT(CRACK(S,B)) will return S provided that S does not end in B. Note also that STRINGOUT(CRACK(S B,B)) will always return S.

Program 4.3 - SEQ   Page 71

```
| STRINGOUT(A,SEP)   will convert from an array of strings to |
| a string.  SEP will serve to separate the strings.          |

        DEFINE('STRINGOUT(A,SEP)I')        :(STRINGOUT_END)

| Entry point:   Initialize I and STRINGOUT.                  |

STRINGOUT           I = 1
                    STRINGOUT  =  A<1>             :F(RETURN)

| Top of loop                                                 |

STRINGOUT_1         I = I + 1
                    STRINGOUT  =  STRINGOUT SEP A<I>
+                                       :S(STRINGOUT_1) F(RETURN)
STRINGOUT_END
```

```
|| Program  ||   Although it is not conceptually difficult to
||   4.3    ||   sequence through an array, it can be a
||   SEQ    ||   tedious exercise if it is required that we
                 do it over and over.  This is especially true
```
in SNOBOL4 which has no DO or FOR statement. SEQ(S,N) provides
a sequencing capability similar to the action of a DO-loop.
For example:

                  SEQ(' A<I> = I ', .I)

will initialize an array A such that the Ith element is assigned the value I. The first argument is a statement or
sequence of statements separated by semicolons. The second
argument is the name of a variable. The variable is assigned
the values 1,2,... and the statement or statements are executed for each such assignment. This is repeated until
failure is detected on the last statement of the sequence.
Thus

        SEQ(" A<K> = TRIM(INPUT) ; DIFFER(A<K>,'STOP') ", .K)

will read cards successively into the array A until either A
has no more room or the word 'STOP' is encountered on the input stream. But note that if an end-of-file is encountered
(INPUT fails) the sequencing will not be stopped. In this
case, if no subsequent file exists, the program will terminate
in error.

If failure is detected on the first attempt to execute the
statements then SEQ will return failure. This permits compounding the iteration as in the following:

          SEQ(" SEQ(' A<I,J> = I * J',.J)", .I)

The above statement will assign a value (as indicated) to each
element of a doubly dimensioned array A.

Chapter 4 - ARRAY FUNCTIONS

> SEQ(S,N) will sequence through a set of statements until failure is detected. The indexing variable is given by the name N.

```
                DEFINE('SEQ(ARG_S,ARG_NAME)')            :(SEQ_END)
```

> Entry point: Initialize indexing variable. Then convert ARG_S to code.

```
SEQ             $ARG_NAME  =  0
                ARG_S  =  CODE(ARG_S  ' :S(SEQ_1)F(SEQ_2)')
+                                                    :F(ERROR)
```

> Increment indexing variable by 1 and spring off to compiled code. Return will be to SEQ_1 or SEQ_2.

```
SEQ_1           $ARG_NAME  =  $ARG_NAME + 1          :<ARG_S>
```

> Control flows to SEQ_2 if a fail was detected. If first time through fail; otherwise succeed.

```
SEQ_2           EQ($ARG_NAME,1)             :S(FRETURN)F(RETURN)
SEQ_END
```

Program 4.4 AOPA	Some languages such as PL/I and APL permit arrays to be arguments to arithmetic operators. SNOBOL4 does not permit such operations, but functions can be written to

serve the same purpose. The resulting function will not be as convenient as the built-in facility but it will be at least, if not more, general and will be programmer-modifiable. AOPA(A1,OP,A2) will return a new array whose elements are the result of applying the indicated operation between corresponding elements of the arrays A1 and A2. Both A1 and A2 are assumed to be singly dimensioned of lower bound 1. Either A1 or A2 or both may be scalar. OP is indicated by a string and can be any SNOBOL4 operator. Thus

```
                A  =  AOPA(A, '+', B)
```

will add the array A to B.

```
                C  =  AOPA(A,' ',',')
```

will concatenate a comma to every element of the array A.

> AOPA(A1,OP,A2) will apply the infix operator OP to corresponding pairs of A1 and A2. An array will be returned unless both are scalars.

```
                DEFINE('AOPA(A1,OP,A2)S1,I,S2,S')         :(AOPA_END)
```

> Entry point: First check datatypes. If neither is an ar-

Program 4.5 - FIND   Page 73

| ray we fall through the two tests, apply the OP to the two |
| scalars and return. |

```
AOPA      IDENT(DATATYPE(A1), 'ARRAY')              :S(AOPA_1)
          IDENT(DATATYPE(A2), 'ARRAY')              :S(AOPA_2)
          AOPA = EVAL('A1 ' OP ' A2')               :(RETURN)
```

| A1 is an array; A2 is in doubt. |

```
AOPA_1    S1 = '<I>'
          S2 = IDENT(DATATYPE(A2), 'ARRAY')   '<I>'
          AOPA = ARRAY(PROTOTYPE(A1))               :(AOPA_COMMON)
```

| A2 is an array; A1 is not. |

```
AOPA_2    S2 = '<I>'
          AOPA = ARRAY(PROTOTYPE(A2))
```

| Common code |

```
AOPA_COMMON
          S = ' AOPA<I> = A1' S1 ' ' OP ' A2' S2
          SEQ(S,.I)                                 :(RETURN)
AOPA_END
```

Names referenced	Name	Type	Where defined
by AOPA:	SEQ	Function	Program 4.3

```
|| Program ||
||   4.5   ||
||  FIND   ||
```
FIND(A,PRED) will search an array for an extreme element. The type of extreme element will be determined by the predicate PRED. Thus

$$FIND(A, 'GE')$$

will find and return the index of the largest element in the array A. Specifically it will return the first element in A which is greater than or equal to all elements of higher index.

$$FIND(A, 'GT')$$

will also return the index of the largest element. If there is a tie, FIND will return the index of the last such element. Thus

$$EQ(FIND(A,'GT') , FIND(A,'GE'))$$

may fail, but

$$EQ(A< FIND(A,'GT') > , A< FIND(A,'GE') >)$$

will succeed.

The predicate may be prefixed with the '¬' operator. Thus

                        A< FIND(A, '¬LGT') >

will return the string lowest in alphabetic order of the strings of the array A.

| FIND(A,PRED)   will return the index of an extreme element
| in the array A as determined by the predicate PRED.

              DEFINE('FIND(A,PRED)EX,I,MAX,TEST')   :(FIND_END)

| Entry Point: Construct an expression for comparing 2
| values. Also initialize FIND and MAX, tentatively.

FIND
          EX   = CONVERT(PRED '(MAX,TEST)' , 'EXPRESSION')
          FIND = 1
          MAX = A<FIND>

| Compare MAX with all elements of higher index than FIND
| until failure is encountered. If no elements remain,
| return.

              I   = 1
FIND_1   I   = I + 1
              TEST = A<I>   :F(RETURN)
              EVAL(EX)   :S(FIND_1)

| A new extreme element has been found.

              MAX = TEST
              FIND = I   :(FIND_1)
FIND_END

Epilogue

Testing of the array is completed when a reference to A<I> (first statement after FIND_1) fails (indicating array reference out of bounds). Note that EX has been assigned an expression to test MAX against TEMP rather than to test MAX against A<I>. The reader might argue that the latter strategy is more efficient since it would save one instruction in the inner loop. That is, failure of EVAL(EX), in this case, would mean either failure of the predicate PRED or array reference out of bounds and the distinction could be made afterwards. But this scheme would not work because ¬LGT(MAX,A<I>) actually succeeds if the array reference A<I> is out of bounds. That is to say the unary ¬ operator does not merely negate the predicate, it negates the entire expression. In any case, the savings would not be very great. As we will see, assignments and statement overhead cost little compared with anything else in the language.

Program 4.7 - TRUNC

	Program	
	4.6	
	AI	

AI(A,I) (Apply Index) - where A and I are arrays will regard I as a set of indices to be applied to the array A. The result is an array. Thus if

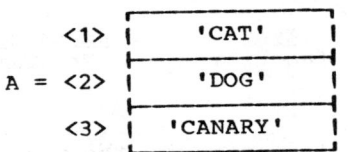

the array returned is

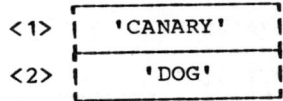

If I is a scalar the result will be A<I>.

AI(A,I) will apply the indices contained in I to the array A.

```
            DEFINE('AI(A,I) J')                       :(AI_END)
```

Entry point: If I is not an array, go to AI_1 where we merely return the Ith element.

```
AI          IDENT(DATATYPE(I), 'ARRAY')               :F(AI_1)
```

Make AI, the array to be returned, look like I. Then apply the indices.

```
            AI  =  ARRAY(PROTOTYPE(I))
            SEQ(' AI<J>  =  A<I<J>> ', .J)            :(RETURN)
AI_1        AI  =  A<I>                               :(RETURN)
AI_END
```

Names referenced	Name	Type	Where defined
by AI:	SEQ	Function	Program 4.3

	Program	
	4.7	
	TRUNC	

TRUNC(A,L,H) will return the truncation of the singly-dimensioned array A. That is, a new array will be created and returned consisting of the elements A<L>, A<L+1>, ..., A<H>.

Chapter 4 - ARRAY FUNCTIONS

```
TRUNC        DEFINE('TRUNC(A,L,H)')                    :(TRUNC_END)
             TRUNC   =   ARRAY(H - L + 1)
             L   =   L - 1
             SEQ('   TRUNC<I>   =   A<L + I> ',.I)
                                                       :(RETURN)
TRUNC_END
```

Names referenced by TRUNC:	Name	Type	Where defined
	SEQ	Function	Program 4.3

```
┌─────────────┐
││  Program  ││   CATA(A1,A2)  will concatenate the two arrays
││    4.8    ││   A1   and   A2.    Both   are  assumed   singly-
││   CATA    ││   dimensioned of lower bound one. The returned
└─────────────┘   array also has lower bound one.

             DEFINE('CATA(A1,A2) I,N1')                 :(CATA_END)
CATA         N1  =   PROTOTYPE(A1)
             CATA =   ARRAY(N1 + PROTOTYPE(A2))
             SEQ('  CATA<I>    =   A1<I> ',  .I)
             SEQ('  CATA<N1 + I>   =   A2<I>'  ,  .I)
                                                        :(RETURN)
CATA_END
```

Names referenced by CATA:	Name	Type	Where defined
	SEQ	Function	Program 4.3

??
?????????????????????????? EXERCISES ???????????????????????????
??

Exercise 4.1 A common problem is to initialize an array with a large number of strings. Commonly this is done with assignment statements but if the list is long this technique can prove wearisome. Using CRACK, assign an array of length 12 to the variable M assigning to M<I> the name of the Ith month (or an acceptable abbreviation). Thus M<1> = 'JAN.', etc.

Exercise 4.2 Modify SEQ so that it accepts 2 additional (optional) arguments. The first will be a lower bound (if not present the lower bound is taken to be 1) and the second will indicate the increment (either positive or negative). The default increment should, of course, be 1.

Exercise 4.3 Let A be an array with lower bound 1.

a) What will be the result of the following 2 statements?

Exercises for chapter 4   Page 77

```
            N = +PROTOTYPE(A)
            SEQ(' SWAP(.A<I>, .A<N + 1 - I>)', .I)
```

b) Modify the second statement above so that the array A is actually reversed.

| Exercise 4.4 | Rewrite STRINGOUT using SEQ.

| Exercise 4.5 | Assume A is an array of strings having a lower bound of 1. Use SEQ to find the index of the first element in A which begins with the character 'M'.

| Exercise 4.6 | Modify AOPA so that if the value of OP syntactically resembles an identifier, it is regarded as a binary function.

| Exercise 4.7 | Is AOPA(A1,,A2) a valid call? If so, what does it do?

| Exercise 4.8 | Write a function OPA(OP,A) which will apply the unary operator OP to every element of the array A.

| Exercise 4.9 | Write BLEND(X,Y) where X and Y are equilength strings by an expression involving functions defined in this chapter.

| Exercise 4.10 | Extend AI to permit I to range over a) 2-dimensional arrays, b) multidimensional arrays, and c) programmer-defined data objects.

| Exercise 4.11 | The statement

            &ALPHABET   BREAK(S)   LEN(1) . T

will assign to T the character in S lowest in the alphabet. Do the same using FIND and other functions defined in this chapter.

| Exercise 4.12 | In TRUNC, the statement L = L - 1 could be removed if the subsequent statement were modified. What modification is needed? Why was it not done this way?

Chapter 4 - ARRAY FUNCTIONS

| Exercise 4.13 | Write a function DO(S,N,L,U,I) where S is a statement sequence, N is a name, L is a lower bound, U is an upper bound, and I is an increment. DO should simulate a Fortran DO-loop.

| Exercise 4.14 | (a) Define a function LBOUNDS(A) which will return an array equal to the sequence of lower bounds of the array A. Define a function UBOUNDS(A) to do a similar thing with upper bounds. For example, LBOUNDS(ARRAY('3:10,-1:1')) will return an array containing two integers, 3 and -1.

(b) Write a function INCREMENT(S,L,U,N) which will increment and return a sequence of subscripts contained in the array S. L is an array of lower bounds as might be obtained from the LBOUNDS function of the previous exercise and U is an array of upper bounds. N is the size of each of these arrays. The function should fail if no more increments remain.

(c) Using the functions INCREMENT, LBOUNDS, UBOUNDS defined above, write a program to print out every item in an array A. A may have any prototype but all of its items may be assumed to be printable.

| Exercise 4.15 | Write a function called PUSH(A,E) which will push an element E onto an array A which is acting like a stack. The first element of A contains the index of the last element pushed. If A runs out of room, double its size. PUSH will return A or the newly created array. Routines in this section may be used if applicable.

CHAPTER FIVE

BASIC

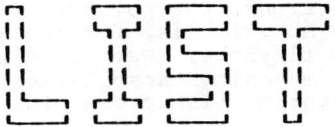

PROCESSING

```
--------------------------------------
|                                    |
|            CONTENTS                |
|                                    |
|   READL ................. 5.1      |
|                                    |
|   READRL ................ 5.2      |
|                                    |
|   REVL .................. 5.3      |
|                                    |
|   LAST .................. 5.4      |
|                                    |
|   PUSH .................. 5.5      |
|                                    |
|   POP ................... 5.6      |
|                                    |
|   TOP ................... 5.7      |
|                                    |
|   COPYL ................. 5.8      |
|                                    |
|   FLD ................... 5.9      |
|                                    |
|   VISIT ................. 5.10     |
|                                    |
--------------------------------------
```

Chapter 5 - BASIC LIST PROCESSING

The SNOBOL series of programming languages through SNOBOL3 had only one datatype, the string. Even the arithmetic facilities of SNOBOL3 were implemented as operations on strings of digits rather than on machine integers. Because of this historical bias, and because the language is extaordinarily rich in string handling, SNOBOL4 is still regarded by some as exclusively a string language. Yet, all the basic facilities which one expects in a list processing language have been incorporated into SNOBOL4; these include the automatic allocation and freeing of storage, recursive functions, the pointer, and the data structure. Moreover, the notation is, for the most part, conventional, convenient and flexible. Were SNOBOL4 suddenly stripped of all its pattern matching capabilities, it would still be a powerful and convenient list-processing language.

What do we mean by list processing? This is the kind of data processing in which associated data is linked together via pointers as opposed to an array organization in which associated data is placed in consecutive locations. List processing is used whenever the association of data is likely to change because such change can be readily accomplished merely be modifying links rather than by moving data.

A list is technically a sequence of items joined together by pointers and is really just a special case of an arbitrary linked structure. Hence 'list processing' is a misnomer for what might be better termed 'link processing'. However, a list may contain items of any kind, including other lists so that arbitrary trees may be formed. Hence, a list is more general than what is at first blush indicated. Nonetheless, it is important to realize that by list processing we mean, really, an arbitrarily interlaced collection of data objects with the possibility of loops and with no restrictions on the number of nodes or the number of links per node. In other words we are really speaking of arbitrary graphs.

The method by which one does list-processing in SNOBOL4 is via the so-called programmer-defined datatype. Calling the function DATA, one can define a new datatype. Instances of this datatype can be created by making what appear to be function calls to the name of the datatype. Thus

```
DATA('LINK(NEXT,VALUE)')
L = LINK('XYZ', 22)
```

will first define a datatype called LINK and then assign to L an object whose 2 fields (viz. NEXT and VALUE) are initialized with the 2 values given as arguments. The result is shown in Figure 5.1.

For convenience we will refer to data objects of this kind as **structures** and to an interlaced set of structures as a data **configuration**. Like arrays, structures consist of a sequence of variables (one created variable for each field) together

Chapter 5 - BASIC LIST PROCESSING

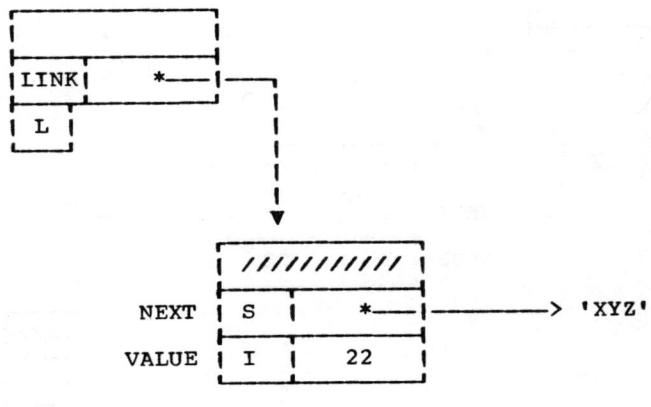

Figure 5.1

with some miscellaneous information denoted by cross hatching in the figure. These fields may be referenced via function notation such as

```
NEXT(L) = 'ABC'
N  = VALUE(L) + 3
```

Such field references may be used wherever a variable may be used, such as on the left hand side of an assignment (as above) or on the right hand side of a variable association operator (binary . or $). As in the case of all variables, the field of a structure may be assigned a data object of any type, including another structure. Thus

```
NEXT(L) = LINK()
```

will allocate a new LINK structure and assign it to the NEXT field of L. This statement will result in the configuration shown in Figure 5.2.

A field of a structure may refer to the structure in which it is embedded or to any part of the configuration. Thus, continuing

```
NEXT(NEXT(L)) = L
```

will produce the configuration shown in Figure 5.3.

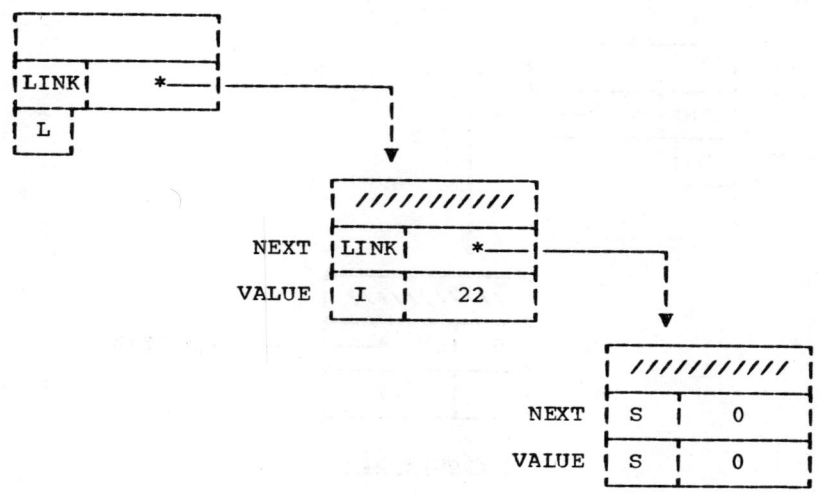

Figure 5.2

There is no intrinsic limit to the number of fields of a structure or to the number of new datatypes that may be created.

It is sometimes required that we obtain a pointer to one of the fields of a structure. This we may do by use of the unary name operator. Thus

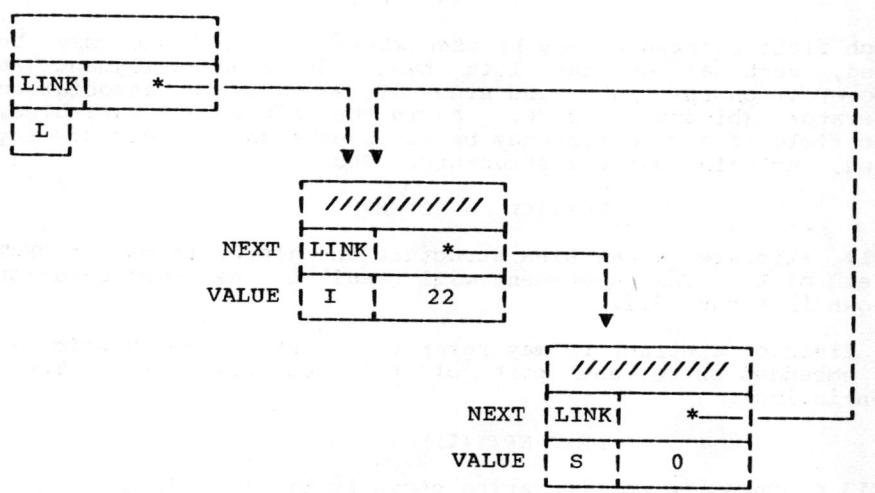

Figure 5.3

Chapter 5 .- BASIC LIST PROCESSING   Page 83

```
        L     = LINK()
        ALPHA = .NEXT(L)
```
will result in the configuration shown in Figure 5.4.

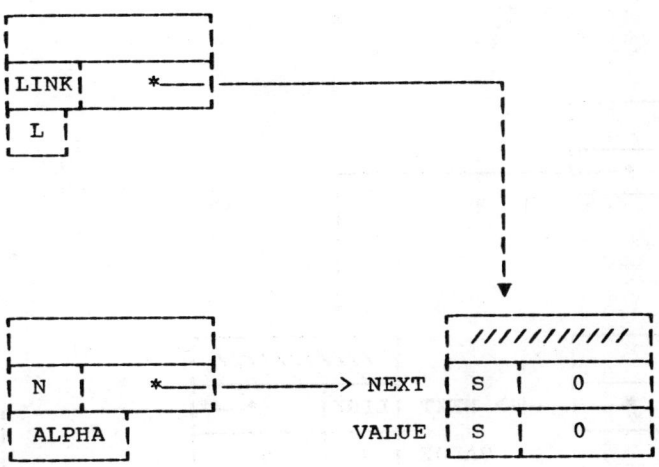

Figure 5.4

Page 84   Chapter 5   -   BASIC LIST PROCESSING

The datatype indicated for ALPHA is 'N' for NAME. We may assign any value to the variable whose name ALPHA contains, by using the unary $ operator. For example:

$$\$ALPHA \quad = \quad LINK()$$

will result in the configuration shown in Figure 5.5.

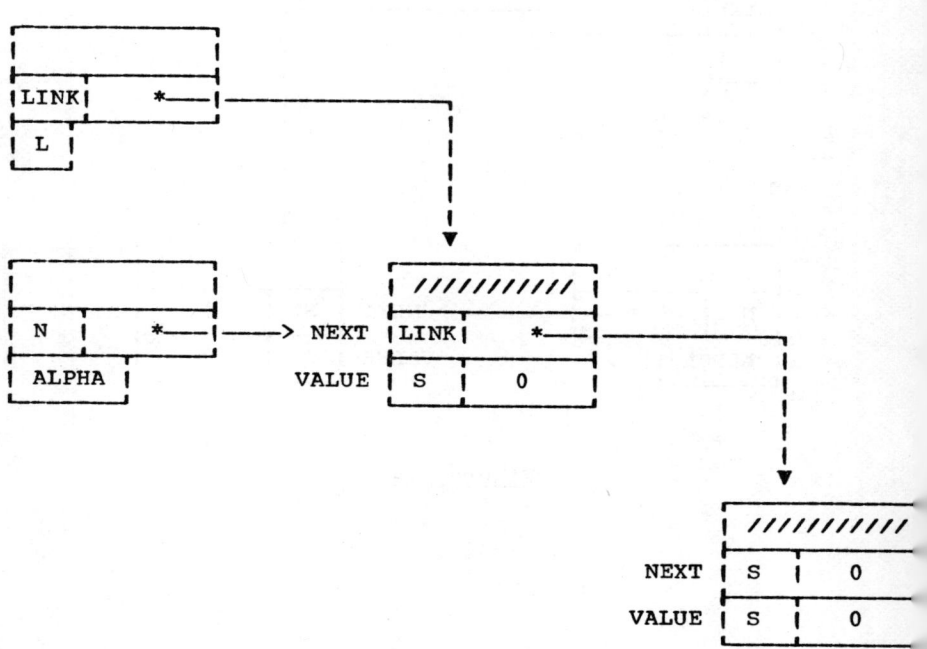

Figure 5.5

Chapter 5 - BASIC LIST PROCESSING

Two different datatypes may have the same field without fear of collision. Thus

DATA('TN(VALUE,NEXT,LSON,RSON)')

will define a new kind of data called TN (for Tree Node). Executing

        T = TN(16, LINK())
        NEXT(NEXT(T)) = .T

will result in the structure shown in Figure 5.6.

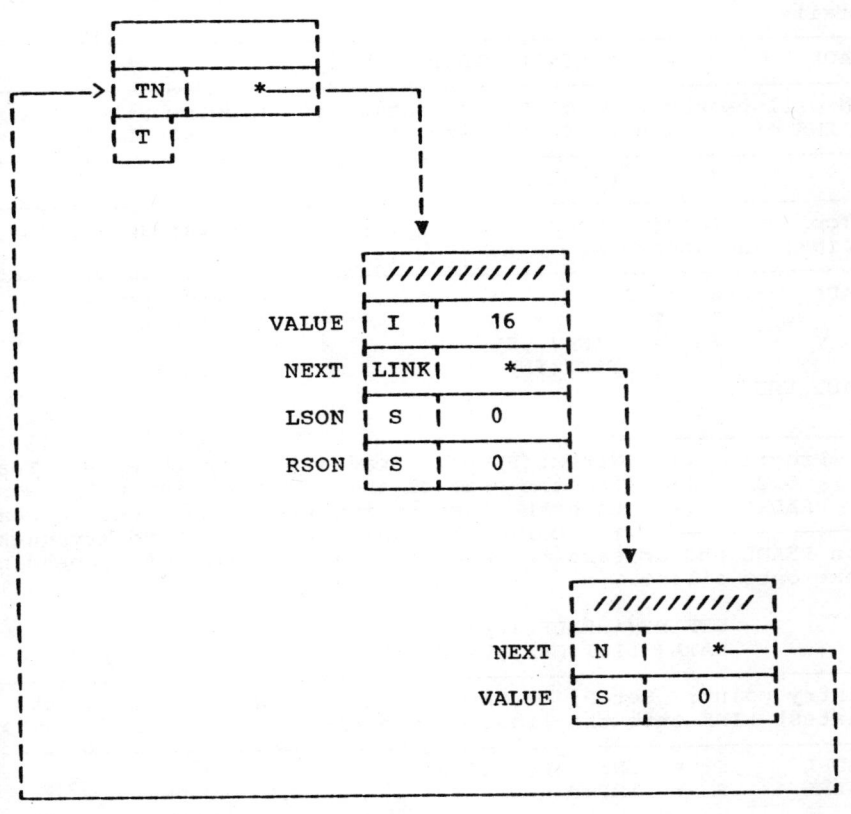

Figure 5.6

Page 86   Chapter 5   -   BASIC LIST PROCESSING

```
|| Program  ||
||   5.1    ||
||  READL   ||
```
The function READL(P) will read in a sequence of items, placing them in a list, and return the head of the list. P is a pattern to indicate the end of the list. If P is null (or equivalently, absent) the list is read in until an end-of-file condition is encountered. Otherwise, it will stop reading when the pattern match succeeds. It will not include the card matched. Thus READL(POS(0) 'STOP') will read a sequence of strings up to but not including the first string having the word 'STOP' in column 1.

```
            DEFINE('READL(P)N,S')
            DATA('LINK(NEXT,VALUE)')                 :(READL_END)
```

| Entry point: If P is null, make sure the pattern will fail.

```
READL     P   =   IDENT(P)   ABORT
```

| N will be the name of the variable to receive the next LINK of the list. Initialize it to point to READL.

```
            N   =   .READL
```

| Top of loop: Read a card; try the pattern; append the LINK; and update N.

```
READL_1   S   =   INPUT                          :F(RETURN)
          S   P                                  :S(RETURN)
          $N  =   LINK( ,S)
          N   =   .NEXT($N)                      :(READL_1)
READL_END
```

```
|| Program  ||
||   5.2    ||
||  READRL  ||
```
READRL(P) will read a list in reverse. That is, the head of the returned list will contain the last string read. The reversed read is curiously easier to write (and keypunch) than READL and appears to be a more natural way of appending items onto a list.

```
            DEFINE('READRL(P)')
            DATA('LIST(NEXT,VALUE)')                :(READRL_END)
```

| Entry point: Set P; go through the loop inserting the latest LINK onto the front of the list.

```
READRL    P   =   IDENT(P)   ABORT
READRL_1  S   =   INPUT                          :F(RETURN)
          S   P                                  :S(RETURN)
              READRL  =  LINK(READRL, S)         :(READRL_1)
READRL_END
```

Program 5.4 - LAST

```
|  Program   |     REVL(L) will reverse a list L. The algorithm
|   5.3      |     works according to the diagram in Figure
|   REVL     |     5.7.  For simplicity the list elements have
                   been denoted by a single cell.
```
Also, an arrow impinging onto the outline of a cell represents a pointer to the data object and not a pointer to any particular field within the data object. REVL and L work their way down the list with L leading the way and REVL right behind. At each step the NEXT field of L is made to point backward to the value of REVL and then the 2 variables are incremented, so that they always span the 'gap' in the chain of links.

```
        DEFINE('REVL(L)T')
        DATA('LINK(NEXT,VALUE)')           :(REVL_END)
```

| Entry point: Return L if it is not a link. Otherwise, |
| initialize REVL and L to span the gap between the first |
| link and the rest of the list. |

```
RE' L       REVL    =  L
            IDENT(DATATYPE(L), 'LINK')         :F(RETURN)
            L   =  NEXT(REVL)
            NEXT(REVL)  =
```

| Go through loop making NEXT(L) point backward to REVL and |
| walk one step forward (T is a temporary to hold NEXT(L)). |
| Quit when L becomes NULL. |

```
REVL_1      IDENT(L)                           :S(RETURN)
            T   =  NEXT(L)
            NEXT(L)    =  REVL
            REVL  =  L
            L   =  T                           :(REVL_1)
REVL_END
```

```
|  Program   |     LAST(L) will return (by name) the name of
|   5.4      |     the last NEXT field of a list.  Thus, if L1
|   LAST     |     and L2 are lists
```

                LAST(L1) = L2

will concatenate the two lists. If the argument to LAST is null the function fails. Thus

        LAST(L1) = L2   :S(LAB1)
        L1 = L2
LAB1

will concatenate L2 to L1 even if one or both of the lists are null. Also

        LAST(L) = L

Page 88   Chapter 5   -   BASIC LIST PROCESSING

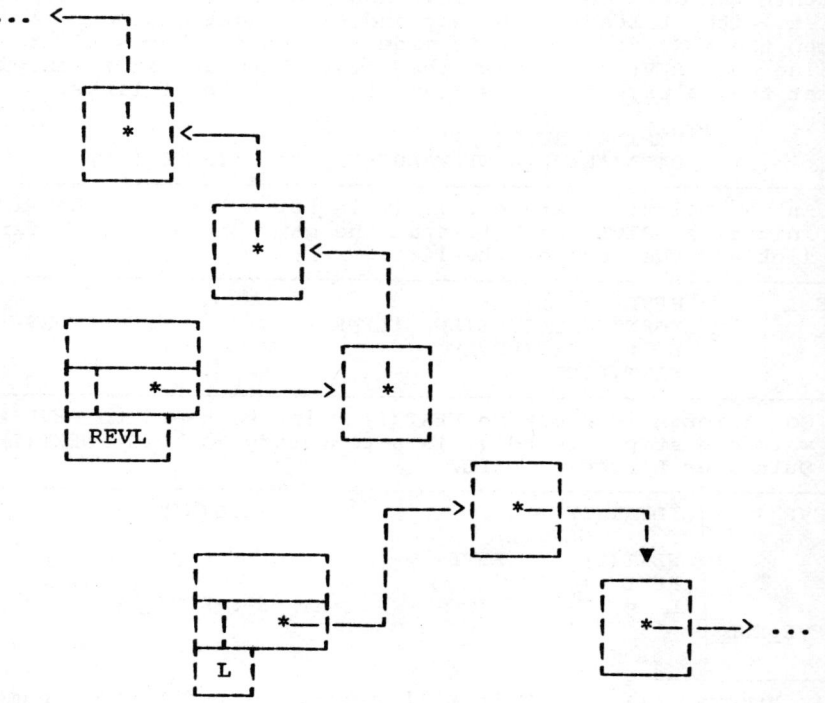

Figure 5.7

creates a circular list.

Programs 5.5, 5.6 & 5.7 - PUSH, POP & TOP

```
            DEFINE('LAST(L)')                :(LAST_END)
```
| Entry point: if L is null, fail. |

```
LAST       IDENT(L)                          :S(FRETURN)
```
| Seek a null NEXT field. |

```
LAST_1     L = DIFFER(NEXT(L))  NEXT(L)      :S(LAST_1)
```
| Return the name of this field by name. |

```
            LAST = .NEXT(L)                  :(NRETURN)
LAST_END
```

|| Programs || These routines are stack manipula-
|| 5.5, 5.6 & 5.7 || tion routines. As their names sug-
|| PUSH, POP & TOP || gest PUSH and POP are used to
                       respectively put on and take off an
item from a stack. TOP is used to examine the last element of
a stack without modifying it. Thus

            PUSH('ABC') ; PUSH(3)

will push 2 items onto a stack.

            K1 = POP() ;   K2 = TOP()
            K3 = POP() ;   K4 = TOP()

will assign to K1 the value 3, to K2 the value 'ABC', to K3
the value 'ABC' and will not modify K4 as the calls to TOP and
POP fail when the stack is empty. As an added bonus, TOP and
POP will return by name. In the case of TOP, this means that
values can be assigned into the top element. For example,

            TOP() = 'XYZ'

will change the value at the top of the stack. PUSH returns
the item pushed; more exactly it returns the _field_ bearing the
item last pushed. Hence,

            PUSH() = S

has the same effect as PUSH(S). Having been written in this
way, PUSH can be used to push matched substrings of a pattern
match onto a stack. For example,

            S   P1 . *PUSH()   P2 . *PUSH()

is a pattern matching statement which, if the match succeeds,
cause two substrings to be pushed onto the stack. We will require this property of PUSH in the chapter on compiling. See
L_ONE, Prog. 18.2.

Page 90   Chapter 5   -   BASIC LIST PROCESSING

```
                DEFINE('PUSH(X) ')
                DEFINE('POP() ')
                DEFINE('TOP() ')
                DATA('LINK(NEXT,VALUE) ')
                                                      :(PUSH_END)
```
```
+--------------------------------------------------------------------+
| Entry  point  for PUSH:  Just allocate a LINK and put it at        |
| the head of the stack pointed to by the  global  variable          |
| PUSH_POP.   Then return the VALUE field by name.                   |
+--------------------------------------------------------------------+
```
```
PUSH            PUSH_POP  =  LINK(PUSH_POP,X)
                PUSH      =  .VALUE(PUSH_POP)        :(NRETURN)
```
```
+--------------------------------------------------------------------+
| Entry  point  for POP:  If the global stack is null, fail.         |
| Otherwise return the element and pop the stack.                    |
+--------------------------------------------------------------------+
```
```
POP             IDENT(PUSH_POP)                      :S(FRETURN)
                POP       =  VALUE(PUSH_POP)
                PUSH_POP  =  NEXT(PUSH_POP)          :(RETURN)
```
```
+--------------------------------------------------------------------+
| Entry point for TOP:  Return name of VALUE field by  name.         |
| Fail if none exists.                                               |
+--------------------------------------------------------------------+
```
```
TOP             IDENT(PUSH_POP)                      :S(FRETURN)
                TOP       =  .VALUE(PUSH_POP)        :(NRETURN)
PUSH_END
```

```
+------------------+
||   Program     ||   COPYL will copy a list.  It makes use of the
||     5.8       ||   built-in function COPY which can be used to
||    COPYL      ||   copy structures (as well as arrays).   Hence
+------------------+   if a list is a chain of LINKs then COPY will
```
be used to copy each LINK in turn.   If it should happen that
the VALUE field of a list points off to some other list, then
a recursive function call is used to copy this subsidiary
list. No difficulty follows from this simple procedure unless
the data configuration has loops. If one of the fields points
back to a node which has already been copied, we need not, and
in fact must not, make a new copy of this node. Hence we must
find a method to indicate which nodes have already been
visited.   This problem is not unique to COPYL. It arises
whenever we wish to process every node of a data configuration
with loops.   We solve the problem here with tables.   Another
method, one involving marking the structure itself is
described in VISIT, Prog. 5.10.

To avoid marking structures, we keep a list of all items already copied paired with copied counterparts. This is most
easily done with a SNOBOL4 <u>table</u>. A table is similar to an
array except that the subscripts are not restricted to integers but may be any value. Thus

                        TBL   =   TABLE(100)
                        TBL<X> =   Y

Program 5.8 - COPYL   Page 91

will assign the Xth element of TBL the value Y, no matter what the datatypes of X and Y are. The value of 100 is an estimate of the number of items to be placed into the table. Thus, a table is a kind of associative array. It is implemented as a collection of descriptor pairs. When items are entered or extracted, a search must be made for the subscript. In SPITBOL the value is hashed so that the search is fairly rapid. In SNOBOL4 the search is linear but is not all that slow because only descriptors need be compared. In both languages the search is quite rapid for small tables.

In our particular application we are interested in the case where X and Y are structures. If L is a LINK then

$$TBL<L> = COPY(L)$$

will associate with that particular LINK a copy of that LINK. In this way, we not only mark that a LINK has been copied but we point directly to the copied LINK.

All this suggests allocating a table when COPYL is first called. But, if COPYL is called recursively, we do not want to allocate a new table but rather retain the old one. This can be done in several ways. Two functions may be defined COPYL and COPYL_INT. COPYL will receive control from external sources; COPYL_INT will be called internally and will not allocate the table.

Another approach, one to be used here, does not require that another function be defined. Rather, the COPYL function is redefined, by itself, twice, once immediately after receiving control, and once immediately before returning.

| COPYL(L) will copy a list of LINKs. The configuration may
| have loops.

```
        DEFINE('COPYL(L)T')
        DATA('LINK(NEXT,VALUE)')
                                        :(COPYL_END)
```

| Entry point: Redefine COPYL to have a new entry point and
| in which T will be treated as global.

```
COPYL   DEFINE('COPYL(L)','COPYL_1')
```

| Allocate a table and call COPYL. 100 is the estimate of
| the number of nodes in the list

```
        T    = TABLE(100)
        COPYL = COPYL(L)
```

| We are done! Redefine COPYL to the original definition
| and return.

```
        DEFINE('COPYL(L)T')             :(RETURN)
```

Page 92   Chapter 5   -   BASIC LIST PROCESSING

```
+---------------------------------------------------------------+
| Internal entry point:  If L is not a link there is no need    |
| to copy it.  Just return L.                                   |
+---------------------------------------------------------------+
COPYL_1     COPYL   =   L
            IDENT(DATATYPE(L), 'LINK')          :F(RETURN)
+---------------------------------------------------------------+
| Have we ever copied this LINK before?  If we have, just       |
| return the copied LINK.                                       |
+---------------------------------------------------------------+
            COPYL   =   T<L>
            DIFFER(COPYL, NULL)                 :S(RETURN)
+---------------------------------------------------------------+
| otherwise copy the LINK and  indicate  this  fact  in  the    |
| table.                                                        |
+---------------------------------------------------------------+
            COPYL   =   COPY(L)
            T<L>    =   COPYL
+---------------------------------------------------------------+
| Now copy the 2 fields.                                        |
+---------------------------------------------------------------+
            VALUE(COPYL)    =   COPYL(VALUE(L))
            NEXT(COPYL)     =   COPYL(NEXT(L))      :(RETURN)
COPYL_END
```

```
+-----------+
|| Program ||   FLD(ST,I) will  return  (by  name)  the  Ith
||  5.9    ||   field  of the structure ST, failing if I ex-
||  FLD    ||   ceeds the number of fields in the  structure
+-----------+   ST.   It  is written using 2 built-in func-
```
tions, APPLY and FIELD.   APPLY may be used with arbitrary
function names as well as with fields of a structure. Note
that APPLY returns by name (where applicable) and also note
that FIELD requires a datatype, not a data object.

```
            DEFINE('FLD(ST,I)')             :(FLD_END)
FLD         FLD =   .APPLY(FIELD(DATATYPE(ST), I), ST)
+                                       :S(NRETURN) F(FRETURN)
FLD_END
```

```
+-----------+
|| Program ||   VISIT  will  visit every structure of a con-
||  5.10   ||   figuration,  once  and  only  once,  calling
||  VISIT  ||   PROCESS(ST)  upon  arrival,  where ST is the
+-----------+   structure visited.   PROCESS represents some
```
activity to be carried out and is left to be defined by the
user.

COPYL, in the process of copying a configuration, had to visit
every node and we could let that function serve as a model
from which to write VISIT. The only basic difference would be
that, in COPYL, we knew the kind of structures we were dealing
with and so we could reference the fields by name.   In VISIT,
the structures are arbitrary and so we must use a function
such as FLD to sequence through every field.

Program 5.10 - VISIT

But we will depart from the COPYL method in two other ways. In the first place, we would like to present a method which avoids recursion. In many languages recursion is either unavailable or inefficient. Also, recursion, if carried to too many levels, will result in stack overflow. Also, we would like to present a method of marking structures which does not depend on tables.

The algorithm, to be presented, was discovered independently in 1965 by Deutsch and Schorr and Waite; see Knuth [Vol.1, p.416-417]. It was developed in connection with garbage collection. One phase of garbage collection is the marking phase when every structure which can be accessed is marked. Subsequent phases insure that the marked structures are saved and the unmarked structures discarded. Avoiding recursion when garbage collecting is highly desirable if the recursion stack is sharing collectable storage.

The algorithm works as follows. SON initially points to the root node of a tree as indicated in Figure 5.8(a), and the node is marked with a 1 (also shown in the figure). All pointers in the structure are examined to see if they point off to any as-yet-unmarked structure. If an unmarked structure is found, it is regarded as the new SON and the old son becomes the FATHER. If, in the new son, there is a pointer off to an unmarked node, the SON and FATHER descend another level. The pointer which had been used to point downward in the tree is redirected <u>upward</u> so that it is possible to determine from whence we came. The situation is depicted in Figure 5.8(b). Note that FATHER and SON span a 'gap' in the structure created by our backward pointer. This is similar to REVL.

The backward pointers permit us to crawl back up the tree when we are through examining all the descendants of SON. The MARK serves also the purpose of denoting which field is being used as backward pointer. For example, Figure 5.8(c) shows the situation a little later in which a mark of 2 on the grandfather indicates that the 2nd field is pointing to the great-grandfather.

When we are done, all the marks will have been set positive. We cannot make all the marks 0 again using our VISIT function but we can make them all negative by setting SIGN = -1. VISIT will work properly if the initial value of the marks is ≤ 0 so that this procedure can be used to restore the state of the configuration to one which will accept subsequent VISITs.

We could use a table to record the marks, as we did with COPYL. However, a more efficient method would be to add a MARK field to each data structure. For example, to add a MARK field to the LINK data type we could execute

DATA('LINK(NEXT,VALUE,MARK)')

It is rather remarkable that we may substitue this DATA call. for the DATA call

Chapter 5 - BASIC LIST PROCESSING

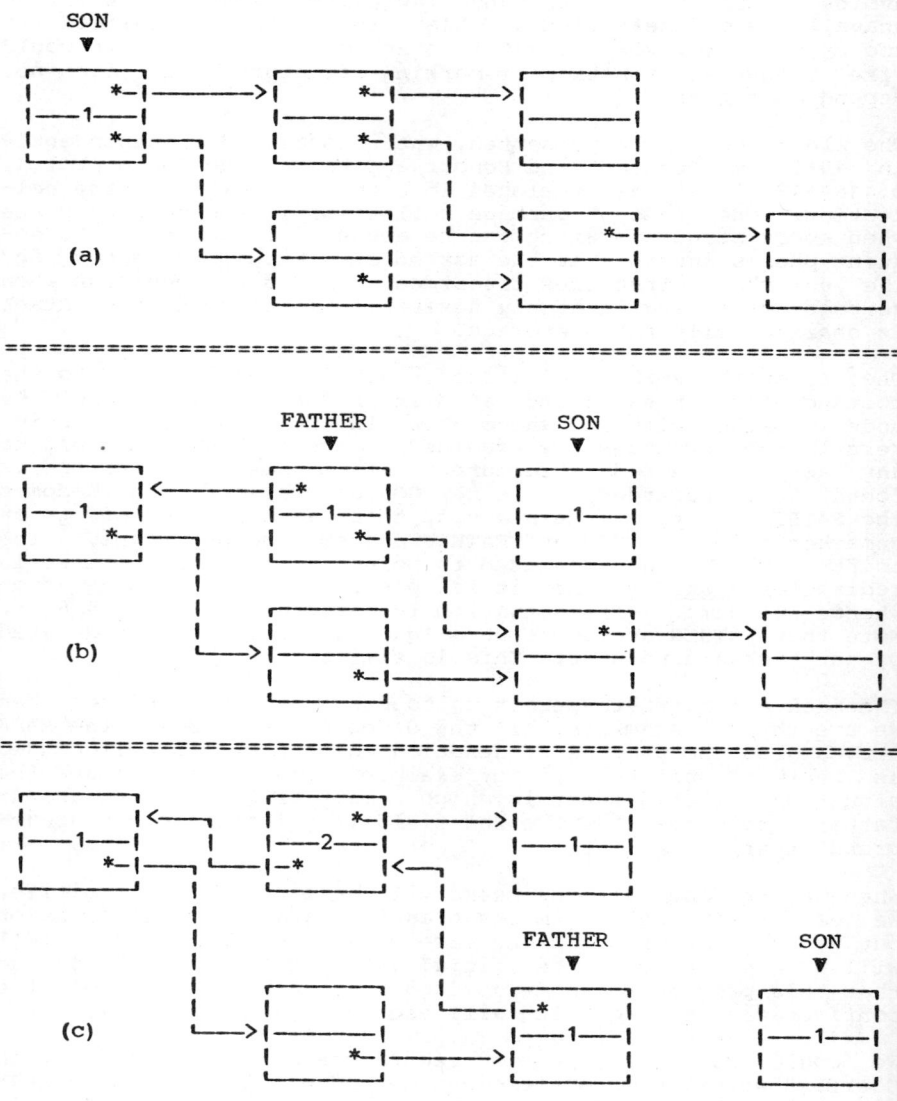

Figure 5.8

Program 5.10 - VISIT

DATA('LINK(NEXT,VALUE)')

in just about any program without modifying its behaviour. But it is at least inelegant, and perhaps impractical, to request users of VISIT to add a MARK field to every structure. Hence we will do this for him by <u>redefining</u> the DATA function. The new data function will capture control of each call to DATA, insert a MARK field, and then call the old original DATA function.

If the user is using the FIELD function, as we do in FLD, he may inadvertently sequence into the MARK field which is supposed to be kept invisible. But we can keep him out of the MARK field by redefining the FIELD function.

```
| VISIT(ST) will visit every node of the configuration
| headed by structure ST.  Visitation consists of calling
| PROCESS(ND) where ND is the node. VISIT(ST,-1) will reset
| the marks.
```

DEFINE('VISIT(SON,SIGN)FATHER,GS,GF,DT,I')

```
| Redefine the DATA function so that a MARK field is inser-
| ted into each new datatype.
```

```
          OPSYN('OLD_DATA', 'DATA')
          DEFINE('DATA(S)')                   :(DATA_END)
DATA      S   ')'  = ',MARK)'
          OLD_DATA(S)                         :(RETURN)
DATA_END
```

```
| Redefine the FIELD function so that the user won't know
| about the MARK field.
```

```
          OPSYN('OLD_FIELD', 'FIELD')
          DEFINE('FIELD(DT,I)')               :(FIELD_END)
FIELD
          OLD_FIELD(DT,I + 1)                 :F(FRETURN)
          FIELD = OLD_FIELD(DT,I)             :S(RETURN) F(FRETURN)
FIELD_END
```

```
| Initialization section for VISIT: STND_DT will match a
| standard datatype.
```

```
          STND_DT = POS(0) ('STRING' | 'INTEGER' | 'REAL'
+                  | 'PATTERN' | 'ARRAY' | 'TABLE' | 'NAME' |
+                  'EXPRESSION' | 'CODE' | 'EXTERNAL') RPOS(0)
                                              :(VISIT_END)
```

```
| Entry point for VISIT: The default value for SIGN is 1.
| If the datatype of the node is standard (i.e. not
| programmer-defined), just return.
```

Chapter 5 - BASIC LIST PROCESSING

```
VISIT       SIGN  = EQ(SIGN,0)    1
            DATATYPE(SON)    STND_DT       :S(RETURN)
```

> Control flows to VISIT_2 whenever a previously unmarked
> SON is found. Here it is processed and marked and I is
> initialized.

```
VISIT_2     PROCESS(SON)
            MARK(SON)  = SIGN
            I = 0
```

> Examine the Ith node of SON (GS means grandson). If GS is
> an unmarked structure, fall through.   Else, loop. If no
> more grandsons remain, go to VISIT_3.

```
VISIT_1     I  =  I + 1
            GS =  FLD(SON, I)                :F(VISIT_3)
            DATATYPE(GS)    STND_DT          :S(VISIT_1)
            GT(SIGN * MARK(GS) , 0)          :S(VISIT_1)
```

> Mark the SON with the current value of I so we can pick up
> later where we left off. Point back to FATHER rather than
> forward to GS.

```
            MARK(SON)  = SIGN * I
            FLD(SON,I) = FATHER
```

> Descend down one level; then go back to PROCESS and MARK
> the new SON.

```
            FATHER = SON
            SON    = GS                      :(VISIT_2)
```

> Here if no grandsons are left. If FATHER is null we are
> done. Otherwise set GF to be the grandfather.

```
VISIT_3     IDENT(FATHER)                    :S(RETURN)
            I  = SIGN * MARK(FATHER)
            GF = FLD(FATHER,I)
```

> Point back toward the SON. Then hoist up one level.

```
            FLD(FATHER,I) = SON
            SON    = FATHER
            FATHER = GF
VISIT_END                                    :(VISIT_1)
```

Names referenced by VISIT:	Name	Type	Where defined
	FLD	Function	Program 5.9

EXERCISES

Exercise 5.1 Rewrite CRACK(S,C) (Prog. 4.1) to return a linked list of strings rather than an array of strings.

Exercise 5.2 A doubly-linked list is one in which, in addition to a NEXT field pointing to the next item on the list, there is a PREV field pointing to the previous item on the list. Let L be a link of such a list. Write code to remove the link from its list.

Exercise 5.3 Write a routine FIRST() which will remove (and return) the _first_ item on the push-down stack maintained by PUSH and POP and fail if no such item exists. Do this (a) without modifying PUSH and POP and (b) modifying PUSH so that the process of getting the first element is more efficient.

Exercise 5.4 Modify COPYL so that it copies a configuration composed of structures of arbitrary types.

Exercise 5.5 As indicated in the text, the assignment LAST(L) = L will create a circular list. What modification to REVL (Prog. 5.3) is required to reverse a circular list (the node returned should be the node originally given).

Exercise 5.6 Write a routine DISPLAY(L) which will display a data configuration headed by L. The type of structures in the configuration may be dissimilar and arbitrary.

Exercise 5.7 Write a function called IFFLD(N,S) which will serve as a predicate to determine whether N is the name of a field of the structure S. The body of the function requires two statements.

Exercise 5.8 Modify DATA and FIELD (subfunctions of VISIT, Prog. 5.10) so that every structure created will have not one but two additional fields MARK and THREAD. Moreover, arrange to sieze control at each request to allocate a new structure so that all structures will be

threaded together via the THREAD field. Rewrite VISIT so that
by chaining down the THREAD field, the MARK field of each
structure is initially set to 0.

| Exercise 5.9 | How would you modify VISIT (Prog. 5.10) in
order to copy an arbitrary configuration?
(Hint: Add a field called NEW to every structure which will
point to the copied version.)

| Exercise 5.10 | Two configurations are said to be isomor-
phic if there is a one-one correspondence
between the structures of the configurations such that if two
structures correspond (a) they have the same type, (b) any
field of one structure that does not have a structure as value
must equal the corresponding field of the other, and (c) if a
field of one has a structure S as value then the field of the
other must have a structure S' such that S corresponds with
S'. Write a subroutine ISO(S1,S2) which will succeed if structures S1 and S2 correspond in an isomorphic configuration.

C H A P T E R   S I X

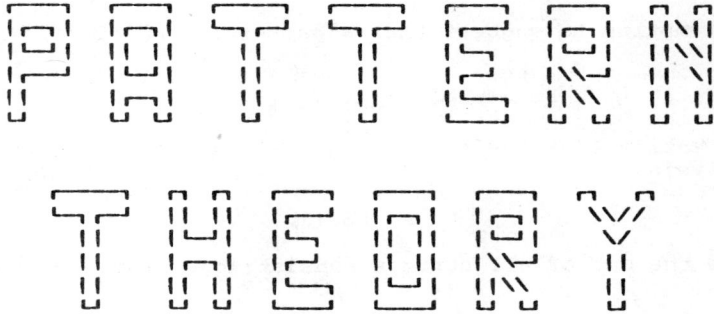

```
                CONTENTS
        Patterns and Cursors
        Nonlinear Patterns
        Fundamental Properties
        Scanning
        ARBNO
        Recursive Patterns
```

Chapter 6 - PATTERN THEORY

What is a pattern? We have used patterns throughout the preceding sections of this book without consciously evoking this question. Indeed it is perhaps not strictly necessary to know what patterns are so long as one knows how they work and what they do. However, patterns play such an important role in SNOBOL4 programming and they provide such a powerful facility for analyzing input data strings that a strong conceptual framework becomes necessary in order to derive clean and efficient implementations, resolve complex and seemingly ambiguous issues and contrive reasonable extensions.

It is tempting to suggest that a pattern is a set of strings. Thus

$$P = 'AB' \mid 'A'$$

would identify P as the two strings 'AB' and 'A'. Continuing in this vein

$$P = LEN(3)$$

would be the set of all strings consisting of three characters and

$$P = ARBNO(ANY('AB'))$$

would be the set of all strings (including the null string) comprised of characters chosen from the set {A,B}. FAIL, of course, would be the empty set.

But what would we make of the patterns POS(n), RPOS(n), TAB(n), RTAB(n), BREAK(s), SPAN(s), FENCE, and ABORT which cannot be uniquely identified with a set of strings. Thus POS(n) matches the null string when it matches but it doesn't match all null strings, only those at position n. If we identified POS(0) with the null string, we would be forced to conclude that POS(0) = POS(1) which is nonsense. By a similar token, BREAK(s), when it matches, will match a string not containing a character of s but it cannot be said to match all such strings, only those followed by a character of s. Hence, although BREAK(s) can match a null string on occasion, it cannot be related uniquely to the null string. The strings that BREAK(s) matches are determined in part by the context in which the strings are embedded and this is true of most of the patterns which cannot be related to string sets.

Another difference between patterns and sets of strings is that a pattern, if it matches more than one string, expresses a preference between any two. Thus

$$'AB' \mid 'A'$$

implies that 'AB' is tried before 'A' and behaves differently from

PATTERNS AND CURSORS

'A' | 'AB'

```
┌──────────────────────┐
│ %%%% ATTERNS AND CURSORS │
│ %  %  ┌──────────────┘
│ %%%%  │
│ %     │
│ %     │
└───────┘
```
Patterns are more accurately thought of as recognition processes operating on cursors. A <u>cursor</u> is a pair (S,I) where S is a string called the <u>subject</u> and I is an integer marking a position in the subject. I is called the <u>cursor position</u>. A cursor points between characters (as opposed to at them) and therefore the cursor position ranges between 0 and the length of the subject inclusive. The cursor ('ABCDEF',2) is depicted in Figure 6.1.

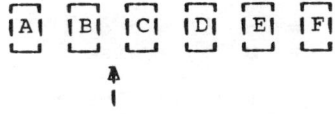

Figure 6.1

A depiction of the cursor ('ABCDEF',2)

When a pattern is called upon to match, it is presented with a cursor called the <u>pre-cursor</u> and the pattern either matches or fails to match at that point. If it matches, there will be a sequence of one or more <u>post-cursor</u> positions to identify the portion of the subject matched. A <u>pattern</u> P can then be defined as a function whose input value is a cursor and whose output value is a sequence of cursors. For reasons which will become apparent later we will use backward notation (c)P or simply cP to represent the application of the pattern P to its cursor argument c. Hence we write

$$cP = [c_1, c_2, \ldots\ ]$$

We will use square brackets as above to represent sequences, reserving braces to represent sets and parentheses for other kinds of scope delimitation.

For example, if the pattern ('CDE' | 'C') is applied to the cursor position of Figure 6.1 we have

$$('ABCDEF',2)('CDE'\ |\ 'C') = [5,\ 3]$$

In the above, the cursor position 5 stands as an abbreviation for the cursor ('ABCDEF',5) and similarly 3 is an abbreviation for ('ABCDEF',3). This represents no ambiguity since the subject does not change during a match.

We will use ∅ to represent the null sequence. Thus

$$('ABCDEF', 1)('CDE' \mid 'C') = \emptyset$$

Two patterns are <u>equal</u> if they represent the same function. That is, if $(c)P_1 = (c)P_2$, for all c then $P_1 = P_2$.

Below are some examples of built-in patterns in SNOBOL4. L is the length of the subject string. When a cursor is used in an arithmetic context it is the cursor position that is implied. For simplicity, the sequence [c] is represented as simply c.

$$\begin{aligned}
c\ POS(n) &= c &&\text{if } n = c \\
&= \emptyset &&\text{otherwise} \\
c\ RPOS(n) &= c &&\text{if } n = L - c \\
&= \emptyset &&\text{otherwise} \\
c\ TAB(n) &= n &&\text{if } n \geq c \\
&= \emptyset &&\text{otherwise} \\
c\ RTAB(n) &= L-n &&\text{if } L-n \geq c \\
&= \emptyset &&\text{otherwise} \\
c\ LEN(n) &= c+n &&\text{if } c+n \leq L \\
&= \emptyset &&\text{otherwise}
\end{aligned}$$

$$('ABCDEF', 1)\,BREAK('TAF') = [5]$$

$$('ABCDEF', 2)\,SPAN('CAT') = [3]$$

$$('A(B())CD', 0)\,BAL = [1, 6, 7, 8]$$

$$('ABCDE', 0)\,ARB = [0, 1, 2, 3, 4, 5]$$

Note that in the above, most built in patterns have at most one post-cursor position. ARB and BAL are exceptions and these are regarded as having 'implicit alternatives'.

Unevaluated expressions within patterns may make their behavior vary during a match. Thus

$$P = BREAK(*S)$$

will succeed or fail depending on the value of S. Any such pattern is termed <u>varying</u>. For the duration of this chapter we will only be concerned with nonvarying patterns.

The <u>alternation</u> (|) of two patterns is defined as:

$$c(P_1 \mid P_2) = (cP_1)(cP_2) \qquad (6.1)$$

where the right hand side indicates the concatenation of the two sequences.

PATTERNS AND CURSORS   Page 103

To define the concatenation of patterns we must extend the definition of pattern to operate on sequences of cursor positions. This is easily done:

$$[c_1, c_2, \ldots\ ]\ P\ =\ (c_1 P)\ (c_2 P)\ \ldots \qquad (6.2)$$

Note that the notation $c_1 P c_2 P$ is ambiguous because it can mean either $((c_1 P) c_2) P$ or $(c_1 P)(c_2 P)$ and so will be avoided. For completeness

$$\emptyset\ P\ =\ \emptyset$$

Pattern concatenation is defined as

$$c(P_1\ P_2)\ =\ (cP_1) P_2 \qquad (6.3)$$

For example

$$('ABCDEF',2)(('CDE'\ |\ 'C')\ LEN(1))\ =\ [5,3]\ LEN(1)$$
$$=\ [6,4]$$

The pattern FAIL is defined as:

$$(c)\,FAIL\ =\ \emptyset$$

for all c. Hence

$$FAIL\ |\ P\ =\ P\ =\ P\ |\ FAIL$$

for all P. That is, FAIL is the identity element under pattern alternation. Note that

$$(c)\,NULL\ =\ c$$

where NULL is the null string. This is the identity mapping for cursors and hence NULL is the identity element for pattern concatenation. That is

$$NULL\ P\ =\ P\ =\ P\ NULL$$

for all patterns P.

A pattern may have a countably infinite number of post-cursor positions. For example:

$$(c)\,SUCCEED\ =\ [c,\ c,\ c,\ \ldots\ ]$$

where the sequence goes on indefinitely. An infinitude of alternates, therefore, produces a well-defined pattern. Thus

$$ARB\ =\ (NULL\ |\ LEN(1)\ |\ LEN(2)\ |\ \ldots\ )$$

may be regarded as a proper definition for ARB. Whereas the number of post-cursor positions of (c)ARB is bounded by the length of the subject and so is always finite, its finiteness is not in general a requirement that the pattern be well-

Chapter 6 - PATTERN THEORY

defined. A pattern whose sequence of post-cursors is finite for all pre-cursors is said to be <u>finite</u>. If there is at least one pre-cursor such that the list of post-cursors is infinite the pattern is said to be <u>infinite</u>. As usual, we will hold that if C is infinite then

$$C = C \ C'$$

for all sequences C'. Thus

$$SUCCEED = SUCCEED \mid P$$

for all patterns P.

It should not be here thought that the definition of pattern is to be restricted in any way to those patterns which are directly available via SNOBOL4 primitives or by combinations of simple operations such as alternation or concatenation. A pattern is any well-defined process which maps a cursor into cursors of the same subject.

ONLINEAR PATTERNS | ABORT is a more pungent form of FAIL. Whereas (c)ABORT, like (c)FAIL, contains no post-cursor positions (ABORT always fails) ABORT differs from FAIL in that it causes an immediate halt of scanning. To include ABORT in the theory it is necessary to annex a new element which is the value of ABORT. We write

$$(c)ABORT = \dagger$$

$\dagger$ is called the <u>abort symbol</u>. When it is concatenated on the left of any sequence of cursors it yields itself. That is

$$\dagger \ [c_1, c_2, \ldots] = \dagger$$

More generally, an <u>extended sequence</u> E is defined as

$$E = C \lambda = [c_1, c_2, \ldots] \lambda$$

where C is a sequence of cursor positions, possibly infinite, possibly null, and λ is either $\dagger$ or $\emptyset$. Concatenation of extended sequences is defined as

$$(C_1\lambda_1)(C_2\lambda_2) = C_1C_2\lambda_2 \quad \text{if} \ \lambda_1 = \emptyset$$
$$= C_1\lambda_1 \quad \text{if} \ \lambda_1 = \dagger$$

it is easy to see that the concatenation of extended sequences is associative (the left most abort symbol is the important one no matter how the sequences are grouped) so that

$$(E_1 \ E_2) \ E_3 = E_1 \ (E_2 \ E_3) \qquad (6.4)$$

We can extend the domain of patterns from mere sequences to extended sequences as follows:

FUNDAMENTAL PROPERTIES   Page 105

$$(C \, \lambda) \, P = (CP) \, \lambda \qquad (6.5)$$

Note that $(\dagger) P = \dagger$.

An extended sequence which does not have a terminal abort symbol is called <u>linear</u>; otherwise it is called <u>nonlinear</u>. If for all cursors c, the value of (c)P is linear then P itself is said to be linear.

The built-in pattern FENCE which matches the null string but causes an immediate halt of scanning (like ABORT) when backed into is defined as

$$(c) \, FENCE = [c] \, \dagger$$

The definition of concatenation and alternation of patterns given above (6.1) and (6.3) are still valid with extended sequences. It follows immediately from the associativity of extended sequences that the alternation of patterns is associative. That is

$$(P_1 \mid P_2) \mid P_3 = P_1 \mid (P_2 \mid P_3) \qquad (6.6)$$

We briefly introduced the notions of transformations and homomorphisms on strings in Chapter 3. It readily follows from (6.2) and (6.5) that patterns are homomorphic transformations on extended sequences. That is

$$(E_1 \, E_2) \, P = (E_1 \, P) \, (E_2 \, P) \qquad (6.7)$$

From this it follows that

$$E \, (P_1 \, P_2) = (E \, P_1) \, P_2 \qquad (6.8)$$

Thus, if a pattern is regarded as a transformation on extended sequences, concatenation becomes function composition. It is an interesting fact that function composition is always associative. Thus

$$(P_1 \, P_2) \, P_3 = P_1 \, (P_2 \, P_3) \qquad (6.9)$$

<u>Proposition</u> Concatenation distributes over alternation from the right. That is

$$(P_1 \mid P_2) P_3 = P_1 \, P_3 \mid P_2 \, P_3 \qquad (6.10)$$

<u>Proof:</u> The left hand side when applied to a cursor c will produce by (6.1) and (6.7) and (6.1) again

$$((cP_1) \, (cP_2)) P_3$$
$$= (cP_1 P_3) \, (cP_2 P_3) = c(P_1 P_3 \mid P_2 P_3)$$

Note that distribution from the left would depend upon $E(P_1 \mid P_2) = (EP_1)(EP_2)$ which is not true for arbitrary E. See Exercise 6.2.

A pattern P is said to be <u>monic</u> if (c) P has at most one post-cursor. Thus 'A' | 'AB' is not monic but 'A' | 'B' is monic since both alternands could not match at the same pre-cursor position. Also, FENCE is monic for although (c) FENCE is c† the abort symbol does not count as a post-cursor position. Note that if M_1 and M_2 are monic patterns then so is their concatenation (M_1 M_2).

<u>Proposition</u> If m is monic and linear then it distributes over alternation from the left. That is

$$m(P_1 \mid P_2) = mP_1 \mid mP_2 \qquad (6.11)$$

The proof of this is simple and will be left as an exercise.

Most of SNOBOL4's built-in patterns are, as has been previously noted, monic. The others are referred to as having implicit alternatives. If a pattern is composed only of monics then it can be decomposed into an alternation of monics as in the proposition below. This yields a kind of <u>canonical form</u> for patterns.

<u>Proposition</u> Let P be any pattern formed by concatenation and alternation of linear monic patterns and ABORT and FENCE. Then P can be written

$$m_1 A_1 \mid m_2 A_2 \mid \ldots \mid m_n A_n \qquad (6.12)$$

where each m(i) is linear monic and where each A(i) is either ABORT or NULL (the null string also serves as the null pattern and both differ from the null sequence, ∅).

<u>Proof</u>: By induction, if P has only one element and since

$$\text{FENCE} = \text{NULL} \mid \text{ABORT}$$

P is of the indicated form. If P is of the form $P_1 \mid P_2$ and both P_1 and P_2 are in the form of (6.12), P is also. If P is of the form, P_1 P_2 and both are of the form (6.12) we have, by right distribution

$$P_1 P_2 = m_1 A_1 P_2 \mid \ldots \mid m_n A_n P_2$$

Focus on only one term, for if we can show that each term reduces to (6.12), their alternation will. Consider

$$m A P_2$$

If A is ABORT, the value is m A and is of the desired form. Otherwise apply left distribution of m over P_2.

```
┌─────────────────┐
│ %%%% CANNING    │   In the normal unanchored mode of scanning
│ %      ┌────────┘   the cursor first presented to the pattern is
│ %%%% │             (Subject,0)  and  upon  failure  is  presented  with
│  %   │             (Subject,1) and so forth until the pattern succeeds.
│ %%%% │             That is, the effect of a pattern match is the  first
└──────┘             cursor position of
```

$$(0\ P)\quad (1\ P)\quad \ldots\quad (L\ P)$$

if any.   Here L is the length of the subject. The string
matched is determined by the first nonempty (c P).   Let (c_1
P) be the first nonempty one. Let c_2 be the first post-cursor
of (c_1 P).   Then the string bounded by c_1, c_2 is the substring
matched.   For example, let the subject be 'ABC' and let the
pattern be 'AB' | 'C'. Then the sequence

$$(0\ P)\quad (1\ P)\quad (2\ P)\quad (3\ P)$$

is

$$[2]\quad \emptyset\quad [3]\quad \emptyset\ =\ [2,\ 3]$$

The first pre-cursor position (0) and the first post-cursor
position (2) determine the string matched ('AB').

If the pattern matcher is in anchored mode then the sequence
of cursor positions of interest is only (0 P).

```
┌─────────────┐
│  %%  RBNO   │   The function ARBNO(P) which may also be written
│ %  %  ┌─────┘   P* is defined as
│ %  % │
│ %%%% │
│ %  % │
└──────┘
```
$$P^* = \text{NULL}\ |\ P\ P^* \qquad (6.13)$$

Since P* is defined in terms of itself we may well ask, is it
well-defined?   That is, does (6.13) specify one and only one
pattern. The answer, as we will see, is yes, but the question
is at least as intriguing as the answer.   Will a pattern, in
general, defined in terms of itself have a unique solution?
the answer is, obviously, no since

$$P = P$$

will be satisfied by any pattern.   Next, we might consider
patterns having the same general form as (6.13), viz.

$$P\ =\ Q_1\ |\ Q_2\ P \qquad (6.14)$$

Will this always uniquely define P where Q_1 and Q_2 are given?
The answer is no, for let Q_1 = FAIL and let Q_2 = NULL.   Then
(6.14) reduces to

$$P\ =\ \text{FAIL}\ |\ \text{NULL}\ P\ =\ \text{NULL}\ P\ =\ P$$

Here, as before, there are an infinite number of solutions to the equation. As a less trivial example, let

$$Q_1 = POS(0)$$
$$Q_2 = POS(1)$$

Then (6.14) has an infinitude of solutions of the form:

$$P = POS(0) \mid POS(1) \; P'$$

where P' is any pattern. (Note that POS(i) POS(j) is either FAIL if the arguments are unequal or POS(i) if i = j.)

For the special case that Q_1 is NULL, however, we have the following

Proposition For any pattern Q the equation

$$P = NULL \mid Q \; P \qquad (6.15)$$

can be satisfied by one and only one pattern P.

Proof: We will prove this by providing a procedure for computing the kth cursor position (if one exists) of (c)P for all c and for all k. Since (c)NULL = c, the first cursor position of (c)P is determinable for all c, viz. c itself. This forms the basis of an inductive proof. Suppose that we can compute the first k-1 cursor positions of (c)P for all c. In some cases there may not be as many as k-1 in which case we would know all of them and also how the sequence terminated (i.e. with an abort symbol or not). Then to compute the k th cursor position of (c)P we note that

$$(c)P = c \; (c \; Q \; P)$$

Letting $(c)Q = [c_1, c_2, \ldots] \lambda$ we have

$$(c)P = c \; (c_1 P) \; (c_2 P) \ldots \lambda$$

Now all that is needed to compute the k th cursor of (c)P is to compute the (k-1)st cursor of $(c_1)P$ if it exists. If it does not and if the sequence is not terminated by an abort symbol, we reduce k-1 by the number of cursor positions in $(c_1)P$ and find the required cursor position of $(c_2)P$. In this way the sequence (c)P can be effectively computed for all k.

If the argument to ARBNO is monic and if ARBNO is anchored a kind of <u>backup-free</u> scanning results which can be useful for selectively scanning over portions of a string. For example,

$$Q = \text{""}$$
$$S \qquad POS(0) \; ARBNO(Q \; BREAK(Q) \; Q \mid NOTANY(Q)) \quad P$$

will scan S for a substring not contained in quotes which will match the pattern P.

A reasonable exercise at this point is to demonstrate that P is applied at all pre-cursors not within quotes. First note that the argument to ARBNO is monic and linear. Next we need a

Proposition Let m be linear monic. Then

$$\text{ARBNO}(m) = \text{NULL} \mid m \mid m^2 \mid m^3 \mid \ldots \qquad (6.16)$$

where m^2 is m concatenated with m, $m^3 = m^2\ m$, etc.

Proof:

$$\begin{aligned}
\text{ARBNO}(m) &= m^* \\
&= \text{NULL} \mid m\ m^* \\
&= \text{NULL} \mid m\ (\text{NULL} \mid m\ m^*) \\
\text{By (6.10)} \qquad &= \text{NULL} \mid m \mid m^2\ m^*
\end{aligned}$$

By induction it can be shown that the ith term is m to the (i-1)st power.

Given (6.16) it should be evident that the sequence of precursors applied to P are monotonically increasing and are applied at all points other than within quotes.

As another example, PL/I comments are delimited by /* on the left and */ on the right. To match pattern P against a string not contained in a comment we can execute:

$$\text{S} \quad \text{POS}(0) \quad \text{ARBNO}('/*' \text{ FENCE ARB } '*/' \text{ FENCE} \mid \text{LEN}(1)) \quad \text{P} \qquad (6.17)$$

Even the most ardent SNOBOL4 enthusiast will admit to being puzzled occasionally over the use of FENCE. It's double application in this example virtually begs for analysis. First note that any pattern of the form P FENCE | M is monic for all patterns P and all monic patterns M. Hence the argument to ARBNO is monic. For any pattern P we have

$$(c) P = C \lambda$$

The **associated linear** pattern, PL, sometimes called the **linear part** of P is defined as

$$(c) PL = C$$

The **associated nonlinear** pattern, PN, sometimes called the **nonlinear part** of P is defined as

$$(c) PN = c \lambda$$

For example, the linear part of (ANY('AB') FENCE) is ANY('AB') and, in general, the linear part of (m FENCE) for any linear monic m is m itself. The nonlinear part is NULL | m ABORT. The linear part of a monic pattern is monic. For example, the linear part of ('/*' | LEN(1)) FENCE is the monic pattern that

Page 110   Chapter 6   -   PATTERN THEORY

matches '/*' if present or a single character if '/*' is not present. Note that

$$(c)(PN\ PL) = (c\ \lambda)PL = (c\ PL)\ \lambda$$
$$= c\ \lambda$$

and hence for all patterns P

$$PN\ PL = P \qquad (6.18)$$

Note too that if PN is the associated nonlinear part of some pattern then

$$FENCE\ PN = FENCE = PN\ FENCE \qquad (6.19)$$

From (6.19) and (6.18) and associativity it follows that

$$FENCE\ P = FENCE\ PL \qquad (6.20)$$

for all patterns P. In what follows, let

$$F = FENCE$$
$$N = NULL$$
$$A = ABORT$$

As stated previously

$$F = N\ |\ A \qquad (6.21)$$

For all patterns P, using (6.21) and right distribution

$$F\ P = P\ |\ A \qquad (6.22)$$

For all P

$$P\ A\ |\ A = A \qquad (6.23)$$

If M is monic, it may easily be shown using (6.23) and (6.21) and right distribution that

$$F\ M\ F = F\ M \qquad (6.24)$$

Proposition If M is monic and if m is the linear part of M then

$$F\ M^* = (F\ M)^* = F\ (M\ F)^* = F\ m^* \qquad (6.25)$$

Proof: To prove the first equality, by (6.22),(6.13), (6.22), and (6.24)

$$F\ M^* = M^*\ |\ A$$
$$= N\ |\ M\ M^*\ |\ A$$
$$= N\ |\ F\ M\ M^*$$
$$= N\ |\ F\ M\ F\ M^*$$

The last equation has the general form

$$P = N \mid F M P$$

Since $(F M)*$ also satisfies this equation we have by (6.15)

$$F M* = (F M)*$$

To prove the second equality, let $M_1 = M F$. M_1 is clearly monic. By the first equality

$$F M_1* = (F M_1)*$$

Replacing M_1 by $M F$ and then using (6.24) we have

$$F(M F)* = (F M F)* = (F M)*$$

To prove the third equality, use the fact that $F M = F m$ (see (6.20)) and the first equality to obtain

$$(F M)* = (F m)* = F m*$$

Let us return to our example of searching for a semi-colon not within comment delimiters. The pattern

$$POS(0)\ ARBNO('/*'\ FENCE\ ARB\ '*/'\ FENCE \mid LEN(1))\ P$$

is of the form $POS(0)\ ARBNO(M)\ P$ where M is monic. This follows from the fact that any pattern of the form $P\ FENCE \mid M$ is monic. Anchoring on the left with $POS(0)$ is equivalent to anchoring on the left with FENCE from the standpoint of global scanning. By (6.25)

$$\begin{aligned} FENCE\ ARBNO(M)\ P &= FENCE\ ARBNO(ML)\ P \\ &= FENCE\ (NULL \mid ML \mid (ML)^2 \mid \ldots)\ P \end{aligned}$$

where ML is the linear part of M. We need only show that ML behaves properly. From its definition there are only 3 cases to consider at any given cursor position.

1) The string '/*' appears at the cursor position and there follows a '*/' in the string. In this case the entire comment is matched by ML.

2) The string '/*' appears but no following '*/' is present. In this case ML fails.

3) The string '/*' does not appear at the cursor in which case a single character is matched.

From this it should be clear that P is applied to all cursors in the order of increasing cursor position except within comments or unclosed comment constructions.

| %%%% ECURSIVE PATTERNS | A pattern P which is defined in
terms of itself is said to be
defined recursively. In the investigation of ARBNO, we have encountered the definition $P = Q_1 \mid Q_2\ P$ where Q_1 and Q_2 were given. Even in this simple case there were values for Q_1 and Q_2 which would lead to an improper definition for P even though the specific case of ARBNO led in all cases to a valid definition. The general case of recursive definition is of interest to the SNOBOL4 programmer because the language permits, via unevaluated expressions, arbitrarily constructed recursive definitions. For example, the SNOBOL4 assignment

$$P = NULL \mid 'A'\ *P$$

assigns to P a pattern which will satisfy the equation

$$P = NULL \mid 'A'\ P$$

From Prop. (6.15) we know that P is well-defined and has a value according to (6.13) of ARBNO('A').

More generally, if P is assigned the value f(*P), where f is some functional form, then the pattern so defined is the one which satisfies the equation

$$P = f(P)$$

It may be that no pattern or more that one pattern satisfies the equation in which case P is not <u>well-defined</u>. The scanner typically loops for not well-defined cases. In SNOBOL4 it is quite easy to write a recursive definition which has more than one solution. For example:

$$P = *P$$

has an infinite number of solutions. It is not quite so easy to find a recursive definition such that there is no solution to P. To do so we make up a primitive pattern function called NOT, defined as:

$$(c)\ NOT(P) = c \text{ if } (c)P = \emptyset$$
$$= \emptyset \text{ if } (c)P \neq \emptyset$$

There surely is no solution to the equation

$$P = NOT(P)$$

and hence the assignment P = NOT(*P) would lead to an ill-defined construct. NOT, however, is not a primitive facility of SNOBOL4 and, moreover, it is not known whether a recursive definition can be written in SNOBOL4 which does not have at least one solution.

RECURSIVE PATTERNS   Page 113

There are many ways in which a recursive definition can be
poorly formed in SNOBOL4 and these usually result in having
more than one possible solution. Frequently the following
principle is violated.

Proposition Let A, B, C and D be patterns. If B does not
match the null string or a string of negative length then

$$P = A \mid B P C \mid D \qquad (6.26)$$

has at most one solution for P.

Proof: Let P_1 and P_2 be different solutions to (6.26). Let S
be a string which is matched differently by P_1 and P_2. Let c
be the cursor in S with the largest cursor position such that
$(c)P_1 \neq (c)P_2$. Then

$$(cA) \; (cBP_1C) \; (cD) \quad \neq \quad (cA) \; (cBP_2C) \; (cD)$$
$$(cBP_1C) \quad \neq \quad (cBP_2C)$$
$$(cBP_1) \quad \neq \quad (cBP_2)$$

Then for some c' in the sequence (cB) we must have

$$(c'P_1) \quad \neq \quad (c'P_2)$$

But by definition of B, c' is greater than c which contradicts
the assumption that c was greatest.

(6.26) can be strengthened a great deal (See Exer. 6.20) but
this simple statement is quite powerful. For example, let

$$P = \text{'B'} \mid \text{'A'} \; P \qquad (6.27)$$

Then by (6.26), P is unique. Now

$$\text{ARBNO('A') 'B'} = \text{(NULL} \mid \text{'A' ARBNO('A')) 'B'}$$
$$= \text{'B'} \mid \text{'A' (ARBNO('A') 'B')}$$

This last equation is in the form (6.27) so that

$$P = \text{ARBNO('A') 'B'}$$

is the unique solution for P.

If P is given as

$$P = A \mid B P$$

where B can match the null string we can frequently formulate
a set of solutions for P which satisfy the equation. First we
define IF(P) as:

$$\text{IF(P)} = \text{NOT(NOT(P))} \qquad (6.28)$$

Then note that from the definition of NOT

Page 114   Chapter 6   -   PATTERN THEORY

$$\text{NULL} = \text{NOT}(P) \mid \text{IF}(P) \tag{6.29}$$

for all patterns P. It follows that for arbitrary patterns P and Q:

$$P = \text{IF}(Q)\ P \mid \text{NOT}(Q)\ P \tag{6.30}$$

In this way we can decompose P into a number of disjoint alternatives from which we may analyze the behavior of P. Note from this last equation, since NOT(P) P = ∅, we have

$$P = \text{IF}(P)\ P \tag{6.31}$$

For example, let P be 'defined' recursively as:

$$P = \text{LEN}(1) \mid \text{POS}(0)\ P \tag{6.32}$$

By considering various disjoint situations we can reason out a behaviour pattern for P as follows:

(c) P = [1, 1, ...]   if POS(0) LEN(1) would succeed
(c) P = c+1   if NOT(POS(0)) LEN(1) would succeed
(c) P = ?   if POS(0) NOT(LEN(1)) would succeed
(c) P = ∅   if NOT(POS(0)) NOT(LEN(1)) would succeed

The question mark (?) indicates that at this set of conditions the equation merely says that P = P and so any pattern would do. Letting X indicate such an arbitrary pattern we have

$$P = \text{POS}(0)\ \text{LEN}(1)\ \text{SUCCEED} \mid \text{NOT}(\text{POS}(0))\ \text{LEN}(1) \mid$$
$$\text{POS}(0)\ \text{NOT}(\text{LEN}(1))\ X \tag{6.33}$$

We will let the reader confirm that any pattern of the form (6.33) is a solution to (6.32) noting that NULL | SUCCEED = SUCCEED, that $P_1 \mid P_2 = P_2 \mid P_1$ if P_1 is mutually exclusive with P_2 and that POS(n) NOT(POS(n)) = FAIL.

Patterns exhibiting left recursion present ambiguous conditions which are resolved when the scanner is in a mode known as QUICKSCAN (the default mode). Consider

$$P = P\ 'A' \mid 'B' \tag{6.34}$$

This equation has a solution P = ABORT. As we will see, however, in QUICKSCAN mode the pattern

$$P = *P\ 'A' \mid 'B' \tag{6.35}$$

operates as if it were defined as

$$P = 'BAA \ldots\ ' \mid \ldots \mid 'BAA' \mid 'BA' \mid 'B'$$

where this indicates that P matches any substring equal to a 'B' followed by an arbitrary number of 'A's matching alternates in the order of decreasing length. The reader may easily confirm that this value for P also satisfies (6.34).

RECURSIVE PATTERNS   Page 115

This is implemented roughly as follows. When *P is called upon
to match in (6.35) the subject is reduced (on the right) by
the minimum number of characters required by *P's subsequent
(1 character in this case). Hence recursive plunges are taken
until no more characters remain which breaks the loop. Some
of the details of this process are described in the next chapter.
To establish the theoretical background for understanding
this heuristic, first note that if A does not match the null
string or a string of negative length, then for any finite sequence C

$$(C)A = C \implies C = \emptyset \qquad (6.36)$$

This is easily seen by considering the smallest cursor position in C and an immediate contradiction results.

Proposition   If A does not match the null string or a string
of negative length and if both A and B are finite linear patterns then

$$P = PA \mid B \qquad (6.37)$$

has exactly one finite linear solution for P, viz.

$$P = \ldots \mid BA^3 \mid BA^2 \mid BA \mid B \qquad (6.38)$$

Proof: We first note that (6.38) is well-defined if A must
match a nonzero length string since we can discard all alternates other than the last L where L is the length of the subject. Using (6.37) we obtain

$$cP = (cPA) (cB) \qquad (6.39)$$

If $(cB) = \emptyset$ then, by (6.36), $(cP) = \emptyset$. Since (cB) is finite
linear it may, by Exer. 6.6, be removed from both sides of
(6.39). Letting C_1 be the result of this removal from cP we have

$$C_1 = cPA = (C_1 (cB))A = (C_1 A) (cBA)$$

Again, by (6.36), if $cBA = \emptyset$ we have that $C_1 = \emptyset$. Otherwise
we may remove cBA from both sides. Assume that C_2 is what
remains after removing cBA from C_1. Then, as before

$$C_2 = (C_2 A) (cBA^2)$$

this process eventually terminates with $C_n = \emptyset$ and this is
ensured by the fact that A does not match the null string.
Hence we have

$$cP = \ldots (cBA^3) (cBA^2) (cBA) (cB)$$

from which we obtain (6.38). We conclude that the QUICKSCAN
heuristic limits the solution space of (6.37) to finite linear
solutions. On the other hand under FULLSCAN, (6.37) loops implying no such restriction on the solution space.

EXERCISES

| Exercise 6.1 | Which of the following are true?

    a) 'A' = 'A' | 'A'
    b) 'A' | 'B' = ANY('AB')
    c) ARBNO('A') = NULL | ARBNO('A')
    d) BREAK(S) ANY(S) = ARB ANY(S)
    e) 'A' | 'B' = 'B' | 'A'
    f) ANY('ABC') = NOTANY(DIFF(&ALPHABET,'ABC'))
    g) FENCE (P_1 | P_2) = FENCE P_1 | FENCE P_2
    h) ('AB' | 'DEF') ('G' | 'H') =
                      'ABG' | 'ABH' | 'DEFG' | 'DEFH'
    i) ARB = ARBNO(LEN(1))
    j) (P_1 | P_2) FENCE = P_1 FENCE | P_2 FENCE

| Exercise 6.2 | While pattern alternation is defined as

$$(c)\,(P_1 \mid P_2) = (c)\,P_1\ (c)\,P_2$$

it is not in general true that

$$(C)\,(P_1 \mid P_2) = (C)\,P_1\ (C)\,P_2$$

where C is a sequence of cursor positions. Find a counter-example.

| Exercise 6.3 | Reduce the following pattern to canonical form

('B' | 'R') ('E' | 'EA') ('D' | 'DS')

Is the pattern monic?

| Exercise 6.4 | In semigroup terminology a left zero z is defined as an element such that z e = z for all elments e of a semigroup. What is a left zero for a) the semigroup of patterns with the alternation operator, b) the semigroup of patterns with the concatenation operator, and c) the semigroup of linear but possibly infinite cursor sequences under concatenation?

| Exercise 6.5 | An idempotent element E for an operator * has the property that

Exercises for chapter 6 — Page 117

$$E * E = E$$

Which of the following are idempotent under concatenation?

a) BREAK(S)   f) NULL
b) SPAN(S)   g) FENCE
c) TAB(N)   h) ABORT
d) POS(N)   i) 'A'
e) FAIL   j) ARB

Exercise 6.6 Let E_1 and E_2 be extended sequences and C a finite linear sequence. Show that any C is left and right cancellative, where left cancellative is defined by a) and right cancellative is defined by b).

a) $\quad C\ E_1 = C\ E_2 \quad \Rightarrow \quad E_1 = E_2$

b) $\quad E_1\ C = E_2\ C \quad \Rightarrow \quad E_1 = E_2$

Show that arbitrary E are not cancellative by finding an E, E_1 and E_2 such that

c) $\quad E\ E_1 = E\ E_2 \quad$ but $E_1 \neq E_2$

d) $\quad E_1\ E = E_2\ E \quad$ but $E_1 \neq E_2$

Demonstrate that if pattern R is finite, linear, then for any two patterns P_1 and P_2

e) $\quad R\ |\ P_1 = R\ |\ P_2 \quad \Rightarrow \quad P_1 = P_2$

f) $\quad P_1\ |\ R = P_2\ |\ R \quad \Rightarrow \quad P_1 = P_2$

Exercise 6.7 What are the first five alternands in the expression:

$$\text{ARBNO(ARBNO(LEN(1)))}$$

Exercise 6.8 Show that if M is monic and P is merely any pattern, then

$$P \quad \text{FENCE} \quad |\quad M$$

is monic.

Exercise 6.9 Let P = ARB ARB. Let L be the length of the Subject. How many post-cursor positions are there in (0)P?

Chapter 6 - PATTERN THEORY

Exercise 6.10 Show that the pattern matching statement

    Subject POS(0) Pattern

is equivalent to the statement

    Subject FENCE Pattern

Exercise 6.11 Let

$$P = ARBNO(LEN(1) \; ARB)$$

How many post-cursor positions are there in (0)P where the size of the subject is L characters?

Exercise 6.12 Prove that if m is linear monic then $m(P_1 \mid P_2) = mP_1 \mid mP_2$.

Exercise 6.13 Which of the following patterns are necessarily monic?

  a) BREAK('ABC')   e) P | ABORT
  b) POS(0) | RPOS(0) f) FENCE P
  c) ANY(S) | BREAK(S) g) P FENCE
  d) POS(N) | TAB(N)   h) FENCE | FENCE

Exercise 6.14 Augment the pattern shown in (6.17) to skip over material in quotes ('...') as well as within comments. Make sure that characters within unclosed quotes are also passed over.

Exercise 6.15 Let P = ARBNO('A' ARB 'B'). What is the sequence of post-cursor positions for

  a) ('AB',0) P
  b) ('ABAB',0) P
  c) (DUPL('AB',K),0) P

Exercise 6.16 Using the technique of Exercise 6.14, write a pattern which will scan for a PL/I statement failing if none exists.

Exercise 6.17 Furnish a counter-example to the following

$$ARBNO(P) = NULL \mid P \mid P^2 \mid P^3 \mid \ldots$$

Exercises for chapter 6   Page 119

| Exercise 6.18 | Using back-up-free scanning, write a pattern which will print out all SNOBOL4 identifiers in a string of SNOBOL4 source. Identifiers within quotes should not be printed. It will be OK to print out the S and F of GOTO's. For example

$$\text{ALPHA} = \text{'ABC'} \; B(\text{"X"}) \qquad :S(\text{SAM})$$

should print the strings 'ALPHA', 'B', 'S' and 'SAM'.

| Exercise 6.19 | Let PL_1 and PL_2 be the associated linear patterns of P_1 and P_2 respectively. Provide a counter-example to the conjecture that $PL_1 \mid PL_2$ is the associated linear pattern of $P_1 \mid P_2$.

| Exercise 6.20 | Let $f(P)$ be an expression involving P composed of constant patterns, alternation and concatenation. Show that $f(P)$ can be written as

$$A_1 \mid B_1 \; P \; f_1(P) \mid A_2 \mid B_2 \; P \; f_2(P) \mid A_3 \ldots$$
$$\ldots A_n \mid B_n \; P \; f_n(P) \mid A$$

where $A, A_1, A_2, \ldots, A_n, B_1, B_2, \ldots, B_n$ are patterns not involving P and $f_1, f_2, \ldots, f_n$ are functions. From this, show that if $B_1, B_2, \ldots, B_n$ do not match the null string and if no pattern primitive matches a string of negative length, then

$$P = f(P)$$

has at most one value for P.

| Exercise 6.21 | Which of the following equations for P uniquely specify a pattern? If P is unique, give its value. Otherwise indicate a class of values (via X) which will satisfy it.

a) P = RPOS(0) | BREAK(S) P
b) P = ANY(S) | SPAN(S) P
c) P = ANY(S) | BREAK(S) P
d) P = TAB(N) | POS(N) P
e) P = TAB(N) | RTAB(N) P

| Exercise 6.22 | let P be a pattern not matching the null string. Define P⁻ recursively as

$$P^- = P \; P^- \mid \text{NULL}$$

Show that P⁻ is well defined. P⁻ is called the negative ARBNO of P.

Let P be given as

Chapter 6 - PATTERN THEORY

$$P = X \mid Y P \mid Z$$

where Y is monic and does not match the null string. Write P explicitly in terms of X, Y, Z and the two ARBNO'S.

CHAPTER SEVEN

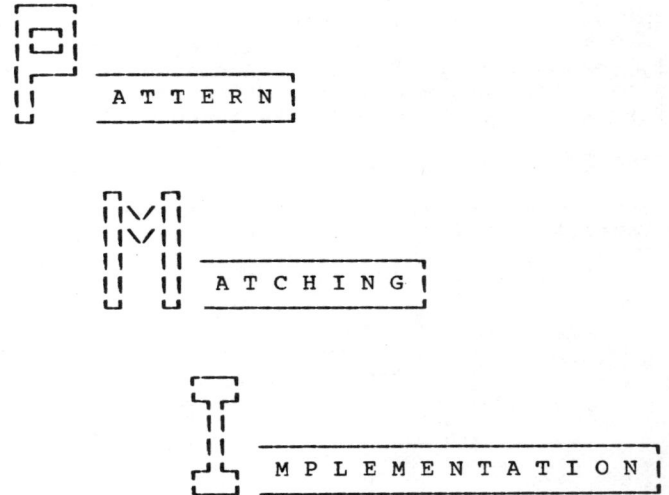

```
┌─────────────────────────────────────────┐
│               CONTENTS                  │
│                                         │
│        Path Diagrams                    │
│                                         │
│        Derived Patterns                 │
│                                         │
│        SCAN                             │
│                                         │
│        Heuristics                       │
│                                         │
│        Compounds                        │
│                                         │
│        Unevaluated Expressions          │
│                                         │
└─────────────────────────────────────────┘
```

Chapter 7 - Pattern Matching Implementation

While it is not strictly necessary to know how pattern matching is implemented in order to use SNOBOL4 patterns, it is necessary to be somewhat aware of the implementation in order to program efficiently and well. This chapter is based on the internals of three independent SNOBOL4 implementations, MAINBOL, SPITBOL, and SITBOL.

The compiler processes all statements in a uniform manner without treating the pattern-matching statement any differently (essentially) than any other statement. Every statement is compiled into a kind of Polish notation which may be visualized as a tree. For example the pattern

('A' BREAK('XY') | 'D') (ANY('ABC') | 'HA' | 'TA')

is depicted in Figure 7.1. An empty box denotes concatenation and the compiler treats | as associating to the left.

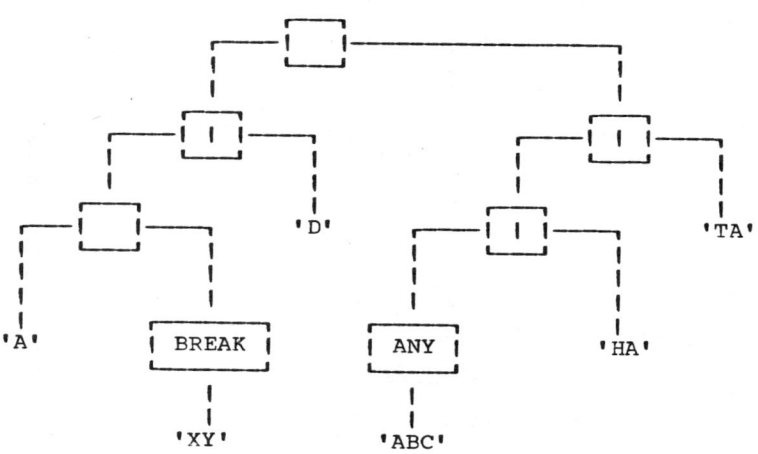

Figure 7.1

The compiled form of
('A' BREAK('XY') | 'D') (ANY('ABC') | 'HA' | 'TA')

Pattern matching operates by the concerted action of a set of built-in monic patterns called _primitives_. Strings used as patterns, and the patterns indicated by BREAK and ANY, fall into this category. Abstracting Figure 7.1 to the point of representing all primitives by single letters we arrive at the diagram in Figure 7.2.

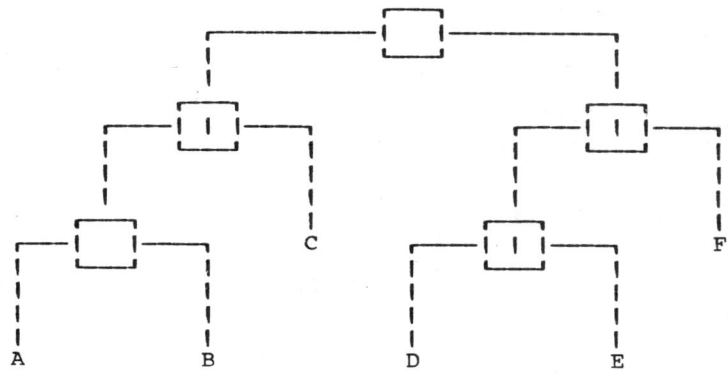

Figure 7.2

The abstract tree of the expression:
('A' BREAK('XY') | 'D') (ANY('ABC') | 'HA' | 'TA')

This form or structure for the pattern is, however, not the most suitable for doing pattern matching. In Figure 7.2 if nodes A and B match successfully, node D is then attempted. But to obtain D the scanner must go up the tree to the top node and back down on the right hand side to find the primitive which is to be matched next. Since ancester information is not present explicitly in the compiled Polish prefix this tree walking would be prohibitively expensive. A similar thing can be said about the events which occur when a primitive fails. The information available from the tree, while complete, does not seem to be in a form most conducive to rapid search. Hence, when the expression represented by the Polish tree is evaluated, an entirely new structure is created. An example of such a structure is shown in Figure 7.3. A solid arrow drawn from a node X to a node Y indicates that if X is successful Y will be matched next. Y is called the subsequent of X. A dotted arrow from X to Y indicates that, if X fails, Y can be tried immediately with the same pre-cursor position. Y is then called the alternate of X.

More formally, a path diagram is an interconnection of nodes. Each node may have a subsequent (indicated by a solid arrow) or an alternate (indicated by a dotted arrow) or both. Each node has an associated primitive which is a monic pattern. An s-vacancy is a node without a subsequent. An a-vacancy is a node without an alternate. The root of a path diagram is the node with no arcs directed into it. (It is easy to show that construction limits the number of root nodes to one.)

Chapter 7 - Pattern Matching Implementation

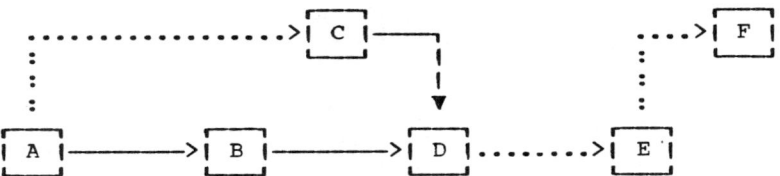

Figure 7.3

The path diagram associated with Figure 7.2.

The path diagram of a pattern consisting only of a primitive p is simply a node without subsequent and without alternate and with p as its associated primitive. The concatenation of two path diagrams D_1 D_2 is found by drawing a solid arrow from every s-vacancy of D_1 to the root of D_2. The alternation of two path diagrams D_1 | D_2 is obtained as follows: starting with the root of D_1, search down the chain of alternates until an a-vacancy is found. Then draw a dotted arrow from this a-vacancy to the root of D_2.

It is interesting to note that the operations of alternation and concatenation of path diagrams are (like patterns) associative. Hence path diagrams form a semigroup under these two operations.

The pattern node contains four essential fields as indicated below (one more field is introduced later).

PROG	program address
SUBS	subsequent
ALT	alternate
ARG	argument

To describe the pattern matching algorithms in SNOBOL4 we would declare a structure of type NODE as

DATA('NODE(PROG,SUBS,ALT,ARG)')

Then, to allocate a node for, say, LEN(13), we may execute

NODE('LENP',,,13)

where the label 'LENP' indicates the location which handles the LEN primitive. Its encoding would be the machine language counterpart of the following SNOBOL4 statements.

PATH DIAGRAMS   Page 125

Is the number of characters remaining in the SUBJECT $\geq$ ARG(NODE)? If not, fail!

LENP   GE(SIZE(SUBJECT) - CURSOR, ARG(NODE))   :F(F)

Otherwise compute the post-cursor position and succeed.

        CURSOR = CURSOR + ARG(NODE)   :(S)

Here F is a label in the scanner where all primitives go to upon encountering failure and S is the label they go to when they encounter success. Note that the primitive bumps the CURSOR.

One may suppose that a routine to concatenate two path diagrams can be written in SNOBOL4 very easily. Consider the following attempt.

        DEFINE('CONCAT(P1,P2)')   :(CONCAT_END)

If P1 is null, just fail!

CONCAT   IDENT(P1, NULL)   :S(FRETURN)

Otherwise fill up the S-vacancies of the alternate and subsequent.

        CONCAT(ALT(P1), P2)
        CONCAT(SUBS(P1), P2)   :S(RETURN)

Failure to CONCAT implies that the subsequent was null. Plug it!

        SUBS(P1) = P2   :(RETURN)
CONCAT_END

The above routine is not valid for several reasons. 1. Path diagrams, as we will see later can have loops and this will possibly ensnare CONCAT in a recursive loop. 2. If the two arguments, P1 and P2, are identical the result is an abomination. 3. The algorithm modifies P1, the first pattern. This is only permissible if it is known that P1 is not to be used for any other purpose. This guarantee, of course, does not exist.

All three problems can be surmounted by copying the first pattern. Copying a graph with loops was treated earlier (COPYL, Prog. 5.8) and that function can be modified to perform the concatenation. See Exercise 7.4. A similar situation prevails with respect to alternation.

A much more practical method, and one that is used by most implementors, is to group all the pattern nodes together in one contiguous block. This not only facilitates the copy operation but increases the speed of sequencing through the nodes of a pattern. (Exercise 7.6 explores this possibility.) Logically, however, it is correct to think of the pattern as being an inter-linked collection of nodes.

```
 _____
| %%%  ERIVED PATTERNS |   Can a pattern be reconstructed from
| %  %  _____|   the path diagram? The answer is yes.
| %  % |   Let p(n) be the primitive associated with node n.
| %  % |   The derived pattern of node n, D(n), is defined in
| %%%  |   terms of its associated primitive and the derived
|_____|   patterns of its subsequent node s and its alternate
a as follows:
```

$$D(n) = p(n)\ D(s)\ |\ D(a) \quad \text{if a and s exist}$$
$$= p(n)\ D(s) \quad \text{if only s exists}$$
$$= p(n)\ |\ D(a) \quad \text{if only a exists}$$
$$= p(n) \quad \text{if neither a nor s exists}$$

The derived pattern of a path diagram is defined as the derived pattern of its root.

When the scanner is defined, it will be seen that it implements the derived pattern. Also, it can be shown [Gimpel, 1971] that any pattern will equal the derived pattern of its path diagram. Together these two observations constitute a proof of the pattern matching algorithm and provides a theoretical basis for the extensions which follow.

```
 _____
| |  Program  | |   The algorithm used internally to do pattern
| |    7.1    | |   matching is illustrated by the function
| |    SCAN   | |   SCAN. SCAN has two arguments, the LENGTH of
|_____|   the subject and a pattern identified by its
```
root node NODE. The subject itself is held by a global variable SUBJECT and the current cursor value is held in a global variable CURSOR. There are good reasons for the selection of which quantities are to be passed to SCAN and which quantites are global. These reasons will be evident when Unevaluated Expressions are discussed.

The initial value of CURSOR is set by a driver program called MATCH (Exercise 7.8). In unanchored mode, if SCAN fails, MATCH increments this pre-cursor by 1 and calls SCAN again. The algorithm requires a stack and the familiar operations of PUSH and POP. The driver program initializes things by pushing a null alternate and a pre-cursor value.

```
 _____
| Basic SCAN function. The pattern identified by its root  |
| node NODE is matched against the SUBJECT at a pre-cursor |
| position given by the global variable CURSOR. CURSOR is  |
| updated on success. The stack is another global quantity |
| which SCAN modifies as a side-effect. If it fails, the   |
| start-up alternate-cursor pair are popped. On success, a |
```

HEURISTICS

    | sequence of alternates may remain on the stack. |

              DEFINE('SCAN(LENGTH,NODE)')
              DATA('NODE(PROG,ALT,SUBS,ARG)')   :(SCAN_END)

    | Entry point and top of loop: If an alternate to the cur- |
    | rent node exists, push the alternate and the current |
    | cursor. |

    SCAN   (DIFFER(ALT(NODE)) PUSH(ALT(NODE)) PUSH(CURSOR))

    | Go to the program label associated with the current node. |
    | Return arrives at either S or F. |

                                            :($PROG(NODE))

    | Here on success. Set NODE to the subsequent. If there is |
    | none, we are done; report success.   Otherwise go back to |
    | SCAN. |

    S   NODE = SUBS(NODE)
              IDENT(NODE,NULL)   :S(RETURN) F(SCAN)

    | Here on failure. Pop the stack for an alternate. If null, |
    | fail. Otherwise attempt to SCAN at this node. |

    F   CURSOR = POP() ;   NODE = POP()
              IDENT(NODE)   :S(FRETURN) F(SCAN)
    SCAN_END

Names referenced   Name   Type   Where defined
by SCAN: PUSH   Function   Program 5.5
                          POP   Function   Program 5.6

    | % % EURISTICS | Each implementation contains a certain
    | % % | number of so-called pattern matching
    | %%%% | heuristics which are intended to increase the speed
    | % % | of matching while having minimal effects upon the
    | % % | success or failure of the match. Generally they fall
                       into two categories, those which speed up matching
without affecting the overall outcome of the match (termed
unobtrusive) and those which may have some effect on the outcome of the match (obtrusive heuristics). The programmer may
turn off all heuristics by setting &FULLSCAN = 1 in which case
he is said to be matching in FULLSCAN mode. Otherwise he is
operating in QUICKSCAN mode. At this writing he cannot selectively turn off individual heuristics or, for example, choose
the unobtrusive but suppress the obtrusive heuristics. There
are four heuristics: futility, length-checking, start-up and
recursive reduction.   None of these heuristics are in-
trinsically obtrusive but under certain assumptions they may
indeed become obtrusive.   There is a fifth heuristic which is
a protection heuristic as opposed to a speed heuristic.   Its
purpose is to catch programming errors. The pattern
ARBNO(NULL) will loop forever in FULLSCAN mode. In QUICKSCAN

Page 128   Chapter 7   -   Pattern Matching Implementation

mode, the scanner checks the number of characters matched by the argument to ARBNO and terminates if 0 characters were matched. Some implementations have not included this heuristic and its inclusion in a language which permits arbitrary statement looping seems questionable. We will not consider it further.

Futility - Under FULLSCAN the driver program successively calls SCAN for all cursor values with the given subject in the order of increasing cursor position. But such a procedure can be woefully time-consuming as in the following common example.

$$S \quad BREAK(';') \ . \ K$$

which causes string S to be scanned for a semicolon and, if found, assigns the initial substring to K. Under FULLSCAN, a failure at CURSOR = 0 will cause a repeat at CURSOR = 1 which will necessarily also result in failure, etc. A total of L + 1 scans will be made where L is the length of the string. The wary user can anchor the scan either by prefixing a POS(0) to the pattern or by using &ANCHOR mode. However under QUICKSCAN mode, the futility heuristic will cause an abrupt halt of scanning after the first failure.

A pattern is said to be <u>futile</u> for a certain cursor c if it fails at this and all advances of the cursor position. That is, if

$$(c')P = \emptyset \quad \text{for all } c' \geq c$$

then P is futile for cursor c. If BREAK(S) fails at cursor c it is also futile at cursor c. Hence, in the above example, additional scanning at advanced cursor positions is not needed. But it is not always possible to make a simple test to determine the futility of a pattern. If the pattern is the string 'XXX' and the subject is 'ABCDE' the pattern is futile for any cursor position but normally this is not discovered until after at least 3 attempts are made to match 'XXX'. Hence, <u>string patterns report futility only when there is insufficient length in the subject string</u>. This is termed <u>length failure</u>. For convenience, whenever a primitive detects futility, it is said to experience length failure, or simply, to length fail. Thus, when BREAK fails, it reports length failure even though, strictly speaking, the futility is not due to an insufficient number of characters.

If a pattern primitive detects that it is futile, it branches to a length-failure exit (LF). Otherwise it branches to match-failure (MF). Both of these are in lieu of the single fail location (F) in the function SCAN. Most pattern primitives can transmit futility detected by a subsequent. This means that if p_2 is the subsequent of p_1, and if p_2 reports length failure, p_1 can also report length failure. More formally, the primitive p is called a <u>transmitter</u> if, whenever any pattern P is futile at cursor c, and if (c')p = c, then (p P) is futile at c'.

HEURISTICS

A necessary and sufficient condition that a monic pattern p be a transmitter is that p be monotonic in the sense that any increase in pre-cursor position brings about a non-decrease in post-cursor position. Virtually all primitives in SNOBOL4 are monotonic. Hence the scanner makes the assumption that all primitives are transmitters. Under the transmitter assumption, if all local failures are length-failures then the overall pattern is futile.

For example, let

```
        Subject:   'ABC..................D'
        Pattern:   'ABC'  BREAK('D')  'DE'
```

Then the 'DE' when matched against the 'D' will length-fail indicating futility. BREAK('D') is a transmitter since its post-cursor position cannot possibly back-up if its pre-cursor advances. Hence (BREAK('D') 'DE') is futile. By a similar line of reasoning, 'ABC' is also a transmitter and hence the entire pattern is futile. The initial cursor position, therefore, need not be advanced beyond 0.

The futility heuristic is implemented by a global flag which is set on at the start of a scan and is turned off at any match-fail or if a non-transmitter succeeds. The flag is called the futility flag. If the futility flag is on when the overall pattern fails, it is useless to go on. The overall pattern is futile.

The futility heuristic is unobtrusive for patterns which are nonvarying. For varying patterns the heuristic becomes obtrusive. For example, the pattern matching statement

```
        'ABXB'    ANY('AB')  $ C  BREAK(*C)
```

will first assign 'A' to C and the pattern BREAK(*C) will fail. BREAK signals length failure and the scanner erroneously concludes that the entire pattern is futile. Should the pattern be matched with a pre-cursor of 1, C would be assigned the character 'B' and the subsequent BREAK would succeed. Hence the pattern was not futile. The difficulty stems from the fact that BREAK lied. If its argument is indeed an unevaluated expression, it should not signal length failure unless there are no characters left in the string.

ARB is a pattern which can use the futility heuristic in two ways to hasten scanning. If the subsequent to ARB is futile at any given cursor then ARB need not extend. Moreover, (ARB P) where P is the subsequent will be futile. For example:

```
        Subject:   'AXXXBXXX'
        Pattern:   'A'  ARB  'B'  ARB  'C'
```

In the above, the 'A' will be matched against the first character. ARB will match 0, then 1, 2, and 3 characters until 'B' succeeds. The second ARB will match 0, 1, 2 characters

until 'C' is futile. Hence, ARB 'C' is detected as being
futile at position 5 and ARB 'B' ARB 'C' is detected as futile
at position 1. The scanner can halt immediately. The futility
heuristic for ARB is implemented by pushing the original state
of the futility flag onto the stack. When the subsequent to
ARB signals futility ARB restores the state of the futility
flag and takes the length-fail exit. If ARB receives no indication of futility for all post-cursor positions up to and
including L, the length of the subject, then ARB should indicate match failure.

Start-up Heuristic - the start-up heuristic permits a pattern
beginning with POS(n) to be applied immediately at CURSOR =
n. The effect is an anchored mode except that the anchoring
is done at a position other than CURSOR = 0. Both SPITBOL and
SITBOL use this heuristic and SITBOL also uses a similar
heuristic for patterns beginning with RPOS(n). Another start-
up heuristic exclusive to SITBOL is so-called contextual
anchoring. Many patterns will only match substrings beginning
with certain letters. For example SPAN('ABC') can only match
a substring starting with one of these 3 letters. The pattern
'CAT' | 'DOG' will match only a string beginning with 'C' or
'D'. Rather than call SCAN at each cursor position, it is
faster if the driver program makes a rapid pre-scan (at BREAK
speeds) to a point where a pattern would find a letter that it
could possibly begin matching. Failure at the first contextual
anchor point implies a repeated attempt to scan for the next
contextual anchor point. The alternation of two patterns
which are both contextually anchored is also contextually
anchored by the union of the anchoring sets. The concatenation
of two patterns is always anchored by the anchoring, if any,
of the left-most pattern. The start-up heuristics in all their
variations are unobtrusive.

Length Checking - This check operates as follows. In the
course of building a pattern the pattern builder deduces a
minimum length for each node. During a match, if the number
of characters remaining in the subject is below this number,
then the node can immediately signal length-failure. The difficulty with this technique is that it takes time to make this
test and it effectively duplicates another test made concur-
rently, the futility check. For example suppose the pattern
is the string 'ABC'. Suppose the subject is '1234567'. The
minimum length required by the pattern is 3. The length check
is made 6 times. The first 5 times indicates that there is
sufficient room in the subject. The last time a check is made,
the length fail exit is given. However if the primitive were
given control it would also have length failed so that the
test is redundant. Moreover the primitive could have deduced
that after the 5th time it was futile. If it signals length
failure when there are 3 characters remaining (which it should
ideally do) then the minimum length check never gets a chance
to signal length failure. All of its activity went to increase
the time of scanning. The length test came historically before
the futility heuristic and its retention is probably for that
reason.

COMPOUNDS   Page 131

Length-checking would not be obtrusive if it were not for the
so-called one-character assumption. Any unevaluated expression
is assumed to match at least one character. For example

    (LEN(1) $ X) (LEN(1) $ Y) *LGT(X,Y)

will look for two characters out of order in a string. Unfortunately, if the two characters are the last two of the
string, it will not find them because the predicate is assumed
(erroneously) to consume one character. This is perhaps the
most obtrusive heuristic of them all since the case of
predicates within a pattern are extremely common and would be
even more so if it were not for this heuristic. The length-
test heuristic appears only in SPITBOL and MAINBOL. SITBOL
and FASTBOL avoid this test for the reasons indicated.

Recursive Reduction - This refers to the scheme whereby
SNOBOL4 is able to break left-recursive loops as in the
pattern:

    P = *P 'A' | 'B'

We will defer a discussion of this heuristic until after the
implementation of recursive patterns is considered.

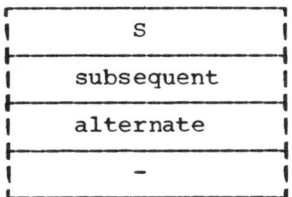

Some built-in patterns are not implemented by a single node, either because they are not monic or because it is more efficient to imple- ment them as several nodes rather than one node. These patterns are predefined by a path diagram of two or more nodes and are called compounds. Examples of compounds are the patterns with implicit alternatives such as ARB, BAL, and ARBNO(p).

ARB

A pattern which does nothing but succeed is called nil. The
node for nil is shown below

S
subsequent
alternate
-

where S refers to that label in the scanner to which control
is passed in the event of a successful match. Since the primitive is effectively short-circuited, this is the fastest
possible successful pattern. The null string may be coded as

the nil node (it is not normally). There is no argument for nil.

ARB can be thought of as being recursively defined as

$$ARB = NULL \mid (LEN(1) \; ARB)$$

and this leads to the compound shown in Figure 7.4. Here, 'a' denotes the alternate to ARB and 's' denotes its subsequent.

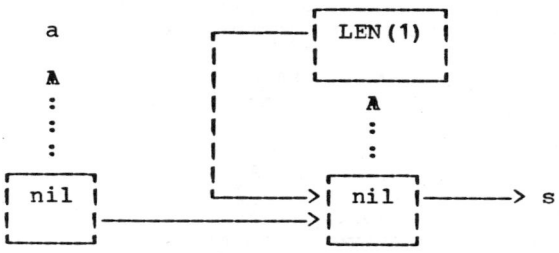

Figure 7.4

A compound for ARB.

Figure 7.4, though conceptually simple, is not the most efficient form of ARB. The futility heuristic as applied to ARB needs to be implemented (see Futility) and more scanner activity can be incorporated within the ARB compound with a consequent gain in efficiency. The more efficient ARB realization is shown in Figure 7.5.

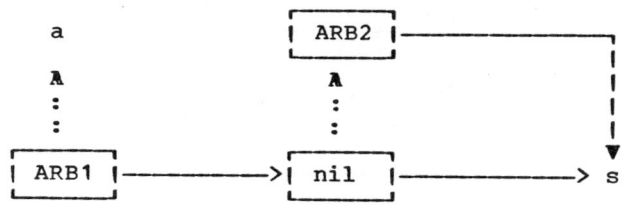

Figure 7.5

An improved version of ARB.

COMPOUNDS   Page 133

The associated primitives ARB1 and ARB2 are defined as:

```
┌─────────────────────────────────────────────────────────────────┐
│ Save the state of the futility flag and set it in order to     │
│ detect it in the subsequent.                                    │
└─────────────────────────────────────────────────────────────────┘
ARB1      PUSH(FUTILITY)
          FUTILITY = 1                                    :(S)
┌─────────────────────────────────────────────────────────────────┐
│ If the subsequent is futile, restore the old futility flag     │
│ and length fail provided we're in QUICKSCAN mode.               │
└─────────────────────────────────────────────────────────────────┘
ARB2      FUTILITY  =   EQ(FUTILITY,1)    EQ(&FULLSCAN,0)
+                       POP()                             :S(LF)
┌─────────────────────────────────────────────────────────────────┐
│ Else bump the cursor and compare with LENGTH of subject.       │
│ If beyond the end of the subject, pop the old futility         │
│ flag and match-fail.                                            │
└─────────────────────────────────────────────────────────────────┘
          CURSOR  =  CURSOR + 1
          (GT(CURSOR, LENGTH)   POP())                    :S(MF)
┌─────────────────────────────────────────────────────────────────┐
│ Otherwise, play scanner by pushing ourself and the current     │
│ cursor onto the stack and succeed.                              │
└─────────────────────────────────────────────────────────────────┘
          PUSH(NODE) ; PUSH(CURSOR)                       :(S)
```

Note the action of ARB if its subsequent is futile. ARB itself is regarded as being futile and it indicates this condition by restoring the state of the futility flag. Note that this algorithm is obtrusive if the subsequent is varying. For example, the pattern matching statement

          'ABCB'   LEN(1) $ X   ARB   'C'   *X

will succeed in FULLSCAN mode with X matching 'B' but will fail in QUICKSCAN mode. In QUICKSCAN mode the 'A' is assigned to X initially; when 'C' match-fails, control arrives at ARB2 which increments the cursor. Ultimately, 'C' length-fails. When control arrives at ARB2, the FUTILITY flag is still on resulting in a length failure and termination of the match. If is important that ARB length-fail if its subsequent is futile. Consider the pattern match

                    S   ARB . T   'CAT'

which scans S for 'CAT' assigning the prefix to T. If no 'CAT' exists in S, the match will require on the order of L^2 matches under FULLSCAN and on the order of L matches under QUICKSCAN where L is the length of the string. Here the desire to have unobtrusive heuristics seems to collide with the need for an intelligent scanner. No completely satisfactory scheme has yet been worked out.

BAL

Define a **balanced string** as any string which either 1) does not contain a parenthesis, or 2) is a balanced string bounded by parenthesis or 3) consists of any sequence of balanced strings. The BAL pattern of SNOBOL4 matches all nonnull balanced strings beginning at a given pre-cursor position. The sequence of post-cursor positions is from smaller to larger. It is relatively straightforward to write a monic pattern to match the earliest (i.e. shortest) balanced string starting at a pre-cursor position. A parenthesis count is maintained. If a left paren is encountered the count is incremented by 1. If a right paren is encountered the count is diminished by 1. If the count ever goes negative the monic fails. If the count reaches 0 (after the first character), a successful match is reported. This monic pattern is available as a primitive (called GBAL) within the implementation and is used to implement BAL. As an example the table below shows the behavior of GBAL on the subject 'A(C()D)'.

Pre-cursor	0	1	2	3	4	5	6	7
Post-cursor	1	7	3	5	-	6	-	-

where a dash (-) indicates failure. BAL can be written in terms of GBAL as

BAL = GBAL ARBNO(GBAL)

and the corresponding BAL compound is shown in Figure 7.6.

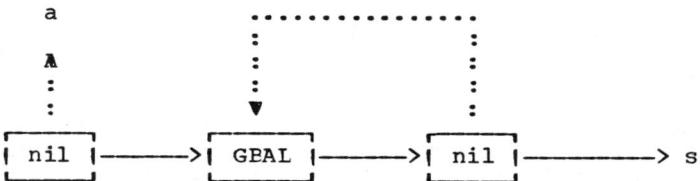

Figure 7.6

The BAL compound.

The GBAL primitive, as the above example illustrated, is not monotonic and hence does not transmit length failure. GBAL, therefore, turns the futility flag off if it succeeds. If the subsequent s is futile, further alternatives need not be taken.

ARBNO(p)

The path diagram for ARBNO(p) is obtained from the path diagram for p in the by-now familiar method suggested by the examples of ARB and BAL. Figure 7.7 indicates how we can form this path diagram from the path diagram for the pattern p.

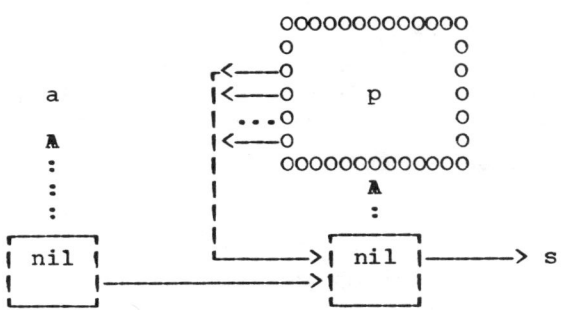

Figure 7.7

A path diagram for ARBNO(p).

Variable Association

An expression of the form p . v where p is a pattern and v is a variable (or an unevaluated expression which will evaluate to a variable) is called a conditional variable association. The variable v is associated with the indicated pattern and will be assigned the substring matched by p on the condition that the overall pattern is successful. An expression p $ v is called an immediate association. Any substring matched by p is assigned immediately to v. The path diagram for p . v can be given in terms of the path diagram for p and is shown in Figure 7.8. A similar diagram could be drawn for p $ v.

The stack which receives alternates and cursor values during the course of the match is called the pattern matching history stack or PM stack for short. To describe the operation of conditional variable association, we postulate the existence of two more stacks which we will refer to as stack Alpha and stack Beta. When VA1 (Variable Association 1) receives control, it pushes the current cursor (pre-cursor position) onto stack Alpha. If p should fail, VAB1 (Variable Association on Backup 1) will receive control and it will pop Alpha. It will then fail forcing control to go to alternate a. Should p succeed, control arrives at VA2. The current cursor and the pre-cursor pushed by VA1 are sufficient to define the string to be assigned to variable v. The two cursor positions and v are

Chapter 7 - Pattern Matching Implementation

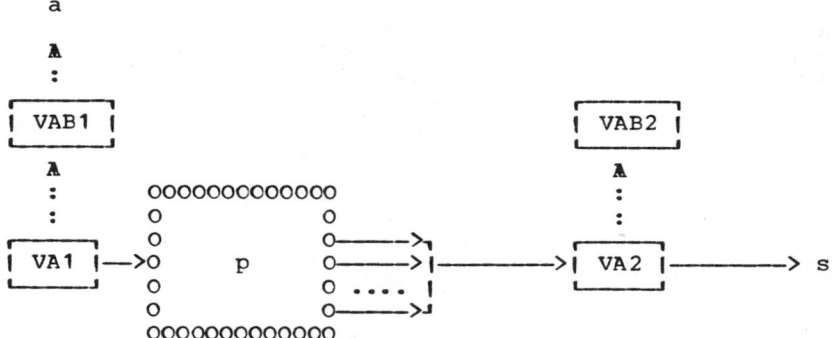

Figure 7.8

A compound for p . v

pushed onto stack Beta and the cursor on stack Alpha is popped. Should the subsequent fail, VAB2 gets control and undoes what VA2 did. That is, the three values on Beta are popped and Alpha is pushed with the original pre-cursor position. VAB2 then fails forcing alternates on the PM stack to be invoked.

If the overall match is successful, Beta is scanned on a FIFO basis (left-to-right) and assignments are made in turn. If the variable is an unevaluated expression, the evaluation is made at this time, by a possibly recursive call.

Stack Beta is normally called the name-list stack. It operates in synchronism with the PM stack and, hence, it would have been possible to use this latter stack to push the two cursor values and the variable. It would not normally be difficult or time-consuming to extract these values from the PM stack at termination of matching. But differences in the way the garbage collector treats each stack may make a separate name-list stack desirable. Here, implementation considerations at the bit level often determine whether 1 or 2 stacks are used for this purpose. Stack Alpha, on the other hand, grows differently than the PM stack. The overall system stack which is employed for expression evaluation and recursive calls is used. The system stack, as we will see, may be active during pattern matching (to implement unevaluated expressions) but its net growth from the beginning of processing of one node to the beginning of processing of its subsequent is always 0 (unless used as the Alpha stack of substring assignment).

Immediate variable association is similar but simpler than conditional association and will be left as an exercise.

UNEVALUATED EXPRESSIONS   Page 137

| % % NEVALUATED EXPRESSIONS | Unevaluated expressions may
be used as patterns and, if
so, are evaluated during a pattern match. The
result of such an evaluation may be any pattern,
even one containing unevaluated expressions. The
difficulty with handling unevaluated expressions,
which can result in arbitrary path diagrams, is to effectively
combine the new path diagram with the old. In principle, this
path diagram could be fused into the overall pattern by means
of the pattern building process discussed earlier. However,
since this pattern is evaluated whenever the scanner is moving
forward through the pattern, this pattern building process may
take place many times during a single pattern match. Worse,
the pattern would have to be detached before the next new patterns
were joined and this would promise more difficulties.
Hence, rebuilding the pattern is not a satisfactory solution.

Let STAR be the program label associated with that part of the
system which is to process unevaluated expressions. The argument
in the node associated with STAR is the unevaluated
expression which we assume that STAR can readily evaluate. We
note that the evaluation of the argument can evoke a
programmer-defined function which can, by virtue of it performing
pattern matching, reenter the scanner. This requires
that, before the unevaluated expression is evaluated, a host
of values such as the cursor position, the subject, the current
value of the push-down list, and the NODE position be
placed in the system stack to be restored after the argument
is evaluated. In our pseudo-implementation of pattern matching
all this is taken care of automatically be declaring the appropriate
variables to be either parameters or temporaries of
the function MATCH.

Assuming that this is done, the result of this evaluation is a
pattern P. What STAR must do is apply this pattern to the
subject at the given pre-cursor position. This can be done by
a call (recursive) to the function SCAN if we first provide
isolation between this call and previous uses of the stack.
This takes the form

    STAR   P = EVAL(ARG(NODE))
            PUSH(NULL)   ;   PUSH(CURSOR)
            SCAN(LENGTH, P)   :F(MF) S(S)

It is a minor detail but if the result of evaluation is an
unevaluated expression it is again EVALed. Assuming that a
pattern P emerges from the evaluation procedure it is applied
to the subject at the current cursor position by means of the
call to SCAN. If P fails, the insulating null-cursor will have
been popped and SCAN will fail. In this case STAR simply
relays the failure. If P succeeds, SCAN will succeed and STAR
reports success. If the subsequent to STAR is ultimately successful,
nothing more need be said. If unsuccessful, the list
of alternates laid down on the stack by P must be invoked. But
they cannot be invoked straight-away as any gyrations of their

Page 138   Chapter 7 - Pattern Matching Implementation

own accord would cause success or failure of the evaluated pattern P to be interpreted as success or failure of the pattern as a whole. Hence a kind of second insulation is set up to receive control should s fail. This comes in the form of the primitive RESTAR shown in Figure 7.9.

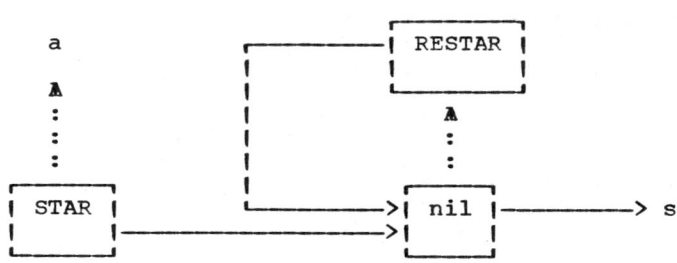

```
STAR      P  =  ARG(NODE)
STAR_1    P  =  EVAL(P)                        :F(MF)
          IDENT(DATATYPE(P),'EXPRESSION')      :S(STAR_1)
          PUSH(NULL)   ;    PUSH(CURSOR)
STAR_2    REDUCTION  =  0
          REDUCTION  =  EQ(&FULLSCAN,0)  RESID(NODE)
          GT(REDUCTION, LENGTH)                :S(LF)
          SCAN(LENGTH - REDUCTION, P)          :F(MF) S(S)

RESTAR    CURSOR  =  POP()
          P  =  POP()
          IDENT(P,NULL)                        :S(MF) F(STAR_2)
```

Figure 7.9

A compound to implement Unevaluated Expressions.

When RESTAR receives control it pops the stack. If the alternate is null, this is the insulating null-cursor pair and RESTAR simply fails. Otherwise it merges with the STAR primitive which calls SCAN with the popped alternate as argument.

The previously cited Recursive Reduction heuristic is shown in Figure 7.9. A fifth field of a pattern node is called the residual. This equals the minimum number of characters required by the node's subsequent to match. The field name used is RESID so that the data statement for a pattern node should really read

DATA('NODE(PROG,SUBS,ALT,ARG,RESID)')

Exercises for chapter 7   Page 139

Residuals are computed by assigning a minimum length string to
each pattern. For example, the minimum lengths of BREAK(S),
TAB(N), POS(N)   and FENCE are each 0. The minimum length of
SPAN(S) and BAL are each 1. The minimum length of a string is
the size of the string, etc. The minimum length of the
concatenation of two patterns is the sum of their minimum
lengths. The minimum length of the alternation of two patterns
is the minimum of their minimum lengths. When two patterns
are concatenated, the residual of each node is incremented by
the minimum length of the second pattern. When two patterns
are alternated, all residuals remain unchanged. The minimum
length of a pattern can either be partially recomputed for
each concatenation from the residual of the root node and the
minimum length of the root or may be stored in a pattern
header where global information about the pattern is kept or
may be retained separately for each node in another field
(MINLEN) of the pattern node.

As an example of the recusive reduction heuristic

             P = *P 'A' | 'B'

will not loop.   Since the residual of *P is 1 (the minimum
length of 'A'), SCAN is called with ever decreasing LENGTH'S.
On the other hand

             P = *P BREAK('A') BREAK('B') | 'B'

will loop because the residual of *P is 0. Note that
BREAK('A') BREAK('B') matches at least one character but the
simple-minded minimum-character algorithm fails to detect
this.

It is not uncommon to experience the BNF-like expression

             P = *P *Q | 'A'

This pattern would loop if it were not for the drastic assumption that unevaluated expressions require a single character
to match. This is the so-called one-character assumption.
Given this assumption, the residual of *P is 1 and so the number of recursive plunges is limited by the length of the
string. Note that the one-character assumption has nothing to
do with the number of characters required by *P but only *Q.

??
????????????????????????   EXERCISES ?????????????????????????
??

| Exercise 7.1 | Implement the BREAK(S) primitive (call it
                 BREAKP) in SNOBOL4 source in a   manner
similar to the way in which the LEN(N) primitive (called

Page 140   Chapter 7   -   Pattern Matching Implementation

'LENP') was implemented in the text.   Assume that ANY(S) and POS(N) are available.

| Exercise 7.2 | There is a single pattern primitive called CHARP which is used in matching any string against the subject. The string is contained in ARG(NODE) while PROG(NODE) contains CHARP. Assuming SUBSTR (Prog. 3.9) is available show how CHARP could be implemented in SNOBOL4 source. Pass control to LF or MF on failure depending on whether or not the pattern is futile.

| Exercise 7.3 | After executing the instructions below, (a) how many s-vacancies will there be in P? (b) how many a-vacancies? Express your answer in terms of N.

```
              P = 'A'
              I = 0
    LOOP      P = (P | P) (P | P)
              I = I + 1   LT(I,N)            :S(LOOP)
```

| Exercise 7.4 | As indicated in the text, to properly concatentate two patterns, the first must be copied.   Assuming the patterns are linked structures as indicated in the function CONCAT, implement CONCAT as a modified form of COPYL (Prog. 5.8).

| Exercise 7.5 | A path diagram is **well-formed** if (1) any sequence of alternates ends in an a-vacancy (i.e. no loop of alternates exist) and (2) no loop of subsequents exist.   Show that any path diagram formed by alternating, concatenating or ARBNO'ing (see Figure 7.7) well-formed (and distinct) path diagrams produces only well-formed path diagrams.

| Exercise 7.6 | One implementation of patterns encodes them as a contiguous set of nodes together with a header to form one large array as shown in Figure 7.10.

The root node is always node 1. The MIN field is the minimum length string that the pattern will match. FLAG and START are used as the anchoring field. If FLAG is 1 and START contains N, then the pattern is anchored in the form POS(N) ... If FLAG is -1 then the pattern is anchored in the form RPOS(N) ... If FLAG is 0, no special anchoring heuristic exists.

The alternate and subsequent fields contain the subscript of the target nodes. If empty, these fields contain some nonpositive integers.

Exercises for chapter 7   Page 141

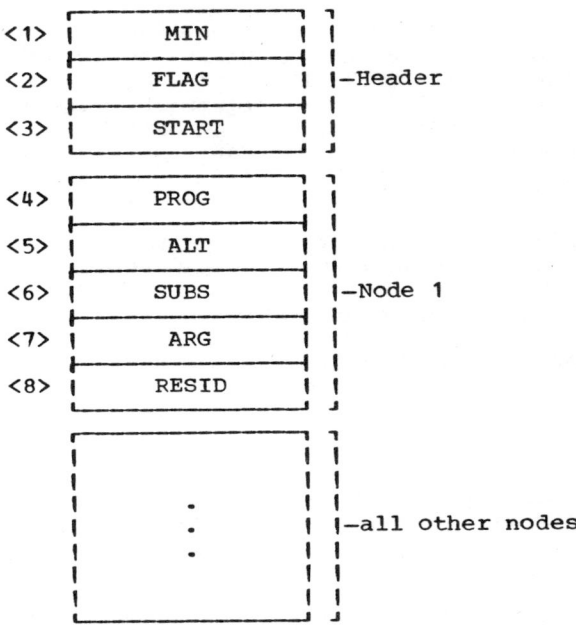

Figure 7.10

The data structure for a practical implementation of patterns.

Write a subroutine to build (a) the alternation and (b) the concatenation of two patterns and (c) find the ARBNO of one pattern.

| Exercise 7.7 | How many primitive matches (successful and unsuccessful) are involved in the following pattern matching statements?

(a)   'ABCDEFGHIJKLMN'   'EF' | 'C'

(b)   DUPL('A',20)   'B' ∂N

(c)   DUPL('A',20)   ∂N 'B'

(d)   'AAEAAACE'   ('C' | 'D') ('E' | 'F')

(e)   DUPL('A',20)   SPAN('A') | BREAK('A')

(f)   'AABAAC'   SPAN('A') 'C'

Chapter 7 - Pattern Matching Implementation

Exercise 7.8 Write the MATCH function which serves to drive the SCANer. Be sure to set and test the futility flag (FUTILITY) if &FULLSCAN is off and check &ANCHOR. MATCH will have two arguments, the subject S and the pattern P. Have MATCH fail if the pattern fails and return the string matched if it succeeds. Be sure to indicate which variables are temporary.

Exercise 7.9 Which of the following monic patterns are transmitters of futility?

(a)   SPAN('AB') | NOTANY('AB')

(b)   TAB(N) | POS(N + 1)

(c)   'ABA' | 'B'

(d)   'ABCD' | 'DCBA'

Exercise 7.10 Which of the following patterns are contextually anchored and what is the character set in each case?

```
(ANY('AB') | SPAN('DE') | 'CAT') LEN(3)
POS(3) BREAK('AB')
('A' | (SPAN('B') | 'CAN'))
ARBNO(ANY('AB'))
```

Exercise 7.11 If the subsequent P to the pattern TAB(N) fails (even if the failure is match-failure) one may presume that TAB(N) P is futile and no increase in cursor position can help. How would we implement TAB(N) to take advantage of this?

Exercise 7.12 If a user requires that BAL match the null string he may very easily create a pattern which will provide this extension. He may write:

NEW_BAL = NULL | BAL

(a) Draw the resulting path diagram.

(b) Design a compound for implementing NULL | BAL directly (using GBAL of course).

Exercise 7.13 In QUICKSCAN mode, if the subsequent to ARBNO(P) is futile, no further extensions need be taken provided P cannot match a string of negative length. The compound shown in Figure 7.11 below is designed to implement this heuristic. Describe the operation of the

Exercises for chapter 7   Page 143

primitives ARBN1 and ARBN2 in SNOBOL4 source, i.e. in a manner
similar to the descriptions of ARB1 and ARB2.

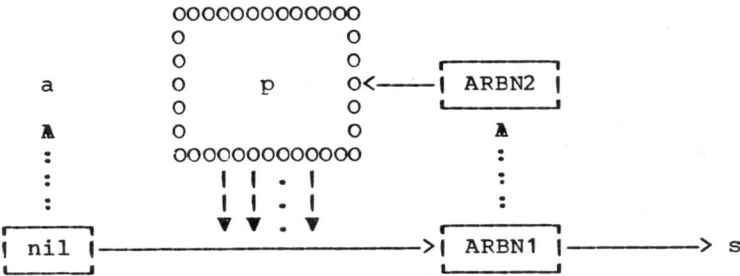

Figure 7.11

A path diagram to implement a futility heuristic
for ARBNO.

| Exercise 7.14 | Design a compound for implementing BREAKX()
(the SPITBOL function, see Prog. 8.2) assuming that the BREAK primitive and LEN(1) are available.

| Exercise 7.15 | Describe how you would implement the pattern NOT(P) defined as matching the null
string if P fails, failing if P succeeds, and aborting if P
aborts.

| Exercise 7.16 | In chapter 6, ARBNO(P) was defined as

ARBNO(P) = NULL | P ARBNO(P)

Show that the derived pattern of the path diagram in Figure
7.7 is

ARBNO(P) D(s) | D(a)

where P is the derived pattern of the path diagram p. You may
assume in your proof that P does not match the null string.

| Exercise 7.17 | The scanner function operates in such a
manner that the pattern implemented is the
derived pattern:

p D(s) | D(a)

Page 144   Chapter 7   -   Pattern Matching Implementation

Rewrite SCAN so that the derived pattern is:

$$D(a) \mid p\ D(s)$$

| Exercise 7.18 | Rewrite SCAN to implement the derived pattern

$$(p \mid D(a))\ D(s)$$

(Hint: study STAR and RESTAR carefully and do not underestimate this problem.)

| Exercise 7.19 | To eliminate one of the nil nodes of Figure 7.4, it is proposed that the alternate be 'hung off' the LEN(1) node, eliminating the first nil entirely. Show that the derived path diagram of this combination does not equal

$$ARB\ D(s) \mid D(a)$$

as it should.

| Exercise 7.20 | Assume that a flag exists called UEFLAG which is set by STAR to indicate that an unevaluated expression was encountered. Modify ARB so that the length fail heuristic is unobtrusive but so that ARB reports length fail if there are no unevaluated expressions encountered in the subsequent to ARB.

CHAPTER EIGHT

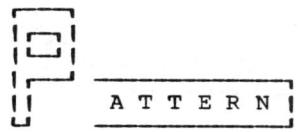

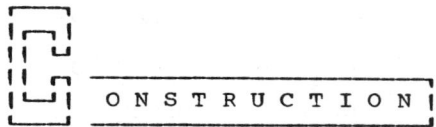

```
CONTENTS

BRKREM .................. 8.1

BREAKX .................. 8.2

BAL ..................... 8.3

FASTBAL ................. 8.4

NOT ..................... 8.5

ONCE .................... 8.6

TEST .................... 8.7

LIKE .................... 8.8

OR ...................... 8.9

PLI.STMT ................ 8.10

ASM360 .................. 8.11
```

Chapter 8 - PATTERN CONSTRUCTION

Patterns are data objects and, as such, enjoy the same rights and priviliges bestowed on objects having the more conventional typings of STRING, INTEGER and REAL. In particular, patterns may be assigned to variables (possibly array elements or field variables) and may be passed to and from functions. This chapter tends to demonstrate these capabilities and describes a number of useful (and not-so-useful) pattern-valued functions and also provides a few very practical patterns for analyzing common linguistic cases.

A word perhaps should be said about the virtue of attempting to solve as much of the problem as possible with one big pattern match. This can obviously be overdone. For example:

```
        S   (REM $ OUTPUT FAIL | LEN(1) . T REM . S)
```

serves to both print the string S and separate it from its first character. This has the same effect as:

```
        OUTPUT = S
        S   LEN(1) . T REM . S
```

The two-line version is clearer and, if anything, more efficient and is easier to type and modify. The one-line version might perhaps be written to be cute or perhaps in the mistaken belief that statement overhead is significant (it is not).

There are, however, often excellent reasons for using one pattern match as opposed to two or more. Consider looking for a quoted literal while analyzing SNOBOL4 source. Assume S contains a valid SNOBOL4 statement and assume we wish to search for the existence of a quoted literal assigning it to the variable X and transferring to NONE if none exists. One poor attempt is:

```
        Q   =   '"'
        QQ  =   ''''
        S   (Q BREAK(Q) Q) . X              :S(AROUND)
        S   (QQ BREAK(QQ) QQ) . X           :F(NONE)
AROUND
```

If the two pattern matches are replaced by:

```
        S  (Q BREAK(Q) Q | QQ BREAK(QQ) QQ) . X        :F(DONE)
```

the result is not necessary clearer or more efficient but does have the beneficial property of not being wrong. If the string S contained

```
                    " ... ' ... " ... '
```

then the two-pattern case would have erred.

Program 8.1 - BRKREM

There are times when a single large pattern can take the place of many lines of code. I have seen a case where a programmer wrote a machine-language subroutine (to be called from SNOBOL4) to parse the 360 assembler language where this parse can be written as one not-too-complex pattern (ASM360, Program 8.11). The reason I saw it at all was because the program became a hopeless jumble and the writer of the program was virtually lost in a sea of complexity. The mistake made here was to assume that because, in assembly language, each step is quite clear, that the composition of an arbitrary number of such steps should also be clear. Programming offers no more vivid testimony than to deny this assumption.

```
|  Program  |
|   8.1     |
|  BRKREM   |
```

There are cases when it is desirous that the pattern BREAK(S) match the entire string if (and only if) there are no break characters found. If it were not for the 'only if' proviso, the pattern

                BREAK(S) | REM

would do. But this pattern has the potentiality of matching 2 strings; i.e. it is not monic.

```
| BRKREM(S) returns a pattern that will behave like BREAK(S) |
| if that pattern would succeed and will match the remainder |
| of the subject string otherwise.                           |
```

    DEFINE('BRKREM(S)CS')   : (BRKREM_END)

```
| If S is null there are no break characters.  Return a pat- |
| tern which will consume the rest of the string.            |
```

BRKREM   BRKREM = IDENT(S)   REM   : S(RETURN)

```
| Find the set complement (CS) of S. If this is null, BRKREM |
| should match the null string.                              |
```

    CS = DIFF(&ALPHABET, S)
    IDENT(CS)   : S(RETURN)

```
| Otherwise return the alternation of 3 mutually exclusive |
| cases.                                                   |
```

    BRKREM = RPOS(0) | SPAN(CS) RPOS(0) | BREAK(S)
                                                    : (RETURN)
BRKREM_END

Names referenced by BRKREM:	Name	Type	Where defined
	DIFF	Function	Program 3.10

Chapter 8 - PATTERN CONSTRUCTION

```
┌─────────────┐
|  Program    |
|    8.2      |
|  BREAKX     |
└─────────────┘
```
The pattern BREAK(S) where S is a string will rapidly scan for one of the characters in S, stopping just short of the found character. The scanning is done as fast as the hardware will allow and, for 360 implementations this is quite rapid. But suppose the problem is not to scan for a character but for a string S. This can be done quite easily by the statement

            SUBJECT   S

To speed up the search, we might think of using BREAK to scan for the initial character of S as follows

         S   LEN(1) . INITIAL
         SUBJECT   POS(0) BREAK(INITIAL) S

this will succeed if S appears at the first instance of its initial character. Otherwise the pattern would fail since BREAK cannot match a string containing INITIAL. If we were to remove the POS(0) the pattern would 'work' in the sense that it would succeed when required but the time required to do so could be worse than before. This is because the scanner would increment the cursor by 1 after each failure and thereby move quite slowly toward its destination. To fix the situation we define a function called BREAKX (BREAK eXtended) which, upon failing, will extend past the break character to find another. Like BAL and ARBNO, BREAKX is said to have implicit alternatives.

BREAKX was first introduced as a built-in function in SPITBOL and appears in SITBOL and FASBOL.

            DEFINE('BREAKX(S)')   :(BREAKX_END)
BREAKX   BREAKX = BREAK(S) ARBNO(LEN(1) BREAK(S))
                                                :(RETURN)
BREAKX_END

```
┌─────────────┐
|  Program    |
|    8.3      |
|  BAL        |
└─────────────┘
```
In analyzing programs BAL can be quite useful but it is also limited in that it cannot be applied freely to expressions which permit quote marks. For example, even though the string

            "ABC(DEF ' (' GHI) JKL"

is balanced in the syntax of SNOBOL4, BAL would not match it. Since most languages have the capability of permitting quoted expressions within an expression, this severely hinders the application of BAL.

Analyzing languages which have bracketing other than, or in addition to, parenthesization also presents a situation in which BAL is inadequate. For example, suppose that a list of

arguments (expressions separated by commas) is contained in
the string LIST and suppose that its initial left parenthesis
were removed. For example

    LIST = '13, A + B(3,4), C)'

In order to pick off arguments from such a list, we may think
of using the pattern matching statement:

    LIST   POS(0)   BAL . ARG   ANY(',)') =

Aside from the problem of quoted literals this statement will
work correctly only if the source language contains no other
kind of bracketing. For example, if the source language were
SNOBOL4 and if LIST contained:

    LIST = '13, A + B<3,4>, C)'

the pattern matching statement described above would find
' A + B<3' as second argument which of course is incorrect.

The function BAL(PARENS,QTS) will return a pattern which will
match all nonnull balanced strings where the first argument is
used to specify paired brackets in nested fashion and the
second argument specifies characters used as quotes. For example BAL('(<>)','"' ''') will match a balanced string in
SNOBOL4 source. Also BAL('()') is equivalent to the built-in
pattern BAL.

Let us consider how we might define the built-in pattern BAL
if it did not exist before proceeding to the more general
case. BAL is a pattern which will match any string balanced
with respect to parenthesis. A balanced string is defined as

1. Any single character not a parenthesis is balanced.

2. If B is balanced or is null then '(' B ')' is balanced.

3. If B_1 and B_2 are balanced, then B_1 B_2 is balanced.

A straightforward translation of this definition could be used
to define BAL and it would have the appearance:

    BAL = NOTANY(')(') | '(' (*BAL | NULL) ')' | *BAL *BAL

The difficulty with this rendition of BAL is twofold. It uses
the stack heavily (even when there are no parentheses in the
subject) and it is inefficient especially if it is headed for
failure. The difficulty in both cases is the third alternative. As discussed in the previous chapter, there are two
kinds of stack usage that we must be concerned with. There is
the relatively mild requirements of the alternatives which
must be placed on the history stack; then there are the more
severe requirements of recursion. This version of BAL uses
the recursion stack quite heavily. Consider the match

Page 150   Chapter 8   -   PATTERN CONSTRUCTION

                    '(XXX ... X)'   '(' BAL ')'

where there are N X's in the subject string. The maximum recursive level is N-1. What's worse, if the pattern BAL does not succeed as in

                    '(XXX ... X'   '(' BAL ')'

the time required rises exponentially with the length of the subject.

Another approach to encoding BAL is as follows: let GBAL match only the first balanced string (as opposed to all balanced strings). Then express BAL in terms of GBAL.

        GBAL = NOTANY(')(') | '(' (*BAL | NULL) ')'
        BAL   = GBAL ARBNO(GBAL)

This reduces BAL to sequential application of GBAL's and the time to determine failure does not rise exponentially. There is still the problem that the amount of stack used rises linearly with the length of the subject. Though this time, the stack used is the history stack and not the recursive stack. An alternate-cursor pair is laid down at each nonparenthesis scanned in the subject string. As this may be disturbing for large strings a better tactic is to reverse the order of alternation in defining GBAL as follows:

        GBAL = '(' (*BAL | NULL) ')' | NOTANY(')(')

There is a time-storage tradeoff here. While this version of GBAL consumes less stack, it requires slightly more time in the event that the pattern is to succeed. We will opt for reduced stack usage.

Another problem associated with writing the BAL function is how do we return a recursively defined pattern from a function. Consider the function F(P) which attempts to return a pattern to match a sequence of P's.

              DEFINE('F(P)')   :(F_END)
F   F = P *F | NULL   :(RETURN)
F_END

F returns a pattern whose definition depends on the current value of F. But Lord knows what the value of F is after the return. It can be anything, since the old value of F is restored. Moreover, even if a global name were used, the name would be reassigned a new value each call. A way to avoid these problems is to create a unique name at each call. Assume for the sake of argument that F1876 is such a unique name. Then if

              F1876 = P *F1876 | NULL
              F =   F1876   :(RETURN)

Program 8.4 - FASTBAL   Page 151

were executed, the desired value would be returned. Code such as this could be created dynamically via the CODE function. A more efficient technique is to convert the unique name to EXPRESSION. This is done in defining BAL.

```
       DEFINE('BAL(PARENS,QTS) Q,GBAL,NAME,STAR,LP,RP')
                                            :(BAL_END)
```

Entry point: Create a unique but uncommon name (NAME) for a variable which is to be assigned the pattern. To use it recursively, we will need the associated unevaluated expression (STAR). Also initialize GBAL.

```
BAL       NAME  =  'BAL_.'  &STCOUNT
          STAR  =  CONVERT(NAME, 'EXPRESSION')
          GBAL  =  NOTANY(PARENS QTS)
```

Loop on quote characters inserting a quoted literal as an optional condidate for a balanced string.

```
BAL_1     QTS   LEN(1) . Q  =                  :F(BAL_2)
          GBAL  =  Q BREAK(Q) Q  |  GBAL       :(BAL_1)
```

Loop on the nested bracketing characters and create a balanced alternate for each pair.

```
BAL_2     PARENS  LEN(1) . LP  RTAB(1) . PARENS  LEN(1) . RP
+                                               :F(BAL_3)
          GBAL  =  LP (STAR | NULL) RP | GBAL   :(BAL_2)
```

Define BAL (the returned string) in terms of GBAL and assign it to the strangely named variable so that recursion works.

```
BAL_3     BAL  =  GBAL  ARBNO(GBAL)
          $NAME  =  BAL                         :(RETURN)
BAL_END
```

Epilogue

Note that the name of the function is the same as the name of a built-in pattern BAL. Both the variable and the function can co-exist and can be entirely unrelated. Note that when the function is called the variable BAL is temporarily assigned a null value and is subsequently assigned the return value. Upon return, the original value of BAL is restored so no difficulty ensues.

	Program	
	8.4	
	FASTBAL	

A criticism that could be leveled against the BAL function is that the pattern it returns creeps along, one character at a time, at speeds determined by ARBNO(NOTANY()). A much faster version can be written which will skip over uninteresting characters at BREAK speeds and

Page 152   Chapter 8 - PATTERN CONSTRUCTION

stop only before parens, quoted-literals and any of a set of
designated characters provided as a third argument. For
example

          SNOARG = FASTBAL('(<>)', '"' '"', ',)') . ARG ANY(',)')

will assign to SNOARG a pattern which can be used to scan for
the arguments of a function call in SNOBOL4 source. If the
string to be scanned is

                    A 'B' + F(')'), X)

then SNOARG will tentatively match "A " and then "A 'B' + F"
before finally matching "A 'B' + F(')')". FASTBAL, like
BREAKX, will continue to take extensions. For example, the
pattern match

          'A/B(/D)/D' POS(0) FASTBAL('()',,'/') '/D'

will succeed with the entire subject being matched.

Like BREAKX and unlike BAL, FASTBAL will not match the entire
string since it requires a break character. Such a modification, however, is easily made and is explored in an exercise.

```
            DEFINE('FASTBAL(PARENS,QTS,S) NAME,IBAL,SPCHARS,ELEM'
+                     ',LPS,Q,LP,RP')        :(FASTBAL_END)
```
┌───┐
│ Entry point: NAME is   a uniquely created name for the │
│ variable that will eventually hold the returned pattern. │
│ IBAL is a pattern to match balanced strings on the in- │
│ terior of brackets.   │
└───┘
```
FASTBAL  NAME   =   'FASTBAL_' &STCOUNT
         IBAL   =   CONVERT(NAME, 'EXPRESSION')
         IBAL   =   DIFFER(S,NULL)  FASTBAL(PARENS,QTS)
```
┌───┐
│ SPCHARS are all the special characters. ELEM is a monic   │
│ pattern to match a balanced string to be built up during   │
│ the subsequent computation.   │
└───┘
```
         SPCHARS =  PARENS QTS S
         ELEM    =  NOTANY(PARENS QTS) BREAK(SPCHARS)
```
┌───┐
│ Loop on quotes, oring in a quoted literal pattern for   │
│ every quote.   │
└───┘
```
FASTBAL_1       QTS   LEN(1) . Q =             :F(FASTBAL_2)
                ELEM  =  Q BREAK(Q) Q | ELEM   :(FASTBAL_1)
```
┌───┐
│ Loop on parens, oring in a balanced form for each pair.   │
└───┘
```
FASTBAL_2       PARENS   LEN(1) . LP   RTAB(1) . PARENS
+                        LEN(1) . RP             :F(FASTBAL_3)
                ELEM  =  LP IBAL RP | ELEM   :(FASTBAL_2)
```

Program 8.5 - NOT   Page 153

> Wrap things up and return.

```
FASTBAL_3      FASTBAL  = BREAK(SPCHARS)   ARBNO(ELEM)
               $NAME    = FASTBAL          :(RETURN)
FASTBAL_END
```

```
|  Program  |
|   8.5     |
|   NOT     |
```
The function NOT(P) returns a pattern which will match the null string provided P would fail and will fail if P would succeed. NOT(P) is undefined if P is nonlinear. As an example of the use of NOT assume we wish to write a pattern which will match a PL/I comment. The pattern '/*' ARB '*/' will not do since it will match other things in addition to comments. For example it will match three strings in the PL/I statement below where only two are comments.

   GOUT /* GARBAGE OUT */ = GIN /* GARBAGE IN */

To match a comment we can write:

   '/*' ARBNO(NOT('*/') LEN(1)) '*/'

Here the ARB is replaced by a pattern constructed from ARBNO which will match an arbitrary string not containing the substring '*/'. To speed up the search for the closing '*/' we can employ BREAK as follows:

   '/*' ARBNO(NOT('*/') LEN(1) BREAK('*')) '*/'

The function NOT is so constructed as to be embeddable in itself. Thus NOT(NOT(P)) will match the null string if P would succeed. Also if C were the comment matcher defined above, NOT(C) would operate correctly.

One drawback of NOT, which is the reason we will not use it more widely in building other patterns, is that it must be used in FULLSCAN mode. The reason for this is the one-character assumption of the recursive reduction heuristic described in the previous chapter. Since mode switching is generally poor programming practice, we will generally avoid the use of NOT.

> NOT(P) will return a pattern which will match the null
> string if P fails and fail if P matches. If P aborts,
> NOT(P) will also abort.

         DEFINE('NOT(P)')   :(NOT_END)

> Entry point: Return a pattern which pushes null onto the
> stack and replaces it with nonnull only if the pattern
> succeeds. The flag is eventually popped and tested by the

Chapter 8 - PATTERN CONSTRUCTION

| alternative.

```
NOT         NOT    =   *PUSH() P *(POP() PUSH(1))   FAIL
 +                     *IDENT(POP())               :(RETURN)
NOT_END
```

Names referenced   Name   Type   Where defined
by NOT: PUSH   Function   Program 5.5
                       POP   Function   Program 5.6

Epilogue

P is assumed not to have side effects which will alter the stack. For example, if

P = NULL | *(POP() PUSH()) FAIL

then P will cleverly undo what NOT was trying to do and cause NOT(P) to succeed where it should always fail. But this amounts to almost deliberate meddling. If P uses the stack normally (i.e. leaving its state the way it was found) then NOT will operate correctly.

| | Program | | ONCE() returns a pattern which will succeed
| | 8.6 | | once and only once and thereafter fail
| | ONCE | | forever. For example the pattern matching
                   statement

              'AAAB'   'A' ONCE() 'B' | 'B'

will result in the 'B' being matched, but not the 'AB', since the first time through the left alternation, 'B' failed, indicating that that path could no longer be taken. Note that ONCE() must return a new and distinct pattern on each call since once it is used it can never be reused.

ONCE() is similar to FENCE in that it matches the null string initially. Unlike FENCE, however, failure in subsequent tries is like FAIL (as opposed to ABORT) which permits other alternates to be taken.

| ONCE() will return a pattern that will succeed just once. |

         DEFINE('ONCE(ID)NAME')   :(ONCE_END)

| Entry point: If the argument is null we return a new pat- |
| tern equal to *ONCE(id) where id is a unique integer. |

ONCE   ONCE   = IDENT(ID,NULL)
 +   CONVERT('ONCE(' &STCOUNT ')' , 'EXPRESSION')   :S(RETURN)

| Otherwise compute a name based on the unique ID. Return |

```
| its value.  It will be initially null.  Set it to FAIL for |
| all subsequent calls.                                      |
```
```
            NAME    =   'ONCE..'   ID
            ONCE    =   $NAME
            $NAME   =   FAIL                          :(RETURN)
ONCE_END
```

Epilogue

the function ONCE() returns an expression of the form *ONCE(n) which will succeed just once and fail forever after. It illustrates several principles. First, a function can return different patterns and each of these patterns can vary their own behavior with time. Second, the function serves both to return a pattern initially and is also the function invoked during the match. Both of these operating principles will be in use in the next function.

The technique used to encode ONCE() can be used to pick off the first match of a pattern and thereby increase efficiency. See Exercise 8.8.

```
|| Program ||    TEST is designed to alleviate some of the
||   8.7   ||    problems involved with the one-character as-
||   TEST  ||    sumption which we have already indicated
                 might be a source of difficulty with the NOT
```
function. TEST will accept an unevaluated expression as argument and return a pattern. When the pattern is encountered by the scanner during a pattern match the original unevaluated expression will be EVALed and the pattern will succeed or fail depending on the outcome of the EVAL. If it succeeds it matches the null string. For example

            TEST(*LGT(A,B))

will return a pattern which, during pattern matching, will succeed or fail depending on whether A is, or is not, lexically greater than B.

Thus TEST(exp) acts like exp. It differs from exp in that its minimum length will be 0 as opposed to 1 and it will match the null string if the evaluation succeeds.

```
            DEFINE('TEST(ARG)NAME')             :(TEST_END)
```
```
| Entry point:  If ARG is an EXPRESSION we will return a   |
| pattern.  The expression is saved in a unique name (NAME)|
| and this name, in the form of a string, is used as an ar-|
| gument on subsequent calls to TEST.                      |
```
```
TEST        IDENT(DATATYPE(ARG),'EXPRESSION')    :F(TEST_1)
            NAME    =   'TEST_'  &STCOUNT
```

Chapter 8 - PATTERN CONSTRUCTION

```
             $NAME   =   ARG
             TEST =  EVAL("NULL $ *TEST('" NAME "')")     :(RETURN)
```
If ARG is not an EXPRESSION we presume that we are dealing with one of those subsequent calls to TEST. In fact, we can conclude that we're in the middle of a pattern match. Retrieve the old expression and evaluate it and return a dummy name.

```
TEST_1     TEST   =   ?EVAL($ARG)    .TEST_      :S(NRETURN) F(FRETURN)
TEST_END
```

```
||   Program   ||      LIKE(S) returns a pattern that will match  a
||   8.8       ||      string  like the one passed as argument.   A
||   LIKE      ||      like string is defined as  anyone  differing
                       from   the   argument by a) a rearrangement of
two characters, b) the deletion  of  a  character or  c)  the
insertion of a character.
```

```
             DEFINE('LIKE(S)C,T1,T2,N')              :(LIKE_END)
```
Entry point: Make sure that S itself is regarded as LIKE S.

```
LIKE       LIKE  =  S
```
Loop on N where N denotes a cursor position within S. Split S into two parts, T1 and T2.

```
LIKE_1     S     TAB(N) . T1  REM . T2           :F(RETURN)
                 N = N + 1
```
First OR in a pattern which matches S with one character inserted at position N.

```
             LIKE  =  LIKE | T1 LEN(1) T2
```
Then OR in the pattern which matches with one character deleted at position N.

```
             T2   LEN(1) . C  =                :F(RETURN)
             LIKE  =  LIKE  |  T1  T2
```
Then OR in the pattern where the two characters at posi- tion N have been rearranged.

```
             T2    POS(1)  =  C                :F(LIKE_1)
             LIKE  =  LIKE  |  T1 T2           :(LIKE_1)
LIKE_END
```

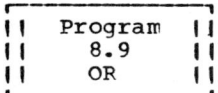

OR(S) is intended to form the OR (in the pattern sense) of several strings contained in S. For example OR(',ABC,DEF,XYZ') IS EQUIVALENT TO

'ABC' | 'DEF' | 'XYZ'

The initial character (in this case a comma) is used to separate elements. For efficiency puroses, OR will factor out like initial characters. Thus

OR(',ABLE,ACTOR,ANCHOR,BAKER,BULL')

is equivalent to

'A' ('BLE' | 'CTOR' | 'NCHOR') | 'B' ('AKER' | 'ULL')

The resulting expression in this example is over twice as fast as alternating 5 strings since for most subjects only 2 checks are needed for every pre-cursor position as opposed to 5. The initial character extraction is done to arbitrary levels so that

OR(',ABC,ABBOT,ACTOR,BAKER')

will return

'A' ('B' ('C' | 'BOT') | 'CTOR') | 'BAKER'

For efficiency purposes, if a factored character contains only one branch, the character is combined with the head of the branch. Thus

OR(',ABC,ABBOT,BAKER')

returns

'AB' ('C' | 'BOT') | 'BAKER'

Characters in parenthesis imply an ANY-like construction. Thus

OR(',C(AO)D,C(AO)ST')

will return

'C' ANY('AO') ('D' | 'ST')

Several examples of the use of OR are given in the initialization section of HYPHENATE (Program 10.7).

> OR(LIST) will return the alternation of the substring of
> LIST separated by the break character determined by the
> first character in LIST. Parenthesized strings are
> regarded as ANY.

```
             DEFINE('OR(LIST) BC,SEIZE,ANC')
```

> OR_EXTRACT() is a function used by OR to extract from the
> global variable LIST, the substrings beginning with the
> same first character (or parenthesized expression).

```
             DEFINE('OR_EXTRACT() COMMON,IC,P,SUBLIST,T,TLIST,C1,C2')
                              :(OR_END)
```

> Entry point for OR. Determine the break character and
> define a pattern to be used throughout to SEIZE all up to
> the next break character. Define ANC as a pattern to
> anchor the scan and match the Break Character.

```
OR           LIST       LEN(1) . BC                :F(FRETURN)
             SEIZE   =  BREAK(BC) | REM
             ANC     =  POS(0)    BC
```

> Or together all extractions.

```
             OR      =  OR_EXTRACT()
OR_LOOP      OR      =  OR | OR_EXTRACT()          :S(OR_LOOP) F(RETURN)
```

> Entry point for OR_EXTRACT(): Set TLIST to be a copy of
> LIST. Extract initial character (IC) and set COMMON equal
> to the first substring. If this pattern fails, no IC could
> be found. This means that LIST is either empty in which
> case we fail, or contains only BC in which case we return
> the null string. Both of these cases are important since
> the former terminates the loop in OR() and the latter
> breaks the recursion of OR_EXTRACT().

```
OR_EXTRACT
             TLIST   =  LIST
             LIST       ANC    (BAL . IC  SEIZE) . COMMON   :S(ORX_1)
             IDENT(LIST, NULL)                              :S(FRETURN)
             LIST    =  NULL                                :(RETURN)
```

> Find the largest COMMON prefix contained in all strings
> beginning with IC.

```
ORX_1        TLIST      ANC    IC                          :F(ORX_3)
ORX_2        TLIST      ANC    COMMON  SEIZE  =            :S(ORX_1)
```

> COMMON was not there. Reduce COMMON by one character and
> try again. This means extract the last balanced string of
> COMMON.

```
             BALREV(COMMON)     BAL  REM . COMMON   :F(ERROR)
             COMMON  =  BALREV(COMMON)              :(ORX_2)
```

Program 8.11 - ASM360

```
┌─────────────────────────────────────────────────────────────┐
│ Now  remove  the  COMMON characters from each string as we  │
│ prepare a SUBLIST to be OR'ed.                              │
└─────────────────────────────────────────────────────────────┘
ORX_3      LIST     ANC   COMMON    SEIZE . T   =   :F(ORX_4)
           SUBLIST  =     SUBLIST   BC    T         :(ORX_3)
```

```
┌─────────────────────────────────────────────────────────────┐
│ Convert any parenthesized expression in COMMON to an  ANY.  │
│ Build up the pattern in a temporary P. Then join this with  │
│ the result of a recursive call to OR.                       │
└─────────────────────────────────────────────────────────────┘
ORX_4      COMMON    BREAK('(') . C1    '(' BREAK(')') . C2
+                               ')'  =                :F(ORX_5)
           P = P  C1  ANY(C2)                         :(ORX_4)
ORX_5      OR_EXTRACT  =  P  COMMON   OR(SUBLIST)     :(RETURN)
OR_END
```

Names referenced   Name   Type   Where defined
by OR: BALREV   Function   Program 3.8


```
┌──────────────┐
││ Program   ││  This  pattern  is  intended to match a PL/I
││  8.10     ││  statement (assigning  to  STMT  the  string
││ PLI.STMT  ││  matched)  and to fail if none exists.   The
└──────────────┘  presumed scenario  is  that  a  program  is
```
reading lines of a PL/I program and continues to apply the
pattern until it succeeds in matching a prefix of the combined
input lines. The pattern need not check for syntactic correct-
ness of the input   and hence it will be sufficient to check
for the   presence of a semicolon provided this character does
not appear within quotes or comments.

```
┌─────────────────────────────────────────────────────────────┐
│ Define  an ELEM as a quoted literal or a comment or a non-  │
│ null sequence containing neither a semicolon nor a comment  │
│ or quote delimeter.                                         │
└─────────────────────────────────────────────────────────────┘
           Q    =  ''''
           QLIT =  Q  FENCE  BREAK(Q)  Q
           CMNT =  '/*'  FENCE  ARB  '*/'
           ELEM =  QLIT | CMNT | LEN(1) BREAK('/;' Q)
```

```
┌─────────────────────────────────────────────────────────────┐
│ Use back-up-free scanning (Chapter 6) to  search  for  the  │
│ statement.                                                  │
└─────────────────────────────────────────────────────────────┘
       PLI.STMT  =  POS(0)   (ARBNO(ELEM FENCE)  ';') . STMT
```

```
┌──────────────┐
││ Program   ││  Many problems involving the  processing  of
││  8.11     ││  assembler  source can be conceptually simple
││ ASM360    ││  and yet provide a challenge to the program-
└──────────────┘  mer.   Consider the problem of reformatting
```
the source so that various syntactic parts such as operations,

Chapter 8 - PATTERN CONSTRUCTION

operands and comments are set to allign at pre-determined card columns. The heart of this problem as well as many others is simply the extraction of the various fields since once these have been obtained it is a relatively simple matter to recast a given line in a new format. Different assembler languages offer different problems to be solved. The OS assembler [IBM360b] is noted for its relative ubiquity and complexity and will offer a fine example to consider.

In the OS assembler there are four fields separated by blanks, viz.

NAME   OPERATION   OPERAND   COMMENT

where the optional NAME field must begin in column 1 if it exists. One is tempted to use BREAK(' ') to separate the fields. This works for the first two fields but the operand field may have blanks embedded in quoted literals and so this simple scheme will not do. Moreover, the quote that appears in an expression beginning with L' is not to be considered for quote-balancing. Thus

L   MVI   3,L'ABC   'THIS IS A COMMENT'

has an operand field (3rd field) that breaks after ABC and not after THIS. The rule for determining whether L' is to be considered specially is given on p. 71 of [IBM360b]

"An apostrophe not within a quoted string immediately followed by a letter and immediately preceded by the letter L (where L is preceded by any special character other than an ampersand) is not considered in determining paired apostrophes."

On page 10 of [IBM360b] we obtain the definitions of 'letter' and 'special character' and so we begin coding ...

```
LETTER = 'ABCDEFGHIJKLMNOPQRSTUVWXYZ$#@'
SP.CH  = "+-,=.*()'/&  "
```

| From this we obtain 'special character other than ampersand' which we will call SCOTA. |

```
SCOTA = SP.CH
SCOTA  '&' =
```

| We consider the line decomposed into disjoint elements where each element is either (in order) a quoted literal, an L' construct, a single SCOTA or a sequence of non-SCOTA's. |

```
Q    =  "'"
QLIT =  Q FENCE BREAK(Q) Q
ELEM =  QLIT | 'L' Q | ANY(SCOTA) | BREAK(SCOTA) | REM
```

| From this we may use back-up-free scanning to define the |

Program 8.11 - ASM360   Page 161

| operand field (F3). B is used to separate fields. The
| first two fields according to p. 8 of [IBM360b] are ter-
| minated by blanks (or the end of the line).

```
        F3 =    ARBNO(ELEM FENCE)
        B  =    (SPAN(' ') | RPOS(0))   FENCE
        F1 =    BREAK(' ')  |  REM
        F2 =    F1
```

| To further complicate the issue, if the operation is one
| of a class of conditional assembly operations defined on
| p. 75 of [IBM360b] as:

```
        CAOP  = ('LCL'  |  'SET')  ANY('ABC')  |
+               'AIF'   |  'AGO'   |  'ACTR'   |  'ANOP'
```

| then the operand is a conditional assembly operand. For
| such operands the number of ways of using the quote
| character in unbalanced situations is increased. For ex-
| ample T'NAME refers to the type attribute of the symbol
| NAME and the quote here is not to be considered as one of
| a pair of balanced quotes. The set of attributes is given
| by the pattern ATTR.

```
        ATTR  = ANY('TLSIKN')
```

| Moreover, the operations SETB and AIF permit 'logical ex-
| pressions enclosed in parenthesis'. Logical expressions
| may contain blanks so we must ignore any blanks contained
| within paired parenthesis. Of course we must ignore any
| parens within quotes and we must continue to ignore quotes
| which occur merely as part of an attribute. Since it can-
| not hurt to ignore blanks within parens in any of the con-
| ditional assembly operations we can treat all of them
| uniformly. ELEMC is an expanded form of ELEM permitting
| the additional attributes and the parenthetical groupings.
| F3C will match an operand field (field 3) if the operation
| is a conditional assembly.

```
        ELEMC =  '(' FENCE *F3C ')'  |  ATTR Q  |  ELEM
        F3C   =  ARBNO(ELEMC   FENCE)
```

| Putting it all together:

```
         ASM360  =  F1 . NAME  B
+          ( CAOP . OPERATION  B  F3C . OPERAND  |
+            F2 . OPERATION    B  F3 . OPERAND)
+            B   REM . COMMENT
```

Chapter 8 - PATTERN CONSTRUCTION

???
?????????????????????????? EXERCISES ??????????????????????
???

| Exercise 8.1 | Assuming S is nonnull, rewrite BRKREM(S) as a single expression involving only (but not necessarily all of) LEN, POS, RPOS, SPAN, BREAK, ANY, NOTANY and ARBNO.

| Exercise 8.2 | Write a version of SPAN(S) (call it SPANULL) which will match the null string in the case that SPAN(S) would fail. Otherwise, SPANULL(S) should behave exactly like SPAN(S). Thus SPANULL(S) must be monic. This can be done in several ways. Try it a) using NOT(P), b) using BRKREM(S) and c) from scratch.

| Exercise 8.3 | Modify BREAKX (call it BRKXREM) so that it will match the remainder of the subject string as its last extension. Thus

```
    'A,B,C'    POS(0) BRKXREM(',')  $ OUTPUT  FAIL
```

will print 'A', 'A,B' and 'A,B,C'.

| Exercise 8.4 | Which of the following assignments would also be valid ways of implementing BREAKX(S)? That is, which of the statements below, if substituted for the one statement in Prog. 8.2, will produce a correct rendition of BREAKX?

```
    BREAKX = ARBNO(BREAK(S) LEN(1)) BREAK(S)
    BREAKX = BREAK(S) (NULL | LEN(1) *BREAKX)
    BREAKX = ARBNO(LEN(1) BREAK(S)) BREAK(S)
    BREAKX = BREAK(S) (NULL | LEN(1) BREAKX(S))
```

| Exercise 8.5 | Given the subject, "AB(C,D')E')GH", which values of pre-cursor position will the pattern

```
    BAL('()' , "'")   ANY(',)')
```

match?

| Exercise 8.6 | Let RULE be string-valued and contain the rule of some SNOBOL4 statement (i.e. the statement without the label and goto fields). Assume the rule is trimmed of leading and trailing blanks. Write code to determine the type of SNOBOL4 statement and branch to one of

Exercises for chapter 8 — Page 163

the following labels: PM for pattern match, PMR for pattern match with replacement, ASGN for assignment and EXP for none of the above (Hint: Using the BAL function, this will require one pattern assignment and three pattern matches).

| Exercise 8.7 | The author once comitted an error similar to the following. Assume that to create a truly unusual name the first statement of FASTBAL (Prog. 8.4) is changed to:

FASTBAL   NAME = 'FASTBAL '   &STCOUNT

Surely, vanishingly few identifiers contain blanks and the &STCOUNT makes it that much more unusual. Why is this an error?

| Exercise 8.8 | Write a function FIRST(P) which will return a monic pattern whose post-cursor position is the first post-cursor position yielded by the pattern P. Note that unlike ONCE(), FIRST(P) should be reset at each cursor position.

| Exercise 8.9 | What is *ONCE() equivalent to ?

| Exercise 8.10 | Write a function NTIMES(N) which will return a pattern which will match the null string exactly N times and thereafter fail forever.

| Exercise 8.11 | Write a function IF(P) which will match the null string if P would succeed and will fail if P would fail. (Hint: you may use functions defined in this chapter).

| Exercise 8.12 | Let the SIZE of a string S be L. How many alternates will LIKE(S) have (Prog. 8.8)? Modify LIKE so that it uses OR (Note: ANY(&ALPHABET) can be used in palce of LEN(1)). How many principal alternates will LIKE then have (assume that S contains at least 3 characters and that the first two characters are different)? What is the fewest number of principal alternates that LIKE could have? Rewrite LIKE to obtain that many.

| Exercise 8.13 | Modify LIKE(S) (Program 8.8) so that, in addition to insertions, deletions and rearragements, any string differing from S in a single character will be matched.

Chapter 8 - PATTERN CONSTRUCTION

Exercise 8.14 LIKE will tolerate just one error. Rewrite LIKE so that it will tolerate K errors (Hint: Rewrite LIKE recursively).

Exercise 8.15 What character(s) could not be used as a break character for OR?

Exercise 8.16 To allow for really rapid scanning for a set of strings, modify OR(S) so that it returns

$$BREAKX(S1) \; OLD\_OR(S)$$

where OLD_OR is the OR function defined in Prog. 8.9 and where S1 is derived from the argument S.

Exercise 8.17 Rewrite PLI.STMT so that it does not use FENCE but NOT instead.

Exercise 8.18 Find a subject for which PLI.STMT will behave incorrectly if any of the following changes are made.

(a) removing the FENCE from QLIT

(b) removing the FENCE from CMNT

(c) removing the FENCE in the argument to ARBNO.

Exercise 8.19 A telephone information service operates by the user dialing (or touch-toning) a party's name using the letters that appear on the dial. This does not uniquely specify a string of letters since each digit has a group of 3 characters associated with it as follows:

```
        ABC - 2        PRS - 7
        DEF - 3        TUV - 8
        GHI - 4        WXY - 9
        LKJ - 5        Z   - 0
        MNO - 6
```

Write a function called NAME which accepts as argument a string of digits and will return a pattern which can be matched against all names in a directory. The pattern should be of the form ANY() ANY() ... ANY() where there are as many ANY's as there are characters in the string. (Hint: the body of the function requires only 3 relatively simple statements.)

Exercises for chapter 8   Page 165

| Exercise 8.20 | Assuming that LEN(N) can have negative arguments we could make a rapid search for the least likely character of a string using BREAKX. For example, to scan for 'EXAMPLE' in a string of text, it would in general be more efficient to use the pattern

BREAKX('X') LEN(-1) 'EXAMPLE'

than a BREAKX('E') construction because of the low frequency of the letter 'X' in English text compared with 'E'. Write a function called SEARCH(S) which will return an optimal pattern in the above form for searching for the string S. Assume that S contains only alphabetics and that the letter frequency is that of English, viz.

FREQ_TBL = 'ETOANIRSHDLCWUMFYGPBVKXQJZ'

(Interesting note: The least-frequent character can be determined in one statement by a simple scan.)

CHAPTER NINE

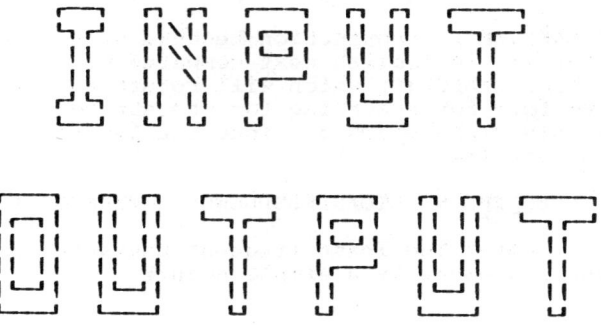

INPUT OUTPUT

```
                CONTENTS

        READ .................. 9.1
        FORTREAD .............. 9.2
        PARAGRAPH ............. 9.3
        SNOREAD ............... 9.4
        TREEREAD .............. 9.5
        MFREAD ................ 9.6
        PUT ................... 9.7
        FORTPUT ............... 9.8
        PEEL .................. 9.9
        SNOPUT ................ 9.10
```

Program 9.1 - READ Page 167

ne of SNOBOL4's many assets is the simplicity and directness of its I/O. One need merely mention the variable INPUT in an expression and, automatically, a card (or card image) is read and the string of characters on the card is used as the value of the variable INPUT. Similarly, the mere assignment of a value to the variable OUTPUT or PUNCH will cause that value to be respectively printed or punched.

In many cases, however, we want something slightly richer than this, as the following programs will illustrate.

```
Program
  9.1
  READ
```

For many applications the basic input process is less than completely ideal. We often would like to read in a card, compare it against a pattern, and, if the card was not what we sought, transfer to another section of the program which will read the same card from the input stream. Our aim could be realized if we had the ability to put something back on the input stream. This act is impossible in SNOBOL4 but it could be effectively done by writing a subroutine which could store things we 'pushed' onto the input stream and yield them up when we sought to read. This we will not do (but leave as an exercise). We will create something which will be less general but simpler and, in most situations, easier to use. We will define a function called READ which will accept one argument, viz. a pattern, which will be matched against the next string on the input stream. If the pattern matches this string, the string will be returned. If the pattern fails to match, the READ function will fail but will save the string for the next time READ is called. In the several programs following this one, we will show how this property can be used.

Another inadequacy with the basic input facility of SNOBOL4 has to do with file sequencing on the IBM 360/370. When no more input remains on the current input file, and an input request is made (by a reference to the variable INPUT) the reference will FAIL (in the SNOBOL4 sense of statement failure). If an input request is made after the initial failure, the next file in sequence will be opened. If this file is not present, the program terminates abnormally.

Unfortunately, this is not what we want most of the time. Often, the reason several files have been placed in sequence is to make them appear to the program as one long file, an appearance which is blemished if failures occur in between. Also we would like the liberty of making several read requests after the final failure without fear of blowing the program.

READ will take care of this file sequencing problem. It will fail only after the last file has been exhausted and subsequent calls thereafter will merely fail.

Page 168   Chapter 9 - INPUT OUTPUT

```
  READ(P) will read in and return a card provided it is mat-
  ched by the pattern P.  If there are no cards remaining or
  if the pattern fails READ will fail.
```

               DEFINE('READ(P)')   :(READ_END)

```
  Check  to see if the number of files beyond the current is
  negative.  If so return failure.
```

READ   LT(NF_INPUT, 0)   :S(FRETURN)

```
  Fill the input buffer if it is empty.
```

               IDENT(INPUT_BUF, NULL)   :F(READ_1)
               INPUT_BUF = INPUT   :F(READ_2)
READ_1

```
  Check the buffer for a successful match against P.   If no
  match, then fail return.   If match, then return the value
  in the buffer (INPUT_BUF) and clear the buffer.
```

               INPUT_BUF P   :F(FRETURN)
               READ = INPUT_BUF
               INPUT_BUF = NULL   :(RETURN)

```
  If the attempt to read resulted in failure,  then  control
  passes  to READ_2.   Deduct 1 from the number of remaining
  files and transfer to label READ.   If this number becomes
  negative, the function will fail continually.
```

READ_2   NF_INPUT = NF_INPUT - 1   :(READ)
READ_END

Epilogue

The variable NF_INPUT (Number of Files on INPUT) is to be set equal to the number of files beyond the current one. Normally NF_INPUT is equal to 0 since the default value of variables is null (which numerically equals 0). Therefore, the programmer normally need not worry about its value. However, he may set this at any time during the running of the program if additional files remain. For example if a special marker is placed at the end of a file to indicate that this was not the last one in a sequence then the appearance of that marker could be used to trigger an assignment of the value 1 to the variable NF_INPUT.

```
||  Program   ||
||    9.2     ||
||  FORTREAD  ||
```
Many string-processing problems involve the analysis of the source language of some other program. FORTRAN is perhaps typical of the kind of language which we might wish to process. Examples include compilation (translation of

Program 9.2 - FORTREAD

FORTRAN programs for sematic errors not discoverable by the compiler), flow charting (describing diagrammatically the flow of control), preprocessing (translation of an extension of FORTRAN into FORTRAN such as SIMSCRIPT [Dimsdale & Markowitz, 1964], and conversion (translating a version of FORTRAN for one machine to a version suitable for another). In addition to these fairly complex undertakings, the processing could be some simple house-keeping chore such as converting every reference of 'ALPHA' to a reference to 'BETA'.

When writing programs to analyze other programs it is usually wise to write a function whose only duty is to collect and return the next statement on the input stream and FAIL if no statement remains. The benefits of doing this are the same as those derived from subroutinizing one's program generally. It saves duplication of code, allows subdivision of labor, the program logic is easier to follow and the program is easier to modify and maintain.

A card with a 'C' in column 1 is regarded as a comment card by the FORTRAN compiler. Comments may appear anywhere, even between a statement and its continuation. These are ignored. A continuation card is indicated by a nonblank in column 6. A blank in column 6 indicates the start of a new statement.

```
| FORTREAD will read in and return the next FORTRAN state- |
| ment on the input stream.                                |
```

```
         DEFINE('FORTREAD()T')
         INPUT(.INPUT,5,72)
         FORT_COMMENT   =  POS(0) 'C'
         FORT_CONTINUE  =  POS(0) LEN(5) NOTANY(' ') REM . T
                                                   :(FORTREAD_END)
```

```
| First pass over any initial comment cards and then read in |
| the first statement.                                       |
```

```
FORTREAD         READ(FORT_COMMENT)              :S(FORTREAD)
                 FORTREAD  =  READ()             :F(FRETURN)
```

```
| Then pass over more comments (if any) and then look for a |
| continue card. If not found we return. But if found, the  |
| variable T will hold the desired value. This is tacked    |
| onto FORTREAD and we renew the search for a continue.     |
```

```
FORTREAD_1       READ(FORT_COMMENT)              :S(FORTREAD_1)
                 READ(FORT_CONTINUE)             :F(RETURN)
                 FORTREAD  =  FORTREAD T         :(FORTREAD_1)
FORTREAD_END
```

Names referenced	Name	Type	Where defined
by FORTREAD:	READ	Function	Program 9.1

Epilogue

The initialization section of FORTREAD reassociates the variable INPUT with the first 72 characters of a card. In this way the identification field of the FORTRAN deck (columns 73 through 80) are ignored.

Two patterns are also set in this initialization section. The first pattern matches successfully any FORTRAN comment card; the second will not only match successfully a FORTRAN continue but will assign the 'meat' of any continue card to the temporary variable T.

One may note the rather heavy use to which READ has been put. It is called at four separate places and has greatly simplified the writing of FORTREAD. The first call represents a rather conventional use of READ. "Give me the next card if it is a comment." It is in fact thrown away immediately. The second call of READ, which is made with no argument, makes use of the fact that a null string will be supplied by default. Since a null string as a pattern will always match, READ() is, in effect, an unconditional grab at the next string on the input stream. It can only fail if there is nothing left.

Another use of READ is in the fourth call in the third last line of the program. This call not only tests the next string but causes a variable (T) to be assigned a subpart of the string. Patterns, in general, can denote arbitrarily complex computations with the subject string as effective argument. This property of patterns imparts to READ a high degree of flexibility.

```
┌─────────────────────┐
| |   Program    | |
| |     9.3      | |
| |   PARAGRAPH  | |
└─────────────────────┘
```
For many of the same reasons that we might want a FORTRAN statement grabber if we were processing FORTRAN decks, we might want a paragraph grabber if we are processing text. A paragraph, here, is assumed to be a sequence of lines down to the next paragraph whose start is designated by a blank in column 1. Since the information on the cards is assumed to be sentences, we will place a blank between lines (after trimming). Moreover, if a line ends in a period, we will place an extra blank between it and the succeeding line, since it is conventional, in typing, to separate sentences with two blanks. If no paragraphs remain, or if the first line to be read does not match the pattern passed to PARAGRAPH as argument, then PARAGRAPH will FAIL.

| PARAGRAPH(p) will read in a paragraph provided the first
| card on input matches the pattern p. The paragraph is as-
| sumed to continue until a blank appears in column 1. It
| will fail if a paragraph is not found.

Program 9.4 - SNOREAD

```
          DEFINE('PARAGRAPH(FIRST_LINE)T,P')
          PARA_CONTINUE = POS(0)  NOTANY(' ')
                                               :(PARAGRAPH_END)
```
┌───┐
│ Read in the first line, provided it is the first line of a │
│ paragraph. If it is not, fail.   │
└───┘
```
PARAGRAPH     P  =  TRIM(READ(FIRST_LINE))       :F(FRETURN)
```
┌───┐
│ Set the variable T equal to 2 blanks or 1 blank depending │
│ on whether or not the paragraph accumulated so far (in P) │
│ ends with a period.   │
└───┘
```
PARAGRAPH_1   T  =  '  '
              P    POS(0)  RTAB(1)    '.'       :F(PARAGRAPH_2)
              T  =  ' '
PARAGRAPH_2
```
┌───┐
│ Now join the next input line provided it is still part of │
│ the paragraph. If so, recycle; otherwise return what is │
│ in P. Note that the blanks in T are not joined to P unless │
│ the READ() is successful.   │
└───┘
```
              P  =  P T TRIM(READ(PARA_CONTINUE))  :S(PARAGRAPH_1)
                    PARAGRAPH  =  P                :(RETURN)
PARAGRAPH_END
```

Names referenced by PARAGRAPH:	Name	Type	Where defined
	READ	Function	Program 9.1

Epilogue

PARAGRAPH, like FORTSTAT, refers to the READ function to do its basic input. The pattern which defines what determines the start of a new paragraph (or more exactly the end of a current paragraph) is contained in PARA_CONTINUE. This pattern can be modified for slightly different paragraph conventions or can be set as an argument.

Note that the temporary variable P was used to accumulate the material in the paragraph. The variable PARAGRAPH could have been used and this would have saved one assignment statement. P was used for brevity and convenience and with the knowledge that straight assignments of the kind indicated are quite fast and their effects on the running time of the overall program are negligible.

┌──────────────┐
││ Program   ││   For many of the same reasons that we would
││   9.4   ││   want statement-gathering activities to be
││ SNOREAD ││   focused in one function in FORTRAN statement
└──────────────┘   processing, we would want to do the same if
we were processing SNOBOL4. A complexity introduced in obtaining SNOBOL4 statements is the possibility of multiple

statements per line (separated by semicolons). Moreover, the
fact that quoted literals may have semicolons embedded within
them means that a blind search for a semicolon will not do. A
further complexity is introduced by the fact that labels may
have quotes embedded within them (only semicolons and blanks
may not appear in labels) so that such quotes are to be
ignored when ignoring semicolons within quotes. But we have
encountered such problems in the preceding chapter and, by now,
they should be routine.

Like FORTSTAT, SNOREAD will ignore comment cards and fail when
no more statements remain.

```
| SNOREAD will read in and return the next SNOBOL4 state- |
| ment.  If no statements remain it will fail.            |
```
          DEFINE('SNOREAD()S,LBL')
```
| Initialization section: Establish I/O and initialize |
| patterns.                                             |
```
          INPUT(.INPUT, 5, 72)
          ALPHA   = 'ABCDEFGHIJKLMNOPQRSTUVWXYZ'
          NUM   = '0123456789'
          CONTINUE.S = POS(0) ANY('+.') REM . S
          SNO_STMTS   = POS(0) ANY(ALPHA NUM ' ')
          SNO_STMT   = (POS(0) BREAK(' ;')
        +   FASTBAL(, '"' '"', ';') ';') . SNOREAD
                               :(SNOREAD_END)
```
| Examine a buffer (SNO_BUFFER) which presumably has charac- |
| ters in it left over from the last read. If a statement   |
| can be pulled out, fine, just return.                     |
```
SNOREAD   SNO_BUFFER   SNO_STMT =   :S(RETURN)
```
| Otherwise check the buffer for null.  If nonnull, then |
| there is a syntactic error in the input.              |
```
          IDENT(SNO_BUFFER)   :F(ERROR)
```
| We now try to fill the buffer. We first make an attempt  |
| to read the first card of a sequence of SNOBOL4 state-   |
| ments.  If this fails, we assume it's a comment or list  |
| control card; in either case we throw the card away and  |
| try again until we succeed in getting a statement or hit |
| an end of file.                                          |
```
SNOREAD_1   SNO_BUFFER = TRIM(READ(SNO_STMTS)) :S(SNOREAD_2)
              READ()   :F(FRETURN) S(SNOREAD_1)
```
| Scoop up all succeeding continue cards and place a     |
| semicolon behind the last card. Then go back to the start |
| of SNOREAD.                                            |
```

Program 9.5 - TREEREAD   Page 173

```
SNOREAD_2          SNO_BUFFER  =  SNO_BUFFER  ' '   ?READ(CONTINUE.S)
+                              TRIM(S)                :S(SNOREAD_2)
                   SNO_BUFFER  =  SNO_BUFFER  ';'     :(SNOREAD)
SNOREAD_END
```

Names referenced   Name   Type   Where defined
by SNOREAD: READ   Function   Program 9.1
                        FASTBAL *   Function   Program 8.4
* indicates name is referenced in the initialization section.

```
┌─────────────────┐
│ │   Program   │ │    A tree, in the context we will be using it,
│ │     9.5     │ │    will be a collection of data in  a hierar-
│ │   TREEREAD  │ │    chical organization.  An example of a tree
└─────────────────┘    is shown in Figure 9.1.
```

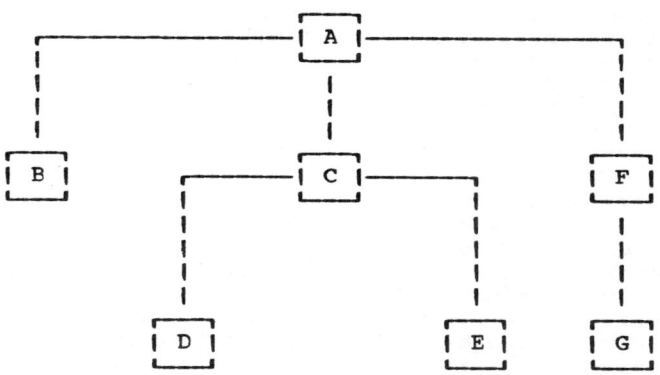

Figure 9.1

An example of a tree.

There is a <u>root</u> node at the top (just the reverse of biological trees which have their roots at the bottom). The root node has 0 or more <u>immediate descendants</u> or <u>sons</u>. Each of these, in turn, have 0 or more immediate descendants. Moreover, each node has a value associated with it which, for the sake of current discussion, we will assume is a string.

In the example shown in Figure 9.1, the root node has the value 'A' and its 3 sons have the values 'B', 'C' and 'F' respectively.

Reading a tree implies both an external form by which the programmer specifies his tree, and an internal form by which the tree will be represented in the machine. These represent

Chapter 9 - INPUT OUTPUT

two decisions which will have to be made before we can progress further.

In general, the representation of computer data is an issue which is perpetually confronted by the computer programmer. His choice can significantly influence the runtime and storage efficiency of the resulting program, as well as the ease with which he can write, debug, modify, and extend his program. In a string language such as SNOBOL4 there is a built-in prejudice to represent data objects as strings, because of the languages's rich string handling capability. That is, one feels that when it comes time to process the data object, in a way or ways not clearly foreseen at the start of the program, the necessary tools will probably be there.

Another strong advantage of using strings to represent data in SNOBOL4 is the relative ease with which one can monitor the changing forms of the data. There are several semiautomatic tracing features available to the SNOBOL4 user (&FTRACE and &TRACE) which print out the values of variables if they are strings, integers or reals but not otherwise. Under such circumstances the advantage of using strings to represent data is more than obvious.* But even if these tracing features were not especially inclined to favor the string, there is nonetheless a convenience in being able to display an entire data object in one fell swoop merely by printing a string.

Another advantage of using a string to represent the data is that (in SNOBOL4 at least) the data within the string will occupy contiguous storage locations. This can mean that certain kinds of analysis can be made very rapidly by a scan. Many machines have built-in mechanisms for quickly scanning contiguous core storage for particular data items. Such efficient machinery can be brought to bear upon a data structure in contiguous core whereas it could not if the data were associated by means, for example, of address links.

One reason for not representing a tree as a string is that the values of the nodes may not be conveniently representable as strings. Another reason may be that the operations that an application will typically make upon a tree may be rather unnatural for a string. We will show in a later chapter how a tree may be represented in SNOBOL4 as a linked structure. For this chapter, we will consider only string representations.

There are many ways in which trees may be represented as strings internally. To visualize one very exotic way, imagine that a tree is elaborately displayed in a printout page with lines of, say asterisks connecting up boxes denoting the nodes, etc. Then the sequence of lines of this printable image

---
* This limitation need not be viewed as a strict one. The discussion surrounding the function FTRACE, Prog. 14.3, describes how the values of data aggregates may be automatically dumped as well.

Program 9.5 - TREEREAD Page 175

will, when concatenated, denote unabiguously a tree. Such an example is a very good one of how not to encode a tree. Not only is the encoding inefficient in terms of storage but it also would prove to be unwieldy in processing (selecting, searching, deleting, adding, etc.).

One sane way of representing a tree is by a LISP-like representation [McCarthy, 1960]. A node is encoded

$$(v, s_1, s_2, \ldots, s_n)$$

where v is the value of the node, and where each s is the representation of a son. For example, the tree in Figure 9.1 is represented as

$$(A, B, (C, (D, E)), (F, G))$$

Using such a representation, the value of nodes are restricted in that they may not contain commas or either of the parentheses (or if they do, three other characters would have to be found at the loss of some notational naturalness). Another disadvantage is that, in many applications, it is convenient to be able to obtain, without an involved computation, the number of sons of a given father node. For both these reasons, we will use a slightly different method which is a variant of polish prefix notation (from Lukasiewicz [195, p. 78] but see Higman [1967, p. 24] for a nice general discussion. We will represent a node as

$$v, n, s_1, s_2, \ldots, s_n$$

where, as before, v is the value of a node, n is the number of sons and s represents a son. The tree in Figure 9.1 would be represented as:

$$A, 3, B,, C, 2, D,, E,, F, 1, G,,$$

Here a node without sons is represented as

$$v,,$$

That is, the null string as well as an explicit 0 can be used to denote 0 sons. This blends well with the SNOBOL convention of regarding null strings as arithmetically equal to 0.

The parenthesis-free or polish notation is somewhat more difficult to analyze visually than the parenthesis notation but it is significantly easier to manipulate and for that reason is a good machine representation.

The external representation of the tree would be that form as it is keypunched onto cards or typed onto a teletypewriter. To be more explicit, we are concerned with an external *input* representation as opposed to an external *output* representation. There are obvious fundamental distinctions between a tree representation which one is willing to type and a tree

Page 176   Chapter 9 - INPUT OUTPUT

which one would like to see.   For the former, we require ease
of typing and ease of modifying which are not considerations
of the latter.

The form of external input representation we will use is
similar to the form used by COBOL and PL/I to represent structures. The root node is said to be on level 1. Its immediate
descendants are on level 2; the immediate descendants of any
node are one level number greater than the level number of
that node.   Thus the representation of any node of a tree is
given as

$$\begin{array}{cc} k & v \\ s_1 & \\ s_2 & \\ \cdot & \\ \cdot & \\ \cdot & \\ s_n & \end{array}$$

where k is the level number of the node, v is the value of the
node and each s represents a son (in the same format).   For
example, the representation of the tree shown in Figure 9.1 is

```
       1 A
         2 B
         2 C
           3 D
           3 E
         2 F
           3 G
```

This form of the tree is not difficult to type or to modify.
It is also not very difficult to read, particularly if the input processor permits indentation (as ours will) so that the
tree may be typed:

```
       1 A
         2 B
         2 C
             3 D
             3 E
         2 F
             3 G
```

The actual program to convert trees from the external input
form into modified polish is given below.

| TREEREAD(level) will read a tree beginning at the given |
| level.   It will fail if this level is not found on the |
| input. |

DEFINE('TREEREAD (LEVEL) SONS,N')

| TR_BC is the tree break character used to separate items |

Program 9.5 - TREEREAD   Page 177

| in the strungout version of the tree. |

                    TR_BC   =   ','

| The pattern LEVEL.TREEREAD tests the level and extracts |
| the value placing this value into TREEREAD. |

              LEVEL.TREEREAD = POS(0)   (SPAN(' ') | NULL) *LEVEL
     +   SPAN(' ') REM . TREEREAD
                                                   :(TREEREAD_END)

| Read in the node at the current LEVEL and assign the value |
| of this node to TREEREAD and tack on the break character. |
| If the LEVEL argument does not match the input level then |
| fail. |

TREEREAD   READ(LEVEL.TREEREAD)   :F(FRETURN)
                TREEREAD = TRIM(TREEREAD)   TR_BC

| Read in the sons of this node by calling TREEREAD recur- |
| sively at a level one higher than the current level. The |
| number of sons is counted in N. |

TREEREAD_1   SONS = SONS   TREEREAD(LEVEL + 1)
     +   :F(TREEREAD_2)
                N = N + 1   :(TREEREAD_1)

| Concatenate the value of the father, the number of sons |
| and the representation of the sons. |

TREEREAD_2   TREEREAD = TREEREAD N TR_BC SONS
                                                     :(RETURN)
TREEREAD_END

Names referenced   **Name**   **Type**   **Where defined**
by TREEREAD: READ   Function   Program 9.1

Epilogue

The first executed statement on entry to TREEREAD calls the
by-now familiar READ, requesting that a card be read only if
it is of the level requested. TREEREAD will then call itself
recursively to obtain trees at levels one deeper. When recursion is called for, the savings in program length can be
dramatic and the subjective effects exhilarating. There are
types of environments in which recursion seems quite well
suited. One of these environments is when the data structure
is organized recursively such as the trees in this example.

The break character is set in the initialization section to be
a comma. This can change at any time by assigning a new break
character to the variable TR_BC.

```
| | Program | |
| |  9.6    | |
| | MFREAD  | |
```
The READ function (Program 9.1) is flexible to the extent that input can be obtained, not merely from the standard card reader, but from any file associated with the variable INPUT. That is, we could reassociate the variable INPUT in order to obtain the INPUT from a source other than the standard input. An example of a reassociation of INPUT was given in the FORTREAD and SNOREAD functions (Programs 9.2 and 9.4); there, INPUT was reassociated not with a nonstandard file (although it could have been) but with a file whose record length was nonstandard (i.e., 72 rather than 80).

It may be, however, that it is desired to read from two or more files simultaneously and then, the original READ would not do. Even if the user would be willing to reassociate the variable INPUT on each shift of the input stream, the scheme would not work because the saved string in INPUT_BUF would become hopelessly mixed between the various streams.

But it is possible to generalize READ to handle multiple streams. Our extended version will allow a second argument to indicate the source. Thus

READ(P, .SYSUT1)

will read from source associated with the variable SYSUT1. Also, a null second argument will imply the stream associated with INPUT. Thus, READ(P) will be equivalent to

READ(P, .INPUT)

In this way our new READ will be upward-compatible with the old READ.

The new READ, while more general, is less efficient than the old READ, and so there are advantages to both. In practice, one can do with the efficient READ until such time as it becomes necessary to read more than one stream; then one can simply 'plug-in' the more general READ.

| MFREAD(P,U,L) will behave like READ(P) except that an op-
| tional second argument (U) can be used to specify a unit
| other than the normal reader. An optional 3rd argument
| can specify a logical record length other than 80 (for the
| first call associated with a given unit).

DEFINE('MFREAD(P,U,L)BUF,NF,NM,DATA')

| Establish structure to hold data on each file.

DATA('RDATA(RNM,RBUF,RNF)')

| Establish table to hold structures.   Establish default

Program 9.6 - MFREAD

| file.

```
                READ_TBL   =   TABLE()
                READ_TBL<> =   RDATA(.INPUT)
```

| Sieze control on calls to the REWIND function. Do a real
| rewind but also discard any file information for unit N.

```
                OPSYN('REWIND.','REWIND')
                DEFINE('REWIND(N)')              :(MFREAD_END)
REWIND          READ_TBL<N> =
                REWIND.(N)                       :(RETURN)
```

| Entry point: Obtain DATA associated with unit U. If DATA
| is null establish an entry for this unit and input-
| associate some contrived name.

```
MFREAD          DATA = READ_TBL<U>
                IDENT(DATA,NULL)                 :F(MFREAD_1)
                NM  =  'READ:' U
                DATA  =  RDATA(NM)
                READ_TBL<U>  =  DATA
                INPUT(NM,U,L)
```

| Arrival here means that DATA contains the data associated
| with our i/o unit. Extract information. If NF is less
| than 0 fail immediately.

```
MFREAD_1        NM  =  RNM(DATA)
                BUF =  RBUF(DATA)
                NF  =  RNF(DATA)
                LT(NF,0)                         :S(FRETURN)
```

| If BUF is null, fill it. Then test it against P. If fail,
| FRETURN. Otherwise return BUF.

```
                IDENT(BUF,NULL)                  :F(MFREAD_2)
                BUF  =  $NM                      :F(MFREAD_3)
                RBUF(DATA)  =  BUF
MFREAD_2        BUF P                            :F(FRETURN)
                MFREAD  =  BUF
                RBUF(DATA)  =                    :(RETURN)
```

| Decrement NF and try again.

```
MFREAD_3        RNF(DATA)  =  NF - 1             :(MFREAD_1)
MFREAD_END
```

Epilogue

The extended version of READ is patterned after the single-file READ. There are several additional statements in the initializing section which set up the names of variables which are to be indirectly referenced. Beyond the label READ_3, things are pretty much the same as the simpler READ with indirect referencing replacing the direct referencing. That is,

Page 180   Chapter 9   -   INPUT OUTPUT

instead of referring for example to the variable INPUT_BUF a
reference to the variable $B is made where B has been assigned
an appropriate name.

The first statement executed (after the entry point) assigns
the name 'INPUT' to the variable F provided F is null. This
is a common way of assigning default values to dummy
parameters in functions.

The reader may be somewhat alarmed as to the amount of overhead associated with each read request. This overhead,
however, may be quite tolerable in a programming situation
which involves relatively few reads compared with other computations or in a situation in which programming the problem
costs more than running it. If the overhead proves excessive,
the reader will find an outline for a faster Multifile READ in
Exercise 4.6.

```
┌──────────────────┐
│ %%%% UTPUT ROUTINES │   As was mentioned in the introductory
│  %   %   ┌──────┘   remarks of this chapter, output in
│  %   %   │ SNOBOL4 is almost magically simple. Assigning a
│  %   %   │ string to the variable OUTPUT or PUNCH will print or
│ %%%%     │ punch the string respectively. Moreover, it does
└──────────┘ not have the problems that input has; i. e. trans-
```
mission is not typically tentative depending on the value of
the string and output files are not sequenced like input files
may be. But there are problems nonetheless. For one thing,
printed output must appeal to the human eye which means vertical as well as horizontal allignment and this generally is
difficult to do when simply outputting strings. For the same
reason, overstriking, which calls for a perpendicular allignment is equally awkward and unnatural. Both of these obstacles
are overcome quite easily with the use of the block datatype,
a discussion of which is deferred until a later chapter.

For this chapter we will consider only basic card output;
i.e., output which is meant to be read by some other computer
program.

```
┌──────────────┐
││  Program  ││   Just as it is good practice to focus input
││   9.7     ││   activities into a single function, so it is
││   PUT     ││   a good idea to do the same for output. PUT
└──────────────┘   is a function which will accept as argument
```
a string (of no greater than 72 characters) and print this
card labeled and numbered in the identification field (columns
73 through 80). It will also punch what is printed.

Labelling is effected by the user of PUT by assigning a string
to the variable PUT_LABEL. Thus

                    PUT_LABEL = 'PUT'

will set this label to equal the indicated 3 letters.

Program 9.8 - FORTPUT   Page 181

Numbering of cards is by increments of 1. Sometimes it is desired to increment by a number other than 1 which is accomplished by setting the value of PUT_INC. Thus

$$PUT\_INC = 10$$

will set the increment to 10.

```
+-----------------------------------------------------------+
| PUT(L) will output L (presumed to be a card image).    It |
| will label the OUTPUTted card starting in column 73.  The |
| user  may  specify  the label by assigning a string to the|
| variable PUT_LABEL.  The cards will be numbered in incre- |
| ments of 1; the increment can be changed by  assigning  an|
| appropriate value to PUT_INC.                             |
+-----------------------------------------------------------+
```

```
              DEFINE('PUT(L)')
              PUT_INC = 1
                                                    : (PUT_END)
PUT           PUT_N  =  PUT_N + PUT_INC
              OUTPUT =  RPAD(L,72)   PUT_LABEL
+                       LPAD(PUT_N, 8 - SIZE(PUT_LABEL))
              PUNCH  =  OUTPUT                      : (RETURN)
PUT_END
```

Names referenced   Name   Type   Where defined
by PUT: LPAD   Function   Program 3.2
                      RPAD   Function   Program 3.3

Epilogue

Note that when OUTPUT is used on the right hand side of the assignment (last executable statement) the value last output is used as value and no OUTPUTing of information is implied or inferred.

For debugging purposes, it is perhaps prudent to turn punching off. This can be done either by removing the assignment to PUNCH or by executing the statement:

DETACH(.PUNCH)

The latter is preferred since when it comes time to actually punch, it will be obvious what to do.

```
+-----------------+
|| Program      ||   In the description of FORTREAD (Program 9.2)
||   9.8        ||   several examples of FORTRAN source proces-
|| FORTPUT      ||   sing were given.  In three of these examples
+-----------------+   (preprocessing, conversion and housekeeping)
```
the output is also FORTRAN and, in such cases, the programming situation can be simplified by writing an output function specially designed for FORTRAN statements.

Chapter 9 - INPUT OUTPUT

| FORTPUT(S) will output a FORTRAN statement S. The card will also be punched, labeled, numbered, and continued if necessary. |

```
                DEFINE('FORTPUT(S)T')                :(FORTPUT_END)
```

| Entry point: Remove initial chunk from S; output it; check for completion, if so return. |

```
FORTPUT         S      (LEN(72) | REM) . T =
                PUT(T)
                IDENT(S,NULL)                        :S(RETURN)
```

| Since something is left in S we must supply a continuation card. The location field of this continuation card (the first 5 characters) must be blank. |

```
                S = DUPL(' ',5)  '1' S               :(FORTPUT)
FORTPUT_END
```

Names referenced   Name   Type   Where defined
by FORTPUT: PUT   Function   Program 9.7

	Program	
	9.9	
	PEEL	

SNOBOL4 statement outputting (which we do next in Program 9.10) is more complex than FORTRAN outputting attributable to the fact that a SNOBOL4 statement cannot be split arbitrarily but only at a point where a blank may appear (but not within quoted literals). The determination of a suitable break point in a SNOBOL4 statement will be done by the function PEEL. This function is being isolated because it can be used for other purposes such as compressing and reformatting SNOBOL4 statements. Also, a slightly modified version of PEEL can be used for finding break points in JCL (Exercise 9.8).

PEEL(name, n) will peel off and return a prefix from the named string. The prefix is to be as large as possible but not longer than n characters. The named string will be modified. The prefix will be broken off from the named string only at a suitable break point defined as follows. The break may never appear within quotes. Given this first condition, it may occur before any of the characters in BEFORE or after any of the characters in AFTER. If no prefix can be found other than the null string then PEEL will fail.

PEEL has a side effect. In addition to returning a value, it will modify a part of the outside world. In particular, it will remove a prefix from the string named by the first argument. The modification of supplied arguments can only be accomplished in SNOBOL4 by passing as argument the name of the variable. Thus to remove a prefix from the string S the call to PEEL must be of the form

Program 9.9 - PEEL   Page 183

PEEL(.S,n)

(the call PEEL('S',n) although equivalent is not recommended because it does not provide as good documentation and in some implementations is less efficient). This method of denoting arguments is a bit unusual inasmuch as the arithmetic languages, FORTRAN, PL/I and ALGOL permit functions to modify argument variables without the encumbrance of an initial period. At first, the initial period appears to be something of a nuisance. As it turns out, however, it has the important advantage of alerting the reader to the possibility of side effects.

```
| PEEL(NAME,N) will peel off and return a prefix from the   |
| named string.  The prefix is to be as large as possible   |
| but not longer than N characters.  The named string will  |
| be modified.  The prefix will be broken off from the named|
| string only at a suitable break point. The break may never|
| appear within quotes.  It may occur before any of the     |
| characters in BEFORE or after any of the characters in    |
| AFTER.  If no prefix can be found other than the null     |
| string then PEEL will fail.                               |
```

```
            DEFINE('PEEL(NAME.,N.)K1.,K2.')
            BEFORE  = ') ,>'
            AFTER   = '( ,<'
        PEEL.K2. = POS(0)  TAB(*K1.)   (ANY(AFTER) @K2.  |
+       BAL(,'"' "'") (@K2. ANY(BEFORE) | ANY(AFTER) @K2. |
+            RPOS(0) @K2.))
                                              :(PEEL_END)
```

```
| If the NAME.ed string is no longer than N. characters, |
| return the value and null out the variable.            |
```

```
PEEL        LE(SIZE($NAME.),N.)                  :F(PEEL_1)
            PEEL = $NAME.
            $NAME. =                             :(RETURN)
```

```
| Otherwise we scan for a break point in the named string. |
| Our search begins after the K1.th character (K1. is ini- |
| tially 0) and assigns the numerical value of the break   |
| point to K2.  Ultimately K2. exceeds the value of N. at  |
| which point we transfer to PEEL_2.                       |
```

```
PEEL_1      $NAME.    PEEL.K2.                   :F(ERROR)
            GT(K2.,N.)                           :S(PEEL_2)
            K1. = K2.                            :(PEEL_1)
```

```
| The breakpoint is now indicated by K1. and provided it is |
| not zero we can return normally.                          |
```

```
PEEL_2      EQ(K1.,0)                            :S(FRETURN)
            $NAME.  LEN(K1.) . PEEL =            :(RETURN)
PEEL_END
```

Chapter 9 - INPUT OUTPUT

Names referenced   Name   Type   Where defined
by PEEL: BAL *   Function   Program 8.3
* indicates name is referenced in the initialization section.

Epilogue

PEEL is not as fast as it could be. The pattern PEEL.K2. advances by 1 character at a time until overflow occurs. The inefficiency is normally not troublesome because PEEL will normally be able to return the entire string without having to search for a break point. Nevertheless, some applications might call for a faster PEEL and Exercise 9.9 outlines a method for increasing the speed as well as increasing the selectivity as to where breaks may occur.

The names of parameters and temporary variables (viz. NAME., N., K1. and K2.) were deliberately made strange so as to reduce the chances of duplicating the name passed as first argument to PEEL. This issue is discussed fully in the Epilogue of the SWAP routine (Program 3.14).


```
|| Program  ||
||  9.10    ||     The function to output SNOBOL4 statements is
|| SNOPUT   ||     shown in Program 9.10.  PEEL has greatly
                   simplified its writing.
```

| SNOPUT(S) will output a SNOBOL4 statement S. It will handle automatically: labeling, numbering, punching, and, if necessary, continuation. |

```
        DEFINE('SNOPUT(S)')
                                                     :(SNOPUT_END)
```

| Output the first 72 characters (breaking appropriately). |

```
SNOPUT      PUT(PEEL(.S,72))                         :F(ERROR)
```

| If S is null we are done, otherwise peel off the next 71 characters and prefix with a continuation (+). Continue to do this until S is null. |

```
SNOPUT_1    IDENT(S,NULL)                            :S(RETURN)
            PUT('+' PEEL(.S,71))          :F(ERROR) S(SNOPUT_1)
SNOPUT_END
```

Names referenced   Name   Type   Where defined
by SNOPUT: PUT   Function   Program 9.7
                      PEEL   Function   Program 9.9

Exercises for chapter 9

Exercise 9.1 — Extend the basic READ routine so that it can operate like a pushdown stack. thus

```
PUSH('ABC')
PUSH('XYZ')
A = READ()
B = READ('S')
C = READ('YZ')
D = READ()
```

when executed will cause the following values to be assigned.

```
A = 'ABC'
C = 'XYZ'
D = the next input card
```

The PUSH & POP routines (Progs. 5.5 & 5.6) may be used. In fact, the PUSH above is assumed to be exactly Prog. 5.5.

Exercise 9.2 — Modify PARAGRAPH so that the start of the next paragraph is denoted by a pattern given to PARAGRAPH as argument. You may use the modified READ given in Ex. 9.1.

Exercise 9.3 — Modify FORTREAD so that it returns the FORTRAN statement with all extraneous blanks removed (i.e., blanks not in positions 1 through 6, not within quotes, and not within a hollerith field (nH...)).

Exercise 9.4 — Modify TREEREAD to accept trees whose structure is denoted by

(a) indentation (allow sons to have any indentation greater than their fathers)

(b) numerical values without the restriction that level numbers increase in steps of 1.

In each case assume that the value of a node is some nonnull quantity.

Exercise 9.5 — Use READ to write a function called ASMREAD which is to read in statements from IBM's OS/360 assembly language [IBM360b]. The fact that a given card is to be continued is denoted by a nonblank in column 72 but

Page 186   Chapter 9 - INPUT OUTPUT

this character is not considered part of the statement. The
next following card (incredibly) must have blanks in columns 1
through 15 and these blanks (but no following blanks) are
ignored when building the statement. ASMREAD should fail if
an inconsistency is encountered in one of the continue
conventions.

┌─────────────┐
| Exercise 9.6 | Write a multifile READ which avoids most of
└─────────────┘ the inefficiencies of multifile reading in
the following way: When READ is called, control is directed to
the label 'READ_' F where F is the file name. The statements
transferred to can be compiled at runtime (using the CODE
function) at the first use of file F and can be 'custom-made'
for the particular file name.

┌─────────────┐
| Exercise 9.7 | Given the tab mechanisms of keypunches and
└─────────────┘ teletypewriters, it is easier, in typing, to
left-justify elements within fields whereas many applications
(especially numerical) call for right justification of elements within fields.

(a)   Given an 80-character string (card image) in the variable
      S, write a single statement to right justify any left-
      justified element in the field which starts in column
      numbered C and whose length is L. You may use LPAD and/or
      RPAD (Progs. 3.2 & 3.3).

(b)   Use (a) as the basis for a program which will right-
      justify elements in a deck of cards. The first input card
      contains a sequence of X's in each field to denote their
      locations. This can be converted to a sequence of number
      pairs and then (a) can be repeated for each number pair
      and each card.

┌─────────────┐
| Exercise 9.8 | (a) Using READ, write a function (called
└─────────────┘   JCLREAD) which will extract a complete JCL
statement [IBM360c] from the input stream (let it pass over
and output all non-JCL). Delete unnecessary blanks between a
control card and the following continue. Remove all comments.

(b)   Write a function to output JCL.   (Hint: PEEL can be
      used.)

(c)   Test the two functions by replacing in a set of JCL
      statements every occurrence of 'DSNAME=' by
      'DSNAME=LIBRARY.'.

┌─────────────┐
| Exercise 9.9 | To improve the operating speed of PEEL
└─────────────┘ (Prog. 9.9) one may search over nonbreaks
and/or decrease the number of break points.

(a) Write a pattern which behaves like PEEL.K2. but which uses FASTBAL, Prog. 8.4, to rapidly scan over characters which are not significant in determining break points (viz. BEFORE, AFTER and the quotes).

(b) If we reduce the break set (say AFTER = '=' and BEFORE = ':') then we will have higher speed and the break points will be more aesthetically placed. There is the danger, however, that a nonnull peel cannot be made. Rewrite PEEL so that if it runs into difficulties with the given BEFORE and AFTER, it temporarily uses a stronger version of PEEL.K2. (richer BEFORE and AFTER) to crack the given statement.

| Exercise 9.10 | (a) Let the variable NAME. have the value

'LABEL   SUBJECT PATTERN = OBJECT : (LABEL) '

What value is returned by the call

PEEL('NAME.',35)

(b) Modify PEEL so that if the name given is a forbidden name, PEEL will go to ERROR.

| Exercise 9.11 | Using SNOREAD and SNOPUT write a SNOBOL4 program to process other SNOBOL4 programs such that every call to the function ALPHA is replaced by a call to the function ALPHANUMERIC.

| Exercise 9.12 | Using SNOREAD and SNOPUT write a program to squeeze out extraneous blanks from another SNOBOL4 program. Be sure to pack as many statements on a line as possible.

CHAPTER TEN

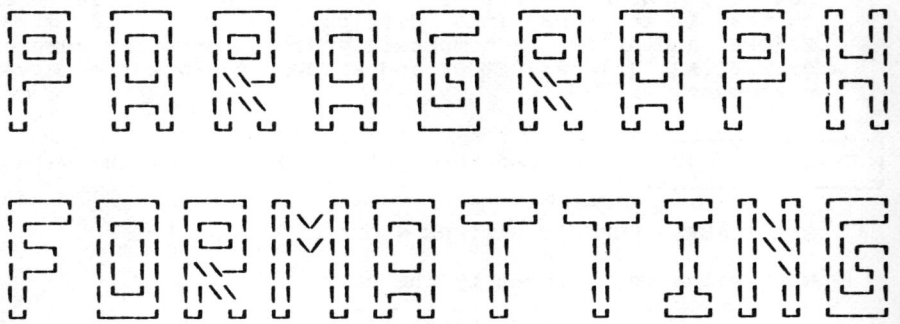

```
                CONTENTS

        BNORM ................ 10.1
        INORM ................ 10.2
        LINE ................. 10.3
        PAD .................. 10.4
        SPACING .............. 10.5
        MINP ................. 10.6
        HYPHENATE ............ 10.7
        IMAGE ................ 10.8
```

Chapter 10 - PARAGRAPH FORMATTING   Page 189

he paragraph you are reading now has been formatted by a computer directed by the very programs we will describe in this chapter. Paragraph formatting is a special case of the more general activity known as text formatting. Whereas the former activity is limited to the shaping of individual paragraphs the latter activity is more open-ended and includes page layout, pagination, etc.

What, the reader may ask, is so complicated about decomposing a paragraph into lines that we must spend an entire chapter in its discussion? If all that were involved in this process were the cutting of lines at convenient blanks and padding with blanks to right-justify margins, then we could dispose of the subject in about a page of text and 6 lines of code. But the task is complicated considerably by the seemingly minor details of backspacing, underscoring and hyphenation. Though the need for overstriking is relatively rare, it does exist and just as much code need be written if we are backspacing occasionally as frequently. In fact, it is quite normal that 90% of execution time of a program is spent in only 10% of it. A grasp of this fact and its implications toward optimum programming is not always fully appreciated. All too often, programmers care only to get the program performing as expected without regard to efficiency considerations or, to the other extreme, have a compulsive urge to optimize every bit of it. Both miss the sound central approach of implementing efficiently that portion which is used most frequently. In this chapter we will have ample occasion to employ this principle

In Program 9.3 we showed how to read in a paragraph and in this section we will format it. Between these two activities, the paragraph may undergo conversions in what we will refer to as the pre-processing stage. If the original input device were a keypunch, then almost certainly some kind of upper to lower case conversion would be necessary. More generally, if characters appear on the printer which are not available on the input device, a conversion is necessary to produce those characters. Another instance in which conversion is used is in the indication of variable information such as figure numbers and exercise numbers. In a sophisticated text processor, these will be given in symbolic form to be converted to actual numbers when the text is printed.

We will assume that, possibly as a result of this preprocessing, the input text will possibly contain the special characters BSPACE and USCORE. BSPACE, as its name implies, will permit the user to overstrike print characters. We will denote this character by backarrow (←) so that 'O←/' will print as 'Ø'. Just what character the user types to obtain a BSPACE in his text is determined by the pre-processor. In the system used to prepare this document, the symbol '¬' was used. Backspacing complicates such issues as separating a paragraph into lines and printing a line on a device which does not directly support the backspace character (such as a printer).

Page 190   Chapter 10   -   PARAGRAPH FORMATTING

It also serves to cloud the issue of when a line equals
another line.

Overstriking can extend the set of characters which one can
print. Several examples of interesting overstruck combinations
are shown in Table 10.1.

```
------------------------------------------------
|  Table 10.1  Characters    obtainable        |
|  via overstriking                            |
|----------------------------------------------|
|   A      B      A + B      Name              |
|----------------------------------------------|
|   c      |       ¢         (cent sign)       |
|   |      -       †         (dagger)          |
|   |      =       ‡         (double dagger)   |
|   =      /       ≠         (not equal)       |
|   :      -       ÷         (division)        |
|   b      /       ƀ         (symbolic blank)  |
|   >      -       →         (right arrow)     |
|   <      -       ←         (left arrow)      |
|   O      -       Θ         (Theta)           |
|   O      /       Ø         (Phi)             |
|   /      )       Γ         (Gamma)           |
|   \      ,       λ         (Lambda)          |
------------------------------------------------
```

USCORE is a character which appears in pairs and indicates
that any material between them is to be underscored. In a
sense, underscoring is a special case of backspacing but, in a
sense it is not. For example, we are permitted to break lines
at blanks and expand lines at blanks for the purpose of formatting paragraphs. But we would also like to be able to break
the line:

"A quick brown fox really did jump over..." after the "really"
so that we might print:

        A quick brown fox really
        did jump over...

Note that not only are we breaking at a nonblank, we are actually discarding a character. If the underscore character
('_') were treated as a break character, then there may be
difficulties with formatting paragraphs which contain '_'. One
example of this is the paragraph you are reading now. Another
example is

        "Printing the string 'A B←←←___' yields 'A B'."

In the above case it becomes not merely awkward but actually
impossible to disentangle that which is regarded as underscoring from that which is overstriking.

Program 10.1 - BNORM   Page 191

The USCORE character is inserted into the text by the pre-
processor and is not actually typed by the user. The way in
which the user will indicate underscoring will depend on the
input device. In the system which formatted this text (and
which is oriented toward key punch input) the underscore
character ('_') is used to denote that the following word is
to be underscored and a sequence of the form __ ... _ indicates underscoring of an arbitrary string of characters. In
a system oriented toward teletype input the sequence

            n-characters   n-backspaces   n-underscores

could be translated by the pre-processor into

                  USCORE   n-characters   USCORE


```
┌─────────────────┐
││   Program    ││    Backspace normalization is the process of
││    10.1      ││    converting a string with backspaces embedded
││    BNORM     ││    in it into a string which prints identically
└─────────────────┘    to the first but in which no 2 backspaces
```
occur consecutively. Thus 'ABCD←←←←1234' is translated into
'A←1B←2C←3D←4'. This serves to localize the effect of
backspacing simplifying later processing. It also serves as a
necessary prelude to image normalization as described in
INORM, Program 10.2.

To describe rigorously what is meant by B-normalization, we
define the _spacing_ of a string as equal to the number of
characters in the string minus twice the number of BSPACE's
and minus the number of USCORE's. Thus, the string 'AB←C' has
a spacing of 4-2(1) = 2. The string 'A_B←C_' (where _ is the
USCORE) has a spacing of 6 - 2(1) - 2 = 2. Informally the
spacing of a string equals the net movement of the type ball
(or equivalent mechanism) when the string is printed on a
teletypewriter. Note that the spacing can be negative as in
the string '←←A'.

We define a _prefix_ of a string as any initial sequence of
characters of the string. Thus, 'PR' is a prefix of the string
'PREFIX'. In general, a string of n characters will have n+1
prefixes including the null string and the string itself.
Similarly, a _suffix_ is any terminal sequence of characters.
More formally, P is a prefix of S if there exists a string T
such that

                        P T = S

and F is a suffix of S if there exists a string T such that

                        T F = S

A string is said to be _balanced on the left_ if the spacing of
each of its prefixes is nonnegative. Informally, if, when
printing the string, we attempt to force the typeball beyond

the left margin of the paper, the string is not balanced on the left. In a similar way, we define a string to be balanced on the right if all of its suffixes have nonnegative spacing. Informally, a string is balanced on the right if its maximum rightward movement is reached at the end of the string. We call a string balanced if it is balanced on the left and on the right.

Examples of strings unbalanced on the left are '←ABC' and 'AB←←__'; such strings cannot generally be printed and are almost certainly errors. Any interpretation short of abnormally terminating the run will probably be an acceptable one. Strings unbalanced on the right such as 'FOB←←/' or 'ABC←' are not errors and have well-defined meanings.

Let a character c which is neither USCORE nor BSPACE be embedded in the string S as

$$S = S_1 \; c \; S_2$$

Then the position number of c is defined as equal to the spacing of S_1 plus 1. We refer to the characters of S other than USCORE and BSPACE as the position characters of S.

Let S be a string without USCORES. Then the B-normalization of S is defined as that string S' such that

1) S' is balanced

2) The position numbers of the characters of S' are monotonically nondecreasing.

3) The position characters of S' are identical to the position characters of S and each such character retains its position number and, moreover, any pair of characters having identical position numbers retain their relative ordering in S' as they had in S.

As an immediate consequence of the definition, all position numbers in the B-normalization of a string are nonnegative. Hence, strings unbalanced on the left having negative position numbers will not have a B-normal form. On the other hand all strings balanced on the left have a unique B-normalization which can be produced by construction. This follows because items 1) and 2) assure us that S' is a sequence of substrings each representing one print position having the form:

$$'c_1 \leftarrow c_2 \leftarrow \ldots \leftarrow c_n'$$

where n≥1 and in general varies with the print position. The characters $c_1, c_2, \ldots, c_n$ each have the same position number. Note that they all must retain their relative ordering. This is done not merely to make B-normalization unique, but also because we do not know the intended purpose of the

Program 10.1 - BNORM Page 193

backspacing. Thus, $c_1 \leftarrow c_2$ is indistinguishable from $c_2 \leftarrow c_1$ when printed but if we choose to interpret '←' as subscript or superscript the ordering is important.

If S contains USCORES the situation is complicated slightly. What are we to make of

'FOM←/RTRANM'

Should it be

'FØRTRAN' or 'FØRTRAN'

Obviously this is a mistake. The string to the right of 'M' should be balanced on the left so that the 'M' is not shifted to the right of characters which appeared after it. Similarly the string to the left of 'M' should be balanced on the right. Hence we define the B-normalization S' of the string S where

$$S = S_1 \text{ M } S_2$$

as

$$S' = S_1' \text{ M } S_2'$$

where S_1' and S_2' are the B-normalized versions of S_1 and S_2 respectively. Of course, S_1 and S_2 may either or both contain USCORE's in which case the definition applies recursively.

Proposition 10.1

If any string S is balanced on the left, then REVERSE(S) is balanced on the right. Conversely, if S is balanced on the right, then REVERSE(S) is balanced on the left.

Proof: The proof is simple but instructive. If S is balanced on the left then all prefixes of S have nonnegative spacing, by definition. If P is a prefix of S then REVERSE(P) is a suffix of REVERSE(S). Since the spacing of REVERSE(P) is the same as the spacing of P the spacing of the suffix is nonnegative. Since all suffixes of REVERSE(S) correspond in this way to some prefix of S, we conclude that S is balanced on the right. In a similar way we can prove the converse.

Proposition 10.2

If S_1 and S_2 are right-balanced then $S_1 S_2$ is right-balanced. Similarly if S_1 and S_2 are left-balanced then $S_1 S_2$ is left-balanced.

Proof: Any suffix of $S_1 S_2$ is either a suffix of S_2 in which case its spacing is nonnegative or is of the form $F S_2$ where F is a suffix of S_1. But the spacing of $F S_2$ = spacing F + spacing S_2 and hence is also nonnegative. Hence $S_1 S_2$ is right balanced. In a similar way $S_1 S_2$ is left balanced.

Chapter 10 - PARAGRAPH FORMATTING

Proposition 10.3

Every suffix of a right-balanced string is right-balanced. Similarly every prefix of a left-balanced string is left-balanced.

Proof: is obvious.

An algorithm to B-normalize a string S containing no USCORE's is given below:

(i)   Reverse S

(ii) Apply the following transformation repeatedly until it can no longer be applied.

$$S \quad NOTANY(B) \cdot X \quad B \quad B \quad ONE\_POS \cdot Y = B \quad Y \quad X \quad B$$

(where B is the BSPACE character and where ONE_POS is a pattern which will match the shortest string whose spacing is 1).

(iii) Remove initial BSPACE's from S.

(iv) Test for double BSPACE or trailing BSPACE. If yes to either question, the original string was not left-balanced, respond appropriately. Otherwise return the reverse of S.

To illustrate the algorithm, let S be the string 'abcd←←←efgh'. By step (i) it is reversed to form 'hgfe←←←dcba'. Step (ii) is a multistepped process illustrated in Figure 10.1, yielding the string shown. Step (iii) does nothing. Step (iv) reverses the string to return 'a←eb←fc←gd←h' which is the result sought.

Step (ii) is the heart of the algorithm and does the following. The spacing of (B B Y) is -1. Hence the position number of X is higher than the position number of all characters in Y. Since in B-normalization the position numbers must be in ascending sequence, the X and the Y are interchanged. It is for this reason too that the transformation of (ii) must terminate since there are only a finite number of inversions in the original string.

Will we be able to reverse all inversions? In order to have an inversion we must have at least one double BSPACE. If the double BSPACE is not removed by (ii) then it either is at the beginning in which case it is removed by (iii) or the sequence

$$NOTANY(B) \quad B \quad B$$

occurs in S but is not followed by ONE_POS. This implies that S is not balanced on the right; the transformation indicated in (ii) preserves right balancing (the proof of which is left as an exercise) so this implies that the original reversed

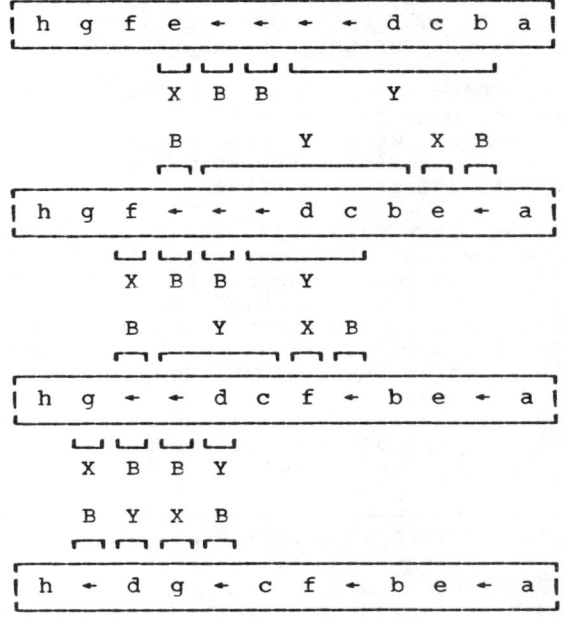

Figure 10.1

string was not right-balanced. This implies by Proposition 10.1 that the original string S was not left-balanced.

The definition of ONE_POS can be given recursively as:

    ONE_POS = NOTANY(B) | B *ONE_POS *ONE_POS

this definition while 'correct' could prove impractical. Let us assume that 100 backspaces appear consecutively. Then ONE_POS will descend to 100 levels before matching. Though there is no inherent limitation on the number of recursive levels to which we can plunge, there are often practical limitations, and this will, in general, depend on the implementation. Since the limit on the recursive depth has been known to be less than 100 for some implementations and since 100 consecutive backspaces, while unusually large, is not an unreasonable quantity, we must seek a solution. We solve our problem by scanning first for a group of BSPACE's (viz. 5 of them) and only if the group is not there do we choose to try the case of one BSPACE. Thus

Chapter 10 - PARAGRAPH FORMATTING

```
        ONE_POS   =  NOTANY(B)     |
+                    DUPL(B,5)  FENCE  *FIVE_POS  *ONE_POS   |
+                    B  *ONE_POS  *ONE_POS
        FIVE_POS  =  ONE_POS ONE_POS ONE_POS ONE_POS ONE_POS
```

The maximum recursive plunge becomes [k/5] + REMDR(K,5) where k is the number of consecutive BSPACE's. If recursive levels of 70 are permitted, we can tolerate k≤338. We can use the same basic scheme to achieve even longer lengths of consecutive BSPACE's but 338 should suffice.

Note the effect of FENCE. If it were not there our clever scheme would be thwarted if a long sequence of BSPACE's appeared in a string which was unbalanced on the left. The reason is that, as we have discussed earlier, the right-most *ONE_POS will fail. Without the FENCE the alternate B *ONE_POS *ONE_POS will be tried. We will ultimately recurse as many levels as there are BSPACE's only it will take longer.

```
┌─────────────────────────────────────────────────────────────────┐
| BNORM(S) will return the B-normalization of the string S.       |
| Blanks will be prepended to S if it is not balanced on the      |
| left.                                                           |
└─────────────────────────────────────────────────────────────────┘

        DEFINE('BNORM(S) B,S1,S2,X,Y,P')
┌─────────────────────────────────────────────────────────────────┐
| Initialize patterns                                             |
└─────────────────────────────────────────────────────────────────┘

        ONE_POS    =  NOTANY(BSPACE)
+                  |  DUPL(BSPACE,5) FENCE *FIVE_POS *ONE_POS
+                  |  BSPACE  *ONE_POS  *ONE_POS
        FIVE_POS   =  ONE_POS ONE_POS ONE_POS ONE_POS ONE_POS
        IF_BSPACE  =  BREAK(BSPACE)
                                                    :(BNORM_END)
┌─────────────────────────────────────────────────────────────────┐
| Entry point:  First make a quick scan to see if any             |
| backspace character exists in S.  If none such, return          |
| immediately.                                                    |
└─────────────────────────────────────────────────────────────────┘
BNORM     S  IF_BSPACE                              :S(BNORM_1)
          BNORM = S                                 :(RETURN)
┌─────────────────────────────────────────────────────────────────┐
| Are there any USCORE's? If so, subdivide and recurse.           |
└─────────────────────────────────────────────────────────────────┘
BNORM_1   S  BREAK(USCORE) . S1 USCORE REM . S2   :F(BNORM_B)
          BNORM = BNORM(S1) USCORE BNORM(S2)        :(RETURN)
┌─────────────────────────────────────────────────────────────────┐
| Reverse the string and apply the transformation described      |
| in the text.                                                    |
└─────────────────────────────────────────────────────────────────┘
BNORM_B   S  =  REVERSE(S)
          B  =  BSPACE
          P  =  NOTANY(B) . X B B ONE_POS . Y
BNORM_2   S  P  =  B Y X B                          :S(BNORM_2)
┌─────────────────────────────────────────────────────────────────┐
| The transformation has been applied as far as it will go.       |
└─────────────────────────────────────────────────────────────────┘
```

Program 10.1 - BNORM

| Remove leading BSPACE's. |

```
            S   POS(0)  SPAN(B)  =
```

| If a double BSPACE or trailing BSPACE remains, add a blank |
| to S and try again. Otherwise reverse and return. |

```
                S    B  B              :S(BNORM_UNB)
                BNORM  =  REVERSE(S)
                BNORM     POS(0)  B    :F(RETURN)
BNORM_UNB       S  =  S   ' '          :(BNORM_2)
BNORM_END
```

Names referenced   Name   Type   Where defined
by BNORM: REVERSE   Function   Program 3.6
                      BSPACE *   Character
                      USCORE   Character
* indicates name is referenced in the initialization section.

Epilogue

BNORM was written under the assumption that most paragraphs do not contain USCORE's or BSPACE's. Such paragraphs are handled as efficiently as possible. Other paragraphs are not treated as quickly as could be done. Specifically, patterns are not predefined where they could be. The scanning for the pattern P could be replaced by a more elaborate process so that double BSPACE would be found rapidly via BREAKX. Similarly, the double BSPACE check at the end could also be done more rapidly using BREAKX. Another improvement might be to handle the special case of

   n-nonBSPACE's   n-BSPACE's   n-nonBSPACE's

by a variant of the BLEND operation. But such sequences are likely to be used in the case of underscoring so that the preprocessor would be expected to catch this special case.

Given our assumptions, however, none of these changes seem warranted, since, for seldom used code, we want to be guided more by the desire to save program space (which is also worth money) than execution time. If the ground rules change, rewriting according to the above principles may be indicated.

Note that if S is not left-balanced, BNORM(S) returns a balanced string which is similar to S. An alternate approach would be to have BNORM fail. In the latter case, however, the calling subroutine would have to specify recovery operations. This can become a continuing nuisance and can be all the more irritating because it involves a case which probably will never occur.

Page 198   Chapter 10   -   PARAGRAPH FORMATTING

```
┌───────────────┐
│ │ Program   │ │
│ │  10.2     │ │
│ │  INORM    │ │
└───────────────┘
```
Image Normalization, or I-normalization is the process of converting a string having a given printed image into a unique representation for that image. Thus, the string '0←/' and '/←0' when printed, will have identical printed images, viz. 'Ø'. Also, the image produced by 'X← ' is the same as the image produced by simply 'X' implying that overstruck blanks may be dropped in I-normalization. The reason for I-normal form is to be able to determine equality of printed images based on the characters used to produce the images. In addition, we would also like to scan a string which produces an image to determine whether a subimage appears within it. For example, suppose, in a time-sharing system, a programmer had typed in the phrase:

"... such a string is called a <u>convoluted rope</u>."

and he wishes to change something in the string. Most time-sharing systems have editors in which one can specify a substring to be searched for and a replacement to be made, so that the user could say in effect

change 'rope' to 'string'

Assuming that USCORE is not being used and that no normalization exists, the above substitution request could result in the string

"... such a string is called a <u>convoluted string</u>."

Since 'rope' has fewer characters than 'string', the underlining is no longer correct. To compensate, we may request the editor to

change 'rope←←←____' to 'string←←←←____'

We may obtain the desired result, but then again we may not. If, in the original, we had typed 'rope' before underscoring 'convoluted' this particular string sequence would not be found. Moreover, if we had typed the period before underscoring 'rope' we also could not make the indicated replacement. If, in the latter case, we made so simple a request as

change '.' to ''

we might obtain

"... such a string is called a<u>_convoluted_rope</u>"

This state of affairs can be quite frustrating, especially when repeated attempts to make replacements result in failure. Image normalization will permit us to escape from this malaise.

Program 10.2 - INORM   Page 199

Earlier we mentioned that B-normalization is a necessary
prelude to I-normalization. That this is true is a deriveable
result.

By an _image_ we mean a configuration of printing on paper, 1
character high and 0 or more characters wide. We may speak of
concatenating images just as we concatenate strings. Let the
image I be produced by each of the set of strings S_1, S_2, ...
where the sequence goes on indefinitely because there is no
limit to the number of backspaced blanks that can be added
without changing the image. Let N(S) be the function which
converts a string to its I-normal form. If N(S) is working as
it should then $N(S_1)$, $N(S_2)$, ... will all produce the same
string. Hence we can meaningfully speak of N(I) where I is an
image. The value of N(I) will be N(S) where S is any of the
strings which produce I. If, for example, N('O←/') happens to
be '/←O', we may say that N('∅') equals '/←O'.

Our intended purpose is to be able to scan a given image I for
a subimage I' by scanning N(I) for N(I'). This implies that

$$N(I_1\ I_2) = N(I_1)\ N(I_2)$$

that is, the function must be homomorphic (with respect to
concatenation of images). This is important because it means
that the function N() is completely specified by a knowledge
of N(I) where I ranges through all single print-position
images. (See Chapter 3 for a further discussion of homomorphic
functions.)

The notion of normal form implies that the thing considered
'normal' is actually a member of the class it represents. That
is, if S_1, S_2, ... is the set of strings corresponding to
image I then

$$N(I) = S_n$$

for some n. If, moreover, we make the normal form irredundant
in the sense that no characters can be removed without
changing the image, we are left with the conclusion that the
normal form of, for example, the overstruck combination A can
either be 'A←_' or '_←A', but nothing else. Hence, the mapping
of a single position must be of the form

$$c_1 \leftarrow c_2 \leftarrow\ \ldots\ \leftarrow c_n$$

where n ≥ 1. This observation coupled with the fact that N()
must be homomorphic implies that a string in I-normal form
must also be in B-normal form.

The order of striking is unimportant in the final image
produced. For example can the reader determine which character
struck first in the set of overstrikes below?

∅ ∅ ∅ ∅ ∅

Chapter 10 - PARAGRAPH FORMATTING

The answer (although not obvious) is that the slash appeared first at positions 1, 2 and 4.

The question of which images are distinguishable is an important one but, unfortunately, is one which depends on the equipment used and, to a certain extent, on the discriminating powers of the individual. Will, for example, a character overstruck with itself produce a different image than if it were not so overstruck. Is, for example, 'A' different from 'A'? We will hold that it is and that use can be made of the resulting **boldface**. However, not all media are like printers in this respect. The all-or-none characteristic of cathode ray displays may prohibit this assumption. Also, some time-shared editors (eg. Saltzer [1964]) have been known to normalize away bold face.

Another source of ambiguity is that different overstruck combinations can resemble each other. For example

$$+ \qquad + \qquad +$$

were produced respectively by the combinations

'⌐ ̅ ̧'   '|←|'   '+'

Though they can be distinguished when compared, they may not be so distinguishable if viewed in isolation.

Another issue is the non-printable character. As mentioned earlier (Chapter 2), most of the 256 EBCDIC characters are non-printing. To be consistent with the previous notions of image identity, each of these should be converted to blank. This we will not do for 2 reasons. Experience has shown that use can be made of a character that prints blank but which really isn't a blank for the purpose of line breaking and padding (so-called hard blanks). Also, the notion of nonprinting character is device dependent. The subscripts (such as '$_1$') are non-printing on most printers (and most devices) but should not be converted to blank each time they appear in text. A program is usually not dedicated to a particular device and in fact may be in simultaneous communication with 2 different devices. In such cases, the notion of non-printing character, loses its significance.

As a result of these considerations, we will assume a string S_1 of overstruck characters can be <u>distinguished</u> from a string S_2 if and only if

$$\text{ORDER}(\text{DIFF}(S_1,' ')) \neq \text{ORDER}(\text{DIFF}(S_2,' '))$$

(See Progs. 3.10 and 3.1). This leads to the following definition. A string is in <u>I-normal form</u> if

(1) it is in B-normal form, and

(2) for every sequence of the form

Program 10.2 - INORM   Page 201

                      $c_1 \leftarrow c_2 \leftarrow \ldots \leftarrow c_n$

where n>1, the characters are in alphabetic order and contain
no blanks.

A string can be I-normalized by placing it in B-normal form,
removing   overstruck   blanks,   and alphabetizing overstruck
characters as is shown below.

```
| INORM(S) will return the Image Normalization of the string |
| S.                                                          |
```

           DEFINE('INORM(S)C,CC,S1,K')
```
| Initialize patterns.   PR_POS will find a   print   position |
| containing backspaces.                                       |
```
           PR_POS = POS(0) ARB . S1   (LEN(1) BSPACE LEN(1)
+   ARBNO(BSPACE LEN(1))) . CC (NOTANY(BSPACE) | RPOS(0)) . C
                                                  :(INORM_END)
```
| Entry Point:  If  no   BSPACE's  are  present, return im- |
| mediately.   Otherwise B-normalize S before going further. |
```
INORM   S   IF_BSPACE   :F(INORM_RET)
          S = BNORM(S)

```
| Look for a print position involving BSPACE.  If none are |
| left, return.  Otherwise, ORDER the overstruck characters. |
```
INCRM_LOOP
          S   PR_POS = C   :F(INORM_RET)
          CC = DIFF(CC, BSPACE ' ')
          CC = IDENT(CC, NULL)   ' '
          CC = BLEND(ORDER(CC) , DUPL(BSPACE, SIZE(CC) - 1))
          INORM = INORM S1 CC   :(INORM_LOOP)

```
| Common return point.                                      |
```
INORM_RET   INORM = INORM S   :(RETURN)
INORM_END

Names referenced   Name   Type   Where defined
by INORM: BNORM   Function   Program 10.1
                      IF_BSPACE   Pattern   Program 10.1
                      ORDER   Function   Program 3.1
                      BLEND   Function   Program 3.7
                      DIFF   Function   Program 3.10
                      BSPACE *   Character
* indicates name is referenced in the initialization section.

Chapter 10 - PARAGRAPH FORMATTING

Epilogue

Here, as in BNORM, we adopt the view that while it is essential to handle the case of no backspace characters rapidly, we can take our time with strings in which they are present. In particular, if no special characters exist in the argument S, control passes to INORM_RET where an exit is made. It seems as if an unnecessary concatenation is performed at INORM_RET but the system is smart enough to return the other argument if one of them is null.

If the assumption that BSPACE's are rare is invalid there are several ways of increasing its speed. One method would be to rewrite PR_POS so that BREAK is used rather than ARB to search for a BSPACE. The writing of PR_POS is complicated by the fact that BREAK carries one further than where one might like to be but this can be handled by failing and alternating. See Exercise 8.5.

Another method of speedup works on the fact that the great majority of overstruck positions have only 2 characters at that position. Handling of this as a special case can avoid the call to ORDER most of the time.

```
┌─────────────────┐
││  Program    ││
││   10.3      ││
││   LINE      ││
└─────────────────┘
```
Given a paragraph stored as one long string, we will need a function to separate the paragraph into lines. LINE(CW) will return the next cluster of words which will just fit within a column width of size CW. To initialize LINE a call is made to LINE_INIT(P) where P is the paragraph to be decomposed. When LINE(CW) fails no more characters remain. Thus

```
        LINE_INIT('A QUICK BROWN FOX JUMPED OVER THE LAZY DOG.')
L       OUTPUT = "'"  LINE(10)  "'"           :S(L)
```

will print

```
                    'A QUICK'
                    'BROWN FOX'
                    'JUMPED'
                    'OVER THE'
                    'LAZY DOG.'
```

If the global variable JUSTIFY is given the value 1 then the right margin is justified. Thus if

```
                    JUSTIFY = 1
```

had been executed prior to the calls to LINE(10) the values printed would have been:

```
                    'A     QUICK'
                    'BROWN   FOX'
```

Program 10.3 - LINE   Page 203

                      'JUMPED'
                      'OVER THE'
                      'LAZY DOG.'

Here, JUSTIFY serves as a switch and follows the same conventions as SNOBOL4 keyword switches (i.e. an integer not equal
to 0 is on; an integer equal to 0 or null is off). No attempt
is made to justify the last line or a line in which no spaces
appear.

In general, justifying text of small line widths suffers from
the possibility of words exceeding the column width and single
word-lines (such as 'JUMPED') not meeting it. These ill effects diminish in significance as the column width increases.
Hyphenation (Program 10.7) also helps in this regard to
produce a document with less white area.

Breaking a line at a suitable break point must seem like sheer
simplicity. If the column width is CW, then go out to that
position + 1 and start marching backward until a blank is
found. This should be our breakpoint. But this doesn't always
work for several reasons. It won't work if we allow the possibility of USCORE's and BSPACE's. Consider the example

               'A ⌴QUICK BRO←/WN⌴ FO←/X'

If the column width is 15, the first 3 words will easily fit
within a column, but the above algorithm will pick up only the
first two. This is because the spacing of a string may be less
than its size.

Another reason that we cannot use the simple algorithm is that
a string may be reduced in size by contracting certain substrings such as converting double blanks to single blanks.
Such a condensation will, in general, be preferable than adding a large number of blanks into the line. In order that
this technique be effective we must include in our consideration enough of the paragraph in order to take advantage of any
conceivable condensation.

A third reason has to do with hyphenation. Hyphenation algorithms are not very good unless the entire word to be
hyphenated is available.

In all of these cases we need to have sufficient context in
order to make an intelligent decision as to how to break a
line.

Another difficulty has to do with the assumption that all
blanks separate words. Consider the string

               'A QUICK BROW←←/ N FOX'

Here a blank is used to get over the 'W' and not to end a
word. But we may convert the string to B-normal form to obtain

Chapter 10 - PARAGRAPH FORMATTING

'A QUICK BRO←/W← N FOX'

From any string we may safely remove either of the combinations '← ' or ' ←' without changing the image printed. Moreover, by making such deletions from the B-normal form we will remove <u>all</u> overstruck blanks. Any remaining blanks will be regarded as true word separators.

There are cases when a user does not wish to have a blank treated as a word separator. (There are some examples of this in the preceding paragraph.) In such instances the user of the system may inject into his text so-called <u>hard blanks</u>. These are any nonprintable character other than blank. As an example, the 0-8-2 punch provides the 029 keypunch user with such a hard blank. For input devices which do not have a special key for this purpose, the system can provide a special character which will be appropriately converted.

The contractions which should be permitted in a line of text will vary with the application, taste and perhaps with the column width. Almost certainly, we should be permitted the freedom to convert the two blanks which normally separate sentences into one blank. Often we may condense strings of the form

> punctuation-mark blank

by removing the blank. For example

> 'A quick, brown, angry fox ...'

could also be rendered

> 'A quick,brown,angry fox'

We can associate with each string S a minimum printing width MINP(S) which is equal to SPACING(S') where S' equals S after all allowable contractions have been made. Then

> MINP(S) ≤ SPACING(S) ≤ SIZE(S)

We define a <u>natural break point</u> as the SIZE of a prefix which ends in a nonblank which immediately precedes a blank. Thus the natural break points of

> 'A ⌫quick, brown, angry fox⌫ jumped ...'

are

> 1 9 16 22 27 34 ...

Associated with each breakpoint is a spacing. For the above example, the spacings are:

> 1 8 15 21 26 32 ...

Program 10.3 - LINE   Page 205

Clearly, if a spacing exists such that it exactly equals CW, there is no problem. Sufficient context is defined as the break-point associated with the smallest spacing equal to or greater than CW. Denote this break-point B_2 and denote its predecessor B_1. Denote the associated spacings (or widths) W_1 and W_2. Then

$$W_1 < CW \leq W_2$$

Denote the associated prefixes X_1 and X_2. Then

$$SIZE(X_1) = B_1$$
$$SIZE(X_2) = B_2$$

Without hyphenation we have 2 choices, either to expand X_1 by inserting blanks or to squeeze X_2. We will assume that the aesthetic liability (termed Ugly Factor (UF) in the program) associated with inserting a blank is equal to that associated with removing a blank (exercises will explore other less simplistic possibilities). Hence we seek the minimum of

$$W_2 - CW \quad \text{and} \quad CW - W_1$$

Of course, if it is not physically possible to shrink X_2 to size, we must use X_1.

If hyphenation is available, we consider each hyphenation point in turn and seek to minimize the contraction or expansion necessary. Also we add an additional cost (of 1) for the aesthetic loss due to hyphenation.

The algorithm to obtain sufficient context (B_2) is simply to look at break-points at CW, CW+1, CW+2, etc. and keep looping until a spacing is found greater than or equal to CW. Since the spacing is less than or equal to the break-point, no break-point below CW is needed. To find a break-point at CW, however, it is necessary to look for blanks beginning at CW-1.

```
| LINE(CW) will return the next line of a paragraph passed |
| to LINE_INIT(). The column width is CW characters. LINE  |
| will fail when no more lines remain. If HYPHENATE is non-|
| zero, words will be hyphenated. If JUSTIFY is nonzero the|
| lines will be right-justified (padded with blanks).      |
```

```
        DEFINE('LINE(CW) B,B2,TRY,X2,W,W2,T,RWORD,UF,UF1,'
+           'K,H,HYPHEN')
        HYPHENATE = 1
        JUSTIFY   = 1

        DEFINE('LINE_INIT(P)T')
        &ALPHABET    LEN(1)  . HARD_BLANK
                                        :(LINE_INIT_END)
```
```
| Entry point for initialization:  B-normalize the paragraph |
```

Page 206   Chapter 10 - PARAGRAPH FORMATTING

| and remove any overstruck blanks from P. |

```
LINE_INIT     P   IF_BSPACE                    :F(LINE_I1)
              P = BNORM(P)
LINE_I2       P   BSPACE ' '  =                :S(LINE_I2)
LINE_I3       P   ' '  BSPACE =                :S(LINE_I3)
```

| Replace leading blanks (if any) by 'hard blanks' (i.e. |
| blanks not subject to reduction or expansion). Append a |
| blank to make scanning easier. U_SAVED contains an under- |
| score if there was an unterminating underscoring left over |
| from the last line. |

```
LINE_I1       P   POS(0) SPAN(' ') @T  = DUPL(HARD_BLANK,T)
                  P_SAVED = P ' '
                  U_SAVED =                    :(RETURN)
LINE_INIT_END
```

| Initialize patterns for LINE. |

```
              SUFFICIENT_CONTEXT.X2 = (LEN(*TRY) BREAK(' ')) . X2
+             @B2 SPAN(' ') @TRY
              FIND.RWORD.T = @T BREAK(' ') . RWORD SPAN(' ') @T
              EXTRACT.LINE = LEN(*B) . LINE (SPAN(' ') | NULL)
              IF_USCORE   = BREAK(USCORE)
                                                    :(LINE_END)
```

| Entry point proper: Obtain sufficient context (B2, X2). |
| If a sufficient context does not exist, go to LINE_SMALL. |
| Keep looping back until a sufficient context is obtained |
| or is determined not to exist. If the spacing, W2, exactly |
| equals CW, this is the desired breakpoint, B. |

```
LINE          TRY = CW - 1
LINE_1        P_SAVED   SUFFICIENT_CONTEXT.X2   :F(LINE_SMALL)
              W2  =  SPACING(X2)
              GE(W2, CW)                        :F(LINE_1)
              B   =  EQ(W2,CW)  B2              :S(LINE_2)
```

| Find the last word RWORD in reversed form from X2. From |
| the breakpoint T, compute a tentative breakpoint B (this |
| is actually B1) and a tentative ugly factor UF (the amount |
| by which X2 must be expanded). |

```
              REVERSE(X2)   FIND.RWORD.T
              B  =  B2 - T
              UF =  CW - SPACING(SUBSTR(X2,1,B))
```

| Starting with no hyphenation (K=0) and looping for |
| increasing degrees of hyphenation , determine a) if the |
| line will fit and b) if the cost of padding plus hyphena- |
| tion (UF1) is less than the lowest so far achieved. W is |
| the spacing of the reduced line. |

```
                    K   =   0
LINE_3              LE(MINP(X2) - K + SIZE(HYPHEN), CW)        :F(LINE_4)
                    W   =   W2 - K + SIZE(HYPHEN)
                    UF1 =   CW - W
                    UF1 =   LT(UF1,0)   -UF1
                    UF1 =   UF1 + SIZE(HYPHEN)
                    GE(UF1,UF)                                 :S(LINE_4)
                    B   =   B2 - K
                    UF  =   UF1
                    H   =   HYPHEN
LINE_4              K   =   NE(HYPHENATE,0)   HYPHENATE(RWORD,K + 1)
+                                                              :S(LINE_3)
```
┌───┐
│ Enter here with B set to break point and with H set to   │
│ null or '-'.   │
└───┘
```
LINE_2              P_SAVED   EXTRACT.LINE =
                    LINE  =   LINE  H
                    LINE  =   NE(JUSTIFY,0)   PAD(LINE, CW)
```
┌───┐
│ If an odd number of USCORE characters appear in LINE, set   │
│ the value of U_SAVED to USCORE to be tacked onto the   next   │
│ line.   │
└───┘
```
LINE_USCORE
                    LINE     =   U_SAVED   LINE
                    LINE         IF_USCORE                     :F(RETURN)
                    U_SAVED  =   DUPL(USCORE, REMDR(COUNT(LINE,USCORE),2) )
                    LINE     =   LINE  U_SAVED                 :(RETURN)
```
┌───┐
│ Entering here means that whatever remains is small enough   │
│ to fit in a line. If nothing remains, FAIL.   │
└───┘
```
LINE_SMALL
                    IDENT(P_SAVED, NULL)                       :S(FRETURN)
                    LINE    =   TRIM(P_SAVED)
                    P_SAVED =                                  :(LINE_USCORE)
LINE_END
```

Names referenced	Name	Type	Where defined
by LINE:	REVERSE	Function	Program 3.6
	PAD	Function	Program 10.4
	SUBSTR	Function	Program 3.9
	MINP	Function	Program 10.6
	BNORM	Function	Program 10.1
	IF_BSPACE	Pattern	Program 10.1
	HYPHENATE	Function	Program 10.7
	USCORE *	Character	
	BSPACE	Character	

* indicates name is referenced in the initialization section.

Chapter 10 - PARAGRAPH FORMATTING

```
 .Program
   10.4
    PAD
```

PAD(S,CW) will add or delete blanks from the string S as necessary to adjust the spacing of S to equal CW. When blanks are added they are not always added from the same direction. Otherwise the process would tend to produce more white area on one side as opposed to the other. White areas running vertically down the page are termed rivers and large bodies of white areas are termed lakes. It is good formatting practice to prevent rivers and lakes from forming.

The writing of PAD is greatly simplified by the assumption that S is B-normalized and contains no overstruck blanks (a fact assured by the activity in LINE_INIT). This implies that every blank separates 2 balanced substrings and so blanks may be inserted without causing misalignment of overstruck characters.

```
| PAD(S,CW) will add or delete blanks to the string S to |
| make it conform to a column width of CW.              |
```

         DEFINE('PAD(S,CW) I,K,T,N')

```
| This pattern looks for the first blank which is not in a |
| sequence of initial blanks.                              |
```

         INTERIOR_BK = ((SPAN(' ') | NULL) FENCE BREAK(' ')) . T
                                                     :(PAD_END)

```
| Entry point: Determine the number of blanks (N) to be ad- |
| ded.  Branch to PAD_REDUCE if N ≤ 0.                      |
```

PAD   N   = CW - SPACING(S)
          PAD = LE(N,0)   S   :S(PAD_REDUCE)

```
| First insert a blank at a statement separator if any |
```

          S   '. ' = '. '   :F(PAD_1)
          N   = N - 1
          PAD = EQ(N,0)   S   :S(RETURN)

```
| PAD_RT is a flag to indicate whether padding should begin |
| from the right (=1) or from the left (=0).                |
```

PAD_1   S   = EQ(PAD_RT, 1)   REVERSE(S)

```
| Inner loop: Remove a prefix from S at an internal blank. |
| Place it onto PAD with an extra blank. Keep looping until |
| N is reduced to 0.                                        |
```

PAD_LOOP S   INTERIOR_BK =   :F(PAD_AGAIN)
          PAD = PAD T ' '
          N   = N - 1   GT(N,1)   :S(PAD_LOOP)

```
| Falling through indicates completion. Append S; reverse |
```

Program 10.5 - SPACING   Page 209

| if necessary; change flag for next time; and return. |

PAD_DONE
          PAD   = PAD S
          PAD. = EQ(PAD_RT,1)   REVERSE(PAD)
          PAD_RT = 1 - PAD_RT   :(RETURN)

| Here if no more holes remain. If PAD is null at this point |
| return; there are no holes. Otherwise restore PAD and S. |

PAD_AGAIN IDENT(PAD)   :S(PAD_DONE)
          S   = PAD S
          PAD =   :(PAD_LOOP)

| Here to remove N characters. |

PAD_REDUCE N = LT(N,0) N + 1   :F(RETURN)
            PAD ' ' = ' '   :(PAD_REDUCE)
PAD_END

Names referenced   Name   Type   Where defined
by PAD: SPACING   Function   Program 10.5
                       REVERSE   Function   Program 3.6

Epilogue

The design of PAD was based on the assumption that N is small
compared with the size of S and indeed that N does not usually
exceed the number of blanks in S. If this were not the case
then a more efficient procedure would be to make one pass
through to determine the number of blanks in S, compute the
number of blanks to be inserted and, in this way, accomplish
the insertion in 2 passes.

The method given saves the initial pass of counting the number
of blanks in S and is very much more efficient when 0, 1 or 2
blanks are to be inserted in S.

| Program || SPACING(S) will determine the spacing of the
| 10.5 || string S. If S has been B-normalized this
| SPACING || will yield the number of print positions oc-
                 cupied by the string.

| SPACING(S) will return the spacing of the string S. |

        DEFINE('SPACING(S)')
        IF_OVERSTRIKE = BREAK(BSPACE USCORE)
                                                   :(SPACING_END)

| If no special characters exist, just return the number of |
| characters in S. |

Chapter 10 - PARAGRAPH FORMATTING

```
SPACING      SPACING  =  SIZE(S)
             S  IF_OVERSTRIKE                         :F(RETURN)
```
| Otherwise deduct 2 for each backspace and one for each underscore. |

```
             SPACING  =  SPACING - 2 * COUNT(S,BSPACE)
+                     -  COUNT(S,USCORE)              :(RETURN)
SPACING_END
```

Names referenced	Name	Type	Where defined
by SPACING:	COUNT	Function	Program 3.4
	BSPACE *	Character	
	USCORE *	Character	

* indicates name is referenced in the initialization section.

Epilogue

The two calls to COUNT do not render the most efficient coding but the convenience and the fact that overstrike characters are relatively rare suggests its use.

```
|  Program  |    MINP(S) will return the minimum number of
|  10.6     |    print positions needed to print the string
|  MINP     |    S.
```

```
             DEFINE('MINP(S)T')                       :(MINP_END)
```

| Entry point: if JUSTIFY is 0, the contraction points are ignored. Just return SPACING in this case. |

```
MINP         MINP = SPACING(S)
             EQ(JUSTIFY, 0)                           :S(RETURN)
```

| Reduce MINP by one for each contraction point found. |

```
             MINP = MINP - COUNT(S,' ')               :(RETURN)
MINP_END
```

Names referenced	Name	Type	Where defined
by MINP:	SPACING	Function	Program 10.5
	COUNT	Function	Program 3.4
	JUSTIFY	Global Flag	

```
| | Program  | |
| | 10.7     | |
| | HYPHENATE| |
```

Hyphenation, while not strictly necessary, serves to eliminate rivers and lakes in documents with right edge allignment. This is particulary true with small column widths in which the same amount of expansion is concentrated in relatively few gaps. An exact algorithm for hyphenating words does not exist short of storing large numbers of special cases. In the extreme, a complete dictionary could be stored but such a massive amount of information would have to be placed on secondary storage since it would be uneconomical, if not impractical, to store the dictionary in high-speed storage. But secondary storage is unsuitable to this problem since accesses must be made frequently (almost once per line).

The algorithm we will present will not depend on dictionary methods other than that a relatively small number of suffixes must be stored. Its error rate is low but not zero. Fortunately, no great tragedy befalls if an occasional word is mishyphenated. In the last analysis it becomes a balance of aesthetics. How many lakes and rivers are worth how many mishyphenated words.

Perhaps the simplest published hyphenation algorithm appears in Rich and Stone [1965]. The basic method involves examining pairs of letters out of context and deciding whether this pair is or is not suitable for hyphenation. This algorithm turns out to be too weak (not enough break points are discovered) if too few , letter pairs are permitted, or too erroneous (producing a break at a non-syllable boundary) if too many letter pairs are dubbed as breakable. Letter pairs do not hyphenate uniformly enough to be used as a sole guide for hyphenation.

The program given here is based on an algorithm developed by M.R. (Molly) Wagner [1971] for incorporation in a text formatting program called Roff [McIlroy 1971]. Wagner extended Rich and Stone's work to include an examination of suffixes before looking for letter pairs and also greatly reduced the number of letter pairs considered breakable. With these improvements, the error rate has been reduced to the neighborhood of 1% and the number of hyphenation points found, while far from total, is nonetheless satisfactory. This book uses the hyphenation algorithm described, with the proviso that the user can override the automatic hyphenation of specific words. Very few overrides were required.

Most hyphenations found are by suffix removal. Three distinct kinds of suffixes are defined. A <u>hyphenating suffix</u> is one before which one can hyphenate. For example 'less' and 'ness' are both hyphenating suffixes. If 'carelessness' is to be hyphenated with room for only 6 characters the 'ness' is stripped off first. There are still too many characters and so the 'less' is stripped off. The word is then hyphenated as 'care-' on one line followed by 'lessness' on the next. An <u>inhibiting suffix</u> is one which is not hyphenated and, moreover, upon encountering one, the suffix hunt is given up and letter-pair (or digram) testing ensues. For example, 'ing' is an inhibiting suffix. If it is detected as in 'winning' the suffix is stripped and digram testing begins with the double-n. This digram is breakable so that the word is hyphenated 'win-ning'. Also, an inhibiting suffix will absolutely prohibit hyphenating at a point where digrams might indicate that hyphenation is allowed. Otherwise 'else' might be hyphenated 'el-se'. A neutral suffix is one which is not hyphenatable but, unlike the inhibiting suffix, does not signal the start of digram testing. More suffix removal can take place. For example 'es' is a neutral suffix. In 'harnesses' the 'es' is stripped and a further suffix search yields 'ness' as a hyphenating suffix. The word can therefore be hyphenated as 'har-nesses'.

The second phase is digram testing. Here we find the interesting phenomenon that most letter-pairs are considered hyphenateable whereas most pairs of letters that actually appear within English text are not. For example, every digram of the form consonant-vowel is non-separable unless the consonant is 'x'. Also every digram of the form vowel-consonant is non-separable unless the consonant is 'q'. But these pairs so predominate in English that it is not hard to find words in which no breakable digram appears; 'hyphenate' itself is one such word.

Finally, we insist on at least one vowel before and after the break. This is so that we do not hyphenate words like 'bless' which only appear to have a hyphenating suffix, or words like 'returns' which would otherwise be hyphenated 'retur-ns'. Also we do not hyphenate words with strange characters in them other than certain leading and trailing punctuation and an initial capital. Otherwise, paragraphs like this and the last 2 might prove awkward to decipher.

```
HYPHENATE(RWORD,MIN) will indicate where within the rever-
sed word (RWORD) a hyphenation point can be found.   MIN
indicates  the number of characters by which the word must
be diminished in order that  the  line  may  include  this
word.  A global variable, HYPHEN, will be set to '-' if a
hyphen must be added to the word.   HYPHENATE will fail if
no hyphenation point is found.   As an example, HYPHENATE(
'niatbo',3) will  just  succeed  and return a value of 4.
HYPHEN will be set to '-'.  The 2nd argument may be ≤ 0 in
which case the first nontrivial hyphenation will be found.
```

  DEFINE('HYPHENATE(RWORD,MIN) K,C,L')

```
Initialize suffix matching patterns.  Construct 3 patterns
INHIB_SUFF, NEUT_SUFF,  and HYPH_SUFF corresponding to the
3 types of suffixes mentioned in the text.  They will  be
applied  to  a  reversed  version  of  the  word to  be
hyphenated.
```

Program 10.7 - HYPHENATE   Page 213

```
         INHIB_SUFF = OR(UPLO(BALREV('ED, (GLSV)E, (GQ)UE,ING,EST,')))
         NEUT_SUFF  = OR(UPLO(BALREV( '(AI)BLE,LY,S,ES,' )))
+                                 |   ANY('.;,:?)')
         HYPH_SUFF  =   OR(UPLO(BALREV(
+         'TURE, (CGST)IVE, (CDMNT)IAL,FUL, (CGST)IAN,'
+         '(CGST)ION,SHIP, (LN)ESS, (CGST)IOUS, (CDGLMNTV)ENT,' )))
```

| DIGRAMS is a string representing all letter pairs which |
| are regarded as breakable. Thus 'xa' is a breakable pair. |
| '∂' stands for the set of vowels (aeiou) and '¬' stands |
| for complementation. Hence '¬(∂)B' means that all |
| consonants followed by a 'b' are breakable; also '¬(∂NS)C' |
| means that any vowel, 's' or 'n', when followed by a 'c' |
| is NOT breakable. |

```
             DIGRAMS =
+         'XA,¬(∂)B,¬(∂NS)C,¬(∂R)D,XE,¬(∂)F,¬(∂N)G,¬(∂CGPSTW)H,XI,'
+         '¬(∂)J,¬(∂CLNS)K,¬(∂BCFGPTY)L,¬(∂Y)M,¬(∂GKSY)N, (AX)O,'
+         '¬(∂SY)P,¬(S)Q, (JKLMNRSVXZ)R,¬(∂KLNWY)S,¬(∂FHSY)T,XU,'
+         '¬(∂)V,¬(∂S)W,¬(∂)X, (QWXY)Y,¬(∂C)Z'
```

| Convert ∂ to vowels, and find complement if ¬ is present. |

```
HYPH_D1   DIGRAMS     '∂'  =  'AEIOU'                   :S(HYPH_D1)
HYPH_D2   DIGRAMS     '¬' BAL . T  =  '(' DIFF(UPPERS_,T) ')'
+                                                        :S(HYPH_D2)
```

| Convert to lower case and reverse to make scanning easier. |
| Then prepare a table (DIGRAM_TBL) of all those breakable |
| digrams. |

```
             DIGRAMS   =   BALREV(UPLO( DIGRAMS ))
             DIGRAM_TBL =  TABLE(30)
HYPH_D3      DIGRAMS   LEN(1) . C
+                  ('(' BREAK(')') . CC ')'   | LEN(1) . CC)
+                  (',' | RPOS(0))  =                   :F(HYPH_D4)
             DIGRAM_TBL<C>  =  ANY(CC)                  :(HYPH_D3)
HYPH_D4
```

| HYPH_PAT is the chief hyphenating pattern combining all |
| previous patterns into one. It will look for a break at |
| least MIN spaces from the back of the string and will set |
| K to equal the break point. |

```
         HYPH_PAT = HYPH_SUFF ∂K (*GT(K,MIN) | FENCE *HYPH_PAT)
+                 | NEUT_SUFF FENCE *HYPH_PAT
+                 | (INHIB_SUFF | NULL) FENCE ARB LEN(1) $ C ∂K
+                 *GT(K,MIN) *DIGRAM_TBL<C>
```

| Other miscellaneous patterns follow. |

```
             TRUE_WORD  =  POS(0)  (ANY('.;),:?') | NULL)
+            SPAN(LOWERS_ '-') (ANY(UPPERS_ '(') | NULL) RPOS(0)
             FIRST_VOWEL  =  BREAK(UPLO( 'AEIOU' ))  LEN(1) ∂L
             FOLLOWING_VOWEL = POS(0) TAB(*K) BREAK(UPLO('AEIOUY'))
                                                     :(HYPHENATE_END)
```

Chapter 10 - PARAGRAPH FORMATTING

| Entry point: Check to see if a normal word is there. Set MIN to be at least beyond the first vowel. |

HYPHENATE
```
          RWORD    TRUE_WORD                    :F(FRETURN)
          RWORD    '-'                          :S(HYPH_1)
          RWORD    FIRST_VOWEL                  :F(FRETURN)
          MIN  =   LT(MIN,L)    L
```

| Scan for a hyphenation point; check for following vowels. Insist on more than one character preceding the hyphenation point. |

```
          RWORD    HYPH_PAT                     :F(FRETURN)
          RWORD    FOLLOWING_VOWEL              :F(FRETURN)
          LE(SIZE(RWORD) - K,1)                 :S(FRETURN)
```

| Return K and set HYPHEN to a '-'. |

```
          HYPHENATE  =  K
          HYPHEN     =  '-'                     :(RETURN)
```

| If the word already contains a hyphen, this is the only point at which it may be hyphenated. |

```
HYPH_1    HYPHEN    =
          RWORD    '-' @K *GT(K,MIN)            :F(FRETURN)
          HYPHENATE =  K - 1                    :(RETURN)
HYPHENATE_END
```

Names referenced | Name | Type | Where defined
by HYPHENATE: | BAIREV * | Function | Program 3.8
                 | OR * | Function | Program 8.9
                 | UPLO * | Function | Program 2.1
                 | DIFF * | Function | Program 3.10
                 | UPPERS_ * | String | Program 2.1

* indicates name is referenced in the initialization section.

Epilogue

The coding of HYPHENATE was based on the desire to make it easy to see and modify the suffixes and letter pairs on which the algorithm is built, but at the same time to produce an efficient subroutine. The suffixes and digrams have therefore been transformed by the initialization section from a viewable format to a swiftly runnable one. The result of the precomputing is a single pattern (HYPH_PAT) used to scan the word in reverse until a hyphenation point is found in which case the variable K is set or is not found in which case the pattern fails. Suffix testing and removal are done by essentially OR'ing the various suffixes together with an appropriate degree of sophistication as contributed by the function OR (Program 8.9). OR contributes to efficiency by consolidating strings beginning with the same first character.

Program 10.8 - IMAGE   Page 215

Digrams are done a little differently. One could have taken
the OR of all breakable digrams to produce a pattern of the
form

           'a' ANY(...) | 'b' ANY(...) | 'c' ANY(...) | ...

This would require 26 tests for each character within the WORD
to be hyphenated until a break point was found. A more direct
approach is a variant on the pattern

                LEN(1) $ C *DIGRAM_TBL<C>

where the search through 26 alternates is replaced by the
lookup in the table. Since the look-up is done by hash coding
it can and is accomplished faster than ORing.

But it is interesting to note that it is not a great deal
faster. Evaluating an unevaluated expression requires sufficient time that the tradeoff in speed occurs at about 10
alternands. If the pattern were intelligent enough not to take
alternatives after once finding a character it would avoid
some needless testing and the average number of trials would
be 13, not 26. Moreover, if the sequence of characters is arranged in order of the frequency of their appearance in
English, we may expect to wait on the average of perhaps only
6 alternands. This suggests a pattern of the form

           'e' FENCE ANY(...) | 't' FENCE ANY(...) | ...

This pattern is slightly more awkward to use since it will
succeed or fail at the first character position. It must be
moved against the subject string by explicit programmer com-
mands. Since the speedup of this approach cannot be great (if
even positive) we leave its encoding as an exercise.


```
|  Program  |
|   10.8    |
|   IMAGE   |
```
Printing a line which contains backspace
characters is not easy using a standard line
printer. In fact, it is not immediately
clear how we can even package this activity.
We certainly would like to focus all print line extraction into a single function. But what is this function to return?
If the function were to go ahead and print the line, complete
with overstrikes, we would not have a very flexible function.
Since we have no idea of the use that is to be made of the
line it would be rather poor practice to commit ourselves in
advance to any particular disposition. We could return a
linked list of lines, one for each overstrike or a string of
consecutive lines (assuming we know the line width these could
be later separated) but these 2 methods imply the necessity of
disentangling the strings once they were brought back, a
process easily enough done but just as soon avoided if
possible. Rather than return all the lines at once we will
have IMAGE return just one particular line, the line numbered
I. This will help us in 2 ways. Not only will it be easier

Page 216   Chapter 10   -   PARAGRAPH FORMATTING

to use in the normal case, but it will provide us with random access to certain levels of lines. If, for example, we interpret the 3rd overstrike as actually a superscript, we could print that line first before going on to the others.

IMAGE(S,I) will return the Ith overstruck image of the B-normalized string S; for I=1 the line proper is returned, for I=2, the set of first overstrikes is returned, for I=3, the set of 2nd overstrikes, etc. For I=0 the underscoring of sections set off by USCORE's is returned. If IMAGE(S,I) does not exist for some I, the function will fail. Note that for I=1 the function never fails.

For example, let

         S = 'THE ⩕QUICK BRO←/WN⩕ FO←/X'

then

         IMAGE(S,0) = '   _____   '
         IMAGE(S,1) = 'THE QUICK BROWN FOX'
         IMAGE(S,2) = '   /   /   '
         IMAGE(S,3)   fails

Printing a line reduces to the following program. First we associate OVER with a format which insures overstriking. (PRINTER is a variable designating the printer unit, is installation dependent, and must be given by the user.) the width of the printer is assumed to be 132.

         OUTPUT(.OVER,PRINTER,'(1H+,132A1)')
         OUTPUT = IMAGE(LINE,1)
         I = 1
  LOOP   I = I + 1
         OVER = IMAGE(LINE,I)
         OVER = IMAGE(LINE,0)   :S(LOOP)

Note that nothing is printed in a statement in which IMAGE fails.

Even this activity, however simple and straightforward, can be avoided if we had the ability to return a data object having more dimensions that the singly dimensioned string. Such data objects exist; for example an extended version of SNOBOL4, called SNOBOL4B [Gimpel 1972], has a 3-dimensional aggregate of characters as a special datatype (called a block). The system which produced this text was written in SNOBOL4B. In this system not only does a function return an overstruck line as a value but there exists a function called TYPSET which returns an entire paragraph complete with overstriking.

Program 10.8 - IMAGE

```
| IMAGE(S,I) will return the Ith print line associated with |
| the string S.  It will fail if there is no Ith line.  S is |
| assumed to be B-normalized.                                |

        DEFINE('IMAGE(S,I)C,BU,T,T1')
        IF_OVERSTRIKE  =  BREAK(BSPACE USCORE)
        IF_BSPACE      =  BREAK(BSPACE)
        IF_USCORE      =  BREAK(USCORE)
                                                :(IMAGE_END)

| Entry  point:    Fan  out to various locations depending on |
| value of I.                                                 |

IMAGE       LE(I,0)                         :S(IMAGE_USCORE)
            GT(I,1)                         :S(IMAGE_BSPACE)

| I = 1:  Ignore USCORE's, BSPACE's and characters following |
| BSPACE's.                                                  |

            IMAGE  =  S
            IMAGE     IF_OVERSTRIKE           :F(RETURN)
IMAGE_1     IMAGE     BREAK(BSPACE USCORE) . T
+                 (USCORE | LEN(2))  =  T   :S(IMAGE_1)F(RETURN)

| For line 0 come here.  Make fast scan for USCORE failing |
| if none exists.  BU will be a convenient abbreviation for |
| BREAK(USCORE).   Replace all up to the first USCORE by   |
| blank.  Replace material between USCORE's by '_'s.       |

IMAGE_USCORE
        S    IF_USCORE                       :F(FRETURN)
        BU = BREAK(USCORE)
IMAGE_UL
        S    BU . T  USCORE  (BU . T1 USCORE | REM . T1)  =
             IMAGE  =  IMAGE  DUPL(' ',SPACING(T))
+                             DUPL('_',SPACING(T1))
        S    BU                               :S(IMAGE_UL)
             IMAGE  =  IMAGE  DUPL(' ',SPACING(S))  :(RETURN)

| For I > 1 come here.  Set up pattern PAT.C specially com- |
| puted for level I.                                        |

IMAGE_BSPACE  S   IF_BSPACE                   :F(FRETURN)
              PAT.C  =  BSPACE LEN(1) . C
IMAGE_B1      I  =  I - 1    GT(I,2)          :F(IMAGE_B2)
              PAT.C  =  BSPACE LEN(1) PAT.C   :(IMAGE_B1)

| See if an Ith overstruck character exists.  Set it to C if |
| it does.                                                   |

IMAGE_B2    S    POS(0)  BREAKX(BSPACE) . T  PAT.C  =
+                                             :F(IMAGE_B3)
             IMAGE  =  IMAGE  DUPL(' ',SPACING(T) - 1)  C

| Now remove any remaining BSPACE's.  If the right neighbor |
```

Page 218   Chapter 10   -   PARAGRAPH FORMATTING

```
|  does not exist we are free to return.                                   |
|_____|
             S    POS(0)    ARBNO(BSPACE LEN(1))    NOTANY(BSPACE) . C = C
+                                                   :S(IMAGE_B2) F(RETURN)
 _____
|  The clue to whether any characters at level I exists is  |
|  found in IMAGE.   If it is still null no Ith level charac- |
|  ters have been found.                                    |
|_____|

IMAGE_B3    IDENT(IMAGE,NULL)                        :S(FRETURN)
            IMAGE = IMAGE DUPL(' ',SPACING(S))       :(RETURN)
IMAGE_END


Names referenced       Name          Type           Where defined
by IMAGE:              BSPACE *      Character
                       USCORE *      Character
                       SPACING       Function       Program 10.5
                       BREAKX        Function       Program 8.2
*  indicates name is referenced in the initialization section.
```

??
??????????????????????? EXERCISES ???????????????????????
??

```
 _____
|  Exercise 10.1  |   Modify BNORM so that it fails if a B-
|_____|   normalized version of the string does not
exist.

 _____
|  Exercise 10.2  |   Prove that if $S_1$ and $S_2$ are B-normalized
|_____|   then the concatenation $S_1$ $S_2$ is B-
normalized.

 _____
|  Exercise 10.3  |   The text says that in order to have an in-
|_____|   version in the print position numbers we
must have at least one double BSPACE.  Intuitively this is ob-
vious.  Can you prove it?

 _____
|  Exercise 10.4  |   Prove that step (ii) of the BNORM algorithm
|_____|   (Prog. 10.1) preserves the property of
being right-balanced.

 _____
|  Exercise 10.5  |   Suppose string $S_1$ prints the image $I_1$ and
|_____|   string $S_2$ prints the image $I_2$.  Write a
pattern-matching statement to determine whether the image $I_2$
is a subimage of $I_1$.
```

Exercises for chapter 10

Exercise 10.6 Modify INORM to process separately the case of a single overstrike.

Exercise 10.7 Rewrite PR_POS (in INORM, Prog. 10.2) to use BREAK rather than ARB to find a BSPACE. Assume the string to be matched is B-normalized.

Exercise 10.8 (a) How would the definition of distinguishable change if overstrikes of the same character are not regarded as different?
(b) How would the definition change if all nonprintable characters were regarded as blank? Assume the nonprintables including blank are contained in the string NONP. Also do not make the assumption in (a).
(c) How would INORM be modified in each instance

Exercise 10.9 (a) Modify LINE so that the cost (UF) of compressing a line be two per char, while the cost of adding a blank and hyphenating remain at 1 (requires modifying one statement). (b) Modify LINE so that the cost (per char) of compressing a line is UF_C, the cost of padding is UF_P and the cost of hyphenating is UF_H.

Exercise 10.10 Modify PAD (Prog. 10.4) and MINP (Prog. 10.6) so that any blank following a special character can be squeezed out. An example of a set of special characters is ',):(;'.

Exercise 10.11 What is the value of HYPHENATE(RWORD, K) for K = 2, 4, 6, 8 where

(a) RWORD = REVERSE('investment')

(b) RWORD = REVERSE('co-operation')

Exercise 10.12 Modify HYPHENATE so that it will use not only '-' as a break character but any of a set of characters in the string BRC. Slash (/), for example, might be such a character to be broken in phrases such as 'input/output'.

Exercise 10.13 Modify the hyphenation algorithm so that digrams are tested in the order of the frequency of letters in English ('etoanirshdlcwumfygpbvkxqjz') and such that testing at a particular position ceases when the letter is found.

Chapter 10 - PARAGRAPH FORMATTING

| Exercise 10.14 | Modify HYPHENATE so that any word consisting entirely of upper case letters will also be hyphenated.

| Exercise 10.15 | (a) Write a function PRIMAGE(S) which will print the image of the B-normalized string S. (b) Given 2 strings, S1 and S2 use PRIMAGE to print them on the same line with S1 beginning in column 10 and S2 beginning in column 60 (assume the spacing of S1 is less than 50).

| Exercise 10.16 | Using PRIMAGE() of the above exercise, print the B-normalized strings S1 and S2 on the same line. That is, overstrike one on the other.

| Exercise 10.17 | Playboy magazine, for reasons best known to itself, wishes the lead page of the Playboy pictorial to be laid out in a 'coke bottle' shape. Assume the line widths, ranging from a maximum of 36 to a minimum of 22 are contained in a string (LENGTHS) separated by commas. Assume the lead paragraph is in a variable P. Assume a page width of 60 with the column centered in the page. Using the function PRIMAGE from Exercise 10.15 write the SNOBOL4 program to satisfy Playboy's request.

| Exercise 10.18 | Suppose that the 3rd overstrike represents superscripting and the 2nd overstrike represents subscripting so that

$$'A \leftarrow 1 = 2 \leftarrow \leftarrow N'$$

prints as

$$A_1 = 2^N$$

Using IMAGE, print such an object.

| Exercise 10.19 | Print a string with exponentiation such as

$$'A**(M+1) = B**N + C**M'$$

in such a way that parenthesis (if any) are stripped from the exponential and the exponents are superscripted such as

$$A^{M+1} = B^N + C^M$$

Assume that the string contains no BSPACE's and whenever '**' appears it means superscript the following character unless a '(' appears in which case the parenthetical expression is superscripted. Assume that the superscript does not itself have superscripting. (Hint: this can be done in four statements using IMAGE and BNORM).

| Exercise 10.20 | Extend the previous exercise to handle arbitrarily nested exponentiation.

CHAPTER ELEVEN

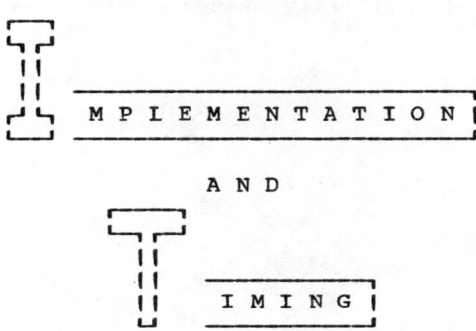

```
CONTENTS

RESOLUTION ............. 11.1
TIMER .................. 11.2
SYSTEM ................. 11.3
TIMEGC ................. 11.4
LPROG .................. 11.5
FPROFILE ............... 11.6
TPROFILE ............... 11.7
```

ne of the reasons for writing in a higher level language is to free oneself from the entanglements of individual bits and the sometimes sordid details of the particular machine on which one is running. A price is normally paid for this in terms of time and/or space efficiency of the resulting program but one is presumably willing to pay this price if the savings in programming time are compensative. Then why, the reader may ask, should we bother about timing and implementation since the former we have agreed is relatively unimportant and the latter represents detail from which we wish to escape? The answer is that although most programs are small and can (and should) be written without regard for the time they consume, most large programs come to grips with the efficiency question sooner or later. Large programs may exceed critical storage bounds or they may consume so much time that their utility is in question. Some knowledge of timing is useful not only to improve the speed of an existing program but to estimate the cost of running programs not yet written. It may well be that a program written in SNOBOL4 will be too slow or inefficient for a given application and it will be helpful to learn this before it is written.

Describing a system as large as an implementation of the SNOBOL4 language can neither be easy nor quick. To make matters even more difficult there are several SNOBOL4 processors. There is the original MAcro ImplementatioN of SNOBOL4 [Griswold 1972] which we refer to as MAINBOL, there is a compiler version for the IBM 360/370 called SPITBOL [Dewar 1971] and a small fast interpreter for the PDP-10 called SITBOL [Gimpel 1972, 1973a]. In addition, the macros of MAINBOL have been expanded to run on several different machines including the IBM 360/370, CDC 6000, Honeywell 635, Univac 1108 and the PDP-10. The process of macro expansion for yet newer machines continues at this writing with unabated ferver so that this list is not, and is not intended to be, exhaustive.

The primary purpose behind SPITBOL was speed and the resulting system is 7-8 times faster than MAINBOL. SITBOL's chief concern was storage and the system is less than one-third the size of MAINBOL. In spite of the differences in design goals, the implementations of these systems are fairly similar.

ymbol Tables | A symbol table is programmer jargon for a table of information that can be referenced on a name basis (the symbol). For example, a telephone directory can be regarded as a symbol table of sorts where the symbol is a person's name and the information to be looked up is his telephone number (and possibly other information such as his address). In principle, a symbol table could be implemented as a long list and a search could be made by comparing a given symbol with every one on the list. This is obviously too inefficient to be practical. In the telephone directory, the symbols are arranged alphabetically to permit rapid searching. In general, a symbol table is organized in such a way as to avoid a lengthy linear search.

A common method of implementing a symbol table is by means of a hashing technique, illustrated in Figure 11.1. The Hash Array is a fixed-length array of pointers to symbol table entries. Each symbol table entry contains the name of the symbol (for comparison purposes), information associated with the symbol and a pointer to the next symbol table entry (if any). Hence, each pointer in the Hash Array may be regarded as heading a list of symbol table entries.

When a symbol such as ALPHA is looked up or entered into the table, a so-called hash number is computed from the characters 'ALPHA' which is a number between 0 and L-1 where L is the length of the Hash Array. This hash number is used to reference into the Hash Array and hence it designates a list of symbol table entries. If a symbol table entry for ALPHA is in the table, it must be in this list. Thus the time to locate ALPHA in the table is reduced by a factor equal to 1/L but is increased by the time needed to compute a hash number.

The hash number must be reproducible so that given the characters 'ALPHA' the same hash number is always produced, but the method for computing the hash is otherwise arbitrary as its name would suggest. It should provide a good mix so that all locations in the Hash Array (sometimes called buckets) are referenced with approximately equal probability. Also the computation should be quick. For example, one may take the first 4 characters exclusive-OR'ed with the last 4 characters and divide by the length L of the array. The remainder is usually an acceptable hash number. Note that the hash number does not uniquely represent the symbol. In Figure 11.1 both ALPHA and GAMMA have the same hash number.

Symbol tables are very important; they form the heart of virtually every assembler, compiler and interpreter. A symbol table provides the link between an external name (symbol) and an internal block of information about that symbol. One need merely reflect on the telephone directory example to see the importance of this. Names in a program remain fairly stable even though they may translate into different internal addresses from run-to-run just as people normally retain their names even though they may be associated with different telephone numbers over the course of their lifetime.

For SNOBOL4 implementations, the information typically retained in the symbol table entry for, say, ALPHA is the value of the natural variable ALPHA, a pointer to function information if ALPHA is a function and a pointer to an internal code location if ALPHA is a label. Also, if ALPHA is a keyword (it is not) information may be present to indicate its value.

For interpreters with the power of SNOBOL4, the symbol table is especially important; it remains in core during execution

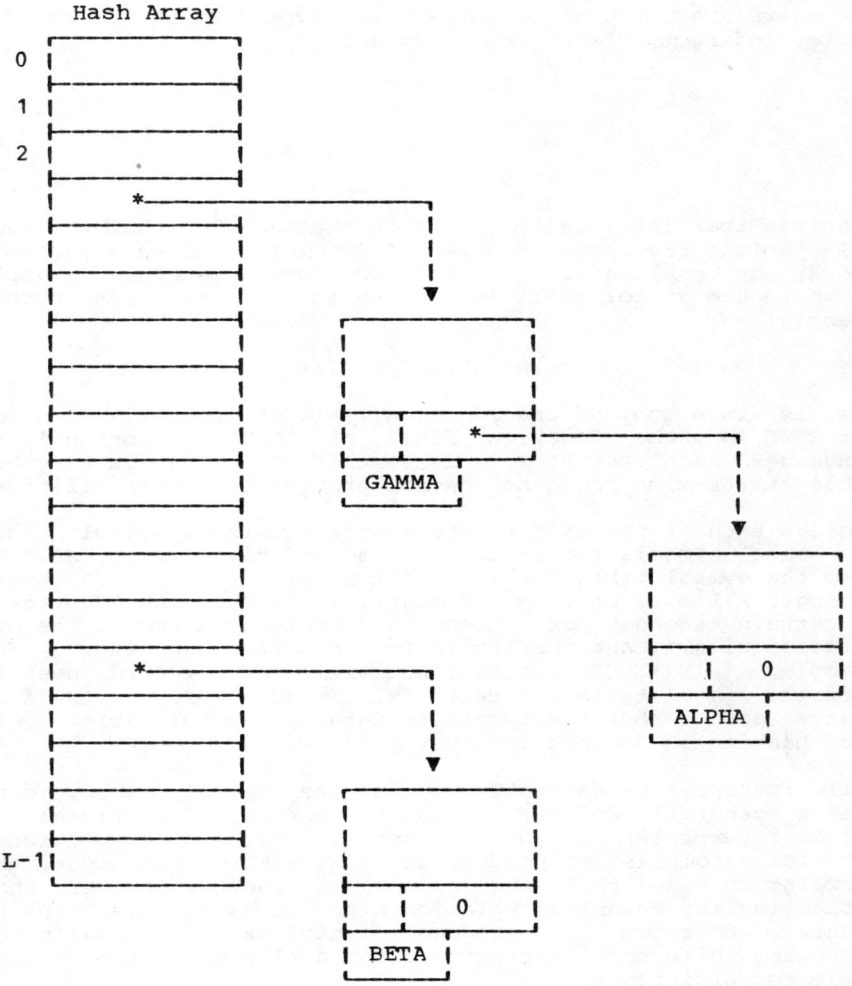

Figure 11.1

A symbol table containing three symbols ALPHA, BETA, and GAMMA.

and there are language features which depend on this. For example, indirect referencing, such as:

$$A = \text{'ABC'}$$

$$\ldots$$

$$\$A = 17$$

requires that 'ABC' be looked up in the table so that the symbol table entry associated with 'ABC' (also called a variable block) can be plugged. The indirect goto is another example of where the symbol table is queried at run-time. As another example:

$$\text{OPSYN('ALPHA', 'SIZE')}$$

results in a copy of the function field of the variable block for SIZE into the function field of ALPHA. Conventional languages such as PL/I and Fortran do not retain a symbol table at run-time and hence cannot provide these capabilities.

Whereas each of the SNOBOL4 processors retains a symbol table to house symbols required for an associative lookup, MAINBOL uses the symbol table for yet another purpose, viz. to store strings. All data strings are stored as symbols table entries. A certain economy of concept is thereby achieved at the expense of significant inefficiencies in string handling. For example, TRIM(INPUT) in MAINBOL will read a record, hash it into the symbol table and call TRIM which deletes trailing blanks and hashes the remainder into the symbol table. All such hashing is avoided in other processors.

While interpreters generally retain the symbol table, compilers generally do not. Since it requires a volitional act for an interpreter to expel the symbol table and a volitional act for a compiler to produce it along with working code, the correlation seems to be the result of inertia rather than reflecting any essential relationship. In fact, exceptions do occur. Some compilers produce a symbol table optionally for debugging while some interpreters optionally expel the symbol table for efficiency.

%%% ypes of Compilers A compiler, in the most general sense of the term, will translate a program written in some language into some intermediate form which can be executed or interpreted by some other program. If the intermediate form can be executed directly, the processor is called a compiler, in the narrow sense of the term. Otherwise it is called an interpreter.

One of the most important questions that can be asked about an implementation is the form of intermediate code. Into what form, for example, will

Types of Compilers   Page 227

ALPHA * BETA + GAMMA

be compiled. Different implementations of the same language may answer this question in different ways. The layman often believes that all SNOBOL interpreters leave the string intact to be interpreted anew each time the expression is evaluated. This is a kind of interpretation called <u>pure interpretation</u> and since the compiler has zero work to do, we will call the compiler a <u>type-0 compiler</u>. Some languages are implemented as pure interpreters (such as GPM, Program 18.8) but SNOBOL4 is not one of them.

A <u>type-1 compiler</u> will convert indivisible syntactic units (called tokens) into pointers into the symbol table. For example, the expression above will be converted into

```
|    ---> ALPHA       |
|----------------------|
|    ---> *(2)        |
|----------------------|
|    ---> BETA        |
|----------------------|
|    ---> +(2)        |
|----------------------|
|    ---> GAMMA       |
```

where ---> ALPHA is a pointer to the symbol table entry for ALPHA, where ---> *(2) is a pointer to the symbol table entry for binary *, etc. LISP [McCarthy, 1960] is an example of a language which employs a type-1 compiler.

The searching for, and the conversion of, tokens into symbol table pointers is called <u>lexical analysis</u>. Most compilers more sophisticated than type-1 nevertheless precede other processing with a lexical analysis.

A <u>type-2</u> compiler will rearrange the pointers into a form more suitable for execution. This can either be a Polish prefix representation in which the functions precede the arguments or a Polish suffix representation in which the function pointers follow the arguments. Each form is illustrated in Figure 11.2.

Most interpreters operate on type-2 code. In particular, MAINBOL uses Polish prefix and SITBOL uses Polish suffix. Polish prefix is slower but more flexible than Polish suffix. It is slower because with prefix code the function is encountered first. When the function gets control it calls the interpreter to obtain its arguments. This call is necessarily recursive and hence slow. In Polish suffix the function is called after the arguments have been evaluated; there is no need for recursion. But Polish prefix is more flexible because certain operators can decide that they do not want to play the same game as other operators. Unary *, for example, does not evaluate its argument but merely returns a pointer to it to be

Page 228   Chapter 11 - Implementation and Timing

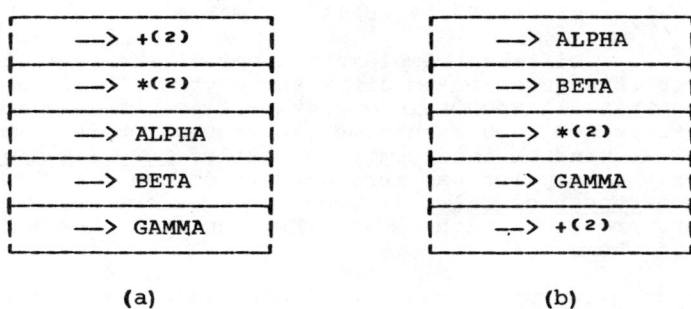

(a)   (b)

Figure 11.2

The result of a type-2 compilation of the expression ALPHA * BETA + GAMMA may be (a) Polish prefix or (b) Polish suffix.

evaluated at some later time. In Polish suffix, unary * can't decide this on its own but needs the co-operation of the compiler. This leads to other problems. For example, unary * cannot be redefined at run-time.

The types 0-2 compilers are regarded as interpreters because the output (intermediate code) is not capable of being executed directly by machine. A type-3 compiler will produce code which can actually be executed. The above expression becomes:

```
            PUSH    —> ALPHA
            PUSH    —> BETA
            CALL    —> *(2)
            PUSH    —> GAMMA
            CALL    —> +(2)
```

where each function finds its arguments on the stack and replaces them with the result of its computation. For efficiency purposes, registers can be used instead of the stack except for very deeply nested expressions.

A type-4 compiler is one which produces optimal (or near-optimal) machine code. The above expression is reduced to:

```
            LOAD    —> ALPHA
            MULT    —> BETA
            ADD     —> GAMMA
```

Most true compilers are combinations of type-3 and type-4. For example, Fortran I/O routines and trigonometric functions are handled with type-3 calls whereas infix operators (+ * - /) and some arithmetic functions such as MAX and ABS are executed in-line in a type-4 manner. SPITBOL is almost entirely Type-3.

Floating Storage

The only operation it does in-line is assignment. The reason that, for example, in-line addition can't be done is because variables are typeless and the compiler has no way of knowing whether A + B is floating point addition, fixed point or mixed mode. Assignment, on the other hand, even for strings and arrays, is comparatively simple since only a pointer and a datatype need be copied.

It should be evident that as the sophistication of the compiler increases (increasing type numbers) the speed of compilation decreases, the speed of execution increases and the flexibility of the run-time system decreases. For example, the type-2 rearrangement of operators is done so that operators will be where they are needed when it comes time to execute. This is faster but less flexible since it means that it is practically impossible to change the precedence of operators at run-time in a type-2 system; an irrevocable decision is made at compile-time.

The lack of declarations in SNOBOL4 (E.g., S is a string whose maximum length is 1000) implies that storage is not preallocated for variables but rather is allocated on demand. When storage is no longer in use it is freed automatically by a so-called garbage collection process.

In SPITBOL, SITBOL and MAINBOL the storage allocation scheme is basically the same. Allocating storage is ultra-simple. When a chunk of storage is needed it is taken from the beginning of a free region and the pointer to the free region is updated. When no free storage is left, the garbage collector is called. The first step of collection is a marking process in which all accessible blocks are marked as such. This is similar in spirit to the function VISIT (Prog. 5.10) and in SITBOL and SPITBOL it is actually implemented in the same way. Once the accessible blocks have been identified, they are moved together so that further allocations can be performed. Before the movement, any pointer pointing into or to a floating block must be adjusted. The term floating is used as it seems to correctly connote the relative ease by which the blocks may be moved about. The incorrect care and feeding of floating addresses while implementing a system such as SNOBOL4 has led to many an implementation disaster. A useful rule of thumb is that one such error will lead to a day's worth of debugging sometime in the future.

It is interesting to note that the predecessor to SNOBOL4, viz. SNOBOL3, implemented its marking phase by means of a use-count. Every time a variable's value is changed under such a system, the use-count on the new object would be augmented and the use-count on the old would be decremented. Marking consists of looking for nonzero use-counts. Where strings are the only datatype, as in SNOBOL3, this is not a bad scheme. If one can have structures pointing to other structures,

Page 230   Chapter 11   -   Implementation and Timing

however, the scheme suffers from the prospect that two structures pointing to each other may be inaccessible from the rest of the world and yet have nonzero use-counts.

The method of implementing the garbage collector in SPITBOL and later copied over into SITBOL was especially clever. After visiting nodes in the manner of the function VISIT, the pointers are left in their reverse direction. This leads to a fast pointer adjustment phase as all the floating addresses which had been pointing to a floating block are then hung off the block in a linked list. The MAINBOL processor uses a more conventional marking phase using recursion much in the manner of COPYL (Prog. 5.8). Also the use of macros produced a slower system. The result is that the garbage collectors of SPITBOL and SITBOL are much faster than SNOBOL4.

```
| %%    natomy of a Processor |
| %  %                        |
| %    %                      |
| %%%%                        |
| %    %                      |
```
This section attempts to describe how a SNOBOL4 processor is organized and which parts of it are exercised most frequently during the course of executing a program. While such an analysis is application and implementation dependent, certain valid conclusions can nonetheless be drawn concerning the running of arbitrary programs against such systems.

Most SNOBOL implementations tend to be implemented as one large assembly program and it is often difficult to breakdown the resource utilization into different functional compartments. The SITBOL implementation is an exception. It consists of 20 separately-assembled files segregated according to function as indicated in Table 11.1. Each section is designated with a two or three-letter mnemonic as well as an indication of space occupied as a percentage of the whole. The approximate number of instructions in each section can be computed by multiplying the percentage by the total number of words (9300).

The 15.5% figure for I/O in Table 11.1 is surprisingly high. It includes code to read and analyze the command string, setup memory, provide a fairly rich collection of system facilities and interpret special i/o formats and make suitable conversions. The space devoted to the interpreter is padded by calls to produce run statistics at job termination plus a message interpreter. Hence the 7.3% figure is larger than what would normally be considered strictly necessary for the interpretation of Polish suffix. Also required in interpretation is all that machinery necessary to provide the correct number of arguments to functions, to evaluate arguments (convert variables such as A to the value of A, or convert INPUT to the next string read, etc.), and to interpret goto's and react correctly to failure.

The compiler consists of a lexical analyzer (LEX) which makes calls on the symbol table manager (SYM) to convert source tokens to pointers into the symbol table which it feeds back

Table 11.1 The Decomposition of SITBOL. Regions are named by a short (2 or 3 letter) mnemonic. The Size is based on the number of words of assembled code and is given as a percentage of the total. The overall size was 9300 (36-bit) words. The storage considered is pure storage and does not include space for stacks, symbol tables, code blocks, etc.

Name	Size(%)	Description
IO	15.5	I/O and system interface
INT	7.3	Interpreter
GC	3.7	Garbage Collector
SYN	4.1	Syntactic Analyzer
LEX	4.4	Lexical Analyzer
SYM	7.9	Symbol table manager
STR	6.1	String handler
SMR	2.1	Streaming (character set searching)
PG	5.7	Patterns Global (pattern building and the scanner)
PL	7.9	Patterns Local (built-in functions and primitives)
NUM	2.1	Numeric functions
CVT	4.4	Datatype conversions (string <==> numeric)
ARY	2.0	Arrays (allocation & referencing)
KW	2.0	Keywords
TBL	2.9	Tables (allocation, referencing and conversion)
DFF	3.5	Defined functions
DFD	1.8	Defined Datatypes
ERR	2.0	Error handling
TRC	7.5	Tracing
DATA	7.1	Assembled in strings, character sets, etc.

to the syntactic analyzer (SYN). LEX makes calls on the streamer (SMR) to search for one of a set of characters. Thus the entire compiler represents 18.5% of the system with the syntactic analyzer only 4%. This is surprising in view of the great attention devoted to syntactic analysis in the literature. The symbol table manager is bloated by an internal symbol table of approximately 450 words (4.8%) and a number of symbol table related functions such as CLEAR() and OPSYN(). The actual machinery for locating and installing names into the symbol table is actually quite small.

The relatively large quantity, 7.9%, of code for PL (Patterns Local) is attributable to the relatively large number of built-in patterns such as POS(n), BREAK(s), BAL, etc.

The SITBOL system has a profiling capability which indicates where the system is spending its time. One can obtain a user-oriented histogram (via statement numbers) or a system-oriented one (via absolute addresses). This, coupled with the physical segregation previously described makes it fairly easy to determine the percentage of time devoted to each subactivity. Table 11.2 summarizes the results of running the profiler for 6 typical string applications. The last column indicates a composite figure obtained rather arbitrarily by averaging the other 6 figures.

Table 11.2 Shows the percentage of time spent in various regions of SITBOL for a variety of string-processing problems.

Region	L^6	Renum	TPST	Pre	Sort	Refm	Comp
IO	3.0	4.5	2.9	20.7		11.8	7.1
INT	27.0	18.1	30.2	38.8	73.6	33.8	36.9
GC	40.2	34.8	20.1	20.1		4.2	19.9
SYN							
LEX							
SYM	.2	.2			.9		.1
STR	13.8	26.3	13.3	5.4	9.8	27.1	15.9
SMR	1.0	1.6	7.0	1.14		2.3	2.3
PG	4.9	7.2	8.1	2.8		5.7	4.8
PL	2.3	4.2	7.6	3.1		1.5	3.1
NUM	.1		1.7		1.7	1.1	.8
CVT	.8	1.8	.8	.5	2.9	1.3	1.5
ARY				1.4			.2
KW							
TBL	.2	1.0	.2				.2
DFF	6.0		7.8	4.3	3.2	10.1	5.2
DFD	.2			1.5	4.3		1.0
ERR							
TRC	.3	.5	.3	.3	2.9	.2	.7
DATA							

L^6 is a compiler. Renum renumbers the statement labels of Fortran programs. TPST (Typeset) is a program to format paragraphs and uses functions virtually identical to those indicated in Chapter 10. Pre is a pre-processor for Fortran which inserts common areas at the beginning of subprograms and does minor data massaging. Sort is a linked-list sort of a kind identical to Prog. 13.3. Refm reads a file with mixed tabs and blanks separating 4 fields and writes out the file with columns alligned using tabs as needed. With one exception (Sort) all programs were complete programs so that time spent in I/O and other necessary but unrelated activity would be included in the timing statistics. Not included as is evidenced from the data itself is the time spent compiling.

The composite figure indicates the rather striking fact that over one-third of the time is spent in the interpreter. Most of this time would drop to nil if SITBOL had been a compiler.

However a compiler version of SITBOL would almost certainly be larger by close to the percentage of time saved so that the cost (measured in core-seconds) would be the same. The important issue is that the interpretive time is not larger than it is. Substantial amounts of time are going to other things such as garbage collection (20%), string processing (15%), pattern matching (FG, PL and SMR, 10%) and IO (7%). It is only in applications such as Sort which use few of the facilities of the language (no storage allocation, no pattern matching) that the interpreter time is really excessive. Thus semantically rich processors such as SNOBOL4 have two reasons for being written as interpreters. The semantical richness is easier to write and there is not that much being lost.

Comparing individual columns it may be seen that the preprocessor Pre spends relatively large amounts of time doing I/O because it has virtually no work to do on most lines read. The relatively low figure of 18% interpreter use in the Fortran renumbering program is probably do to the heavy use of concatenation and pattern matching and the rest of the data bears this out. TPST spends by far more time in SMR than do the other routines and this is because it is continually scanning for USCOREs and BSPACEs as was pointed out in Chapter 10. The PDP-10 has no automatic scan instruction like the IBM 360 but nonetheless even in this exagerated use of the BREAK function, relatively little time (7%) is spent streaming. The DFF entry indicates the amount of time spent in function calls and is relatively small even for heavily recursive applications such as Sort. The amount of time spent in this category had more to do with the structuredness of the program. TPSET, as a look at Chapter 10 would reveal, is well-modularized and a certain price must be paid, but the cost is not excessive. It is somewhat surprising that areas such as numerics, conversions, tables, arrays, defined-datatypes, and keywords represent so little of the total time (3.7%). Even, for example, when the defined datatypes are used rather heavily as in Sort, the amount of time spent in DFD is relatively small (4.3%).

How do these figures compare with the corresponding figures for MAINBOL and SPITBOL? Since SPITBOL is type-3, the time spent in INT would be reduced substantially and, to a first approximation, all other activities would experience a proportional increase (just to make up the 100%). The Garbage Collection time would be reduced somewhat because SITBOL, operating in a time-sharing environment, deliberately keeps a 'low profile' to keep a relatively good priority. This results in garbage collections every 1500 words or so which is quite frequent compared with batch-oriented systems such as SPITBOL. The STR (String Handling) area would also be reduced in SPITBOL because the IBM 360 is a byte-orented machine with certain built-in string operations. The result is that SPITBOL should be more nearly balanced in its overall profile with much of its time being spent in pattern matching, defined functions, IO and garbage collection. This, however, will depend considerably on the application. MAINBOL has an interpretive loop about twice as slow as SITBOL and has a much slower garbage collection, pattern matcher and I/O. Since overall program time goes up by more than a factor of 2, the time spent in the interpreter for MAINBOL would actually decrease (to say 25%). IO, GC, PL, PG and SMR times would increase whereas other times would likely remain roughly the same.

```
|| Program    ||
||   11.1     ||
|| RESOLUTION ||
```

To accumulate his own timing statistics, the programmer will make calls on the built-in function TIME(). The value returned is not uniformly increasing, but rather rises in steps which are sometimes rather large. On many systems the step size, called the resolution, is one-sixtieth of a second which is fairly large as many things can happen during this time period. It is essential to know or be able to compute this resolution to obtain accurate timings. Fortunately, this is rather easily done.

       DEFINE('RESOLUTION() T')   :(RESOLUTION_END)

| Entry point: Initialize T to the current time. Then
| repeatedly set RESOLUTION to the difference between the
| current time and this initial time. When it goes positive,
| the smallest resolution is obtained.

```
RESOLUTION      T = TIME()
RESOLUTION_1    RESOLUTION = TIME() - T
                GT(RESOLUTION,0)   :S(RETURN) F(RESOLUTION_1)
RESCLUTION_END
```

Epilogue

Since TIME() returns an integer in milliseconds, it is possible that the resolution may be off by as much as a millisecond. For example, on the IBM 370 Mod 165 the interval timer resolution is 3.3 and RESOLUTION returns 3 two-thirds of the time and 4 one-third of the time. In such cases, RESOLUTION could be modified to return a constant known value. But it should be remarked that only an approximate value for the resolution is ever needed. Exercise 11.6 explores another possibility for improving the behavior of RESOLUTION.

```
|| Program ||
||  11.2   ||
||  TIMER  ||
```

The timer routine shown below will time a statement (or statements) passed to it as arguments. Thus

              TIMER(' A = B + C ')

will determine how much time is required to execute the given assignment statement and will print appropriate statistics.

Program 11.2 - TIMER   Page 235

If more than one statement is to be timed they should be
separated by semicolons.

To time a statement it is placed in a loop and executed for
several times longer than the resolution of the clock. In
order to deduct the time required to increment a counter and
test, the loop is executed twice, once with the statement in
and once with it out.

```
                DEFINE('TIMER(S_,N_)C_,T_,I_')     :(TIMER_END)
```
```
| Entry Point:  On first call, fall through.  When TIMER is |
| called  recursively,  N_  is nonzero and control passes to |
| TIMER_N.                                                   |
```
```
TIMER           EQ(N_,0)                           :F(TIMER_N)
```
```
| Starting with 10 executions, double the number until  the |
| difference  between  the times required to execute and not |
| execute the given statement is 20 ticks of the clock.      |
```
```
                N_ = 10
TIMER_1         T_ = TIMER(' ;' S_,N_) - TIMER(,N_) :F(FRETURN)
                N_ = LT(T_,20 * RESOLUTION())  N_ * 2  :S(TIMER_1)
```
```
| Now print the results.                                     |
```
```
                T_ = CONVERT(T_, 'REAL')
                OUTPUT =
                OUTPUT = 'THE STATEMENT'
                OUTPUT = S_
                OUTPUT = 'REQUIRED ' (T_ / N_) ' MILLISECONDS +/- 10%'
+                        ' TO EXECUTE IN ' SYSTEM()   :(RETURN)
```
```
| Here if N_ is nonzero.  Prepare a string C_ which will be |
| compiled and executed and will contain the statement to be |
| measured together with a control loop.                     |
```
```
TIMER_N         I_ = 1
                C_ = ' COLLECT()   ; TIMER = TIME()  ;'
+              'TIMER_3'   S_    ';'
+              ' I_ = I_ + 1 LT(I_,' N_ ')'           :S(TIMER_3);'
+              ' TIMER = TIME() - TIMER              :(RETURN)'
```
```
| Compile the string and, if successful, execute it.         |
```
```
                C_ = CODE(C_)                      :S<C_>F(FRETURN)
TIMER_END
```

Names referenced	Name	Type	Where defined
by TIMER:	SYSTEM	Function	Program 11.3
	RESOLUTION	Function	Program 11.1

Page 236   Chapter 11 - Implementation and Timing

Epilogue

Note that the temporaries and arguments are given 'funny' names, i.e. ending with the underscore (_) character. This is to avoid conflict with variables in the statement being timed.

```
|  Program  |
|  11.3     |
|  SYSTEM   |
```
SYSTEM() is a function which will attempt to determine which of the various SNOBOL4 processors it is running under. For example, under SPITBOL, SYSTEM() will return 'SPITBOL'. The function is not easy to write because if there is a difference between any two processors this may be regarded as a deficiency and may get fixed sometime in the future rendering the function we're about to write invalid.

One of the main differences between the various systems is in functions and/or keywords implemented. Unhappily, one cannot test directly for the existence of such functions or keywords so knowing about such differences does us no good.

SYSTEM() was used to identify which implementation was being measured by TIMER and is provided more for its intrinsic interest than its necessity.

```
          DEFINE('SYSTEM()K')              :(SYSTEM_END)
```

| Entry point: First separate out MAINBOL from the other |
| processors.   Only MAINBOL regards .X as a string. |

```
SYSTEM    IDENT(DATATYPE(.X),'STRING')        :F(SYSTEM_2)
```

| Falling through implies MAINBOL. Now separate out the |
| various systems on the basis of the SIZE of &ALPHABET. The |
| Honeywell 635 uses a 9-bit code. IBM equipment uses an |
| 8-bit character while the PDP-10 uses 7-bit ASCII. |

```
          K   =   SIZE(&ALPHABET)
          SYSTEM = EQ(K,512)   'HONEYWELL MAINBOL'   :S(RETURN)
          SYSTEM = EQ(K,256)   'IBM MAINBOL'         :S(SYSTEM_1)
          SYSTEM = EQ(K,128)   'PDP-10 MAINBOL'      :S(RETURN)
```

| Both CDC and UNIVAC MAINBOL's use 6-bit codes. We can |
| distinguish between these two systems by the order of |
| characters in &ALPHABET. Only CDC contains () as adjacent |
| characters. |

```
          SYSTEM    =   'CDC MAINBOL'
          &ALPHABET     '()'                   :S(SYSTEM_1)
          SYSTEM    =   'UNIVAC MAINBOL'       :(RETURN)
```

| Here to test if the system also contains blocks. The |
| operator sharp (#) will have a lower precedence than blank |
| if the blocks extension is available. If the value of T is |
| 1 (5 + 5) then we're in pure MAINBOL. Otherwise we've got |

Anatomy of a SNOBOL4 Statement   Page 237

| blocks. |

```
SYSTEM_1        OPSYN('OLD_SHARP','#',2)
                OPSYN('#','+',2)
                T  =  1  5 # 5
                OPSYN('#','OLD_SHARP',2)
                EQ(T,110)                         :S(RETURN)
        SYSTEM = SYSTEM ' WITH BLOCKS'            :(RETURN)
```

| Here if not MAINBOL. FASBOL has an unorthodox SUBSTR func- |
| tion. |

```
SYSTEM_2
        SYSTEM = DIFFER(SUBSTR('ABC',2,1),'B')   'FASBOL'
+                                                 :S(RETURN)
```

| SITBOL, running on the PDP-10, can easily be distinguished |
| from the IBM SPITBOL by the size of &ALPHABET. |

```
        SYSTEM = EQ(SIZE(&ALPHABET),128) 'SITBOL'  :S(RETURN)
        SYSTEM = 'SPITBOL'                         :(RETURN)
SYSTEM_END
```

Epilogue

The above function is obviously incomplete as it does not include all machines for which MAINBOL has been expanded. If your favorite processor is not among the group you are encouraged to modify the program to include it.

| %% natomy of a SNOBOL4 Statement | In this section we
| % % | will study the time
| % % | requirements of SNOBOL4 statements. Such an analysis
| %%%% | may at first blush seem rather difficult because in
| % % | a language as rich as SNOBOL4 there is 'so much
| | going on'. But just the reverse is the case. For
example, Table 11.3 shows the times required to execute in SPITBOL and MAINBOL a sequence of four statements in ascending order of complexity. TIMER, Program 11.2, was used to time these statements and is responsible for other similar timing figures given in this section. All times in this section were made (or normalized to) an IBM 360 Mod 65. For possible comparison with other processors, some representative instruction times are given in Table 11.4.

In Table 11.3, we see that the null statement (statements which do nothing) consume relatively little time; i.e. statement overhead is relatively small. Assignment is fairly fast since, for all datatypes, it is merely a descriptor (two 32-bit words) copy. But the most notable thing about Table 11.3 is that there is a linear relationship of time with the number of arithmetic operators.

This relationship is more nearly linear in an interpreter or type 3 system because the various operations are 'packaged'

> Table 11.3 Time in milliseconds required to execute a sequence of arithmetic assignment statements.
>
> | Statement | SPITBOL | MAINBOL |
> |---|---|---|
> | A | .0012 | .02 |
> | A = I1 | .004 | .10 |
> | A = I + J | .009 | .30 |
> | A = I + J + K | .015 | .50 |
> | A = I + J + K + L | .021 | .70 |

more so than in a type-4 compiler. In a type-4 system, code optimization techniques render more interaction between operations of the same expression so that the time of a statement is not simply the sum of the times of the component operations.

Measuring the time of an operation which does not generate storage is fairly straightforward as the direct measurement by TIMER may be used. If the operation generates storage which must later be collected, an additional increment of time should be charged to such an operation. We will see later how this can be done.

Arithmetic Table 11.5 shows the time required for arithmetic operations. In MAINBOL the time is dominated by overhead so that all operations, even exponentiation, take pretty much the same time (about .2 milliseconds). This even includes the case where one of the operands must be converted to string or real.

> Table 11.4 Selected instruction times for the IBM 360/65. (N is the number of characters involved in a multiple-character operation.)
>
> | Operation | Time (microseconds) |
> |---|---|
> | Load (1 word) | .95 |
> | Store (1 word) | .93 |
> | Add (storage-to-register) | 1.65 |
> | Floating add (storage-to-register) | 1.68 |
> | Multiply (storage-to-reg.) | 4.45 |
> | Divide (storage into reg.) | 9.00 |
> | Compare (reg. with storage) | 1.40 |
> | Branch | 1.10 |
> | MVC (storage-to-storage move) | 3 + .3N |
> | CLC (storage-to-storage compare) | 2.9 + .3N |
> | TRT (SPAN & BREAK) | 4.1 + 1.2N |
> | TR (REPLACE) | 1.9 + 1.8N |

In SPITBOL, as may be expected, the overhead has been reduced to the point where variations in the natural execution times do show up in the time for the overall operations. Thus, integer division (.019) is longer than integer multiplication (.014) which in turn is longer than addition (.007) which reflect differences in the absolute times to perform these instructions (.009, .005, and .001 respectively).

```
Table 11.5  Time in milliseconds to carry out selec-
ted arithmetic operations in SPITBOL and MAINBOL on
the IBM 360/65.
```

Data Type	Operation	Data Type	SPITBOL	MAINBOL
integer	+	integer	.007	.2
integer	-	integer	.007	.2
integer	*	integer	.014	.2
integer	/	integer	.019	.2
integer	**	integer	.039	.2
integer	REMDR	integer	.035	.18
integer	+	real	.061	.2
real	+	integer	.067	.2
real	+	real	.016	.2
integer	+	string(2)	.084	.22

Table 11.5 shows a ratio of improvement of SPITBOL over MAINBOL which varies from about 25:1 in the case of integer arithmetic to about 2.5:1 in the case of addition with one argument a string. This is because, in the latter case, the time is dominated by the conversion, and this MAINBOL does within a single macro, so that the SPITBOL approach grants no advantage.

Flow of Control Various operations associated with flow of control are given in Table 11.6. These figures should be sufficient to predict the time of simple looping control instructions.

For example, the standard method of implementing a loop in SNOBOL4 is some variant of

```
         N = 0
LOOP     N = N + 1  LT(N,100)         :F(LOOP_OUT)
         ...
                                      :(LOOP)
LOOP_OUT
```

which will execute the inner part of the loop 100 times. The statement labeled loop will be executed 100 times before failing. Predicates such as LT() will return the null string when they succeed as this is the least flagrant value they can

Table 11.6 shows time in milliseconds of flow-of-control type operations for SPITBOL and MAINBOL.

Operation	SPITBOL	MAINBOL
GT,LT,EQ,LE,GE,NE	.02	.2
IDENT, DIFFER	.02	.2
LGT	.05	.35
Null Concatenation	.02	.2
Label Goto	.027	.17
Code Goto	.037	.20
Function call (N = # of args and temps)	.09+.012N	.40+.03N

return. Concatenation treats null as a special case simply returning the other value and hence is very fast.

The time to execute the statement labeled LOOP can be obtained by adding the times for assignment, addition, LT() and null concatenation which yields .70 for MAINBOL and .051 for SPITBOL. To this should be added the time to execute a label goto which brings the total control overhead to .87 and .078 milliseconds respectively.

The time to execute a goto is influenced slightly by whether its a fail goto, success goto, and the actual configuration of the goto portion of the statement. The figure given in Table 11.6 is simply an estimate usable mainly because the transfer of control consumes, normally, a very small portion of the total time. The total time required by a function is found by adding the function overhead time, given in Table 11.6 to the time required to execute the function's statements. The time of a RETURN (or FRETURN) is absorbed in the function overhead.

Miscellany   Table 11.7 contains a miscellaneous collection of times for a number of different operations. Some of the operations generate storage which will lengthen subsequent garbage collections but the times given do not reflect this cost (see the Epilogue of TIMEGC, Prog. 11.4). It is interesting to note that with the indirect reference (unary $) the time required by SPITBOL and MAINBOL are almost the same. Because MAINBOL hashes all data strings it does not have to hash for indirect reference. SPITBOL does, but the hashing does not take as long as MAINBOL's interpretive loop. Pattern Matching   The execution of a pattern matching statement consists of five distinct parts: subject evaluation, pattern evaluation (pattern building), pattern matching proper (scanning), object evaluation and replacement. Not all of these operations need be present. The time to execute such a statement is the sum of the times of its component parts. The subject and object evaluation are in the same category as ordinary expression evaluation. The replacement operation is approximately equiva-

Anatomy of a SNOBOL4 Statement

Table 11.7 shows timings of miscellaneous operations. N, where indicated, is the number of characters involved in the operation. Times do not include garbage collection overhead.

Operation	SPITBOL	MAINBOL
Concatenation	.05+.0005N	.35+.0005N
SIZE	.023	.13
DUPL (of a single char)	.045+.0003N	.6+.027N
$ (indirect reference)	.09	.12
PROTOTYPE	.016	.13
A<I>	.03	.30
A<I,J>	.07	.45
ARRAY(N)	.06+.03N	.7+.03N
CODE(' X = Y + Z :(LA)')	1.53	3.7
EVAL('LGT(S1,S2)')	1.2	3.1

lent in time to two concatenations and is given in Table 11.10.

The time required to build a pattern is, to a first approximation, proportional to its size. Table 11.8 contains some representative times for the construction of patterns. Variables A, B and AB are used rather than constants 'A', 'B' and 'AB' because SPITBOL precomputes any constant-valued expression such as 'A' | 'B'. As indicated in the table, the time is measured in the absence of garbage collection. As we will see, garbage collection will approximately double this figure.

Table 11.8 indicates timings (in milliseconds) of selected pattern-building operations. Times do not include that attributable to garbage collection.

Pattern expression	SPITBOL	MAINBOL	No. of Primitives
A | B	.167	.80	2
(A | B) . X	.466	1.1	4
(A | B) . X (A | B) . Y	1.16	2.7	8
BREAK(A)	.07	.36	1
BREAK(AB)	.12	.36	1
BREAK(AB) . X	.41	.93	4
BREAK(AB) . X LEN(1)	.57	1.78	5

where: A = 'A', B = 'B', AB = 'AB'

Chapter 11 - Implementation and Timing

To a first approximation the time required for pattern matching proper (scanning) is some fixed overhead given by Table 11.10 plus the total attributable to individual primitive matches (and failures) as given by Table 11.9. Thus the pattern match below

```
S  = DUPL('A',100)
S     ('A' | 'B')  'C'
```

will have approximately 3N primitive matches, N successful matches by 'A', and N failures each by 'B' and 'C'. Table 11.9 indicates that in SPITBOL it requires .04 milliseconds per string primitive resulting in a total time of 12 milliseconds plus overhead.

Table 11.9 Primitive matching time in Milliseconds per Character for selected primitives. N indicates the number of characters matched for multi-character operations.

Primitive	SPITBOL	MAINBOL
String	.040	.18
RPOS(N)	.020	.20
LEN(N)	.020	.20
POS(N)	.020	.20
NOTANY(S)	.028	.24
NOTANY(*S)	.071	.42
SPAN(S)	.040+.0014N	.25+.0014N
BREAK(S)	.040+.0014N	.25+.0014N

Table 11.10 Other miscellaneous timings associated with pattern matching. Times are in milliseconds and are approximate.

Operation	SPITBOL	MAINBOL
Matching Overhead	.09	.5
Replacement	.082+.0005N	.42+.0005N
Pure String Scanning Rate (per character)	.0014	.04
ARBNO, per iteration	.010	.26
GBAL	.043+.017N	.22+.033N

The reader is cautioned that this analysis is approximate. The time required to scan (P1 | P2) will be less than the sum of the separate scanning times. Also failure will be slightly different than success. If differences on the order of 20 % or so are significant the reader is urged to make his own timing tests of time-critical statements.

The reader should also note that pattern matching heuristics play a significant role in affecting the overall time. Thus the pattern

$$POS(143) \quad \text{'CAT'}$$

will result in two primitive matches in SITBOL AND SPITBOL because of the POS heuristic (see Chapter 7) but will require 145 primitive matches in MAINBOL (assuming the subject is long enough). Also, the futility heuristic can greatly reduce the number of primitives matched.

When the pattern is a simple string, SPITBOL and MAINBOL treat it as a special case resulting in a faster scan as indicated in Table 11.10. If ARBNO appears in a pattern, then to the time required for all primitive matchings must be added the sum of all ARBNO extents multiplied by the given weighting factor given in Table 11.10. BAL, as indicated in Chapter 7, is implemented by the repeated use of a primitive GBAL which matches the shortest nontrivial balanced string. Thus BAL will match the string '(XXXX)' with one application of the primitive GBAL and will match 'XXXXXX' with 6 applications of GBAL. Hence it requires much less time to match the former than it does the latter. For example, in MAINBOL, it requires .22 + (.033)(6) MSEC. to match '(XXXX)' whereas it requires (.22)(6) MSEC. to match 'XXXXXX'.

I/O Timing When INPUT is mentioned in the source program, a line is read. How long does it take? This has no easy answer. Clearly different devices require different times. Even if we restrict our attention to one device, such as the disk, the issue is compounded by a host of factors. As a rough rule of thumb the total time required to move the arm of a disk drive into position (seek time) and wait for the information to come under the read heads (latency) plus the amount of time to actually read is, to grossly simplify, in the order of 100 milliseconds. This figure is not normally charged directly to the user since the operating system can direct the cpu to do other things during the interim. This represents an extraordinarily complex situation not made less so by a variety of charging algorithms and scheduling philosophies. A rule of thumb is that the effective cost is equivalent to half the elapsed time. Hence, for disk, one may assume 50 milliseconds per transmission. Since the time of transmission is relatively independent of the amount transmitted it pays to transmit more than one line at a time. Hence, lines are transmitted in what is called a block. The number of lines per block is called the blocking factor. Typical blocking factors for efficient disk I/O is on the order of 100 which converts the effective transmission time to .5 milliseconds per line.

Chapter 11 - Implementation and Timing

To this we must add the processing time to extract a given line from a buffer. This again will require rule of thumb estimates. In MAINBOL a rather slow Fortran conversion routine causes an I/O operation to require 5 milliseconds per line (IBM 360 Mod 65). Hence if the file is properly blocked, I/O times are dominated by this figure. In SPITBOL, Fortran I/O is sidestepped and the required processing takes about half a millisecond. Hence, in SPITBOL, an I/O reference requires a total of approximately one millisecond.

```
|| Program  ||
||   11.4   ||
||  TIMEGC  ||
```

The following program will permit the caller to time a 'typical' garbage collect. Strings, array elements and programmer-defined datatypes are strewn about in rather chaotic fashion and a call is made to clean some of it up. An argument to TIMEGC can be given which will alter the amount and somewhat the type of litter. The caller may experiment with other values of this number as well as with different kinds of allocation to see if the garbage collect time significantly varies.

```
            DEFINE('TIMEGC(N)I,S,A,L,T,K,FREED')
            DATA('LINK(VALUE,NEXT)')                  :(TIMEGC_END)
```

| Entry point and top of loop. Free everything and issue a garbage collect.

```
TIMEGC     I = ;  S = ;  A = ;  L =
           COLLECT()
           N = IDENT(N)  25
           A = ARRAY(N)
```

| Allocation loop: For each I from 1 through N allocate ap-
| proximately one length-80 string, assign a length I string
| to A<I> and add one element to the linked-list L.

```
TIMEGC_1           I   = I + 1
                   $I  = DUPL(' ',78)  I
                   A<I> = DUPL('*',I)
                   L   = LINK(NULL,L)
                   GE(I,N)                            :F(TIMEGC_1)
```

| Determine the storage remaining. Then loosen about half of
| it and issue a garbage collect. Determine how much was
| collected and how long it took to make the collection.

```
           STREM = COLLECT()
TIMEGC_2
           $I    = ;  A<I> = ;  L = NEXT(L)
           I     = I - 2  GT(I,2)                     :S(TIMEGC_2)
           T     = TIME()
           FREED = FREED + (COLLECT() - STREM)
           TIMEGC = TIMEGC + (TIME() - T)
           K     = K + 1
```

Program 11.4 - TIMEGC   Page 245

```
|   If  not  significantly  more  than  the  resolution of the  |
|   clock,  go  back  for  more.      Otherwise  produce  some  |
|   statistics.                                                 |

            LT(TIMEGC,50 * RESOLUTION())            :S(TIMEGC)
            OUTPUT  =
            OUTPUT = 'IN ' SYSTEM() ' ' K ' GARBAGE COLLECTS'
+           REQUIRED A TOTAL OF ' TIMEGC ' MILLISECONDS TO FREE '
+           FREED ' STORAGE UNITS.'
            TIMEGC  =  CONVERT(TIMEGC,'REAL')
            OUTPUT = 'THIS AVERAGES TO ' (TIMEGC / K) 'MSEC. PER'
+           ' GARBAGE COLLECT AND ' (TIMEGC / FREED) ' MSEC. PER'
+           ' STORAGE UNIT.'                        :(RETURN)
TIMEGC_END
```

Names referenced   Name   Type   Where defined
by TIMEGC: RESOLUTION   Function   Program 11.1

Epilogue

TIMEGC(N) was called for various values of N and the results
are given in Table 11.11.

Table 11.11 Data obtained by calling TIMEGC with a variety of arguments.						
	SPITBOL			MAINBOL		
N	Ave GC Time (MSEC)	Storage Coll. per GC	Time per byte (Mcrsec)	Ave GC Time (MSEC)	Storage Coll. per GC	Time per byte (Mcrsec)
50	17	3.4K	5.0	98	5.8K	17.0
100	27	8.1K	3.3	105	13.5K	8.9
150	41	14.0K	2.9	144	21.6K	6.7
200	51	21.3K	2.4	196	31.5K	6.3
250	77	30.0K	2.6	220	42.6K	5.2
300	104	39.4K	2.6	224	55.0K	4.1
350	138	50.0K	2.8	256	68.4K	3.9
400	183	62.4K	2.9	304	83.3K	3.5
450	210	76.0K	2.8	343	100 K	3.5

As might be expected, the time to garbage collect is a function of how many allocated objects are lying about in core. For small collections, SPITBOL has a clear advantage over MAINBOL; but this advantage curiously diminishes as the collections become larger. (This anomaly has yet to be explained.) Also, as collections get larger, the time required per byte collected seems to converge to about three microseconds. This figure is not absolute since garbage collections in which very little storage as a fraction of the whole is retrieved can require much more than this. Nevertheless, it serves as a useful rule of thumb for estimating the garbage collection overhead attributable to an operation that allocates storage. For example Table 11.7 indicates the time for concatenation to be .05+.0005N milliseconds in SPITBOL. To this we must add a factor attributable to later garbage collection. In SPITBOL, a string requires 6 + N bytes of storage as indicated in Table 11.12. Using a figure of 3 microseconds per byte, the real cost of concatenation is .068 + .0035N milliseconds.

Table 11.12 shows the amount of storage required for a variety of datatypes. Storage is given in bytes.

Datatype	SPITBOL	MAINBOL
String (N is no. of chars.)	6 + N	32 + N
Variable (N is number of characters in name)	38 + N	32 + N
Patterns (N is no. of primitives, A is no. of ANY, NOTANY's, B is no. of BREAK & SPAN's*, figure is approximate)	16 + 16N + 32A + 256B	8 + 32N
Arrays (N is no. of elements and D is no. of dimensions)	20+8N+8D	16+8N+16D
Prog. Defined Data Object (N is no. of fields)	8 + 8N	8 + 8N
Table (E is no. of items in the table and I is the initial first argument to the TABLE function)	12+24E+4I	8+16E

* If the argument to BREAK or SPAN is only one character, no additional storage is required (B is 0).

Program 11.6 - FPROFILE

```
┌─────────────────┐
│ %%% he Inner Loop │   It is characteristic of  many  programs
│  %   ┌──────────┘   that  approximately  90% of the time is
│  %   │ spent in 10% of the program.  This is true of SNOBOL4
│  %   │ itself and it tends to be true of programs written in
│  %   │ the language.   Whether or not the  topology  of  the
└──────┘ program  merits   the   epithet,   the   point  or points
```
within the program where most of the time is spent is called
the 'inner loop'.   While the SITBOL system has an automatic
method for determining which statements are responsible for
the most time, most SNOBOL4 systems do not.   There do exist,
however, certain tracing tools which may be used to examine a
program's behaviour   and   extract at least approximate timing
information.

```
┌─────────────────┐
││  Program    ││   LPROG() will return  the  length  (i.e.  the
││   11.5      ││   number of statements) in the SNOBOL4 program
││   LPROG     ││   in which it is called.   LPROG will actually
└─────────────┘   cause  one   more statement to be compiled at
```
run-time so that its repeated use will return slightly dif-
ferent values.   If new code is compiled in the interim, the
value returned by LPROG will be augmented by the number of new
statements

       DEFINE('LPROG()')   :(LPROG_END)

| Entry point: Compile a statement and return 1 less than |
| its statement number. |

LPROG   :<CODE(' LPROG = &STNO   : (RETURN)')>
LPROG_END

Epilogue

LPROG has intrinsic interest of its own as well as being a
useful, if not essential, tool in constructing an array to
record a program's profile (as we shall see).

```
┌─────────────────┐
││  Program    ││   FPROFILE is a program which determines   the
││   11.6      ││   number  of times each statement is executed
││  FPROFILE   ││   in the program in  which  it  is  embedded.
└─────────────┘   This is called the frequency profile of the
```
program.   The statistics gathering begins when the initializa-
tion section of FPROFILE is executed and tracing is turned on.
Hence FPROFILE is   normally   placed before the program to be
monitored but must be placed after the LPROG function which it
calls during initialization. For each statement executed after
tracing has been established, FPROFILE is called and a tabula-
tion is made in an array (FP_ARY). At any given time during
the course of execution, statement number N will have been executed FP_ARY<N> times.

Chapter 11 - Implementation and Timing

```
               DEFINE('FPROFILE()')
```

Allocate an array to gather statistics and set up tracing on the keyword &STCOUNT.

```
        FP_ARY  =  ARRAY(LPROG())
        TRACE(.STCOUNT, 'KEYWORD',,'FPROFILE')
        &TRACE  =  1000000                        :(FPROFILE_END)
```

Entry point of FPROFILE (called at each executable statement).

```
FPROFILE    FP_ARY<&LASTNO> = FP_ARY<&LASTNO> + 1    :(RETURN)
FPROFILE_END
```

Names referenced   Name   Type   Where defined
by FPROFILE: LPROG *   Function   Program 11.5
* indicates name is referenced in the initialization section.

```
┌─────────────┐
││ Program  ││
││  11.7    ││
││ TPROFILE ││
└─────────────┘
```
A time profile of a program indicates the relative time spent in each statement. In a language like SNOBOL4, where there is a relatively high variation in the time required to execute any given statement, a time profile is much more desirable than a frequency profile.

TPROFILE, a modification of FPROFILE, allocates to the statement just executed the difference between the current time and the last previous time. Unhappily, the time required to gather the statistic may be as large or even larger than the time being measured. However it is likely to be more valuable an indicator than FPROFILE and in many cases can give a surprisingly accurate time profile.

```
               DEFINE('TPROFILE() S,T')
```

Set up tracing. Times are tabulated in TP_ARY. TPROFILE will be called at the start of each statement to be executed.

```
        TP_ARY  =  ARRAY(LPROG())
        TRACE(.STCOUNT,'KEYWORD',,'TPROFILE')
        &TRACE  =  1000000                        :(TPROFILE_END)
```

Entry point: Save the statement number (S) of the statement about to be executed and quickly obtain the time (T). Augment TP_ARY according to the last interrupted statement.

```
TPROFILE        S  =  &LASTNO
                T  =  TIME()
        TP_ARY<LAST_STNO> = TP_ARY<LAST_STNO> + T - LAST_TIME
                LAST_STNO  =  S
```

Exercises for chapter 11   Page 249

TPROFILE_END   LAST_TIME = TIME()   : (RETURN)

Names referenced   Name   Type   Where defined
by TPROFILE: LPROG *   Function   Program 11.5
* indicates name is referenced in the initialization section.

Epilogue

To test the two profiling programs, the function BNORM (Prog.
10.1) was used. It was passed a string of approximately 120
characters containing 10 BSPACEs and two USCOREs. To average
out noise effects, BNORM was called 250 times. The results of
applying FPROFILE and TPROFILE to the program are shown in
Figure 11.3.

The data was collected on the SITBOL system so that a
comparison could be made with a 'true' time profile as
provided by a built-in facility. Figure 11.4 shows the results
of turning on the built-in profiler. As might be expected,
the times are a little higher for TPROFILE than they are truly
since each statement executed is accredited with a little of
the overhead used to gather the statistic. But the results
are surprisingly close due to the relatively small amount of
time required to execute a simple assignment statement.

For running TPROFILE on SPITBOL it is imperative to obtain the
TIME() before &LASTNO because the latter represents a relatively slow operation. Exercise 11.11 provides a method of
doing this.

???
???????????????????????? EXERCISES ????????????????????????????
???

| Exercise 11.1 | Which   of   the   following   linguistic
                    facilities require a run-time symbol table?

(a)   Pattern Matching
(b)   a Sort facility
(c)   Run-time compilation
(d)   Redefinition of functions
(e)   Go to a label whose name is computed
(f)   call a function whose name is computed
(g)   Linked-list operations

| Exercise 11.2 | Each method below for computing hash num-
                    bers has at least one flaw.   Indicate
whether it is too time-consuming (T), does not provide a good
spread (S) or is not repeatable (R).   More than one letter
might be applicable. Assume each character is an 8-bit code

Page 250   Chapter 11 - Implementation and Timing

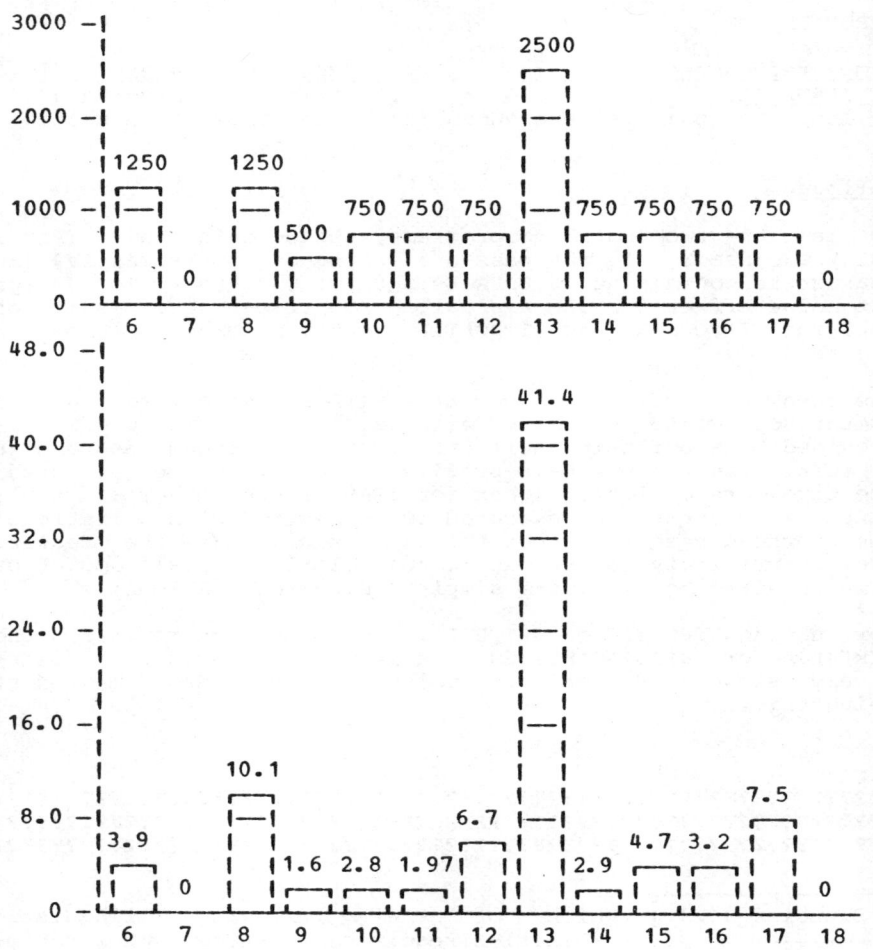

Figure 11.3

The result of applying FPROFILE (above) and TPROFILE (below) to 250 calls to the BNORM function. The numbers below the bars refer to statement numbers in BNORM. Times are in seconds.

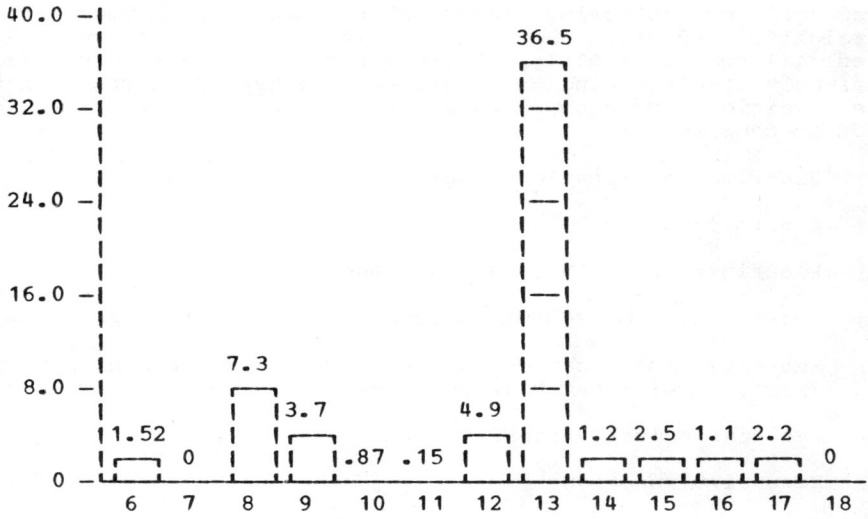

Figure 11.4

The histogram above shows the 'true' time profile of the program run to produce the histograms in Figure 11.3. Times are given in seconds.

which represents some integer between 0 and 255. L is the length of the Hash Array.

(a) Multiply all the characters together ignoring overflows. Then divide by L and use the remainder.

(b) Divide the size of the string by L and use the remainder.

(c) Let L be 256 and choose simply the first character as the hash number.

(d) Let L be 256 and Exclusive-OR all the characters together.

(e) Add the size of the string to the last previous hash number and divide by L, using the remainder.

(f) Use the machine address of the first character of the string.

| Exercise 11.3 | As indicated in the text, compilers can be ranked from Type 0 to Type 4. Each increase in compilation complexity brings about a decrease in run-time

Chapter 11 - Implementation and Timing

flexibility. What type of compiler is required to implement each of the following language features in a reasonably straightforward way. For example, if your answer is Type 2, then all compilers of Type 2 and lower should have no special difficulty implementing the feature. By type 3 assume that the decision to push a value or a pointer to a variable is made at compile time.

(a) Run-time modification of operator precedence

(b) A Sort function.

(c) Redefinition of SNOBOL4 functions

(d) Redefinition of SNOBOL4 operators

(e) Run-time modification of the meanings of characters (E.g., hereinafter R is an operator).

(f) Declarationless variables

(g) Recursive functions

(h) Run-time trace requests on variables

(i) Run-time macros (hereafter all strings in the text of the program of the form X shall be regarded as string Y).

| Exercise 11.4 | Which of the following facilities are more likely to be associated with a floating form of storage management and which with fixed storage?

(a) Declaring a variable to be string and giving it a maximum length.

(b) Arrays containing arbitrary and mixed datatypes.

(c) Garbage Collection.

(d) Functions which return arrays.

(e) String assignment implemented via copying.

| Exercise 11.5 | Give an example of a statement which if timed using TIMER would result in an infinite loop.

| Exercise 11.6 | Modify RESOLUTION (Prog. 11.1) so that it averages ten attempts to obtain the resolution. Make sure the computation is done once and not at each call.

| Exercise 11.7 | One can define the factorial of n (normally written n!) as follows:

```
        DEFINE('F(N)')           :(F_END)
F       F  =  LE(N,1)   1        :S(RETURN)
        F  =  N + F(N - 1)       :(RETURN)
F_END
```

Estimate the time required (in SPITBOL) to compute F(1), F(2) and F(n) for arbitrary n. Compare the time required for this recursive program with the following iterative version of the factorial function.

```
        DEFINE('F(N)')           :(F_END)
F       F  =  1
F_1     F  =  GT(N,1)  F * N     :F(RETURN)
        N  =  N - 1              :(F_1)
F_END
```

| Exercise 11.8 | You are writing a pre-processor in SNOBOL4 statement for the occurence of a special character (say %). If the special character is there, the program will do something interesting. Otherwise it copies the line intact. Write an 'inner loop' that does nothing but read and write and check for the existence of the special character. Assuming the lines containing the special character are relatively rare, the speed of processing approximates the speed of the inner loop. Compute the speed of your pre-processor in statements per minute operating in SPITBOL. Assume I/O time is one millisecond per line.

| Exercise 11.9 | Since error and trace messages are given in terms of SNOBOL4 statement numbers it is helpful to have a method of producing such numbers for statements compiled via the CODE function. Redefine the CODE function in an upward compatible way so that in addition to compiling code it sets the global variable CODENO to the number of the statement (or first statement of a sequence) being compiled. (Hint: Look at the LPROG function and use the fact that SNOBOL4 assigns statement numbers sequentially without breaks. Only two statements are required in the body of the function.)

| Exercise 11.10 | Modify LPROG (Prog. 11.5) so that it will always return the value it returned when it was first called. (Hint: This can be done by the insertion of 5 characters.)

> **Exercise 11.11** TPROFILE (Prog. 11.7) attempts to obtain the TIME() as quickly as possible but is torn by the fact that the first statement executed must capture the &LASTNO. Suggest how TPROFILE can be improved so that the TIME() is captured as quickly as possible in the first statement without losing the value of &LASTNO.

CHAPTER TWELVE

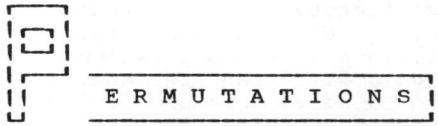
ERMUTATIONS

```
                CONTENTS

        PERMUTATION ............ 12.1
        PERM ................... 12.2
        PERMS .................. 12.3
        REORDER ................ 12.4
        LPERM .................. 12.5
        IP ..................... 12.6
```

Chapter 12 - Permutations

 here are n! ways of rearranging (or permuting) n objects and these are referred to as permutations. For example, there are 3! (=6) ways of permuting the 3 characters of the string 'ABC' as follows

```
ABC
ACB
BAC
BCA
CAB
CBA
```

There is a body of literature on the subject of permutations [Algorithms, 1968, p. 829] owing, perhaps, more to the value of studying permutations as a computational exercise rather than for strictly utilitarian reasons. Yet, the study of techniques employed to solve this problem is undoubtedly useful in discovering techniques for solving more practical problems.

Permutation routines are subject to a variety of different ground rules. The object to be permuted may be an array, a list or a string. The array may be an array of integers $\{1, 2, \ldots, n\}$ or an arbitrary array. The permutation may be lexicographic; in the case of strings this would imply that the permutations are produced in alphabetic order. In general, if the objects to be permuted can be compared relative to each other (well-ordered in mathematical parlance) a lexicographic order is defined on the permutation, and some algorithms are constrained to produce the permutations in this order. Sometimes the objects to be permuted contain duplicates such as the characters of 'MISSISSIPPI' and the permutation program is required to produce only those permutations which are truly distinct. These are sometimes known as "permutations with repetitions" or, as we will call them, reorderings. Finally, the permutation wanted may be a purely random one and the algorithm for doing that is included in the section on Stochastic Strings.

| %%%% ERMUTATION RECORDS | We will speak in this section of permuting n+1 objects. This may seem more awkward than speaking of permuting n objects but it will have the advantage of making our notation simpler. The number of permutations of n+1 objects is (n+1)! and the reasoning is as follows. Assume that the objects are selected one at a time in an arbitrary sequence to be placed in some permutation. The first object drawn can be placed in only one way. The second object drawn can be placed to the left or the right of the first object; the 3rd object can be placed to the left, between, or the the right of the previous 2 objects. In general, the ith object can be placed in any of i different positions and a little reflection will reveal that each position will lead to

a different permutation. Moreover, every permutation can be obtained by this means. Hence, the total number of permutations can be obtained by multiplying all these combinations which yields the result (n+1)!.

This reasoning leads naturally into the idea of a **permutation record** which is important computationally, because most algorithms depend on some form of this record to record past history. Let

$$i_1 \; i_2 \; \ldots \; i_n$$

be a sequence of integers obeying the following inequalities

$$0 \leq i_1 \leq 1$$
$$0 \leq i_2 \leq 2$$
$$\vdots$$
$$0 \leq i_n \leq n$$

For example:

$$1 \; 0 \; 2 \; 4 \; 2$$

is a permutation record for n = 5. A permutation record of length n can be thought of as representing a permutation of n+1 objects as follows: the first object is placed down. The second object is placed to the left or right of the first object depending on whether i_1 is a 0 or a 1. This process is continued until the (n+1)st object is placed in the position indicated by i_n.

For some applications it is convenient to speak of the "Ith permutation" of n+1 objects where I ranges from 0 to (n+1)!-1. The integer I can be related to a permutation record as follows:

$$I = i_1 + i_2(2!) + i_3(3!) + \ldots + i_n(n!) \qquad (12.1)$$

Such an I will be called the **permutation number** of the given record. The permutation record may be regarded as a representation in the factorial number system of the permutation number [Knuth, Vol.2, 175 and Pager, 1970]. For example, let i_1 i_2 i_3 = 1 0 2. Then

$$I = 1 + 0(2!) + 2(3!)$$
$$= 1 + 0 + 12 = 13$$

Thus every permutation record yields some permutation number. But is that number unique, or will two different records lead to the same number? We will show that not only is there a unique record for each number but that the record is easily reconstructed. First, note that 2 divides every term on the right hand side of (12.1) except the first so that

Page 258   Chapter 12 - Permutations

$$i_1 = \text{REMDR}(I,2)$$

To determine the remaining n-1 elements of the permutation record, set $I_1 = (I - i_1)/2$ so that

$$I_1 = i_2 + i_3(3!/2) + \ldots + i_n(n!/2)$$

In this equation, each term is divisible by 3 except the first so that

$$i_2 = \text{REMDR}(I_1,3)$$

This process of division and remaindering can be repeated until all coefficients have been obtained. Hence, given a number I, the permutation record can be deduced.

```
|¦     Program     ¦|
|¦      12.1       ¦|
|¦   PERMUTATION   ¦|
```
PERMUTATION(S,I) will return the Ith permutation of the string S where I is a permutation number as defined above. If I is 0 then the permutation is equal to S itself. If I ≥ N! where N = SIZE(S), then PERMUTATION will fail. Note that we can obtain all permutations of a given string in this way provided N!-1 ≤ the maximum integer. On the IBM 360, with a maximum integer of $2^{31}-1$, this amounts to the restriction that N≤12. This seems rather severe and Exercise 12.11 suggests a remedy. Note that if one were cycling through each permutation of a set of objects one would be better advised to use a routine specially designed for that purpose (such as PERM, Program 12.2).

| PERMUTATION(S,I) will return the Ith permutation of the |
| string S. |

DEFINE('PERMUTATION(S,I)RADIX,T,S1,N')
                    :(PERMUTATION_END)

| Entry point and top of loop: If I is 0 or drops to 0 as a |
| result of repeated division, return the value remaining in |
| S and the characters already accumulated in PERMUTATION. |

PERMUTATION
    PERMUTATION = EQ(I,0)   PERMUTATION S   :S(RETURN)

| Otherwise remove the next character of S (calling it T) |
| and insert it into the position determined by the next |
| value (N) of the permutation record. If no T could be |
| found then fail because this means I was too big. |

        S   LEN(1) . T =   :F(FRETURN)
        RADIX = RADIX + 1
        N   = REMDR(I,RADIX)
        PERMUTATION   RTAB(N) . S1 = S1 T

```
        I = I / RADIX                 :(PERMUTATION)
PERMUTATION_END
```

Epilogue

Characters are inserted one at a time into the string PERMUTATION in a position depending on the value of the permutation record. The value indicates a number of characters from the right because in this way a 0 permutation and only a 0 will result in an identity operation.

PERMUTATION is not well suited for arrays (as it stands) because insertion of an object into an array (while neighbors are moved apart) is not a natural operation. Instead of interpreting each element of the permutation record as an insertion point, each value can be regarded as an interchange distance, as follows. Interchange A<2> and A<1> according to the value of i_1. That is, interchange

$$A<2> \text{ and } A<2-i_1>$$

Then interchange A<3> with A<3-i_2>. Continue in this way until A<n+1> and A<n+1-i_n> are interchanged.

Can all permutations be obtained in this way? By a bit of backward reasoning we can conclude that they can. From the position in the permuted array of the last element of the original array one can determine the value of i_n. Hence the scene as it existed prior to the last interchange can be reconstructed. Continuing in this way, the entire permutation record can be reconstructed. That means that every different permutation record gives rise to a different permutation. But there are n+1! permutation records and hence all permutations must be obtainable.

```
┌─────────────────┐
|| Program     ||
||   12.2      ||
||   PERM      ||
└─────────────────┘
```
Although the function PERMUTATION can yield a particular one of a class of permutations, it is not particularly well suited for cycling through all permutations of a given set of elements. This is because each permutation is generated freshly. It is more efficient to continually modify the last permutation to obtain the next. Trotter [1962] produced a scheme in which only one interchange per call was necessary to obtain each permutation. His method is basically as follows. Imagine the objects to be permuted to be arranged from left to right and numbered from 1 to n. Interchange objects 1 and 2 to produce a new permutation. Then interchange objects 2 and 3, 3 and 4, etc. In this way the object which had been on the left will swing in daisy chain fashion over to the right. When it reaches the right side it stops, the n-1 objects to its left are permuted once and, on subsequent calls, the last element is daisy-chained back from right to left. When it reaches the left, the other elements are again permuted and the process repeats. One needs a permutation record of sorts to

Page 260   Chapter 12   -   Permutations

record this movement and this is done as follows. I_1 contains
the position of the   1st element among the other (n-1) elements. I_2 holds the position of the 2nd element among the
other   (n-2)   elements,   etc. (A separate array can hold ±1 to
denote direction of movement.) This system has the nice
property that most permutations are done by a single test,
increment, and interchange. The programming can be simplified
by the use of recursion (not originally given by Trotter)
without significantly adding to the time (see Exercise 12.12).

PERM(A) uses Trotter's algorithm to cycle through every permutation of a singly dimensioned array with lower bound 1. The
first time PERM is called the array is not modified but
initialization is made. The initial value of A is regarded as
the first permutation. On subsequent calls, the argument to
PERM (presumably the same array) is permuted. Finally, when
no more permutations remain, PERM will fail and reset itself
to its initial state awaiting a new array.

```
| PERM(A)  will permute the elements of the array A, failing |
| when no more permutations remain.  A is assumed to have at |
| least 2 elements.                                          |

            DEFINE('PERM(A)','PERM_INIT')    :(PERM_END)

| PERM_INIT is the entry point on the first  call  to  PERM. |
| First obtain the size of A (by converting prototype to in- |
| teger)  and  retain  it for future reference in the global |
| variable SIZE_A.                                           |

PERM_INIT     SIZE_A  =  +PROTOTYPE(A)

| Set up arrays to indicate location and direction of  move- |
| ment of elements.  Initialize location arrays to 1 because |
| every element starts in 1st position relative to remaining |
| members.   Initialize  direction  array  to 1 to indicate  |
| rightward movement.  -1 indicates leftward movement.       |

              LOC_ELEMENT  =  ARRAY('0:' SIZE_A - 2, 1)
              DIR_ELEMENT  =  ARRAY('0:' SIZE_A - 2, 1)

| Redefine the entry point.  All outside calls will have one |
| argument so that I and  OFFSET  will  initially  have  the |
| value null.   When PERM is called recursively I and OFFSET |
| are  given different values.  I represents the item to be  |
| permuted and OFFSET represents the  extent  to  which  the |
| subpermutation  of elements I, I + 1, ..., N - 1 is offset |
| from the overall permutation.                              |

         DEFINE('PERM(A,I,OFFSET)RL,D,LIMIT,AL')    :(RETURN)

| Steady state entry point: Determine the relative location  |
| (RL) of the Ith element in the subarray and the  direction |
| (D)  in  which it is moving.  Also determine the LIMIT of  |
| travel in this direction.   If the limit has been reached, |
```

Program 12.3 - PERMS

```
| go to PERM_1.                                                        |

PERM         RL    =  LOC_ELEMENT<I>              :F(FRETURN)
             D     =  DIR_ELEMENT<I>
             LIMIT =  EQ(D,1)     SIZE_A - I
             LIMIT =  EQ(D,-1)    1
             EQ(LIMIT, RL)                        :S(PERM_1)
| Determine the absolute location (AL) of the Ith   element, |
| swap elements, update location vector, and return.         |

             AL  =  RL + OFFSET
             SWAP(.A<AL>, .A<AL + D>)
             LOC_ELEMENT<I>  =  RL + D            :(RETURN)
| Reverse  the  direction  of  movement  of the Ith element. |
| Determine the OFFSET of the subpermutation and attempt  to |
| make  the  permutation; if success return; otherwise, reset|
| entry point and fail.                                      |

PERM_1       DIR_ELEMENT<I>  =  -D
             OFFSET  =  EQ(D,1)    OFFSET + 1
             PERM(A, I + 1, OFFSET)               :S(RETURN)
PERM_F       DEFINE('PERM(A)', 'PERM_INIT')       :(FRETURN)
PERM_END
```

Names referenced   Name   Type   Where defined
by PERM: SWAP   Function   Program 3.14

Epilogue

The program is written recursively because this is the way the algorithm is described, and because the inefficiencies of recursion will not manifest themselves in substantially slower programs. A difficulty involved in specifying the function recursively was that the recursive call is to permute an array which does, not exist in isolation but only as part of a larger array. Hence, we must give additional information such as the OFFSET of the start of the array with respect to the larger array and I, the level of the item to be moved. The OFFSET and level have been defined in such a way that the outer call should be made with these values equal to 0. Hence if the user ignores them which he is instructed to do and passes only one argument, the array, he will get the correct results.

```
|| Program ||
||  12.3   ||
||  PERMS  ||
```

Although PERM can be modified to permute strings, we here seek an algorithm specifically intended for use with the string data type in hopes of obtaining something simpler if not more efficient. As we recall from Chapter 3, a permutation can be regarded as a positional transformation and hence can be programmed to run rapidly via the REPLACE function. Thus if P(S) is a permutation of the

Page 262   Chapter 12 - Permutations

string S and if X is the first n characters from &ALPHABET where n is the size of S, then

$$\text{REPLACE}(P(X), X, S)$$

will be equal to P(S). The difficulty, it would seem, is that in order to obtain P(S) we need construct the permutation first. But this difficulty can be surmounted by the following consideration. Let

$$S_1 = \text{REPLACE}(P(X), X, S)$$
$$S_2 = \text{REPLACE}(P(X), X, S_1)$$
$$S_3 = \text{REPLACE}(P(X), X, S_2)$$

etc. Each consecutive permutation is obtained by permuting according to P the last previously obtained permutation. It is customary to denote the compounding of permutations in this way by product notation and the repeated application of the same permutation therefore is denoted by exponential notation as:

$$S_1 = P(S)$$
$$S_2 = PP(S) = P^2(S)$$
$$S_3 = P^3(S)$$

etc. One interesting question is: does there exist a permutation P for which its various powers cycle through all the permutations. This question is answered by group theory. The set of permutations of n objects can be regarded as the elements of a group (of cardinality n!) where the group operation is the "multiplication" described above. The question becomes, is the Permutation group of n elements cyclic? The answer is readily given as no (see, for example, Zassenhaus [1958]), but we can produce almost as good a result by obtaining a small set of basic permutations, from which we can produce all the others.

In what follows we will speak of <u>rotating the first k characters of a string one place</u> or simply <u>rotating the first k characters</u> to mean the transformation:

$$S \text{ LEN}(1) . C \text{ LEN}(K - 1) . S1 = S1 C$$

In words, the first k characters are picked up, rotated once to the left and set down again. Thus, rotating the first 3 characters of 'ROTATE' yields 'OTRATE'. Rotating the first k characters of a string is a positional transformation and can be done at high speed provided appropriate REPLACE arguments have been set up in advance. Let R(k) denote the operation of rotating the first k characters of a string. Then R(n) will rotate all the characters, and R(1) will do nothing. All permutations of a string can be obtained by a suitable combination of R(i)'s as follows.

To produce the first permutation apply R(n). To obtain the 2nd apply R(n) again. Upon applying R(n) for the nth time, we

Program 12.3 - PERMS

will have produced the original string which of course we cannot return. At this point we apply R(n-1) and return the resulting string. On subsequent calls R(n) is applied until the nth time thereafter at which point R(n-1) is again applied. Upon n-1 repetitions of this sequence of events we will have returned to the starting point at which time we apply R(n-2). So the sequence continues until, at last, there emerges an attempt to apply R(1). R(1) is a 'no-op' and this is the signal that all permutations have been produced. A permutation record is used to record the number of applications of each type of rotation.

The idea of obtaining the sequence of permutations by a suitable number of rotations was suggested by Peck and Schrack [1962] and suffered from the fact that Trotter's algorithm (which appeared later) produced a superior result for arrays. But in the case of strings, rotations can be programmed to be as efficient as interchanges. Since the computational backdrop is simpler for the Peck and Schrack algorithm we will use it to write PERMS. We have come full cycle on this one.

```
| PERMS(S) will permute the characters of the string S.  S |
| is assumed to be at least 2 characters long and no greater |
| than the size of &ALPHABET.  The argument S should be the |
| string which had been returned by PERMS on the last call. |
| When no more permutations remain, PERMS will fail.        |
```

          DEFINE('PERMS(S)T,N,C,K','PERMS_INIT')   :(PERMS_END)

```
| Initialization entry point: N_R<I> will record the number |
| of applications of R(I).  FIRST_OP is an array such that |
| REPLACE( FIRST_OP<I>, SECOND_OP, S) will be equivalent to |
| applying R(I) to S.                                       |
```

PERMS_INIT
          N   = SIZE(S)
          N_R = ARRAY('2:' N, 0)
          &ALPHABET   LEN(N) . SECOND_OP   :F(ERROR)
          FIRST_OP =   ARRAY('2:' N, SECOND_OP)
          K   = N + 1
PERMS_I1 K   = K - 1
          FIRST_OP<K>   LEN(1) . S1 TAB(K) . S2 = S2 S1
+   :S(PERMS_I1)
          DEFINE('PERMS(S)I,K')
          PERMS = S   :(RETURN)

```
| Steady state entry point: Initialize K to the size of the |
| string.                                                   |
```

PERMS   K   = SIZE(S)

```
| Apply R(K); failure implies that K=1 in which case we |
| branch to PERMS_1.                                    |
```

Page 264   Chapter 12 - Permutations

PERMS_1
         S   =   REPLACE(FIRST_OP<K>, SECOND_OP, S)   :F(PERMS_2)
┌───┐
│ Bump N_R<K>; if this number equals 0 mod K we have come   │
│ full cycle; decrement K and repeat. Otherwise return S.   │
└───┘
         N_R<K> =   N_R<K> + 1
         K   =   EQ(REMDR(N_R<K>, K), 0)   K - 1   :S(PERMS_1)
         PERMS   =   S   :(RETURN)
┌───┐
│ If K is 1 no more permutations remain.   Fail but ready   │
│ PERMS for next set of permutations.   │
└───┘
PERMS_2 DEFINE('PERMS(S)T,N,S1,S2','PERMS_INIT')   :(FRETURN)
PERMS_END

┌──────────────┐
││ Program   ││   We define a <u>reordering</u> of a string S as a
││   12.4   ││   permutation which produces a new string. For
││ REORDER   ││   example, the string 'AAB' has 6 permutations
└──────────────┘   but only 3 are distinct (determined by the
position of 'B') and so has only 3 reorderings.   Reorderings
are usually more significant than permutations in string
processing where repeated elements are more common than in,
say, arrays of numbers.

REORDER(S,OS) will produce a reordering of the characters of
the string S where OS is an ordered version of the string S.
REORDER can be used to cycle through every different string
composed of the characters of a given string, starting with
the ordered string OS. It will FAIL when no more strings
remain. Thus, using Program 3.1, ORDER, to order the string S
we can print every reordering of S by the statements

              OS =   ORDER(S)
              OUTPUT =   OS
LOOP   OUTPUT =   REORDER(OUTPUT, OS)   :S(LOOP)

Note that in the above, the previously generated string is
used as the next input.

It so happens that ORDER(S) will place the characters of S in
alphabetic order. It is not necessary to be so strict. In
fact, all that is necessary is that the ordered string contain
like characters in adjacent positions. Thus if the string is
'MISSISSIPPI', then 'SSSSIIIIPPM' will be a suitably ordered
version.

The number of reorderings of a string can be substantially
less than the number of permutations. Let N be the length of
a string S having n different characters. Let there be k_1
instances of the first character, k_2 instances of the second,
etc. Then the number of reorderings is

Program 12.4 - REORDER

$$\frac{N!}{k_1! \; k_2! \; \ldots \; k_n!}$$

For 'MISSISSIPPI' the number of reorderings is

$$\frac{11!}{4! \; 4! \; 2!} = 34650$$

It would take about 48 pages to print all the reorderings of 'MISSISSIPPI'. To print the permutations would require about 50,000 pages.

```
┌─────────────────────────────────────────────────────────────┐
│ REORDER(S,OS) is used to produce the next permutation       │
│ (with repetitions) of the string S.  OS is an ordered ver-  │
│ sion of the string S.  It is called recursively.            │
└─────────────────────────────────────────────────────────────┘
```

          DEFINE('REORDER(S,ORDERED_S)C,FRONT,S1,LAST,D,OS')
                                    :(REORDER_END)

```
┌─────────────────────────────────────────────────────────────┐
│ Entry Point:  Obtain in C the last character of ORDERED_S.  │
│ If no such character exists, S must be the null string.     │
│ Since this has no reordering, we fail.                      │
└─────────────────────────────────────────────────────────────┘
```

REORDER   ORDERED_S   RTAB(1) LEN(1) . C   :F(FRETURN)

```
┌─────────────────────────────────────────────────────────────┐
│ Then work any character of type C toward the front of S.    │
│ First remove the characters of type C (if any) that al-     │
│ ready are at the front of S.                                │
└─────────────────────────────────────────────────────────────┘
```

           S   (SPAN(C) | NULL) . FRONT =

```
┌─────────────────────────────────────────────────────────────┐
│ Look for an interior C and interchange it with its          │
│ predecessor, grouping in with C all the characters ob-      │
│ tained previously in FRONT.  If an interior C cannot be     │
│ found, go to REORDER_1.                                     │
└─────────────────────────────────────────────────────────────┘
```

           S   ARB . S1 LEN(1) . D C =   :F(REORDER_1)
           REORDER = S1 FRONT C D S   :(RETURN)

```
┌─────────────────────────────────────────────────────────────┐
│ If all characters of type C have been worked toward the     │
│ front, control flows to REORDER_1.  Here we recursively     │
│ obtain a new sub-ordering and put all the characters of     │
│ type C on the back end.                                     │
└─────────────────────────────────────────────────────────────┘
```

REORDER_1 ORDERED_S   BREAK(C) . OS
           REORDER = REORDER(S,OS) FRONT :S(RETURN) F(FRETURN)
REORDER_END

Epilogue

We normally make concessions to the aim of providing the simplest possible calling sequence, feeling that simplicity and convenience are two of the most desirable qualities that a

Page 266   Chapter 12   -   Permutations

program have. Strictly speaking, the second argument to
REORDER is unnecessary inasmuch as the second argument can be
reconstructed unambiguously from the first. But in the interest of avoiding gross inefficiencies the second argument is
made mandatory.

```
┌─────────────────┐
│ │   Program    │ │
│ │    12.5      │ │
│ │    LPERM     │ │
└─────────────────┘
```
As we have stated earlier, some applications
require permutations to be lexically
ordered. This added restriction complicates
the problem of permuting slightly; several
solutions have been proposed. One by Shen [1963] has been
found [Ord-Smith 1967] to be the "best and fastest" of a number of lexical permutation algorithms. It operates as follows.
Obviously the first permutation is the string in lowest alphabetical order, i.e. the one produced by ORDER. The next
permutation is obtained by interchanging the last 2 characters. It is also clear that the last permutation will be the
one in reversed lexical ordering as shown below:

               ABCDEF
               ABCDFE
                  .
                  .
                  .
               FEDCBA

To obtain the next higher lexical ordering we find the smallest sized suffix that can be increased lexically. This is
done by scanning from right to left looking for a character
smaller than the previous character. This we call the pivotal
character. All characters to its left must remain unchanged.
The character moved in (from the right) to take the place of
the pivotal character must be the next higher character to the
right of the pivotal character. This is called the replacement
character. All other characters in the suffix must be placed
into the lowest lexical state. This is most easily done by
interchanging the pivotal character with its replacement and
reversing all characters other than the replacement. An example of this operation is shown in Figure 12.1.

LPERM(S) will return the reordering of S next higher in lexical order. It uses the Shen algorithm modified for SNOBOL4.
If no lexically greater permutation exists for S, LPERM will
fail. to obtain all reorderings of a string the previously-
returned string must be passed as argument; the initial argument must equal ORDER(S).

```
┌─────────────────────────────────────────────────────────────┐
│ LPERM(S) returns the next reordering in lexicographic       │
│ order of the string S.                                      │
└─────────────────────────────────────────────────────────────┘
```

           DEFINE('LPERM(S) P,T,X,R,Y,HIGHS')

Program 12.5 - LPERM   Page 267

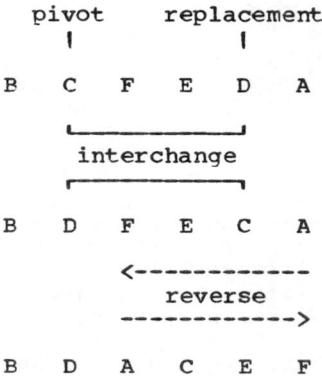

Figure 12.1

An example illustrating the method used by LPERM
to obtain the next permutation in lexical order.

```
| Find the alphabetically highest character.                          |

          &ALPHABET    RTAB(1)    LEN(1)  .  HIGH_CHAR
                                             :(LPERM_END)

| Entry point: Reverse the string to make scanning from the |
| back  end  easier.   Also place dummy character onto end so |
| that unevaluated expressions work.                          |

LPERM      S  =  REVERSE(S)    HIGH_CHAR

| Look for pivot character (P).   If none can be  found  the  |
| argument  was in its highest lexical state.   We therefore  |
| fail.                                                       |

          S   LEN(1) $ T   LEN(1) $ P   *LGT(T,P)    :F(FRETURN)

| Search &ALPHABET for the set of all characters > P.  Call |
| them HIGHS.   Then search S for the replacement  character |
| (R).                                                       |

          &ALPHABET    BREAK(P)   LEN(1)    REM . HIGHS
          S    BREAK(HIGHS) . X    LEN(1) . R   BREAK(P) . Y   LEN(1)
+            =    REVERSE(X P Y)    R

| Reverse the entire string back, remove the dummy character |
| and return.                                                |
```

```
        LPERM   = REVERSE(S)
        LPERM   HIGH_CHAR  =              :(RETURN)
LPERM_END
```

Names referenced	Name	Type	Where defined
by LPERM:	REVERSE	Function	Program 3.6

Epilogue

The most single interesting part of LPERM, from the implementation point of view is the search for the pivot element. Here a search is made for 2 consecutive characters such that the first is lexically greater than the second. This is done using dynamic assignment (the binary $ operator) and an unevaluated expression (*LGT(,)).   To make this work under the normal quick-scan mode, a character had to be appended to S. This is because the scanner assumes that *LGT will match at least one character (which it does not) and would prematurely fail without testing if no more characters remained. The character appended (viz. HIGH_CHAR) was chosen in such a way that the algorithm will work whether or not the one-character assumption is made.

```
┌─────────────────┐
││  Program   ││
││   12.6     ││
││    IP      ││
└─────────────────┘
```
A permutation vector is a sequence i_1 i_2 ... i_n containing one each of the numbers $\{1,2,\ldots,n\}$. If P is a permutation vector (in the form of an array) then AI(A,P), where AI is Prog. 4.6, will return an array in which the elements of A have been permuted according to P. That is, the element in position P<i> will be moved to position i. Let

$$B = AI(A,P)$$

If P is a permutation vector there must be another permutation vector Q such that A = AI(B,Q). Q is called the inverse of P. One description of Q is as follows

$$Q<j> = k \quad \text{if and only if} \quad P<k> = j$$

This suggests that Q can be created as follows

```
          Q  = COPY(P)
          SEQ('   Q<P<K>> = K',  .K)
```

(SEQ is defined in Prog. 4.3).   For very large arrays we may find that it is necessary, or at least highly desirable, to invert the permutation vector in place and thus avoid the creation of additional storage.   One way to do this is to recognize that every permutation consists of a sequence of cycles.   Thus, the permutation vector (5,3,1,6,2,4,7) will have cycles as indicated in Figure 12.2.

Program 12.6 - IP

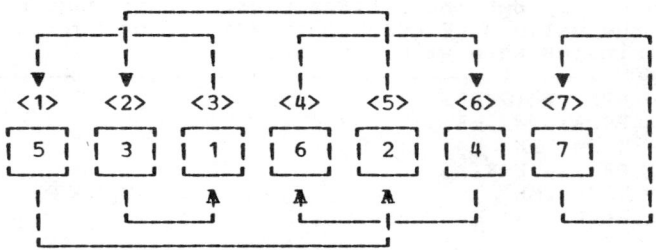

Figure 12.2

Figure 12.2 is drawn by directing an arrow from box i to box P<i>. For example P<1> is 5 so that an arrow is drawn from the first box to the fifth. A permutation vector has the property that each box will have exactly one such arrow directed in and one directed out. From this it follows that each arrow will form part of a closed loop and that the entire graph is a collection of non-intersecting closed loops. Thus, permutations can be completely characterized by their loops. The vector of Figure 12.2, for example, can be described as:

(5, 2, 3, 1) (6, 4) (7)

The inverse permutation can be obtained by reversing all arrows. This is most conveniently done by reversing all the arrows in a given loop much in the manner used to reverse a list (REVL, Prog. 5.3). When elements in a given loop are reversed they are made negative to indicate their reversal.

| IP(P) will invert a permutation vector contained in the array P. No additional storage is consumed. |

```
        DEFINE ('IP(P) M, PM, K, PK, PPK')          : (IP_END)
```

| Entry point and outer loop: Bump M by 1 looking for a non-negative value in P<M>. Such a value indicates the start of a cycle. Array elements already inverted are denoted by negative values. When M runs out, we are done. |

```
IP        M   = M + 1
          IP  = ¬P<M>   P                          :S(RETURN)
          P<M> = LT(P<M>,0)  -P<M>                 :S(IP)
```

| If PM = M then we have a trivial cycle. Go back. Otherwise, we let K sequence through the cycle starting at M. |

```
          EQ(P<M>,M)                               :S(IP)
          K = M   ;   PK = P<M>
```

Chapter 12 - Permutations

```
| Go through loop setting P<P<K>> = -K.    Care must be taken |
| to save the value of P<P<K>> before it is overwritten. The |
| loop terminates when we arrive back at M.                   |

IP_LOOP     PPK    =   P<PK>
            P<PK>  =   -K
            K   =  PK
            PK  =  PPK
            EQ(PK,M)                    :F(IP_LOOP)
            P<PK>  =   K                :(IP)
IP_END
```

Epilogue

IP has been adapted for SNOBOL4 from an algorithm by Medlock [1965] and Boonstra [1965]. See also Knuth [Vol.1, 175] for another inverse permutation algorithm.

???
??????????????????????????? EXERCISES ?????????????????????????
???

| Exercise 12.1 | Give the permutation numbers for the records below (provided they are valid permutation records).

a) (0 1 2 1)
b) (1 2 1 0)
c) (0 1 2 3)
d) (1 3 2 4)
e) (0 0 0 1)

| Exercise 12.2 | Compute the permutation record of the following permutation numbers: (a) 6, (b) 3, (c) 13, (d) 26.

| Exercise 12.3 | Write a SNOBOL4 program to convert a permutation record in V to a permutation number I. Assume the record is a string containing numbers separated by commas as in '1,2,1,3,'.

| Exercise 12.4 | Define the sum of 2 permutation records as the permutation record of the sum of the associated permutation numbers. Write a SNOBOL4 program to determine the sum of 2 such records. Assume the records are in the form indicated by the previous exercise.

Exercises for chapter 12

Exercise 12.5 — Prove that the permutation number of $(1,2,3,\ldots,n-1)$ is $n!-1$.

Exercise 12.6 — The permutation number can alternatively be defined as

$$I = i_1(n!/1!) + i_2(n!/2!) + \ldots + i_n(n!/n!)$$

Devise an algorithm to extract the record given I.

Exercise 12.7 — On the first time through the loop of PERMUTATION what will be the values assigned to RADIX, N, S1 and I?

Exercise 12.8 — What is the associated permutation record of I and what value is returned by PERMUTATION('ABC', I) as I ranges from 0 through 5?

Exercise 12.9 — Let S be a string of 6 characters. Obtain the reverse of S by a call to PERMUTATION.

Exercise 12.10 — Rewrite PERMUTATION to operate on arrays.

Exercise 12.11 — In the call to PERMUTATION, one may escape the problem of limited arithmetic precision by denoting the permutation number as one long string as in

PERMUTATION(S, '32564117246785')

Assuming that the length of a string is no greater than the largest integer what statements within PERMUATION would have to be modified to permit these extended integers? modify them!

Exercise 12.12 — Let C(n) be the average number of calls to PERM (both external and internal) per permutation of an array of n elements. For example, if PERM were non-recursive, C(n) would be 1.

(a) Write an expression for C(n) in terms of C(n-1).

(b) Assuming that C(1) = 1, use a) to compute C(2), C(3) and C(4).

(c) Prove that if C(n) < C(n-1) then C(n+1) < C(n).

Chapter 12 - Permutations

(d) On the basis of (a), (b) and (c) what value does C(n) approach as n approaches infinity?

(e) What conclusions can you draw with respect to the use of recursion to program PERM.

| Exercise 12.13 | PERM can be extended to handle the special case of arrays of length 1 by the insertion of a single instruction. What is the instruction and where should it be placed?

| Exercise 12.14 | what error in PERM will arise if its argument is an array with only one element?

| Exercise 12.15 | PERM may be modified to permute a global string (say G_S) rather than an array by changing only two statements (in addition to perhaps adding temporary variables). What are they and suggest modifications.

| Exercise 12.16 | Modify PERMS so that if it is called with the null string it will be reset.

| Exercise 12.17 | In using PERMS to permute the string 'LEMON', let us denote 'LEMON' itself as the 0th permutation. The next value returned is called the first permutation, etc. What number permutation is (a) 'MELON' and (b) 'EMLON'?

| Exercise 12.18 | Give the smallest sequence of k-rotations (denoted R(k)) to permute the characters 'LEMON' to 'MELON'.

| Exercise 12.19 | How can REORDER be modified so that it requires only one argument. Assume that the first string given is in alphabetic order (as returned from the ORDER function).

| Exercise 12.20 | Write a function REORDERING(S,I) which will return the Ith reordering of the string S. That is REORDERING(S,0) will return ORDER(S), etc. Pattern the function after PERMUTATION(S,I). Do not merely call REORDER I times as this would be grossly inefficient. Hint: the number of ways of interspersing K identical characters into the n+1 positions of a string of length n is given by the binomial coefficient:

Exercises for chapter 12   Page 273

$$C_k^{n+k} = \frac{(n+k)!}{n!\,k!}$$

Exercise 12.21 Will the function LPERM (Prog. 12.5) produce all permutations or all reorderings of a string with repeated characters? Why?

Exercise 12.22 Permutation vectors may be regarded as elements of a group under what operation?

Exercise 12.23 Let I be the identity permuation of n elements. That is I = {1, 2, ... ,n}. Let P be an arbitrary permutation vector and Q be its inverse. What is the value of (a) AI(P,I), (b) AI(I,P), (c) IP(I), and (d) AI(P,Q)?

CHAPTER THIRTEEN

```
CONTENTS

BSORT ................. 13.1
HSORT ................. 13.2
LSORT ................. 13.3
MSORT ................. 13.4
FRSORT ................ 13.5
TSORT ................. 13.6
SSORT ................. 13.7
INSERT ................ 13.8
LINEARIZE ............. 13.9
INSERTB ............... 13.10
```

Chapter 13 - SORTING   Page 275

orting on a digital computer covers a wealth of applications, can involve a variety of data structures and devices, and has been met with a host of techniques. Sorting has been widely used in business applications where payrolls, accounts, inventories and lists of all kinds must be sorted by name, number, address, etc. But, in addition, many other data processing applications find a need for sorting. Examples include compiler writing where symbols are sorted in alphabetic order, in computational linguistics where dictionaries, indexes and concordances are prepared, and in systems programming where libraries are alphabetized for rapid searching. When the items to be sorted can fit entirely in core storage, the process is called **internal sorting**. When secondary storage is required, it is called **external sorting**. This chapter is concerned with internal sorting methods only. External sorting is generally only done when the amount of data to be sorted is large. Under these circumstances, SNOBOL4 is not the ideal language for efficiency reasons.

The aggregate of things to be sorted internally may be an array, a list, a string, a tree or a table. The ordering may be on the basis of numerical value, lexicographic value or number of occurrences and the ordering may be forward or reverse. A routine may be required to actually sort an array or merely return an array of indices that could then be applied to one or more arrays. For these reasons and others to follow there is no one universal sort routine. Rather, each situation tends to be special and tends to require a sort tailored for the application.

The distribution of the input items may not be very uniform. There may, in fact, be strong correlations present in the to-be-sorted aggregate which, if taken into account, could improve the sorting time. Not all algorithms are equally adept at taking advantage of an almost-ordered input array. With some algorithms, almost-ordered data can actually adversely affect sorting time.

Another factor associated with the distribution which can influence the choice of sorting algorithm is the degree to which there is repetition in the data to be sorted. For example, in the preparation of a book index or a word concordance, the number of repeated items is high. There are sorting techniques which work quite well in such circumstances and their use can reduce sorting times substantially for this kind of problem.

The sorting situation is somewhat influenced by the nature and amount of so-called **passive** information which must undergo the same permutation as the input array, but which does not participate in the determination of the new order. For example, if we are sorting the payroll by location we presumably want to bring along with the location other passive information such as name, payroll number, salary, etc. Such ancillary information may take many forms. The passive information may

Chapter 13 - SORTING

appear in a separate array. Or the active information may be embedded in the passive information as for example when card-image strings are to be sorted on the basis of certain columns. Or the passive and active information may appear as fields of programmer-defined data objects. The way in which a sorting method handles equal items may be crucial in certain applications where passive information is present.

The reason that sorting is done at all is usually to facilitate later lookup by either man or machine. Imagine the difficulty one would have if all the names in the telephone book were scrambled chaotically. To search the telephone book for an entry we would have to make what is called a linear search comparing each name one after the other until the desired entry was found. The time required would be, on the average, the time to make n/2 comparisons, where n is the number of items in the book. On the other hand, if the book is alphabetized we can do a so-called binary search. We can look at the middle item and decide whether the desired name occurs after or before this middle item. Regardless of the outcome of this initial test, we can again probe the middle element in the segment known to contain the name and, in such a way, narrow the search by half at each comparison. The number of comparisons in this latter case is $log_2 n$. When n is large the difference between $log_2 n$ and n/2 is truly impressive. For n equal to 10000, $log_2 n$ is only 13 whereas n/2 is 5000.

An appreciation of the difference between a quantity which grows linearly (such as n/2) and a quantity which grows logarithmically is needed to understand the significance of some sorting methods and some formulas expressing their computational requirements. To further underscore the distinction between linear and logarithmic growth, the latter quantity grows only as fast as the number of digits needed to express the former. Thus $log_2 n$ not merely grows more slowly than n but becomes extremely sluggish as n grows large.

As we have outlined here, there is a rich variety in the kinds of sorts that one might be called upon to make. We will not try to give a complete and exhaustive set of programs which could handle every conceivable situation. We will, rather, present a few general methods, and give a few specific examples and hope that either these, or suitable modifications of them, will serve any given sorting need.

More complete sources of information on sorting are available. Flores [1969] and Knuth [Vol. 3] have written books on the subject. An entire CACM issue has been devoted to sorting [Sorting Issue, 1963]. An excellent early summary of sorting techniques is given by Friend [1956]. A recent bibliography is given in Lorin [1971].

Sorting methods generally subdivide into two categores, internal and external. The internal sorts are subdivided again into two categories, comparison sorts and distributive sorts. Generally speaking, comparison sorts sort on the basis of pairwise comparisons between elements. Distributive sorts are anything else.

```
┌─────────────┐
│ %%%% OMPARISON SORTS │
│ %           │
│ %    │ be sorted.
│ %    │ other than
│ %%%% │ Thus, a
└─────────────┘
```
A comparison sort works by successively comparing pairs of items to be sorted. The values of the items are irrelevant other than as to how they compare with each other. Thus, a comparison sort will operate in precisely the same way if one is sorting strings or numerical values. Indeed, a comparison sort can be used effectively to sort data objects of any kind provided an operation can be written which compares the two items.

Before considering the various methods of sorting it will be well to obtain some idea of the basic computational necessities involved in a comparison sort. If we assume that every permutation of the input array is equally likely, then we can use an information-theory argument to determine a lower bound on the average number of comparisons needed. There are n! ways of permuting n objects. Therefore the input array (of length n) can be thought of as encoding a message containing $\log_2 n!$ bits. Since one comparison yields one bit of information and since in order to sort we need complete information concerning the permutation, we may loosely conclude that at least $\log_2 n!$ comparisons are needed on the average. Using Stirling's approximation formula [Knuth, Vol.1, p.46] we obtain

$$\log_2 n! \text{ (appr.)} = \log_2 (2 \text{ PI } n^{.5 n + .5} e^{-n})$$

$$= 1.33 + n \log_2 n + .5 \log_2 n - 1.43 n$$

$$\text{(appr.)} = n (\log_2 n - 1.43)$$

Moreover, for large n (say n > 1000)

$$\log_2 n! \text{ (appr.)} = n \log_2 n$$

The information theory argument may be made rigorous by the following line of reasoning. Suppose we wanted to communicate to a distant location the contents of a permutation vector P. If P has n elements and if all permutations are equally likely then this will require $\log_2 n!$ bits (on the average). That this is true is intuitively plausible. For a more general and rigorous treatment of the subject consult any textbook on information theory. For example, see Reza [1961], p.148. This granted, assume that we have a comparison sorting algorithm (Algorithm S) which uses a predicate COMPARE(X,Y) to obtain information about the array it is sorting. But no other information about the value of the elements of the array are available to S. If we allow Algorithm S to sort P it will transform P into I, the identity permutation vector 1,2,...,n. Now at a distant location set up Algorithm S to sort the elements of I using the comparison bits tapped from the sorting of P. This setup is shown in Figure 13.1. The result of this

Chapter 13 - SORTING

is that I is transformed into the inverse of P so that we have effectively transmitted P. Since the information transmitted must be at least $\log_2 n!$ bits on the average we know that we must have at least $\log_2 n!$ comparisons on the average.

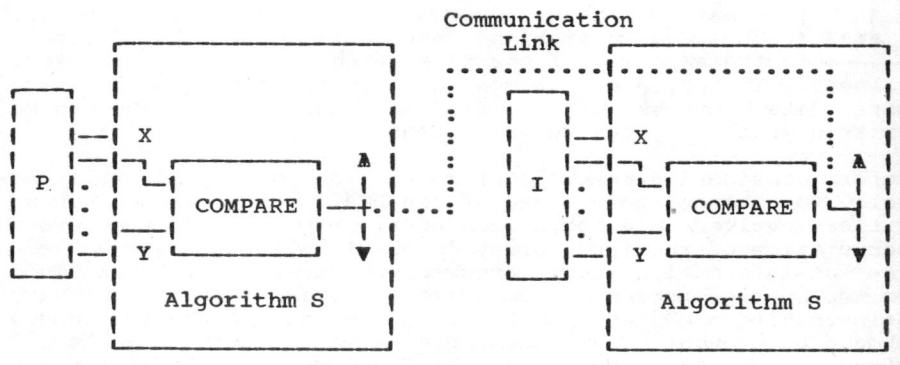

Figure 13.1

An information theoretic argument for showing that sorting requires $\log_2 n!$ comparisons.

It is important to understand what the formula says. It does not say that we must necessarily make this many comparisons in any given instance. We must, rather, make this many comparisons on the _average_ if the permutations are equally likely. From this observation we can deduce that if the number of comparisons which are to be made is independent of the distribution and only dependent on n (the number of items) then the method must make at least $\log_2 n!$ comparisons if it is to work for all possible distributions.

There are four principal kinds of comparison sorts:

Interchange
Merging
Selection
Insertion

Program 13.1 - BSORT   Page 279

| % NTERCHANGE SORTING | Given an array, the elements of the
| % _____| array can be pair-wise interchanged
| % | until the elements are sorted. This has the advantage
| % | that no additional storage need be allocated. Moreover
| % | no other sort type has this property. But every inter-
|___| change sort has some flaw which makes it unacceptable
for some applications.

| | Program | | The simplest kind of interchange sort which
| | 13.1 | | is of any interest is the so-called bubble
| | BSORT | | sort. In the bubble sort the first and
|__|_____|_| second items are compared; if they are out
of order they are interchanged. This sorts the first 2 items.
To sort the first K items assuming the first K-1 items are
sorted we 'bubble' the Kth item down through the sorted list
of K-1 items searching for its correct insertion point. This
takes an average of approx. K/2 comparisons to insert the Kth
item and approximately N(N/4) comparisons to sort N items.
This is really too many, yet the popularity of the bubble sort
persists. This is due to several factors. The bubble sort is
easy to program and understand. Also for small N the figure
N(N/4) is not much greater than N $\log_2$ N. Hence the bubble
sort is reasonably fast for N = 25 or so. But as the number
of items increases the bubble sort departs severely from the
ideal. At N = 100, the bubble sort requires 4 times as many
comparisons. For N = 1000 the ratio is 25.

Sorting routines, like the bubble sort, whose comparisons are
dominated by the factor N^2 are called <u>quadratic</u>. Sorting algorithms which obey an N $\log_2$N law or differ by a propor-
tionality constant are called <u>logarithmic</u>. Though inefficient
for large N, a quadratic sort can be more efficient than a
logarithmic sort for small values of N (less than 10 or so).
For this reason a logarithmic sort may use a quadratic sort as
a utility routine for the purpose of handling small arrays.

For medium values of N the bubble sort can save time if the
array is almost sorted to begin with. The bubble sort, more
than most, takes advantage of any pre-existing order in the
array.

| BSORT(A,I,N) will sort (via a Bubble sort) in ascending |
| lexical order the strings in the subarray A<I>, A<I + 1>, |
| ..., A<N>. CAUTION: Bubble sorts may be time consuming |
| for large arrays. |

        DEFINE('BSORT(A,I,N)J,K,V')   :(BSORT_END)

| Entry point: J will hold the index of the item to be |
| bubbled. |

BSORT   J = I

Chapter 13 - SORTING

| Outer loop: Loop on J. V is the value of the bubble. |

BSORT_1   J = J + 1   LT(J,N)   :F(RETURN)
          K = J
          V = A<J>

| Inner loop: Loop on K. We bubble down into the lower |
| portion of the array looking for a place to insert V. |

BSORT_2   K = K - 1   GT(K,I)   :F(BSORT_RO)
          A<K + 1> = LGT(A<K>,V) A<K>   :S(BSORT_2)
          A<K + 1> = V   :(BSORT_1)

| On runout, plunk bubble into bottom and go back to outer |
| loop. |

BSORT_RO A<I> = V   :(BSORT_1)
BSORT_END

	Program	
	13.2	
	HSORT	

An interchange sort which is logarithmic rather than quadratic is one introduced by Hoare [1961] and improved by Hoare [1962] and Scowen [1965]. It is frequently called QUICKSORT. The basic idea is to interchange the elements of the array until they are partitioned into two groups, A and B, such that

(i) Each element in group A lies lower (i.e. has lower index) than every element in group B.

(ii) Every element in group A ≤ every element in group B.

Note that A and B need not be equal in size. If groups A and B are then sorted separately the entire array will be sorted. The sort routine therefore consists of partitioning the array followed by two recursive calls to sort the partitions.

One method of partitioning is to pick the middle element and use this as a criterion to separate the lows from the highs. The elements of lower index are examined one by one for an element that is ≥ this criterion. The elements of higher index are searched from the top down to determine if any are ≤ this criterion. When found the elements are interchanged and the search goes on. Eventually the two pointers cross at which point the partitioning is completed.

For each partition there are approximately n comparisons where n is the size of the array to be partitioned. Hence the number of comparisons is n times the average depth of the recursion. Ideally this is $\log_2 n$. Hence, ideally the number of comparisons approaches $n \log_2 n$. But this ideal is reached only if the criterion is always chosen so that it partitions the array in half. For randomly chosen criterion the figure for the number of comparisons is approximately $1.4\, n \log_2 n$ [Hoare

Program 13.2 - HSORT   Page 281

1962]. This factor of 1.4 also shows up in the analysis of
one of the insertion sorts. (See Exercise 13.13).

HSORT is not particularly fast for arrays with a small number
of items. Ideally, when the array is small, BSORT should be
called. This is explored in an exercise.

The algorithm given here differs somewhat from Hoare [1961]
and is such as to reduce the size of the program at the expense of a small increase in running time.

```
| HSORT(A,I,N)    will   sort the strings in array A<I>, A<I + |
| 1>, ..., A<N> in ascending sequence.   HSORT calls   itself  |
| recursively.                                                 |
```
          DEFINE('HSORT(A,I,N)J,K,CRITERION')   :(HSORT_END)
```
| Entry point: If more than 2 items remain skip.  If only 1 |
| item is to be sorted, just return.                        |
```
HSORT   GT(N - I, 1)   :S(HSORT_LARGE)
              GE(I,N)   :S(RETURN)
              (LGT(A<I>, A<N>)   SWAP(.A<I>, .A<N>))   :(RETURN)
```
| Obtain  CRITERION  to  be used for partioning array into 2 |
| groups.                                                    |
```
HSORT_LARGE
              CRITERION = A<(I + N) / 2>
```
| J will move through the array from the bottom looking  for |
| an element ≥ CRITERION. K will move through the array from |
| the top looking for an element ≤ CRITERION.                |
```
              J = I - 1
              K = N + 1
HSORT_UP   J = J + 1
              ¬LGT(CRITERION, A<J>)   :F(HSORT_UP)
HSORT_DOWN   K = K - 1
              ¬LGT(A<K>, CRITERION)   :F(HSORT_DOWN)
```
| If J is still < K, interchange and go back. |
```
              (LT(J,K) SWAP(.A<J>, .A<K>))   :S(HSORT_UP)
```
| Otherwise, we are done partitioning the elements.  K will  |
| serve as a convenient dividing line.  Sorting will be ac-  |
| complished by sorting the 2 subarrays.  Might as well use  |
| HSORT to do this.                                          |
```
              HSORT(A,I,K)
              HSORT(A, K + 1, N)   :(RETURN)
HSORT_END

Chapter 13 - SORTING

Names referenced by HSORT:	Name SWAP	Type Function	Where defined Program 3.14

Epilogue

A difficulty with the Hoare sort is the possibility that equal items will not retain their relative order. In the subroutine given, this makes no difference since such an inversion will be undetectable by the user. But in sorting structures, for example, this property could prove to be a critical defect.

```
┌─────────────┐
│ %   % ERGING │  Merging is not strictly a sorting technique.
│ %% %%       │  It is a technique whereby two sorted ag-
│ % % %       │  gregates can be combined into one sorted  aggregate
│ %   %       │  by the simple process of selecting and incrementing
│ %   %       │  the aggregate showing the current least value. But,
└─────────────┘  merging may be converted into a sorting technique
```
in the following way. Let the final sorted aggregate of length n be the result of merging two sorted aggregates of length n/2. Let each of these be the result of merging two aggregates of length n/4, etc. Ultimately we reach a point at which the aggregates have length 1 and can be regarded as being sorted. The merged sort is quite efficient and approaches the theoretical lower limit on the number of comparisons needed.

```
┌───────────┐
││ Program ││  The aggregate merged in the merge sort can
││   13.3  ││  be any collection of information accessible
││  LSORT  ││  in serial fashion and hence it is a favorite
└───────────┘  way of sorting such serial aggregates as
```
files and lists. LSORT will sort a linked-list in ascending sequence according to the value contained in the VALUE field. If HEAD is the head of the linked list then LSORT(HEAD) will sort the list and return the new head. LSORT does not allocate new storage; it just rearranges pointers.

┌───┐
│ LSORT will sort a linked list L using a merge sort. The   │
│ caller may specify the name of the value field, the next   │
│ field and the predicate. Default names are VALUE, NEXT   │
│ and LGT.   │
└───┘

   DEFINE('LSORT(L,VFLD,NFLD,PRED) L1,L2,PTR')

┌───┐
│ LSORT uses the auxiliary function LSORTA which is called   │
│ recursively.   │
└───┘

   DEFINE('LSORTA(N) I')   :(LSORT_END)

┌───┐
│ Entry point for LSORT: Give default names. Then make the   │
│ fields used in the program synonymous with these.   │
└───┘

Program 13.3 - LSORT

```
LSORT         VFLD    =   IDENT(VFLD)     'VALUE'
              NFLD    =   IDENT(NFLD)     'NEXT'
              PRED    =   IDENT(PRED)     'LGT'
              OPSYN('VFLD', VFLD)
              OPSYN('NFLD', NFLD)
              OPSYN('PRED', PRED)
```

Calling LSORTA with an argument of 0 will sort the entire list.

```
              LSORT   =   LSORTA(0)                   :(RETURN)
```

Entry point for LSORTA: LSORTA(N) where N is a power of 2 will return a sorted list comprised of the first N links of the list L (or all of the list if fewer than N links remain). The variable L is treated as global and is altered. If N is 0 the entire list will be sorted and returned.

```
LSORTA        IDENT(L)                                :S(FRETURN)
```

Remove exactly one link from the head of the list. If N = 1, then we return immediately.

```
              LSORTA  =   L
              L       =   NFLD(L)
              NFLD(LSORTA) =
              I       =   1
LSORT_1       EQ(N,I)                                 :S(RETURN)
```

Otherwise our list is not sufficiently long. Let us obtain another list of length I and merge the two. If L is null, we are done.

```
              L2      =   LSORTA(I)                   :F(RETURN)
              L1      =   LSORTA
```

Merging begins here. PTR will point to the receptacle which will receive the next item. Flow goes to LSORT_L1 if the next item is to come from list L1; otherwise, flow falls through.

```
              PTR     =   .LSORTA
LSORT_C       PRED(VFLD(L1),VFLD(L2))                 :F(LSORT_L1)
```

Choose L2; update PTR and L2; loop unless runout in which case the entire L1 list is appended.

```
              $PTR    =   L2
              PTR     =   .NFLD(L2)
              L2      =   NFLD(L2)
              IDENT(L2)                               :F(LSORT_C)
              $PTR    =   L1                          :(LSORT_DONE)
```

Choose L1; similar comments as above apply.

Page 284   Chapter 13 - SORTING

```
LSORT_L1      $PTR   =   L1
              PTR    =   .NFLD(L1)
              L1     =   NFLD(L1)
              IDENT(L1)                          :F(LSORT_C)
              $PTR   =   L2
```

> Our list (beginning at LSORTA) is now twice as long as it
> was.   Record   this   in   I   and   loop back to see if this
> suffices.

```
LSORT_DONE    I = I * 2                          :(LSORT_1)
LSORT_END
```

┌─────────────────┐
││   Program   ││   The   function   MSORT   is a sort based on the
││   13.4   ││   merging principle. A call to MSORT requires
││   MSORT   ││   only one argument, the array of strings to
└─────────────────┘   be sorted. It assumes the array has a lower
bound of 1 and obtains the upper bound by a call to the
prototype function.

MSORT(A) will not sort the array A but will return an array of
integers (i.e. a permutation vector) which can then be applied
to the array A and any passive array by using AI (Prog. 4.6).
Thus if A is an array of names and if B is an array of (associated) salaries then

                         I   =   MSORT(A)
                         A   =   AI(A,I)
                         B   =   AI(B,I)

will sort A and B according to alphabetic order of A.   MSORT
will sort numerical items if a second argument denoting the
comparison predicate is given.   Thus

                         I   =   MSORT(B, 'GT')
                         B   =   AI(B,I)
                         A   =   AI(A,I)

will sort the two lists by salary (in increasing order). More
exactly, an element X in the array B which appears before an
element Y will be placed after this element if and only if the
predicate GT(X,Y) holds.

The coding of MSORT is based on the sorting algorithm designed
for APL as described by Woodrum [1969]. He defines the notion
of a chain of subscripts as follows. Let P be an array of integers.   Then,   for   any   integer   K we have the sequence of
integers (called a chain)

                    K, P<K>, P<P<K>>, ...

We will assume the sequence terminates by the appearance of a
0 subscript which will cause failure in the reference. In the
cited   paper, the sequence terminates by two consecutive equal

Program 13.4 - MSORT   Page 285

subscripts.   Such a sequence of integers can represent a list
of elements of the array A as

$$A<K>, A<P<K>>, A<P<P<K>>>, \ldots$$

Whereas it seems to be always necessary to allocate fresh
storage in order to do a merge sort, the method of chaining
permits us to merge without allocating any more storage than
needed to contain the permutation vector. The behavior of
MSORT is such as to form increasingly longer chains representing sorted lists of elements of A.

```
| MSORT(A,OP)   uses a merge sort to return an array   of in- |
| dices  which can then be used to sort the array A.    OP is |
| the operation to be used to indicate ordering.              |
```

                DEFINE('MSORT(A,OP) U,P,I,K,SAVE,AI,AJ')

```
| CHAIN is an auxiliary function called by MSORT to chain |
| the  indices  in  the  global  array P<L>, ..., P<U>. It |
| returns the top of the chain. It calls itself recursively. |
```

                DEFINE('CHAIN(L,U) I,J,MIDDLE,K')
                                                    :(MSORT_END)

```
| CHAIN entry point:  If the number of items to be sorted is |
| 1, just return the index.                                   |
```

CHAIN   CHAIN = EQ(L,U) L   :S(RETURN)

```
| Otherwise split the array into 2  parts,  and  chain  each |
| part separately.                                            |
```

          MIDDLE = (L + U) / 2
          I = CHAIN(L, MIDDLE)
          J = CHAIN(MIDDLE + 1, U)

```
| Now merge the 2 chains.  The value to be returned will be |
| either I or J depending upon which should come first. This |
| is determined by  the  function CHAINOP  which  must be |
| defined by the caller.                                     |
```

          CHAIN = I
          AI = A<I>
          AJ = A<J>
          CHAIN = CHAINOP(A<I>,A<J>)   J

```
| K will point to the last element in the chain being built. |
| Then branch to  increment  one  or  the  other  of  the  2 |
| indices.                                                    |
```

          K = CHAIN
          EQ(K,I)   :S(CHAIN_I1) F(CHAIN_J1)

Chapter 13 - SORTING

| Come here to make all subsequent comparisons. |

```
CHAIN_COMP     CHAINOP(AI,AJ)              :S(CHAIN_J)F(CHAIN_I)
```

| The I-chain has won; Place I on the chain and update the last-element pointer. |

```
CHAIN_I        P<K>   =   I
               K      =   I
```

| Obtain next element from I chain and go back for a comparison; if no more elements are left, fall through, concatenate the remainder of the J chain and return. |

```
CHAIN_I1       I    =   P<I>
               AI   =   A<I>                :S(CHAIN_COMP)
               P<K> =   J                   :(RETURN)
```

| The following code is analogous to the code above; J and I have been interchanged. |

```
CHAIN_J        P<K>   =   J
               K      =   J
CHAIN_J1       J    =   P<J>
               AJ   =   A<J>                :S(CHAIN_COMP)
               P<K> =   I                   :(RETURN)
```

| Entry point for MSORT: Obtain comparison expression. Then allocate a permutation vector (P) and form a chain. |

```
MSORT          OP    =   IDENT(OP)  'LGT'
               OPSYN('CHAINOP',OP)
               U     =   +PROTOTYPE(A)
               P     =   ARRAY(U)
               I     =   CHAIN(1,U)
```

| Convert chain by replacing in P<I> the value K where A<P<I>> is the Kth element of the sort. |

```
MSORT_1        K      =   K + 1
               SAVE   =   P<I>              :F(MSORT_2)
               P<I>   =   K
               I      =   SAVE              :(MSORT_1)
```

| We now have the inverse of a permutation vector. Invert it and return it. |

```
MSORT_2        IP(P)
               MSORT  =   P                 :(RETURN)
MSORT_END
```

Names referenced by MSORT:	Name	Type	Where defined
	IP	Function	Program 12.6

SELECTION SORTING   Page 287

Epilogue
─────────

Merge sorting is quite fast. It not merely betters the figure
of n log₂n comparisons (but of course not less than log$_2$ n!)
but will take advantage of any pre-ordering that exists in the
data. Its popularity for sorting arrays has been inhibited by
the necessity of allocating additional storage.

```
┌─────────────────┐
││   Program    ││   A frequency sort on a string will   return   a
││    13.5      ││   string where the characters have been sorted
││    FRSORT    ││   on the basis of the number of occurrences in
└─────────────────┘   the  string.   Each character will appear at
most   once   in    the   returned    string.    For    example,
FRSORT('MISSISSIPPI') will return 'ISPM'.
```

This is an example of a sorting application which makes use of
a passive array of information (the characters) while sorting
on an array of numbers. It also serves to demonstrate the use
of MSORT.

```
┌──────────────────────────────────────────────────────────────┐
│ FRSORT(S)   will do a frequency sort on the  characters  of  │
│ the  string  S.   The most frequent character will appear    │
│ first in the string returned.                                │
└──────────────────────────────────────────────────────────────┘
```

           DEFINE('FRSORT(S) SC,C,N,I')   :(FRSORT_END)

```
┌──────────────────────────────────────────────────────────────┐
│ Entry point:  Obtain in the array C the set of  characters   │
│ of which S is composed.   Then allocate an array N to hold   │
│ the  number  of  occurrences  in  S  of  the corresponding   │
│ characters of C.                                             │
└──────────────────────────────────────────────────────────────┘
```

FRSORT   C = CRACK(SKIM(S))
            N = ARRAY(PROTOTYPE(C))
            SEQ('   N<I> = COUNT(S,C<I>) ' , .I)

```
┌──────────────────────────────────────────────────────────────┐
│ Sort the indices of N and apply these indices to the array   │
│ C.  Then convert the array to a string.                      │
└──────────────────────────────────────────────────────────────┘
```

            FRSORT = STRINGOUT(AI(C,MSORT(N,'LT')))   :(RETURN)
FRSORT_END

Names referenced	Name	Type	Where defined
by FRSORT:	SKIM	Function	Program 3.11
	COUNT	Function	Program 3.4
	AI	Function	Program 4.6
	MSORT	Function	Program 13.4
	STRINGOUT	Function	Program 4.2
	CRACK	Function	Program 4.1
	SEQ	Function	Program 4.3

```
|%%%% ELECTION SORTING |
| %                    |
| %%%%   ┌─────────────┘
|  %   | selected
| %%%% |
└──────┘
```
In selection sorting the least element of the input aggregate is selected and is placed into the output aggregate. This element can be chosen in the straightforward way of making one pass through the array to determine the least element. When an element is chosen, its position can be filled with a special marker to avoid selecting that element in the future. To select the least element in this way requires n-1 comparisons and hence this form of selection sort requires a total of n(n-1) comparisons. This is unfortunately far more than the theoretical minimum of $n \log_2 n$.

But selection sorting can be continually refined until this lower limit is approached. For example, the n items can be subdivided into SQRT(n) groups of SQRT(n) items each. Assume that for each group a least item is known. Then a selection consists of first selecting the least of these least items. Then only the selected candidate's group must be searched for a least item to recompose the original situation. This kind of selection will be called order-2 selection and requires

$$2(n^{1/2} - 1)$$

comparisons for each item obtained. We may decompose our array into a group of groups of groups and so have order-3 selection. Assuming each group has the same number of members (the cube root of n) then a selection would require

$$3(n^{1/3} - 1)$$

comparisons. For a level k hierarchy we would need

$$k(n^{1/k} - 1)$$

comparisons per item. This value monotonically decreases as k increases and so it pays to make k as large as possible. In the limit the hierarchy becomes a binary tree. The 'winner' of each subgroup 'plays' the 'winner' of the adjacent subgroup to determine the winner of the group, etc. This method of sorting has the suggestive name <u>tournament sort</u>. The number of levels k becomes $\log_2 n$ and plugging this value in for k we obtain

$$\log_2 n (2 - 1) = \log_2 n$$

comparisons per extraction which is close to the theoretical limit.

Program 13.6 - TSORT

	Program
	13.6
	TSORT

TSORT stands for Tournament sort; it also stands for Table sort since it can be used to sort tables as well as one- and two-dimensional arrays. The method by which tournament winners are recorded is by an auxiliary array of subscripts. Consider a typical tournament where the winner is decided by lexical ordering (first in alphabetical order wins). The playoff of such a tournament is shown in Figure 13.2.

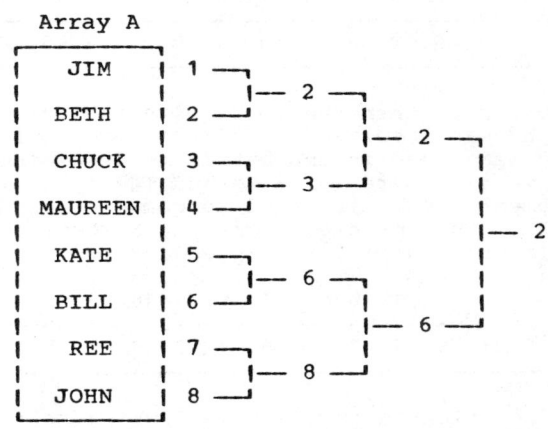

Figure 13.2

Here, subscripts, rather than actual values, are used to denote players in the tournament. Assume that the number of players N in the tournament is a power of 2. Then the tournament can be recorded in an array T of length 2 * N - 1. For example the above tournament is represented as:

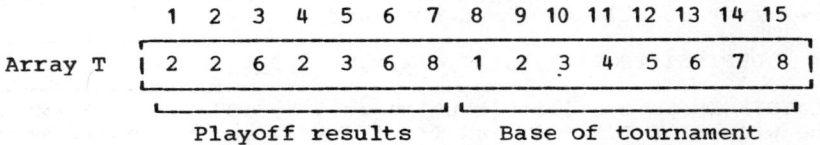

Here the elements T<8> through T<15> (in general, T<N> through T<2 * N - 1>) hold the base of the tournament. The rest of array T is filled in as follows. To determine which subscript (of array A) should be placed into T<I>, a playoff is arranged between T<I * 2> and T<I * 2 + 1>. This method of recording

Chapter 13 - SORTING

the tournament is adopted from a tree-sorting algorithm by
Floyd [1964], and can generally be used to encode a balanced
binary tree. T<I> has sons T<I * 2> and T<I * 2 + 1> and has
father T<I / 2>.

The value found in T<1> is the subscript in A of the overall
tournament winner. To find the runner-up, the winner is
'disqualified' by assigning a zero subscript into his original
slot. This is found by adding N - 1 to the subscript in A.
Thus if A<2> is the winner, T<2 + N - 1> is set to 0 to
produce:

```
              1  2  3  4  5  6  7  8  9 10 11 12 13 14 15
   Array T  | 2  2  6  2  3  6  8  1  0  3  4  5  6  7  8 |
```

A series of events is then run to resolve the outcome of games
in which only he was involved. This is done as follows. The
element T<9> was used in the battle to determine T<9 / 2> =
T<4>. Hence we recompare T<2 * 4> and T<2 * 4 + 1>. The
resulting element T<4> is used to compute the new entry in
T<4 / 2> = T<2>. This proceeds for Log_2 N steps until T<1> is
determined. In our example, this produces:

```
              1  2  3  4  5  6  7  8  9 10 11 12 13 14 15
   Array T  | 6  3  6  1  3  6  8  1  0  3  4  5  6  7  8 |
```

The new winner, indicated by T<1>, is 6 which refers to 'BILL'
in the original array A. This process is repeated until the
winning index is a zero.

```
| TSORT(A,F,P) will use a tournament sort to sort the ele- |
| ments of the array or table A according to predicate P. P |
| may be absent in which case the assumed predicate is LGT. |
| A may be singly-dimensioned in which case F, if nonnull, |
| will indicate the field of a programmer-defined datatype |
| on which the sort is based.  A may also be a table or a |
| doubly dimensioned array.  In these cases, F may be an in- |
| teger indicating the column on which to sort.  If F is |
| null, it is taken to be 1.  The array A is not modified; a |
| new array is allocated and returned.                     |
```

            DEFINE('TSORT(A,F,P) I,J,X,N,TS,T,P_I_J,K,II,W')

```
| PLAYOFF(K) is a utility routine used by TSORT to determine |
| the winner of T<K * 2> and T<K * 2 + 1> and to modify T<K> |
| accordingly.  It will fail if K is < 1.  The array T con- |
| tains subscripts; some of these are 0 indicating open |
| slots.                                                   |
```

                DEFINE('PLAYOFF(K)')   :(PLAYOFF_END)
PLAYOFF   LT(K,1)   :S(FRETURN)

Program 13.6 - TSORT   Page 291

```
                I    =  T<K * 2>                    :F(PLF_J)
                J    =  T<K * 2 + 1>                :F(PLF_I)
                LE(I,0)                             :S(PLF_J)
                LE(J,0)                             :S(PLF_I)
                EVAL(P_I_J)                         :S(PLF_J)
PLF_I           T<K> =  I                           :(RETURN)
PLF_J           T<K> =  J                           :(RETURN)
PLAYOFF_END
```

┌───┐
│ TS will compute a tournament size needed for N elements;   │
│ i. e. the smallest power of 2 ≥ N.   │
└───┘

```
                DEFINE('TS(N)')                     :(TS_END)
TS              TS   =  1
TS_1            TS   =  LT(TS,N)    TS * 2         :S(TS_1)F(RETURN)
TS_END
                                                    :(TSORT_END)
```

┌───┐
│ TSORT entry point: Compute the size of the tournament   │
│ (TS). Allocate the tournament array (T) and the array to   │
│ be returned.   │
└───┘

```
TSORT           A    =  CONVERT(A,'ARRAY')
                TSORT =  ARRAY(PROTOTYPE(A))
                N    =  PROTOTYPE(A)
                N       BREAK(',') . N              :F(TSORT_1)
                F    =  IDENT(F)    1
TSORT_1         TS   =  TS(N)
                T    =  ARRAY(TS - 1 + N)
```

┌───┐
│ Initialize base of the tournament.   │
└───┘

```
TSORT_2         I    =  I + 1
                T<TS - 1 + I>  =  I                 :S(TSORT_2)
```

┌───┐
│ Obtain comparison expression.   │
└───┘

```
                P    =  IDENT(P)    'LGT'
                X    =  F  '(A<I>),' F  '(A<J>)'
                X    =  IDENT(DATATYPE(F),'INTEGER')
           +         'A<I,' F  '>,A<J,' F  '>'
                P_I_J  =  CONVERT(P '(' X ')', 'EXPRESSION')
```

┌───┐
│ Now run a complete tournament determining an absolute win-   │
│ ner (in T<1>).   │
└───┘

```
                K    =  TS
TSORT_3         K    =  K - 1
                PLAYOFF(K)                          :S(TSORT_3)
```

┌───┐
│ Transfer the winning structure to TSORT. For a one-   │
│ dimensional array, this is simple. For a two-dimensional   │
│ array, we must go through a loop.   │
└───┘

```
TSORT_4         II   =  II + 1
                W    =  T<1>
```

Chapter 13 - SORTING

```
              .EQ(W,0)                              : S (RETURN)
              TSORT<II DIFFER(DATATYPE(F),'INTEGER')>  =  A<W>
+                                                   : S (TSORT_7)
              J = 0
TSORT_6       J = J + 1
              TSORT<II,J> = A<W,J>                  : S (TSORT_6)
```
| 'Disqualify' the winner. Replay all matches in which he was involved. |

```
TSORT_7       K = TS - 1 + W
              T<K> = 0
TSORT_5       K = K / 2
              PLAYOFF(K)                            : S (TSORT_5) F (TSORT_4)
TSORT_END
```

Epilogue

The tournament sort as given uses a near minimum number of comparisons but unfortunately allocates two additional arrays. For sorting structures, strings or two-dimensional arrays, the additional allocation is probably not harmful since it will be small compared to the storage already allocated. Minimum core sorting of arrays such as HSORT (Prog. 13.2) and Treesort 3 [Floyd 1964] have the unfortunate property of inverting equal elements and this, we will see, can be bad for sorting arrays of structures. Other minimum storage sorting algorithms such as BSORT (Prog. 13.1) and one by Shell [1959] have the property of not being minimum time. There appears to be, at this writing, no minimum-core sorting algorithm (i.e. an in-place sort) which is minimum time and inversion free.

| % NSERTION SORTING | In an _insertion sort_ the next available element to be sorted is placed in the correct relative position in the output aggregate. This requires that the number of elements in the output aggregate be adjustable and suggests the use of a list, a string or a tree. A simple-minded insertion sort will compare the next item on the input list with each item in sequence on the output list until the correct place is found at which point an insertion is made. This would require, on the average, n/4 comparisons for each inserted item. This is too many for large n. But for small n, where time is not an issue, this simple scheme has the advantage of providing a very simple sort.

| Program 13.7 SSORT | SSORT(SS,S) is a string sort (or short sort or simple sort). The string S is inserted into a string of strings (separated by commas) in SS. The augmented list is returned as value. For example, if the items in the input stream are being read in and are to be sorted one may execute

Program 13.8 - INSERT

```
LOOP    LIST  =  SSORT(LIST, TRIM(INPUT))           :S(LOOP)
```

If the input contained the names 'PAT', 'JOE', 'TOM' then the
resulting LIST would contain ',JOE,PAT,TOM,'. Note that
leading and trailing commas form part of the resulting string.

```
            DEFINE('SSORT(SSORT,S)T')
            SS_PAT = ',' (BREAK(',') $ T *LGT(T,S) | RPOS(0)) . T
                                                    :(SSORT_END)
SSORT       SSORT SS_PAT  =  ',' S ',' T            :S(RETURN)
            SSORT  =  ',' S ','                     :(RETURN)
SSORT_END
```

Epilogue

SSORT was written to be as short and as convenient as
possible. Its major failing is that it is slow. Not only is
it a quadratic sort, but the data structure holding the sorted
items is not the most conducive to high speed insertion. On
the other hand, many if not most sort applications require
only something 'quick and dirty' and for such applications
SSORT is recommended since it is not only easy to type but it
saves on program space.

```
| |  Program  | |
| |  13.8     | |
| |  INSERT   | |
```
The insertion sort, like the other sorts,
can be refined to the point where it becomes
a logarithmic sort. To find the correct
position of the ith element we ought to com-
pare it with the middle item. If it is > than this middle item
it is compared with the middle item in the upper half, and so
forth. Thus, to insert the ith item requires approximately
$\log_2 i$ comparisons. The total number becomes (approximately)

$$\log_2 1 + \log_2 2 + \ldots + \log_2 n = \log_2 n!$$

which is the theoretical lower limit.

This sounds attractive, but how does one find the middle element in each of these lists. The middle element of an array
(or subsection of an array) can be easily computed but an array is not adjustable and its use would prove awkward in an
insertion sort. That is, although the sort would prove
logarithmic with respect to compares it would be quadratic
with respect to moves. A list, on the other hand, is adjustable and an element can easily be inserted within it, but
the central element is not easily found. The solution is to
use a tree as the receiving data aggregate.

For example, assume that the following strings are to be
inserted.

```
            NOW IS THE TIME FOR ALL GOOD MEN
```

If these strings are inserted into a binary tree, the result
is depicted in Figure 13.3.

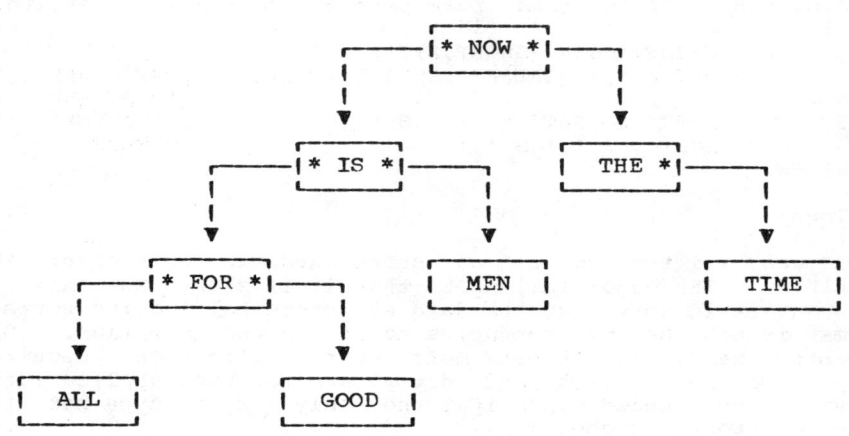

Figure 13.3

The first string is associated with the root node. The second
string is lexicographically less than the first and so is associated with the left branch of the binary tree. Each
additional string is compared with the node and successive
descendents until an opening in the tree is found at which
point the string is inserted. A trace through the tree will
readily indicate the nature of this process.

```
| INSERT(T,S)   will insert the string S into the tree T and |
| return the modified tree.  If T is null a  root  node   is |
| created and returned.                                      |
```

```
            DEFINE('INSERT(T,S) V')
```

```
| BTNODE is the datatype of a single node of a binary tree. |
```

```
          DATA('BTNODE(VALUE,NO,LSON,RSON)')   :(INSERT_END)
```

```
| Entry point: If T is null, return immediately with a fresh |
| node.   Else we prepare to return T and go on to modify it. |
| Get VALUE(T) out for fast and easy reference.  If S equals |
| value, increment count by 1 and return.                    |
```

```
INSERT      INSERT  =  IDENT(T)   BTNODE(S,1)      :S(RETURN)
            INSERT  =  T
```

Program 13.10 - INSERTB

```
            V    = VALUE(T)
            NO(T) = IDENT(S,V)    NO(T) + 1        :S(RETURN)
```
| If S > value, insert S into right half of tree; otherwise into left half. |

```
            RSON(T) = LGT(S,V)    INSERT(RSON(T),S) :S(RETURN)
            LSON(T) = INSERT(LSON(T), S)            :(RETURN)
INSERT_END
```

Epilogue

Note that we do not create separate nodes for duplicate items but record a count in a field of the node. This saves on storage if the percentage of duplicate items is 20% or so. It also saves on compute time, especially if there are many duplicate items. For this reason, the binary insertion sort is ideal for preparing a word concordance which is a word-frequency analysis of a piece of text.

```
|| Program  ||
|| 13.9     ||
|| LINEARIZE||
```
LINEARIZE(T) will linearize a binary tree of the kind used in INSERT (Program 13.8). The tree will be strung via its right sons. The value returned will be the first node of the tree. If T is null, LINEARIZE will fail.

```
            DEFINE('LINEARIZE(T)')                  :(LINEARIZE_END)
```

| Entry point: |

```
LINEARIZE   IDENT(T)                                :S(FRETURN)
```

| Linearize the left side and attach on node T (LAST_NAME is a global variable set to equal the name of the last link on the chain). |

```
            LINEARIZE = IDENT(LSON(T))  T           :S(LIN_1)
            LINEARIZE = LINEARIZE(LSON(T))
            $LAST_NAME = T
```

| Now linearize the right-hand side. |

```
LIN_1       RSON(T) = LINEARIZE(RSON(T))            :S(RETURN)
            LAST_NAME = .RSON(T)                    :(RETURN)
LINEARIZE_END
```

```
|| Program  ||
|| 13.10    ||
|| INSERTB  ||
```
With some sorting procedures, an almost-sorted input will serve to decrease sorting time. The speedup is most pronounced with the bubble sort but pre-ordering will favorably affect the merge and Hoare sort as well. With the tree insertion sort we have the reverse phenomenon. If the

Page 296   Chapter 13   -   SORTING

elements inserted are already in alphabetic order the number
of comparisons to insert the Ith element is I-1, the worst
case. The logarithmic sort becomes a quadratic sort. Perversely, if the elements are initially in reverse alphabetic
order, we also achieve the worst case of I-1 comparisons for
the Ith element.

But the insertion sort can be modified slightly to not only
avoid the inefficiencies of almost-ordered data but to actually
take advantage of any ordering that exists. The trick is to
grow the tree backward! that is, the last node to be inserted
should become the root of the tree.

For example, if the sequence of strings is

                NOW   IS   THE   TIME   FOR   ALL   GOOD

the tree grown backward becomes as shown in Figure 13.4. A
rough rule for growing the tree backward is the following.
Draw an imaginary line down the middle of the tree separating
all nodes < the new root from all nodes > than it. Any path
broken by such a line should be 'short circuited' so that all
pointers from any node are directed to nodes in the same half
of the tree. As an example, the result of adding the string
'MEN' to the diagram in Figure 13.4 is shown in Figure 13.5.

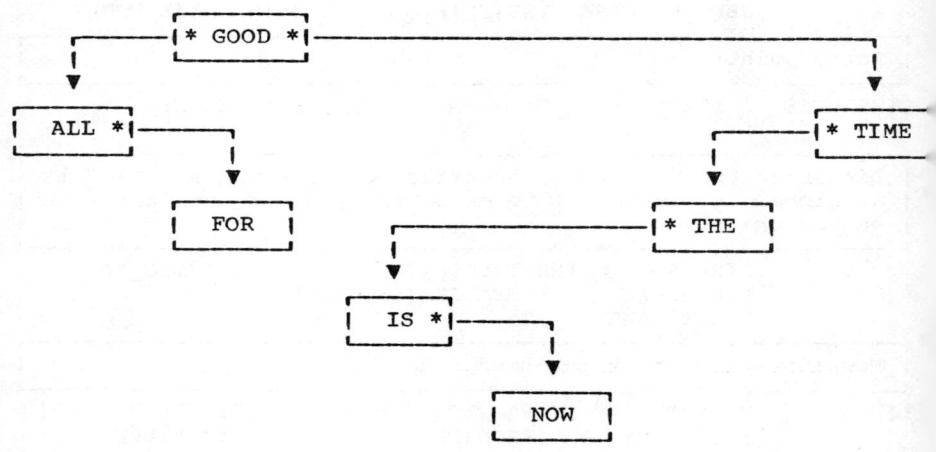

Figure 13.4

Program 13.10 - INSERTB   Page 297

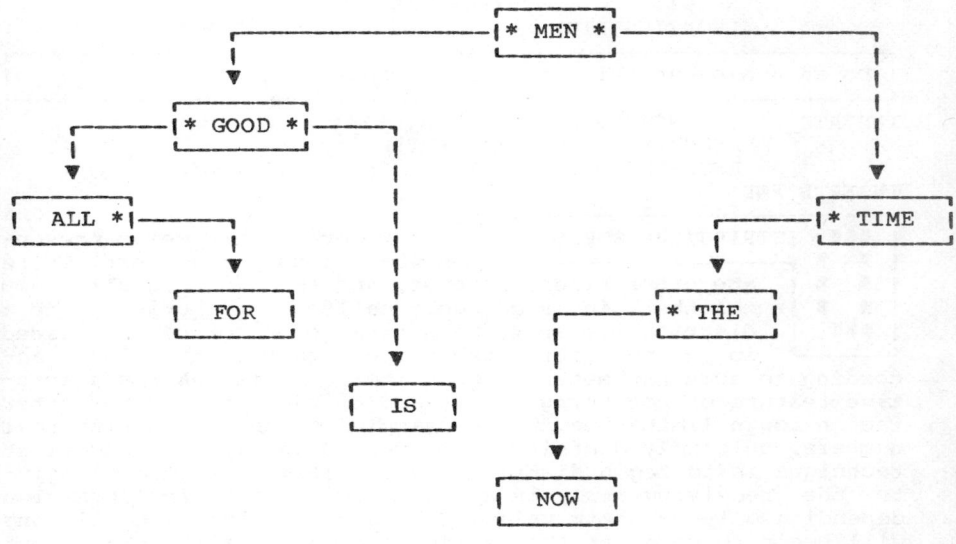

Figure 13.5

```
| INSERTB(T,S)  will insert the string S into the backward- |
| growing binary tree T.  The root of the returned tree will |
| contain S.                                                 |

          DEFINE('INSERTB(T,S)V')
          DATA('BTNODE(VALUE,NO,LSON,RSON)')
                                         :(INSERTB_END)
| Entry point:  The first part is similar to INSERT.  Com- |
| ments there are appropriate here.                         |

INSERTB      INSERTB  =  IDENT(T)   BTNODE(S,1)    :S(RETURN)
             V  =  VALUE(T)
             NO(T)   =   IDENT(S,V)    NO(T) + 1    :S(RETURN)

| If S > value, insert S into the right half of the tree.  |
| The  root node of the returned tree will have a VALUE of S |
| and will become the root node of the tree we will be     |
| returning.                                                |

             LGT(S,V)                         :F(INSERTB_L)
             INSERTB   =   INSERTB(RSON(T), S)

| Include the rest of T under the left side of this new |
| root.                                                  |
```

Page 298   Chapter 13   -   SORTING


```
              RSON(T)      =  LSON(INSERTB)
              LSON(INSERTB) =  T              :(RETURN)
```
| Do an analogous thing for the opposite side. |

```
INSERTB_L       INSERTB    =  INSERTB(LSON(T), S)
                LSON(T)    =  RSON(INSERTB)
                RSON(INSERTB) = T              :(RETURN)
INSERTB_END
```

| %%%   ISTRIBUTIVE SORTS | So far, every sort we've presen-
| % % | ted was a comparative sort. There
| % %   are other kinds, however, and these we can all lump
| % %   together in a category called distributive. In a
| %%%   distributive sort, each item to be sorted is placed
           in a position with respect to the other items ac-
cording to some parameter of that item. This has the attractive feature of not being binary and thereby one can better
the n $\log_2$n limitation. For example, if one is sorting real
numbers, uniformly distributed between 0 and 1, an excellent
technique is to begin distributing the items one at a time into the receiving array in approximately their final position
depending only on their value. Unless one is lucky, collisions
will begin to occur as the receiving array is filling up, but
the time to patch up such discrepancies is assumed to be small
compared with the time saved by the almost-one-pass nature of
the sort. The effectiveness of such a sort is highly data
dependent, however, and for this reason is not very popular.

A more familiar distributive sort is the radix sort. This is
the sort used on mechanical sorters which distribute cards into bins. Assuming n cards are to be sorted on a field containing k characters, a distribution over the least
significant character is made first. The clumps are gathered
together and passed through the machine again, this time on
the next least significant character. After k passes, the entire deck is sorted. the number of operations is n k rather
than n $\log_2$n because each operation involves pitching a card
into one of several bins and such an operation yields more information than a binary choice.

We do not have space to describe a SNOBOL4 rendition of the
radix sort but happily refer the reader to the original SNOBOL
article [Farber, et al 1964] where it appeared as an example.

???
????????????????????????? EXERCISES ???????????????????????????
???

| Exercise 13.1 | What two instructions constitute the inner
                    loop of BSORT? Can the reader recommend a
slightly faster version?

| Exercise 13.2 | Prove that in HSORT the value of K when the
recursive call HSORT(A,I,K) is made is always less than N thereby removing the possibility of an infinite loop.

| Exercise 13.3 | Write a non-recursive version of HSORT using PUSH and POP (Programs 5.5 and 5.6).
Hint: This can be done by modifying 2 go-to fields and adding 5 very simple instructions in place of the 2 recursive calls.

| Exercise 13.4 | Given 3 items to sort, what is the average number of comparisons required by BSORT and by HSORT. Note, as a consequence, that BSORT will actually be faster than HSORT for small arrays. Estimate the crossover point at which the number of comparisons are the same. Then modify HSORT so that it calls BSORT for arrays smaller than this. (The estimate may be made on analytical or empirical grounds.)

| Exercise 13.5 | The elements of an array A are to be sorted numerically in ascending sequence but all numbers within a certain range R of each other are to be regarded as numerically equal and are to retain their relative ordering. Using MSORT, define an appropriate predicate and sort A accordingly.

| Exercise 13.6 | Assume we wish to sort an array of strings, A, alphabetically as defined by the predicate AGT (Prog. 3.13). We could call MSORT(A, 'AGT'). What is a more efficient procedure?

| Exercise 13.7 | Both MSORT(A, 'LT') and MSORT(A, 'LE') can be used to sort A in decreasing numerical order. The difference between the two is in the way equal elements are treated. Which should be used so that the relative order of equal items is retained.

| Exercise 13.8 | SSORT can be speeded up considerably by the following technique. Represent a binary tree as a string by the following method. The null string is the null tree. A tree with root R is represented as:

(LSON) R (RSON)

where LSON is the string representation of the left son of the tree and RSON is the representation of the right son. Then BAL can be used to rapidly scan for an insertion point. A tree is built up much in the manner of INSERT. Rewrite SSORT so that the string returned is this tree.

Page 300   Chapter 13   -   SORTING

| Exercise 13.9 | The body of SSORT (Prog. 13.7) need only be
                   one statement. Modify the pattern SS_PAT
so that the :S(RETURN) can be changed to :(RETURN) and the
second statement deleted entirely.

| Exercise 13.10 | One can enhance the speed of INSERT by
                    periodically balancing the tree. Write a
function TREEBAL(N) which will balance a tree beginning at
node N and return the root of the balanced tree. The use of
LINEARIZE to write this function is optional.

| Exercise 13.11 | Modify LINEARIZE so that the LSON fields
                    are cleared.

| Exercise 13.12 | Modify LINEARIZE so that it counts the
                    number of nodes in the tree. Assume some
global variable exists (say N) which is initially 0.

| Exercise 13.13 | The average number of comparisons of a
                    logarithmic insertion sort was estimated
in the text to be $\log_2 n$! This average would be achievable by
INSERT only if the tree is always kept perfectly balanced. But
for random data this will not be the case and the expected
degree of unbalance can be computed.

a) Determine the average number of comparisons required by
the tree-insertion sort. Assume that every input permutation
is equally likely and that no two items are identical.

b)   As n approaches infinity, what is the ratio between this
number an n $\log_2 n$.

| Exercise 13.14 | What does the tree resemble when the fol-
                    lowing strings are placed into a) INSERT
and b) INSERTB?

        A QUICK BROWN FOX JUMPED OVER THE LAZY DOG

CHAPTER FOURTEEN

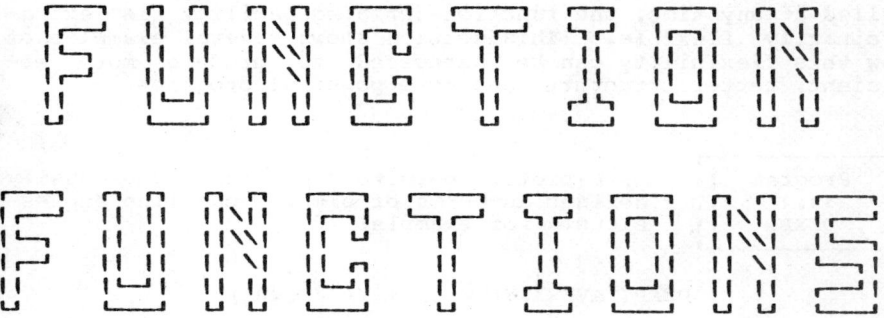

FUNCTION FUNCTIONS

CONTENTS

DEXP	14.1
DEXTERN	14.2
FTRACE	14.3
INSULATE	14.4
REDEFINE	14.5
PHYSICAL	14.6
STATEF	14.7
STACK	14.8

Chapter 14 - FUNCTION FUNCTIONS

The function definition facility in SNOBOL4 is somewhat unorthodox. In conventional languages, a function (or its equivalent) is defined at compile time. Thus, its entry point, number and type of arguments, temporaries, etc. are fixed for the duration of the program. In SNOBOL4, these are governed by arguments to the DEFINE function. Since these arguments can be the product of an arbitrary computation, and since the DEFINE function can be called at any time, the function-defining facility is extraordinarily flexible. This section shows several examples of how this flexibility can be harnessed to produce more efficient, better structured and more powerful programs.

```
Program     DEXP(proto) permits functions to be easily
  14.1      defined in terms of simple, one-line expres-
  DEXP      sions. For example:
```

         DEXP('AVE(X,Y) = (X + Y) / 2.0')

will define the function AVE(X,Y) to be equal to half the sum of X and Y. It thus mimics the Fortran arithmetic function facility. It is, however, much more powerful, since any sequence of statements separated by semicolons may be used to specify a function. In fact, arbitrary functions may be defined in this way.

         DEFINE('DEXP(PROTO)NAME,ARGS')   :(DEXP_END)

| Entry point: First remove leading blanks, just in case. Next obtain the name of the new function (NAME) and its argument list (ARGS), removing the latter.

DEXP   PROTO   POS(0)   SPAN(' ') =
         PROTO   BREAK('(') . NAME BAL . ARGS = NAME

| Create code which will be the body of the new function.
| Then DEFINE it.

         CODE(NAME ' ' PROTO ' :S(RETURN) F(FRETURN)')
         DEFINE(NAME ARGS)   :(RETURN)
DEXP_END

Epilogue

Care must be taken in the use of DEXP. If the last statement of a sequence fails, the entire function might inadvertently fail. This can be cured by placing a semi-colon after the last statement (null statements always succeed). For example, we can define SIGN(X) which returns +1 if $X > 0$ and -1 if $X < 0$ and null if $X = 0$ as:

         DEXP('SIGN(X) = GT(X,0) 1 ; SIGN = LT(X,0) -1 ;')

Program 14.2 - DEXTERN

```
| |  Program  | |    One of the most frequent requests that
| |   14.2    | |    SNOBOL4 users make is for more space.  If
| |  DEXTERN  | |    lack of main storage is due to the size of
                     the program, then this next function, or
```
some variant of it, can be used to obtain more core. The
function DEXTERN (Define EXTERNal function) will allow for the
dynamic loading of SNOBOL4-coded functions. The arguments to
DEXTERN(proto,label) are identical to those of the built-in
DEFINE function. DEXTERN will create a small provisional
function body for each such function. This will cause the
first call on that function to result in the function being
loaded from an external file, compiled and executed. Subsequent calls go straight into execution with no overhead.

```
           DEFINE('DEXTERN(PROTO,LBL) NAME')
           DEFINE('LOADEX(LBL) PAT,X,CODE')
           LIB_   = Some Library File Designator    : (DEXTERN_END)
```

| Entry point for DEXTERN. Determine the label (LBL) and |
| compile code which serves as the function body until the |
| first call. Then define the function. |

```
DEXTERN    PROTO  IDENT(LBL)   BREAK('(') . LBL
           CODE(LBL  "  LOADEX('" LBL "')  ;  :(" LBL ")" )
           DEFINE(PROTO, LBL)                       :(RETURN)
```

| Entry point for LOADEX(LBL). LOADEX will load an external |
| segment of code beginning with label LBL and ending with |
| LBL_END. |

```
LOADEX     REWIND(LIB_)
           INPUT(.LIB_FILE, LIB_)
```

| Loop to look for function |

```
           PAT    =  POS(0)    LBL    (' ' | RPOS(0))
LOADEX_1   CODE   =  LIB_FILE                        :F(ERROR)
           CODE   PAT                                :F(LOADEX_1)
```

| Loop to process statements. Note conventional continuation |
| and comment characters. |

```
           PAT    =  POS(0)    LBL    '_END'  (' ' | RPOS(0))
LOADEX_2   X      =  LIB_FILE                        :F(LOADEX_3)
           X      PAT                                :S(LOADEX_3)
           X      POS(0)   ANY('*-')                 :S(LOADEX_2)
           X      = ';'  X
           X      POS(0)   ';'  ANY('.+')  =  ' '
           CODE   =  CODE  X                         :(LOADEX_2)
```

| Now code it up and return. |

```
LOADEX_3   CODE(CODE)                                :(RETURN)
DEXTERN_END
```

Page 304   Chapter 14   -   FUNCTION FUNCTIONS

Epilogue

One reason for the DEXTERN function is convenience. Frequently-used subroutines need not be copied into a given program but may be kept in a file which serves as a library. In this way several programs may share a common library and may be assured of up-to-date copies.

Another reason for DEXTERN is that it permits the running of many large programs which would otherwise not fit into core. Most large programs have significant portions that are infrequently used and it is extremely rare to encounter an application which requires all the facilities of the large program.

The text processing system used to write this book is a good example of this. There are approximately 1200 statements in the main program and approximately 1500 in an external library. Each chapter of the book may be processed within prime-shift limits since no chapter uses all the facilities of the text processor. However, the entire book requires an evening run.

It is not necessary to dynamically load source programs on a per-function basis. See Exercise 14.5.

```
|¯¯¯¯¯¯¯¯¯¯¯¯¯¯¯¯¯|
|| Program      ||
||   14.3       ||
||   FTRACE     ||
|_____|
```
One advantage of decomposing a large program into functions is that the values passed to a function and the value returned can be easily monitored by means of the &FTRACE switch. Unfortunately, only strings, reals and integers are printed explicitly. Other data objects such as patterns, arrays, tables, etc. result in only the datatype being printed (with possibly an identification number as in SITBOL). This deficiency can be corrected by the programmer, however, by using the available trace facilities. In particular

TRACE(NAME, 'CALL', , FNAME)

will cause the function named FNAME to be invoked when the function named NAME is called. FNAME can determine sufficient information about the called function (such as its arguments via the ARGS function) to produce an elaborate display of any aggregate passed as argument. The second argument to TRACE can be the string 'RETURN' which can enable a similar function to display the returned value.

One weakness of the scheme is that unlike the &FTRACE switch which affects all function calls, the TRACE function requires two explicit calls for each function traced. The FTRACE function defined here is designed to automate this process. It is simply placed once in the program before all functions which are to be traced. FTRACE will redefine the DEFINE function and thereby sieze control at each function definition. The

Program 14.4 - INSULATE   Page 305

functions actually called to do the tracing (FTR_CALL and FTR_TRC) are left as exercises.

```
        DEFINE('FTRACE(PROTO,LABEL)NAME')
        OPSYN('DEFINE.','DEFINE')
        OPSYN('DEFINE','FTRACE')
        &TRACE  =  10000                         :(FTRACE_END)
```
| Entry point: Define the function, issue the trace requests and return. |

```
FTRACE  DEFINE.(PROTO, LABEL)
        PROTO    BREAK('(')  .  NAME
        TRACE(NAME, 'CALL', , 'FTR_CALL')
        TRACE(NAME, 'RETURN', , 'FTR_RET')      :(RETURN)
FTRACE_END
```

| | Program | | This routine can protect other routines
| | 14.4 | | from possible malfunction owing to an unan-
| | INSULATE | | ticipated modification of some global
                     variable or keyword. As written, protection
from modification of the &ANCHOR keyword is obtained, but this
protection could be extended to include other keywords and
global variables as well.

While it is held in these pages that modification of the
&ANCHOR keyword is seldom warranted and is inconsistent with a
general functional scheme of decomposing and structuring a
large program, it is nonetheless true that occasionally one
encounters two separately written sections of code that in-
teract with each other and that depend on opposite values for
the &ANCHOR keyword. For example, if routines in this book
were called from a main program which assumed anchored mode,
then pandemonium would be the general result.

To rectify the situation short of recoding one or the other of
the two ill-fitting sections one may insert the INSULATE
function.

| INSULATE will cause each function following it to trap to INS_CALL() when called and to INS_RET() on return. This requires redefining DEFINE to point to INSULATE. |

```
        DEFINE('INSULATE(PROTO,LABEL)NAME')
        DEFINE('INS_CALL() ')
        DEFINE('INS_RET() ')
        OPSYN('DEFINE.', 'DEFINE')
        OPSYN('DEFINE',  'INSULATE')
        &TRACE  =  100000                       :(INSULATE_END)
```

| Entry point for INSULATE. Define the function and set up tracing. |

```
INSULATE    PROTO  BREAK('(') . NAME
            DEFINE.(PROTO, LABEL)
            TRACE(NAME, 'CALL',, 'INS_CALL')
            TRACE(NAME, 'RETURN' ,, 'INS_RET')      :(RETURN)
```
| The two routines. |

```
INS_CALL   PUSH(&ANCHOR)  ;   &ANCHOR = 0          :(RETURN)
INS_RET    &ANCHOR = POP()                         :(RETURN)

INSULATE_END
```

Names referenced   Name   Type   Where defined
by INSULATE: PUSH   Function   Program 5.5
                    POP   Function   Program 5.6

Epilogue

Note that when a routine is called and INS_CALL gains control it calls the routine POP(). If tracing were on, at this point, POP would presumably be traced sending control to INS_CALL again; an infinite loop would be the sad result. But the &TRACE switch is conveniently turned off at this point and restored on return. As Dickman and Jensen (the original implementors of the SNOBOL4 trace facility) put it, the 'stout of heart' can turn tracing on after the function receives control.


```
 ┌───────────┐
 |  Program  |     SNOBOL4 has the ability to redefine built-
 |   14.5    |     in operators and functions.  Thus we may
 |  REDEFINE |     write
 └───────────┘
```

OPSYN('+','*',2)

indicating that the binary operator '+' is made equivalent to binary '*'. All additions thereafter become multiplications. OPSYN can be used for named functions as well as operators and user-defined functions as well as built-ins.

While the basic facility exists, we are here concerned with its proper and effective use as a programming tool. Undoubtedly it has already occurred to the reader that he can play 'fool the counselor' with an OPSYN as above. Let us assume, however, that we are above such pranks. A semi-legitimate use of redefining an existing facility is as follows. Being unfamiliar with the language, and in particular unaware of the built-in function REPLACE, a programmer writes a user-defined function REPLACE as part of a larger program. Subsequently he learns of this built-in facility and wants to use it. He may write

Program 14.5 - REDEFINE   Page 307

before defining REPLACE and use REP() to obtain the built-in facility.

This use is only semi-legitimate for if the program is to have a long life, he would be better off redefining his original function, even if more painful, than in redefining a built-in.

Redefining a built-in is normally only justifiable as a design objective if one is writing a facility designed to be upward compatible with an existing one. For example, one may redefine the operator '+' to sum arrays, complex numbers or physical quantities but in that case it should treat conventional objects (integers, reals, strings) as it did prior to the redefinition.

REDEFINE(OP,PROTO,LABEL) is intended to make such upward compatible extensions. The first argument is an operator to be redefined, or, if a function is redefined the first argument is null. The name of this function can be taken from the second argument which is the function prototype normally given to DEFINE.

```
        DEFINE('REDEFINE(OP,DEF,LBL) NAME,N,FLAG')
                           :(REDEFINE_END)
```
|---|
| Entry point: Extract the function's name (NAME) and deter- |
mine the number of arguments (N = 1 or 2).

```
REDEFINE  DEF   BREAK('(') . NAME '(' BREAK(')',') LEN(1) . FLAG
          N  =  1
          N  =  IDENT(FLAG, ',')  2
```
|---|
| But if the first argument is null, we are not talking |
about an operator (OP) at all but a named function.

```
          N  =  IDENT(OP)
          OP =  IDENT(OP) NAME
          OPSYN(NAME '.', OP, N)
          DEFINE(DEF, LBL)
          OPSYN(OP, NAME, N)                    :(RETURN)
REDEFINE_END
```

Epilogue

In order to avoid defining away the built-in facility irretrievably, REDEFINE will OPSYN to it a created name formed by appending a period to the function's name. For example,

              REDEFINE('+','SUM(X,Y)I')

will cause SUM.() to be defined and equivalenced to the old binary + while binary + will now be equivalenced to SUM().

REDEFINE can substantially simplify the task of extending a range of built-in operators. This is best illustrated by example as in the next program.

Chapter 14 - FUNCTION FUNCTIONS

```
|  Program   |
|   14.6     |   To illustrate the redefinition facility and
|  PHYSICAL  |   to create a possibly useful extension to
```
SNOBOL4 we will define the four fundamental operators of arithmetic to operate on 'physical' quantities. For example, a quantity such as four meters divided by a quantity such as two seconds produces a speed of two meters-per-second. Normally, physical quantities are represented by some combination of units of length, mass, time and charge. We will illustrate our system with the near-standard MKS system (Meters-Kilograms-Seconds-Coulombs) but it should be obvious that any other system can be employed. Indeed, the subroutines, as written, depend in no way on our particular universe; any type and number of physical quantities may be employed (up to the size of &ALPHABET).

Physical quantities will be represented by a programmer-defined datatype defined as

DATA('PHYS(VAL,NUM,DEN)')

where VAL is the numerical value, NUM is the numerator of the units field and DEN is the denominator. Units are represented by single letters. For example, 3.5 meters/second^2 may be represented as:

PHYS(3.5, 'M', 'SS')

DATA('PHYS(VAL,NUM,DEN)')

| The following operators and one function are redefined.

```
        REDEFINE('-', 'MINUS(X)')
        REDEFINE('+', 'SUM(X,Y)')
        REDEFINE('-', 'DIFF(X,Y)')
        REDEFINE('*', 'MULT(X,Y)')
        REDEFINE('/', 'DIV(X,Y)')
        REDEFINE( , 'EQ(X,Y)')
```

| NORM(X) will normalize a physical quantity, meaning that
| we obtain a unique specification for comparison purposes.
| This is done by sorting the physical units and canceling
| common factors across the division bar.

```
        DEFINE('NORM(X)C')                      :(NORM_END)
NORM    X = DIFFER(DATATYPE(X), 'PHYS')   PHYS(X)
        NORM = X
        DEN(X) = ORDER(DEN(X))
        NUM(X) = ORDER(NUM(X))
NORM_1  IDENT(DEN(X))                           :S(RETURN)
        NUM(X) ANY(DEN(X)) . C =                :F(RETURN)
        DEN(X) C =                              :(NORM_1)
NORM_END
```

| XY() will normalize the two arguments of an arithmetic
| operation (assumed to be X and Y). As an added bonus, XY()

Program 14.6 - PHYSICAL   Page 309

| will succeed if neither argument is a physical quantity |
| (the old operation can be applied). |

```
        DEFINE('XY()')                          :(XY_END)
XY      (DIFFER(DATATYPE(X), 'PHYS')
+       DIFFER(DATATYPE(Y), 'PHYS'))            :S(RETURN)
        X = NORM(X) ; Y = NORM(Y)               :(FRETURN)
XY_END                                          :(PHYSICAL_END)
```

| The definitions of the separate functions are now greatly |
| simplified because of the utilities written above |

```
MINUS   MINUS  = XY()  MINUS.(X)                :S(RETURN)
        MINUS  = PHYS(-VAL(X),NUM(X),DEN(X))    :(RETURN)

SUM     SUM    = XY()  SUM.(X,Y)                :S(RETURN)
        SUM = PHYS(VAL(X) + VAL(Y), NUM(X), DEN(X))  :(RETURN)

DIFF    DIFF   = X + -Y                         :(RETURN)

MULT    MULT   = XY()  MULT.(X,Y)               :S(RETURN)
        MULT   = PHYS(VAL(X) * VAL(Y), NUM(X) NUM(Y),
+              DEN(X) DEN(Y))                   :(RETURN)

DIV     DIV    = XY()  DIV.(X,Y)                :S(RETURN)
        DIV    = PHYS(VAL(X) / VAL(Y), NUM(X) DEN(Y),
+              DEN(X) NUM(Y))                   :(RETURN)

EQ      XY()                                    :F(EQ_1)
        EQ.(X,Y)                                :S(RETURN) F(FRETURN)
EQ_1    (EQ(VAL(X),VAL(Y)) IDENT(NUM(X),NUM(Y))
+              IDENT(DEN(X),DEN(Y)))            :S(RETURN) F(FRETURN)
PHYSICAL_END
```

Names referenced   Name   Type   Where defined
by PHYSICAL: REDEFINE *   Function   Program 14.5
                    ORDER   Function   Program 3.1
* indicates name is referenced in the initialization section.

Epilogue

As an example of the use of physical arithmetic, we may assign:

```
                    MET. = PHYS(1, 'M')
                    SEC. = PHYS(1, 'S')
                    KG.  = PHYS(1, 'K')
```

and from now on we need not so much as employ the PHYS() functional form as it will be called implicitly. Thus a Newton is a Met.^{2}/Sec.^{2} so we write:

```
                    NEWT. = (MET. * MET.) / (SEC. * SEC.)
```

Chapter 14 - FUNCTION FUNCTIONS

and a Joule is a Newton-Meter:

$$JL. = NEWT. * MET.$$

Though we are using an MKS system as a base for our physical quantities, we can specify any given problem and perform all calculations in thoroughly colloquial units. For example, we can express foot, mile and acre as:

$$IN. = MET. / 39.4$$
$$FT. = 12 * IN.$$
$$MI. = 5280 * FT.$$
$$ACRE = (MI. * MI.) / 640$$

We may then express computations entirely in the new units. For example, to print the acreage of a plot of ground 200' by 250' we write:

$$OUTPUT = VAL(200 * FT. * 250 * FT. / ACRE) \ ' \ ACRES'$$

We may even dispense with the asterisk between 200 and FT. but this is left as an exercise.

| %%%% o-routines and state functions | The notion of co-routine is of interest from several standpoints. In theoretical circles, it is as worshiped a programming practice as the goto is deplored. However, this theoretical enthusiasm does not carry over to the practical world. Practical programmers shun co-routines to a greater extent than they embrace goto's. Nonetheless, techniques for the construction of well-formed programs are not very well developed nor understood at this writing and study of the co-routine protocol is warranted merely for the light it can shed on this other, more general, issue.

As remarked by Knuth [Vol. 1, p. 191], small examples of co-routines do not seem to exist and so we must construct a somewhat elaborate situation merely to demonstrate what it is. The best example seems to be one furnished by a compiler. As we have discussed previously (Chapter 11), a compiler is frequently decomposed into lexical analysis and syntactic analysis. The purpose of lexical analysis is to decompose a string into a sequence of discrete non-decomposible objects frequently represented by pointers into a symbol table. Thus, the portion of SNOBOL4 program:

$$(ALPHA + BETA \ \ GAMMA)$$

will be analyzed by the lexical analyzer into seven components, i.e., left parenthesis, ALPHA, binary plus, BETA, binary blank, GAMMA and right parenthesis. It may be seen from this example that the output of the lexical analyzer is not determined completely from the characters which appear before it on the input stream but is also based on characters which

Co-routines and state functions   Page 311

have previously been processed. Thus, if the last token passed back had been a binary operator, then a blank preceding an identifier (such as BETA) is ignored, but if the last token had been an identifier (or constant, right parenthesis, etc.) then the blank preceding another identifier is interpreted as an operator.

The lexical analyzer can most naturally be described by state transitions. For example, after having processed a left parenthesis, the lexical analyzer is in the same state as after it has processed a binary operator. Also, after having processed a right parenthesis it is in the same state it is in when it has processed an identifier. Though this simple example only depicts two such states there are in fact several others.

States are most naturally represented by a location within the program which is currently being executed. Now this presents an anomaly if, as frequently happens, the syntactic analyzer calls the lexical analyzer for each token. This is because called functions do not normally 'remember' their state but rather begin each computation afresh from some fixed entry point.

We may at this point wonder if we had not got things backward. Maybe the lexical analyzer should call the syntactic analyzer each time it wants to dispose of one of its tokens. But then the shoe is on the other foot. The state of the syntactic analyzer is also best recorded by means of a location.

This dilemma is resolved by a co-routine linkage. The jump-and-set-link instruction, common in most machines, can jump to a location and simultaneously set a register to the current location. By means of this instruction the lexical analyzer, when it wishes to return to the syntactic analyzer, can jump to a common return point which can save the contents of this register and use this as the start up point when the lexical analyzer is reentered. From the point of view of the lexical analyzer, it is like <u>calling</u> the syntactic analyzer. Actually, a little section of code is needed to make it seem as though each is calling the other in an entirely symmetric way.

We may at this point step back and wonder why the need for co-routines is not felt more frequently than it is. Certainly it cannot be the inappropriateness of modeling computational behavior by state transitions as this is very common. The answer must lie in the fact that few functions require shifts in entry point to operate effectively. A shift in entry point implies that the next computation will depend on the ones which went before; that is, the function is non-homomorphic.*

Non-homomorphic transformations are frequently homomorphic if the units are made large enough. Thus, lexical analysis, when

---

*Recall from Chapter 3 that a homomorphic string transformation T is one such that $T(S_1 S_2) = T(S_1) T(S_2)$.

Page 312   Chapter 14   -   FUNCTION FUNCTIONS

considered on a token basis, is non-homomorphic but is
homomorphic on a per-statement basis. This is, in fact, one
of the advantages of a string language (or a list language).
Entire sequences may be ported across functional boundaries
which may then be aligned with the natural decomposition of a
problem into homomorphic transformations.

Such decompositions alone, however, are not sufficient, necessarily, to reduce the complexity of large practical problems
simply because the natural homomorphic transformation may be
considerably complex (as is the case with a compiler). This,
incidentally, is why simple co-routine examples don't exist.
Simple examples tend to be homomorphic or at least expressible
as simple homomorphic transformations.

As stated above, the conventional co-routine protocol requires
a jump-and-set-link instruction. No such facility exists in
SNOBOL4 nor can one be programmed. The main reason for this
is that in order for a statement to be pointed to, it must
have a label; the 'pointer' is a string (identical to the
label) and goto's are permitted by indirection (unary $). The
&STNO and &LASTNO keywords provide statement numbers which
could be quite useful in this regard except for the fact that
these numbers are entirely descriptive. No mechanism exists
for going to a statement with some given number.

In any event, it is not clear that a direct translation from
assembly language is the form most useful to the SNOBOL4
programmer. It is, in fact, more likely that we would want
something closer to the normal function mechanism in which arguments are passed, values returned and temporaries saved.
This is provided by the state function.

```
||  Program   ||
||   14.7     ||
||  STATEF    ||
```
A _state function_ is one whose next entry
point (its state) is determined by the
return. In particular, in our rendition, if
the next entry point is to be label ENTRY_2,
then the goto should take the form

:(RET('ENTRY_2'))

Returning from a state function is done only by calling
RET(label).

```
| A State function is defined by a call to STATEF.  It must |
| not execute a RETURN but must pass control back via a call |
| to RET(NEXT) where NEXT is the next entry point.          |
```

        DEFINE('STATEF(PROTO,LBL)NEWL')
        DEFINE('RET(NEXT)NAME')   :(STATEF_END)

| Entry point for STATEF. Determine the nominal entry point
| (LBL) for the state function. Then create a new label

Program 14.8 - STACK

| (NLBL) which will serve as the real entry point for the |
| function. |

```
STATEF   PROTO   IDENT(LBL)   BREAK(' (')  . LBL
         NLBL  = LBL  '_ENTRY'
         DEFINE(PROTO, NLBL)
```

| At this entry point we push our name so that upon return |
| we know what function we were in. |

```
         CODE(NLBL  " PUSH('" NLBL "')  :($" NLBL ")" )
         $NLBL  = LBL                              :(RETURN)
```

| Entry point for RET: Get the name pushed on entry. Assign |
| our argument (NEXT) to this name so that we know where to |
| come back to next time. Then indicate a return. |

```
RET      NAME  = POP()
         $NAME = NEXT
         RET   = .RETURN                          :(NRETURN)
STATEF_END
```

Names referenced	Name	Type	Where defined
by STATEF:	PUSH	Function	Program 5.5
	POP	Function	Program 5.6

Epilogue

An example of the use of STATEF is given in Exercise 14.18.

	Program	
	14.8	
	STACK	

The functions PUSH, POP and TOP (Progs. 5.5, 5.6 and 5.7) are fine if you only need one stack. What should one do if one requires more than one stack? We could provide an optional second argument to designate which of several stacks are intended. For example, PUSH(V,N) could push an item V onto a stack designated by N. The principle disadvantage of this approach is that it produces code which lacks clarity. Another disadvantage is that an extra instruction must be executed in a rather simple function resulting in inefficiencies. To correct these deficiencies,, we will incorporate the name of the stack into the name of the function. For example, PUSHA(V) will push onto stack A the value V. In general any string may take the place of 'A' as a stack designator.

To automate the process of creating the stack functions, we will write a function STACK(suffix). STACK will define three stack-manipulation functions, POPsuffix, PUSHsuffix, and TOPsuffix. For example, STACK('A') will define the three functions, PUSHA(V), POPA() and TOPA().

Chapter 14 - FUNCTION FUNCTIONS

```
            DEFINE('STACK(SUF) S')
            DATA('LINK(VALUE,NEXT)')              :(STACK_END)
```
┌───┐
│ Entry point: Assign to S a long string equal to the code   │
│ we have to create except that the string 'SUF' is used   │
│ where the suffix will eventually be placed.   │
└───┘
```
STACK      S    =
+         'PUSHSUF      STACK_SUF = LINK(V,STACK_SUF)           ;'
+         '             PUSHSUF = .VALUE(STACK_SUF)   :(NRETURN);'
+         'POPSUF       IDENT(STACK_SUF)              :S(FRETURN);'
+         '             POPSUF = VALUE(STACK_SUF)                ;'
+         '             STACK_SUF = NEXT(STACK_SUF)   :(RETURN)  ;'
+         'TOPSUF       IDENT(STACK_SUF)              :S(FRETURN);'
+         '             TOPSUF = .VALUE(STACK_SUF)    :(NRETURN) ;'
```
┌───┐
│ Now we create the required code and define functions.   │
└───┘
```
            CODE(REPL(S,'SUF',SUF))
            DEFINE('PUSH'  SUF  '(V)')
            DEFINE('POP'   SUF  '()')
            DEFINE('TOP'   SUF  '()')                   :(RETURN)
STACK_END
```

Names referenced   Name   Type   Where defined
by STACK: REPL   Function   Program 3.15

Epilogue

Note the use of the REPL function to create code. It is possible to avoid the use of REPL by a judicious concatenation of string constants and variables (try it) but it is impossible to avoid going mad in the process.

???
????????????????????????? EXERCISES ???????????????????????????
???

┌─────────────────┐
│ Exercise 14.1   │ If we attempted to define MAX(X,Y) by means
└─────────────────┘ of:

            DEXP('MAX(X,Y) = X ; MAX = GT(Y,X) Y ')

we would experience a difficulty. (a) What is it? (b) What simple change in this call will correct things?

┌─────────────────┐
│ Exercise 14.2   │ Modify DEXP (Prog. 14.1) so that iden-
└─────────────────┘ tifiers following the argument list are regarded as function temporaries (requires modifying one statement).

Exercises for chapter 14

Exercise 14.3 The encoding of LOADEX (in Prog. 14.2) assumes no syntax error in the external code.
(a) Modify LOADEX so that if the external code contains a syntax error it will print out the code and establish a function body which will always fail.

Exercise 14.4 Rewrite DEXTERN so that it operates by tracing. That is, on first call of the indicated function, a routine is called which loads the function (you may use LOADEX to simplify matters). Be sure to issue a STOPTR after loading the function.

Exercise 14.5 A particularly long program consists of sections labeled L1, L2, ..., L100. Not all of these sections are in use in any given run. But, depending on the data, any section <u>could</u> be reached. Using LOADEX, how could you replace these sections with something smaller?

Exercise 14.6 Encode FTR_CALL and FTR_TRC to trace functions as required by FTRACE (Prog. 14.3).

Exercise 14.7 Should the definition of FTR_CALL and FTR_RET precede or follow the definition of FTRACE or does it not make any difference?

Exercise 14.8 Modify INSULATE (Prog. 14.4) so that it doesn't depend on TRACE to obtain control on calls or returns.

Exercise 14.9 How could INSULATE be used to guard against modifications of the ARB variable?

Exercise 14.10 Define a complex number by the structure

DATA('COMPLEX(R,I)')

where R is the real part and I is the imaginary part. With the help of REDEFINE (Prog. 14.5) extend the binary operators +, -, *, / and the binary functions GT, GE, LE, LT, EQ, NE to operate on complex numbers if <u>one</u> or both of the arguments are complex. To simplify things, write a generalized argument processing function which will succeed if both arguments are <u>not</u> complex and will otherwise fail converting any non-complex argument to complex.

Chapter 14 - FUNCTION FUNCTIONS

| Exercise 14.11 | Assuming that the binary arithmetic operators have been redefined to operate on COMPLEX quantities as in the previous exercise, can the PHYSICAL package also be used with the VAL field a possibly complex quantity? Said another way, what trouble spots are there in compounding redefinitions along the lines suggested?

| Exercise 14.12 | Redefine the arithmetic operators to operate on identically-dimensioned arrays.

| Exercise 14.13 | Ordinarily a function such as F() cannot set the variable F as a side effect since the value of F is saved at the call and restored on return. Strange as it seems, however, a technique exists to do precisely that. In particular, it is possible that F(X) will assign the value of X to the variable F. Define such an F.

| Exercise 14.14 | Generalize the previous exercise. That is, define a function DEF(NAME) such that, for example, DEF('F') will establish F(X) as equivalent to:

$$F = X$$

| Exercise 14.15 | Rewrite STATEF (Prog. 14.7) such that on a return via the call RET(LABEL) the function DEFINE is called with LABEL the new entry point.

| Exercise 14.16 | In the epilogue to PHYSICAL (Prog. 14.6) we expressed the quantity 200 FT. with an intervening asterisk (denoting multiplication). This could have been avoided by redefining concatenation (a purifying experience). What four statements need be added to PHYSICAL so that concatenation as well as multiplication form the product of physical units. (Hints: Be cautious of a circular definition, i.e. using concatenation to define concatenation, unless the recursion stops. Don't worry about the various predicate uses of concatenation since your program won't get control if one of the items to be concatenated fails.)

| Exercise 14.17 | Add an FRET(NEXT) function to provide an FRETURN facility to STATEF (Prog. 14.7).

| Exercise 14.18 | Draw a state transition table for a lexical analysis of SNOBOL4 expressions (i.e., assume no labels, no pattern matching, no goto-fields, just expressions) as follows. For each state and each token (left parenthesis, identifier, number, operator, etc.) direct

an arrow to the next state and indicate what, if anything, is to be returned. Implement this as a state function.

| Exercise 14.19 | Write a function FUNCTION(NAME) that will succeed returning the null string if NAME is the name of a programmer-defined function. Otherwise it should fail. Hint: the definition of function should appear before every other function. For extra credit, any name OPSYN'ed to some other name should also be regarded as a programmer-defined function.

CHAPTER FIFTEEN

CONTENTS

COMB	15.1
DECOMB	15.2
INFINIP	15.3
FLOOR	15.4
CEIL	15.5
SQRT	15.6
TRIG	15.7
ARC	15.8
LOG	15.9
RAISE	15.10

Program 15.1 - COMB   Page 319

~~ven special-purpose programming languages require arithmetic. The original SNOBOL contained the five arithmetic operators (+, -, /, *, **) which operated only on strings (that resembled integers) within a limited form of expression (eg. no parentheses). SNOBOL3 allowed more freedom (e.g., parenthetical groupings were permitted) in forming expressions but retained the string format for representing integers. SNOBOL4 broke with the tradition of the single datatype and introduced both INTEGER and REAL as separate types. Moreover, it represented these objects internally as machine integers and reals (i.e. floating point numbers) respectively. Hence, a study of SNOBOL4 numbers, in contrast to previous SNOBOL's, is very much a study of how they are represented on most machines.

Most machines for which SNOBOL4 has been implemented are binary machines representing integers in base-two notation. In every case known to the author, the negatives are represented in two's complement form. This is the binary equivalent of representing, say, -2 by a number of the form 999...99998. Hence, the range of integers is usually

$$[-2^{W-1}, 2^{W-1} - 1] \qquad (15.1)$$

where W is the number of bits in the field allowed for integers. Usually, W is the word size of the machine. For example, on the IBM 360/370 implementation of both SNOBOL4 and SPITBOL, the range of integers is $[-2^{31}, 2^{31}-1]$.

The first several programs offer some examples of integer manipulation, the last of which (INFINIP) being aimed at overcoming the restrictions imposed by a finite word size.

	Program	
	15.1	
	COMB	

The function COMB(N,M) will return the number of combinations of N things taken M at a time, usually written in 'over' notation as shown and defined below:

$$COMB(N,M) = \begin{bmatrix} N \\ M \end{bmatrix} = \frac{N!}{(N-M)!\, M!} \qquad (15.2)$$

where $N \geq M \geq 0$. By convention $0! = 1$. For N < M the value of COMB, by convention, is 0. COMB(N,M) may also be regarded as the coefficient of $X^{**}M$ in the expansion of $(X + Y)^{**}N$ and is therefore called the binomial coefficient. It is illustrated by the easily remembered Pascal's triangle:

Page 320   Chapter 15 - NUMBERS

```
                    1
                  1   1
                1   2   1
              1   3   3   1
            1   4   6   4   1
          1   5  10  10   5   1
                  ...
```

in which N corresponds to the row (starting with 0) and M corresponds to the position within the row (starting with 0). Note that each term may be found by adding the two elements immediately above it. Hence we have a simple recursive method for computing COMB(N,M). A slightly more efficient method is used below which is based on the identity:

$$\begin{bmatrix} N \\ M \end{bmatrix} = \frac{N}{M} \begin{bmatrix} N-1 \\ M-1 \end{bmatrix} \qquad (15.3)$$

provided M > 0.

```
┌─────────────────────────────────────────────────────────────────┐
│ COMB(N,M)  returns  the number of combinations of N things     │
│ taken M at a time.                                              │
└─────────────────────────────────────────────────────────────────┘
```

```
              DEFINE('COMB(N,M)')                    :(COMB_END)
COMB     COMB    =  EQ(M,0)   1                      :S(RETURN)
         COMB    =  COMB(N - 1,M - 1) * N / M        :(RETURN)
COMB_END
```

Epilogue

Note that we do not write COMB in terms of factorials as this may needlessly result in integer overflow during the calculation of intermediate results. An alternative approach is to write COMB iteratively and is to be recommended if time is an issue. This is left as Exercise 15.1. A rather bizarre method for computing COMB relies on pattern matching. This too is left as an exercise.

```
┌──────────────────┐
││   Program    ││
││    15.2      ││
││   DECOMB     ││
└──────────────────┘
```
We have seen several methods of representing numbers, the Roman system, the positional number systems (BASEB and BASE10, Progs. 2.4 and 2.5) and the factorial number system (PERMUTATION, Prog. 12.1 and its prologue). The <u>combinatorial number system</u> is yet another number system where a sequence of integers can be used to represent a presumably larger integer. Given a fixed number n called the <u>nome</u>, one can represent <u>any</u> positive integer K by a vector $K_n, \ldots, K_2, K_1$ such that

$$K = \begin{bmatrix} K_n \\ n \end{bmatrix} + \ldots + \begin{bmatrix} K_2 \\ 2 \end{bmatrix} + \begin{bmatrix} K_1 \\ 1 \end{bmatrix} \qquad (15.4)$$

Moreover, if we add the restriction that:

$$K_n > \ldots > K_2 > K_1 \geq 0 \qquad (15.5)$$

the representation is unique. The values $K_n, \ldots, K_2, K_1$ are called <u>cogets</u> (as opposed to digits). The combinatorial number system can be used to find a uniformly distributed evaluation of poker hands (POKEV, Prog. 17.6) and this relies mainly on the fact that cogets are monotonically decreasing.

To see that the representation is unique (for a fixed nome) note that if the cogets assume their least value ($K_1=0$, $K_2=1$, ..., $K_n=n-1$) we obtain $K=0$. Next, we assert that if the cogets assume their largest value with $K_n=M$, then K will be incremented by exactly one if K_n is increased by one (to M+1) and all other cogets are made as low as possible. That is:

$$\begin{bmatrix} M \\ n \end{bmatrix} + \begin{bmatrix} M-1 \\ n-1 \end{bmatrix} + \ldots + \begin{bmatrix} M-n+1 \\ 1 \end{bmatrix} + 1 = \begin{bmatrix} M+1 \\ n \end{bmatrix}$$

That this is true follows from the rule of forming Pascal's triangle, viz.

$$\begin{bmatrix} M+1 \\ n \end{bmatrix} = \begin{bmatrix} M \\ n \end{bmatrix} + \begin{bmatrix} M \\ n-1 \end{bmatrix} \qquad (15.6)$$

The second of the two terms on the right is decomposed according to this formula and this is continued until the '1' is reached.

Finally note that increasing K_1 by 1 increases K by 1. From these three observations, it follows that all integers are representable and that their representation is unique.

DECOMB(S) will regard S as a sequence of cogets, i.e. a number in the combinatorial number system, and will return its corresponding integer value. Cogets are represented as characters from an alphabet (COMB_ALPHA) much as we have previously done with positional representations.

| DECOMB(S) returns the decimal number equivalent of the ar-
| gument S regarded as a representation in the combinatorial
| number system.

```
            DEFINE('DECOMB(S)T')
            COMB_ALPHA  =   '0123456789ABCDEFGHIJKLMNOP'
                                                            :(DECOMB_END)
DECOMB    S  LEN(1) . T =                                   :F(RETURN)
          COMB_ALPHA  @K  T                                 :F(FRETURN)
          DECOMB = DECOMB + COMB(K,SIZE(S) + 1)             :(DECOMB)
DECOMB_END
```

Names referenced   Name   Type   Where defined
by DECOMB: COMB   Function   Program 15.1

Epilogue

For additional information concerning the combinatorial number system see Lehmer [1964] or Whitehead [1973].

| | Program | | INFINIP is a package of infinite precision
| | 15.3 | | arithmetic (i.e. integer) functions. Large
| | INFINIP | | integers are represented by strings of
                       digits and so the size of integers permitted
is not quite infinite but is limited by the maximum length of strings. This is generally quite large so that for all intents and purposes the precision may be regarded as infinite.

INFINIP redefines virtually all arithmetic operators to handle large integers in an upward compatible way. This facilitates their use, and makes them plug-in-able to routines that have already been written using conventional facilities. It also serves to make the algorithms themselves clearer, since they are written, in part, recursively.

INFINIP has applications in addition to generating numerical wall-paper. For example, it can alleviate some rather severe restrictions encountered in base conversions (BASEB and BASE10, Progs. 2.4 and 2.5) and permutation generation (PERMUTATION, Prog. 12.1).

Our basic operating philosophy in writing INFINIP was not speed. A linked-list approach would probably have been considerably faster. Our main goal was to produce a legible and flexible package that could serve (a) to produce the effect and (b) as a kind of extended precision laboratory in which different algorithms could be tested. Techniques used to implement infinite-precision arithmetic can also be found in Knuth [Vol. 2], Blum [1965], and Collins [1966].

Program 15.3 - INFINIP

```
    INFINIP - an infinite (just about) precision arithmetic
    package.   The following operators and built-in functions
    are redefined.
```

```
        REDEFINE('-','MINUS(X) Y')
        REDEFINE(    ,'GT(X,Y)')
        REDEFINE(    ,'EQ(X,Y)')
        REDEFINE(    ,'GE(X,Y)')
        REDEFINE(    ,'NE(X,Y)')
        REDEFINE(    ,'LT(X,Y)')
        REDEFINE(    ,'LT(X,Y)')
        REDEFINE(    ,'LE(X,Y)')
        REDEFINE('-','DIFF(X,Y)')
        REDEFINE('+','SUM(X,Y) X1,X2,Y1,Y2,K')
        REDEFINE('*','MULT(X,Y) X1,X2,K')
        REDEFINE('/','DIV(X,Y) X1,X2,Y1,Y2,T,T1,T2,KX,KY')
        REDEFINE(    ,'REMDR(X,Y)')
```

    Pattern definitions:

```
        SIGN_OFF   =  POS(0)     '-'
        LDG_ZEROS  =  BREAK('123456789') | RTAB(1)
        NO_DIGITS  =  8
```

    Utility functions

```
        DEFINE('SMALL()')
        DEFINE('SPLIT(NAME,PAT)')                    :(INFINIP_END)
```

    SMALL() will succeed if X and Y are small integers defined
    strategically as integers whose sum or difference will not
    cause overflow. Tactically, they are defined as numbers
    whose digits do not exceed NO_DIGITS.

```
SMALL      (LE.(SIZE(X),NO_DIGITS)
+           LE.(SIZE(Y),NO_DIGITS))       :S(RETURN) F(FRETURN)
```

    SPLIT(NAME,PAT) will split the named string into two
    parts, NAME1 and NAME2 (after removing leading zeros). It
    returns the amount of the split measured from the right.
    The split is determined by the incoming pattern (PAT); if
    this is null the split is approximately half.

```
SPLIT      PAT    =  IDENT(PAT) LEN(SIZE($NAME) / 2)
           $NAME     (PAT | '') . $(NAME 1) @SPLIT (SPAN('0') | '')
+                  REM . $(NAME 2)
           SPLIT  =  SIZE($NAME) - SPLIT          :(RETURN)
```

    Unary minus - Remember, REDEFINE establishes MINUS. as the
    old MINUS built-in.

```
MINUS      MINUS  =  SMALL()   MINUS.(X)          :S(RETURN)
           MINUS  =  X
           MINUS     SIGN_OFF  =                  :S(RETURN)
           MINUS  =  '-'  X                       :(RETURN)
```

Page 324   Chapter 15 - NUMBERS

```
┌─────────────────────────────────────────────────────────────────┐
│ The predicates - They assume integers in normal form (i.e.      │
│ no leading zeros).                                              │
└─────────────────────────────────────────────────────────────────┘
GT      SMALL()                             :F(GT_1)
        GT.(X,Y)                            :S(RETURN) F(FRETURN)
GT_1    X    SIGN_OFF  =                    :F(GT_2)
        Y    SIGN_OFF  =                    :F(FRETURN)
        SWAP(.X,.Y)
GT_2    Y    SIGN_OFF  =                    :S(RETURN)
        LGT(LPAD(X,SIZE(Y),'0'),
+            LPAD(Y,SIZE(X),'0'))           :S(RETURN) F(FRETURN)

EQ      SMALL()                             :F(EQ_1)
        EQ.(X,Y)                            :S(RETURN) F(FRETURN)
EQ_1    IDENT(X,Y)                          :S(RETURN) F(FRETURN)

GE      ¬(¬GT(X,Y)  ¬EQ(X,Y))               :S(RETURN) F(FRETURN)
NE      EQ(X,Y)                             :S(FRETURN) F(RETURN)
LT      GE(X,Y)                             :S(FRETURN) F(RETURN)
LE      GT(X,Y)                             :S(FRETURN) F(RETURN)
┌─────────────────────────────────────────────────────────────────┐
│ DIFF(X,Y)   -   Let SUM(X,Y) handle it.                         │
└─────────────────────────────────────────────────────────────────┘
DIFF    DIFF  =  X + -Y                     :(RETURN)

┌─────────────────────────────────────────────────────────────────┐
│ SUM(X,Y)  -  There are essentially two cases: plus plus         │
│ and plus minus.  We first reduce to cases.                      │
└─────────────────────────────────────────────────────────────────┘
SUM     SUM  =  SMALL()  SUM.(X,Y)          :S(RETURN)
        SUM  =  LT(X,0)  -(-X + -Y)         :S(RETURN)
        Y    SIGN_OFF  =                    :S(SUM_1)

┌─────────────────────────────────────────────────────────────────┐
│ Here is plus plus.  Simply divide and conquer.                  │
└─────────────────────────────────────────────────────────────────┘
        (LT(X,Y)   SWAP(.X,.Y))
        K    =   SPLIT(.X)
        Y    =   Y + X2
        SPLIT(.Y,RTAB(K))
        SUM  =   (Y1 + X1) LPAD(Y2,K,'0')   :(RETURN)

┌─────────────────────────────────────────────────────────────────┐
│ Here is plus minus.  Make sure X ≥ Y.  Then add the 10's        │
│ complement of Y.                                                │
└─────────────────────────────────────────────────────────────────┘
SUM_1   SUM  =  GT(Y,X)   -(Y - X)          :S(RETURN)
        Y    =  LPAD(Y,SIZE(X),'0')
        SUM  =  X + 1 + REPLACE(Y,'0123456789','9876543210')
        SUM  '1'  LDG_ZEROS  REM . SUM      :(RETURN)

┌─────────────────────────────────────────────────────────────────┐
│ MULT(X,Y)  -  Multiply is fairly simply written especially      │
│ if we concentrate on reducing the size of one argument at       │
│ a time.  Note that the test for small size is somewhat          │
│ different here.                                                 │
└─────────────────────────────────────────────────────────────────┘
MULT    MULT  =  LE(SIZE(X) + SIZE(Y),NO_DIGITS)
+                MULT.(X,Y)                 :S(RETURN)
```

REALs and Mixed Mode   Page 325

```
        MULT    =   LT(X,0)     -X * -Y              :S(RETURN)
        MULT    =   LT(Y,0)     -(X * -Y)            :S(RETURN)
        (GT(Y,X)    SWAP(.X,.Y))
        MULT    =   EQ(Y,0)     0
        K       =   SPLIT(.X)
        MULT    =   (Y * X1)    DUPL('0',K)
        MULT    =   MULT    +   X2  *   Y            :(RETURN)
```

| DIV(X,Y) -   First we handle negative arguments much as we
| did with multiply. The next part, more than any other
| section requires some explanation. Imagine a long division
| operation with two (rather large) digits Y1, Y2 being
| divided into two other large digits X1, X2. The trial
| divisor T1 (on top of the line) is multiplied by the
| divisor Y and subtracted from the left end of X to produce
| error term T. This term is then divided by Y to obtain a
| final adjustment.

```
DIV     DIV     =   SMALL()     DIV.(X,Y)            :S(RETURN)
        DIV     =   LT(X,0)     -(-X / Y)            :S(RETURN)
        DIV     =   LT(Y,0)     -(X / -Y)            :S(RETURN)
        DIV     =   GT(Y,X)     0                    :S(RETURN)
        KY      =   SPLIT(.Y,LEN(NO_DIGITS / 2)  | REM)
        KX      =   SPLIT(.X,LEN(NO_DIGITS))
        T1      =   X1 / Y1
        T2      =   DUPL('0', KX - KY)
        T       =   X   -   ((T1 * Y)   T2)
        DIV     =   T1  T2
        T       =   LT(T,0)     T + 1 - Y
        DIV     =   DIV +   (T / Y)                  :(RETURN)
```

| And last but not least, REMDR.

```
REMDR       REMDR   =   X   -   (X / Y) * Y          :(RETURN)
INFINIP_END
```

Names referenced   Name   Type   Where defined
by INFINIP: REDEFINE   Function   Program 14.5
                     SWAP   Function   Program 3.14
                     LPAD   Function   Program 3.2

```
┌─────────────────────────┐
| %%%% EALs and Mixed Mode |   REALs consist of three fields,
|  %  %                    |   a sign bit, the _exponent_ (or
| %%%% |  characteristic) and the _mantissa._ The exponent in-
|  % % |  dicates the extent that an assumed base must be
|  %  % |  raised whereas the mantissa represents the most
└──────┘  significant bits of the number.  In symbols:
```

$$NUMBER = mantissa * base^{exponent}$$

REALs, of course, vastly increase the range of numbers representable at the sacrifice of precision. While the particular details of representing floating point numbers differ from machine to machine, there are none-the-less a few general practices which most machine manufacturers adhere to:

The three fields of a floating point number are arranged in their order of significance and adjusted so that comparison of two quantities can be made using the <u>same arithmetic comparator as integers</u>. This places the sign bit in the first position, followed by the exponent and then the mantissa. To facilitate comparisons, the exponent is represented in so-called <u>excess notation</u> with the most negative exponent represented as 00...0 and the highest as 11...1. Also, the mantissa is normalized to produce, for any given number, a unique exponent, again, so that the comparison can be carried out. The mantissa is normalized by shifting it to the left and decreasing the exponent until further shifting destroys information. The mantissa is generally assumed to represent a fraction just less than 1. With a binary base, the lead digit of the normalized number is always 1 and so represents redundant information. It can, and actually has been, omitted on at least one machine (the PDP-11). By convention, a floating point 0 is represented as an all-0 word. On the PDP-11 it is the only bit pattern not otherwise used.

The IBM 360 uses a base of 16 and hence the normalization process may not produce, in the mantissa, a leading bit of 1. Rather, the leading four bits must contain a 1. For this reason, numbers whose leading hexadecimal digit is low (such as 1 or 2) cannot be represented very accurately (the error as a fraction of the number is relatively large) and hence the need exists on the 360, more than on most other machines, for double and quadruple precision.

We will speak (loosely) of the <u>range</u> of REAL numbers and by this we will mean roughly the extremes of values the REALs can achieve. These can be very high, very low or very negative and are governed almost solely by the base and the maximum exponent. We will speak of the precision P as meaning the binary precision given generally as:

$$P = M - Log_2 B$$

where M is the size of the mantissa in bits (including invisible bits) and B is the base of the exponent. Approximately, the precision is the negative log (to the base 2) of the relative error of a number due to the finite resolution of the representation.

It should be noted that integers up to 2**M, or so, can be represented exactly as REALs and that operations such as plus, minus and multiply are exact provided no intermediate results exceed this limit.

The rules governing mixed expressions in SNOBOL4 are similar to those in Fortran. If the two operands of a binary arithmetic operator (other than **) or a binary comparator (GE, EQ,

Programs 15.4 & 15.5 - FLOOR & CEIL   Page 327

etc.) have different types (one INTEGER and the other REAL)
then the integer is converted to REAL before the operation
proceeds. SPITBOL contains a DREAL type (double precision)
and if one of the arguments to such an operation is DREAL then
the other is converted if necessary to DREAL.

One important difference with Fortran (or PL/I for that matter) is that the types are not declared but are contained as
part of the value. This means that it is possible to write a
routine which can accept either type as argument and return a
correct result. For example, assuming we wish to write a
routine RECIP(X) which will return the reciprocal of the number X, we can simply write:

```
RECIP         RECIP = 1.0 / X              :(RETURN)
```

This routine will operate correctly whether the argument is
INTEGER, REAL, or DREAL.

```
┌─────────────────────┐
||   Programs       ||   FLOOR(X)  is defined as the largest in-
||   15.4 & 15.5    ||   teger not greater than X.   CEIL(X)  is
||   FLOOR & CEIL   ||   the  smallest  integer not less than X.
└─────────────────────┘   They are both related (nonlinearly) to
the integer conversion facility which truncates toward zero.
```

```
          DEXP('CEIL(X) = -FLOOR(-X)')

          DEFINE('FLOOR(X)')                       :(FLOOR_END)
FLOOR     FLOOR = CONVERT(X,'INTEGER')
          GE(X,0)                                  :S(RETURN)
          FLOOR = NE(X,FLOOR) FLOOR - 1            :(RETURN)
FLOOR_END
```

Names referenced	Name	Type	Where defined
by FLOORCEIL:	DEXP	Function	Program 14.1

Epilogue

FLOOR and CEIL, in addition to illustrating how
CONVERT(,'INTEGER') behaves, are of interest in their own
right. Below, let N be an integer and let X be a real. Then:

```
          N ≥ CEIL(X)      <==>     N ≥ X
          N < CEIL(X)      <==>     N < X              (15.7)
          N ≤ FLOOR(X)     <==>     N ≤ X
          N > FLOOR(X)     <==>     N > X
```

These identities can be used to solve some interesting integer
inequalities in a straightforward fashion. (See Exercise
15.9.)

Transcendental Functions A transcendental function is one that cannot be written (finitely) using the four fundamental operations of addition, subtraction, multiplication and division. Examples include the sine and other trigonometric functions, logarithms, etc. These may be represented as an infinite series (power series, Taylor series) of terms involving $X^{**}n$ where $n = 0, 1, 2, \ldots$ and X is the argument. This represents a readily available computational method which is often the best technique if the precision of the machine is unknown; i.e. if the computation is to be machine-independent or if it is to be equally valid for single and double precision.

Where the precision is known, a much more efficient technique is the so-called Chebyshev interpolation method. Since most libraries are written for a specific machine, this method is widely used and a little knowledge is helpful if only for the purpose of pirating existing code. Let us assume that we wish to approximate the function f(x) with an nth degree polynomial p(x) and, moreover, suppose that we wish p(x) to be the best such approximation in the so-called mini-max sense. That is, the maximum deviation from f(x) in some fixed range should be a minimum for all polynomials of that degree. We can immediately deduce a property that p(x) must have. Suppose some polynomial q(x) existed which had the same degree as p(x) and had the same lead coefficient of $x^{**}n$ and was such that the error of this approximation, f(x) - q(x), varied from a maximum of +M to a minimum of -M back to +M, to -M, etc. Suppose that there are exactly n+1 such maxima. Such polynomials can always be constructed, as we will see. Now suppose that q(x) is not as good an approximation as p(x). Then each of the local maxima are greater deviations than the largest deviation of f(x) - p(x). That means that

$$(f(x) - p(x)) - (f(x) - q(x)) = q(x) - p(x)$$

must oscillate back and forth across the abscissa; this means that there are n solutions to an (n-1) degree equation. This is impossible and hence we conclude that q(x) had to be at least as good in the mini-max sense as p(x). This is quite startling in view of the fact that no assumptions at all about the magnitude of M were made. Polynomials which oscillate about the axis n times over a given interval are derived from the oscillatory nature of the sine wave and are known as Chebyshev polynomials. We have no time or space to pursue this fascinating topic in greater detail but we may recommend Fox and Parker [1968] or Hastings [1955] for further reading.

The result of a Chebyshev approximation is a polynomial of the form

$$C + C_1 X + C_2 X^2 + \ldots + C_n X^n \qquad (15.8)$$

which is actually computed as:

$$C + X * (C_1 + X * (C_2 \ldots))$$

to minimize operations.

It is interesting to note that approximations of this kind can be found by an adaptive process in which successive approximations converge to the desired polynomial. Fox and Parker [1968, p.74] describe such a procedure originally due to Novodvorskii and Pinsker. Hence it would be possible to write a SNOBOL4 program to produce coefficients automatically for any given function, range and desired accuracy.

For a known function and a fixed precision, the Chebyshev interpolation coefficients can usually be looked up. Hastings [1955] is an excellent source. If unavailable, Handbook [NBS] should be adequate. For any specific machine, there has probably been some work done towards constructing a mathematical library, and such sources, if they exist, can often provide routines carefully tailored for a specific environment. One excellent source for the IBM 360 is IBM [360f].

The functions to follow are machine independent programs for computing many of the common transcendental functions. The results returned should be as precise as the arguments given, with the exception that DREAL precision in some cases may not obtain merely because one or more internal constants have less than DREAL precision. This difficulty is easily overcome and some exercises explore such modifications.

One problem that arises in writing machine-independent algorithms is determing the proper accuracy. For example, suppose we wish to compute the sum of the series:

$$\text{SUM} = X + X^2 + X^3 + \ldots \qquad (15.9)$$

where $0 < X < 1/2$. Ignore for the moment that the sum of the series is $1/(1-X)$ and suppose that we wish to calculate the same result in brute force fashion. How do we know when to stop adding new terms. We might think of setting up a PRECISION variable (adjusted for each machine) such that when the terms of the series fall below the quantity PRECISION * SUM, where SUM is the partial sum so far computed, we quit. This method has the disadvantage of being machine-dependent and does not give double precision results if X is DREAL. Hence we will avoid this method and employ a scheme to let the machine tell us when to quit. This will have the happy property of adapting to any machine and any precision. Our test is, in effect:

$$\text{EQ(SUM , SUM + X ** n)}$$

which means that in order to add X**n to our number we have to shift is so far to the right that all its '1' bits are lost. This is implemented by saving the old value of SUM in a tem-

Page 330   Chapter 15   -   NUMBERS

porary (T) and comparing, updating and branching all in the same statement at the base of the loop. The following statements compute the SUM of (15.9) according to this method.

```
          T    =  0
          SUM  =  0
          TERM =  1.0
LOOP      TERM =  TERM * X
          SUM  =  SUM + TERM
          T    =  NE(SUM, T) SUM                   :S(LOOP)
```

The reader is cautioned that this stopping test is not equivalent to:

$$EQ(TERM, 0)$$

If continually multiplied by X, TERM will ultimately become 0 (or raise machine underflow which many SNOBOL4's regard as an error) but not before it falls below the range of small numbers (a typical value is 2^{-128}) whereas to be <u>negligible</u> in the computation it need merely be below $X * 2^{-25}$ or so. Hence, even if underflow were not raised, the test would be quite inefficient.

```
┌─────────────────┐
││   Program    ││    SQRT(Y)  will   return the square root of the
││    15.6      ││    REAL number Y.  The returned precision will
││    SQRT      ││    equal the precision of Y. The algorithm used
└─────────────────┘    is an excellent example of  Newton's  Method
```
for solving implicit equations, which goes as follows. Suppose we wish to solve the equation:

$$f(x) = 0$$

for x, and suppose further that, given x, we can compute f(x) and the derivative f'(x). Starting with an estimate, x_1, for x, we can compute $f(x_1)$. Since this is supposed to be zero, we can estimate how far we are off by dividing this number by the slope $f'(x_1)$. We can then modify x_1 to obtain a new, and closer, estimate x_2 according to the formula:

$$x_2 = x_1 - f(x_1) / f'(x_1)$$

With the new estimate, a new error and slope are calculated and the process is repeated until the desired accuracy is obtained. In many cases, the computation converges rapidly to a correct solution. The rate of convergence and the question of convergence are decided by algebra for any particular case. To determine if the desired accuracy has been reached, we will wait until

Program 15.6 - SQRT

$$EQ \left[x_n , x_n - \frac{f(x_n)}{f'(x_n)} \right]$$

As previously stated, this will adapt to any machine and any argument.

To obtain the initial estimate, x_1, we draw a line tangent to the curve, $x = y^2$ at the point $(1,1)$. This curve, $y = (x+1)/2$, yields an estimate of the square root which is good for x close to 1, but quite poor for very large or very small values of x. While Newton's method will eventually converge on the correct value, the error is reduced by only a factor of 2 for large errors; this contrasts with a factor of 2/e for small errors (See Exercise 15.11). Hence, for efficiency purposes, the numbers are brought into an acceptable range by (a) inverting, (b) dividing by 4096, and (c) dividing by 16. Powers of two are used for range reduction, as opposed to powers of 10, as these operations can be done exactly on a binary machine. On the IBM 360/370, the exponent is a power of 16 (for this reason, it is sometimes regarded as a hexadecimal machine) and hence, powers of 16 are used where possible.

```
        DEFINE('SQRT(Y) T,ERR,SLOPE')          :(SQRT_END)
```

| Entry point: Range reduction and initialization.

```
SQRT    LT(Y,0)                                 :S(FRETURN)
        EQ(Y,0)                                 :S(RETURN)
        SQRT = LT(Y,0.05)  1. / SQRT(1. / Y)    :S(RETURN)
        SQRT = GT(Y,4096)  SQRT(Y / 4096.) * 64.:S(RETURN)
        SQRT = GT(Y,16)    SQRT(Y / 16.) * 4.   :S(RETURN)
        SQRT = (Y + 1.) / 2.
        T    = SQRT
```

| Successively increase the precision of our estimate

```
SQRT_1  ERR   = SQRT * SQRT - Y
        SLOPE = 2. * SQRT
        SQRT  = SQRT - (ERR / SLOPE)
        T     = LT(SQRT,T)   SQRT           :S(SQRT_1) F(RETURN)
SQRT_END
```

Epilogue

The speed of SQRT can be increased (by about 30%) by an algebraic condensation of the inner loop. This is left as an exercise.

```
|  Program  |    By elementary trigonometry, if we can obtain
|   15.7    |    any one of the six trigonometric  functions,
|   TRIG    |    viz.  sine,  cosine,  tangent,  cotangent,
                 secant or cosecant, we can obtain them  all.
```
Cotangent, secant and cosecant are merely reciprocals of tangent, cosine and sine respectively and are therefore not represented as functions here. Tangent and cosine are given in terms of the sine.

The algorithm for sine is from Beeler, et al [1972, p. 75] and relies on the following trigonometric identity:

$$\sin A = 3 \sin(A/3) - 4 \sin^3(A/3)$$

The identity is normally given as sin 3A and we speak of 'triple-angle' formulas. Collections of such identities are available in many handbooks such as Handbook [CR] and Handbook [NBS]. This formula is a recursive formula for obtaining the sine of an angle in terms of a smaller angle. If the angle ever becomes small enough we can say it equals itself (the angle is presumed to be given in radians and we assume the reader knows that one radian is 57.3° or 180/PI degrees). Again, the issue of when to terminate arises and this is done when subtracting off $4*\sin^3(A/3)$ does not modify $3*\sin(A/3)$. But this test must be made before sin(A/3) is called or else we will have an infinite recursive plunge. Hence we do the test on A/3. If equality obtains for A/3 it must also obtain for the slightly smaller value sin(A/3). Thus the algorithm terminates when $4*(A/3)^3$ is insignificant compared with $3*(A/3)$, or, equivalently, when $4*A^2$ is insignificant compared with 27. With 25 bits of precision, for example, this happens if A is 2^{-12} or so. Since A decreases by thirds, we will require eight recursive calls or so before the function is evaluated. This will depend somewhat on the original argument. By using other identities, the amount of recursion required can be considerably reduced. See Exercise 15.12.

```
          DEFINE('SIN(A) K')
          DEFINE('SIN.(A) ')
          PI. = 3.14159265358979                       :(SIN_END)
```
| Entry point: reduce range to [0, 2 PI.) |

```
SIN       SIN  = LT(A,0)     -SIN(-A)                  :S(RETURN)
          SIN  = LT(A,2 * PI.)  SIN.(A)                :S(RETURN)
          K    = CONVERT(A / (2 * PI.) , 'INTEGER')
          SIN  = SIN.(A - K * 2 * PI.)                 :(RETURN)
```
| Test and return or plunge recursively and adjust. |

```
SIN.      SIN. = EQ(27., 27. - 4 * A * A)  A           :S(RETURN)
          A    = SIN.(A / 3.)
          SIN. = A * (3 - 4 * A * A)                   :(RETURN)
SIN_END
```

> Standard identities yield other trigonometric functions.

```
DEXP('COS(A) = SQRT(1 - SIN(A) ** 2)')
DEXP('TAN(A) = SIN(A) / COS(A)')
```

Names referenced   Name   Type   Where defined
by TRIG: SQRT   Function   Program 15.6
    DEXP   Function   Program 14.1

Epilogue

The reason for the separate recursive routine (SIN.) is to save time (no need for range checking after its done originally) and space on the recursive stack (no need to continually push K).

> Program 15.8 ARC

The functions ASIN(X), ACOS(X) and ATAN(X) will return respectively the arc sine, arc cosine and arc tangent in radians. As was the case with the trig functions, a nonobvious computation is required for one of the functions, and standard trig identities produce the other two. Since we already have sine and cosine we could use Newton's method to compute the arcs. Alternatively, we could invert the recursive procedure used to compute the sine. For variety, however, we will leave these options as exercises and consider yet another method for producing a machine-independent computation of the arcs.

A power series expansion for arc sine X is [Handbook, NBS, p. 81]:

$$X + \frac{X^3}{2*3} + \frac{1*3*X^5}{2*4*5} + \frac{1*3*5*X^7}{2*4*6*7} + \ldots \quad (15.10)$$

While this series converges for all $|X| < 1$, convergence is slow if X is near one. For $X < 0.5$, however, the convergence rate is quite acceptable requiring at most about P/2 terms where P is the precision in bits.

A power series expansion for arc cos(1-Z) [Handbook, NBS, p. 81] is

$$(2Z)^{.5} \left[1 + \frac{Z}{4^1(3)} + \frac{(1)(3) Z^2}{4^2(5)(2!)} + \frac{(1)(3)(5) Z^3}{4^3(7) 3!} + \ldots \right]$$

This series converges more rapidly in the worst case that the previous one. It makes use of the fact that the parabolic curve of the general form $y = x^2$ is a close fit to the bend in the sine curve. The power series expansion is actually for the deviation between the two. After range reduction, the worst case value is $Z = 1$ and convergence may be expected in about $P - \log_2 P$ steps. Hence, we will define the arcs in terms of the power series for arc cosine.

The two methods actually complement each other and together can provide a method of keeping the number of iterations below P/2. This is left as Exercise 15.16.

```
        DEFINE ('ACOS(X) K,TERM,T')
        PI.  =  3.14159265358979                    :(ACOS_END)
```
```
| Entry point:  Reduce the range to consider only quantities |
| in the first quadrant.                                     |
```
```
ACOS    ACOS  =  LT(X,0)   PI. - ACOS(-X)          :S(RETURN)
```
```
| Initialize for the loop starting with label ACOS_1.  This |
| is a power series for arc cosine.                         |
```
```
        ACOS  =  1.0
        TERM  =  1.0
        X     =  1.0 - X
        K     =  1
ACOS_1  TERM  =  TERM * (2 * K - 1) * X / (4 * K)
        ACOS  =  ACOS + TERM / (2 * K + 1)
        K     =  K + 1
        T     =  NE(ACOS,T)   ACOS                 :S(ACOS_1)
        ACOS  =  SQRT(2 * X) * ACOS                :(RETURN)
ACOS_END
```
```
| Arc sine and arc tangent are defined in terms of arc |
| cosine.                                              |
```
```
        DEXP('ASIN(X) = (PI. / 2) - ACOS(X)')
        DEXP('ATAN(X) = ACOS(1. / SQRT(1 + X * X))')
```

Names referenced by ARC:	Name	Type	Where defined
	SQRT	Function	Program 15.6
	DEXP	Function	Program 14.1

```
|  Program  |
|   15.9    |
|   LOG     |
```
LOG(X,B) will return the log of X to the base B. If B is null (or absent), the natural log is returned. Given a method of obtaining logs to some base B, one can obtain a log to an arbitrary base B1 by the identity:

        LOG(X,B1) = LOG(X,B) / LOG(B1,B)

and so the problem reduces to finding logs to some base B.

Program 15.9 - LOG

If one were coding in assembly language, a natural choice on a
binary machine would be base 2. This is because the exponent
part of the real number is the integer part (actually the
floor plus one) of the logarithm and is available with no computation. Moreover, the fractional part of the logarithm can
also be plucked out of the exponent after successive squarings
of the mantissa in a method described by Gosper in Beeler
[1972, p.76].

Unfortunately, SNOBOL4 cannot generally 'get at' the exponent
of a floating point number (except for SITBOL). An integer
approximation to the base 10 logarithm can be found by counting the number of characters in a string representation of
the number. Thus SIZE(CONVERT(X, 'INTEGER')) returns the
ceiling of LOG10 X. If X is larger than the largest integer,
however, it must be divided down. One can translate Gosper's
method to operate on a decimal machine (which is what we have
at this point) by raising the remainder to the 10th power for
each succeeding digit. This is the method actually used.

```
| LOG(X,B) will return the logarithm of X to the base B. |
| LOG(X)   will return the natural logarithm of X.       |

        LN_10 = 2.3025850929940456840
        DEXP('LOG(X,B) = NE(B,0) CLOG(X) / CLOG(B) ;'
      +      ' LOG      = EQ(B,0) CLOG(X) * LN_10  ;' )
```

```
| CLOG will return the common log (base 10) of X. |

        DEFINE('CLOG(X) FACTOR,T,K')              :(CLOG_END)
```

```
| Entry point: FACTOR is initialized to 1.0 with a precision |
| equal to the precision of the argument X.  Here we handle  |
| fractional  cases (negative logs) in the event that either |
| the original number was below 1.0 or the number  X  goes   |
| fractional as a result of the division at CLOG_4.          |

CLOG    FACTOR = X / X
CLOG_1  X      = LT(X,1)  1 / X           :F(CLOG_2)
        FACTOR = -FACTOR
```

```
| Here's the main loop.  We determine the number of digits |
| (minus one) to the left of the decimal (K), which we may |
| regard as  a crude approximation of the log.  Reduce the |
| log of X by this much by dividing by 10 ** K.  Then find |
| the log of this reduced quantity.                        |

CLOG_2  EQ(X,1.0)                         :S(RETURN)
        K    = SIZE(CONVERT(X,'INTEGER')) - 1  :F(CLOG_4)
        EQ(K,0)                           :S(CLOG_3)
        CLOG = CLOG + K * FACTOR
        T    = NE(CLOG,T)  CLOG           :F(RETURN)
        X    = X / 10. ** K
```

Page 336   Chapter 15   -   NUMBERS

```
CLOG_3   FACTOR = FACTOR / 10.
         X = X ** 10                                    :(CLOG_1)
```
| If X is larger than the largest integer, we come here. |
```
CLOG_4   K = 10
         X = X / 10. ** K
         CLOG = CLOG + K * FACTOR                       :(CLOG_2)
CLOG_END
```

Names referenced   Name   Type   Where defined
by LOG: DEXP   Function   Program 14.1

Epilogue

Since the characteristic of a number to the base 10 can be obtained by inspection, the method above is suitable for computing logorithms on the four-function desk calculator. The reader is invited to try a few examples for himself.

Another method for computing log is the power series:

$$\ln 1+x = x - x^2/2 + x^3/3 - x^4/4 + \ldots \qquad (15.11)$$

To use this power series one must reduce large x until they come close to 0. This can be done in part by the SIZE method. To bring x yet closer to 0, the identity:

$$LOG(X) = 2 * LOG(SQRT(X))$$

can be used.

```
| | Program | |
| |  15.10  | |
| |  RAISE  | |
```
RAISE(X,Y) will raise X to the power Y. This function is entirely redundant if the second operand of the ** operator is permitted to be REAL. It is not in many versions of the language and so RAISE must be included in our set. Indeed, its presence may suggest alternative methods for computing some of our functions (certainly SQRT).

If one can raise some number, Z, to an arbitrary power, one can then define RAISE(X,Y) as:

$$RAISE(Z, LOG(X,Z) * Y)$$

The number we will choose as Z is the base of the natural logs (normally designated e) and a special function EXP(X) will return e raised to the Xth power; EXP is normally called the exponential function.

EXP(X) can be written as a Taylor series:

$$1 + X + X^2/2! + X^3/3! + \ldots$$

which converges rapidly for X ≤ 1. For X > 1, we simply obtain
the integer part (the floor) I and use the rule:

$$e^X = e^{X-I} * e^I$$

    DEXP('RAISE(X,Y) = EXP(Y * LOG(X))')

    DEFINE('EXP(X)TERM,K,T')
    NAT_BASE   =   2.718281828459045   :(EXP_END)

| Entry point for EXP.   Reduce the range to [0,1]. |

EXP   EXP = LT(X,0) 1. / EXP(-X)   :S(RETURN)
        K   = GT(X,1)   CONVERT(X,'INTEGER') :F(EXP_1)
        EXP = EXP(X - K) * NAT_BASE ** K   :(RETURN)

| Initialize for the power series which is summed in the |
| loop headed by EXP_2. |

EXP_1   TERM = 1.
EXP_2   EXP = EXP + TERM
        K   = K + 1.
        TERM = TERM * X / K
        T   = NE(T,EXP)   EXP   :S(EXP_2)F(RETURN)
EXP_END

Names referenced	Name	Type	Where defined
by RAISE:	LOG	Function	Program 15.9
	DEXP	Function	Program 14.1

??
????????????????????????? EXERCISES ?????????????????????????
??

| Exercise 15.1 | Rewrite COMB (Prog. 15.1) so that it com-
putes iteratively. Do not separately com-
pute numerator and denominator as this may result in an
unnecessary overflow. Also do not divide numbers that are not
divisible.

| Exercise 15.2 | A rather unusual method for computing some
combinatorial functions was shown to the
author by Dennis Allen. It uses pattern matching to count
combinations. The pattern matcher will undergo a number of
attempts to match and this can be used (in fullscan mode) to
compute (however inefficiently) some combinatorial functions.
For example, let INC(.N) increment the variable N by 1. Then,

       &FULLSCAN = 1
       N = 0
       S   LEN(1) *INC(.N)   FAIL

Page 338   Chapter 15   -   NUMBERS

will count the number of characters in the string S.   Rewrite COMB(N,M) so that it computes the function this way.

| Exercise 15.3 | What is the maximum number representable in the combinatorial number system with nome N where SIZE(COMB_ALPHA) = L.

| Exercise 15.4 | Write a function COMBDE(K,N) which converts integer K into a representation in the combinatorial number system with nome N. If there are insufficient characters in COMB_ALPHA, COMBDE should fail.

| Exercise 15.5 | Since SPITBOL does not allow redefinition of operators, the INFINIP package (Prog. 15.3) must be modified to run under that processor. (a) What, for example, would DIFF look like under such a modification? (b) How many statements in DIV would require modification?

| Exercise 15.6 | Augment the INFINIP package by adding the ** operator. Do not multiply out the indicated number of times but use the rule:

$$X^N = X^{N/2} * X^{REMDR(N,2)} \qquad (15.12)$$

| Exercise 15.7 | In the DIV procedure of the INFINIP package, a better estimate of the trial quotient can be obtained by making the first digit of Y higher (better to be 9 than 1). This can be done by multiplying both X and Y by the same quantity. See Knuth [Vol. 2, p. 235]. Implement a scheme to make sure that the first digit of Y is at least 5 (requires only one additional statement if SUBSTR (Prog. 3.9) is used).

| Exercise 15.8 | Write a function ROUND(X) which will return the nearest integer to X (on ties, pick either). This requires three statements.

| Exercise 15.9 | Let X, Y and Z be positive real numbers. For what values of X will

$$FLOOR(Y / X) \leq Z$$

Using the relationships in (15.7) and the fact that

$$N > M \iff N \geq M + 1$$

for all integer N and M, give a step-by-step proof of your answer.

Exercises for chapter 15 — Page 339

| Exercise 15.10 | To improve the speed of SQRT (Prog. 15.6), replace the three statements at label SQRT_1 by one.

| Exercise 15.11 | Let e represent the error of an approximation $\hat{x}$ to the square root of the quantity x^2. That is

$$e = \hat{x} - x$$

One iteration of Newton's method produces a new error.   (a) Derive a formula which yields the new error E in terms of the old error e.   (b) Assuming an initial error of 0.1, how many iterations will produce an error less that 10^{-20}?

| Exercise 15.12 | Given the formula for sine 3A, deduce a formula for sine 9A.   Recode the SIN routine of TRIG (Prog. 15.7) accordingly.   Can the same stopping criterion be used?

| Exercise 15.13 | If the second statement of SIN.() had been:

$$A = SIN.(A / 3)$$

a bug would have been introduced. For which values of argument A would SIN(A) then yield an incorrect value?

| Exercise 15.14 | Compute ASIN(X) using SIN(A), COS(A) and Newton's method in a manner similar to SQRT. Use X as the original estimate of ASIN(X).

| Exercise 15.15 | To express arc sine recursively, one may use a half-angle (or fractional angle) formula in order to reduce the range. One such is:

$$SIN(A / 2) = SQRT((1 - SQRT(1 - SIN^2 A)) / 2)$$

(a) Express ASIN(X) in terms of ASIN(X / 2).   (b) If one were to use the recursive formula to implement ASIN(X), what stopping criterion would one use?

| Exercise 15.16 | Using the power series of (15.10), modify ACOS as suggested in the text.

| Exercise 15.17 | In LOG (Prog. 15.9) we depend on being able to convert REALs to INTEGERs for all reals in the range (0, M). That is, we suppose that the max-

Page 340   Chapter 15   -   NUMBERS

imum integer is greater than M. What is M?   (Hint: the answer is not 10^{10}.)

| Exercise 15.18 | It is not strictly necessary to insert numeric constants into the programs TRIG, ARC, LOG and RAISE. Rather, they may be computed by appropriate calls on the defined routines. Modify the routines so that they compute the constants.

| Exercise 15.19 | Assume you are writing an assembler and must construct a real number in its machine form for a binary machine with 27 bits of precision. Given other functions in the book (Chapter two), this reduces to the following problem: given a non-zero real number X, find the exponent N and integer I such that $2^{26} \le I < 2^{27}$ and

$$X = (\text{approx.}) \ 2^N * \frac{I}{2^{27}}$$

Using LOG (Prog. 15.9), N and I can be computed in three statements. What are they?

| Exercise 15.20 | In order to make the random number generator (RANDOM, Prog. 16.1) go backward, we need to be able to find the inverse of a multiplier. That is, we need to solve for X in:

$$X * R = 1 \quad (\text{Mod } M)$$

This can be done by noting that:

$$X = R^{M-2} \quad (\text{Mod } M)$$

Assuming that M-2 multiplications may be too time-consuming, work out a method whereby only $2*\text{Log}_2(M-2)$ multiplications are required.

| Exercise 15.21 | If RAISE (Prog. 15.10) is used in SPITBOL and if a DREAL argument is given to the function EXP, the returned value will be DREAL but will not have DREAL accuracy. Why? How can one correct this deficiency and still return a single-precision result if a REAL is given as argument? (Hint: the answer requires modifying one statement.) Starting with an estimate,

CHAPTER SIXTEEN

STOCHASTIC STRINGS

CONTENTS

RANDOM	16.1
RAMM	16.2
RPERMUTE	16.3
ONEWAY	16.4
RCHAR	16.5
RWORD	16.6
RSELECT	16.7
RSENTENCE	16.8
RPOEM	16.9
RSEASON	16.10
RSTORY	16.11

Chapter 16 - STOCHASTIC STRINGS

Stochastic or random strings have many applications within the computing sphere of activity. Some exotic uses include poetry, choreography, play and brand-name generation, cryptographic and linguistic analysis, and even police-patrol scheduling [Aberg 1974]. Simulations and game-playing also make critical use of the computer's ability to generate near random sequences. More mundane applications include algorithm testing and timing.

Digital computers have the power to produce prodigious quantities of what appear to be random strings and/or random numbers. However, if pressed to define precisely what is meant by the term 'random' one must be careful. For example, Table 16.1 contains two groups of 'random' English words. One group was formed by selecting words at random from a novel. The other group was formed by selecting dictionary entries at random. It should be immediately evident which source produced which group. Yet both groups have at least some claim to being called 'random English words'.

Table 16.1 One of the groups of words shown below was obtained by randomly selecting from entries in a dictionary and the other by selecting words from a novel. Is it obvious which is which?

Source A	Source B
your	dialectition
a	Jemappes
the	profligate
and	disenfranchise
Hell	opaque

To make the notion of randomness more precise we speak of a _sample space_ containing a possibly infinite collection of things. A _random selection_ is a selection of a single item from the sample space with the proviso that all items have an equal chance for selection. In the example above, one sample space was the set of dictionary entries which approximates the set of distinct words of the English language. The other sample space was the set of words in a novel which approximates the totality of all words actually used to communicate thought using the English language. Note that a sample space may have repeated items such as the novel or they may all be distinct as in the dictionary case. Note too that a sample space may be completely unstructured as in the two examples given. This may be contrasted with a sample space obtained by five tosses of a coin in which the sample space is a well-structured set

Program 16.1 - RANDOM Page 343

containing 32 combinations, each describable by a sequence of five binary digits.

```
|| Program ||
||  16.1   ||
||  RANDOM ||
```
Random strings are constructed from random numbers and so this is what we must obtain first. RANDOM(N), where N is a positive integer, will return a 'random' number from the sample space {1, 2, ..., N}. For example, if RANDOM(3) were called 10 times the sequence produced could be:

$$1 \; 3 \; 3 \; 2 \; 3 \; 1 \; 2 \; 1 \; 1 \; 3$$

If the argument N is 0, the number returned will be of type REAL chosen from the sample space [0,1) which is the interval on the real line from 0 [inclusive] to 1 (exclusive).* Calls to RANDOM with different arguments may be intermixed without adversely affecting the generating process.

Since the numbers are produced by a deterministic process they are not truly random but only apparently random. It is conventional to term such processes <u>pseudo-random</u>. Pseudo-random sequences have the very convenient property of being repeatable. This can be important in debugging or in studying certain effects in greater detail. If one wishes to obtain a different sequence one can set the variable RAN_VAR to some other value in the range {1, 2, ..., 414970}. For game playing, it is sometimes necessary to initialize the random number generator to a value which is indeed unpredictable. For such purposes one can use the clock.

```
| RANDOM(N) will return an integer uniformly distributed on |
| 1,2,...,N.  If N=0, it will return a real uniformly       |
| distributed in the interval [0,1).                        |
```

```
          DEFINE('RANDOM(N)')
          RAN_VAR = 1                              : (RANDOM_END)
```

```
| The REAL is produced in any case. If an integer is wanted, |
| the REAL is multiplied by the proper range. Note that      |
| CONVERT Truncates rather than rounds.                      |
```

```
RANDOM
          RAN_VAR = REMDR(RAN_VAR * 4676, 414971)
          RANDOM  = RAN_VAR / 414971
          RANDOM  = NE(N,0) CONVERT(RANDOM * N,'INTEGER') + 1
                                                   : (RETURN)
RANDOM_END
```

---

*Actually, this is a slight fiction. The number of reals representable by the machine is finite, whereas the number of reals in the interval is (uncountably) infinite. The intent is to approximate this interval.

Epilogue

RANDOM(N) belongs to a class of generators called the congruential type first proposed by Lehmer [1951]. Given some integer R in the range $0 \leq R \leq M$ where M is some integer called the __modulus__, the next value of R (which we denote by R') is obtained by the computation

$$R' = R * A \quad (\text{Mod } M)$$

or, in SNOBOL4 notation

$$R' = \text{REMDR}(R * A, M)$$

where A is some positive integer called the __multiplier__. The numbers will begin to repeat themselves after a certain period governed by R, A and M. For example, if M=10, A=7 and R=3 (thoroughly impractical values) the sequence of R's becomes

$$3 \quad 1 \quad 7 \quad 9 \quad 3 \quad 1 \quad 7 \quad 9 \quad 3 \quad \ldots$$

repeating themselves every four numbers (the period is said to be four). A random real number in the interval is then obtained by dividing R by M.

The congruential method is extremely important historically because the operation

$$R' = \text{REMDR}(R * A, M)$$

can be accomplished with one multiply instruction where M is the natural modulus of the machine (For example on the IBM 360 the natural modulus is 2^{31}). Use of the natural modulus is attractive from an efficiency standpoint but is machine dependent and can't be used in SNOBOL4 anyway because the computation will be regarded as an error (arithmetic overflow).

The sequence of R's will consist only of integers relatively prime to M. This means that a period equal to M where M is a natural modulus is impossible. A way around this is to use the so-called mixed congruential generator first proposed by Greenberger [1961] in which the formula

$$R' = R * A + C \quad (\text{Mod } M)$$

is used. For correctly chosen values of A and C, the R's will range through every number in the set $\{0, 1, \ldots, M-1\}$.

Another method of obtaining long periods is to use a prime modulus. If M is prime, then for certain values of A the generator:

$$R' = R * A \quad (\text{Mod } M)$$

will cause the R's to cycle through every integer in the range $\{1, 2, \ldots, M-1\}$. Such an A is called a __primitive__ element of

Program 16.1 - RANDOM   Page 345

the field of integers modulo M (see for example, Barnard and
Child [1955], p. 438).

The prime-primitive pair must be such that the A*R never overflows the machine. If the maximum integer is, for example,
$2^{31}-1$ (as it is for most 32-bit machines), then it will be
sufficient that A*M < 2^{31}. A list of prime-primitive pairs is
given in Table 16.2 together with an indication of the number
of bits of arithmetic required to avoid overflow. The choice
of prime-primitive pair for the function RANDOM was based on
the observation that most SNOBOL4's can represent all positive
integers below 2^{31}.

Table 16.2 This table provides prime-primitive pairs and
an upper bound in terms of a power of 2.

Prime Modulus M	Primitive Element P	Smallest Power of 2 > M*P	Prime Modulus M	Primitive Element P	Smallest Power of 2 > M*P
127	12	2^{11}	10657	735	2^{23}
127	29	2^{12}	10657	824	2^{24}
211	35	2^{13}	4409	4035	2^{25}
211	41	2^{14}	19423	3088	2^{26}
491	59	2^{15}	10657	7367	2^{27}
491	84	2^{16}	24281	9713	2^{28}
1103	117	2^{17}	29443	13300	2^{29}
1103	156	2^{18}	39971	20411	2^{30}
1223	421	2^{19}	414971	4676	2^{31}
1987	451	2^{20}	532333	8705	2^{33}
1987	1017	2^{21}	1299709	16322	2^{35}
2741	1148	2^{22}	1798963	160658	2^{39}

Tests for Randomness

One might suppose that there existed a single, simple test for
randomness which could be applied to some psuedo-generator to
determine a coefficient of randomness. Unfortunately, no such
single test exists. It is interesting to note that if one had
a test to determine whether a sequence was truly random that
test could be used to produce, by elimination, a truly random
sequence. We would then have a contradiction in terms, since
an algorithmic process can never produce truly random numbers.
Rather than a single, all-powerful test for randomness, there
exists many tests each oriented toward detecting violations of
important characteristics of random behavior. Knuth [Vol. 2]
and Canavos [1967] describe a number of such tests. Those
outlined here are from Canavos and have actually been applied
to the generators mentioned in this chapter.

Chapter 16 - STOCHASTIC STRINGS

The most common test seems to be the <u>bins test</u> and seeks to answer the most obvious question: Is each of the B integers from RANDOM(B) equally likely? RANDOM(B) is called successively N times where B is the number of bins. The number of numbers appearing in each bin should average out to N/B. But the distribution over the bins cannot be expected to be perfectly flat or one would suspect nonrandom behavior. One can measure the extent to which the distribution deviates from perfection and the deviation proper for a random generator is given by the so-called Chi-squared distribution. The number of bins, B, is selected so as to maximize the power of the test and depends upon the number of samples taken. For example, for N = 1000, the number of bins suggested is 50.

Another popular test for randomness is the <u>correlation test</u> which determines whether numbers a given fixed distance apart are correlated. For example, in the Canavos series, correlation is tested for distances of 1 through 8. The extent to which the numbers are correlated in any given sequence can be calculated. Random generators would tend to produce zero correlation in the long run, but in the short run they are expected to produce a small correlation. Observed correlations above or below this level are suspicious.

When RANDOM(2) is called repeatedly, the binary sequence produced can be considered to be like the head-tail sequence produced by flipping a coin. Questions one might ask are: Is heads just as likely as tails? This is answered by the bins test. Another question is: Will heads follow heads as often as it follows tails? This is answered by the correlation test. A classic coin-tossing question not answered by these tests is the following: If K heads in a row are produced, is the next toss more likely to be a head or a tail? One might fear that an artificial system of producing random numbers might be too 'round' and not produce enough long sequences or be too 'angular' and produce too many. Such questions are settled by the so-called <u>runs test</u>. A run is a sequence of heads bounded on both sides by a tail or a sequence of tails bounded by heads. The number of runs of length 1, 2, 3, ... is measured and the resulting distribution should close to that obtained from a random distribution. Like the bin test, the chi-square formula is used to determine if the distribution is 'too good' or 'too bad'.

Other Generators

It is frequently useful to know of other genrators so that if the results of one generator or type of generator becomes suspect, another may be plugged in. The following extremely portable generator was suggested by Kruskal [1969].

$$R' = R * 125 \pmod{2^{13}}$$

The one multiplication by 125 can be replaced by three multiplications by 5 so that provided the machine can contain 5 *

Program 16.2 - RAMM

2^{13} as an integer, the computation can be done without overflow. Unfortunately the period is short.

Another method is to construct a random number generator according to a recipe suggested by Knuth [Vol. 2, p. 155-156]. One such generator is:

$$R' = R * 3141 + 110795 \pmod{524288 = 2^{19}}$$

Another approach is to use a standard generator with multiple precision arithmetic. One generator endorsed by Coveyou and Macpherson [1967] (they do not endorse many) is:

$$R' = R * 25214903917 \pmod{2^{35} = 34359738368}$$

To perform the arithmetic within SNOBOL4 on the IBM 360, three integers are needed to contain the multiplication. This will slow the computation and increase the complexity on the program but the random numbers should be quite random.

```
||  Program  ||
||   16.2    ||
||   RAMM    ||
```
There are techniques for combining random number generators to produce degrees of randomness higher than either operating alone. One method, proposed by MacLaren and Marsaglia [1965] is to let one random generator shuffle the output of a second random generator. This is done in RAMM(N) below which will behave like RANDOM(N) except that its statistics will be better. It uses a Knuth generator to shuffle the output of RANDOM.

```
        DEFINE('RAMM(N)K')
```

| The following two OPSYN's make the subroutine plug-in-able to any routine already using RANDOM. |

```
        OPSYN('RANDOM.','RANDOM')
        OPSYN('RANDOM','RAMM')
```

| Initialize the RAMM array (RAMM_A) with random numbers obtained from RANDOM.(). |

```
        I = 0
        RAMM_A = ARRAY('0:99')
RAMM_1  RAMM_A<I> = RANDOM.(0)              :F(RAMM_END)
        I = I + 1                           :(RAMM_1)
```

| Entry point: Select an element K of RAMM_A at random. Return this value and fill up the entry with a new RANDOM value. |

```
RAMM    RAM_VAR = REMDR(RAM_VAR * 3141 + 110795, 524288)
        K = CONVERT((RAM_VAR / 524288.) * 100,'INTEGER')
        RAMM = RAMM_A<K>
        RAMM_A<K> = RANDOM.(0)
```

Page 348   Chapter 16 - STOCHASTIC STRINGS

            RAMM   =   NE(N,0) CONVERT(RAMM * N, 'INTEGER') + 1
RAMM_END   :(RETURN)

Names referenced   Name   Type   Where defined
by RAMM: RANDOM *   Function   Program 16.1
* indicates name is referenced in the initialization section.


```
|  Program  |    A  natural   application  of a random  number
|   16.3    |    generator  is  to  produce  random   permuta-
|  RPERMUTE |    tions.   This  is  easy  to do in  SNOBOL4.
                 RPERMUTE(S) will return a  random  permuta-
tion of the string S.
```

            DEFINE('RPERMUTE(S)T')   :(RPERMUTE_END)
RPERMUTE   S   LEN(1) . T =   :F(RETURN)
            RPERMUTE   POS(RANDOM(SIZE(RPERMUTE)) + 1) - 1)
+   = T   :(RPERMUTE)
RPERMUTE_END

Names referenced   Name   Type   Where defined
by RPERMUTE: RANDOM   Function   Program 16.1


```
|  Program  |   A  one-way  cipher  is  a  notion of Needham
|   16.4    |   first introduced in published form by Wilkes
|  ONEWAY   |   [1972].   The function ONEWAY(S) where S  is
                some  string  will  return  a string the same
size as S having the property that it would be computationally
prohibitive to compute S or some other value S' such that:
```

                    ONEWAY(S) = ONEWAY(S')

That is, even knowing **everything about** ONEWAY to the extent of
having a listing of ONEWAY in front of you, it is still impractical to compute the original argument from the output
obtained.

One-way ciphers are used in password protection schemes as
follows. A user types in his password S. The system applies
ONEWAY(S) to obtain a cipher C. C is then looked up in a
table. If a match is found the user is identified and appropriate privileges are assumed. This protects against
accidental or malicious revelation of the table's contents.
That is, if one, or even all, such ciphers were revealed it
would not help a thief. He must know the original password or
any password that would yield the same cipher as the original,
but this he presumably cannot obtain.

Without such a protection scheme, the collection of passwords
is always in jeopardy. In one instance, the message of the
day for a time-sharing system that will go nameless became,
quite by accident, the list of passwords. As one wag put it,

Program 16.4 - ONEWAY   Page 349

the most confidential file in the system suddenly became the most public file.

Other applications of ONEWAY are indicated in the chapter on games.

| ONEWAY(S) will return a one-way cipher of the alphabetic
| string S.

            DEFINE('ONEWAY(S)A,SIZE,C,K,SB')   :(ONEWAY_END)

| Entry point: Initialize the random number generator (by
| setting RAN_VAR) and set the alphabet A. The length of A
| must be a power (PWR) of 2.

ONEWAY   RAN_VAR = 1
         A   =   'ABCDEFGHIJKLMNOPQRSTUVWXYZ012345'
         PWR =   5

| Now, for each character (C) within (S) determine its posi-
| tion (K) in the alphabet (A). Obtain K's binary equivalent
| and append it to the growing string of bits, SB. Also,
| use K to modify the 'seed' of the random generator.

ONEWAY_1 S LEN(1) . C =   :F(ONEWAY_2)
          A   @K C   :F(ERROR)
          SB = SB LPAD(BASEB(K,2),PWR,'0')
          RAN_VAR = REMDR(RAN_VAR * 2 ** PWR + K, 414971)
                                                     :(ONEWAY_1)

| Now we replace each '0' by a '01' and each '1' by a '10',
| randomly permute the string, and extract the first half of
| it.

ONEWAY_2
          RPERMUTE(BLEND(SB,REPLACE(SB,'01','10')))
     +   LEN(SIZE(SB)) . SB

| Now repack the string from its 1-0 form into something
| more amenable.

ONEWAY_3
          SB   LEN(PWR) . S =   :F(RETURN)
          A POS(BASE10(S,2))   LEN(1) . C
          ONEWAY = ONEWAY C   :(ONEWAY_3)
ONEWAY_END

Names referenced   Name   Type   Where defined
by ONEWAY: LPAD   Function   Program 3.2
                    BASEB   Function   Program 2.4
                    RPERMUTE   Function   Program 16.3
                    BASE10   Function   Program 2.5
                    BLEND   Function   Program 3.7

Page 350   Chapter 16   -   STOCHASTIC STRINGS

Epilogue

How difficult is it to break the cipher? No one knows. There
is no guarantee that someone will not come up with an algorithm to quickly find the inverse of ONEWAY, it is just not
very likely.

Essentially the initial argument regarded as a bit string is
both used to 'seed' a random generator and is permuted by the
generator. The straightforward way of cracking the cipher is
to assume a final value for the generator and work RPERMUTE in
reverse by running RANDOM in reverse. If the results are found
to agree, the cipher is cracked. This points up a weakness of
ONEWAY as presented here. We normally wish the number of
guesses required to be of the order of the number of combinations of the original string. If this were the case, longer
passwords would prove to be more difficult to discover. But
the number of different modes of operation for RANDOM are
relatively small (414970). Hence, if added security is wanted,
a generator with a longer cycle time (such as RAMM) should be
used. Even so, the computation required to permute a half
million strings in the manner indicated is sufficiently formidable that the writer is confidant that no one will discover
the original string used to produce:

                        'BFDDGL'

Of course, other techniques can be used to produce one-way
ciphers. See Evans, et al [1974] and Purdy [1974].


```
┌─────────────────────┐
||  Program    ||        RCHAR(CONTEXT) will return a random charac-
||    16.5     ||        ter. The intended sample space is the set
||    RCHAR    ||        of all characters following the CONTEXT
└─────────────────────┘  provided as argument. For example,
```
RCHAR('BR') will return 'A' much more frequently than, say,
'B' because 'A' is much more likely to follow the characters
'BR'.

In order to write RCHAR we could pump it full of statistical
information concerning the English language. A more flexible
(and easier) approach is to let the user supply his own
language sample (called the corpus) and use pattern matching
to search for a likely subsequent character. In this way we
do not limit ourselves to English nor, indeed, even to natural
languages.

To obtain a likely successor to, say, 'BR' within a language
corpus, we may look up each occurrence of 'BR' and choose randomly from among each successor. Another approach is, starting
at some random point within the string, to scan for the first
occurrence of 'BR' and then return the character which follows. This latter technique is much faster than the former,
but will produce statistically incorrect results. Thus, if
the corpus is 1000 characters long, and if 'BR' occurs three

Program 16.5 - RCHAR

times in positions 500, 510 and 910, then the random probe and forward scan would mean that the 500 or the 910 would be picked up relatively frequently, but that the 510 would have an extremely small chance of being selected.

A compromise between these two choices is to scan the string for the first K instances of the CONTEXT and to choose a random character from among the K characters which followed. This greatly reduces the time required to process CONTEXT's which occur frequently, such as RCHAR('E'), while maintaining good statistics for other kinds of CONTEXT's. The encoding of RCHAR given below will use a compromising value for K of 2.

```
| RCHAR will return a random character following the CONTEXT |
| given as argument.  If none such exists, RCHAR will fail.  |

            DEFINE('RCHAR(CONTEXT)BX,C,P,N,RC1')

| Initialization:  Read into R_CORPUS the language corpus on |
| which  the  statistical  characteristics  of RCHAR will be |
| based.                                                      |

RCHAR_1    X   =   TRIM(INPUT)                    :F(RCHAR_END)
           IDENT(X, 'END')                        :S(RCHAR_END)
           R_CORPUS  =  R_CORPUS X ' '            :(RCHAR_1)

| Entry point: Prepare in P a pattern suitable for  scanning |
| the  text  beginning  at  cursor  position  N  looking for |
| CONTEXT.  BREAKX is used to make the scan rapid.           |

RCHAR      CONTEXT LEN(1) . C                      :F(RCHAR_2)
           BX  =  BREAKX(C)
RCHAR_2    P   =   POS(0) TAB(*N) BX CONTEXT LEN(1) . RCHAR

| Pick up the first random character  fitting  the  context. |
| Scanning begins at some arbitrary point N.                  |

           N  =  RANDOM(SIZE(R_CORPUS)) - 1
           R_CORPUS  P                             :S(RCHAR_3)
           N  =  0
           R_CORPUS  P                             :F(FRETURN)

| Here  to pick up the next adjacent random character.  The |
| first is saved in RC1.                                    |

RCHAR_3    N  =  N + 1
           RC1  =  RCHAR
           R_CORPUS  P                             :S(RCHAR_4)
           N  =  0
           R_CORPUS  P

| Here to select from between these two.                    |

RCHAR_4    RCHAR = EQ(RANDOM(2),1)  RC1           :(RETURN)
RCHAR_END
```

Chapter 16 - STOCHASTIC STRINGS

Names referenced Name   Type   Where defined
by RCHAR: RANDOM   Function Program 16.1
                  BREAKX   Function Program 8.2

```
| Program |
|  16.6   |
|  RWORD  |
```
RWORD is an obvious application of RCHAR. RWORD(K) will return a random word with characteristics similar to other words in the given corpus. K is a small whole number indicating the extent to which context is used in forming the result. That is, the next character chosen depends on at most the last K characters already chosen. Selection begins with RWORD 'seeded' with a blank.

Table 16.3 Below is a list of random names produced by RWORD(K) from a list of 700 names (R_CORPUS in RCHAR). Words chosen were in the range of 5 - 10 characters but were otherwise not pre-selected.

K = 0	K = 1	K = 2	K = 3
Rnztn	Faundobr	Joher	Alton
Eebfer	Einakicl	Thelmsti	Vigan
Uoaer	Kolin	Gringtock	Young
Earlho	Fssmched	Clouth	Rosen
Meeofr	Paubin	Mcdorg	Haekstra
Asnegrmnmh	Mormer	Jordawm	Repsherty
Ckwaig	Feymet	Paudelly	Haekstraun
Kninhaaf	Madicos	Franic	Walton
Agajfoope	Halitun	Cloobs	Bartoliti
Hfhclunc	Mchoskyr	Panscher	Thatchek
Usirollbh	Ralmrollan	Thaman	Caseyman
EEdhmeucc	Ffrrr	Mowski	Walker
Lasdctn	Linestz	Spaglema	Lopiparo
Ghsiafee	Reawstz	Loobs	Shallisi
Riesl	Gellar	Eiter	Ruscher

Table 16.3 contains a number of random words generated by RWORD when RWORD was given a corpus of 700 surnames culled from an addressing list. One can see clearly the effects of increasing K as well as the influence of the type of corpus chosen. The names for K=2, for example, would be quite acceptable in outer galactic society. RWORD, using a different corpus, could be used for brand-name generation. The name EXXON was purportedly chosen in this way.

Program 16.7 - RSELECT   Page 353

```
        DEFINE('RWORD(K)CONTEXT')        :(RWORD_END)
```
| Entry point: Initialize RWORD with a blank. |

```
RWORD          RWORD = ' '
```
| Use the last K characters of RWORD (or all of RWORD if it |
| fails to contain K characters) as context for the next |
| character. |

```
RWORD_1 CONTEXT = RWORD
        RWORD   RTAB(K)   REM . CONTEXT
        C   =   RCHAR(CONTEXT)                :F(RETURN)
        RWORD   =   DIFFER(C,' ')   RWORD C   :S(RWORD_1)
```
| Falling through means we encountered a blank. Remove the |
| initial blank from RWORD. If RWORD is null, try again. |

```
        RWORD ' ' =
        IDENT(RWORD)                          :S(RWORD) F(RETURN)
RWORD_END
```

Names referenced	Name	Type	Where defined
by RWORD:	RCHAR	Function	Program 16.5

		Program			RSELECT will make a random selection of one
		16.7			of a sequence of strings passed to RSELECT
		RSELECT			as argument. The first character is taken

strings in the sequence. Thus, RSELECT('|A|BIG|CAT') will
return each of 'A', 'BIG' and 'CAT' with probability one-
third. An optional integer weight enclosed in sharp signs may
be placed at the beginning of any alternation. Thus,

```
              RSELECT('|A|#3#BIG|CAT')
```

will select 'BIG' three times out of five.

RSELECT will be used as a utility routine by several programs
which follow.

```
        DEFINE('RSELECT(S) WT,WTS,ALT,CODE,I,CODE,SSAVED,BC')
        RSEL_TBL = TABLE()                    :(RSELECT_END)
```
| Entry point: All previously-seen arguments had been placed |
| in a table (RSEL_TBL) together with code to be executed. |
| In this case we simply execute the code. |

```
RSELECT CODE = RSEL_TBL<S>
        DIFFER(CODE,NULL)                     :S<CODE>
```
| If S had not been seen before, we fall through here. We |
| first save the string (SSAVED) and determine the break |
| character (BC). For each alternate (ALT), its weight (WT) |

Page 354   Chapter 16   -   STOCHASTIC STRINGS

| is determined and added to a subtotal (WTS).   CODE is |
| produced which will assign the alternative to RSELECT if |
| the numbers are right. |

```
          SSAVED  =  S
          S      LEN(1) . BC  =                   :F(RETURN)
RSELECT_1
          WT   =  1
          S    POS(0)  '#' BREAK('#') . WT '#' =
          S    (BREAK(BC) | REM) . ALT  =
          WTS  =  WTS + WT
          CODE =  CODE ' ;  RSELECT = LE(I,' WTS ') '
+                            QUOTE(ALT)    '  :S(RETURN)'
          S    BC  =                         :S(RSELECT_1)
```

| Falling through means we're done.   We simply prefix the |
| code to assign a random number to I, fill the table and |
| try again. |

```
          CODE  =  '  I = RANDOM(' WTS ') '  CODE
          S  =  SSAVED
          RSEL_TBL<S>  =  CODE(CODE)        :S(RSELECT) F(ERROR)
RSELECT_END
```

Names referenced   Name   Type   Where defined
by RSELECT: QUOTE   Function   Program 3.16
                      RANDOM   Function   Program 16.1

Epilogue

An interesting implementation aspect of RSELECT is that it
compiles code the first time through for any given argument.
This makes sense for a random generator since it may be called
many times with the same argument and compiling code, as shown
here, greatly increases the speed of subsequent calls.
Moreover, the program is not made very much more complicated
because of this; in fact, the construction of CODE actually
saves a second pass over the string and in this sense serves
to produce a more simple program.   If space is a greater
consideration than time, See Exercise 16.5.


```
||   Program    ||    RSENTENCE(ARG) will generate and return  a
||    16.8      ||    random sentence according to a grammatical
||  RSENTENCE   ||    description read in during initialization.
```
                      The argument ARG represents a string pos-
sibly containing syntactic variables which are expanded
according to the grammar.   As a simple example, let the input
be

<SENT>::=the <NOUN> <VERB> the <NOUN>
<NOUN>::=boy|man|dog|<NOUN> who <VERB>s the <NOUN>
<VERB>::=bite|walk|pet|lick|smack
END

Program 16.8 - RSENTENCE   Page 355

Then a call such as RSENTENCE('<SENT>.') will generate, among an infinite number of sentences,

the dog bites the man.
the man walks the dog.
the man who walks the dog who licks the boy smacks the boy
      who bites the dog.

Identifiers in pointed brackets (here shown in uppercase for ease of distinction) are termed **syntactic variables**. Alternates are separated by vertical bar (|). Though these special characters may not appear within the text it is not difficult to provide an escape convention so that they can be (See Exercise 16.9).

When a syntactic variable is **expanded** it is replaced by one of its alternates randomly and this alternate may in turn contain other syntactic variables which are also expanded. This process may never halt (see the Epilogue).

The meta-language used for describing the grammar is the so-called Backus Normal Form (BNF) which is also referred to as Backus-Naur Form since the form is not normal (non unique) and since Naur was a cohort of Backus. The meta-language is a bit awkward (the first four meta-characters are redundant provided syntactic variables do not contain ='s) but has the convenient property of being commonly understood.

Another feature of RSENTENCE is that an expression in parentheses is treated as a SNOBOL4 expression. It is evaluated and inserted into the text stream. Also, an identifier between ='s is expanded like a syntactic variable but will also have the side-effect of assigning the result of the expansion to the indicated variable. Thus

```
<THING>::=rose|tree|turkey
<SENT1>::= A =THING= is a (THING) is a (THING).
<SENT2>::= The word '=THING=' has (SIZE(THING)) letters.
```

will produce for <SENT1>:

        A rose is a rose is a rose.

with probability one-third. An example of <SENT2> is

        The word 'turkey' has 6 letters.

Other miscellaneous features of the program are as follows. Continuation is represented by a line not beginning with a '<'. Weights can be associated with alternation using the #n# notation of RSELECT.

One application of RSENTENCE is test-data generation for compilers and other processors expecting stylized input (an early version of RSENTENCE was used to find bugs in SNOBOL4 itself). Another application is in producing nonrepetitive messages in

an interactive environment. For example, in game playing, a
variety of sarcastic remarks can provoke an otherwise
apathetic player into a competitive state. RSENTENCE has been
used in the production of prospective topics for a discussion
group.   While not all topics randomly generated are directly
usable, they are often sufficiently suggestive and sufficiently numerous that random generation followed by a cul-
ling process, such as the previously described brand-name
selection, becomes an effective technique.

Yngve [1962a] suggests that such programs coupled with a full
and valid grammar, solve one aspect of the problem of machine
translation, viz. the target-language generation end. One must
realize, however, that RSENTENCE, by itself, is limited almost
exclusively to context-free generations and hence to very
restrictive grammars. To aid in the machine translation study,
RSENTENCE must be considerably enhanced. One such enhancement,
suggested by Yngve is given in Exercise 16.8. It must also be
realized that it is not merely sufficient to generate sentences having a variety of syntactic constructs, one must
actually be able to perform transformations from one form into
another. This is considered more fully in RSTORY (Prog.
16.11).

```
            DEFINE('RSENTENCE(STACK)VAR,EXP,S,TEXT')
```

| Pattern initialization: |

```
          SYN.VAR    = POS(0)      '<'   ARB . VAR    '>'
          SNOBAL.EXP =  POS(0)  ' (' BAL(' (<>)','"' "'") . EXP ')'
          ASGN.VAR   = POS(0)      '='   ARB . VAR    '='
          LITERAL.TEXT          =  BREAK('<=(') . TEXT
```

| Read in the grammar and enter the alternative lists into a |
| table (RSENT_TBL). |

```
          RSENT_TBL  =   TABLE()
          SS    =   TRIM(INPUT)
RSI_1     S     =   TRIM(INPUT)
          S    POS(0)  ('<' | 'END' RPOS(0))         :S(RSI_2)
          SS   =   SS S                              :(RSI_1)
RSI_2     SS      '<' ARB . NM '>::=' =
          RSENT_TBL<NM>   =   '|' SS
          IDENT(S,'END')                             :S(RSENTENCE_END)
          SS   =   S                                 :(RSI_1)
```

| Entry point: The string named STACK will contain all not- |
| yet processed information. The string S will contain the |
| random sentence being formed. We examine the STACK for a |
| syntactic variable, a SNOBOL4 expression in parenthesis, |
| an assignment operation enclosed in ='s, or, if none of |
| these, arbitrary text. |

```
RSENTENCE
          STACK SYN.VAR = RSELECT(RSENT_TBL<VAR>)    :S(RSENTENCE)
```

Program 16.8 - RSENTENCE

```
          STACK    SNOBAL.EXP  =                :F(RSENT_1)
          S      = S  EVAL(EXP)                 :(RSENTENCE)
RSENT_1   STACK    ASGN.VAR    =                :F(RSENT_2)
          $VAR   = RSENTENCE('<' VAR '>')
          S      = S  $VAR                      :(RSENTENCE)
RSENT_2   STACK    LITERAL.TEXT =               :F(RSENT_3)
          S      = S  TEXT                      :(RSENTENCE)
RSENT_3   RSENTENCE = S  STACK                  :(RETURN)
RSENTENCE_END
```

Names referenced by RSENTENCE:	Name	Type	Where defined
	BAL *	Function	Program 8.3
	RSELECT	Function	Program 16.7

* indicates name is referenced in the initialization section.

Epilogue

A curiosity of sentence generators such as RSENTENCE is that it is possible to write a grammar with a chance of looping forever. Pohl [1967] gives the following examples:

```
<S1>::= A | B <S1>
<S2>::= A | <S2> A <S2> | <S2> B <S2>
<S3>::=#2# A | <S3> A <S3> | <S3> B <S3>
```

Whereas <S1> will always halt, <S2> has only a probability of 1/2 of halting (unlike normal loops, the program will not actually run forever because storage requirements will ultimately be exceeded; in practice, however, the program will _appear_ to be looping because the storage growth rate is small). <S3> represents a 'fixed-up' version of <S2> which, like <S1>, will halt with probability 1.

The analysis of this phenomenon is based on the notion of random walks with ruin and is treated in detail by Feller [1957]. Let a particle on each step move either to the left or to the right. Let it move to the left with probability p and to the right with probability q so that p+q = 1. Let P be the probability of moving one step to the left, ever. Then P^{**n} is the probability of ever moving n steps to the left. Hence

$$P = p + q P^2$$

This equation has exactly two solutions, viz. P = 1 and P = p/q. Curiously, the correct choice does not seem to be deducible by a simple argument. It happens to be 1 if $p \geq q$ and is p/q if $p \leq q$. The dividing line of p = q = 1/2 is of interest in that the walk is certain to ultimately reach any point but the expected waiting time is infinite.

In the examples above, <S2> loops because, effectively, q = 2/3 and p = 1/3. On the other hand <S3> has p = 1/2 and Q = 1/2 and so the probability of halting is 1 (but just barely). In <S1>, we may throw out any alternation that leads to the same state so that, effectively, p = 1 and q = 0.

Chapter 16 - STOCHASTIC STRINGS

```
|| Program  ||
||  16.9    ||
||  RPOEM   ||
```

One use (one hesitates to say application) of RSENTENCE is in poetry generation (See Milic [1970, 1971] for a general discussion of this topic and other references). For example, if the following were the input to RSENTENCE:

```
<PROP>::=action|duration|hunger|feeling|activity|movement|
motion|notion|endurance|tenderness|age|taste|bounty|goodness
<GEN>::=time|nature|age|wisdom|war|peace|power|energy|earth|
love|beauty|charity|faith|hope|thought|strength|night|
piety|heart|land|evil
<SPEC>::=flower|tree|dove|star|cloud|twig|pond|dog|goat|
muffin|petal|wagon wheel|gate|trap|lark|raven|drop|dish|spoon|
spark|bone|brain|tooth|face|rake|shovel|book|cover|whistle
<PREP>::=on|up|over|under|within|beside|of|in
<TVERB>::=revere|worship|understand|beseech|control|provoke|
heal|pursue|strengthen|become|kill|arouse|becalm|ensnare
<IVERB>::=sing|talk|run|aspire|twiddle|think|gurgle|ponder|
wiggle|bend|simmer|bask|break|tumble|dance|whistle|squawk
<ADJ>::=gentle|frail|happy|sorrowful|mournful|gay|rusty|
frolicking|wonton|lustful|timid|pensive|timorous|moody
<AUX>::=may|can|shall|should|must|doth
<NOUN>::=a <ADJ> <SPEC>|a <SPEC> of <GEN>|the <PROP> of a
<SPEC>|the <SPEC> <PREP> <NOUN>|<GEN> <PREP> <GEN>|<GEN>'s
<PROP>|<ADJ> <GEN>|the <PROP> of <GEN>
<RPOEM>::=A =ADJ= =SPEC= <AUX> <IVERB> <PREP> =NOUN=/And <AUX>
<TVERB> <NOUN>./But <NOUN> <TVERB>s <NOUN>/While (NOUN)
<TVERB>s the (ADJ) (SPEC)./
END
```

The first four calls to RSENTENCE('<RPOEM>') (with RAN_VAR set to 1) produces:

```
| A lustful twig can twiddle up the tenderness of a spoon
| And can kill the motion of wisdom.
| But the brain beside gay power heals the action of earth
| While the tenderness of a spoon heals the lustful twig.
|
| A happy muffin shall bask under earth of night
| And can ensnare the pond up charity of earth.
| But the activity of charity strengthens sorrowful faith
| While earth of night beseechs the happy muffin.
|
| A wonton gate may gurgle under the gate of the age of a star
| And should worship a gay shovel.
| But frail wisdom ensnares the endurance of night
| While the gate of the age of a star pursues the wonton gate.
|
| A moody cloud shall ponder over the motion of a shovel
| And should beseech the goodness of beauty.
| But war over nature worships a wonton goat
| While the motion of a shovel strengthens the moody cloud.
```

where the lines are broken at slashes. Notice that an effort was made to produce sentences which would be syntactically correct and also have some semantic soundness. For example, there are three types of nouns, GENeral, SPECific and PROPerty. One of the noun phrases is <PROP> of <SPEC>, i.e. a property of a specific thing, but <SPEC> of <PROP> is not allowed.

One reason that the random generation of poems has been popular is that context-free generators produce very little semantic connectivity between words. Since the poet is granted license to break such rules we naturally interpret text in which such rules are broken as poetry. As Milic [1970] has observed, we readily "... accept metaphor as an alternative to calling a sentence nonsensical." Hence, in generating random text it is much easier to randomly generate 'poetry' than prose just as it is easier to randomly generate 'abstract art' than good pictures. One conceivable application of random poetry is as an initial exercise in a poetry-appreciation course. The exercise of explaining the 'meanings' of some of the computer renderings can be a mind-expanding experience.

RSENTENCE may, as we will see, be also used for story generation. There are, however, definate limitations in this direction. Mendoza [1968] describes one effort to improve somewhat on the semantic soundness of the generated sentences. Essentially his method applied weights to different noun-verb combinations so that a squirrel would munch and crunch with a greater likelyhood than crawl and swim. This technique produced sentences which were internally sound but which had very little relation to other sentences. Hence, when Mendoza read sets of such sentences to his children as stories, the children complained because the stories never got anywhere.

Using a vocabulary heavily sprinkled with chemical terms, Mendoza reported on attempts to pass off randomly-generated sentences in a chemistry examination. It is perhaps a plus for higher education that the teacher not only did not give a high grade to the computer but actually stormed into the Director's office shouting "Who the hell is this man - why did we ever admit him?" Perhaps what is of interest in these stories is that the individuals involved did not see the computer behind the gibberish but accepted is as very bad human products. This is an advance of sorts. The problem of providing inter-sentence connectivity is a challenging one and will be considered after taking up the next topic.

Chapter 16 - STOCHASTIC STRINGS

```
  ****  IMULATION
  *
  ****           outcome
  *
  ****
```
The computer may be used to simulate real events and, in so doing, may determine the outcome of certain strategies or actions far less expensively and more quickly than by concocting the event physically. Simulation is used where the events to be predicted are not amenable to mathematical analysis but where the underlying stochastic structure is well-established. Simulations are used in business where transport networks, factories and shops, trading centers, etc. may be analyzed, in the study of warfare, cities, traffic, demography, biological adaptation and many other large and complex situations. Simulations are sometimes referred to as Monte Carlo techniques, but this latter term is more likely to be reserved for more mathematically-oriented situations. As a crude example, the area under a curve can be approximated by generating random number pairs (See Exercise 16.13) and testing to see if they fall above or below the curve of interest. Other areas where simulations can be used is in game-playing, sports and gambling. For a specific simulation we choose the game of baseball.

```
  ||  Program  ||
  ||   16.10   ||
  ||  RSEASON  ||
```
The function RSEASON(NG) is intended to simulate a random season of baseball. The number of games is given by the argument NG. The value returned is the number of runs scored in the simulation. The simulation is governed by statistics read in at initialization time. One example of input that could be given is shown in Table 16.4.

Table 16.4 Shows the line-up and statistics for the 1927 New York Yankees. Source is BB [1969]. Only the data shown in lower center was actually input to RSEASON.

Name	AB	H	DB	TR	HR	BB	BA
Combs	648,	231,	36,	23,	6,	62	.356
Koenig	526,	150,	20,	11,	3,	25	.285
Ruth	540,	192,	29,	8,	60,	138	.356
Gehrig	584,	218,	52,	18,	47,	109	.374
Meusel	516,	174,	47,	9,	8,	45	.337
Lazzeri	570,	176,	29,	8,	18,	69	.309
Dugan	387,	104,	24,	3,	2,	27	.269
Collins	251,	69,	9,	3,	7,	54	.275
Pitcher	500,	50,	5,	1,	2,	10	.100

Table 16.4 shows the lineup and statistics of the 1927 New York Yankees, perhaps the most powerful hitting aggregation in

Program 16.10 - RSEASON — Page 361

the history of baseball. The statistics given for the pitcher
are not those of any given player but are an estimated composite of the entire pitching staff.

The program is in a sense the simplest possible simulation
since only offensive data are given for only one team. A perfect simulation would perhaps require that every blade of
grass be taken into account and is completely out of the question from the standpoint of human effort let alone the fact
that baseball records, complete as they are, do not show all
such minutiae. Between these extremes, the pitcher on the
defensive team and to a lesser extent the fielders do affect
the performance of the offensive team as a whole and may
peculiarly effect individual hitters. Another weakness of the
simulation is that every player's performance is independent
of his previous performances and, more severely, of the game
situation. Some players are considered 'clutch hitters' and
pitchers tend to 'bear down' on hitters in tight situations.
All of these factors are worth a study of their own to anyone
interested in a serious simulation of the game. We will be
content with exploring the principles of simulation. As it
stands, however, RSEASON could be used to determine the gross
effects due to line-up changes and permutations in order to
determine optimal line-ups or to evaluate trades, the effect
of pinch hitters, etc.

```
          DEFINE('RSEASON(GAMES) INNING,RUNS,BASES,OUTS,K')
```

A structure, RECORD, is defined to contain the statistics of one player. STATS is an array, filled during the initialization period with statistics of the players in the simulated lineup.

```
              DATA('RECORD(AB,H,DB,TR,HR,BB)')
              STATS = ARRAY(9)
              I = 0
RS_INIT       I = I + 1
              STATS<I> = EVAL('RECORD(' INPUT ')')   :S(RS_INIT)
                                                      :(RSEASON_END)
```

Entry point and outer loop: Control returns here after each complete game. Control arrives at RS_1 for each new inning. BASES will contain the men on base in the form of a string and OUTS is an integer recording the number of outs.

```
RSEASON  GAMES = GT(GAMES,0)   GAMES - 1         :F(RETURN)
         BATTER = 0
RS_1     OUTS = 0
         BASES =
```

Here for each new batter. His statistics are obtained in S. A random number K is obtained based on his total at-bats. The variable ADV is set according to how his performance would advance runners from bases 0, 1, 2, and 3. The actual advancement is done at RS_4. An exception is

Page 362   Chapter 16 - STOCHASTIC STRINGS

| the walk (BB) in which advancement is context sensitive |
| and so must be treated as a special case at RS_BB. |

```
RS_2      BATTER  =  EQ(BATTER,9)   0
          BATTER  =  BATTER + 1
          S       =  STATS<BATTER>
          K       =  RANDOM(AB(S) + BB(S))
          ADV     =  GT(K,AB(S))         '1223'              :S(RS_BB)
          OUTS    =  GT(K,H(S))          OUTS + 1            :S(RS_OUT)
          ADV     =  LE(K,HR(S))         'RRRR'              :S(RS_4)
          ADV     =  LE(K,HR(S) + TR(S))      '3RRR'         :S(RS_4)
          ADV     =  LE(K,HR(S) + TR(S) + DB(S))  '23RR'     :S(RS_4)
          ADV     =  '12RR'
RS_4      BASES   =  REPLACE(BASES 0, '0123', ADV)           :(RS_2)
RS_BB     BASES   '321'  =  '421'
          BASES   '21'   =  '31'                             :(RS_4)
```

| If there are not three outs, determine the number of RUNS |
| scored this inning by scanning BASES. Add to total |
| (RSEASON). Then check to see if we've completed 9 INNINGS.|

```
RS_OUT    EQ(OUTS,3)                                         :F(RS_2)
          RUNS    =  0
          BASES      SPAN('R') @RUNS
          RSEASON =  RSEASON + RUNS
          INNING  =  INNING + 1   LT(INNING,9)               :S(RS_1)
          INNING  =  0                                       :(RSEASON)
RSEASON_END
```

Names referenced   Name   Type   Where defined
by RSEASON: RANDOM   Function   Program 16.1

One of the most important aspects of a simulation is how to
interpret the numbers. For example, to simulate a season we
may call RSEASON(154) and find that 978 runs were scored. But
repeated calls to RSEASON(154) will produce slightly different
numbers. An actual sequence obtained was:

         978   1013   1068   1004   886   999   1053   1039

These eight numbers average to 1005. In general, the more
numbers we obtain the closer these numbers approach some
limiting value. Since computation can be expensive and time-
consuming, we may well ask how far we must pursue the
statistic-gathering before the average settles down to
something reasonable. Said another way, how can we estimate
the error of such a computed average?

Let M be the mean of n numbers X_1 X_2 ... X_n. That is

$$M = (X_1 + X_2 + \ldots + X_n) / n \qquad (16.1)$$

It is well known [Feller 1957] that if the $X_1, X_2, \ldots, X_n$ are
independent then no matter what their distribution (assuming
their means and variances are not infinite), their sum S

Program 16.10 - RSEASON   Page 363

$$S = X_1 + X_2 + \ldots + X_n$$

approaches a Gaussian distribution whose standard deviation (or standard error) E can easily be estimated from the formula:

$$E^2 = (X_1 - M)^2 + (X_2 - M)^2 + \ldots + (X_n - M)^2 \qquad (16.2)$$

The sum S will be in error by about E. Moreover, we may be 95% confident that S is within ± 2E from the average value. Hence we may with the same confidence (95%) expect that the asymptotic average will be in the range:

$$S/n \pm 2E/n$$

As an example, given the previous 8 numbers, we obtain

$$E^2 = 729 + 64 + 3969 + 1 + 14161 + 36 + 2304 + 1156$$
$$= 22420$$
$$E = 150$$
$$S/n \pm 2E/n = 1005 \pm 37.5$$

For long sequences of numbers, (16.2) is not in the most convenient form, since the mean M is not available until the last number X_n is seen. Rewriting (16.2) using (16.1) we obtain:

$$E^2 = (X_1^2 + X_2^2 + \ldots + X_n^2) - n M^2 \qquad (16.3)$$

Note that E^2 varies roughly as n and so E/n varies inversely as the square root of n. Hence in order to reduce our range of error by a factor of K we must gather K^2 times as many statistics. Hence, precision is expensive and, for this reason, simulations are used only when analytical techniques are not available.

To determine the effect of modifying the batting order, RSEASON(154) was called 45 times with the lineup as indicated in Table 16.4 and 45 times with Ruth and the pitcher interchanged. In the first case the average runs scored per season was 1009 ±14 where 14 is the 95% confidence interval. In the second case the average was 971.5 ±14. The experiment clearly shows the efficiency of the given lineup over the postulated one.

One curiosity remains however. The number of runs the Yankees actually scored that season was 975. This in spite of the fact that pinch hitters, clutch hitting, extra-inning games, errors and better pitcher-hitting than .100 would have made the actual figure higher than the simulated figure. On the other hand, the Yanks won 110 games that year. If say 70 were won at home then they missed one inning out of twenty which would account for 50 runs. Almost certainly, good clutch pitching, if not choke hitting, could account for the rest.

Page 364   Chapter 16   -   STOCHASTIC STRINGS

```
||  Program  ||
||   16.11   ||
||  RSTORY   ||
```
As indicated by Mendoza (Epilogue to RPOEM, Prog. 16.9) sequences of sentences which bear little coherence one to the other are not particulary interesting even to children let alone the flabergasted professor. At first sight, the ability to produce an actual story may seem quite beyond the state of the computer art. However, it is not essentially difficult to supply the desired connectivity by using some underlying simulation to form a developing plot and use the random sentence generator to supply verbal 'suguring'. This is amply illustrated by the baseball simulation (RSEASON) which would be quite easy to modify to produce a 'meat and potatoes' narration such as: "... Ruth makes out, Gehrig hits single, Meusel makes out, End of inning, no runs ... ", etc. For the purpose of story-generation, descriptive phrases, chosen at random could further embellish the tale adding needed color (See Exercise 16.16).

For the generation of stories which may appeal to children, a child's game may be simulated. There are many games on the market in which tokens moving over a board carry the child through a sequence of adventures often with a competitive element thrown in which would make the story interesting. Board games, such as Monopoly, have been programmed and most children's games are considerably less complicated than this.

One method of producing random stories which only vary weakly from each other is to locally perturb certain variables of a given pre-concocted story. There are children's books on the market which utilize this principle in producing personalized books. In addition to using this principle, RSTORY, below, attempts to utilize a collection of semantically rich (or at least richer) information of the form <agent> <adversely operates upon> <agent>. RSTORY draws upon these relationships in order to produce a simple 'actor-action' chain which this classic children's story requires.

```
| Process phrases - We assume that RSENTENCE has read in all |
| syntactic variable definitions. All phrases are of the    |
| form SUBJECT VERB OBJECT. For each object expressed or    |
| implied in a phrase, we make an entry in the table ACTIONS|
| which will contain the subject and object.                |
```

```
            ACTIONS  =  TABLE()
            BB = BREAK(' ')
            SB = SPAN(' ')
READ_PHRASE
            X  =  TRIM(INPUT)                        :F(BEGIN_STORY)
            IDENT(X,'END')                           :S(BEGIN_STORY)
            X  (BB SB BB) . SUBJ_VERB  SB  REM . OBJS
            OBJS  =  OBJS  '|'
READ_PH1
            OBJS  POS(0)  '<' ARB . VAR '>'  =  RSENT_TBL<VAR>
            OBJS  POS(0)  '|'  =                     :S(READ_PH1)
```

Program 16.11 - RSTORY

```
           CBJS      BREAK('|')  .  OBJ   '|'   =        :F(READ_PHRASE)
           ACTIONS<OBJ>   =  ACTIONS<OBJ>  '|'  SUBJ_VERB
                                                         :(READ_PH1)
```
┌───┐
│ The story's setting and the principal characters are in-   │
│ troduced here.   │
└───┘
```
BEGIN_STORY        RSTORY   =   RSENTENCE('<OPENING>')
                   LIST  =  '  ' PET " won't jump over the " BARRIER
                   LAST  =  PET
                   &MAXLNGTH   =   30000
```
┌───┐
│ Find a new agent; we will try ten times to produce a   verb   │
│ and an agent that we haven't seen before.   │
└───┘
```
NEW_AGENT
           TRY   =   0
RETRY      TRY   =   TRY + 1   LT(TRY,10)            :F(REQUEST)
           ALTS  =   ACTIONS<LAST>
           RSENTENCE(RSELECT(ALTS))   BB . SUBJ  SB  REM . VERB
           RSTORY    ' ' SUBJ ' '                    :S(RETRY)
           RSTORY    ' ' VERB ' '                    :S(RETRY)
```
┌───┐
│ Here the refusal is added to the story as well as descrip-   │
│ tive text relating to finding a new agent and making a   │
│ request.   │
└───┘
```
REQUEST    RSTORY   =   RSTORY  RSENTENCE('<REFUSAL>')
           LIST  =   '  ' SUBJ " won't " VERB ' the ' LAST ", " LIST
           LAST  =   SUBJ
```
┌───┐
│ If the agent complies freely with the request, control   │
│ falls through the next test and the story is essentially   │
│ over.   │
└───┘
```
           LT(SIZE(LIST),  175)                      :S(NEW_AGENT)
FIN1       LIST   "won't"   =   "began to"           :S(FIN1)
FIN2       LIST   ','       =   "; the"              :S(FIN2)
           RSTORY   =   RSTORY  RSENTENCE('<PERSUADED>')
```
┌───┐
│ Now output the story.   │
└───┘
```
OUT        RSTORY   (LEN(50) BB) . OUTPUT  SB  =     :S(OUT)
           OUTPUT   =   RSTORY
```
┌───┐
│ Below find the input data to the program. The first half   │
│ (up to END) is processed by RSENTENCE. Following this we   │
│ find the phrases on which the story is based.   │
└───┘
```
END
<OPENING>::=<TIME> there was a =CHAR= who went to <PLACE> and
bought a =PET=.  On the way home they came upon a =BARRIER=
which the (PET) was afraid to cross.  The (CHAR) said "(PET),
(PET), jump over the (BARRIER) or I won't get home tonight."
<TIME>::=Once upon a time|Once|Long ago in a small village|
In days gone by in a little town by the river
```

Chapter 16 - STOCHASTIC STRINGS

```
<PLACE>::=market|a pet store|a super market|town|the city
<BARRIER>::=fence|ditch|fallen tree|large rock|stream|brook
<PET>::=dog|cat|parrot|pony
<REFUSAL>::=  But the (LAST) would not. The (CHAR)
<EXCURSION> and she met a (SUBJ). She said, "(SUBJ), (SUBJ),
  (VERB) (LAST), (LIST) and I shan't get home tonight."
<EXCURSION>::=went down the path|went over a hill|went by
  <OBJECT> and then <EXCURSION>|went toward <OBJECT>|
went over hill and dale|went near <OBJECT>|went on the road to
  <OBJECT>|went for (RANDOM(20) + 1) miles
<OBJECT>::=the <COLOR> <THING>
<COLOR>::=white|blue|red|yellow|grey|black|dark|green|orange
<THING>::=mill|tavern|church|school|house|meadow|rock|barn
<PERSUADED>::=  The (SUBJ) knew the (CHAR) and, in fact,
  had been saved by her from a wild <WILD_AN>. So the (LIST)
  and the (CHAR) got home that night.
<CHAR>::=little old woman|little old lady|kind grandmother|
  kind old aunt|little girl dressed in red|retired seamstress|
  nice old lady|little girl green
<DOM_AN>::=cow|pig|horse|sheep|chicken
<WILD_AN>::=lion|giraffe|tiger|camel|ostrich|rhinoceros
<ANIMAL>::=<DOM_AN>|<WILD_AN>|<PET>
<HUMAN>::=farmer|girl|policeman|hunter|man|boy
<A>::=<HUMAN>|<ANIMAL>
<CUT>::=cut|slice|snip|slash
<CUTTER>::=knife|scissor|sword|dagger
<BEE>::=bee|wasp|horse-fly
<HURT>::=bite|frighten|scare|kick|eat
END
<ANIMAL> <HURT> <HUMAN>
<CUTTER> <CUT> <A>
<A> break <CUTTER>
water drown <A>
<A> drink water
fire burn <A>
smoke suffocate <A>
<BEE> sting <A>
<A> swat <BEE>
wind blow-out fire
wind disperse smoke
smoke pollute wind
smoke smother fire
<HUMAN> disperse smoke
<A> spill liquor
liquor intoxicate <A>
<HUMAN> slay <WILD_AN>
<WILD_AN> eat <HUMAN>
END
```

Names referenced by RSTORY:	Name	Type	Where defined
	RSENTENCE	Function	Program 16.8

Epilogue

One example of a story produced by the program (untouched by human hands) is:

> Long ago in a small village there was a little old lady who went to a pet store and bought a cat. On the way home they came upon a ditch which the cat was afraid to cross. The little old lady said "cat, cat, jump over the ditch or I won't get home tonight." But the cat would not. The little old lady went over hill and dale and she met a water. She said, "water, water, drown cat, cat won't jump over the ditch and I shan't get home tonight." But the water would not. The little old lady went on the road to the red school and she met a man. She said, "man, man, drink water, water won't drown the cat, cat won't jump over the ditch and I shan't get home tonight." But the man would not. The little old lady went toward the blue church and she met a lion. She said, "lion, lion, eat man, man won't drink the water, water won't drown the cat, cat won't jump over the ditch and I shan't get home tonight." But the lion would not. The little old lady went toward the yellow rock and she met a smoke. She said, "smoke, smoke, suffocate lion, lion won't eat the man, man won't drink the water, water won't drown the cat, cat won't jump over the ditch and I shan't get home tonight." But the smoke would not. The little old lady went toward the blue house and she met a girl. She said, "girl, girl, disperse smoke, smoke won't suffocate the lion, lion won't eat the man, man won't drink the water, water won't drown the cat, cat won't jump over the ditch and I shan't get home tonight." The girl knew the little old lady and, in fact, had been saved by her from a wild ostrich. So the girl began to disperse the smoke; the smoke began to suffocate the lion; the lion began to eat the man; the man began to drink the water; the water began to drown the cat; the cat began to jump over the ditch and the little old lady got home that night.

The reader will note that the story tends to be repetitious which is somewhat the point since small tots have a penchant for this sort of thing.

In order to extend the robustness of the given program (where robustness is defined as the degree to which the stories vary) one may, of course, extend the vocabulary. One of the limitations so encountered, is the necessity within English to observe certain grammatical niceties such as using 'she' to refer to a woman. This single fact, incidently, is the reason that the principal character in the story has feminine gender. To include any gender, one would at least need a function PRONOUN(W) which will return the third person singular personal pronoun for any word given as argument. While this task

Chapter 16 - STOCHASTIC STRINGS

is not formidable (with a limited vocabulary) a complete set of grammatical transformations which would include, for example, present tense to past and future, active voice to passive, indicative mood to subjunctive, singular to plural, represents a considerable undertaking. Thus, with story generation, as opposed to mere sentence generation we come to grips with much more severe syntactic problems.

The semantic difficulties involved in considerably extending the robustness of the story generator are also of interest. It should be clear that the vocabulary section of RSTORY can be completely overhauled to produce stories in such diverse settings as the wild west, interplanetary travel, the Jurassic period (dinosaur days), etc. A weakness of the system is that one could not place the union of all such information into the story since, for example, the <excursion> variable might produce "the cowboy drove his spaceship past the red pterodactyl." We should want to at least draw actors and actions into the story on a logical, though perhaps probabilistic, basis. The problem seems somewhat similar to the Analogy Problem [Tuggle 1973] in which a program attempts to fill in the blank in a sentence of the form

A is to B as C is to ___

Here, a sufficiently rich data base makes such problems tractable. Returning to our story, if CHAR is our principal character and we wish her (him) to travel we may say:

"cowboy is to horse as CHAR is to ___"

in order to find an appropriate means of transport. We can see a bit of this in the specialized data section of RSTORY (the second set of data) which sets forth relations between individuals and specialized groups to obtain greater realism at the expense of robustness. These relations are, of course, all of a certain kind, viz. of the form <agent> <affects> <agent>. Increasing the kinds of relations is essentially what is required to solve the Analogy Problem. Thus, RSTORY may be augmented by the possibility of having one or more of the chain of agents wander off (after having been lined up) in a manner consistent with the agent (water might evaporate, fire burn out, lion be distracted by game, etc). This would add another dimension to the story.

On a deeper level, one may wonder whether it is possible for the computer to play a greater role in the formation of the plot and deciding on the 'point' of the story. Would computer-generated stories always remain in the entertainment category or could they serve some useful function such as describing some complex event within, say, an operating system? The question of randomly generated stories is currently a topic of considerable interest. See AI FORUM [1974] for a vigorous discussion and several other references. Also Knuth [Vol. 2] describes a random western which was used as the basis for a television film.

Exercises for chapter 16   Page 369

??
???????????????????????   EXERCISES ???????????????????????
??

┌─────────────────┐
│ Exercise 16.1   │ RANDOM(0) has a distribution which is
└─────────────────┘ uniform over the interval (0,1). It is
sometimes required to have other kinds of distributions.
Define the <u>distribution function</u> (sometimes called the cumula-
tive distribution function) D(X) of a random number generator
R() as the function

$$D(X) = \text{Prob}\{ R() < X \}$$

For example, the distibution function assocated with the
uniform distribution slopes between 0 and 1 in the range (0,1)
and is 0 below and 1 above this rannge. Given an arbitrary
distribution function D(), write the random generator R() in
terms of the uniform generator RANDOM() and the inverse of
D(), call it ID(), which is presumed to exist.

┌─────────────────┐
│ Exercise 16.2   │ Suppose that a program requires random num-
└─────────────────┘ bers between 0 and 1 in such a way that x
is x/y times more likely to occur as y. Thus 1/2 is twice as
likely to occur as 1/4. Write the distribution function D()
for the generator. Write a program to produce the random numbers (functions in the ARITHMETIC chapter can be used).

┌─────────────────┐
│ Exercise 16.3   │ Let a deck of cards be represented by 52
└─────────────────┘ separate characters, say:

$$\text{DECK} = \text{'ab ... zAB ... Z'}$$

In one statement, deal out four 5-card poker hands to players
P1, P2, P3 and P4. (Any function(s) in this chapter may be
used.)

┌─────────────────┐
│ Exercise 16.4   │ A well-known game is to find, for a given
└─────────────────┘ telephone number, a sequence of letters
which (1) when dialed will produce the same number and (2) are
a pronouncable sequence. For example, 233-6874 can perhaps
more easily be remembered as 'BEDMUSH' or 'ADDNURI'. The correspondence is:

2	ABC	6	MNO
3	DEF	7	PRS
4	GHI	8	TUV
5	JKL	9	WXY

(1's and 0's create problems).

Page 370   Chapter 16   -   STOCHASTIC STRINGS

Write a function RPHONE to accept a telephone number and return a random sequence of letters associated in the above sense with the number. The sequence should bear some similarity to English; to do this, use RCHAR for probable next characters.

| Exercise 16.5 | What single statement can be modified so that RSELECT (Prog. 16.7) saves space rather than time?

| Exercise 16.6 | Augment the assignment interpreter in RSENTENCE so that the variable assigned into need not also be the name of the syntactic variable expanded. One way to do this is to let

=var/s=

be interpreted as:

var = RSENTENCE(s)

| Exercise 16.7 | If the argument to RSENTENCE is not well formed, the function can loop. Give an example of a string which will have this effect. What modificaiton to RSENTENCE can correct this. (Requires the addition of six characters and a blank).

| Exercise 16.8 | This exercise is based on a suggestion by Yngve [1962]. In the input to RSENTENCE let /text/ indicate that the result of evaluating text (via RSENTENCE(text)) is to be placed in the stack after the next item. An item is defined as either a syntactic unit or a sequence of non-blanks. Thus

<SENT>::= <NOUN> <VERB-PHRASE> <NOUN>
<VERB-PHRASE>::=<VERB>/ <ADVERB>/

can result in " He called her up". Incorporate Yngve's suggestion into RSTENTENCE.

| Exercise 16.9 | In RSENTENCE, there are several characters which can't be used directly within alternatives because they have some meta-meaning (such as <>| etc.) Define an 'escape' convention so that any special character can be incorporated in the final text. Implement your scheme (Hint: this can be implemented by modifying one pattern).

| Exercise 16.10 | For which of the following definitions will <S> have a probability of looping greater than 0.

(a)   <S>::=A|<S>A|<S><S>A
(b)   <S>::=#2#A|<S>A|<S><S>A|<S><S><S>A
(c)   <S>::=A|<T><T>
      <T>::=B|<S>C

| Exercise 16.11 | What is the probability that

<S>::=A|<S>A<S>B<S>

as input to RSENTENCE will halt?

| Exercise 16.12 | The 'one-arm bandits' of gambling fame (also known as slot machines) have three windows in which one of 20 pictures can appear as follows [Spencer 1968]:

Symbol	Wheel 1	Wheel 2	Wheel 3
Cherry (C)	4	6	0
Orange (O)	5	4	7
Bell (E)	4	6	5
Lemon (L)	3	2	4
Watermelon (W)	3	1	3
Bar (B)	1	1	1

Payoffs are as follows:

```
        C - -   3        W W B   15
        C C -   5        O O O   18
        O O B   6        W W W   20
        E E O   8        B B B   200
        L L L  10
```

Identify the sample space. Determine the total input to the machine and the total return if each item in the sample space is hit once and only once. What percentage of total bets is taken by the machine? Write a program to simulate the slot machine (can be done in as few as 10 statements using SUBSTR (Prog. 3.9) and RANDOM).

| Exercise 16.13 | (a) Write a program to compute the area under the curve $Y = X^2$ on the interval $[0,1)$ by Monte Carlo techniques. Print out this area every 100 samples so that you can observe the rate at which the answer converges to its correct value (1/3). (Hint: this requires a total of three statements). (b) Compute the 95% confidence interval after N trials and compare this figure with the experimental results.

Page 372   Chapter 16 - STOCHASTIC STRINGS

| Exercise 16.14 | To speed up the previous exercise, DUPL and CODE can be used so that the inner loop of three statements is reduced effectively to one. How can this be done?

| Exercise 16.15 | Modify RSEASON (Prog. 16.10) so that with probability E a batsman will advance to first by means of an error where otherwise he would simply have made an out. All other runners should advance one base.

| Exercise 16.16 | Write a program called RGAME which will behave like RSEASON except that RSENTENCE is used to supply running commentary of the events which transpire. Include names of players in the input data. Make your game colorful. Don't have a player merely make an out, have him hit a sharp drive to center which is speared by the centerfielder.

| Exercise 16.17 | Sagasti and Page [1970] describe an effort to program and actually stage a computer-generated dance routine. The stage is divided up into 13 areas roughly as shown in Figure 16.1

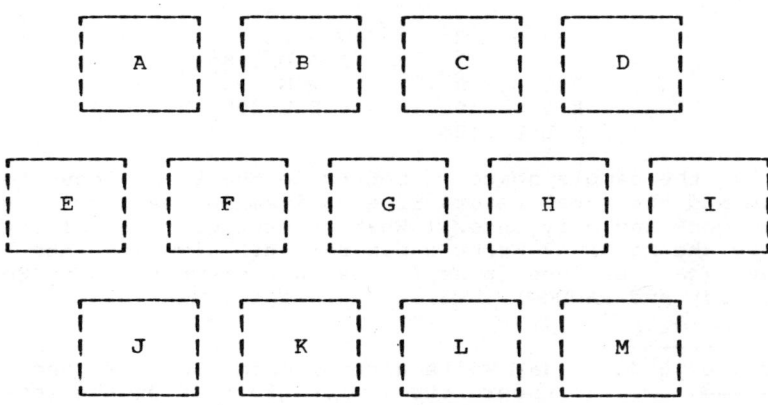

Figure 16.1

The decomposition of the stage to produce a random dance.

A dancer is permitted to move from one circle to an adjacent one; for example, in Figure 16.1 a dancer at F can move to any of A, B, E, G, J, or K; of course, the dancer may also remain at the same position. Dancers may exit and enter at random times but only to or from what may be called terminal nodes. For the exercise, let E, J, K, L, M and I be the terminals. Also, no two dancers may occupy the same spot at the same time.

Implement a program to produce a random dance with the additional constraint that there be left-right symmetry. That is, for example, if a dancer moves from A to B then another dancer must move from D to C. To allow movement into the center position, create a new position Y which is offstage center. If a dancer at K goes to G then the dancer at L must go to Y, etc. Also, permit dancers at G and Y to change places. Denote offstage left as position X and offstage right as position Z. The output of the program should be a list of instructions for each of eight dancers.

Be careful! Sagasti and Page describe their initial efforts as resulting in "pandemonium on stage" until a slower tempo was found. They also described one dancer as "mildly bitter" being forced to leave early.

| Exercise 16.18 | Change the story given by RSTORY to one involving a space motif. Use RWORD to provide stange-sounding names of people and planets.

CHAPTER SEVENTEEN

GAMES

CONTENTS

PHRASE 17.1

QUEST 17.2

STONE 17.3

TICTACTOE 17.4

CARDPAK 17.5

POKEV 17.6

POKER 17.7

Chapter 17 - GAMES   Page 375

Games are artificial environments frequently abstracted from reality intended to amuse and/or exercise the cranium. The computer (and computer programmers) are quite proficient at simulating such abstractions, much more so than the reality backdrop, so that there has for a long time been a happy marriage between computers and game playing (frequently to the chagrin of management intent on putting the high-priced piece of equipment to better use than amusing its high-priced employees). As the cost of computation diminishes, however, the recreational or game-playing applications of digitial computers may be expected to increase, and surely any survey of SNOBOL4 applications would not be complete were it to ignore this area entirely. The computer is, after all, the ultimate game if not the ultimate player.

We almost, but not quite, include under the heading of games, attempts to make the computer behave (i.e. converse) like a human. Weisenbaum [1966] made a notable attempt in this direction with his program ELIZA. ELIZA will converse with the user in a form characteristic of a script given to it as data. The most familiar and popular script makes ELIZA behave like a psychiatrist. Though ELIZA was originally written in Fortran, Duquet [1970] has written a 'dramatically shorter' version in SNOBOL4. In SNOBOL4, the program is actually smaller than the psychiatrist script (two pages versus four). While we do not include the program here, we note in passing that dialogue is a necessary aspect of most games and a snappy dialogue can add an appeal to an otherwise not-too-exciting game. We will return to this issue later.

For good or ill, many games have been programmed on the computer. At a nearby PDP-10 time-sharing computer there exists twenty-some games including Chess, Go, Black Jack, Go-Moku, Monopoly, Tick-tack-toe (two and three dimensions), Nim and games based on football, golf and Startrek to mention only those names that are immediately recognizable. There are many other games which have been, or will be, written for a digital computer; see Spencer [1968], Ball [1962] and especially Ahl [1973].

A game may be <u>concealed</u> or <u>open</u>. In an open game, such as Chess or Checkers, all information concerning the state of the game is available to both players. In concealed games, such as in many card games or in penny matching, each player may have information unavailable to the other. This is clearly the case if one is holding cards unseen by one's opponent. With penny matching, the concealed information is the player's strategy. In a concealed game, the player must play in such a way as not to reveal his hidden information and therefore the techniques and analysis are quite different from the open game.

In concealed games, there seems to be a problem involving player and computer credibility which does not exist with the

Page 376   Chapter 17   -   GAMES

open game. Consider the game of penny-matching in which both
players choose a side of a penny; one player wins (the other
player's penny) if there is a match; otherwise the other
player wins. With a computer there is a problem. If the computer
goes first, there is the possibility that the player
will cheat. If the player goes first, he may suspect the
machine of cheating. Hagelbarger [1956] built a penny-matching
machine, called SEER which 'solved' this problem by the human
saying aloud his choice of head or tail and the machine
(sensitive only to sound) would indicate its choice whereupon
the player would tell the machine, by a push button, who won.
The machine can't cheat under these circumstances but the
human certainly can. A counter was wired up to accumulate
total wins and losses for the machine. Though the machine won
most of its games, the results are clouded by the fact that
some players would deliberately lie to the machine to see how
it would operate in stressful situations.

One solution to the concealment problem lay in the use of a
one-way cipher (See ONEWAY, Prog. 16.4). Recall that given
the returned value of ONEWAY(S) it is impractical to compute
the original S or, indeed, any S which would yield the same
returned value. Hence the computer can choose a random string
R (possibly based on the clock) and then call ONEWAY(R 'H') if
it chooses a head or call ONEWAY(R 'T') if it chooses a tail.
The computer prints the returned value. Then the player plays.
The machine then reveals its move together with R. The player
can check, if he cares to, whether the previously printed
value corresponds to the given value of R. Spot-checking a
machine for fraudulent behavior should, in this way, be fairly
easy.

A one-way cipher can also be used to make sure that a computer
is giving you a fair deal. See Exercise 17.1.

Decision Trees and Decision Graphs

A decision tree exists, at least conceptually, for any
discrete open game. The top node, or root of the tree,
represents the decision node of the first player and has a
branch descending down for each possible choice of the first
player on his first move. Each such branch descends to a node
representing the decision node of the second player, etc. An
actual decision tree is produced for a simple version of the
stone game (see Figure 17.1).

Decision trees grow exponentially and hence tend to be large.
A complete decision tree for the game of Tick-tack-toe is forbidding
enough. One for the game of Chess is so large as to
be meaningless. For example, at 10 moves per play and for 70
plays, the number of nodes in the tree exceeds the number of
atoms in the earth.

It is more convenient to think of an open game as a collection
of states where each move carries the play to a different

Program 17.1 - PHRASE   Page 377

state. There are terminal states which end the game and indicate a winner for one of the players. If every different move sequence leads to a different state, then the decision tree is equivalent to the decision graph. But in many games, the number of different states is far fewer than the number of nodes in the decision tree and the problem becomes amenable with a graph even though it appears to be impossible with a tree.

One of the appeals of the decision tree is that it leads conceptually to a solution by means of the <u>minimax</u> process. The first player (A) selects that node which will maximize the outcome for him assuming that the second player will respond with the move that will minimize the output for A assuming that the first player responds with the move ... , etc. This strategy may be carried over to the decision graph as follows. Label all terminal states as +1 if a victory for the first player and -1 if a loss and 0 if a tie. Find a state that is directed only to terminal states. If it is a move by A, mark it with the maximum of the values of all states reachable from it. If it is a move by player B, mark it with the least such value. Each state will be thus marked with the value of the state to player A (assuming both players play optimally). If there is no state which is directed only to states already marked, then the game is not well-formed as it contains loops (or, what is equivalent, infinite paths).

It will clearly be impossible to present a large number of intricate game-playing programs in this section. One complete chess program could perhaps occupy the better part of this book. What we can do is present a few games illustrative of their type and also give some commonly useful functions.

```
|| Program  ||
||  17.1    ||
||  PHRASE  ||
```
For many computer-game players it is necessary to provide a carrot and a stick; otherwise, they will simply lose interest and quit. For the carrot we will issue a random compliment and, for the stick, we will generate an insult. These are illustrated by the two functions PRAISE() and INSULT(). There is also a function to mark time called LETMESEE(). Using RSENTENCE (Prog. 16.8) the dialogue is always fresh and lively.

```
DEXP("PRAISE()  = RSENTENCE('<PRAISE>')")
DEXP("INSULT()  = RSENTENCE('<INSULT>')")
DEXP("LETMESEE() = RSENTENCE('<LETMESEE>')")
```

<u>Names referenced</u>   Name   Type   <u>Where defined</u>
<u>by PHRASE:</u>   DEXP   Function   Program 14.1
                    RSENTENCE   Function   Program 16.8

The input for RSENTENCE is:

Chapter 17 - GAMES

```
<GOOD>::=excellent|wonderful|nice|careful|impeccable|shrewd|
clever|nifty|good|smart|skillful|cunning|witty|fine|
splendid|elegant|#5#very <GOOD>|bright|brainy|brilliant|sharp|
keen|nimble-witted|slick|sly|astute|penetrating
<LETMESEE>::=<THOUGHT>|<MUMBLE>|<MUMBLE> <THOUGHT>|<THOUGHT>
   <MUMBLE>
<MUMBLE>::=Hmmm|Ahh|Well Well|Gosh|Gee|OK|Oh man|Let's see|
Wait a minute|Interesting|Wow|Wowee|Yipes|Zowee|Whoosh|
#5#<MUMBLE> <MUMBLE>|#6#<MUMBLE>...
<THOUGHT>::=<LETME> <CONSIDER> <THIS>
<LETME>::=I think I'll|let me|I need time to|I'm going to
   have to
<CONSIDER>::=consider|contemplate|mull over|#4#<THINK> about
<THINK>::=think|see|cogitate|meditate
<THIS>::=this|this one|the situation|this problem|this here
<P1>::=maneuver|strategem|tactic|play|move
<P2>::=performance|game|effort
<P3>::=play|strategy
<P13>::=<P1>s|<P3>
<P23>::=<P2>|<P3>
<P123>::=<P1>s|<P2>|<P3>
<PRAISE>::=<THANKS> for the game, <NICEGAME>
<THANKS>::=Thanks|Thank you|Thank you very much
<NICEGAME>::=I admired the <GOOD> <P123> on your part|
that was <GOOD> <P3> on your part|your <P1>s were quite
   <GOOD>|it was a pleasure to play against one so <GOOD>|I
   enjoyed your <GOOD> <P123>|I enjoyed particularly that last
   <GOOD> <P1>
<STUPID>::=stupid|dumb|blundering|thick-headed|sad|
thick-skulled|silly|ludicrous|witless|poor|ponderous|
brainless|foolish|bungling|heavy-handed|graceless|clumsy
<FOOL>::=fool|dolt|idiot|oaf|blockhead|chump|ass|moron|ninny|
nincompoop|chump|dunce|bonehead|fathead|imbecile|jerk|baboon
<INSULT>::=You <STUPID> <FOOL>|I have never seen such <STUPID>
   <P13>|Your <STUPID> <P23> befits a <STUPID> <FOOL>|
Your <STUPID> <P1>s indicate that you are a <STUPID>
   <FOOL>|A <STUPID> <FOOL> is not so <STUPID> as you|
Your <P23> marks you as a <STUPID> <FOOL>|Your <P1>s are
   less than <GOOD>
END
```

Epilogue

While random sentence generation has been around for quite some time, it generally comes in the form of a program which prints something. It is then neither obvious nor easy to harness the sentence generation for other than demonstrating the effect. It was for this reason that RSENTENCE was written as a function.

Some sample phrases are:

   "Thanks for the game, that was nice strategy on your part"
   "You dumb idiot"
   "Interesting Hmmm..."
   "I'm going to have to consider this"

Program 17.2 - QUEST   Page 379

"I have never seen such thick-headed strategems"
"Thank you for the game, your plays were quite shrewd"

It should be obvious which phrases were respectively returned
by INSULT(), PRAISE() and LETMESEE().

| | Program | | QUEST is intended to save some of the
| | 17.2 | | routine problems and house-keeping chores
| | QUEST | | associated with a dialogue system. For ex-
                   ample, all game routines will request num-
bers and/or strings from the player. The system must then
check if these arguments are valid and, if not, indicate what
is expected.   If valid, the argument must be interpreted or
assigned to a variable and an appropriate branch must be
taken.   Certainly, none of these chores are difficult to do,
but it will be more convenient to combine them into one
routine. For example,

        QUEST('How much do you wish to bet?/BET(1...10) | (DROP)DR')
       +   :S($LABEL)

will print the message:

                How much do you wish to bet?

(i.e. all characters up to the slash) and then either accept
an integer in the range 1...10 and assign it to BET or accept
the literal input DROP and transfer to label DR. The transfer
is accomplished by having QUEST assign the string 'DR' to the
global variable LABEL; if such an assignment is made, the
RETURN exit is taken; otherwise the FRETURN exit is taken. In
this way, the actual transfer takes place outside the function
as shown.

In general, the string following the slash is called the QUEST
pattern and is a sequence of descriptors separated by bars.
Each descriptor is of the form:

                    variable(values)label

The variable, if any, is assigned the value (if accepted) and
the label is assigned as described above. Values may be of
the form:

                       number...number

or some string constant, or the string ARB implying that any
string of characters will be accepted.

If the user types something that doesn't match, an error message (including a random insult) is given. Using the above
example, the message (among other things) that will be typed
is:

Page 380   Chapter 17 - GAMES

                The correct form is: 1...10|DROP

In general, the message will contain the QUEST pattern with
labels, variables and parentheses stripped off.

As a final bonus, if the user ever types question mark (?), a
friendly reminder of the correct form is given.

            DEFINE('QUEST(QS)QP,QPA,QN,QVP,QL,QLOW,QHI,QI')
┌───┐
│ First   define   a utility function QUESTP(QS,QP) which will │
│ analyze the argument string QS according to the QUEST pat- │
│ tern given by QP. It will fail if no match is found.   │
└───┘
            DEFINE('QUESTP(QS,QP)QP1,QS1')   :(QUESTP_END)
┌───┐
│ Entry point: Break on an alternative and if one is found │
│ call QUESTP recursively.   │
└───┘
QUESTP   QP   BREAK('|') . QP1   '|'   =   :F(QUESTP_1)
          QUESTP(QS,QP1)   :S(RETURN) F(QUESTP)
┌───┐
│ In QP we now have a single QUEST descriptor. Obtain the   │
│ variable name (QN), the label name (QL) and the value pat- │
│ tern (QVP).   │
└───┘
QUESTP_1   QP   BREAK('(') . QN   '('   =   :F(FRETURN)
           QN = IDENT(QN)   'QDUMMY'
           QP   BREAK(')') . QVP   ')' REM . QL
┌───┐
│ If QS matches the value pattern, branch to QUESTP_3 for │
│ the assignment.   Convert   QS if necessary to the proper │
│ type.   │
└───┘
              IDENT(QVP,'ARB')   :S(QUESTP_3)
              QVP   ARB . QLOW '...' REM . QHI   :S(QUESTP_2)
              IDENT(QS,QVP)   :S(QUESTP_3) F(FRETURN)
QUESTP_2   QLOW = ¬INTEGER(QLOW)   EVAL(QLOW)
              QHI   = ¬INTEGER(QHI)   EVAL(QHI)
              QS   = CONVERT(QS,'INTEGER')   :F(FRETURN)
              (LE(QLOW,QS) LE(QS,QHI))   :F(FRETURN)
QUESTP_3 $QN =   QS
              LABEL = DIFFER(QL)   QL   :(RETURN)
QUESTP_END
┌───┐
│ Define a pattern (QUEST.QPA) which will extract from a │
│ QUEST descriptor, the inner QUEST pattern. ID.V will match │
│ an identifier assigning it to V.   │
└───┘
              NEUT   =   BREAK('|()')
              QUEST.QPA =   NEUT '(' NEUT . QPA ')' (NEUT | REM)
              A   =   'ABCDEFGHIJKLMNOPQRSTUVWXYZ'
              ID.V   =   (ANY(A) (SPAN(A '0123456789_.') | '')) . V
                                                     :(QUEST_END)
┌───┐
│ Entry   point: After   printing the message, interpret the │

Program 17.3 - STONE

| input. Errors are processed at QUEST_1. |

```
QUEST       LABEL  =
            QS    BREAK('/')  . OUTPUT   '/'  REM . QP
            QI   =  TRIM(INPUT)   ;   OUTPUT  =  QI
QUEST_1     QP   ID.V '...'   =   EVAL(V)  '...'        :S(QUEST_1)
QUEST_2     QP   '...' ID.V   =   '...'  EVAL(V)        :S(QUEST_2)
            (DIFFER(QI,'?')   QUESTP(QI,QP))            :F(QUEST_3)
            DIFFER(LABEL)                    :S(RETURN) F(FRETURN)
```

| Extract and print the pattern and also indicate our |
| feelings. |

```
QUEST_3     QP   QUEST.QPA   =   QPA               :S(QUEST_3)
            OUTPUT   =   DIFFER(QI,'?')
+                    RSENTENCE('Bad input, you <STUPID> <FOOL>')
            OUTPUT   =   'The correct form is '  QP    :(QUEST)
QUEST_END
```

Names referenced	Name	Type	Where defined
by QUEST:	STUPID	Syntactic Variable	Program 17.1
	FOOL	Syntactic Variable	Program 17.1

```
||  Program  ||
||   17.3    ||
||   STONE   ||
```

Let there be N stones in a pile (where N is odd) and let each player take, on each move, either 1, 2, ... , or K stones from the pile. When the pile is exhausted, the player with an odd number of stones wins. For example, if N=5 and K=2 we have a very simple game for which we can portray a complete decision tree as shown in Figure 17.1.

By applying the previously described minimax procedure (or by using common sense) the tree indicates a victory for the first player, A. If the rules of the game are changed to make the winner the one with even parity, the game is victory for B, no matter what A does on the first move.

The decision tree algorithm can be employed if the tree is sufficiently small but becomes quite impractical as soon as the game becomes nontrivial. To see this, let us fix K=2 and let N vary. The number of branches, E(N), in the tree is given by the formula:

$$E(N) = 2 + E(N - 1) + E(N - 2)$$

which is immediately evident from the figure. While it may be an interesting exercise to solve this recurrence relation our purpose is served by simply noting that:

$$E(N) > 2 * E(N - 2)$$

so that

$$E(N) > 2 ** (N/2)$$

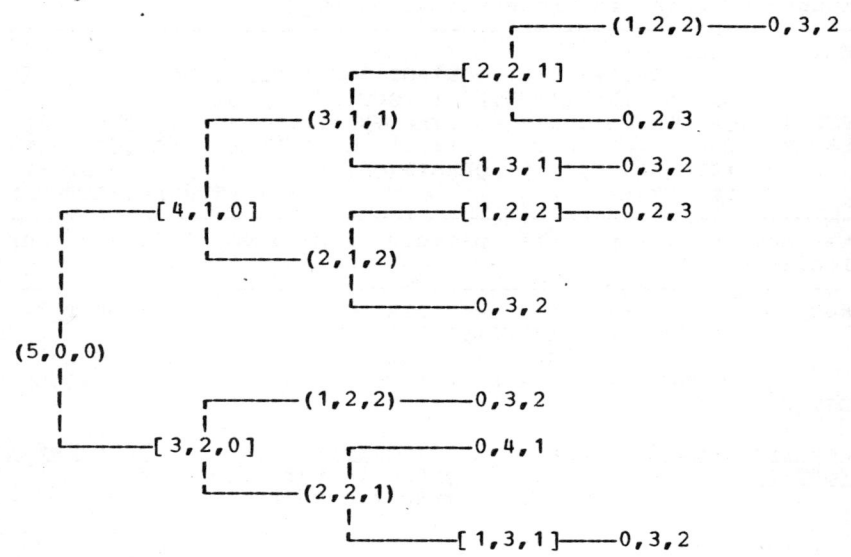

Figure 17.1

The decision tree for the stone game with N=5 and K=2. Player A goes first. At each node, three numbers indicate the number of stones left in the pot, the number of stones in A's possession and the number of stones in B's possession. Parens indicate a decision node for A, brackets indicate a decision node for B.

which implies that E(N) is exponential.

The decision graph on the other hand is quite well-behaved especially if we combine all nodes with the same parities for the two players. That is, for a given number of stones in the pot, we can group all nodes together such that the player about to pick has an even parity. In this way the number of nodes is only 2N and the number of branches is bounded by 2NK. Figure 17.2 indicates (within the limits of our artistry) the decision graph for the stone game (with K=2 and N=5).

From the decision graph it is an easy matter for a program to compute an optimal strategy for a game of any N and any K and for either victory parity. A 2 X N decision array is allocated which corresponds to the nodes of Figure 17.2. The rest is a simple matter of using the QUEST routine.

Program 17.3 - STONE   Page 383

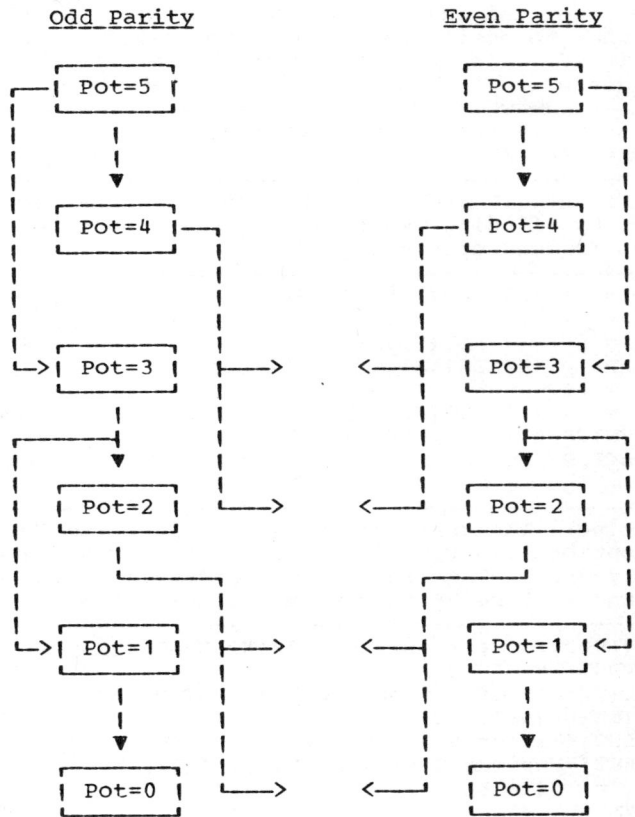

Figure 17.2

A decision graph for the stone game with K=2 and N=5. The nodes on the left are associated with Odd parity and those on the right with even parity. Parity refers to the parity of the player about to move.

The function SDA(NSTONES,PARITY,MAX) will create a Decision Array for the Stone game for a given number of stones (NSTONES). PARITY (0 or 1) indicates which parity wins and MAX indicates the maximum number of stones that may be taken per step.

DEFINE('SDA(NSTONES,PARITY,MAX)A,I,OPAR,P,J')
                                          :(SDA_END)

Chapter 17 - GAMES

---

* Allocate and initialize the array (SDA). SDA<N,P> indicates what to do if there are N stones left and you've got parity P. If there is no right decision, an 'L' for lose is given.

```
SDA        SDA     =  ARRAY('0:' NSTONES ',0:1' , 'L')
           SDA<0,PARITY>  =  'W'
```

---

* For each stone (I) and for each parity (P), determine the strategy by finding which move (J) will end in a losing situation for the opponent.

```
SDA_1      I   =   I + 1    LT(I,NSTONES)               :F(RETURN)
           P   =   -1
SDA_2      P   =   P + 1    LT(P,1)                     :F(SDA_1)
           OPAR =  REMDR(NSTONES - I - P, 2)
           J   =   0
SDA_3      J   =   J + 1    LT(J,MAX)                   :F(SDA_2)
           IDENT(SDA<I - J, OPAR>, 'L')                 :F(SDA_3)
           SDA<I,P>  =  J                               :(SDA_2)
SDA_END
```

---

* Main routine: The rules of the game follow the END label and are optionally printed (no sense boring the expert, he may be you). The rest of the program should be self-evident and will be given without further comment.

```
           QUEST('Do you want the rules?/(NO)NEWG|(YES)')  :S($LABEL)
STONE_1    OUTPUT   =   INPUT                              :S(STONE_1)
NEWG       QUEST('No. of stones (odd) = /NSTONES(1...1000)')
           EQ(REMDR(NSTONES,2),0)                          :S(NEWG)
           QUEST("Winner's Parity (0...1) = /P(0...1)")
           QUEST("Maximum Take = /MAX(2...1000)")
OLDG       NS   =   NSTONES
           MAXA =   MAX
           A    =   SDA(NS,P,MAX)
           HIM  =   0
           ME   =   0
HIS_TURN
           OUTPUT   =   'There are ' NS ' stones in the pile.'
           MAXA =   GT(MAXA,NS)   NS
           QUEST('How many do you want? /K(1...MAXA)')
           NS   =   NS - K    ;    HIM  =  HIM + K
           EQ(NS,0)                                        :S(TOTALIZE)
MY_TURN
           K    =   A<NS,REMDR(ME,2)>
           K    =   IDENT(K,'L')    1
           NS   =   NS - K
           ME   =   ME + K
           OUTPUT   =   LETMESEE()
           S    =   K ' stones.'
           S    =   EQ(K,1)   'just one.'
           OUTPUT   =   "I think I'll take " S
           EQ(NS,0)                                        :F(HIS_TURN)
TOTALIZE
```

```
                  Program 17.3 - STONE                          Page 385


         OUTPUT = 'You have ' HIM ' stones and I have ' ME ' stones'
         EQ(REMDR(HIM,2),P)                           :S(HE_WINS)
         OUTPUT   =  'That means I win'
         OUTPUT   =  INSULT()                         :(CHANGE)
HE_WINS
         OUTPUT   =  'That means you win'
         OUTPUT   =  PRAISE()
CHANGE
         QUEST('Would you like to change the game? /'
+                ' (YES)NEWG|(NO)OLDG')               :($LABEL)
END

Names referenced        Name        Type        Where defined
by STONE:               QUEST       Function    Program 17.2
                        PHRASE      Package     Program 17.1
```

Epilogue

It is necessary to be as complete as possible in the processing of input information when the user of the system is someone other than the person who wrote the program. This is especially true here where presumably the user is the playful sort anyway. This was the reason for the creation of the variable MAXA whose purpose is to limit the value of the selection to the maximum of the stated limit and the pile.

An example of a typical session with the STONE game is shown below. Underlined sections indicate the machine's responses.

```
Do you want the rules? NO
No. of stones (odd) = 13
Winner's parity (0...1) = 0
Maximum Take = 3
There are 13 stones in the pile.
How many do you want? 3
Let me contemplate this one
I think I'll take 2 stones.
There are 8 stones in the pile.
How many do you want? 1
OK Yipes... Gee Yipes I need time to see about this one
I think I'll take 3 stones.
There are 4 stones in the pile.
How many do you want? 3
Ahh... Wow
I think I'll take just one.
You have 7 stones and I have 6 stones
That means I win
Your dumb maneuvers indicate that you are a
                    thick-skulled moron
Would you like to change the game? 1
Bad input, you brainless ninny
```

Page 386   Chapter 17   -   GAMES

```
┌─────────────────┐
| |   Program   | |
| |    17.4     | |
| |  TICTACTOE  | |
└─────────────────┘
```
The reader is presumed familiar with the game of Tick-tack-toe whose popularity is itself a puzzle since it is hard to do anything but tie. Nonetheless, it is interesting enough to illustrate several game-playing techniques.

A complete decision tree for the game has nine possible choices for the first move, eight for the second, seven for the third, etc. Hence there are 9! (= 362,888) branches in the decision tree. Using SNOBOL4 and spending 10 milliseconds on each branch, one must spend 10 minutes of machine time to analyze the game, which is a bit much. When one considers the decision graph, however, there are only 3^9 = 19,683 possible boards and not every board is reachable by the rules of the game. Thus, there is a great deal of folding back.

The pure tree-searching algorithm is actually quite simple since one need only know how to make a move and how to detect victory. That is, assume we write a routine, TTTV, to determine the value of a board to, say, Player X (i.e. the one who marks X's in squares as opposed to O's) and another routine TTTM, which determines an optimal move for X. An arbitrary board is given to TTTV which first tests whether a winning combination exists. If so, the value of the board is self-evident. If not, it asks TTTM for the best move for player X. Upon getting it, TTTV evaluates the board from the point of view of player O. It does this by interchanging O's and X's and calling itself recursively. It then returns the negative of the number so returned. The coding of TTM is even simpler. TTTM simply tries each move and asks TTTV to evaluate it (from the standpoint of player O). This is not super efficient but it works.

An algorithm based on the decision graph, on the other hand, may at first sight appear to be much more complicated requiring a complete graph description of the game. But we can let the computer do most of our graph-building as follows. Record each new state (new board position) that we come to in a table allocated for that purpose, and record with the table the move made. At each new situation, the table is consulted to see whether we've been there before.

While these techniques are suitable for Tick-tack-toe, the search times become impractical for more complicated open games such as Chess and Checkers. To a first approximation, these games can be played with a truncated decision tree which means that the tree is searched to a limited depth and only a limited number of alternative moves at each level are considered. Samuel [1963] describes a Checker-playing program which also stores boards as in the decision graph algorithm. This permits the program to learn as it continues to play. Note that storing a particular state helps not only when returning to that state but in resolving the value of all states which can reach the remembered state. In the game of

Program 17.4 - TICTACTOE   Page 387

Checkers the number of states that need be remembered can be reduced by considering all symmetries of a given board position. This is fully illustrated with the game of Tick-tack-toe. Thus if the proper response to:

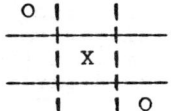   is remembered
            to be: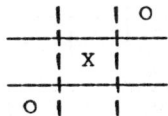

then we should not have to recompute if

```
   |   | O
---+---+---
   | X |
---+---+---
 O |   |
```

is encountered.

Assume that boards are represented as strings, so for example the last board above is represented as:

'   O X O   '

We can permute such a string very efficiently using positional transformations. But how many symmetries are there? Figure 17.3 below illustrates the eight symmetries of the two-dimensional Tick-tack-toe board.

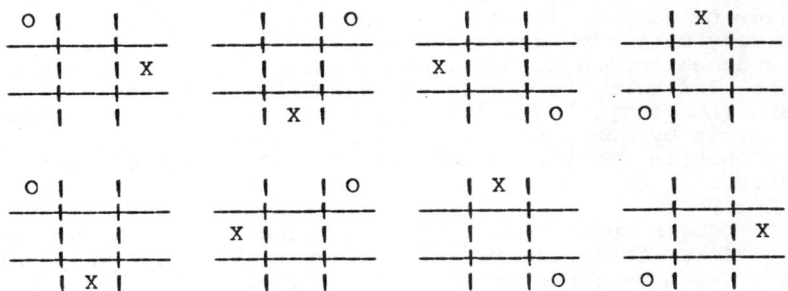

Figure 17.3

The eight symmetries of the Tick-tack-toe board.

A method for producing these symmetries is found by noting that the upper four are 90° clockwise rotations of each other as are the bottom four. The first of the bottom group is found by flipping one of the top group completely over so that we

Page 388   Chapter 17   -   GAMES

are looking at its underside.   Thus, with two basic permutations we are able, with the help of a little counting, to produce all eight.

It is not always easy to determine the number of symmetries for some arbitrary board game. A method that may prove helpful is to consider the number of equivalent serializations of the points of the board. For example, we can serialize the points of Tick-tack-toe in the order indicated in the diagram below:

```
1 | 2 | 3
--+---+--
4 | 5 | 6
--+---+--
7 | 8 | 9
```

An equivalent serialization would require that we begin at some corner (there are 4) and that we proceed along some edge (given the corner, there are 2 possibilities) and sweep the square one line at a time until all points have been touched. There are therefore 8 in all.

Whereas before we could count approximately 20,000 different Tick-tack-toe boards, there are far fewer if we take into account symmetries.   Unfortunately, if we wanted to determine exactly how many we could not simply divide 20,000 by 8 to obtain 2,500 as this would not allow for the fact that some boards rotate or flip into themselves. Though 2500 is a good lower bound, to find the exact number one must use Polya's theory of counting. See for example Harrison [1965]. We will be content with letting the program do the counting.

In what follows we will define the functions TTTV and TTTM for the game of Tick-tack-toe. Given these functions, it should be an easy matter to write a complete program to play the game with a human opponent. Also, the program will play other games on the 3X3 board by simply changing the definition of losing pattern (LOS_PAT).   It will play other O-X games on different size boards by changing the definition of equivalent board (the function NEXTBD) as well as LOS_PAT. These are left as exercises.

TTTM remembers board positions by storing them in the table TTT. This table can be initialized with boards which block opponent victory (increasing efficiency) or with boards indicating heuristic plays or standard openings. These options, too, are explored in the exercises.

```
┌─────────────────────────────────────────────────────────────┐
│ We first define a utility routine which cycles through all  │
│ the boards equivalent to a given Tic-tac-toe board.  It     │
│ expects as argument the last board returned.  NEXTBD can    │
│ always be initialized by setting NEXT_N to 0.               │
└─────────────────────────────────────────────────────────────┘
```

            DEFINE('NEXTBD(B)')   :(NEXTBD_END)

Program 17.4 - TICTACTOE   Page 389

```
*------------------------------------------------------------------*
| Entry point: The first REPLACE is a clockwise rotation           |
| (done each time). The second REPLACE is a flip (done every       |
| four times).                                                     |
*------------------------------------------------------------------*
NEXTBD      NEXT_N    =   EQ(NEXT_N,8)                        :S(FRETURN)
            NEXT_N    =   NEXT_N + 1
            NEXTBD    =   REPLACE('741852963','123456789',B)
            NEXTBD    =   EQ(REMDR(NEXT_N,4))
+                         REPLACE('321654987','123456789',B)
                                                              :(RETURN)
NEXTBD_END
*------------------------------------------------------------------*
| TTTV(B) will determine the value of the board B to player        |
| X given that it is his move.  It is presumed that he does        |
| not yet have a winning combination.                              |
*------------------------------------------------------------------*
            DEFINE('TTTV(BOARD)')
            LOS_PAT   =   POS(0) ('OOO'  |  'O' LEN(3) 'O' LEN(3) 'O'
+                                |  LEN(3) 'OOO')
                                                              :(TTTV_END)
TTTV        NEXT_N    =   0
            TTTV      =   -1
TTTV_1
            BOARD     =   NEXTBD(BOARD)                       :F(TTTV_2)
            BOARD     LOS_PAT                     :S(RETURN) F(TTTV_1)
TTTV_2
            TTTV      =   0
            TTTV      =   -TTTV(REPLACE(TTTM(BOARD),'XO','OX')) :(RETURN)
TTTV_END
*------------------------------------------------------------------*
| TTTM will find the best move that player X can make on the       |
| given board.  It first checks to determine whether it or         |
| any board similar to it was processed before.  Old boards        |
| are kept in the table TTT.  TTTM actually returns the new        |
| game state.                                                      |
*------------------------------------------------------------------*
            DEFINE('TTTM(BOARD)T,N,MAX,V')
            TTT       =   TABLE()
                                                              :(TTTM_END)
TTTM        NEXT_N    =   0
            MAX       =   -2
            BOARD     '  '                                    :F(FRETURN)
TTTM_1      BOARD     =   NEXTBD(BOARD)                       :F(TTTM_2)
            TTTM      =   TTT<BOARD>
            DIFFER(TTTM)                          :S(RETURN) F(TTTM_1)
TTTM_2      BOARD     (TAB(N) ARB) . T ' ' @N = T 'X'         :F(TTTM_4)
            V         =   -TTTV(REPLACE(BOARD,'OX','XO'))
            MAX       =   GT(V,MAX) V                         :F(TTTM_3)
            TTTM      =   BOARD
TTTM_3      BOARD     POS(N - 1) LEN(1)    =   ' '            :(TTTM_2)
TTTM_4      TTT<BOARD> =  TTTM                                :(RETURN)
TTTM_END
```

Page 390   Chapter 17   -   GAMES

Game Theory In concealed games, we have the added complexity that our strategy may tip off our opponent to our disadvantage. In any of the varieties of the game of poker, for example, aggressive betting may scare off an opponent who might otherwise stick and, in this way, fail to seduce him into betting more of his funds in a losing cause. It therefore pays to vary one's strategy and either not always bet aggessively with a good hand or bet aggressively with a bad hand occasionally (the so-called bluff). Many people feel that behavior such as bluffing is incompatible with machine play. But as we will see, machines can do very well in a game such as poker and in fact can play truly optimal strategies.

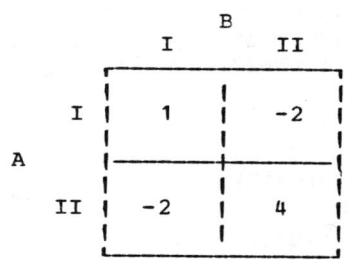

Figure 17.4

A two-person zero-sum game

Let us take a hypothetical situation shown in Figure 17.4. There are two players, A and B, each with two possible moves, I and II. Each selects a move (unbeknownst to the other) and the matrix indicates how much B should pay A for each of the four possible outcomes. If the amount indicated is negative then the transfer of funds is in the direction from A to B. The game is called zero-sum because whatever one player wins the other loses; a situation which does not always exist in real life when, for example, a nuclear holocaust could be disastrous for both sides.

How should A play the game? If he tries for the big payoff of 4 by always selecting move II, B will catch on eventually and begin playing move I exclusively. Then A, seeing that he is losing 2 on each turn will begin selecting move I until B catches on to that. Clearly both sides must play a so-called <u>mixed strategy</u> wherein their selection of I and II is unpredictable. Neither player should base their move on a strictly deterministic basis as this strategy may be uncovered by the opponent and exploited. This conclusion is perhaps intuitively implausible but one need only reflect on the penny-

Program 17.5 - CARDPAK   Page 391

matching game to see the importance of not developing easily detectable patterns of play.

```
┌─────────────────┐
││ Program     ││
││ 17.5        ││
││ CARDPAK     ││
└─────────────────┘
```
As a fairly complicated example of a game-theoretic approach, we will present a program which will play an optimal game of poker. Prior to presenting the game we will establish certain utility functions which may be useful not only in other forms of poker but perhaps in other card games as well.

An important initial consideration is the choice of data representation. How should a card be represented? In SNOBOL4, with its wealth of string operations, a natural choice is a single character. We will represent the 52 cards of the deck by the letters of the alphabet:

'ABCDEFGHIJKLMNOPQRSTUVWXYZabcdefghijklmnopqrstuvwxyz'

The assumed ordering is:

(2C 3C ... AC) (2D 3D ... AD) (2H 3H ... AH) (2S 3S ... AS)

In principle, any 52 characters could have been used such as the first 52 characters of &ALPHABET. In practice, debugging is easier if one uses printable characters.

```
        DEFINE('RHAND(K,FLAG)')
        DEFINE('SUITS(H)')
        DEFINE('VALS(H)')
        DEFINE('DISPLAY(H)VALS,SUITS,V,S')
```

| Initialization of constant strings. |

```
        FULL_DECK   =
+       'abcdefghijklmnopqrstuvwxyzABCDEFGHIJKLMNOPQRSTUVWXYZ'
        ALL_VALS    =   'ABCDEFGHIJKLM'
        JUST_VALS   =   DUPL(ALL_VALS,4)
        JUST_SUITS  =   DUPL('C',13) DUPL('D',13) DUPL('H',13)
+                       DUPL('S',13)
                                                    :(CARDPAK_END)
```

| RHAND(K,FLAG) will return a random hand with K cards in |
| it. If FLAG is nonnull, the deck will be reshuffled. If |
| an insufficient number of cards remain, RHAND will fail. |

```
RHAND    RANDOM_DECK =  DIFFER(FLAG) RPERMUTE(FULL_DECK)
         RANDOM_DECK LEN(K) . RHAND =  :F(FRETURN)S(RETURN)
```

| SUITS(H) will return just the suits for the hand H. |

```
SUITS    SUITS = REPLACE(H,FULL_DECK,JUST_SUITS)    :(RETURN)
```

```
| VALS(H) will return just the values of the hand H.                   |

VALS    VALS  = REPLACE(H,FULL_DECK,JUST_VALS)       :(RETURN)

| DISPLAY(H) will return a string representing the hand H in |
| a form consistent with conventional representations.       |

DISPLAY VALS = REPLACE(VALS(H),ALL_VALS,'23456789TJQKA')
        SUITS = SUITS(H)
DISPLAY_1
        VALS    LEN(1) . V =                    :F(RETURN)
        V   = IDENT(V,'T')    '10'
        SUITS   LEN(1) . S =
        DISPLAY = DISPLAY V S ' '                :(DISPLAY_1)
CARDPAK_END
```

Names referenced	Name	Type	Where defined
by CARDPAK:	RPERMUTE	Function	Program 16.3
	ORDER	Function	Program 3.1

| | Program | | As a prelude to finding an optimal strategy
| | 17.6 | | of a game of poker we will write a function
| | POKEV | | POKEV(HAND) which will evaluate a poker hand
                   (5 cards) producing a number (very nearly)
uniformly distributed in the range (0,1) and monotonically
increasing with the strength of the hand. Thus, hand H1 is
stronger than H2 if POKEV(H1) > POKEV(H2). The constraint that
the numbers be uniformly distributed is very important to the
successful operation of the optimal POKER-playing program.
That is, the percentage of times that a hand H will be such
that POKEV(H) < X must be X or close to it. This is perhaps
the trickiest part of the program.

To begin with we find, via pattern matching, which of the
several categories the hand falls into, eg. bust, pair, two-
pair, three-of-a-kind (trips), etc. We set an array (POKEV_A)
to contain probabilities that such hands are dealt. The
probabilities can be computed or looked up in a source such as
Epstein [1967]. We then need to resolve the question of where
a given hand falls with respect to all other hands in its
category (the variable FRACTION). This may be done crudely by
regarding the values of the hand, sorted in descending order,
as a number in a base-13 radix system. Unfortunately (as the
author learned by experience) the result is too inaccurate to
lead to optimal play. Consider for example, bust hands. Few
hands would have a lead value of 10 or less and no hands would
have a lead value of 6 or less. Hence no hands would evaluate
to .15 or less, a severe distortion.

A solution is to consider the hand as representing a number in
the combinatorial number system (see DECOMB, Prog. 15.2). This
system has the property that the digits descend, just as re-

Program 17.6 - POKEV   Page 393

quired. Were it not for straights, the representation for bust
hands would be exact.

For hands such as pairs, trips, two-pairs, fours, and full-
houses we take the most significant designator (one or two
cards) as a base-13 number and combine this with the remaining
cards in a mixed residue fashion to obtain a final evaluation.

          DEFINE('POKEV(H) VALS,SUITS,V,W')

| Define patterns to detect major poker categories |

          STRAIGHT_SEQ = REVERSE(ALL_VALS) SUBSTR(ALL_VALS,13,1)
          PAIR.V   = LEN(1) $ V *V
          TRIPS.V = PAIR.V *V
          FOURS.V = TRIPS.V *V
          FLUSH.V = FOURS.V *V

| The following array gives the probability that a hand will |
| fall within or lower than the indicated level.   0 is a |
| bust, 1 is a pair, etc. |

          POKEV_A   = ARRAY('-1:8')
          POKEV_A<0> = 0.501
          POKEV_A<1> = 0.924
          POKEV_A<2> = 0.971
          POKEV_A<3> = 0.9924
          POKEV_A<4> = 0.9963
          POKEV_A<5> = 0.9983
          POKEV_A<6> = 0.99974
          POKEV_A<7> = 0.999985
          POKEV_A<8> = 1.0

| PR(L,PREFIX) is a utility function used by POKEV to com- |
| pute the actual evaluation of the poker hand, assign it to |
| POKEV and return. L is the level of the hand as in the |
| above array. PREFIX is the secondary evaluation parameter |
| and consists of zero, one or two cards (e.g., the 6 of |
| trip 6's). For further resolution, the variable VALS con- |
| tains the rest of the values in order of significance. |
| These are regarded as a combinatorial representation of |
| some number. |

          DEFINE('PR(L,PREFIX) COMBS,FRACTION,A') : (POKEV_END)
PR
          COMBS   = COMB(13,SIZE(VALS))
          BASEB_ALPHA = ALL_VALS
          COMB_ALPHA = ALL_VALS
          FRACTION = (BASE10(PREFIX,13) * COMBS + DECOMB(VALS))
     +   /   (13. ** SIZE(PREFIX) * COMBS)
          A   = POKEV_A
          POKEV = A<L - 1> + (A<L> - A<L - 1>) * FRACTION
          PR   = .RETURN   : (NRETURN)

| Entry point for POKEV. Thanks to PR, our job reduces to a |

Page 394   Chapter 17   -   GAMES

| simple matter of pattern matching. |

```
POKEV    VALS     =    REVERSE(ORDER(VALS(H)))
         SUITS    =    SUITS(H)
         STRAIGHT_SEQ  VALS  | ROTATER(VALS,-1)     :F(POKEV_3)
         SUITS         FLUSH.V                      :S(PR(8))F(PR(4))
POKEV_3
         SUITS         FLUSH.V                      :S(PR(5))
         VALS          PAIR.V                       :F(PR(0))
         VALS          FOURS.V   =                  :S(PR(7,V))
         VALS          TRIPS.V   =                  ;F(POKEV_5)
         W    =   V
         VALS          PAIR.V    =                  :S(PR(6,W V))F(PR(3,W))
POKEV_5
         VALS          PAIR.V    =
         W    =   V
         VALS          PAIR.V    =                  :S(PR(2,W V))F(PR(1,W))
POKEV_END
```

Names referenced   Name   Type   Where defined
by POKEV: ORDER   Function   Program 3.1
                      ROTATER   Function   Program 3.5
                      REVERSE   Function   Program 3.6
                      COMB   Function   Program 15.1
                      BASE10   Function   Program 2.5
                      CARDPAK   Package   Program 17.5
                      DECOMB   Function   Program 15.2

```
,----------,
||  Program ||
||   17.7   ||
||   POKER  ||
'----------'
```
As the reader may be aware, there are many forms of the game of poker; Draw, Stud (5 and 7 cards), Baseball, Blind, etc. There may be wild cards and there may be any number of players. We will pick the simplest game, viz. cold-hand five-card poker between two players with nothing wild. This choice is dictated by the simple fact that it is the only poker game that has been fully analyzed [Cutler 1975] and for which an optimal strategy exists. The reader may obtain additional references to the analysis of this game from Cutler's paper or from a cited bibliography, Findler [1972].

In cold-hand poker, each player enters an *ante* into the pot and is dealt a hand (best thought of as a number in the range (0,1)) and the players take turns betting, checking, calling, raising and folding. Briefly, checking and betting are done when the pot contains equal contributions from both players (such as at the start or after a check). Calling, raising and folding are done when it is up to one of the players to equalize the pot. If he does not, he folds, forfeiting his right to the pot. If he calls, there is a showdown. A raise is a call followed by a bet. The set of possibilities are shown in Figure 17.5 where the first player is designated X and the second is Y. Note that Check-raises are not permitted.

Program 17.7 - POKER   Page 395

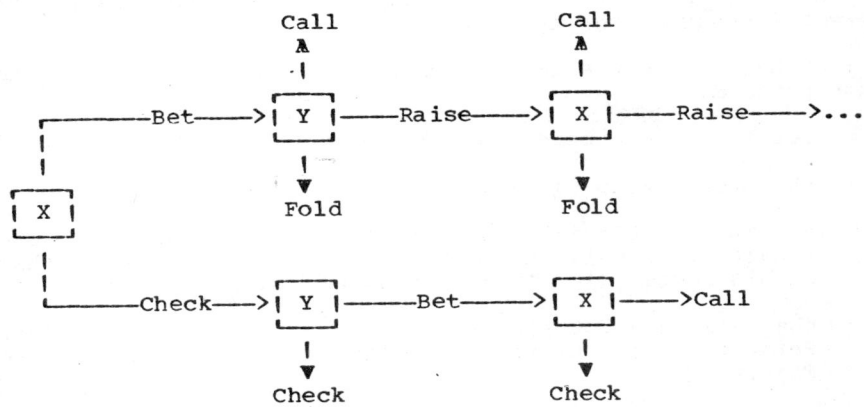

Figure 17.5

The allowable bet sequences of cold-hand poker.

In the game given by Cutler, the value for all bets is the current value of the pot. The value of a raise is found by decomposing the raise into a call followed by a bet. We will extend the game somewhat by allowing the player to set the value of the bet (before-hand) to any fraction of the pot. Whereas all poker games require some limit, most games do permit players to bet any amount up to this limit. It has been conjectured that any bet short of the limit is suboptimal so that it might be reasonable to allow the player to make submaximal bets. But then the strategy, particularly when to fold, would have to be changed.

The derivation of the optimal strategy is beyond the scope of the current discussion. To obtain a flavor for the analysis, consider only the case where the first player, X, may check or bet and the second player, Y, either calls or folds. Since Y's move ends the game, he has nothing to conceal from X and so he plays a pure strategy of calling on all good hands (anything above a certain value called the <u>call line</u>) and folding on poor hands (anything else). Now consider X's situation. On very strong hands, X has nothing to lose by betting. On his average hands he has very much to lose if he bets since he would have to square off against Y's better hands. On the other hand, if he has an absolutely rotten hand, his only hope of winning is to bluff Y. Though he stands to lose more if caught bluffing, his expectation, it can be shown, is larger than if he stood the certain loss of a showdown with Y. The pattern of this simple situation holds in all the more complex cases, viz. a bet on all hands above a certain level and a bluff on all hands below a certain level. Also the bluff must

Chapter 17 - GAMES

be in a fixed ratio R of the percentage of legitimate bets where R depends on the bet limit.

We list here for convenience, various parameters used by the poker program.

L = bet limit as a percentage of the pot.

R = the bluff ratio (L / (1 + L))

A = the initial betting line for player X. X bets on hands greater than this. He checks on hands worse, except that on his lowest (1 - A) * R hands he bluffs.

B = the call line for player X after the sequence Check-Bet. Below this line he folds. He has no other options. See Figure 17.5.

C = the betting line for player Y after X checks. Below this line, player Y calls except for the lower R * (1 - C) hands which he bluffs.

D = The call line for player Y after X bets. Above this line, he will call (except for the very good hands which he bets) and below this level he will fold (except for the bluffs).

The astute reader will note that the game can go on indefinitely whereas we have provided parameters for only a finite number of situations. The parameters ALPHA and BETA below serve to bridge the gap between the finite and the infinite as they provide rules for extrapolating out to the Nth raise.

ALPHA = the <u>raise attenuation</u> factor. Given that the opponent's best strategy is to raise with his best P hands, then our best strategy is to respond by raising on our best P * ALPHA hands. Note that the raise attenuation factor for a round trip is ALPHA^2 and this factor is actually used in the program.

BETA = the <u>lion factor</u>. Given that my optimal strategy is to bet (or raise) in the upper P hands, then, if my opponent responds by raising, I will fold below the BETA * P line (unless I'm bluffing). (1 - BETA is sometimes called the chicken factor.)

```
The function ABCDR(L) will set the global variables A, B,
C, D and R as well as the parameters ALPHA and BETA. It
is assisted in this by the functions ALPHA(L) and BETA(L)
which compute ALPHA and BETA respectively.
```

```
DEFINE('ABCDR(L) THETA,PHI,TAU,TTR')
DEFINE('ALPHA(L) T')
```

Program 17.7 - POKER

```
            DEFINE('BETA(L) T')
                                                    :(ABCDR_END)
+-----------------------------------------------------------------+
| Entry point for ALPHA:                                          |
+-----------------------------------------------------------------+
ALPHA       T     =   1 + 2 * L
            ALPHA = -(T + 1) + SQRT(T ** 2 + 6 * T + 1)
            ALPHA =  ALPHA / (2 * T)                 :(RETURN)
+-----------------------------------------------------------------+
| Entry point for BETA:                                           |
+-----------------------------------------------------------------+
BETA        T    =  1 + 2 * L
            BETA =  -(T ** 2) + 2 * T + 1 + (T - 1) *
+                    SQRT(T ** 2 + 6 * T + 1)
            BETA =  BETA / (2 * T ** 2)              :(RETURN)
+-----------------------------------------------------------------+
| Entry point for ABCDR:                                          |
+-----------------------------------------------------------------+
ABCDR       ALPHA  =  ALPHA(L)
            BETA   =  BETA(L)
            PHI    =  L / (1 + 2 * L)
            THETA  =  1 - PHI
            TAU    =  1 + 2 * L
            R      =  L / (1 + L)
            TTR    =  TAU * THETA / R
            A = -1 + 2 * PHI + ALPHA + TTR * (4 * PHI + 2 * ALPHA)
            A = A / (TAU * THETA + ALPHA + TTR * (2 * ALPHA + 1))
            B = 4 * PHI + 2 * ALPHA - (2 * ALPHA + 1) * A
            C = 2 * PHI + ALPHA - A * ALPHA
            D = R * (1 + ALPHA) - R * ALPHA
                                                     :(RETURN)
ABCDR_END
+-----------------------------------------------------------------+
| BET() will compute the amount which can be bet with a           |
| given limit L.                                                  |
+-----------------------------------------------------------------+
            DEFINE('BET()')                          :(BET_END)
BET         BET = CONVERT(POT * L, 'INTEGER')
            BET = GT(BET,HIM)   HIM
            GT(BET,0)                          :S(RETURN) F(FRETURN)
BET_END
+-----------------------------------------------------------------+
| Now for the POKER program proper.  Given the mnemonic           |
| labels, the use of QUEST, and the discussion in the text,       |
| comments are virtually unnecessary.  The request for the        |
| lucky number is simply a device to warm up our random num-      |
| ber  generator  so that identical hands will not always be      |
| dealt.                                                          |
+-----------------------------------------------------------------+
            OUTPUT  =  'Welcome to Cold-hand Poker'
            QUEST('Would you like to know the rules? /'
+            '(YES)|(NO)INIT')                       :S($LABEL)
PLOOP       OUTPUT  =  INPUT                         :S(PLOOP)
INIT
           .QUEST('What is your lucky number today?/RAN_VAR(1...1000)')
            HIM  =  RANDOM(100) + 20
```

```
Page 398                     Chapter 17  -  GAMES


            OUTPUT  =  "We'll start you off with " HIM " chips"
NEWP        QUEST('Bet limit (% of pot) = /L(10...1000)')
            L  =  L / 100.
            ABCDR(L)
ANTE        QUEST("What's the ante? /ANTE(1...HIM)")
START       GT(ANTE,HIM)                              :S(ANTE)
            POT  =  2 * ANTE
            HIM  =  HIM - ANTE
            OUTPUT = 'With a ' ANTE ' chip ante the pot has '
+                                    POT ' chips'
            HX  =  RHAND(5,1)
            X   =  POKEV(HX)
            HY  =  RHAND(5)
            Y   =  POKEV(HY)
            OUTPUT  =  'You are dealt ' DISPLAY(HX)

            RAISE  =  (1 - A) * ALPHA
            CALL   =  1 - D
            QUEST('Would you like to bet(B) or check(-)? /'
+                  '(B)HE_BETS|(-)HE_CHECKS')         :S($LABEL)

HE_CHECKS          OUTPUT  =  LETMESEE()
        (LE((1 - C) * R,Y)  LT(Y,C))                  :S(I_CHECK)

I_BET    BET  =  BET()                                :F(CANT_BET)
         POT  =  POT + BET
         OUTPUT  =  "I guess I'll bet " BET " chips."
         QUEST('How about you, call(C) or fold(F)? /'
+               '(C)|(F)I_WIN')                       :S($LABEL)

HE_CALLS           POT  =  POT + BET
                   HIM  =  HIM - BET                  :(COMPARE)

I_CHECK            OUTPUT = "I'll check too"          :(COMPARE)

HE_BETS            BET  =  BET()                      :F(CANT_BET)
                   POT  =  POT + BET
                   HIM  =  HIM - BET
                   OUTPUT  =  'You bet ' BET ' chips.'
                   OUTPUT  =  LETMESEE()
                   GT(Y,1 - RAISE)                    :S(I_RAISE)
                   GT(Y,1 - CALL)                     :S(I_CALL)
                   LT(Y,R * RAISE)            :S(I_RAISE) F(I_FOLD)

I_RAISE            OUTPUT = "I'll see your " BET " chips"
                   POT  =  POT + BET
                   BET  =  BET()                      :F(CANT_BET)
                   OUTPUT  =  " and raise you " BET
                   POT  =  POT + BET
        QUEST('You must now raise(R), call(C) or fold(F) /'
+              '(R)|(C)HE_CALLS|(F)I_WIN')            :S($LABEL)

HE_RAISES          OUTPUT  =  'You call my ' BET ' chips and'
                   HIM  =  HIM - BET
                   POT  =  POT + BET
                   CALL  =  RAISE * BETA
```

```
                    RAISE   =   RAISE * ALPHA * ALPHA  :(HE_BETS)

I_CALL              OUTPUT  =  'OK, I call'
                    POT     =   POT + BET                     :(COMPARE)

CANT_BET            OUTPUT  =  'Since you have no money left we '
+                             'have to stop here'

COMPARE             OUTPUT  =  "Let's see, I have "  DISPLAY(HY)
                    GT(X,Y)                                 :S(HE_WINS)

I_WIN     OUTPUT  =  'I guess I take all ' POT ' chips in the pot'
          OUTPUT  =  INSULT()                                :(SUMMARY)

I_FOLD              OUTPUT  =  'I fold'
HE_WINS             HIM     =  HIM + POT
          OUTPUT  =  'You win the ' POT ' chips in the pot'
          OUTPUT  =  PRAISE()                                :(SUMMARY)

SUMMARY   OUTPUT  =  'You now have ' HIM ' chips'
          OUTPUT  =  EQ(HIM,0)  'So Long'           :S(END)
          QUEST('Same game (S) or new parameters (N)? /'
+                 '(S)START|(N)NEWP')                        :($LABEL)
END
```

Names referenced by POKER:	Name	Type	Where defined
	QUEST	Function	Program 17.2
	SQRT	Function	Program 15.6
	POKEV	Function	Program 17.6
	CARDPAK	Package	Program 17.5

Epilogue

The following session was actually obtained using the above poker program. As usual, underscored items indicate responses by the machine.

```
Welcome to cold-hand poker
Would you like to know the rules? nope
Bad input, you stupid dunce
The correct form is YES|NO
Would you like to know the rules? NO
What is your lucky number today? 177
We'll start you off with 120 chips
Bet limit (% of pot) = 100
What's the ante? 10
With a 10 chip ante the pot has 20 chips
You are dealt 7D 4C 8D 6D AD
Would you like to bet(B) or check(-)? -
I need time to meditate about this problem
I'll check too
Let's see, I have 10D 9S 2D QC JD
You win the 20 chips in the pot
Thank you very much for the game, I enjoyed your brilliant
                                                     effort
```

Page 400   Chapter 17   -   GAMES

```
Same game (S) or new parameters (N)? S
With a 10 chip ante the pot has 20 chips
You are dealt  9D 6D JD 5S 2H
Would you like to bet(B) or check(-)? B
You bet 20 chips
interesting...... I think Ill cogitate about this
OK, I call
Let's see, I have JS 8D KC 5H 5D
I guess I take all 60 chips in the pot
Your heavy-handed performance befits a silly ass
```

Not all games are this brief. With lower betting limits, optimal play calls for generally more betting. The most complex bidding sequence resulted with a bet limit of 10% of the pot. The player was dealt two-pair and bet ruthlessly. The machine also bet heavily raising three times before calling. The machine had a full house. In general, however, the machine is very conservative and most bidding sequences are quite short.

The use of the 'lucky number' ruse to initialize the random number generator is common but entirely unnecessary if one has the time-of-day available to him. The time of day is actually available in many SNOBOL's, though not in the original.

Though the reader may be expected to understand most of the routines in this book, the equations used in the function ABCDR to compute these parameters are probably not in this category. At this writing, this is their only appearance in print.

???
??????????????????????? EXERCISES ??????????????????????
???

| Exercise 17.1 | Assume a machine and a player would like to play cards. If the player shuffles and deals, the machine may be cheated. If the machine randomly generates hands, the player could be cheated. How can a one-way cipher be used to ensure a fair deal?

| Exercise 17.2 | Assume one had a program to play penny-matching such that the program attempted to find patterns in the play of the opponent. Assume that there were no randomizing component in the program but that it was strictly deterministic. Is there a strategy which will beat such a program?

| Exercise 17.3 | Categorize and describe the decision graph for the following game. Player A places $10 in the pot and player B places $1 in the pot. First it is player A's turn and he can bet $1 whereupon B must call or

fold. If B folds, A takes the pot. If he calls, he matches A's $1 and it remains A's turn. The procedure continues until A choses not to bet whereupon they roll a die. 1 or 2 is victory for B; 3, 4, 5 or 6 is victory for A.

| Exercise 17.4 | Write a function PHRASE(LIST) where LIST is a list of names separated by commas which will, for each name NM in the list, (1) define a function by that name and (2) compile code so that the function returns RSENTENCE('<NM>'). In this way, for example,

PHRASE('INSULT,PRAISE,LETMESEE')

could take the place of the function definitions given in Prog. 17.1.

| Exercise 17.5 | Some variables cannot be used in a QUEST descriptor (Prog. 17.2). Give a simple rule to prospective QUEST users so that they may avoid any difficulties. How would you modify QUEST so that a diagnostic can be given.

| Exercise 17.6 | One of the reasons that QUEST was written with a separate utility function QUESTP was so that it could be easily modified to handle extensions of the following kind. Extend QUEST so that several arguments may be supplied separated by commas. QUEST patterns are then any combination of QUEST descriptors joined by the operators comma(,) and alternation(|) with comma having higher precedence. Also allow parenthesis in such expressions.

| Exercise 17.7 | Extend QUEST so that it accepts, in addition to number ranges, letter ranges of the form (C_1-C_2) where C_1 and C_2 are single characters.

| Exercise 17.8 | The game of NIM is such that there are four piles of 1, 3, 5, and 7 stones. Each player may take any number, including all, of any one pile. He must take at least one stone, however. The person forced to remove the last stone loses. There is an optimal strategy for NIM which guarantees a win for the first player which is based on converting the numbers to binary and exclusive-ORing on a digit-by-digit basis. There are also optimal strategies if the game is extended to selecting from any K piles; one then uses a K+1 system; see Ball [1962].

But the game can easily be perturbed so that the optimal strategies can't be used. Examples include placing a limit on the number of stones or requiring that an even number be followed by an odd. Of course, such rule changes do not invalidate a decision graph approach. For these reasons, if not for the sheer joy of doing so, write a function NDA(S) which will prepare and return a NIM decision array. S will be a string of initial-pile numbers such as '1,3,5,7'. Assume the one-pile no-limit restriction on betting.

| Exercise 17.9 | Modify the function SDA (of STONE (Prog. 17.3)) so that the variable MAX designates a list of possible moves separated by commas. For example, MAX = '1,3,5' means that 1, 3 or 5 stones may be selected.

| Exercise 17.10 | Amaze your friends with this one. Modify STONE so that the player can insert, in place of the parity, a predicate P(N) which will determine whether or not the player (opposing the machine) wins. Thus:

EQ(REMDR(N,2))

as the predicate P(N) indicates that the player will win if he has an even number of stones. Also

(GE(N,5) LE(N,10))

indicates that the player will win if his total is within the range (5,10).

| Exercise 17.11 | How many symmetries are there to the 4X4X4 Tick-tack-toe game (i.e. classic 3-D Tick-tack-toe)? How about a 3X3X3 board?

| Exercise 17.12 | Modify TTTM and TTTV and rewrite NEXTBD for the following game. The board is 3X3X3, moves are like Tick-tack-toe and a winning pattern is:

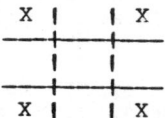

on any of the 6 sides or in any of the 3 slices parallel to a side through the middle or in any of the 6 slices through the diagonal.

| Exercise 17.13 | Consider a three-dimensional cube, 3X3X3 with one corner subcube removed leaving exactly 26 subcubes. How many symmetries of this cube are there?

Exercises for chapter 17

Exercise 17.14 With the help of QUEST and a nice board-printout function, complete the Tick-tack-toe game (Prog. 17.4).

Exercise 17.15 One way of speeding up TICTACTOE is to not look further when a move is found which results in victory. Implement this (Hint: it requires adding one instruction to TTTM.)

Exercise 17.16 To play 3D Tick-tack-toe on a 4X4X4 board, one needs to limit somehow the depth of search. If the depth of search is limited, one needs a heuristic for evaluating a board. Use the following scheme. Assume that it is X's move. For every X find the lines passing through it not already blocked by an O. If it stands by itself in a line add 1. If it stands with another add 3. If it stands with two others, add 10000 or some other such large number as this would imply victory. Do a similar evaluation for O and subtract the two amounts. Modify TTTV to use this evaluation whenever the global variable FNCLEVEL reaches the value of the keyword &FNCLEVEL. The global variable is of course set by the main program.

Exercise 17.17 Let H be a hand of cards as in CARDPAK. Suppose we wish to sort the cards in the order of increasing value (ignoring suits). How could the function ORDER be modified to accomplish this?

Exercise 17.18 Modify the CARDPAK functions so that they are operative with a pinochle deck (48 cards, Ace-9 (twice) of each suit).

Exercise 17.19 A bridge hand is evaluated for high-card points by assigning 4, 3, 2, 1 points respectively to the A, K, Q, J. In two statements, randomly shuffle and deal a hand, and determine and print its value. You may use COUNT (Prog. 3.4).

Exercise 17.20 Modify POKEV (Prog. 17.6) so that it evaluates a three-card poker hand. Note that straights and flushes do not count extra but that a straight-flush counts higher than either a pair or trips. Use the values 0.83, 0.955, and 0.978 as the probabilities of getting a bust, a pair or lower, and three-of-a-kind or lower respectively.

> **Exercise 17.21** If we were playing with three decks, so that duplicate and triplicate cards could actually be obtained in a single hand, POKEV would no longer be monotonic. Why? How would you modify POKEV so that it would work with any number of decks?

> **Exercise 17.22** Write a function POKUNVAL which will be an approximate inverse of POKEV. That is, given a real number in the range (0,1), POKEV(POKUNVAL(X)) should approximate X.

> **Exercise 17.23** POKEV is not especially uniform over the range of hands categorized as two-pairs. Fix up POKEV so that it regards (W V) as a number in a combinatorial number system rather than in a radix system.

> **Exercise 17.24** Assuming that both players are playing optimally, label the branches of the flowchart for cold-hand poker (Figure 17.5) with comparisons of the values of their hands against expressions involving the parameters A, B, C, etc. Modify POKER so that it plays an optimal game for X, rather than Y.

> **Exercise 17.25** If we were not concerned with losing optimal behavior, we could, by adding just one statement to POKER (Prog. 17.7), permit the player to bet any amount up to the maximum allowed. Give an example of such a statement and indicate where it should be placed.

CHAPTER EIGHTEEN

ASSEMBLERS

COMPILERS

AND MACROS

```
              CONTENTS

     ASM  ....................  18.1
     L_ONE  ..................  18.2
     BLANKS  .................  18.3
     POL  ....................  18.4
     TREE  ...................  18.5
     TR  .....................  18.6
     TUPLE  ..................  18.7
     GPM  ....................  18.8
```

Chapter 18 - Assemblers, Compilers and Macros

　　　he development of the stored-program machine is thought to be of importance because it allows a program to modify itself. Today, index registers obviate the necessity for a program to be self-modifying so that the practice is not only considered non-important (witness the growth of pure procedure) but is considered harmful as an obscuring practice. The real and lasting significance of stored program is that it allows programs to produce other programs (if most machines still had plug-board control, the output of a 'compiler' would have to be a wired-up plug-board or a wiring diagram and a congenial and dextrous computation staff).

It is therefore no coincidence that assemblers began appearing at about the time of the first installations of stored-program machines (circa 1950) and compilers (originally called automatic coders) and interpreters began to be developed shortly thereafter. This marked for the first time in the history of mankind the development of artificial languages; languages which would be literally and unfailingly obeyed by a mechanical servant; languages whose constructs and convolutions are subject only to the requirement that a translation algorithm be written for the language. Alas, this turns out to be one of the major obstacles to creating languages which are powerful and congenial, since it is no simple task to describe how to convert an arbitrary language into efficient code. This not only makes it difficult to implement large languages efficiently, but also makes it difficult to formally describe a large language.

This chapter is devoted primarily to the task of describing how language translators of one kind or another can be written using the SNOBOL4 language. Compiling and assembling are primarily string processing activities and so it is not surprising that SNOBOL4 should be particulary helpful along these lines. But actually it is by no means obvious how to employ the powerful pattern matching operations to parse languages. In fact, Griswold [1974, p. 11] says that "patterns derived from grammars are of little use in such [i.e., parsing] problems." We will show, on the contrary, that we can almost directly map a formal grammar into a parsing pattern and that SNOBOL4 patterns are particularly applicable to the parsing task.

Traditionally, SNOBOL processors have had a tendency to be big and slow and for this reason applications have tended to hover about the periphery of linguistic translation in such chores as bootstrapping, pre-processing, macro pre-passes and in general software which has a small user population and high development costs. But the more recent implementations of SNOBOL4 (viz. SPITBOL, SITBOL and FASBOL) have greatly extended the practical application of SNOBOL4 while the great proliferation of languages and machines has extended the need for such applications. Also, SNOBOL4 has often been used to teach compiler-writing because it simplifies the task suf-

Chapter 18 - Assemblers, Compilers and Macros

Machine M is a word-addressable machine with 32 bits per word. All instructions have the format:

OP-code	AC	X	A
Bits 0-7	8-11	12-15	16-31

There are sixteen general purpose registers which can serve both as accumulators for arithmetic and as index registers for address modification. The AC (accumulator) and X (index register) fields are four bits for the purpose of specifying one of these sixteen registers. The maximum number of words for the machine is 2^{16} so that the A (address) field can specify absolutely any address in the machine. The effective address, E, for any instruction is the sum of the index register (X) plus the value of the A field. We will refer to the contents of location E as C(E). If E is less than 16, a register is the assumed location. If the X field is 0, no indexing is assumed. Thus, Reg. 0 cannot be used as an index register. In the description of OP-codes which follow, AC will refer to the accumulator referenced by the AC field.

Mnemonic	Code (Hex)	Instruction
LOAD	21	Load C(E) into AC
STORE	22	Store AC into location E
ADD	31	Integer add C(E) to AC
SUB	32	Integer subtract C(E) from AC
MUL	33	Multiply C(E) to AC (Overflow lost)
DIV	34	Integer divide C(E) into AC
FADD	71	Floating add C(E) to AC
FSUB	72	Floating subtract C(E) from AC
FMUL	73	Floating multiply C(E) to AC
FDIV	74	Floating divide C(E) into AC
LOADA	2A	Load effective address E into AC
LOADN	2F	Load -C(E) into AC
BR	A0	Branch to location E
BRGT	A1	Branch to E if AC is > 0
BRLT	A2	Branch to E if AC is < 0
BREQ	A3	Branch to E if AC is = 0
BRNE	A4	Branch to E if AC is ≠ 0
BRGE	A5	Branch to E if AC is ≥ 0
BRLE	A6	Branch to E if AC is ≤ 0

Figure 18.1

A description of machine M.

Chapter 18 - Assemblers, Compilers and Macros

ficiently to allow the student to complete a compiler in a term. By using SNOBOL4 many of the by-now routine tasks of lexical and syntactic analysis are quite easily accomplished permitting attention to be focused on more difficult aspects of the translation task.

Since we will be involved in this chapter with assembling and compiling it will be helpful to fix on a particular machine. The machine whose instruction set is described in Figure 18.1 will be referred to as machine M. It will be used as an example machine throughout.

```
┌─────────────────┐
││   Program    ││
││    18.1      ││
││    ASM       ││
└─────────────────┘
```

ASM is an assembler for machine M. Each word of the machine can be represented by 32 bits or 8 hexadecimal digits or, if &ALPHABET has size 256, 4 characters. We will presume that our assembler is only required to punch hexadecimal digits on cards, one word per card. Other output formats are rather easily obtained using conversions from Chapter 2. Our assembly language will consist of instructions in the following format:

Label   Op   AC,A(X)   Comment

The four fields indicated are separated by blanks. Absence of a label is denoted by a blank in column 1. If AC (and/or the comma) is missing, 0 is assumed. If the '(X)' is missing, 0 is assumed. The comment may be missing; if the Op field is present, the operand (3rd) field must also be present. If the Op field is missing, no instruction is generated; thus labels may appear on separate lines. The Op field may contain any Mnemonic shown in Figure 18.1.

Perhaps the most important single observation one can make about an assembler is that it is inherently a two-pass system. This is because it is impossible to assert a maximum length for the sequence:

        STORE   ALPHA
        .
        .
        .
ALPHA

Hence addresses such as ALPHA are resolved in the first pass based on their location; instructions are translated on the second pass.

The essence of assembling is associative look-up. There are two distinct reasons for this. It is (by definition) easier to remember a mnemonic such as 'LOAD' than an op-code such as '21'. But aside from this it is necessary to have symbols (such as ALPHA in the above sequence) whose meaning is resistant to perturbations of the program (such as insertions or deletions of instructions). The associative lookup is nor-

mally accomplished in most assemblers with the help of some
form of symbol table as described in Chapter 11. In SNOBOL4,
we will use the TABLE datatype to serve this purpose.

| This is a simple assembler for the machine M (Figure 1).
| First we initialize a table (OPS) with the operators and
| their codes.

```
            LIST = 'LOAD 21,STORE 22,ADD 31,FADD 71,SUB 32,'
+          'FSUB 72,MUL 33,FMUL 73,DIV 34,FDIV 74,LOADA 2A,LOADN 2F,'
+          'BR A0,BRGT A1,BRLT A2,BREQ A3,BRNE A4,BRGE A5,BRLE A6,'

            OPS = TABLE()
OPS_INIT   LIST BREAK(' ') . OP ' ' BREAK(',') . CODE ','    =
+                                                       :F(INIT1)
            OPS<OP> = CODE                              :(OPS_INIT)
```

| Initialization for Pass 1. SYMS is a table to hold user
| symbols. LOC is our location counter. We assume I/O unit
| no. 10 is available for scratch storage.

```
INIT1      SYMS = TABLE()
            LABEL.L = BREAK(' ') . L SPAN(' ')
            LOC = 0
            OUTPUT(.DISK,10)
```

| Loop for pass 1. Evaluate all symbols.

```
PASS1      X = INPUT ' '                               :F(INIT2)
            DISK = X
            X LABEL.L =
            SYMS<L DIFFER(L)> = BASEB(LOC,16)
            LOC = DIFFER(X) LOC + 1                    :(PASS1)
```

| Initialization for pass 2: set up a big pattern
| (P.OP.AC.A.X) to crack fields.

```
INIT2      REWIND(10)
            DETACH(.DISK)
            INPUT(.DISK,10)
            NO_OP = POS(0) BREAK(' ') SPAN(' ') RPOS(0)
            P.OP.AC.A.X = NULL $ OP $ AC $ A $ X    NULL . CAUSE
+          POS(0)   BREAK(' ')    SPAN(' ')
+          BREAK(' ') . OP   SPAN(' ')
+          (BREAK(' ,') . AC   ','  |  NULL)
+          BREAK('( ') . A
+          ('(' BREAK(')') . X ')'  |  NULL)
```

| We define a generalized convert-symbol routine (CVTSYM)
| which converts a symbol according to a given symbol table
| (TABLE) producing a hex string of length LENGTH. TYPE in-
| dicates the type of symbol for diagnostic purposes. CAUSE
| is a global error-bearing variable which is printed on the
| listing.   'Uf' means undefined symbol in field f.   'Lf'

| means length of field f is too long.

```
           DEFINE('CVTSYM(SYM,TABLE,LENGTH,TYPE)')   :(CVTSYM_END)
CVTSYM     SYM   =  INTEGER(SYM)    BASEB(SYM,16)    :S(CVTSYM_1)
           SYM   =  TABLE<SYM>
           CAUSE =  IDENT(SYM,NULL)  'U' TYPE ' '
CVTSYM_1
           SYM   =  LPAD(SYM,LENGTH,'0')
           CVTSYM = LE(SIZE(SYM), LENGTH)     SYM    :S(RETURN)
           CAUSE =  CAUSE    'L' TYPE ' '
           SYM   =                                   :(CVTSYM_1)
CVTSYM_END
```

| We now go into the pass 2 loop. We tentatively set our |
| error indicator (CAUSE) to syntax error (S). |

```
PASS2      CAUSE =  'S '
           LINE  =  DISK  ' '                        :F(END)
           LINE     NO_OP                            :S(PASS2A)
           LINE     P.OP.AC.A.X
           OP    =  CVTSYM(OP,OPS,2,'O')
           AC    =  CVTSYM(AC,SYMS,1,'R')
           X     =  CVTSYM(X, SYMS,1,'X')
           A     =  CVTSYM(A, SYMS,4,'A')
           PUNCH =  OP  AC   X   A
           OUTPUT = RPAD(CAUSE,15)   OP ' ' AC ' ' X ' ' A
+          '        '  LINE                          :(PASS2)
PASS2A     OUTPUT = DUPL(' ',32)   LINE              :(PASS2)
END
```

Names referenced   Name   Type   Where defined
by ASM: RPAD   Function   Program 3.3
                    BASEB   Function   Program 2.4

Epilogue

Note that when an error occurs an instruction is generated in any case with one or more fields zeroed. This is so that symbols that are resolved by the assembler will have their correct value and that an assembly with one or two small errors may nonetheless be a valid assembly for debug purposes.

The assembler is a very primitive one lacking many 'bells and whistles' of a commercial product. Extensions such as data generation statements, expressions, relocatability, psuedo-ops, conditional assembly and multiple-location counters can be added, however, without a major overhaul of the program structure. For a more detailed discussion of assembler implementation, see Donovan [1972].

¶¶¶¶ ompiling using SNOBOL4
¶
¶ and parsing in the past several years. Much of this
¶ writing is theoretical and most is devoted to a
¶¶¶¶ thorough analysis of parsing; i.e., the decomposition of an input into its linguistic components. For example, the recognition that the source language string:

There has been much written on the subject of compilation

$$A = BETA + C * DELTA$$

is of the form:

$$VARIABLE = EXPRESSION$$

and that EXPRESSION is of the form TERM1 + TERM2 and that TERM2 is of the form FACTOR * FACTOR, may be regarded as parsing the original string. Parsing is an essential component in the translation not only of computer languages but of natural languages as well.

It has long been recognized, however, that parsing comprises only a portion of the compilation process and not the dominant portion by any means. This is especially true in SNOBOL4 where pattern matching makes parsing quite automatic, as we will see. On the other hand, techniques for generating efficient object code from a fully parsed statement are not well understood and are often embedded in compiler listings and nowhere else. Some of these methods have been distilled into English and can be found in Gries [1971], Donovan [1972], Graham [1975] and McClure [1972].

We have introduced in a previous chapter the BNF (Backus Normal Form) for representing sets of strings or languages. As an example, the grammar shown in Figure 18.2 can be used to define a simple language which we will refer to as L_1. L_1 contains only assignment statements, the four fundamental (binary) arithmetic operations, and negation. Identifiers within pointed brackets are designated syntactic variables.

```
<IDEN>::=<LETTER>|<IDEN><LETTER>|<IDEN><DIGIT>
<INTEGER>::=<DIGIT>|<INTEGER><DIGIT>
<PRIMARY>::=<IDEN>|<INTEGER>|(<E>)
<FACTOR>::=<PRIMARY>|-<PRIMARY>
<TERM>::=<TERM>*<FACTOR>|<TERM>/<FACTOR>|<FACTOR>
<E>::=<E>+<TERM>|<E>-<TERM>|<TERM>
<STMT>::=<IDEN>=<E>
```

Figure 18.2

A BNF description for the language L_1.

Chapter 18 - Assemblers, Compilers and Macros

We will assume that the reader is already acquainted with BNF. He has undoubtedly been exposed to this or similar notation when learning the constructs accepted by a programming language or indeed any other linguistic system such as an operating system command language or an editor's command language. This notation can be directly mapped into SNOBOL4 patterns so that any syntactic variable is associated with some pattern. In fact Exercise 18.9 invites you to write a program to carry out this translation automatically.

One difficulty with a BNF description is that languages that it is used to describe are typically not context free. Thus

$$A(3) = 17$$

may or may not be valid in Fortran depending on declarations for A. Pure BNF cannot be used to decide the issue. Such context dependencies are generally treated by the addition of a symbol table, with appropriate insertions and checks; in this way the language can be treated as context free, even though it is in fact not. Dynamic function evaluation can be used in SNOBOL4 to make these checks. Thus, for example, if the function ATEST(X) will test to see if its argument is an array and if ID is a pattern to match identifiers, then

$$ID \ \$ \ X \quad *ATEST(X)$$

will match only array identifiers. The function ATEST() can be written using symbol tables as were needed in ASM. Routines such as ATEST() are often erroneously referred to as semantic routines. They are not, for their purpose is to extend a context free formalism to handle context sensitive situations. It would be more correct to use the term <u>syntactic routine</u> for any routine used to decide syntax. We will reserve the term <u>semantic routine</u> for routines which have a side-effect other than recognition such as code production or error-message generation.

The semantics of a language described using BNF, i. e. the meaning of the various linguistic constructs, are seldom defined formally. For the language L_1, for example, we may say that all arithmetic operations represent operations on integers of a precision equal to that of the target machine. Most readers, especially those already exposed to Fortran-like languages, will then understand the meaning of L_1. While this is true of a simple algebraic language it may not be true if the language is neither algebraic nor simple. Formal systems to describe semantics are of two kinds, concrete and theoretical. A concrete system is one which has been subject to the rigors of machine implementation; a theoretical system is one which purportedly could be, but which for some reason has not. Concrete systems (listings) are messy; theoretical systems are at least buggy and at worst severely distorted. The answer to this dilemma may lay in the development of compiler-compilers which compile inefficiently and produce inefficient code but which yield sufficiently simple listings

that they may be understood. Much of this chapter is dedicated
to the ultimate fullfillment of this pious hope.

```
┌──────────────┬──┐
││  Program   ││.
││   18.2     ││
││   L_ONE    ││
└──────────────┴──┘
```
L_ONE is a compiler for the language L_1
(Figure 18.2). The output is in the form of
assembly language (accepted by ASM) for
machine M (Figure 18.1). The implementation
of L_ONE is based on a method of employing <u>semantic routines</u>
during a pattern match, a technique suggested to the author by
M. J. Rochkind (Bell Laboratories, Raritan River, N.J.). This
method is based on the observation that a routine invoked to
generate code (as opposed to one used to supplement the match
as given above in the case of ATEST) is best done using conditional assignment. This defers any code production until
after the match thus guarding against premature production.
For example, consider the pattern

$$P1 \ . \ *A() \quad P2 \ . \ *B() \quad | \quad P3 \ . \ *C() \qquad (18.1)$$

If P1 and P2 match, then A() and B() are called. If P1 matches and P2 fails but P3 matches, then only C() is called. A()
is not called in this case because backup on failure removes
the conditional assignment as was fully described in Chapter
7. This is, of course, exactly what we want and will greatly
reduce the complexity of a compiler written in SNOBOL4. The
reduction in complexity is worth the fact that we are using
conditional assignment in a way completely unintended by the
originators of the language. Functions called in this way are
supposed to be returning names and receiving values; they do,
but the names are dummy names and the values assigned are
irrelevant.

It will be more convenient to have only one semantic routine,
viz. S_(name), where name is the name of a routine. Thus,
instead of writing

$$P1 \ . \ *A()$$

we will write

$$P1 \ . \ *S\_('A')$$

But this is a bit messy, so we will write a routine S(name) to
return NULL . *S_(name) so that we may write

$$P1 \quad S('A')$$

to achieve the same effect with a cleaner appearance. The
above pattern (18.1) is then written:

$$P1 \quad S('A') \quad P2 \quad S('B') \quad | \quad P3 \quad S('C')$$

Finally, we can scan and push an element all in the same pattern by the construction:

Page 414   Chapter 18   -   Assemblers, Compilers and Macros

                         PAT . *PUSH()

where PAT matches the string pushed (See PUSH, Prog. 5.5). The
semantic routines produce code by popping the stack for the
location of the previous result, producing code to compute a
new result, and pushing onto the stack the location of the new
result.

| The program L_ONE will compile statements of L_1 into as-
| sembly language for machine M. In the semantic routines
| below, there is a label S_op for each operation op.

```
         DEFINE('S(NAME)')
         DEFINE('S_(NAME)T')               :(S_END)
S        S  = EVAL("NULL . *S_('" NAME "')")  :(RETURN)
S_       S_ = .DUMMY                       :($('S_' NAME))

S_NEG    OUTPUT = ' LOADN ' POP()
         OUTPUT = ' STORE ' PUSH(TEMP())   :(NRETURN)

S_ADD ;S_SUB ;S_MUL ;S_DIV
         T      = POP()
         OUTPUT = ' LOAD ' POP()
         OUTPUT = ' ' NAME ' ' T
         OUTPUT = ' STORE ' PUSH(TEMP())   :(NRETURN)

S_ASGN   OUTPUT = ' LOAD ' POP()
         OUTPUT = ' STORE ' POP()          :(NRETURN)
S_END
```

| The following patterns will match the syntactic variables
| of the language L_1 and call the appropriate semantic
| routines.

```
         LET     = 'ABCDEFGHIJKLMNOPQRSTUVWXYZ'
         DIGITS  = '0123456789'
         IDEN    = (ANY(LET) (SPAN(LET DIGITS) | '')) . *PUSH()
         INTEGER = SPAN(DIGITS) . *PUSH()
         PRIMARY = IDEN | INTEGER | '(' *E ')'
         FACTOR  = PRIMARY | '-' PRIMARY S('NEG')
         TERM    =   *TERM '*' FACTOR S('MUL')   |
+                    *TERM '/' FACTOR S('DIV')   | FACTOR
         E       =   *E '+' TERM S('ADD')   |
+                    *E '-' TERM S('SUB')   | TERM
         STMT    = POS(0) IDEN '=' *E S('ASGN')  RPOS(0)
```

| TEMP() is always ready to provide us with a new temporary
| location.

```
         DEFINE('TEMP()')                  :(TEMP_END)
TEMP     TEMP_NO = TEMP_NO + 1
         TEMP    = 'TEMP' TEMP_NO          :(RETURN)
TEMP_END
```

> The main program is essentially a single pattern match.

```
READ        S    =    TRIM(INPUT)                      :F(END)
REMOVE_BLANKS    S  ' '  =                             :S(REMOVE_BLANKS)
            TEMP_NO   =   0
            S    STMT                                  :S(READ)
            OUTPUT = '*** ERROR IN ' S                 :(READ)
END
```

Names referenced   Name   Type   Where defined
by L_ONE: PUSH   Function   Program 5.5
                    POP   Function   Program 5.6

As a simple example, the input

$$A = B - C * D$$

will produce the output

```
        LOAD    C
        MUL     D
        STORE   TEMP1
        LOAD    B
        SUB     TEMP1
        STORE   TEMP2
        LOAD    TEMP2
        STORE   A
```

The resulting code is clearly non-optimal but it gets the job done. There are numerous extensions that one can incorporate into L_ONE to produce more efficient code and to provide more features. Some of these have been left as exercises.

The reader should not be misled by the simplicity with which L_ONE was written into believing that full-fledged compilers for complete languages can be had cheaply. In general, the complexity of a compiler will grow nonlinearly with the introduction of new features. The world is full of compiler-compilers that look good for toy languages but which don't quite stand up to the hammering of a full scale language such as, for example, PL/I. The mere fact that declarations in PL/I can follow use is enough to discourage the one-pass approach used in L_ONE. For big compiling, we must step back a bit and proceed in stages.

> **%%%%** artitioning the compiler
> **%   %**
> **%%%%**
> **%**
> **%**

A compiler is generally decomposed into lexical analysis, syntactic analysis, code optimization and code generation. The latter two are often intertwined in more than two passes for good reasons, as we shall see later. The first two of these phases is indicated in Figure 18.3.

(a)   ALPHA = BETA + GAMMA ** 2

(b) | ALPHA | | = | | BETA | | + | | GAMMA | | ** | | 2 |

(c)
```
                    | = |
                   /     \
              | ALPHA |   | + |
                          /   \
                    | BETA |  | ** |
                              /    \
                       | GAMMA |   | 2 |
```

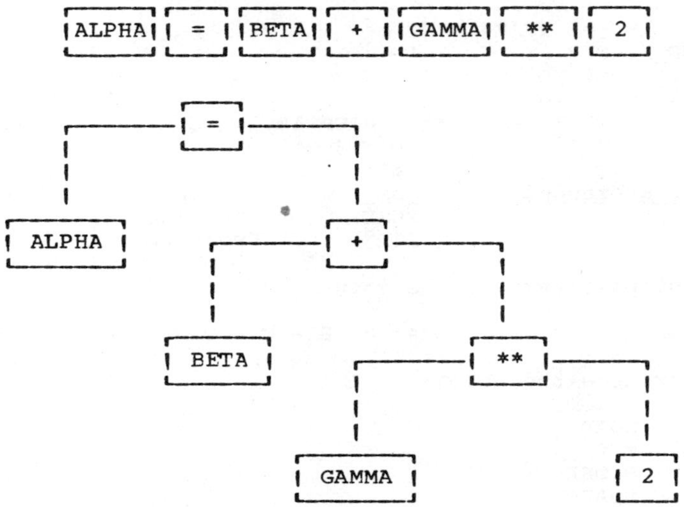

Figure 18.3

A lexical analysis (b) and a syntactic analysis (c) of an input string (a).

Lexical analysis decomposes the source string into indivisible tokens (or atoms). These tokens are, of course, not literally indivisible since they are, after all, composed of characters, but they are indivisible in the sense that no further decomposition has any meaning with respect to compilation. Thus, the meaning of 'ALPHA' is not a composition (homomorphism) of the meanings of its individual characters (though its sound may be). On the other hand, the meaning of 'ALPHA + BETA' can be interpreted as a composition of the meanings of the three tokens 'ALPHA', '+' and 'BETA'. The distinction is very much like the distinction between morpheme and phoneme in the study of natural languages. It is actually a kind of mixed radix system whereby a relatively small number of different symbols (letters or phonemes) is used to compose a fairly large (but finite) number of different notions (words or morphemes). Sentences are then built from the words. Evidently there are more ideas than sounds.

When SNOBOL4 is used to compile a programming language, no distinct lexical pass is required. On the other hand, the input may have to be massaged (pre-processed). In L_ONE this amounted to removing blanks. In a real language such as Fortran, blank removal is not nearly so simple as we will see (BLANKS, Prog. 18.3). In PL/I the pre-processing may consist of the extraction of the next statement (see PLI.STMT, Prog. 8.10) and the removal of comments. Redundant blank removal is not nearly so necessary for PL/I as it is for Fortran (since identifiers cannot be split in PL/I).

The result of a syntactic analysis is the tree structure shown in Figure 18.3. This tree structure may be represented in any of a variety of ways, most commonly as a linked structure. In SNOBOL4 the tree is perhaps best represented as a string in Polish prefix form (as described in Chapter 9) because pattern matching may then be exploited to effect desired transformations.

It is convenient to separate out that portion of a compiler which is machine-dependent simply to avoid duplication of effort if the same compiler is needed for a different target machine. The tree structure of Figure 18.3 is clearly machine independent, and code generation is clearly machine-dependent. What of code optimization?

According to McClure [1972], the two most effective means of code optimization are common subexpression removal (from address calculations) and register allocation. An example of the first is the removal of the common subscript calculation in:

$$A(I,J) = A(I,J) + 1$$

Removal of common subexpressions is machine independent and can be effected by transformations applied to the tree structure. On the other hand, register allocation is clearly machine dependent and must be done at some later stage.

It is very common to have some intermediate machine-independent form between the tree structure and the resulting code. This is to push the machine independence as far as possible. Hence the intermediate form is a kind of least common multiple of all machine languages. The original macro implementation of SNOBOL4 was actually written in such a language. The most extensive (or perhaps intensive would be a better word) of this kind known to the author is being developed by Robert Dewar (Ill. Inst. of Tech., Chi., Ill.) in connection with a machine-independent implementation of SPITBOL. Dewar's motivation is to produce a macro language which will lose little to efficiency when expanded on a given machine.

One of the more common intermediate forms is the four-tuple. Four-tuples consist of an operation followed by two operands followed by a destination all separated from each other by a convenient break character such as a comma. For example:

ADD,L1,L2,L3

would mean add the contents of L1 and L2 and store the result into L3. We will assume that the locations can be indexed by other locations. For example:

MUL,A(TEMP2),TEMP3,TEMP4

would reference as the first argument the location A offset by the current value of TEMP2. This could be rendered in machine M code as:

```
LOAD    1,TEMP2
LOAD    A(1)
MUL     TEMP3
STORE   TEMP4
```

An optimized version of this code may not actually contain the initial LOAD or the STORE. This will depend on the origin of TEMP2 and the destination of TEMP4.

Hence we may decompose a large processor into the following phases (as opposed to passes since several phases may actually go on in the same pass).

1. Pre-processsing
2. Syntactic analysis
3. Tree transformations and global optimization
4. Intermediate language production
5. Final expansion and detailed optimization

```
| Program |
|  18.3   |
|  BLANKS |
```
The function BLANKS is an example of pre-processing that may be required when compiling a full language. BLANKS(S) will remove blanks from a Fortran statement provided as argument. We assume a function such as FORTREAD (Prog. 9.2) is available to read in a statement and handle continuation. Removing blanks sounds simple but is complicated by the fact that blanks within string literals may not be removed. A string literal in ANSI Fortran has the form

nH<n-characters>   (eg. 3HCAT)

String literals may only appear in FORMAT and CALL statements. But we cannot simply go looking for this pattern in such statements because the indicated pattern may appear as part of an identifier (which may also be an argument of a subroutine call). For example:

CALL ALPHA(A1H)

contains no literal. Hence we must ignore such sequences which follow alphabetics. Another problem is that blanks may be interspersed in and around the length indicator. For example:

1   2   HABCDEFGHIJKL

is a valid literal. This makes it difficult (but, as we will see, not impossible) to write a single pattern to match a literal.

If we depart from the relatively rarified air of the ANSI standard and enter the domain of a practical compiler, we encounter more problems. IBM's OS/360 Fortran [IBM 360j] is typical of many Fortrans and so we will assume this to be our source language. With respect to blank removal, this Fortran has the following additional properties:

(1) A literal may be designated by the sequence '...' as well as by the nH<n-character> sequence.

(2) Function calls (as well as subroutine calls) may contain literals.

(3) The READ and WRITE statements may be direct access in which case they have the form:

    cmnd(f ' exp ...

    where cmnd is READ or WRITE, where f is an integer or an identifier designating a file and where exp is an arbitrary expression designating a record number.

Now (2) implies that all arithmetic expressions (including the exp portion of (3)) can potentially contain literals. Therefore READ and WRITE statements must be handled specially. A logical IF statement has the form:

    IF(exp) stmt

Here we must check to see if stmt is a READ or WRITE statement but our check is complicated by the fact that in order to find stmt we must determine where exp ends. To do this we must maintain a parenthesis count ignoring parentheses that are within literals. This can be done by recursion in a manner reminiscent of the BAL function (Prog. 8.3).

We might say a word at this point as to why we wish to go through so much trouble to remove blanks. For one thing, the blank removal process can be used not only for compiling but for many other kinds of pre-processing, data laundry, etc. that require pattern matching of Fortran programs. Hence it saves duplication of effort if it can be done once and for all. Another reason is that keywords, identifiers and many other non-decomposible units can have blanks interspersed within them (however improbable that may be) which will prove difficult to pattern match. For example, the keyword READ may be written as 'R EA D'; to match this we may write:

    OPTB = SPAN(' ') | NULL
    READ = 'R' OPTB 'E' OPTB 'A' OPTB 'D'

but this is as troublesome as it is inefficient.

Chapter 18 - Assemblers, Compilers and Macros

BLANKS(S) will return the result of removing blanks from a
Fortran statement provided in S. BLANKS(S) will operate
correctly for OS/360 Fortran [IBM 360g]. The statement is
presumed to have had its label removed by previous
processing.

```
        DEFINE('BLANKS(S)IF,KW,STMT,IO')
        Q     = ''''
        ALPHA = 'ABCDEFGHIJKLMNOPQRSTUVWXYZ'
        NUM   = '0123456789'
```

FBAL will match a string balanced with respect to parentheses but will ignore parentheses within literals. We
will use backup-free scanning (i.e. the ARBNO(P FENCE)
construct) as established in Chapter 6.

```
        BLINT       = ANY(NUM)  (SPAN(NUM ' ') | NULL)
        F.LIT       = BLINT $ N 'H' LEN(*DIFF(N,' ')) . LIT
+                   | Q BREAK(Q) . LIT Q
        ITEM1       = F.LIT  |  SPAN(' ')  |  SPAN(ALPHA NUM ' ')
+                   | LEN(1)
        SEARCH.LIT  = POS(0) ARBNO(ITEM1 FENCE) . TEMP F.LIT
        ITEM2       = '(' *FBAL ')' | ITEM1
        FBAL        = ARBNO(ITEM2 FENCE)
```

The function BL(S) will remove all blanks from S except
those in literals.

```
              DEFINE('BL(S)LIT,TEMP')                  :(BL_END)
BL            S SEARCH.LIT =                           :F(BL_1)
              BL = BL DIFF(TEMP,' ') '''' LIT ''''     :(BL)
BL_1          BL = BL DIFF(S,' ')                      :(RETURN)
BL_END
```

Define some patterns to scan statements containing
critical keywords.

```
        KWORD.KW = POS(0) SPAN(ALPHA ' (') . KW
        IF.STMT  = POS(0) ('IF(' FBAL ')') . IF REM . STMT
        IO.STMT  = POS(0) (('READ' | 'WRITE') '('
+       BREAK(ALPHA NUM) SPAN(ALPHA NUM ' ')) . IO Q REM . STMT
                                                       :(BLANKS_END)
```

Entry point for BLANKS(S) ; First remove blanks from the
keyword to test statement type.

```
BLANKS     S KWORD.KW   = DIFF(KW,' ')
           BLANKS       = S
           BLANKS IF.STMT = BL(IF) BLANKS(STMT)        :S(RETURN)
           BLANKS IO.STMT = DIFF(IO,' ') '''' BL(STMT) :S(RETURN)
           BLANKS       = BL(S)                        :(RETURN)
BLANKS_END
```

Names referenced by BLANKS:	Name	Type	Where defined
	DIFF	Function	Program 3.10

```
| | Program | |
| |  18.4   | |
| |   POL   | |
```

The method of invoking semantic routines used in the coding of L_ONE is general enough but not sufficiently convenient for very large languages of, say, PL/I size. To see this, consider the tree decomposition of a language statement as shown in Figure 18.3. By means of S() a function may be called before and after each node of the tree with the sequence of calls being made in left-to-right order. Moreover, every leaf of the tree may be pushed and these pushes are interspersed between calls also in a left-to-right fashion. We could hardly ask for anything better, or could we?

The reader will find, if he does the exercises involving extensions to L_ONE, that he will be forced to push and pop many different items in order to preserve quantities from the start of a syntactic unit across to its termination. For example, to produce code for IF<E>THEN<S> we must create a conditional branch across the THEN-clause. For this we will need to create a label which will be used in two places, before and after the <S>. Since <S> may be arbitrary including another IF<E>THEN<S> sequence the label cannot be assigned to a variable but must be pushed and popped. Now if the functional relationship followed the structural relationship we would regard IFTHEN as a single node of a tree with two arguments <E> and <S>. The IFTHEN function would call the functions for <E> and <S> to obtain translations. This will prove to be more natural. The temporary-variable facility built into the function mechanism can be used instead of stacks and a somewhat cleaner implementation results. In order to achieve a functional relationship conforming to the structural relationship the source string is converted into a tree form; our tree will be Polish prefix.

To obtain a slightly richer language to illustrate the conversion process, we define an upward compatible superset of L_1 called L_2. This is defined in Figure 18.4. Unlike L_1, we must allow blanks as separators (not shown in the BNF) but we do not permit blanks within identifiers and numbers. This is much like the PL/I convention whereas L_1 followed the Fortran convention.

The form of Polish prefix for any non-leaf (a node containing at least one descendent) is:

$$\text{operator}:n,\text{operand}_1,\text{operand}_2,\ldots,\text{operand}_n$$

where each operand is itself a valid tree. The operator may not contain either of the two special characters colon or comma. For a leaf, the :n is absent and, of course, there are no operands. Thus:

```
       A + B * C   becomes   +:2,A,*:2,B,C
                 and
       A * (-B)    becomes   *:2,A,-:1,B
```

```
<ELIST>::=<E>,<ELIST>|<E>
<REF>::=<IDEN>(<ELIST>)
<PRIMARY>::=<IDEN>|<INTEGER>|(<E>)|<REF>
<FACTOR>::=<PRIMARY>|-<PRIMARY>
<TERM>::=<TERM>*<FACTOR>|<TERM>-<FACTOR>|<FACTOR>
<E>::=<E>+<TERM>|<E>-<TERM>|<TERM>
<RELOP> is one of  '>'   '<'   '<='   '>='   '='   '¬='
<BOOL>::=<E><RELOP><E>
<IFSTMT>::=IF<BOOL>THEN<STMT>ELSE<STMT>|IF<BOOL>THEN<STMT>
<VAR>::=<IDEN>|<REF>
<ASGNSTMT>::=<VAR>=<E>
<STMT>::=<IFSTMT>|<ASGNSTMT>
```

Figure 18.4

The language L_2. The definitions for <IDEN> and <INTEGER> are the same as for L_1 (Figure 18.2).

This seems ugly but it will be easy to produce, scan and expand.

A functional form such as A(B,C,D) will translate into:

REF:2,A,COMMA:2,B,COMMA:2,C,D

No distinction is made, at least initially, between an array and a function since declarations may follow first use. Note that the argument list is a sequence of 2-ary functions rather than a single n-ary. This form is easier to produce and just as easy to scan.

To transform infix to prefix, we will use the conditional invocation of semantic routines as in L_ONE. Only two routines need be defined; CPUSH(STR) will conditionally push the string STR onto the stack (conditional upon the pattern being a part of an overall successful match). CPUSH(STR) actually returns:

NULL . *S_('CPUSH', STR)

where S_() is now written expecting an extra argument. The other routine is POL(N) which causes N+1 items on the stack to be popped and replaced by one larger item, viz.

OP:N,ARG_1,ARG_2,...,ARG_n

The operator is assumed to be the second last item on the stack. N is at least 1.

Once the machinery of POL(N) and CPUSH(STR) have been set up, very large languages can be compiled with no additional semantic routines except error messages and routines to handle declarations. These we ignore for simplicity. We will illustrate the method by writing a pattern which will transform sentences of L_2 into Polish prefix.

```
 This program illustrates how to convert L₂ into Polish
 prefix using special semantic routines, viz. POL(N) and
 CPUSH(S) for the purpose. We first define the semantic
 routines.
```

```
            DEXP("POL(N) = S('POL',N)")
            DEXP("CPUSH(ARG) = S('CPUSH',ARG)")
            DEFINE('S(NAME,ARG)')
            DEFINE('S_(NAME,ARG)T1,T2')                    :(S_END)
S           S = EVAL("NULL . *S_('" NAME "','" ARG "')")  :(RETURN)

S_          S_ = .DUMMY                                   :($('S_' NAME))
S_POL       T2 = POP()
            T1 = POP() ':' ARG ','
S_POL1      (EQ(ARG,1) PUSH(T1 T2))                       :S(NRETURN)
            ARG = ARG - 1
            T2 = POP() ',' T2                             :(S_POL1)

S_CPUSH     PUSH(ARG)                                     :(NRETURN)
S_END
```

```
 We now write our patterns. Interspersed blanks are handled
 by placing an optional blank pattern at the end of each
 pattern primitive. Patterns formed from other patterns
 then need not worry about blanks.
```

```
            AL = 'ABCDEFGHIJKLMNOPQRSTUVWXYZ'
            NU = '0123456789'
            BL = SPAN(' ') | NULL
            IDEN = (ANY(AL) (SPAN(AL NU) | '')) . *PUSH()   BL
            INTEGER = SPAN('0123456789') . *PUSH()   BL
            ADDOP = ANY('+-') . *PUSH()   BL
            MULOP = ANY('*/') . *PUSH()   BL
            RELOP = (ANY('=<>') | ANY('¬><') '=') . *PUSH()   BL
            LP = '(' BL
            RP = ')' BL
            ELIST = *E (',' BL CPUSH('COMMA') *ELIST POL(2) | '')
            REF = IDEN LP CPUSH('REF') ELIST RP POL(2)
            PRIMARY = IDEN | INTEGER | LP *E RP | REF
            FACTOR = PRIMARY | '-' . *PUSH() BL PRIMARY POL(1)
            TERM = *TERM MULOP FACTOR POL(2) | FACTOR
            E = *E ADDOP TERM POL(2) | TERM
            BOOL = *E RELOP *E POL(2)
            IFSTMT = 'IF' BL BOOL 'THEN' BL
+              (*STMT 'ELSE' BL CPUSH('IFELSE') *STMT POL(3) |
+               CPUSH('IFTHEN') *STMT POL(2) )
            ASGNSTMT = (IDEN | REF) '=' . *PUSH() BL *E POL(2)
            STMT = IFSTMT | ASGNSTMT
```

Names referenced	Name	Type	Where defined
by POL:	DEXP *	Function	Program 14.1
	PUSH	Function	Program 5.5
	POP	Function	Program 5.6

* indicates name is referenced in the initialization section.

Epilogue

For example, if we execute:

```
    'IF A(I) > 6 THEN I = 2'    STMT
     OUTPUT  =  POP()
```

we will print:

IFTHEN:2,>:2,REF:2,A,I,6,=:2,I,2


```
,----------------,
|| Program      ||
||   18.5       ||
||   TREE       ||
'----------------'
```
With a statement cast as Polish prefix we may enter the optional tree-adjustment phase in which the tree is scanned looking for patterns which may be pruned, modified or rearranged. There are several reasons for doing this, some of which are listed below:

1. To insert explicit conversions (for mixed mode arithmetic, array references, etc.).

2. To remove ambiguities (such as floating versus integer addition, binary versus unary minus, function references versus array references).

3. Code optimization such as common subexpression removal or such as replacing <VAR> = <VAR> + 1 by a single operator.

Other uses for the tree adjustment phase will occur to the writer of a practical compiler. An important point to note is that the scan is generally easier to apply to the tree than to any other form because it is quite easy to specify a pattern to match a tree. The following function, TREE(P,N), will return a pattern that will do precisely that. For example,

            TREE('+',2) $ OUTPUT   FAIL

is a pattern that will scan for and print all binary sums in Polish prefix form.

> TREE(P,N) will match a tree in Polish prefix form whose
> node value matches the pattern P and where N is the number
> of branches. The tree is assumed to be a non-leaf. If N
> is 0, then an arbitrary number of nodes (up to some max-
> imum) is implied.

```
           DEFINE('TREE(P,N)')
           ARB_TREE  =  TREE(BREAK(':,'))  |  BREAK(':,') ','
+                                                          :(TREE_END)
TREE       TREE  =  EQ(N,0)  P
+          (TREE(,1)  |  TREE(,2)  |  TREE(,3)  |  TREE(,4))
+                                                          :S(RETURN)
           TREE  =  P  ':'  N  ','
TREE_1     N  =  N - 1    GT(N,0)                          :F(RETURN)
           TREE  =  TREE  *ARB_TREE                        :(TREE_1)
TREE_END
```

Epilogue

The alert reader will note that the pattern requires a terminating ','. Thus, to use TREE on the Polish notation
described above would require appending a comma to the total
string. It may also be necessary to prepend a comma. For example, ARB_TREE is a variable which was set as a side-effect
of initializing TREE to equal a pattern which will match an
arbitrary tree. Then:

```
           POLISH  =  ','  POLISH  ','
           POLISH     ','  ARB_TREE $ T  ARB  *T
```

will scan the Polish for a pair of identical expressions. (For
this pattern match to work it will be necessary to use
FULLSCAN mode; in QUICKSCAN mode, ARB indicates futility as
was discussed in Chapter 7). Several examples of the use of
TREE have been left as exercises.

> | Program |
> | 18.6 |
> | TR |

Given a statement in Polish prefix, we can
generally produce compiled code by recursive
invocation of a single translate function.
We will not produce code directly but will
create four-tuples as described previously. The set of acceptable 4-tuples is indicated in Figure 18.5.

Certain semantic ambiguities in the description of L_2 need be
resolved before TR can be written. Floating point as well as
integer arithmetic will be permitted. We assume that identifiers beginning with ANY('IJKLMN') are integer; all others
are real (floating point). Mixed-mode arithmetic is not permitted. The functional forms specified in the syntax of L_2
refer to array references; function calls are not permitted
(but are left as an exercise). Finally, for simplicity, array
references are assumed to be one-dimensional. The extension
to multi-dimensioned arrays is relatively straightforward

4-tuple	Description
ADD,arg1,arg2,arg3	Place arg1 plus arg2 into arg3
Seven similar operations for SUB, MUL, DIV, FADD, FSUB, FMUL and FDIV.	
ASGN,arg1,,arg3	Move the quantity from arg1 to arg3.
MNS,arg1,,arg3	Store -arg1 into arg3
BR,,,arg3	branch to arg3
BRGT,arg1,arg2,arg3	Branch to arg3 if arg1 is greater than arg2.
Five similar operations for BRGE, BREQ, BRNE, BRLT and BRLE	
LBL,arg1	Insert a label here

argn is of the form ID or ID(ID) where ID is an identifier.

If identifiers are of the form TEMPn they are considered volatile; i. e., they may be destroyed after first use.

Figure 18.5

The tuple language.

given the standard multiplier technique [Gries 1971, Sect.
8.4] but is beyond the scope of the present discussion.

| TR() will return a translation of a polish string con-
| tained in the global variable POLISH which is modified
| (and reduced to null) in the process. A trailing comma is
| appended to the Polish string to permit easier pattern
| matching. The translation is in the form of 4-tuples
| separated by '//'. The language is L_2.

```
          DEFINE('TR(ARG)OP,N,P,T,ID,L1,L2')
```

| Pattern definitions: ITREE will match an integer tree.
| RTREE will match a real tree.

```
          ITREE  =  ANY('+-*/') ':' ANY('12') ',' *ITREE     |
+                   ANY('IJKLMN') BREAK(',:') ','  |   'REF:2,' *ITREE
          RTREE  =  ANY('+-*/') ':' ANY('12') ',' *RTREE     |
+                   NOTANY('IJKLMN') BREAK(',:') ','  |   'REF:2,' *RTREE
                                                    :(TR_END)
```

| Entry point: if an operator, fan out; otherwise push the
| leaf.

```
TR        POLISH  POS(0)  BREAK(':,') . OP ':' BREAK(',') . N
+                 ','  =                         :S($('TR_' OP))
          POLISH  BREAK(',') . *PUSH() ','  =    :(RETURN)
```

| Arithmetic operators.

```
TR_+ ;TR_- ;TR_* ;TR_/
          TR = EQ(N,1) TR() 'MNS,' POP() ',,' PUSH(TEMP()) '//'
+                                                :S(RETURN)
          '+ADD-SUB*MUL/DIV'  OP  LEN(3) . OP
          POLISH  POS(0)  ITREE                  :S(TR_1)
          OP  =  'F' OP
TR_1      T  =  TR()
          P  =  POP()
          TR = T TR() OP ',' P ',' POP() ',' PUSH(TEMP()) '//'
+                                                :(RETURN)
```

| Array references

```
TR_REF    POLISH  BREAK(',') . ID ','  =
          TR  =  TR()
          TOP()   '('                            :S(TR_REF1)
          PUSH(ID '(' POP() ')')                 :(RETURN)
TR_REF1   T  =  TEMP()
          TR  =  TR  'ASGN,' POP() ',,' T '//'
          PUSH(ID '(' T ')')                     :(RETURN)
```

| Relations are handled here. Note that '=' has been trans-
| lated by the TR_IF... processor to 'EQ' to avoid ambiguity
| with assignment. An argument, ARG, contains the fail
| label. Success implies a no-op. Hence we need the com-

Page 428   Chapter 18   -   Assemblers, Compilers and Macros

| plement of the given operation. |

```
TR_>  ;TR_>=  ;TR_<  ;TR_<=  ;TR_¬=  ;TR_EQ
         'EQNE ¬=EQ <GE >LE <=GT >=LT'    OP   LEN(2)  .  OP
         T   =   TR()
         P   =   POP()
         TR  =   T  TR()  'BR' OP ','  P  ','  POP()  ','  ARG  '//'
+                                                              :(RETURN)
```

| Assignment |

```
TR_=     TR  =   TR()  TR()  'ASGN,'  POP()  ',,'  POP()  '//'
+                                                              :(RETURN)
```

| The IF's |

```
TR_IFTHEN
TR_IFELSE       L1  =   LABEL()
        POLISH    POS(0)    '=:2'   =   'EQ:2'
        TR   =   TR(L1)   TR()
        TR   =   EQ(N,2)  TR  'LBL,'  L1  '//'        :S(RETURN)
        L2   =   LABEL()
        TR   =   TR  'BR,,,'  L2  '//'
+                'LBL,'  L1  '//'  TR()  'LBL,'  L2  '//'    :(RETURN)
TR_END
```

| LABEL() is like TEMP(). |

```
        DEFINE('LABEL()')                              :(LABEL_END)
LABEL   LABEL_NO  =  LABEL_NO + 1
        LABEL  =  'LBL.' LABEL_NO                      :(RETURN)
LABEL_END
```

Names referenced   Name   Type   Where defined
by TR: PUSH   Function   Program 5.5
                    POP   Function   Program 5.6
                    TOP   Function   Program 5.7
                    TEMP   Subfunction   Program 18.2

| | Program | | TUPLE(OP,ARG1,ARG2,ARG3) will expand a
| | 18.7 | | 4-tuple (as described in Figure 18.5) into
| | TUPLE | | reasonably optimized machine code. It does
                   this by being 'aware' at all times of the
state of the registers and allocates and frees registers according to a primitive priority scheme. For example, the
tuples produced (by POL and TR) for the two statements:

                X = X + 1
                IF X > Y THEN X = X + A(I+1) + Z

are shown in Figure 18.6 together with the instructions
generated by TUPLE. Note that spurious LOAD's and STORE's
which were present in L_ONE are gone. TUPLE assumes that any

temporary variable (of the form TEMPn) is only referenced once
and is not used across statement boundaries.

```
| FADD,X,1,TEMP1           |  LOAD   1,X        |
|                          |  FADD   1,=1       |
|                          |                    |
| ASGN,TEMP1,,X            |  STORE  1,X        |
|                          |                    |
| BRLE,X,Y,LBL.1           |  SUB    1,Y        |
|                          |  BRLE   1,LBL.1    |
|                          |                    |
| ADD,I,1,TEMP2            |  LOAD   1,I        |
|                          |  ADD    1,=1       |
|                          |                    |
| FADD,X,A(TEMP2),TEMP3    |  LOAD   2,X        |
|                          |  FADD   2,A(1)     |
|                          |                    |
| FADD,TEMP3,Z,TEMP4       |  FADD   2,Z        |
|                          |                    |
| ASGN,TEMP4,,X            |  STORE  2,X        |
|                          |                    |
| LBL,LBL.1                |  LBL.1             |
```

Figure 18.6

The tuples produced by TR (on the left) and the
corresponding code generated by TUPLE (on the
right) for the statement sequence: X = X + 1 ;
IF X > Y THEN X = X + A(I+1) + Z.

The register allocation schemes used in actual compilers seem
to be 'always messy'. TUPLE was written in a highly structured
top-down fashion to avoid this. Note that the higher level
routines have no notion at all of what the data structure to
associate registers with locations looks like. Only low-level,
caretaker routines, know this. This is an example of
'information hiding' as advocated by Parnas [1972].

```
           DEFINE('TUPLE(OP,ARG1,ARG2,ARG3)R')       : (TUPLE_END)
TUPLE                                                :($('TU_' OP))

TU_ADD  ;TU_FADD ;TU_SUB ;TU_FSUB
TU_MUL  ;TU_FMUL ;TU_DIV ;TU_FDIV
           R   =  LOAD(ARG1)
           OUTPUT =  ' ' OP ' ' R ','  ADDR(ARG2)
           DEASSOC(R)
           STORE(R,ARG3)                             : (RETURN)

TU_ASGN R  =  LOAD(ARG1)
           STORE(R,ARG3)                             : (RETURN)
```

```
TU_MNS      R    =    REG()
            OUTPUT  =   ' LOADN '  R  ','  ADDR(ARG1)
            STORE(R,ARG3)                              :(RETURN)

TU_BR       ARG3  =  INDEX(ARG3)
            OUTPUT  =  ' BR '  ARG3                    :(RETURN)

TU_BRGT ;TU_BRGE ;TU_BRLT ;TU_BRLE ;TU_BREQ ;TU_BRNE
            R    =    LOAD(ARG1)
            OUTPUT  =  ' SUB '  R  ','  ADDR(ARG2)
            FREE(R)
            OUTPUT  =  ' '  OP  ' '  R  ','  ARG3      :(RETURN)

TU_LBL      OUTPUT  =  ARG1
            REG_LIST  =  ','                           :(RETURN)
TUPLE_END
```

LOAD(LOC) will load the indicated location (if not already
loaded) into a register and return the register.

```
            DEFINE('LOAD(LOC)')                        :(LOAD_END)
LOAD        LOAD  =  ISREG(LOC)                        :S(RETURN)
            LOC   =  ADDR(LOC)
            LOAD  =  REG()
            ASSOC(LOC,LOAD)
            OUTPUT  =  ' LOAD '  LOAD  ','  LOC        :(RETURN)
LOAD_END
```

STORE(REG,LOC) is a generalized store operation storing a
given register REG into a given location LOC updating the
register assignment list.

```
            DEFINE('STORE(REG,LOC)')                   :(STORE_END)
STORE       LOC  =  INDEX(LOC)
            FREE(REG)
            ASSOC(LOC,REG)
            LOC    TEMP_LOC                            :S(RETURN)
            OUTPUT  =  ' STORE '  REG  ','  LOC        :(RETURN)
STORE_END
```

ADDR(LOC) will return a usable address designating the
possibly subscripted location LOC. The address returned
will be a register number if LOC is contained in a
register. If LOC is subscripted, a register number
replaces the subscript. If LOC is a constant, the symbol
'=' is prepended.

```
            DEFINE('ADDR(LOC)')                        :(ADDR_END)
ADDR        ADDR  =  LOC
            ADDR  =  INDEX(ADDR)
            ADDR  =  ISREG(ADDR)                       :S(RETURN)
            ADDR  POS(0)  SPAN('0123456789')  RPOS(0)  =
+                                   '='  ADDR          :(RETURN)
ADDR_END
```

Program 18.7 - TUPLE

> INDEX(LOC) will load the subscript (if any) of the given
> location into a register and return the same expression
> with the index replaced by a constant.

```
            DEFINE('INDEX(LOC)S')                    :(INDEX_END)
INDEX       INDEX   =   LOC
            INDEX   '('   BREAK(')')'  .  S  =  '('  LOAD(S)  :(RETURN)
INDEX_END
```

> The following five functions are low-level basic routines
> used to associate registers with locations. A string of
> register-location pairs is kept in the order of increasing
> priority in REG_LIST. If a register is associated with a
> location then the value normally found at that location
> will be in the register. Also, if the location is a tem-
> porary, the location will not contain that value; other-
> wise the location will also contain the value.

```
            DEFINE('REG()LOC')
            DEFINE('FREE(REG)')
            DEFINE('ISREG(LOC)')
            DEFINE('ASSOC(LOC,REG)')
            DEFINE('DEASSOC(REG)')

            NO_REGS  =  16
            REG_LIST =  ','
            TEMP_LOC =  POS(0) 'TEMP' SPAN('0123456789') RPOS(0)
                                                        :(REG_END)
```

> REG() will return an available register. If all registers
> are associated with locations, it will free up the
> register with the lowest priority.

```
REG         REG  =  LT(REG,NO_REGS)  REG + 1          :F(REG_1)
            REG_LIST    '('  REG  ')'                 :F(RETURN) S(REG)
REG_1       REG_LIST    ','  BREAK('(')  .  LOC  '('
+                                BREAK(')')'  .  REG  ')'  =  ','
            LOC    TEMP_LOC                           :F(RETURN)
            OUTPUT  =  ' STORE ' REG ',' LOC          :(RETURN)
```

> FREE(REG) will free a register for other associations.

```
FREE        REG_LIST  ','  BREAK('(')  '('  REG  ')'  =  :(RETURN)
```

> ISREG(LOC) is a predicate which will determine if LOC is
> currently associated with a register. If so it will boost
> its priority.

```
ISREG       REG_LIST  ','  LOC  '('  BREAK(')')'  .  ISREG  ')'  =
+                                                        :F(FRETURN)
            REG_LIST  =  REG_LIST  LOC  '('  ISREG  '),'  :(RETURN)
```

> ASSOC(LOC,REG) will associate an unsubscripted location
> with a register.

Page 432   Chapter 18   -   Assemblers, Compilers and Macros

```
ASSOC     LOC    '('                          :S(RETURN)
          REG_LIST = REG_LIST LOC '(' REG '),'    :(RETURN)
```
┌───┐
│ DEASSOC(REG) will remove any association a register has   │
│ with a location but will not free the register.   │
└───┘
```
DEASSOC    REG_LIST  ','  BREAK('(') '(' REG ')' =
+                         ',(' REG ')'            :(RETURN)
REG_END
```

Epilogue

Note that a distinction is made between a register which is free and one which is merely disassociated. This distinction is necessary because when a register is about to be stored it is not yet free (for use as an index register for example) and yet it may unrelated to any given variable. Note also that although a register could theoretically be associated with two different location (such as after A = B), TUPLE allows only one such association.

No distinction is made between fixed and floating point operands of the relational operators. We are here assuming that floating numbers operate on the same equality scale as integers (a common case).

┌──────────────┐
│ │ Program │ │   A macro system is basically a method whereby
│ │   18.8   │ │   the user of the system may define and employ
│ │   GPM   │ │   abbreviations. GPM stands for General Pur-
└──────────────┘   pose Macro processor and was developed by
Strachey [1965]. GPM is general purpose in two ways; it can be employed as a preprocessor for an arbitrary language and it can produce arbitrary string computations.

Macros first grew into prominence with the development of assemblers. Initially they were mere abbreviations for instruction sequences but soon grew more sophisticated with the introduction of arguments, conditional assembly instructions, repeat and sequencing facilities. Macros were able to define other macros and redefine themselves. McIlroy [1960] describes many of these techniques.

It was soon realized that a complete computational facility could be implemented relatively easily based on little more than the ability to define a macro and GPM was one of the first complete languages to be based on a macro system. But whereas GPM is complete, as we shall see later, one must almost stand on one's computational head to perform certain common operations (e.g., see Exers. 18.25 and 18.27).

We will write GPM as a function GPM(S) which will return a translation of string S. If S does not contain either of the two special characters '#' or '<', it will be returned intact. A sequence of the form:

Program 18.8 - GPM Page 433

#name,arg$_1$,arg$_2$, ... , arg$_n$;

is considered to be a <u>macro call</u>. Macro calls within the string S will be replaced by an <u>evaluation</u>. Every macro call <u>returns</u> a string (which is possibly null). This returned string is again passed through GPM by a recursive call to obtain the macro's evaluation.

The built-in macro DEF allows macros to be defined.

#DEF,name,pr;

will define a macro by the given name and associate it with a prototype pr. It returns the null string. For example,

#DEF,M,STRING;

will define a macro M whose prototype is 'STRING'. When M is called as in:

#M;

the value returned is 'STRING'. Hence:

GPM('#DEF,M,STRING;x#M;y')

will return 'xSTRINGy'.

In some respects, the DEF function may be thought of as assigning a string to a name. But a macro may also have arguments which may be embedded within the prototype. The position of the first, second, third, etc. argument is indicated by the position of the symbols &1, &2, &3, etc. Thus:

#DEF,SQUARE,&1*&1;

defines the macro SQUARE with one argument. The macro call:

#SQUARE,(X+Y);

returns '(X+Y)*(X+Y)'. Within the argument list of a macro call there may be other macro calls and these are evaluated to obtain the actual arguments. For example,

#SQUARE,#M;Y;

returns 'STRINGY*STRINGY'. The macro call may be suppressed by surrounding a string with pointed brackets. Thus GPM('AA<#>AA') returns 'AA#AA'. Pointed brackets are stipped off in pairs. Thus, GPM('A<B<C>D>E') returns 'AB<C>DE'. Pointed brackets may be used to defer evaluation of macro calls until some later time. Thus

#DEF,A,<#M;>;

will associate with A the prototype '#M;'. When A is called as in #A; the returned string is evaluated leading to a call on #M; which returns 'STRING'.

Were the returned values merely substituted for the macro call without again being evaluated, the macro system we have described so far would only be useful as a system of forming abbreviations. But by the simple act of reevaluating the returned value, we obtain a general purpose computational language, a language capable of expressing anything computable. This is a remarkable fact. To see that this is so, consider defining a conditional macro #COND,X,Y,Z; which evaluates to Z if X equals Y and evaluates to null otherwise. On the one hand, if the returned string were not reevaluated it would be impossible to write COND (should it be written as the null string or as &3 ?) and hence GPM would not be completely general. On the other hand, a conditional allows one to simulate a Turing machine and hence perform arbitrary computations. To see this reflect that a state-transition table (as in a Turing machine) may be implemented as a collection of conditionals (one for every combination of states and inputs).

We may write #COND,X,Y,Z; as:

   #DEF,COND,<#DEF,<&1>,;#DEF,<&2>,<&3>;#<&1>;>;

In the above, the first argument is defined as a macro which evaluates to null. The second argument is also defined as a macro and this definition overrides the first if and only if the first two arguments are equal (a macro name need not be an identifier but may be any string of symbols). Finally, the macro named by the first argument is called. The returned value is the third argument if the second definition overrode the first. Programming in this language is opaque but is perfectly general. If the argument to GPM is not well-formed, meaning that if a '#' is not followed by a corresponding ';' or that a '<' is not followed by a corresponding '>', GPM will fail. This fact can be used to apply GPM to a program without reading it into main storage in its entirety. Only a sufficient amount of it need be read to enable GPM to succeed. Said another way, if GPM(S1) succeeds then GPM(S1) GPM(S2) equals GPM(S1 S2).

There is one point in which the implementation given departs from official GPM as defined by Strachey. Macro definitions here are global and not local to the evaluation of a specific macro. Assume the following definition occurs.

   #DEF,X,Initialization <#DEF,X,Action; #X; >;

In our system, #X; will evaluate to 'Initialization Action' on the first call and to 'Action' on all subsequent calls. This is because the macro X redefines itself. In Strachey's system the macro definitions are pushed so that when return is made to the outer level the original definitions remain intact. Hence a macro could not redefine itself. There are

advantages and disadvantages to both. As a computation tool,
Strachey's system is perhaps superior since macro names can
serve as temporary variables. For a practical macro processor,
however, it is better to have global macro names.

```
          DEFINE('GPM(S) PREFIX,BOD,ARG,NAME,N,PUSH_POP')
```
```
| Initialization section for GPM: FORB_CH (forbidden charac- |
| ter) is assigned a character not permitted in  the  source |
| string.  GPM_BAL is assigned a pattern which will match a  |
| string  balanced in the GPM sense.  Note that although <>  |
| and #; both serve as a kind of parenthesis  they  are  not |
| symmetric.                                                 |
```
```
          &ALPHABET    LEN(1)  .  FORB_CH
          MAC_TBL  =  TABLE()
          ITEM    =   '<' BAL('<>')  '>'   |   '#' *GPM_BAL ';'
+                   | NOTANY('<#')  BREAK('<#>;,')
          GPM_BAL  =  ARBNO(ITEM)
```
```
| This is the basic pattern used to process strings.  PREFIX |
| is the string up to a macro call or a <...> literal.  BOD  |
| will   be  either  the  literal  body  or  the  result  of |
| evaluating the macro                                       |
```
```
          GET.PREFIX.BOD  =  POS(0) BREAK('<#')  .  PREFIX  FENCE
+         ('<' BAL('<>')  .  BOD '>'    |
+         '#' GPM_BAL . NAME . *PROC('NAME')
+         ARBNO(',' GPM_BAL . ARG . *PROC('ARG'))
+         ';' . *PROC('MEND')   )         |
+         REM . PREFIX    NULL . BOD              : (GPM_END)
```
```
| Entry point:                                                |
```
```
GPM       IDENT(S)                              : S (RETURN)
          S  GET.PREFIX.BOD  =                  : F (FRETURN)
          GPM  =  GPM  PREFIX  BOD              : (GPM)
GPM_END
```
```
| The routine PROC will process macro names (at PNAME) macro |
| arguments (at PARG), and macro terminations (at PMEND).    |
```
```
          DEFINE('PROC(TYPE)')                  : (PROC_END)
PROC      PROC  =  .DUMMY                       : ($('P' TYPE))

PNAME     NAME  =  GPM(NAME)
          N  =  0
          PUSH_POP  =
          PUSH(NAME)                            : (NRETURN)

PARG      PUSH(GPM(ARG))
          N  =  N + 1                           : (NRETURN)

PMEND     BOD = IDENT(NAME,'DEF')  POP()        : F(PMEND_2)
          MAC_TBL<POP()>  =  BOD
          BOD  =                                : (NRETURN)
```

Page 436   Chapter 18 - Assemblers, Compilers and Macros

```
PMEND_2 BOD  =  REPLACE(MAC_TBL<NAME>,'&',FORB_CH)
PMEND_1 BOD     FORB_CH N  =  TOP()                  :S(PMEND_1)
        N  =  N - 1
        POP()                                        :S(PMEND_1)
        BOD  =  GPM(BOD)                             :(NRETURN)
PROC_END
```

Names referenced   Name   Type   Where defined
by GPM: BAL *   Function   Program 8.3
                        PUSH   Function   Program 5.5
                        POP   Function   Program 5.6
* indicates name is referenced in the initialization section.

??
?????????????????????? EXERCISES ?????????????????????????
??

┌─────────────────┐
│ Exercise 18.1   │ Suggest a method (or methods) whereby the
└─────────────────┘ OPS and SYMS tables of ASM (Prog. 18.1) can
be made smaller at the expense of time. Implement one of your
plans.

┌─────────────────┐
│ Exercise 18.2   │ Add expressions to ASM (binary +, -, * and
└─────────────────┘ / and unary -) by modifying the semantic
routines of L_ONE for the purpose. Let the period (.) mean
the current address.

┌─────────────────┐
│ Exercise 18.3   │ Assuming there are eight bits per charac-
└─────────────────┘ ter, how would you modify ASM to output (on
the PUNCH file) a 32-bit word as four characters.

┌─────────────────┐
│ Exercise 18.4   │ Modify ASM to allow symbols of the form
└─────────────────┘ =<constant>. For example, =37 implies the
address of the constant 37. (This convention was actually assumed by TUPLE, Prog. 18.7.) Be sure to avoid generating
duplicate constants. All such literals should be placed after
the last instruction of the program being assembled.

┌─────────────────┐
│ Exercise 18.5   │ What character is not permitted in the ar-
└─────────────────┘ gument to S(name), the semantic subfunction
of L_ONE, Prog. 18.2? How can S(name) be modified to avoid
this restriction?

┌─────────────────┐
│ Exercise 18.6   │ Augment Language L_1 (Figure 18.2) by al-
└─────────────────┘ lowing subscripted expressions.   Modify
L_ONE accordingly.

Exercises for chapter 18   Page 437

| Exercise 18.7 | Identifiers seen by L_ONE are passed on to the assembler untouched. This is not always desirable. Modify L_ONE so that each identifier is replaced by a unique 'internal' name.

| Exercise 18.8 | Extend L_ONE to handle real arithmetic. An identifier is assumed to be integer or real (floating point) depending on whether or not it begins with one of the letters 'IJKLMN'. Allow mixed expressions both in binary operations and across an assignment. Assume two additional instructions for machine M, viz. CIR which converts from integer to real (loading into the target register) and CRI which converts from real to integer.

| Exercise 18.9 | Write a program which will read in a BNF grammar and produce for each syntactic variable <V> a pattern named V that will match it. Assume there are no extraneous blanks. (This requires about eight instructions.)

| Exercise 18.10 | It has been observed that well over half of all Fortran programs appearing on listings dumped into a certain trash can contain no interior blanks. Use this observation to improve the speed of blanks.

| Exercise 18.11 | If BLINT (a pattern in BLANKS, Prog. 18.3) is simplified to SPAN(NUM ' ') then BLANKS will operate incorrectly in some cases. Furnish such a case.

| Exercise 18.12 | A squemish programmer, wishing to avoid left-recursion writes, for the definition of E (a pattern in POL, Prog. 18.4):

E = TERM ADDOP *E POL(2) | TERM

What error has been introduced? Give an example of a statement which would yield incorrect results.

| Exercise 18.13 | Modify POL so that a null statement is allowed. This would permit, for example, the sequence:

IF A=1 THEN ELSE X = 2

| Exercise 18.14 | Modify POL, Prog. 18.4, to allow IF ... THEN ... ELSE type _expressions_. An example is:

$$A = IF\ A > 0\ THEN\ 1\ ELSE\ -1$$

Transform this syntax into Polish using a 3-ary operator called EIF (Expression IF).

| Exercise 18.15 | This exercise indicates how error messages may be incorporated into POL(). Write a function DNF(S1,S2) (Did Not Follow) which will form the message:

A valid ... S1 ... was encountered but
this was not followed by a valid ... S2 ...

This is to be appended onto a global error message string (MESSAGE) which is printed if the statement cannot be matched. Using DNF, modify the patterns of POL, Prog. 18.4, to issue error messages in the following cases: (1) an expression doesn't follow an '=' in assignment. (2) a Boolean doesn't follow an IF. (3) a statement doesn't follow a 'THEN'. (4) a primary doesn't follow a unary minus. (5) an expression doesn't follow a '('.

| Exercise 18.16 | This exercise indicates how SNOBOL4 pattern matching can be used on the intermediate form to achieve a degree of machine-independent code optimization. Scan a Polish string (as output by POL, but with a trailing comma) for a pattern which resulted from an assignment of the form

$$<VAR> = <VAR> + <E>$$

where <VAR> is the same (possibly subscripted) variable. Transform this into the 2-ary form:

$$AUG:2,<VAR>,<E>$$

Do the same for an assignment in which the <E> is the first operand.

| Exercise 18.17 | Write a pattern to match an arbitrary tree with no upper limit on the number of leaves.

| Exercise 18.18 | Modify TREE to accept N additional arguments, NAME1, NAME2, ..., NAMEn which are to be associated with the various leaves of the tree. Thus

TREE('+', 2, .NAME1, .NAME2)

will return, in effect,

'+:2'   ARB_TREE . NAME1   ARB_TREE . NAME2

Exercises for chapter 18   Page 439

To do this exercise, you must assume some maximum N (already assumed anyway in the coding of TREE). For extra credit, make your program entirely dependent on the parameter MAX_N.

| Exercise 18.19 | In POL, Prog 18.4, argument lists were compiled into a Polish notation having the form:

$$COMMA:2,arg_1,COMMA:2,arg_2,COMMA:2 \ldots$$

Use pattern matching to convert this into the form:

$$COMMA:n,arg_1,arg_2, \ldots$$

| Exercise 18.20 | Modify TR, Prog. 18.6, to handle mixed expressions, both in the binary arithmetic operations and relations and across assignments. Assume tuples

$$CVTIR,Arg_1,,Arg_3$$
$$CVTRI,Arg_1,,Arg_3$$

exist to convert from integer to real and real to integer respectively.

| Exercise 18.21 | The following exercise extends TR (Prog. 18.6) to include functions. Assume that the tuples required for output for the function reference:

$$FUNC(Arg_1, Arg_2, \ldots , Arg_n)$$

are

$$ARG,Arg_1$$
$$ARG,Arg_2$$
$$\ldots$$
$$ARG,Arg_n$$
$$CALL,FUNC,,RES$$

where RES is the location in which the result is deposited. Assume that the function ATEST(ID) exists which is a predicate to determine whether ID is an array. If ID is not an array, it must be a function.

| Exercise 18.22 | Modify L_ONE to call TUPLE rather than producing unoptimized code.

| Exercise 18.23 | TUPLE (Prog. 18.7) is stupid in not optimizing the case where the 2nd argument is already in a register and the first argument is not and the operation is (F)ADD or (F)MUL. Modify TUPLE to handle this.

Chapter 18 - Assemblers, Compilers and Macros

> **Exercise 18.24** The action taken by TUPLE for a label is rather ruthless (removing all previous register associations). For labels generated as a result of IF processing, only those symbols need by disassociated that are actually modified by one of the clauses. Write a routine that will scan the output of TR to determine which symbols are modified and arrange to have only these disassociated when IF-type labels are encountered.

> **Exercise 18.25** The following formula from Strachey [1965] defines a macro S with one argument.
>
> #DEF,S,<#1,2,3,4,5,6,7,8,9,10,#DEF,1,<&>&1;;>;
>
> What is the result of (a) #S,2; (b) #S,5; (c) In words, what does S do?

> **Exercise 18.26** Modify ASM so that it uses GPM as a macro processor. Allow macro prototypes to contain more than one line. This can be done by encoding line boundaries as a special character sequence.

> **Exercise 18.27** It is sometimes required to build up a large string at assembly time. Write a macro #CS,S; (Concatenate String) such that when #S; is called all the strings so far passed to CS will be returned concatenated together.

FOR ODD-NUMBERED EXERCISES

```
=================================================================
=====================   Solutions   =====================
=====================      for      =====================
=====================   Chapter 2   =====================
=================================================================
```

2.1 The body of the function UP(ARG) is
UP   UP = REPLACE(ARG,LOWERS_,UPPERS_)   : (RETURN)

2.3
L   P (POS(0) (SPAN(' ') | '') | '. ') . T
+   ANY(UPPERS_) . C = T   UPLO(C)   :S(L)
          P = UPLO(P)

2.5
          SIZE(BASEB(K,2))
          SIZE(BASEB(K,n))

2.7
          DEFINE('V(ARG) B,S,E,F')   : (V_END)
V   B = BASEB(BASE10(ARG,16),2)
          B LEN(1) . S LEN(10) . E REM . F
          V = (-1) ** S CONVERT(BASE10(F,2),'REAL')   *
+   2 ** (BASE10(E,2) - 1045)
                                                         : (RETURN)
V_END

2.9 Those involving built-in numerical operators: EQ, REMDR,
/, * and + (four statements in all).

2.11 Initialize H with '01234567'; then replace all   16's   by
8's and replace all HEX's by OCT's.

SOLUTIONS

2.13 After doing the obvious checks on the month being in the range 1-12 and the day being in the range 1-31, see if the day is either the 29th, 30th or 31st. If so, and the DAY (of the week) is equal to the DAY of the first, second or third of the following month, the day is invalid.

2.15 M = CEIL((5 * D - 150) / 153.) (See the chapter on arithmetic for an analysis of this); then take the number of days and subtract off 31+28 (or 31+29 in a leap year); if this number is negative, add the number of days in the year (365 or 366). Use the formula above to determine M. Then REMDR(M + 2, 12) + 1 is the month.

2.17 Insert a test and branch at the entry point of SPELL and insert a section of code labeled SPELL_LONG as follows:

```
SPELL      LE(SIZE(N),6)                          :F(SPELL_LONG)
           ...
SPELL_LONG         N   RTAB(6)  .  M =
           SPELL = SPELL(M)
           SPELL  'SEPT'     =  'OCT'
           SPELL  'SEXT'     =  'SEPT'
           SPELL  'QUINT'    =  'SEXT'
           SPELL  'QUADR'    =  'QUINT'
           SPELL  'TRILLION' =  'QUADRILLION'
           SPELL  'BILLION'  =  'TRILLION'
           SPELL  =  SPELL  ' BILLION'
           SPELL  =  NE(N,0)  SPELL ' ' SPELL(N)  :(RETURN)
```

===
====================== Solutions   ======================
====================== for   ======================
====================== Chapter 3   ======================
===

3.1 RPAD(S,N,C) = REVERSE(LPAD(REVERSE(S),N,C))

3.3 RPAD(LPAD(S,(N - SIZE(S)) / 2,C),N,C)

3.5 (a) REPLACE('CXCB','BBCD',S);   (b) 4

3.7 (a)
```
           DEFINE('TPOS(S,H,W)K,C')                :(TPOS_END)
TPOS       S    POS(K) LEN(1) . C                  :F(TPOS_1)
           TPOS =  TPOS  C
           K  =  K + W                             :(TPOS)
TPOS_1     GE(SIZE(TPOS), H * W)                   :S(RETURN)
           K  =  REMDR(K,W) + 1                    :(TPOS)
TPOS_END
```

(b)
```
           &ALPHABET     LEN(H * W)  .  S1
           S2  =  TPOS(S1)
```
(c)

```
             DEFINE ('ENCODE (S) T')
             &ALPHABET  LEN (H * W) . S1
             PS1   =   TPOS (S1,H,W)                  : (ENCODE_END)
ENCODE       S     LEN (H * W) . T =                  :F (ENCODE_1)
             ENCODE  =  ENCODE REPLACE (PS1, S1, T)   : (ENCODE)
ENCODE_1
             S  =  S  DUPL (':', H * W - SIZE (S))
             ENCODE  =  ENCODE REPLACE (PS1,S1,S)
             ENCODE  =  DIFF (ENCODE| ':')            : (RETURN)
ENCODE_END
```

3.9 Do a positional transformation to obtain the odd characters in the string (H1). Then do a similar transformation to obtain the even characters (H2). Transliterate H1 so that digit k goes to the (16 * k)th character of &ALPHABET. Transliterate H2 so that digit K goes to the Kth character. Then OR the resulting strings.

3.11 '0011223344556677889'

3.13 IDENT (SKIM (S), S)

3.15 (a)
REVERSE (REPLACE (TRIM (REPLACE (REVERSE (S), '0', ' ')), ' ', '0'))
(b) +S

3.17 SWAP, SWAP_ARG1 and SWAP_ARG2

3.19 a-ht, b-ht, d-h

3.21 (X Y)   X . Y   Y . X

==
==================== Solutions   ======================
====================   for   ======================
==================== Chapter 4   ======================
==

4.1 M = CRACK ('JAN.,FEB.,MARCH,APRIL,...', ',')

4.3 (a) opposite pairs are swapped twice resulting in a mutual cancellation. A remains unchanged, I is set to N + 1.
  (b)   SEQ(' J = N + 1 - I ; (GT(J,I) SWAP(.A<I>,.A<J>))',.I)

4.5 SEQ(" A<I> POS(0) NOTANY('M') ", .I)

4.7 It is equivalent to AOPA(A1,' ', A2)

4.9 STRINGOUT (AOPA (CRACK (X),' ',CRACK (Y)))

4.11 A<FIND (A, '¬LGT') >

4.13 A practical version of the following function would use 'funny' names for temporaries and parameters.

```
            DEFINE('DO(S,N,L,U,I)')                      :(DO_END)
DO          S   =   CODE(S  '  ;  :(DO_1)')              :F(FRETURN)
            $N  =   L                                    :<S>
DO_1        $N  =   $N + I
            LE($N,U)                                     :S<S>F(RETURN)
DO_END
```

4.15

```
            DEFINE('PUSH(A,E)')                          :(PUSH_END)
PUSH        PUSH  =  A
            A<1>  =  A<1> + 1
PUSH_1      A<A<1>>  =  E                                :S(RETURN)
            A     =  CATA(A,A)
            PUSH  =  A                                   :(PUSH_1)
PUSH_END
```

===
====================   Solutions   =======================
====================   for   =======================
====================   Chapter 5   =======================
===

5.1

```
            DEFINE('CRACK(S,B) N,V,PAT')                 :(CRACK_END)
CRACK       IDENT(B,NULL)                                :S(CRACK_1)
            S   RTAB(1) B ABORT | REM . S   =   S B
            PAT  =  BREAK(B) . V  LEN(1)
CRACK_2     S  PAT  =                                    :F(RETURN)
            $N  =  LINK(,V)
            N   =  .NEXT($N)                             :(CRACK_2)
CRACK_1     PAT  =  LEN(1) . V                           :(CRACK_2)
CRACK_END
```

5.3 (a)

```
            IDENT(PUSH_POP)                              :S(FRETURN)
            NM  =  .PUSH_POP
FIRST_1     NM  =  DIFFER(NEXT($NM)) .NEXT($NM)          :S(FIRST_1)
            FIRST  =  VALUE($NM)
            $NM  =                                       :(RETURN)
```

(b) Use a doubly-linked list as in Ex. 5.2.

5.5 No modification to REVL is required.

5.7

```
            DEFINE('IFFLD(N,S) I,F')                     :(IFFLD_END)
IFFLD       F  =  FIELD(DATATYPE(S),I + 1)               :F(FRETURN)
            I  =  DIFFER(F,N)  I + 1                     :S(IFFLD)F(RETURN)
IFFLD_END
```

5.9 (1) Insert the four characters ',NEW' behind 'MARK' in the DATA function.   (2) Use the constant 2 rather than 1 in FIELD.   (3) The third statement after VISIT_1 should read:
```
    FLD(SON,I)  =  GT(...)  NEW(GS)                      :S(VISIT_1)
```

(4) Change VISIT_2 to:
VISIT_2   NEW(SON) = COPY(SON) ; SON = NEW(SON)
(5) Return the copied configuration by modifying VISIT_3 to:
VISIT_3   VISIT = IDENT(FATHER) SON   :S(RETURN)

===
=====================   Solutions   ====================
=====================   for   ====================
=====================   Chapter 6   ====================
===

6.1 a-F, b-T, c-F, d-F, e-T, f-T, g-F, h-T, i-T, j-T.

6.3 The canonical form is 'BED' | 'BEDS' | 'BEAD' | 'BEADS' | 'RED' | 'REDS' | 'READ' | 'READS'. The pattern is not monic.

6.5 a-Y, b-N, c-Y, d-Y, e-Y, f-Y, g-Y, h-Y, i-N, j-N.

6.7 NULL | NULL | NULL | NULL | NULL | ...

6.9 $(L^2+3L+2)/2$

6.11 2 ** L

6.13 a-Y, b-N, c-N, d-N, e-Y, f-N, g-Y.

6.15 a) [0, 2] b) [0, 2, 4, 4] c) 2**K

6.17 ARBNO('AA' | 'A') will match all even-length sequences of A's before matching odd sequences.

6.19 P_1 = FENCE 'ABC', P_2 = FENCE 'XYZ'.

6.21
    a) RPOS(0) | BREAK(S) SUCCEED
    b) ANY(S)
    c) ANY(S) | BREAK(S) ANY(S) SUCCEED
    d) POS(N) SUCCEED | TAB(N)
    e) P = TAB(N) | RTAB(N) TAB(N) SUCCEED | RTAB(N) X

===
=====================   Solutions   ====================
=====================   for   ====================
=====================   Chapter 7   ====================
===

7.1
```
BREAKP       C = CURSOR
BREAKP.1     SUBJECT   POS(CURSOR)   ANY(ARG(NODE))    :S(S)
             CURSOR  =  GE(CURSOR, LENGTH) C           :S(F)
             CURSOR  =  CURSOR + 1                     :(BREAKP.1)
```
Full credit if LF is used instead of F; half credit if MF is used. If the pattern match and test are inverted, take 3/4 credit.

SOLUTIONS

7.3 (a) 2 ** N   (b) (4 ** N + 2) / 3

7.5 To form a loop of alternates by alternation or a loop of subsequents by concatenation would require that the loop go through the root of the second argument since this is the only kind of arrow added by these operations. But since the second argument does not impinge on the first, no loop can be formed. If a loop was formed via ARBNO(P) it must go through P. But it could not be a loop of alternates since only solid arrows are added out of P and it could not be a loop of subsequents because only a dotted arrow enters P.

7.7 a-9, b-20, c-40, d-14, e-1, f-7

7.9 a-Yes, b-Yes, c-No, d-Yes

7.11 Design TAB(N) as a compound consisting of a node TAB1 and an alternate TAB2. TAB1 pushes the futility flag, TAB2 restores it and fails.

7.13
```
ARBN1    PUSH(FUTILITY)
         FUTILITY = 1                                    :(S)
ARBN2    FUTILITY = EQ(FUTILITY,1) EQ(&FULLSCAN,0) POP() :S(LF)
         POP()                                           :(S)
```

7.15 Create a compound similar to Figure 7.8 with NOT1, NOT1B and NOT2 in place of VA1, VAB1 and VA2 and with no VAB2. NOT1, like VA1, pushes a nonnegative value onto Stack Alpha. NOT2 changes this to a negative value and fails. NOT1B (NOT1 on Backup) pops the value and succeeds or fails depending on whether the value is positive or negative.

7.17 Call the root node r. Then
$$D(r) = D(s) \mid LEN(1) \, D(r) \mid D(a)$$
Since D(r) is <u>supposed</u> to equal ARB D(s) | D(a) we may plug this trial value into the right hand side and after some manipulation we obtain
$$ARB \, D(s) \mid LEN(1) \, D(a) \mid D(a)$$
which does not equal the trial value.

7.19
```
SCAN     IDENT(ALT(NODE))                       :($PROG(NODE))
         PUSH(NODE) ; PUSH(CURSOR)
         NODE = ALT(NODE)                        :(SCAN)

S        NODE = SUBS(NODE)
         IDENT(NODE)                             :S(RETURN) F(SCAN)

F        CURSOR = POP() ; NODE = POP()
         IDENT(NODE)                             :S(FRETURN) F($PROG(NODE))
```

===
====================   Solutions   ====================
====================   for   ====================
====================   Chapter 8   ====================
===

8.1 ARBNO(NOTANY(S)) RPOS(0) | BREAK(S)

8.3 Replace calls to BREAK by calls to BREAKREM.

8.5 3,4,5,6

8.7 When NAME is converted to expression the result is not EVAL'ed as an identifier but as a concatentation.

8.9 NULL

8.11 IF(P) = NOT(NOT(P))

8.13 In the fourth line following LIKE_1 add a third alternative to produce:
```
         LIKE   =   LIKE  |  T1 T2  |  T1 LEN(1) T2
```

8.15 either parenthesis

8.17
```
        QLIT = Q BREAK(Q) Q
        CMNT = '/*' ARBNO(NOT('*/') LEN(1)) '*/'
        ELEM = QLIT | CMNT | NOT(Q | '/*') LEN(1) BREAK('/;' Q)
        PLI.STMT = POS(0) (ARBNO(ELEM) ';') . STMT
```

8.19
```
         DEFINE('NAME(NO) D,X')                    :(NAME_END)
NAME     NO LEN(1) . D =                           :F(RETURN)
  '2ABC3DEF4GHI5JKL6MNO7PRS8TUV9WXY0ZZZ1***'  D LEN(3) . X
         NAME = NAME ANY(X)                        :(NAME)
NAME_END
```

===
====================   Solutions   ====================
====================   for   ====================
====================   Chapter 9   ====================
===

9.1
```
         DEFINE('READ(P)')                   :(READ_END)
READ     LT(NF_INPUT,0)                      :S(FRETURN)
         READ = POP()                        :S(READ_1)
         READ = INPUT                        :F(READ_2)
READ_1   READ P                              :S(RETURN)
         PUSH(READ)                          :(FRETURN)
READ_2   NF_INPUT = NF_INPUT - 1             :(READ)
READ_END
```

9.3 The following will remove blanks except within string literals as defined in the exercise. To handle 'real' Fortran we must be a bit more sophisticated. See BLANKS, Prog. 18.3.

Before returning, execute the following code. The patterns can (and perhaps should be) defined out of line.

```
                   Q = "'"   ;    QQ = '"'
                   QLIT = Q BREAK(Q) Q | QQ BREAK(QQ) QQ
                   HOL  = SPAN('0123456789') $ N  'H' LEN(*N)
                   PAT  = POS(0) ARB . T1 NULL . T2
+                       (SPAN(' ') | (QLIT | HOL) . T2)
                   FORTREAD  LEN(6) . T =
FORTREAD_2         FORTREAD  PAT =                    :F(FORTREAD_3)
                   T = T T1 T2                        :(FORTREAD_2)
FORTREAD_3         FORTREAD = T FORTREAD              :(RETURN)
```

The above will not handle the rare case that the integer preceding the H in a holerith literal contains interspersed blanks. This can be handled as follows (take extra credit if you did this):
   HOL = SPAN('0123456789 ') $ N 'H' LEN(*DIFF(N,' '))

9.5 The following rendition of ASMREAD assumes that the READ routine removes comments.

```
              DEFINE('ASMREAD()A,T')
              CONTINUE    = TAB(71) . T  NOTANY(' ')
              CONTINUE16  = DUPL(' ',16) CONTINUE
              ORDINARY    = TAB(71) . T
              ORDINARY16  = DUPL(' ',16) ORDINARY    :(ASMREAD_END)
ASMREAD    A = READ(CONTINUE) T                      :S(ASM_1)
           ASMREAD = READ(ORDINARY) T   :S(RETURN) F(FRETURN)
ASM_1      A = READ(CONTINUE16) A T                  :S(ASM_1)
           A = READ(ORDINARY16) A T                  :F(RETURN)
           ASMREAD = A                               :(RETURN)
ASMREAD_END
```

9.7 (a)   S POS(C - 1) LEN(L) . A = LPAD(TRIM(A),L)

(b) To convert X's in S to number pairs write:

```
LOOP    S BREAK('X') @K SPAN('X') . X @L        :F(DONE)
        PAIRS = PAIRS '(' N + K ',' SIZE(X) ')'
        N = N + L                               :(LOOP)
DONE
```

The rest is straightforward.

9.9 (a)
```
          PEEL.K2. = POS(0) TAB(*K1.) (ANY(AFTER) @K2. |
+         LEN(1) FASTBAL(,'"' "'", BEFORE AFTER)
+         (@K2. ANY(BEFORE) | ANY(AFTER) @K2.)
+         | REM @K2.)
```

(b) Make AFTER, BEFORE and C temporaries to PEEL. Define PEEL.K2. with unevaluated expressions *AFTER and *BEFORE in place of AFTER and BEFORE respectively. Replace the branch to

Solutions for Chapter 10   Page 449

PEEL_1 in the first statement of PEEL to PEEL_3; also change
the branch to ERROR by a branch to PEEL_3. PEEL_3 is defined
as:
```
PEEL_3    K1. = 0
          ':  ,)>'    BEFORE   LEN(1) . C          :F(ERROR)
          BEFORE   =  BEFORE   C
          '=  ,(<'    AFTER    LEN(1) . C
          AFTER    =  AFTER    C                   :(PEEL_1)
```

9.11
```
          NONID = NOTANY('ABCDEFGHIJKLMNOPQRSTUVWXYZ0123456789_.')
L1        X  =  SNOREAD()                          :F(END)
L2        X  (NONID ARBNO('_.')) . N  'ALPHA(' =
+                               N  'ALPHANUMERIC(' :S(L2)
          SNOPUT(X)                                :(L1)
END
```

==
==================== Solutions   ====================
==================== for   ====================
==================== Chapter 10   ====================
==

10.1 In the line after BNORM_1 change the go-to field to
:(FRETURN)S(RETURN) and in the line labeled BNORM_UNB change
the go-to field to :(FRETURN).

10.3 If there is an inversion then the spacing between the
two characters must be ≤ -2. But no string can have a spacing
this negative unless it contained a double BSPACE.

10.5
```
          NB  =  NOTANY(BSPACE)
          INORM(S1)    (POS(0) | NB)   INORM(S2)    (NB | RPOS(0))
```

10.7
```
          PR_POS  =  POS(0) @N BREAK(BSPACE) @N FAIL  |
+                    POS(0) *NE(N,0) TAB(*(N - 1)) . S1
+                    (LEN(1) ARBNO(BSPACE LEN(1)) . C1
+                    (NOTANY(BSPACE) | RPOS(0)) . C
```

10.9 (a) Change the line UF1 = LT(UF1,0) -UF1
             to UF1 = LT(UF1,0) (-2 * UF1)
(b) Modify
```
          UF1  =  CW - W
          UF1  =  LT(UF1,0)  -UF1
          UF1  =  UF1 + SIZE(HYPHEN)
```
to
```
          UF1  =  UF_P * (CW - W)
          UF1  =  LT(UF1,0) - (UF_C * (UF1 / UF_P))
          UF1  =  UF1 + UF_H * SIZE(HYPHEN
```

Page 450   SOLUTIONS

10.11

| | (a) | (b) |
k =	value HYPHEN	value HYPHEN
2	4 -	9 null
4	8 -	9 null
6	8 -	9 null
8	fails not set	9 null

10.13
```
Replace     DIGRAMS    =   'XA,¬(@)B, ...
by          DIGRAMS    =   'XE,¬(@FHSY)T ...

Replace     DIGRAM_TBL =   TABLE(30)
by          DIGRAM_PAT =   ABORT

Replace     DIGRAM_TBL<C> = ANY(CC)
by          DIGRAM_PAT =   C FENCE ANY(CC) | DIGRAM_PAT
```
In the pattern HYPH_PAT:
```
Replace     FENCE  ARB  LEN(1) $ C ...
by          @K  ABORT


Replace     RWORD  HYPH_PAT                       :F(FRETURN)
by
            RWORD     HYPH_PAT                    :S(HYPH_3)
HYPH_2      K = K + 1  LT(K, SIZE(RWORD) - 1)     :F(FRETURN)
            RWORD  TAB(K - 1)  DIGRAM_PAT         :F(HYPH_2)
HYPH_3
```

10.15
(a)
```
         DEFINE('PRIMAGE(S) I')
         OUTPUT(.OVER, ... )                      :(PRIMAGE_END)
PRIMAGE     OUTPUT  =  IMAGE(S,1)
            OVER    =  IMAGE(S,0)
PRIMAGE_1   I       =  I + 1
            OVER    =  IMAGE(S,I + 1)             :S(PRIMAGE_1) F(RETURN)
PRIMAGE_END
```

(b)
```
         S1 = BNORM(S1)  ;  S2 = BNORM(S2)
         PRIMAGE(DUPL(' ',9) S1 DUPL(' ',50 - SPACING(S1)) S2)
```

10.17
```
         P = BNORM(P)
         LINE_INIT(P)
LOOP     LENGTHS    BREAK(',') . CW  ','  =         :F(DONE)
         PRIMAGE(DUPL(' ', (60 - CW) / 2) LINE(CW))  :(LOOP)
```

10.19
```
L        S  '**' ('(' BAL . K ')' | LEN(1) . K)
+           = DUPL(' ', SIZE(K)) DUPL(BSPACE, SIZE(K))  K
+                                                :S(L)
         S = BNORM(S)
```

```
              OUTPUT   =   IMAGE(S,2)
              OUTPUT   =   IMAGE(S,1)
```

==
====================   Solutions   =====================
====================   for   =====================
====================   Chapter 11   =====================
==

11.1 a-No, b-No, c-Yes, d-Yes, e-Yes, f-Yes, g-No

11.3 a-1, b-3, c-3, d-2, e-0, f-3, g-4, h-2, i-0

11.5 '   I_ = 0'

11.7 Recursive: $F(1) = .164$, $F(n) = .140n + .006$
Iterative: $F(1) = .126$, $F(n) = .096n + .030$

11.9
```
              OPSYN('CODE.','CODE')
              DEFINE('CODE(S)')                          :(CODE_END)
CODE               :<CODE.('    CODENO = &STNO + 1   :(CODE_1)')>
CODE_1   CODE  =   CODE.(S)                              :(RETURN)
CODE_END
```

11.11 Write a routine CAPTURE(T1,S1) which is called by TPROFILE upon entry as CAPTURE(TIME(), &LASTNO)

==
====================   Solutions   =====================
====================   for   =====================
====================   Chapter 12   =====================
==

12.1 (a-e) 38,11,86,-,24

12.3
```
              RADIX  =  0
              I  =  0
              FACTOR  =  1
LOOP     V    BREAK(',') . V1  LEN(1)  =              :F(DONE)
              RADIX  =  RADIX + 1
              FACTOR  =  FACTOR * RADIX
              I  =  V1 * FACTOR + I                    :(LOOP)
```

12.5 Add 1 to the number associated with the record 1, 2, 3, ..., n-1 to obtain
$$1 + 1*1! + 2*2! + 3*3! + \ldots + (n-1)*(n-1)!$$
Note that $k! + k*k! = (k+1)!$ so that the first two terms keep collapsing until only one term is left, viz. n!

12.7 1,0,null string, I

12.9 PERMUTATION(S, 6 * 5 * 4 * 3 * 2 - 1)

Page 452   SOLUTIONS

12.11 (a) The statements which need modification are:

         N = REMDR(I,RADIX)
         I = I / RADIX

(b) Perform 'short division' on the string. The function below will divide a string by an integer and return the quotient. R is a global variable set to equal the remainder.

```
           DEFINE('DIVIDE(S,I)')                    :(DIVIDE_END)
DIVIDE      R  =
DIVIDE_1    S   LEN(1)  .  T  =                     :F(RETURN)
            R  =  R T
            DIVIDE  =  DIVIDE  (R / I)
            R  =  REMDR(R, I)                       :(DIVIDE_1)
DIVIDE_END
```

So the two statements may be replaced with:
         I = DIVIDE(I,RADIX)
         N = R

12.13 After PERM_INIT insert the statement:

   (EQ(SIZE_A,1)   DEFINE('PERM(A)','PERM_F'))   :S(RETURN)

12.15
Change: SIZE_A = +PROTOTYPE(A)
To: SIZE_A = SIZE(G_S)

Change: SWAP(.A<AL>, .A<AL + D>)
To: G_S   POS(AL + D - 1) LEN(2) . T = REVERSE(T)

12.17 (a) 100,   (b) 20

12.19 (1) At the entry point, put in an explicit check for the null string in order to break recursion. (2) Obtain C from &ALPHABET as follows:
                   REVERSE(&ALPHABET) ANY(S) . C
(3) Remove the statement at REORDER_1 and shift the label to the next statement. (4) Remove the second parameter from the function definition and from the recursive call.

12.21 All reorderings. The function has no memory so that if it produced, say, 'ABBC' twice, as it would have to do if it produced all permutations of 'ABBC', then it would never produce anything else.

12.23 (a) P, (b) P, (c) I, (d) I.

===
==================== Solutions   ====================
====================   for   ====================
==================== Chapter 13   ====================
===

13.1 The 2 instructions starting with BSORT_2 constitute the inner loop. An improvement is to add an instruction
$$V1 = A<K>$$
and use V1 in place of A<K> in two places. This saves one array reference but adds an assignment statement; it is faster but just barely.

13.3 Replace the two RETURN's by transfers to HSORT_X. Then replace the two calls to HSORT by the following instructions:
```
          PUSH(I)   ;   PUSH(K)
          I  =  K + 1                        : (HSORT)
HSORT_X   N  =  POP()                        :F(RETURN)
          I  =  POP()                        : (HSORT)
```

13.5
```
            DEFINE('GRTH(X,Y)')
GRTH        GT(X,Y + R)              :S(RETURN) F(FRETURN)
GRTH_END
            I  =  MSORT(A,'GRTH')
            A  =  AI(A,I)
```

13.7 MSORT(A, 'LT')

13.9 Add one more alternand:
```
    SS_PAT = ... | RPOS(0) . T
```

13.11 Add the statement LSON(T) = NULL before LIN_1.

13.13 (a) $2(n+1)(1/2 + 1/3 + \ldots + 1/(n+1)) - 2n$
(b) $2 \ln 2 = 1.38$

===
==================== Solutions   ====================
====================   for   ====================
==================== Chapter 14   ====================
===

14.1 (a) MAX(X,Y) will fail if X < Y. (b) Append a semicolon (;) to the argument.

14.3 Change the :(RETURN) to :S(RETURN) and add the following two statements:
```
            OUTPUT = CODE
            CODE(LBL  '     :(FRETURN)')              : (RETURN)
```

14.5

```
        <Definition of LOADEX function>
                                            :(START)
L1      LOADEX('L1')                        :(L1)
L2      LOADEX('L2')                        :(L2)
           .
           .
           .
L100    LOADEX('L100')                      :(L100)
START
```

14.7 Makes no difference.

14.9 Replace
```
    PUSH(&ANCHOR) ... &ANCHOR = 0 ... &ANCHOR = POP() ...
by
    PUSH(&ARB) ... &ARB = &ARB ... &ARB = POP() ...
```

14.11
The names used by both packages to name identical operations must not be the same. Thus REDEFINE('+','CSUM(X,Y)') would be OK for complex sum, but not REDEFINE('+','SUM(X,Y)').

14.13
```
        DEFINE('F.(X)')
        OPSYN('F','F.')                     :(F_END)
F.      F = X                               :(RETURN)
F_END
```

14.15
```
        REDEFINE(' ', 'CAT(X,Y)')
           .
           .
           .
CAT     CAT = ¬XY() X * Y                   :S(RETURN)
        CAT = CAT.(X,Y)                     :(RETURN)
```

14.17
```
            OPSYN('OPSYN.','OPSYN')
            DEFINE('OPSYN(NAME1,NAME2)')
            OPSYN('DEFINE.','DEFINE')
            DEFINE.('DEFINE(PROTO,LBL) NM')
            DEFINE('FUNCTION(NAME)')
            FUNC_LIST = ',OPSYN.,OPSYN,DEFINE,'
                                            :(FUNCTION_END)
DEFINE      PROTO BREAK('(') . NM
            FUNC_LIST = FUNC_LIST NM ','
            DEFINE.(PROTO,LBL)              :(RETURN)

FUNCTION    FUNC_LIST ',' NAME ','          :S(RETURN) F(FRETURN)

OPSYN       FUNC_LIST = FUNC_LIST NAME1 ','
            OPSYN.(NAME1,NAME2)             :(RETURN)

FUNCTION_END
```

===
==================== Solutions   ====================
==================== for   ====================
==================== Chapter 15   ====================
===

15.1
```
              DEFINE('COMB(N,M)K')                  :(COMB_END)
COMB          COMB  =  1
COMB_1        EQ(K,M)                               :S(RETURN)
              K  =  K + 1
              COMB  =  COMB * ((N - M) + K) / K     :(COMB_1)
COMB_END
```

15.3 COMB(L,N) - 1

15.5 (a) DIFF   DIFF = SUM(X,MINUS(Y)) :(RETURN)   (b) 5

15.7 Before the first of the SPLITs insert
DIV = LE(SUBSTR(Y,1,1), 5)   X * 2 / Y * 2

15.9 X > Y / (CEIL(Z) + 1)

15.11 (a) E = e^2 / 2(e + 1)   (b) 5

15.13 A = 1, 2, 4, 5 (integers).

15.15 (a)
ASIN(X) = 2 * ASIN(SQRT((1 - SQRT(1 - X^2)) / 2))
(b) the same as the stopping criterion for SIN(A)

15.17 10^5

15.19
```
N  =  CONVERT(LOG(X,2), 'INTEGER') + 1
X  =  X / (2 ** N)
I  =  CONVERT(X * 2 ** 27, 'INTEGER')
```

15.21 The difficulty is that NAT_BASE is single precision. Replace the second occurrence of NAT_BASE by EXP(X / X).

===
==================== Solutions   ====================
==================== for   ====================
==================== Chapter 16   ====================
===

16.1 ID(RANDOM(0))

16.3 Let HA = LEN(5). Then the following statement will execute the deal.
RPERMUTE(DECK) HA . P1 HA . P2 HA . P3 HA . P4

16.5 The last one. Instead of assigning CODE(CODE) to a table, simply go to it. The first two statements could also be eliminated.

16.7 In general, any string not containing a balancing right bracket to a left bracket will cause looping. One example is '('. The cure is to prefix the pattern LEN(1) to LITERAL.TEXT.

16.9 Let %C be equivalent to C where C is some character. Thus %| is equivalent to | and %% is equivalent to %. Implementation is simple:
```
         LITERAL.TEXT = POS(0)  '%' LEN(1) . TEXT    |
+                      BREAK('<=(%')  . TEXT
```

16.11 The probability P must satisfy the equation: $2P = 1 + P^3$. The solutions to this equation are 1, .616, and -1.62. The value 1 is unsuitable because the situation is clearly worse than the case where it just barely halts. -1.62 is not a probability. Hence, by elimination, P = .616

16.13   (a)
```
LOOP     N = N + 1
         NUM = LT(RANDOM(),RANDOM() ** 2) NUM + 1.0
         OUTPUT = EQ(REMDR(N,100),0) N ': ' (NUM / N) :(LOOP)
```
(b) $\pm .94/SQRT(N)$

16.15 Replace the rule that begins 'OUTS = GT(' by simply the predicate to obtain the statement:
```
         GT(K,H(S))                                  :S(RS_OUT)
```
Then at RS_OUT insert:
```
RS_OUT   ADV = LT(RANDOM(),E) '123R'                 :S(RS_4)
         OUTS = OUTS + 1
         ...
```

16.17 In the program which follows, FORMAT will format a string for output; MIRIM will return the mirror image of any given sequence of positions and RSTEP will move half the dancers one random step forward making sure no conflicts occur among the dancers or their mirror images.
```
         DEFINE('FORMAT(S)C')                        :(FORMAT_END)
FORMAT   S LEN(1) . C =                              :F(RETURN)
         FORMAT = FORMAT ' ' C                       :(FORMAT)
FORMAT_END
         DEFINE('MIRIM(POS)')                        :(MIRIM_END)
MIRIM    MIRIM = REPLACE(POS,'ABCDEFGHIJKLMXYZ',
+                              'DCBAIHYFEMLKJZGX')   :(RETURN)
MIRIM_END
         DEFINE('RSTEP(CPOS) P,NPS,NP')
         NEXT_POS = 'A(ABEF) B(ABCF) E(AEFJX) F(ABEFJK) J(EJFKX) '
+                   'K(JFKXGL) X(EJXK) Y(KYL) '
         NEXT_POS = NEXT_POS MIRIM(NEXT_POS)         :(RSTEP_END)
RSTEP    CPOS LEN(1) . P =                           :F(RETURN)
         NEXT_POS P '(' ARB . NPS ')'
         NPS = RPERMUTE(NPS)
RSTEP_1  NPS LEN(1) . NP =                           :F(FRETURN)
```

```
               'XZ'     NP                                      :S(RSTEP_2)
               (RSTEP MIRIM(RSTEP))          NP                 :S(RSTEP_1)
RSTEP_2 RSTEP    =    RSTEP    NP                               :(RSTEP)
RSTEP_END
         OUTPUT   =    FORMAT('12345678')
         POS      =    'XXXX'
LOOP     OUTPUT   =    FORMAT(POS    MIRIM(POS))
         POS      =    RSTEP(POS)
         N    =   LT(N,100)    N + 1                            :S(LOOP)
END
```

==
=====================   Solutions   =====================
=====================   for   =====================
=====================   Chapter 17   =====================
==

17.1 Assume for the moment that ONEWAY maps integers to integers. The machine obtains a random number N1 and prints ONEWAY(N1). The player thinks of a number N2 and types it in. The machine initializes a random number generator with the sum N1 + N2. After the hand is completely over and before the start of a new deal, the machine prints out N1 which enables the player to check on the machine's honesty.

17.3 The game is ill-formed. From a decision graph standpoint there are an infinitude of nodes and every terminal state is avoided by A whose best interests lie in prolonging the game until B's wallet is exhausted.

17.5 Variables which can't be used are those indicated as temporary. They all begin with 'Q' so that programs using QUEST should avoid them. As a precaution to their forgetting, one can insert
```
         QN    POS(0)   'Q'                       :S(ERROR)
```
after label QUESTP_1.

17.7 After the check for '...' insert:
```
         QVP   POS(0)   LEN(1) .  QC1 '-'  LEN(1) . QC2  RPOS(0)
+                                                 :F(QUESTP_4)
               &ALPHABET    BREAK(QC1) BREAK(QS)  :F(FRETURN)
      REVERSE(&ALPHABET)    BREAK(QC2) BREAK(QS)  :F(FRETURN)
               EQ(SIZE(QS),1)               :S(QUESTP_3) F(FRETURN)
QUESTP_4
```

17.9 Replace J = 0 by LIST = MAX. Replace:
         J = J + 1   LT(J,MAX)
by
         LIST BREAK(,) . J , | (LEN(1) REM) . J =
As a matter of aesthetics, the name 'MAX' could be changed.

17.11 For both cases, 8 X 3 X 2 = 48

17.13 3 X 2 = 6

17.15 Add: EQ(V,1) :S(TTTM_4) immediately before TTTM_3.

17.17 Replace &ALPHABET by ORD_ALPHA which is defined as:

```
         FULL_DECK    LEN(13) . SA    LEN(13) . SB
+                     LEN(13) . SC    LEN(13) . SD
         ORD_ALPHA  = BLEND(BLEND(SA,SB),BLEND(SC,SD))
```

17.19
```
LOOP    H  =  VALS(RHAND(13,1))
        OUTPUT  =  4 * COUNT(H,'M')  +  3 * COUNT(H,'L')  +
+                  2 * COUNT(H,'K')  +      COUNT(H,'J')    :(LOOP)
```

17.21 The problem lies with the FLUSH test. It should properly go after the test for a full house. Thus 2H 2H 2H 3H 3H should be interpreted as a full house. The initial pairs test was inserted for speed. This could be left out simplifying the result.

17.23 Setting VALS = W V and doing a :(PR(2)) is good enough for a uniform distibution but won't distinguish between hands that contain the same pairs but differ in only the fifth card. Hence, replace the W V in the call to PR by the expression:
```
        BASEB(CONVERT((CONVERT(DECOMB(W V),'REAL') / COMB(13,2))
+             * 13 ** 2, 'INTEGER'), 13)
```

17.25 After HE_BETS insert:
```
             QUEST('How much? /BET(1...BET)')
```

===
====================   Solutions   =====================
====================   for   =====================
====================   Chapter 18   =====================
===

18.1 One method is to insert integers rather than strings into the table. Thus, instead of inserting '2F', insert BASE10('2F',16). Another, perhaps extreme, method is to combine all elements of a table into a long string and use pattern matching to extract an element.

18.3 PUNCH = CH(OP AC X A)   (Using Prog. 2.7).

18.5 The single quote (') cannot be used. The solution is to use the QUOTE function (Prog. 3.16).

18.7 Assuming CRNAME() returns a unique created name:
```
        IDTBL  =  TABLE()
        ...
        IDEN = ...   S('ID')
        ...
S_ID    T  =  POP()
        (DIFFER(IDTBL<T>) PUSH(IDTBL<T>))         :S(NRETURN)
        IDTBL<T>  =  CRNAME()
        PUSH(IDTBL<T>)                            :(NRETURN)
```

Solutions for Chapter 18

18.9
```
            Q   =   ''
L2          X   =   INPUT                        :F<CODE(S ' ;  :(DONE)')>
            X   '<' BREAK('>') . K '>' = K
            X   '::=' = ' = ' Q
L           X   '<' BREAK('>') . K '>' = Q ' *' K ' ' Q        :S(L)
            X   =   REPLACE(X,'|','<') Q
L1          X   '<' = Q ' | ' Q                                :S(L1)
            S   =   S X ';'                                    :(L2)
DONE
```

18.11
ALPHA(H) would be converted to ALPHA('').

18.13
```
            NLSTMT = '' . *PUSH()   BL
            STMT   = IFSTMT | ASGNSTMT | NLSTMT
```

18.15
Writing DNF is obvious. We then replace *E of ASGNSTMT by

(*E | *DNF('assignment operator (=)', 'EXPRESSION')

Replace the BOOL of IFSTMT by
(BOOL | *DNF('IF keyword', 'relation'))
etc.

18.17
```
ATREE = BREAK(':,') (',' | ':' SPAN('0123456789') $ N
+  ',' *EVAL(DUPL('*ATREE ',N)))
```

18.19
```
        POLISH 'COMMA:' SPAN('0123456789') . N ','
+       ARB_TREE . T 'COMMA:2' = 'COMMA:' (N + 1) T
```

18.21
At TR_REF, after extracting the ID, apply the predicate ATEST(ID). If this fails, branch to TR_FREF defined as follows.

```
TR_FREF      POLISH POS(0) 'COMMA:2,' =             :F(TR_FREF1)
             TR = TR TR() 'ARG,' POP() '//'  :(TR_FREF)
TR_FREF1     TR = TR TR() 'ARG,' POP() '//'
             TR = TR 'CALL,' ID ',,' PUSH(TEMP()) '//'
                                                    :(RETURN)
```

18.23
```
TU_ADD ;TU_MUL ;TU_FADD ;TU_FMUL
        ISREG(ARG1)                             :S(TU_SUB)
        R = ISREG(ARG2)                         :F(TU_SUB)
        OUTPUT = ' ' OP ' ' R ',' ADDR(ARG1)
        DEASSOC(R)
        STORE(R,ARG3)                           :(RETURN)
TU_SUB ;TU_DIV ;TU_FSUB ;TU_FDIV
```

18.25
(a) 3, (b) 6, (c) Returns the successor of a number.

18.27
#DEF,CS,<#DEF,S,#S;%1>;

APPENDIX

Cross-reference Listing of Functions

Program	Number	References	Is referenced by
AGT	3.13	UPLO	
AI	4.6	SEQ	FRSORT
AOPA	4.4	SEQ	
ARC	15.8	SQRT DEXP	
ASM	18.1	BASEB RPAD	
ASM360	8.11		
BAL	8.3		PEEL RSENTENCE GPM
BALREV	3.8	REVERSE	OR HYPHENATE
BASEB	2.4		ONEWAY ASM
BASE10	2.5		CH ONEWAY POKEV
BCD_EBCDIC	2.2		
BLANKS	18.3	DIFF	
BLEND	3.7		HEX LEXGT INORM ONEWAY

Cross-reference of functions   Page 461

Program	Number	References	Is referenced by
BNORM	10.1	REVERSE	INORM
			LINE
BREAKX	8.2		COUNT
			REPL
			IMAGE
			RCHAR
BRKREM	8.1	DIFF	
BSORT	13.1		
CARDPAK	17.5	RPERMUTE	POKEV
		ORDER	POKER
CATA	4.8	SEQ	
CEIL	15.5	DEXP	
CH	2.7	BASE10	
COMB	15.1		DECOMB
			POKEV
COPYL	5.8		
COUNT	3.4	BREAKX	CRACK
			SPACING
			MINP
			FRSORT
CRACK	4.1	COUNT	FRSORT
DAY	2.8		
DECOMB	15.2	COMB	POKEV
DEXP	14.1		CEIL
			TRIG
			ARC
			LOG
			RAISE
			PHRASE
			POL
DEXTERN	14.2		

Program	Number	References	Is referenced by
DIFF	3.10		SKIM LEXGT BRKREM INORM HYPHENATE BLANKS
FASTBAL	8.4		SNOREAD
FIND	4.5		
FLD	5.9		VISIT
FORTPUT	9.8	PUT	
FLOOR	15.4		
FORTREAD	9.2	READ	
FPROFILE	11.6	LPROG	
FRSORT	13.5	SKIM COUNT AI MSORT STRINGOUT CRACK SEQ	
FTRACE	14.3		
GPM	18.8	BAL PUSH POP	
HEX	2.6	BLEND	
HSORT	13.2	SWAP	
HYPHENATE	10.7	BALREV OR UPLO DIFF	LINE
IMAGE	10.8	SPACING BREAKX	
INFINIP	15.3	REDEFINE SWAP LPAD	

Cross-reference of functions

Program	Number	References	Is referenced by
INORM	10.2	BNORM ORDER BLEND DIFF	
INSERT	13.8		
INSERTB	13.10		
INSULATE	14.4	PUSH POP	
IP	12.6		MSORT
L_ONE	18.2	PUSH POP	TR
LAST	5.4		
LEXGT	3.12	BLEND UPLO DIFF	
LIKE	8.8		
LINE	10.3	REVERSE PAD SUBSTR MINP BNORM HYPHENATE	
LINEARIZE	13.9		
LOG	15.9	DEXP	RAISE
LPAD	3.2		PUT ONEWAY INFINIP
LPERM	12.5	REVERSE	
LPROG	11.5		FPROFILE TPROFILE

Program	Number	References	Is referenced by
LSORT	13.3		
MDY	2.9		
MFREAD	9.6		
MINP	10.6	SPACING COUNT	LINE
MSORT	13.4	IP	FRSORT
NOT	8.5	PUSH POP	
ONCE	8.6		
ONEWAY	16.4	LPAD BASEB RPERMUTE BASE10 BLEND	
OR	8.9	BALREV	HYPHENATE
ORDER	3.1		INORM CARDPAK POKEV PHYSICAL
PAD	10.4	SPACING REVERSE	LINE
PARAGRAPH	9.3	READ	
PEEL	9.9	BAL	SNOPUT
PERM	12.2	SWAP	
PERMS	12.3		
PERMUTATION	12.1		
PHRASE	16.1	DEXP RSENTENCE	STONE QUEST
PHYSICAL	14.6	REDEFINE ORDER	
PLI.STMT	8.10		

Cross-reference of functions

Program	Number	References	Is referenced by
POKER	17.7	QUEST SQRT POKEV CARDPAK	
POKEV	17.6	ORDER ROTATER REVERSE COMB BASE10 CARDPAK DECOMB	POKER
POL	18.4	DEXP PUSH POP	
POP	5.6		SCAN NOT INSULATE STATEF L_ONE POL TR GPM
PUSH	5.5		SCAN NOT INSULATE STATEF L_ONE POL TR GPM
PUT	9.7	LPAD RPAD	FORTPUT SNOPUT
QUEST	17.2	PHRASE	STONE POKER
QUOTE	3.16	REPL	RSELECT
RAISE	15.10	LOG DEXP	
RAMM	16.2	RANDOM	

Appendix A

Program	Number	References	Is referenced by
RANDOM	16.1		RAMM RPERMUTE RCHAR RSELECT RSEASON
RCHAR	16.5	RANDOM BREAKX	RWORD
READ	9.1		FORTREAD PARAGRAPH SNOREAD TREEREAD
READL	5.1		
READRL	5.2		
REDEFINE	14.5		INFINIP PHYSICAL
REORDER	12.4		
REPL	3.15	BREAKX	QUOTE STACK
RESOLUTION	11.1		TIMER TIMEGC
REVERSE	3.6		BALREV BNORM LINE PAD LPERM POKEV
REVL	5.3		
ROMAN	2.3		
ROTATER	3.5		POKEV
RPAD	3.3		PUT ASM
RPERMUTE	16.3	RANDOM	ONEWAY CARDPAK

Cross-reference of functions   Page 467

Program	Number	References	Is referenced by
RPOEM	16.9		
RSEASON	16.10	RANDOM	
RSELECT	16.7	QUOTE RANDOM	RSENTENCE
RSENTENCE	16.8	BAL RSELECT	RSTORY PHRASE
RSTORY	16.11	RSENTENCE	
RWORD	16.6	RCHAR	
SCAN	7.1	PUSH POP	
SEQ	4.3		AOPA AI TRUNC CATA FRSORT
SKIM	3.11	DIFF	FRSORT
SNOPUT	9.10	PUT PEEL	
SNOREAD	9.4	READ FASTBAL	
SPACING	10.5	COUNT	PAD MINP IMAGE
SPELL	2.10		
SQRT	15.6		TRIG ARC POKER
SSORT	13.7		
STACK	14.8	REPL	
STATEF	14.7	PUSH POP	

Program	Number	References	Is referenced by
STONE	17.3	QUEST PHRASE	
STRINGOUT	4.2		FRSORT
SUBSTR	3.9		LINE
SWAP	3.14		HSORT PERM INFINIP
SYSTEM	11.3		TIMER
TEST	8.7		
TICTACTOE	17.4		
TIMEGC	11.4	RESOLUTION	
TIMER	11.2	SYSTEM RESOLUTION	
TOP	5.7		TR
TPROFILE	11.7	LPROG	
TR	18.6	PUSH POP TOP L_ONE	
TREE	18.5		
TREEREAD	9.5	READ	
TRIG	15.7	SQRT DEXP	
TRUNC	4.7	SEQ	
TSORT	13.6		
TUPLE	18.7		
UPLO	2.1		HYPHENATE
VISIT	5.10	FLD	

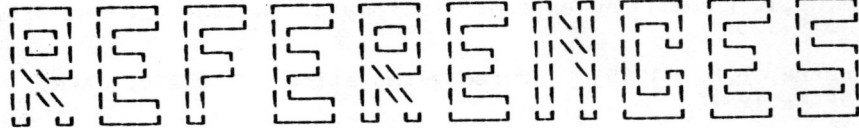

REFERENCES

Aberg, G. [1974] Computer program to add 'true randomness' into police patrol schedules. Computers & People, 23:1, 42-43.

Abrahams, P.W. [1974] Improving the control structure of SNOBOL4. Sig. Not., 9:5, 10-12.

ACM Forum [1974-1975] CACM, 17:9, 541-542 and CACM, 18:1, 63-64.

ACM Algorithm Letters [1966] CACM, 9:4, 243, and CACM, 9:9, 653-654.

Ahl, D.H. [1973] <u>101 BASIC Computer Games</u>. Software Distribution Center, Digital Equip. Corp., Maynard, Mass.

Aho, A.V., J.E. Hopcroft and J.D. Ullman [1974] <u>The Design and Analysis of Computer Algorithms</u>. Addison-Wesley, Reading, Mass.

Algorithms [1968] Index by subject to algorithms, 1960-1968. CACM, 11:12, 827-830.

Alt, F.L. [1972] Archaeology of computers. CACM, 15:7, 693-694.

AI Forum [1974] Sigart Newsletter, No. 45, ACM, New York, 3-5.

[ASCII] American Standard Code for Information Interchange. CACM, 6:8 (Aug. 1963), 422-426.

Ball, W.W. [1962] <u>Mathematical Recreations and Essays</u>. Revised by H. Coxeter, Macmillan, N.Y.

Barnard S. and J. Child [1955] <u>Higher Algebra</u>. MacMillan, London.

References

BB [1969] Baseball Encyclopedia. Macmillan, New York.

Beeler, M., R.W. Gosper and R. Schroeppel [1972] HAKMEM, A.I. Memo 239, AI Laboratory, MIT, Cambridge, Mass.

Blum, B.I. [1965] An extended arithmetic package. CACM, 8:5, 318-320.

Boonstra, B.H. [1965] Inverse permutation. Alg 250, CACM, 8:2, 104.

Canavos, G. [1967] A comparative analysis of two concepts in the generation of uniform pseudo-random numbers. Proceedings of the 22nd National Conference of the ACM, 485-502.

Collins, G.E. [1966] PM, a system for polynomial manipulation. CACM, 9:8, 578-589.

Crissman, P. [1962] CTSS Programmer's Manual. Continually updated from 1962-1967, MIT, Project MAC, Cambridge, Mass.

Coveyou, R.R. and R.D. MacPherson [1967] Fourier analysis of uniform random number generators. JACM, 14:1, 100-119.

Cutler, W.H. [1975] An optimal strategy for pot-limit Poker. To be published, Am. Math. Monthly.

de Bruijn, N.G. [1946] A combinatorial problem. Neder. Aked. Wetensch., 49, 758-764.

Dewar, R.B.K. [1971] SPITBOL Version 2.0. Document S4D23, Illinois Institute of Tech., Chicago, Ill.

Dijkstra, E.W. [1968] Goto statement considered harmful. Letter to the editor, CACM, 11:3, 147-148.

Dimsdale B. and H.M. Markowitz [1964] A description of the SIMSCRIPT language. IBM Systems Journal, 3:1, 57-67.

Donovan, J.J. [1972] Systems Programming. McGraw Hill, N.Y.

Dunn, R. [1973] SNOBOL4 as a language for bootstrapping a compiler. Sig. Not., 8:5, 28-32.

Duquet, R.T. [1970] Eliza in SNOBOL4. Sigplan Notices, 5:12, ACM, New York, 50-59.

Edmonds, J. and E.L. Johnson [1973] Matching, Euler tours and the Chinese postman. Math. Prog., 5:1, 88-124.

Epstein, R.A. [1967] The Theory of Gambling and Statistical Logic. Academic Press, N.Y.

Evans, A., W. Kantrowitz and E. Weiss [1974] A user authentication scheme not requiring secrecy in the computer. CACM, 17:8, 437-442.

Farber, D.J., R.E. Griswold and I.P. Polonsky [1964] SNOBOL, a string manipulation language. JACM, 11:1, 21-30.

------- [1966] The SNOBOL3 programming language. BSTJ, XLV:6, 895-944.

Feigenbaum, E.A. and J. Feldman [1963] <u>Computers and Thought</u>. McGraw-Hill, N.Y.

Feller, W. [1957] <u>An Introduction to Probability Theory and Its Applications</u>. John Wiley, N.Y.

Findler, N.V., et al [1972] Studies on decision making using the game of Poker. Information Processing, 71-North-Holland Publishing Company.

Floyd, R.W. [1964] Treesort3. Alg 245, CACM, 7:12, 701.

Flores, I. [1969] <u>Computer Sorting</u>. Prentice-Hall, Englewood Cliffs, N.J.

Fox, L. and I.B. Parker [1968] <u>Chebyshev Polynomials in Numerical Analysis</u>. Oxford Univ. Press, London.

Friend, E.H. [1956] Sorting on electronic computer systems. JACM, 3:3, 134-168.

Freiburghouse, R.A. [1969] The Multics PL/I compiler. AFIPS, FJCC, 35, 187-199.

Gimpel, J.F. [1971] The theory and implementation of pattern matching in SNOBOL4 and other programming languages. SNOBOL4 Document S4D24, Bell Laboratories, Holmdel, N.J.

Gimpel, J.F. [1972] A design for SNOBOL4 for the PDP-10. Document S4D29, Bell Laboratories, Holmdel, N.J.

Gimpel, J.F. [1972a] Blocks - A new datatype for SNOBOL4. CACM, 15:6, 438-447.

Gimpel, J.F. [1973] A theory of discrete patterns and their implementation in SNOBOL4. CACM, 16:2, 91-100.

Gimpel, J.F. [1973a] SITBOL - Version 3.0. Document S4D30b, Bell Laboratories, Holmdel, N.J.

Gimpel, J.F. [1974] Some highlights of the SITBOL language extensions to SNOBOL4. Sig. Not., 9:10, 11-20.

Goetz, M.A. [1965] Internal and tape sorting using the replacement selection scheme. CACM, 6:5, 201:206.

References

Good, I.J. [1946] Normal recurring decimals. J. London Math. Soc., 21, 169-172.

Graham, R.M. [1975] *Principles of Systems Programming*. John Wiley, N.Y.

Greenberger, M. [1961] Notes on a new pseudorandom number generator. JACM, 8:2, 163-167.

Gries, D. [1971] *Compiler Construction for Digital Computers*. Wiley, N.Y.

Griswold, R.E., J.F. Poage and I.P. Polonsky [1971] *The SNOBOL4 Programming Language*. Second Edition, Prentice-Hall, Englewood Cliffs, N.J.

Griswold, R.E. [1972] *The Macro Implementation of SNOBOL4*. Freeman, Chicago.

Griswold, R.E. [1974] Suggested revisions and additions to the syntax and control mechanisms of SNOBOL4. Sig. Not., 9:2, 7-23.

Griswold, R.E. [1974a] *String and List Processing in SNOBOL4*. Prenctice-Hall, Englewood Cliffs, N.J.

Hagelbarger, D.W. [1956] SEER - a sequence extrapolating robot. IRE - Trans on Elec Comp, EC-5:1, 1-7.

Hammersley, J.M. and D.C. Handscomb [1964] *Monte Carlo Methods*. Methuen & Co., London.

Hamming, R. [1962] *Numerical Methods for Scientists and Engineers*. McGraw Hill, New York.

Hanson, D.R. [1973] Correspondence to the Editor. Sig. Not., 8:8, 3-8.

Handbook [CR] *Handbook of Chemistry and Physics*. The Chemical Rubber Publ. Co., Cleveland, Ohio.

Handbook [NBS] *Handbook of Mathematical Functions*. Ed. by M. Abramowitz and I. Stegun, National Bureau of Standards, U.S. Government Printing Office, June, 1964.

Harrison, M.C. [1971] Implementation of the substring test by hashing. CACM, 14:12, 777-779.

Harrison, M.A. [1965] *Introduction to Switching and Automata Theory*. McGraw-Hill, N.Y.

Hastings, C. [1955] *Approximations for Digital Computers*. Princeton Univ. Press, Princeton, N.J.

Hays, D.G. [1967] *Computational Linguistics*. American Elsevier, New York.

References

Higman, B. [1967] *A Comparative Study of Programming Languages*. American Elsevier, New York.

Hoare, C.A.R. [1961] QUICKSORT and PARTITION. Algs 63 and 64, CACM, 4:7, 321.

Hoare, C.A.R. [1962] QUICKSORT. British Computer Journal, 5;1, 10-15.

IBM [1965] *Sorting Techniques*. Form C20-1639, IBM Data Processing Division, White Plains, New York.

IBM [360a] *IBM System/360 Principles of Operation*. Form A22-6821-6, IBM System Reference Library, Jan. 13, 1967.

IBM [360b] *IBM System/360 Operating System, Assembler Language*. File No. S360-21, Order No. GC28-6514-7, IBM Systems Reference Library, Dec. 1970.

IBM [360c] *IBM System/360 Operating System, Job Control Language*. Form C28-6539, IBM Systems Reference Library.

IBM [360d] *IBM System/360 Model 65 Functional Characteristics*. Form A22-6884-1, IBM Systems Reference Library.

IBM [360e] *System/360 Scientific Subroutine Package*. Form H20-0166-5, Aug. 1968, p 77.

IBM [360f] *Fortran IV Library Subprograms*. Form C28-6596, IBM Systems Reference Library, Oct, 1968.

IBM [360g] *IBM System/360 and System/370 FORTRAN IV Language*. File No. S360-25, Order No. GC28-6515-8, IBM Systems Reference Library, Dec. 1971.

Irwin, L. [1967] Implementing phrase structure productions in PL/I. CACM, 10:7, 424.

Knuth, D.E. [Vol. 1] *The Art of Computer Programming - Fundamental Algorithms*. Addison-Wesley, 1968.

Knuth, D.E. [Vol. 2] *The Art of Computer Programming - Seminumerical Algorithms*. Addison-Wesley, 1969.

Knuth, D.E. [Vol. 3] *The Art of Computer Programming - Sorting and Searching*. Addison-Wesley, 1973.

Knuth, D.E. [1971] An empirical study of Fortran programs. Software Practice & Exp., 1:2, 105-133.

Knuth, D.E. [1972] Ancient Babylonian algorithms. CACM, 15:7, 671-677.

Kruskal, J. [1969] Extremely portable random number generator. CACM, 12:2, 93:94.

References

Lawson, H.W. [1967] PL/I list processing. CACM, 10:6, 358-367.

Lee, C.Y., D.C. Leagus, H.M. Vellenzer, I.P. Polonsky, L.P. White and R.E. Griswold [1962] A language for symbolic communication. Bell Laboratories, Murray Hill, N.J.

Lehmer, D.H. [1951] Mathematical methods in large scale computing units. Ann Comp Lab, Harvard Univ, 26, 141-146.

Lehmer, D.H. [1964] The machine tools of combinatorics. in Applied Combinatorial Mathematics, E. Beckenback (Ed.), Wiley, N.Y.

Lorin, H. [1971] A guided bibliography to sorting. IBM System J, 10:3, 244-254.

Luce, R.D. and H. Raiffa [1958] Games and Decisions. Wiley, N.Y.

Lukasiewicz, J. [1951] Aristotle's Sylogistic From the Standpoint of Modern Formal Logic. Clavendon Press, Oxford England.

Maclaren, M.D. and G. Marsaglia [1965] Uniform random number generators. JACM, 12:1, 83-89.

Madnick, S.E. [1967] String processing techniques. CACM, 10:7, 420-424.

Markov, A.A. [1954] Theory of Algorithms. Academy of Sciences of the USSR, Moscow, Document TT 60-51085, National Tech Inf Services, Springfield, Va.

Marsaglia, G. and T.A. Bray [1968] One-line random number generators and their use in combinations. CACM, 11:11, 757-759.

McCarthy, J. [1960] Recursive functions of symbolic expressions and their computation by machine. CACM, 3:4, 184-195.

McClure, R. [1972] An appraisal of compiler technology. Spring Joint Comp. Conf., AFIPS, 1-9.

McIlroy, M.D. [1960] Macro instruction extensions of compiler languages. CACM, 3:4, 214-220.

McIlroy, M.D. [1971] Roff. Internal memorandum, Bell Laboratories, Murray Hill, N.J.

Medlock, C.W. [1965] Inverse Permutations. Remark on Alg 250, CACM, 8:11, 670.

Mendoza, E. [1968] in Computer poems and texts. in Cybernetic Serendipity, London, 53-62.

Milic, L.T. [1970] The possible usefulness of poetry generation. Internal report, Dept. of English, Cleveland St. Univ.

Milic, L.T. [1971] The RETURNER poetry program. Internal report, Dept. of English, Cleveland St. Univ.

Moore, F. [1974] PCC Games. People's Computer Co., 1921 Menalto Ave., Menlo Park, Calif.

Morley, S.G. [1956] The Ancient Maya. Third Ed., Revised by W. Brainerd, Stanford Univ. Press, Stanford, Calif., p 256.

Newell, A., and J.C. Shaw [1957] Programming the logic theory machine. Proceedings of the Western Joint Computer Conference, 1957, I.R.E., N.Y., 1957, 230-240.

Newell, A., Ed. [1967] Information Processing Language-V Manual. Prentice-Hall, Englewood Cliffs, N.J.

Ord-Smith, R.J. [1967] Remarks on: Algorithm 87, CACM, 10:7, 452.

Pager, D. [1970] A number system for the permutations. CACM, 13:3, 193.

Parnas, D.L. [1972] On the criterion to be used in decomposing systems into modules. CACM, 15:12, 1053-1058.

Peck, J.E.L. and G.F. Schrack [1962] Permute. Alg 86, CACM, 5:4, 208.

Pohl, I. [1967] Phrase structure productions in PL/I. CACM, 10:12, 757.

Purdy, G.B. [1974] A high-security log-in procedure. CACM, 17:8, 442-445.

Reed, S.L. [1967] TEXT360. Share Document 360D29.5.002.

Reza, F.M. [1961] An Introduction to Information Theory. McGraw Hill, N.Y.

Rich, R.P. and A.G. Stone [1965] Method for hyphenating at the end of a printed line. CACM, 8:7, 444-445.

Sagasti, F. and W. Page [1970] Computer choreography. Computer Studies, III:1, 46-49.

Saltzer, J. [circa 1964] TYPSET. Computer program, CTSS, Project MAC, MIT, Cambridge, Mass.

Samuel, A.L. [1959] Some studies in machine learning using the game of checkers. IBM Journal of R & D, 3 (July), 211-229. Also in Feigenbaum and Feldman [1963].

Santos, P. [1971] FASBOL, A SNOBOL4 Compiler. Memo No. ERL-M314, Electronic Research Lab., Univ. of Calif., Berkeley.

Scowan, R.S. [1965] QUICKERSORT. Alg 271, CACM, 8:11, 669-670.

Shell, D.L. [1959] A high speed sorting procedure. CACM, 3:1, 30-32.

Shell, D.L. [1971] Optimizing the polyphase sort. CACM, 14:11, 713-719.

Shen, M.K. [1963] Generation of permutations in lexicographical order. Alg 202, CACM, 6:9, 517.

Smith, L.D. [1955] *Cryptography.* Dover.

Sorting Issue [1963] CACM, 6:5.

Spencer, D. [1968] *Game Playing with Computers,* Spartan, N.Y.

Strachey, C. [1965] A general purpose macro generator. Comp. Journal, 8, 225-241.

Tantzen, R. [1963] Conversions between calendar date and Julian day number. Alg 199, CACM, 6:8, 444.

Tou, J.T. (Ed.) [1969] Proceedings of the Third Symposium on Computer and Information Sciences. Academic Press, 1971.

Trotter, H.F. [1962] PERM. Alg 115, CACM, 5:8, 435.

Tuggle, F.D., et al [1973] Computer solution of verbal analogy problems. Computer Studies, IV:2, 97-111.

Von Hagen, V.W. [1960] *World of the Maya.* Mentor, 199.

Wagner, M.R. [1971] The search for a simple hyphenation scheme. Internal Memorandum, Bell Laboratories, Murray Hill, N.J., June 29.

Weizenbaum, J. [1966] ELIZA--a computer program for the study of natural language communication between man and machine. CACM, 9:1 (Jan), 36-45.

Whitehead, E.G. Jr. [1973] *Combinatorial Algorithms.* Courant Institute Lecture Notes, New York Univ., N.Y.

Wilkes, M.V. [1972] *Time-Sharing Computer Systems.* American Elsevier, N.Y.

Woodrum, L.J. [1969] Internal sorting with minimal comparing. IBM Syst J, 8:3, 189-203.

Yngve, V.H. [1962] COMIT as an IR Language. CACM, 5:1, 19-28.

Yngve, V.H. [1962a] Random generation of English Sentences. 1961 International Conference of Machine Translation and Applied Language Analysis, London, Vol. I, 66-80.

Yngve, V.H. [1974] COMIT. in Encyclopedia of Computer Science and Technology, J. Belzer, A.G. Holzman and A. Kent (Eds.), Marcel Dekker, New York, in press.

Yngve, V.H. [1975] Introduction to Human Linguistics. Notes from a book in progress.

Zassenhaus, H.J. [1958] The Theory of Groups. Chelsea, New York, p 16. f

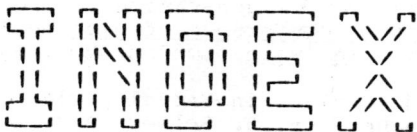

INDEX

Aberg, G.: 342
ABORT: 104
abort symbol: 104
ABORT, difficulty with: 17
Abrahams, P.W.: 15
ACOS: 333, 339
acreage: 310
active information: 276
AGT: 55
Ahl, D.H.: 375
Aho, A.V.: 2
AI: 75, 284
AI FORUM: 368
ALGOL: 183
algorithm: 2
Allen, D.: 337
allocation of registers: 429
ALPHABET: 24, 30, 31, 54
Alt, F.L.: 4
alternate pattern: 123
alternation: 102
analogy problem: 368
anatomy of a processor: 230
anatomy of a SNOBOL4 statement: 237
ANCHOR: 19, 305
AOPA: 72, 77
APL: 18, 72
ARB: 103, 131
ARB_TREE: 425
ARBNO
  definition: 107, 143
  implementation: 135, 143
  ,negative: 119
ARC: 333, 340
arithmetic in SNOBOL4: 319
arithmetic timings: 237
array: 293
  functions: 63
  representation: 66
  ,sorting an: 279, 280, 284
arrays

,initialization of: 76
,permutation of: 259
,truncation of: 75
ASCII: 24
ASIN: 333
ASM: 408, 436, 440
ASM360: 147, 159
assembler: 224
  for machine M: 408
  source, processing: 159
assignment timings: 237
associated linear pattern: 109, 119
associated nonlinear pattern: 109
ATAN: 333
average, error of: 362

B-normal form: 192, 204
B-normalization: 191, 192, 208-9, 218
backup-free scanning: 108, 119, 159
Backus Normal Form: 355, 411
BAL function: 148, 151, 163
BAL pattern: 134, 142, 243
balanced
  (by spacing): 192
  binary tree: 290
  on the left: 191
  on the right: 192
  string, parenthetically: 134, 149
  ,right-: 218
Ball, W.W.: 375, 401
BALREV: 51
base conversions: 27
base of a real number: 325
BASEB: 27, 38, 322
baseball lineup: 360
BASE10: 27, 38, 322
BB: 360

Index

BCD: 25
BCD_EBCDIC: 25, 46, 61
Beeler, M.: 335
binary
  search: 276
  tree: 294
  tree, balanced: 290
binomial coefficient: 319
bins test: 346
BLANKS: 417, 418, 436
blanks, ambiguous use of: 16
BLEND: 31, 50, 58, 77
block: 216
block structure: 14
Blum, B.I.: 322
BNF: 355, 411, 436
BNORM: 191, 218, 249
Boesch, F.: viii
boldface: 200
Boonstra, B.H.: 270
Bosack, L.: viii
brand-name generation: 352, 356
BREAK 44: 43
break-point
  determination: 182
  of a paragraph: 203
  ,natural: 204
BREAKX: 43, 148, 151, 162, 162, 165
British system (of illions): 39
BRKREM: 147, 162
BRKXREM: 162
Brophy, F.: viii
BSORT: 279, 292, 298
BSPACE: 189, 233
bubble sort: 279
buckets: 224

calendar, Gregorian: 32
Canavos, G.: 344
cancellative, left: 117
cancellative, right: 117
canonical form of patterns: 106
CARDPAK: 391, 403
caretaker routine: 429
CATA: 76
CEIL: 327
CENTER: 58
CH: 31, 59, 61
chain: 284
character
  ,pivotal: 266
  ,position: 192

,random: 350
,replacement: 266
Chebyshev approximation: 328
Chebyshev polynomials: 328
Checker-playing program: 386
Chen, S.: viii
chess: 376
chi-square formula: 346
children's game: 364
Churchill: 11
cipher: 59
  ,one-way: 348, 376, 400
  ,transpositional: 59
co-routines: 310
COBOL: 176
CODE: 372
code
  creation: 314
  optimization, machine-
    dependent: 425
  optimization, machine-
    independent: 438
CODENO: 253
cogets: 321
collection, garbage: 93, 229
Collins, G.E.: 322
COMB: 319, 337
combinatorial number system: 320
combinatorial pattern matching: 337
COMIT: 6, 7
comparison sorting: 276, 277
compiler: 224
  ,partitioning of a: 415
  ,phases of a: 418
  ,tree adjustment phase of
    a: 424
  ,type-0: 227
  ,type-1: 227
  ,type-2: 227
  ,type-3: 228
  ,type-4: 228
compilers, types of: 226, 251
compiling
  in SNOBOL4: 411
  using pattern matching: 406
  ,error messages in: 438
complex numbers: 315
compound patterns: 131
concatenation of patterns: 103
concealed game: 375
concordance, word: 295
concrete formal systems: 412
confidence interval, 95%: 363

configurations: 80
 ,copying of: 98
 ,isomorphism of: 98
control structures: 12
conversions: 22
converting from infix to
    Polish prefix: 421
COPY function: 66
copying of configurations: 98
COPYL: 90, 97, 230
correlation test: 346
COUNT: 43, 57, 210, 403
Coveyou, R.R.: 347
CR: 332
CRACK: 69, 76, 97
cursor: 101
  position: 101
  ,post-: 101
  ,pre-: 101
Cutler, W.H.: 394

dance, random: 372
DAY: 32, 39
decision
  graph: 377
  graph for the stone game: 381
  tree: 376
  tree for the stone game: 381
  tree for tick-tack-toe: 386
DECOMB: 320, 392
decomposition of a rule: 162
derived pattern: 126, 143, 144
descriptor: 66
Dewar, B.: viii
Dewar, R.B.K.: 11, 223, 417
DEXP: 302, 314
DEXTERN: 303, 315
Dickman: 305
DIFF: 52
digram: 212
Dijkstra, E.W.: 17
Dimsdale, B.: 169
DISPLAY: 97
distinguishability, of strings: 200
distribution function: 369
distributive sorting: 276, 298
DIV: 338
DO-loop: 71, 78
Donovan, J.J.: 410, 411
DREAL: 327, 340
DUMP convention: 21

Dunn, R.: 12
Duquet, R.T.: 375
Dwyer, T.: viii
dynamic loading of programs: 303

EBCDIC: 24, 25, 200
Edmonds, J.: 3
ELIZA: 375
English letter frequency: 165, 219
ENIAC: 4
Epstein, R.A.: 392
equality of patterns: 102
ERROR label: 21
error messages in compiling: 438
estimation of error: 362
Euler: 3
Evans, A.: 350
excess notation: 326
EXP: 336, 340
exponent: 325
exponentiation: 220
extended sequence: 104, 117
external sorting: 275
EXXON: 352

factorial number system: 257
Farber, D.J.: 7
FASBOL: 11, 148, 406
FASTBAL: 151, 163, 187
Feller, W.: 357, 362
FENCE: 105
FENCE, difficulty with: 17
FIND: 73, 77
Findler, N.V.: 394
finite patterns: 104
FIRST: 163
fixed storage: 252
FLD: 92
floating point number: 38
floating storage: 229, 252
FLOOR: 327, 338
FLOORCEIL: 327
Flores, I.: 276
flow-of-control timings: 240
Floyd, R.W.: 292
foibles of SNOBOL4: 11
formatting, paragraph: 232
FORTPUT: 181
Fortran: 5, 18, 60, 169, 181, 183, 327, 375, 416, 436
Fortran, OS/360: 419
FORTREAD: 168, 185
four-tuple: 417

four-tuples: 426
Fox, L.: 329
FPROFILE: 247
frequency
  profile: 247
  sort: 287
  ,English letter: 165, 219
Friend, E.H.: 276
FRSORT: 287
FTRACE: 174, 304
FULLSCAN: 13, 19, 127
function
  definition: 15
  definition facility in SNOBOL4: 302
  functions: 301
  predicate: 316
  ,sine: 332
functions, trigonometric: 332
futility: 13
FUTILITY flag: 133, 142
futility heuristic: 127, 143, 243

game
  theory: 390
  ,children's: 364
  ,concealed: 375
  ,open: 375
  ,random: 372
  ,zero-sum: 390
games: 374
garbage collection: 93, 229
garbage collection timing: 244
Gaussian distribution: 363
GBAL primitive: 134, 243
Gimpel, J.F.: 11, 15, 216, 223
Gosper, R.W.: 335
goto controversy: 18
GPM: 432, 440
Graham, R.M.: 411
graph, decision: 377
Greenberger, M.: 344
Gregorian calendar: 32
Gries, D.: 411, 427
Griswold, R.: viii
Griswold, R.E.: 2, 10, 12, 223, 406
Guthrey, kS.: viii

Hagelbarger, D.W.: 376
hand evaluation for poker: 392
Hanson, D.: viii

Hanson, D.R.: 12
hard blanks: 204
Harrison, M.A.: 388
Harrison, M.C.: 9
hash number: 249
hashing: 224
Hastings, C.: 328, 329
heuristic
  ,futility: 127, 143, 243
  ,length-checking: 127
  ,POS: 243
  ,recursive reduction: 115, 131, 138
  ,start-up: 127
heuristics: 127
  ,obtrusive: 127
  ,unobtrusive: 127
HEX: 30, 38, 46, 61
high-level language: 223
history stack: 135, 149
Hoare, C.A.R.: 280
homomorphic: 199
homomorphism: 46, 61, 311, 416
hop-around convention: 20
HSORT: 280, 292, 299
HYPHENATE: 157, 211, 219
hyphenating suffix: 211

I-normalization: 198
I/O timing: 243
IBM
  1403: 30
  360: 9, 10, 11, 23, 25, 30, 223, 258, 319, 331
  360 timings: 237
  7090: 7
IBM360a: 23, 25
IBM360b: 156, 185
IBM360c: 186
IBM360f: 329
IBM360j: 419
idempotent pattern: 116
identity permutation: 273
IF: 163
IFFLD: 97
image: 199, 215
Image normalization: 198
implementation of patterns: 121
implementation, recursive pattern: 137
implicit alternative: 102
implicit alternatives: 148
INCREMENT: 78
INFINIP: 322, 338

Index

infinite patterns: 104
information theory: 277
inhibiting suffix: 211
initialization of arrays: 76
initialization section: 20
INORM: 191, 219
INPUT/OUTPUT: 166
INPUT/OUTPUT, difficulty
    with: 15
INSERT: 293, 300
INSERTB: 295, 300
insertion sorting: 292
INSULATE: 305, 315
interchange sorting: 279
internal sorting: 275, 276
interpreter: 224
interpreter, pure: 227
inverse, permutation: 258, 269
inversion of equal elements: 282
IPL: 5
isomorphism of configura-
    tions: 98

JCL: 182
JCLREAD: 186
Jensen: 305
Johnson, E.L.: 3
JUSTIFY flag: 202

k-transformation: 47
Knuth, D.E.: 2, 257, 270, 276, 277, 310, 322, 338, 344, 347, 368
Kruskal, J.: 346

L_ONE: 89, 413, 421, 436, 439
L_2: 421
L_1: 411, 436
L^6: 232
lake: 208, 211
language
  clutter: 17
  , high-level: 223
  , tuple: 426
LAST: 87, 97
last element of a list: 87
LBOUNDS: 78
leading 0's: 60
Lee, C.Y.: 6
left
  cancellative: 117
  recursion: 114, 436
  zero: 116
Lehmer, D.H.: 322

length failure: 127
length-checking heuristic: 127
Lewart, kC.: viii
LEXGT: 54
lexical
  analysis: 227, 415
  analyzer: 311
  comparison: 60
  ordering: 54
LGT: 54, 155
LIKE: 156, 163
LINE: 202, 219
linear pattern, associated: 109
linear search: 276
LINEARIZE: 295, 300
lines of a paragraph: 202
lineup, baseball: 360
LISP: 6, 175, 227
list: 293
List processing: 79
list
  , last element of a: 87
  , reversing a: 87
  , sorting a: 282
lists, reading of: 86
LOADEX: 303, 315
LOG: 334, 339, 340
logarithmic growth: 276
logarithmic sorting: 279
Lorin, H.: 276
LPAD: 43, 57
LPERM: 266
LPROG: 247, 253
LSORT: 232, 282

machine M: 407
machine M, assembler for: 408
machine-dependent code op-
    timization: 425
machine-independent code
    optimization: 438
MacLaren, M.D.: 347
MacPherson, R.D.: 347
macro call: 433
macro system: 432
Madnick, S.E.: 8
MAINBOL: 10, 223, 226, 229, 233, 237
mantissa: 325
marking phase: 93
Markov languages: 6
Markowitz, H.M.: 169
Marsaglia, G.: 347
MAX: 314

Mayan Indians: 27, 37
McCarthy, J.: 6, 227
McClure, R.: 411, 417
McIlroy, M.D.: 211, 432
MDY: 34, 39
mean: 362
Medlock, C.W.: 270
Mendoza, E.: 359, 364
merge sorting: 282
MFREAD: 178
Milic, L.T.: 358, 359
minimax process for game
 playing: 377
MKS system: 308
modulus: 344
 , natural: 344
 , prime: 344
monic pattern: 106
Monte Carlo technique: 371
Morley, S.G.: 32
morpheme: 416
MSORT: 284, 299
Multi-file reading: 178
multiplier: 344
musical scale: 40

name-list stack: 136
natural break-point: 204
natural modulus: 344
NBS: 329, 332
Needham: 348
negative ARBNO: 119
neutral suffix: 212
New York Yankees: 360
Newton's method: 330, 339
nil pattern: 131
Nim: 401
Noll, J.C.: viii
nome: 320
nonlinear pattern, as-
 sociated: 109
nonlinear patterns: 104
normal form, B-: 192, 204
normalization
 , B-: 191, 192, 208-9, 218
 , I-: 198
 , Image: 198
NOT: 112, 153
Novodvorskii: 329
number system, combinatorial:
 320
number system, positional: 27

obtrusive heuristics: 127
ONCE: 154, 163

one-character assumption: 13,
 131, 139, 155, 258
one-way cipher: 348, 376, 400
ONE_POS: 194-196
ONEWAY: 348, 376
OPA: 77
open game: 375
optimal poker strategy: 394
OR: 59, 157, 164, 214
Ord-Smith, R.J.: 266
ORDER: 42, 403
OS/360: 34
 assembler: 156
 assembly language: 185
 Fortran: 419
overstriking: 190

PAD: 208, 219
Page, W.: 372
Pager, D.: 257
PARAGRAPH: 170, 185
paragraph formatting: 188,
 232
paragraph, lines of a: 202
parenthetically balanced
 string: 134, 149
Parker, I.B.: 328, 329
Parnas, D.L.: 429
parsing: 411
partitioning of a compiler:
 415
Pascal's triangle: 319
passive sorting information:
 275
password protection: 348
path diagram: 124, 140
pattern
 building: 13
 matching a tree: 438
 matching, combinatorial:
 337
 matching, compiling using:
 406
 matching, difficulties in:
 12
Pattern Theory: 99
pattern-building timings: 241
pattern-matching timings: 242
pattern/152, SNOARG: 151
pattern
 , alternate: 123
 , associated linear: 119
 , definition of: 101
 , derived: 126
 , idempotent: 116
 , monic: 106

,nil: 131
,root of a: 123
,subsequent: 123
,varying: 102
patterns
  ,canonical form of: 106
  ,compound: 131
  ,concatenation of: 103
  ,equality of: 102
  ,finite: 104
  ,infinite: 104
  ,nonlinear: 104
  ,primitive: 122
  ,recursive: 112, 144
  ,representation of: 140
PDP-10: 223, 233, 375
Peck, J.E.L.: 262
PEEL: 182, 186, 187
penny-matching: 376
PERM: 258, 259, 271, 272
PERMS: 261, 272
permutation: 50, 258, 271, 277, 320, 322
  inverse: 258, 269
  number: 257, 270, 271
  of arrays: 259
  of strings: 261
  record: 256, 270
  vector: 258, 273, 277, 284
  ,identity: 273
permutations: 255
phases of a compiler: 418
phoneme: 416
PHRASE: 377, 401
PHYSICAL: 308, 316
physical arithmetic: 308
piglatin: 47
Pinsker: 329
pivotal character: 266
PL/I: 9, 52, 72, 159, 176, 183, 327, 415, 417, 421
  comment: 153
  comments: 109
Playboy: 220
PLI.STMT: 159, 164
plug boards: 4
Pohl, I.: 357
POKER: 394, 404
poker strategy, optimal: 394
poker, hand evaluation for: 392
POKEV: 392, 403, 404
POL: 421, 436, 438, 439
Polish
  notation: 122, 175
  prefix: 227, 417

prefix, converting from infix to: 421
prefix, form of: 421
suffix: 227, 228, 230
Polonsky, I.: viii
polynomials, Chebyshev: 328
POP: 89, 97, 299, 305, 313
portable generator: 346
POS heuristic: 243
position character: 192
position number: 192
positional number system: 27, 37
positional transformation: 47, 58, 261, 262
post-cursor: 101
pre-cursor: 101
pre-processing stage: 189
precedence anomalies: 17
PRECISION: 329
prefix: 191
PRIMAGE: 220
prime modulus: 344
prime-primitive pairs: 344
primitive
  element: 344
  matches: 141
  patterns: 122
processing assembler source: 159
processor, anatomy of a: 230
profile, frequency: 247
profile, time: 231, 232, 248
program library: 304
programs: 2
programs, dynamic loading of: 303
PROTOTYPE function: 66
pseudo-random: 343
Purdy, G.B.: 350
pure interpreter: 227
PUSH: 78, 89, 97, 299, 313, 414
PUT: 180

quadratic sort: 296
quadratic sorting: 279
QUEST: 379, 401, 403
quick and dirty sort: 292
QUICKSCAN: 114, 127
QUOTE: 57, 61, 62

radix sort: 298
.RAISE: 336, 340
RAMM: 347, 347
RANDOM: 340, 343, 369, 371

random
　character: 350
　compliment: 377
　dance: 372
　game: 372
　insult: 377
　names: 352
　poetry: 358
　selection: 342
　sentence: 354
　stories: 364
　string: 353
　strings: 342
　word: 352
range of real numbers: 326
RCHAR: 350, 370
READ: 167, 178, 185
reading of lists: 86
reading, Multi-file: 178
READL: 86
READRL: 86
real numbers: 325
recursion stack: 149
recursion, left: 114
recursive
　pattern implementation: 137
　pattern, returning a: 150
　patterns: 112, 144
　reduction heuristic: 115, 131, 138
REDEFINE: 305
redefining functions: 95
redefinition of operators and functions in SNOBOL4: 305
registers, allocation of: 429
removing blanks from Fortran: 418
REORDER: 264, 272
reordering: 256, 264
REPL: 56, 314
REPLACE function: 25
replacement character: 266
representation
　of a tree: 417
　of patterns: 140
　of strings: 42
　of structures: 80-85
　of trees: 174
　,array: 66
RESOLUTION: 234, 252
returning a recursive pattern: 150
REVERSE: 45, 57
reversing a list: 87
REVL: 269
Reza, F.M.: 277

Rich, R.P.: 211
right cancellative: 117
right-balanced: 218
river: 208, 211
Rochkind, M.: viii
Rochkind, M.J.: 413
Roff: 211
ROMAN: 25, 61
root of a pattern: 123
root of tree: 173
ROTATER: 43, 57
ROUND: 338
routine, caretaker: 429
RPAD: 43, 57
RPERMUTE: 348
RPHONE: 370
RPOEM: 358
RSEASON: 360, 372
RSELECT: 57, 353, 370
RSENTENCE: 354, 371
RSTORY: 364, 373
rule, decomposition of a: 162
runs test: 346
RWORD: 352

s-vacancy: 123
Sagasti, F.: 372
Saltzer, J.: 200
Samberg, L.: viii
sample space: 342
Samuel, A.L.: 386
Santos, P.: 11
SCAN: 126
scanning: 107
scanning, backup-free: 108
Schrack, G.F.: 262
SCL: 6
Scowen, R.S.: 280
search, binary: 276
search, linear: 276
SEER: 376
selection sorting: 286
semantic routine: 412, 436
SEQ: 71, 76, 77, 258
set of strings model: 100
set operations: 52, 60
Shell sort: 292
Shen, M.K.: 266
short sort: 292
Siegel, M.: 46
SIGN: 302
simple sort: 292
SIMSCRIPT: 169
simulation: 360
SIN: 339
sine function: 332

Index

SITBOL: 11, 12, 52, 148, 223, 229, 230, 231, 406
SITBOL, decomposition of: 231
SKIM: 53, 60
SNOARG pattern/152: 151
SNOBOL3: 7, 229
SNOBOL4: 237
  statement, anatomy of a: 237
  ,arithmetic in: 319
  ,compiling in: 411
  ,function definition facility in: 302
  ,redefinition of operators and functions in: 305
SNOBOL4B: 216
SNOPUT: 187
SNOREAD: 171, 187
sort
  ,frequency: 287
  ,quadratic: 296
  ,quick and dirty: 292
  ,radix: 298
  ,Shell: 292
  ,short: 292
  ,simple: 292
  ,tournament: 286, 289
sorting: 274
  a list: 282
  an array: 279, 280, 284
  an array of structures: 289
  ,comparison: 276, 277
  ,distributive: 276, 298
  ,external: 275
  ,insertion: 292
  ,interchange: 279
  ,internal: 275, 276
  ,logarithmic: 279
  ,merge: 282
  ,quadratic: 279
  ,selection: 286
  ,table: 289
space, more of: 303
spacing: 191, 209
SPANULL: 162
SPELL: 35, 39
Spencer, D.: 371, 375
SPITBOL: 11, 12, 52, 148, 223, 228, 229, 233, 237, 253, 319, 327, 338, 406, 417
SQRT: 330, 339
SSORT: 292, 299, 300
STACK function: 313
stack
  operations: 89

,history: 135, 149
,name-list: 136
,recursion: 149
standard deviation: 363
start-up heuristic: 127
state function: 312
state functions: 310
STATEF: 312, 316
Stirling: 277
stochastic strings: 341
STONE: 381, 402
stone game, decision graph for the: 381
stone game, decision tree for the: 381
Stone, A.G.: 211
Stone, D.: viii
storage requirments: 246
stored-program machines: 406
Strachey, C.: 432, 440
string
  functions: 41
  representation: 42
  transformation: 46, 311
  ,random: 353
STRINGOUT: 70, 77
strings
  ,permutation of: 261
  ,random: 342
  ,stochastic: 341
structure: 80
structured programming: 3, 17
structures, representation of: 80-85
structures, sorting an array of: 289
subject: 101
subscripting: 220
subsequent pattern: 123
SUBSTR: 52, 140, 371
sufficient context: 203, 205
suffix: 191, 266
  ,hyphenating: 211
  ,inhibiting: 211
  ,neutral: 212
superscripting: 220
SWAP: 56, 61, 184
symbol table: 223, 249
symmmetries of the cube: 402
syntactic
  analysis: 415
  analyzer: 311
  routine: 412
  variable: 355, 411
SYSTEM: 236
system, factorial number: 257

TAB(*R): 29
table datatype: 90
table sorting: 289
Tantzen, R.: 33
Taylor series: 336
telephone: 276
  directory: 223
  information: 164
  number: 369
TEST: 155
test
  ,bins: 346
  ,correlation: 346
  ,runs: 346
text formatting: 189
theoretical formal systems: 412
tick-tack-toe: 376, 386, 402
  ,decision tree for: 386
  ,3D: 403
TICTACTOE: 386, 403
time profile: 231, 232, 248
TIMEGC: 244
TIMER: 234, 252
timing, garbage collection: 244
timing, I/O: 243
timings
  ,arithmetic: 237
  ,assignment: 237
  ,flow-of-control: 240
  ,IBM 360: 237
  ,pattern-building: 241
  ,pattern-matching: 242
token: 227, 416
TOP: 89, 313
tournament sort: 286, 289
TPROFILE: 248, 253
TR: 425, 439
transcendental functions: 328
transformation
  ,k-: 47
  ,positional: 47, 58, 261, 262
  ,string: 46, 311
transliteration: 46, 61
transmitter: 127
transpositional cipher: 59
tree: 173, 424, 438
  adjustment phase of a compiler: 424
  ,binary: 294
  ,decision: 376
  ,pattern matching a: 438
  ,representation of a: 417
  ,root of: 173

TREEBAL: 300
TREEREAD: 173, 185
trees, representation of: 174
TRIG: 340
trigonometric functions: 332
Trotter, H.F.: 259
TRT: 9
TRUNC: 75, 77
truncation of arrays: 75
TSORT: 289
Tuggle, F.D.: 368
TUPLE: 428, 439, 440
tuple language: 426
two's complement: 319
type-0 compiler: 227
type-1 compiler: 227
type-2 compiler: 227
type-3 compiler: 228
type-4 compiler: 228
types of compilers: 226, 251

UBOUNDS: 78
ugly factor: 205
underscoring: 190
unevaluated expressions: 137
unobtrusive heuristics: 127
UPLO: 23, 36, 46, 61
USCORE: 189, 233
use-count: 229

vacancy, s-: 123
Variable association: 135
varying pattern: 102
VISIT: 90, 92, 97
Von Hagen, V.W.: 27
Von Neumann machine: 5

Wagner, M.R.: 211
Walsh, J.: viii
Weizenbaum, J.: 375
Whitehead, E.G. Jr.: 322
Wilkes, M.V.: 348
Woodrum, L.J.: 284
word concordance: 295

Yankees, New York: 360
Yngve, V.H.: 356, 370

Zassenhaus, H.J.: 262
zero-sum game: 390
zero, left: 116

RAYMOND H. FOGLER LIBRARY
DATE DUE

**BOOKS ARE SUBJECT TO
RECALL AFTER TWO WEEKS**

DEC 2 3 1983
DEC 2 3 1983
FEB 2 4 1984
MAY 1 1 1984
MAY 3 1985
SEP 0 6 1985
RENEW OCT 1 1 1985

JAN 1 0 1986
FEB 0 4 1986